# BEHIND
# CLOSED
# DOORS

# BEHIND
# CLOSED
# DOORS

## THE POWER
## AND INFLUENCE OF
## SECRET SOCIETIES

## MICHAEL STREETER

NEW
HOLLAND

First published in 2008 by New Holland Publishers (UK) Ltd
London • Cape Town • Sydney • Auckland

1 3 5 7 9 10 8 6 4 2

www.newhollandpublishers.com

Garfield House, 86–88 Edgware Road, London W2 2EA, UK

80 McKenzie Street, Cape Town 8001, South Africa

Unit 1, 66 Gibbes Street, Chatswood, NSW 2067, Australia

218 Lake Road, Northcote, Auckland, New Zealand

ISBN 978 1 84537 937 7

Editorial Director: Rosemary Wilkinson
Editors: Giselle Osborne, Steffanie Brown, Julia Shone
Editorial Assistant: Nicole Whitton
Design and cover design: Ian Hughes, Mousemat Design Ltd
Production: Melanie Dowland

Front cover image © Greg Blomberg

Printed and bound in India by Replika Press

Note: The author and publishers have made every effort to ensure that the information given in this book is accurate, but they cannot accept liability for any resulting loss or damage to either property or person, whether direct or consequential and howsoever arising.

# Contents

# Introduction

HUMAN BEINGS HAVE ALWAYS HAD a penchant for concealment and secrets. The saying that 'information is power' may seem like a modern one, but it is something our ancestors understood as well – though they may have used the word 'knowledge' rather than information. Even as children our desire to keep secrets from others is a powerful one. The capacity and desire to guard secrets, conceal information and limit the amount of information given is part of the human condition.

It should thus come as no surprise that when we look back into the furthest reaches of human society, to the limits of known history, we find people gathering into exclusive groups and protecting or hiding knowledge from others. As the esoteric scholar and author Manly P. Hall noted in his book, *The Secret Destiny of America* (Philosophical Research Society, 1944): 'Secret societies have existed among all peoples, savage and civilized, since the beginning of recorded history. It is beyond question that the secret societies of all ages have exercised a considerable degree of political influence, usually directed against despotism, intolerance and religious fanaticism.'

It should be stated from the outset – and as Hall's quotation makes clear – that just because people choose to set up private, covert or secretive organizations does not mean that these organizations are *de facto* malevolent in purpose. Concealing information is not inherently evil. Furthermore, as we shall see in the course of this book, people have often joined together behind closed doors to protect themselves and certain knowledge from potential persecution or misuse. Secrecy is not always wrong, and secret organizations are not necessarily dangerous.

There are, however, dangers involved when people and information that touch on important issues such as political power, faith and money are kept concealed from society. The British historian Lord Acton, well known as a defender of liberty for both the individual and society, is remembered for his much-repeated saying about the tendency for power to corrupt, and for 'absolute power to corrupt absolutely', but Lord Acton was also vigilant about the dangers of secrecy. In 1861 he warned that 'everything secret degenerates, even the administration of justice; nothing is safe that does not show how it can bear discussion and publicity.' There are also dangers when organizations conceal or distort information when dealing with existing members or potential recruits.

Throughout history, organizations and movements have remained, or tried to remain, secret for various purposes. The purpose is often to preserve knowledge, perhaps because that knowledge has been deemed too explosive to be made public, yet too important to be allowed to vanish. Sometimes the reason for secrecy is that the knowledge being preserved is counter to the prevailing views of the particular period or society, and concealment is carried out to protect the keepers of that information from being attacked as heretics or criminals.

Other covert organizations are undoubtedly formed to promote a particular political aim, or set of ideas, and the members wish – or feel the need to – hide the true purpose of their intentions. There are, of course, other secretive groups that exist to further criminal purposes in pursuit of wealth and power. The Mafia and the Chinese Triads (organized criminal groups) are two examples of this last kind.

It might be thought that secret societies are essentially a phenomenon of the past; that such groups flourished when communications were slow, when the flow of information was controlled by a few, and when there was no mass media to throw a relentless spotlight on persons and organizations. Surely societies and people cannot remain secretive at a time when millions of emails are constantly sweeping around the planet, when endless websites exist, and when cameras of all kinds – TV, CCTV, mobile phone and video – seemingly cover our every move? In fact, paradoxically, the sheer volume of information with which we are all confronted nowadays may make it easier for secret organizations to flourish. Indeed, there's an old saying amongst journalists that the problem with the British authorities' attitude to information is that they give you too little, while the problem with that of the American authorities lies in the fact that they give you too much. In other words, amid a blizzard of words, facts and figures, it's often hard to find what you're looking for, especially if you don't really know what it was you were looking for in the first place.

Indeed, the evidence seems to suggest that in the midst of today's deluge of information and access to media, people are more likely than ever to believe in the existence and threat of secret societies and covert organizations. In fact, the briefest of trawls through any search engine reveals an amazing variety and breadth of some truly incredible conspiracy theories. In many parts of the world, for example, it is accepted as 'fact' that Diana, Princess of Wales, was murdered; that the 9/11 bombings were carried out by the Americans and/or the Israelis; and that astronaut Neil Armstrong got no closer to the moon than a TV studio. Claims, allegations and casual speculation quickly become accepted as 'evidence', and are lapped up by the gullible and by those who are desperate to hear anything that will back up their own point of view.

A world where facts and evidence can be treated so casually is one in which organizations that want to conceal their activities or their true goals can flourish. If they so choose, they can flood websites, emails, the airwaves and other forms of media with the messages they want listeners to hear, confident that their true purpose will be drowned out in the process, or won't be taken any more seriously than are thousands of other agendas. As the volume of information rises, so perhaps our ability to sift and make sense of it falls. And as traditional media outlets are either ignored or regarded as part of a conspiracy of their own, we lose some of our best allies in our attempt to understand the world and to apply real standards of evidence to the countless claims and rumours swirling around us.

An alternative view is that the Internet can be used to 'expose' the curious claims of some groups to the full glare of publicity, thereby insuring they are ridiculed, thus losing their ability to influence. This may, however, be a rather optimistic view of how people react to 'exciting' claims and conspiracy theories. We often like to believe the outlandish simply because doing so makes life more exciting.

A good recent example of our desire to believe in secrets, and as a result to suspend our critical judgement, can be seen in the reaction by some to the hugely successful novel *The Da Vinci Code* (Doubleday, 2003), by Dan Brown. While a very enjoyable novel, it is a work of fiction – yet various claims made on its behalf have suggested that some of it is based in reality.

The novel's basic storyline – that Jesus and Mary Magdalene had a family whose descendants were the Merovingian royal dynasty of France, and whose secret was later kept by a mysterious group called the Priory of Sion – became accepted as 'fact' by some readers of the book and viewers of the subsequent film. Indeed, as this book will show, the truth often matters less than that which people *believe* to be true.

There is no doubt that secretive societies do exist, and that some of them have been perceived as a real threat. Authorities throughout history have attempted to ban those organizations they saw as threatening. One prominent example was Freemasonry, which was viewed with growing alarm by Catherine the Great, Empress of Russia, towards the end of her reign at the end of the 18th century. Similarly, General Franco ranted and raved about the group's influence and, rightly or wrongly, credited the Freemasons with considerable influence. Even today certain countries have enshrined laws prohibiting secret societies. For example, Article 13 of the Polish Constitution, written in 1997, reads:

Political parties and other organizations whose programmes are based upon totalitarian methods and the modes of activity of nazism, fascism and communism, as well as those whose programmes or activities sanction racial or national hatred, the application of violence for the purpose of obtaining power or to influence the State policy, *or provide for the secrecy of their own structure or membership,* [author's italics] shall be forbidden.

Others take the opposite view, finding the importance accorded to secret or covert organizations to be laughable. They dismiss such bodies as groups of men (and they are indeed often comprised mainly of men) indulging in silly but harmless fantasies, and whom the rest of us should just ignore.

The truth, as it does so often, probably lies somewhere in between these two extreme positions. There are undoubtedly many shadowy and secretive organizations whose membership is unimportant, whose influence is miniscule and whose ideas will remain forever in the obscurity to which they belong. Others, however, are less easy to dismiss. Whatever one thinks of its purpose, for example, the stellar membership of the Bilderberg Group demands our attention. As we shall see, (*see page 164–175*) this body cannot be called a classic secret society, but it is nonetheless an organization with secrets, and serious observers consider it to be potentially dangerous to modern democracy. Indeed, whenever powerful people meet behind closed doors we should all sit up and take notice.

It is similarly difficult to cast aside the influence of two other prominent organizations: the Church of Scientology and Opus Dei. Their many supporters claim that they are forces for good in an uncertain world, while their many detractors see them as harmful. But how much do any of us who are not members really know about these groups, their core beliefs and, above all, their ultimate aims?

The goal of this book is not to evaluate the 'truth' behind the beliefs of these organizations. Rather, it is to examine how these sorts of groups have helped shape the modern world – and to what extent they continue to do so. We will deliberately employ a very wide definition of what is meant by 'secret', as a number of the groups discussed in this book cannot truly be called secret societies, though there is an element of secrecy about each of them. The label they go under is less important than their impact upon the modern world.

Some of the groups we will discuss in this book have their roots in the past. Indeed, a key feature of many secret societies is the claim that they are directly descended from ancient forebears. We will thus begin by looking at the secret ideas, organizations and movements that helped shape the ancient world and, as a result, the world we live in now.

# 1

## The Dawn of Time

HIRAM ABIFF HAD JUST FINISHED his noon prayers, as was his custom. Having completed his devotions, the Master Builder strolled towards the south entrance of the temple that he had helped to build, and which by now was almost complete. As he approached the entrance Hiram was confronted by a priest, who demanded to be told the secret of how the temple had been constructed. Hiram refused, pointing out that he was one of only three people who knew the secret, and that he had sworn never to divulge it. Enraged, the priest lifted his weapon, a piece of lead used as a measuring rule, and aimed a blow at Hiram's head. The priest only managed to strike a glancing blow, however. After recovering from the shock, Hiram made his way towards the temple's north entrance, and to what he hoped was safety.

At the north entrance, however, Hiram encountered another priest, who also demanded that he be told the secret of the temple's construction. Once more Hiram refused, and the priest struck him with his weapon. This time the Master Builder was injured, but bleeding and shaken he managed to make his way towards the temple's east entrance. Here he was confronted by a third priest who, when Hiram once more refused to divulge the secret of the temple, struck the Master Builder a terrible blow with a hammer. Hiram fell dead on the spot. The three priests, who had been working in collusion, then grabbed the dead man's body and took it away to a desolate spot, where it was buried in a grave marked only by an acacia bush. The great architect of King Solomon's Temple was no more.

This striking account concerns the celebrated temple built by King Solomon in Jerusalem, a feat described in some elaborate detail in the Old Testament. The story's principal importance today is that it forms the first major ritual of modern-day Freemasonry. In the so-called Third Degree rite, Masons act out the murder of Hiram, with the candidate for the Third Degree taking the role of the Master Builder. The two others who supposedly knew the Temple's jealously guarded secret are King Solomon himself, and his ally, King Hiram of Tyre (Tyre is now a city in today's Lebanon).

While the story of Hiram's murder does not appear in the Old Testament, a 'Huram' is mentioned in 1 Kings 6:13:

> King Solomon sent to Tyre and brought Huram, whose mother was a widow from the tribe of Naphtali and whose father was a man of Tyre and a craftsman in bronze. Huram himself was highly skilled and experienced in all kinds of bronze work. He came to King Solomon and did all the work assigned to him.

In 2 Chronicles 2:13, King Hiram describes the same man as 'Huram Abi'. The monarch describes him further as a person of 'great skill', and whose mother was from Dan and whose father was from Tyre. In a letter to King Solomon, King Hiram states: 'He will work with your craftsmen'.

One mystery of the story of Hiram's supposed murder at the start of the first millennium – when the temple is believed to have been built – is how the story came to be adopted into modern Masonic ritual. Was it, as most people suppose, just a symbolic story that sprang from the imagination of a Mason in the early 18th century, the time from which modern Freemasonry dates? Or was it a story that had been passed down from generation to generation, through secret organizations and traditions, until it ended up a part of modern Freemasonry? In either case the story is a good example of how a 'modern' secretive group such as the Freemasons can draw inspiration from a biblical character thought to have lived some 3,000 years ago.

The murder of Hiram Abiff is not the end of the story in Masonic legend. After the three priests had murdered and secretly buried Hiram, they fled, but the disappearance of the Master Builder of the Temple was soon discovered. At this time, 12 other priests who had originally been part of the plot to kill Hiram, but who had pulled out at the last minute, confessed what had been planned. Solomon dispatched his men to find the missing Master Builder, not knowing whether he was still alive. During the search, one of Solomon's men came across an acacia bush, which to his surprise came out of the ground easily when he grabbed hold of it. He soon found Hiram's body buried beneath the bush. Solomon was distraught and angry at the news of the murder and ordered the capture of the three priests, who were apparently found in a cave, weeping with sorrow over what they had done to Hiram. They were subsequently executed for their crime. According to legend, the secret of the Temple, kept safe by Hiram Abiff, King Hiram and King Solomon, was never discovered by anyone else.

The story of Hiram Abiff's murder is not the only tradition relating to the Temple's Master Builder that has survived. In one Jewish story, all those who had worked on the building's construction were subsequently killed in order to prevent anyone else from building a temple that could rival the original, or to stop anyone constructing one dedicated to other (non-Jewish) gods. In this tale, Hiram alone escaped when God raised him into the heavens to safety. Another account suggests that after he had completed his great mission, Hiram returned safely to Tyre, where he lived in some comfort. Yet another account given by the Jewish historian Josephus (not always the most reliable of sources) relates that a wise man called Abdemon would help King Hiram solve riddles that King Solomon used to send to him. One Masonic tradition suggests that Hiram Abiff and Abdemon are the same person.

Some scholars have noted the similarity between the story of the death of Hiram Abiff and that of Polydorus in the epic Roman poem, the *Aeneid*, written by Virgil in the 1st century BC. Polydorus was the son of the Trojan king Priam. According to Virgil, the ageing king, fearing the destruction of Troy, sent the young man away for his own safety to Thrace. Once Troy was finally toppled, however, the Thracian king treacherously switched sides and had Polydorus murdered. Later, Aeneas, the hero of the *Aeneid*, finds the buried body of Polydorus while pulling up clumps of myrtle wood on a hillside. (This is similar to the way in which Hiram was discovered under an acacia bush.) Again, as with Hiram, Polydorus was later reburied with honours worthy of his status.

Others have seen strong parallels between the story of Hiram Abiff and the Egyptian legend of the death of Osiris, who was killed by Seth and whose body was later torn to pieces and scattered. At one point in the story, Isis, Osiris's consort, finds his body encased inside a tamarisk tree. This similarity is not surprising: Freemasonry claims to be able to trace its roots back to Ancient Egypt, so it would be perfectly natural for it to incorporate a story with strong echoes of Egyptian mythology. One version of the story even sites the tamarisk tree on the Phoenician coast (modern-day Lebanon), the region in which Hiram Abiff is said to have lived.

## Solomon and Sheba

Just as the legend of Hiram Abiff is central to the beliefs held by the Freemasons, so the story of Solomon and the building of the Temple plays a central role in the beliefs of other occult and secret societies. In the Jewish faith, Solomon is admired as the son of the great King David, and also for creating the temple that once stood in Jerusalem, and which was at the heart of the religion. In Islam, too, Solomon is held in great esteem through his reputation as a just ruler. The powerful 16th century leader of the Ottoman Empire, Suleyman the Great, was, in fact, named after Solomon, and was even regarded by Muslims as the 'second Solomon'.

Yet it was Solomon's supposed links with magic, other gods, sacred geometry and the Ark of the Covenant that have made him such an important figure in the world of arcane knowledge and secret societies. Solomon is thought to have been born c.1000 BC, the son of David and Bathsheba, and to have died around 70 years later. Solomon ruled over the kingdom of Israel for approximately 40 years, and this period is associated with stability and prosperity. The name 'Solomon' means 'peaceful', but he was also known by the name 'Jedidiah', which means 'beloved of God'.

Solomon was married to a daughter of the Egyptian pharaoh. It is interesting that neither she nor the pharaoh is named in the Bible, yet this has not stopped considerable speculation about their identity. Some historians have even questioned whether the story is true, pointing out that it was not customary at that time for pharaohs to allow their daughters to marry foreign rulers. According to one theory, the claim that the king had married a pharaoh's daughter was simply an invention to enhance the prestige of both Solomon and Israel itself. In any case, Solomon was rarely alone, for according to the Bible he had a total of 700 wives, plus some 300 or so concubines. Many of these were described as foreign wives from cultures who worshipped other gods. Indeed, it is the influence of some of these women, especially his Egyptian wife, which is blamed for Solomon having strayed from the path of true faith in his later years.

The best known of the women with whom Solomon is linked is the mysterious Queen of Sheba. The Queen is said to have been so impressed by the King's wisdom that she wanted to see it for herself. It is written in I Kings 10:1–13 (*New International Version*):

> When the Queen of Sheba heard about the fame of Solomon and his relation to the name of the Lord, she came to test him with hard questions. Arriving at Jerusalem with a very great caravan – camels carrying spices, and large quantities of gold, and precious stones – she came to Solomon and talked with him about all that she had on her mind. Solomon answered all her questions; nothing was too hard for the king to explain to her...she said to the king... 'In wisdom and in wealth you have far exceeded the report I have heard.' King Solomon gave the Queen of Sheba all that she desired and asked for, besides what he had given her out of his royal bounty. Then she left and returned with her retinue to her own country.

This is the last biblical reference we hear of the Queen of Sheba. (Sheba is not clearly located in the scriptures; it is thought to have possibly been located in the Arabian peninsula in what is now Yemen, or further away in Ethiopia.) Other stories, however, including those from Arabic and Ethiopian sources, relate more than the tantalizing glimpse we are given in the Old Testament about the relationship between Sheba and the King, where we simply learn that Solomon '...gave the Queen of Sheba all that she desired and asked for, besides what he had given her out of his royal bounty.' According to these other traditions, during the course of her six-month-long stay at the court of King Solomon, the young virgin queen Sheba, noted for her beauty as well as her love of knowledge and learning, became the King's lover. Moreover, Makeda (as the Queen was apparently called, though she is not so named in the Bible) became pregnant with Solomon's child and gave birth to a son. She called him Ibn al-Hakim, meaning 'son of the wise man', though he was also known as Menelik. (According to local Ethiopian tradition Menelik became the first emperor of Ethiopia.)

## Solomon's Seal

Yet another story concerning King Solomon that is of great importance to certain organizations and secret groups is that of Solomon's Seal. This legendary signet ring, made of brass and iron, is said to have been a gift from heaven, upon which was inscribed the sacred name of God himself. With this ring Solomon is said to have been able to command 'devils' to do his bidding, and this is one of the origins of his reputation as a great magician.

In more recent years, Solomon's Seal has come to refer to the six-pointed star, or hexagram, also known as the Star of David and the modern symbol of Israel. Confusingly, the five-sided star or pentagram has also become known as Solomon's Seal. In Western magical tradition, the pentagram is reputed to have the power to ward off evil spirits, rather as the signet ring worn by Solomon was supposed to have given him great powers. Both geometric symbols are said to celebrate the union of heaven with Earth, the divine with the human and spirit with matter – the harmony of the universe. The Pythagoreans also adopted the pentagram as their symbol, and it appears in Arabic legends as well. In one story, Solomon loses the ring when it is thrown into the sea by the evil spirit Asmodeus, and thus is temporarily deprived of his great powers. Solomon eventually finds the ring inside a fish.

## King Solomon's Temple

Most important of all, perhaps, to the stories of many secret societies is that of the temple that Solomon had built, known in the history of Judaism as the First Temple. Solomon's father, David, had planned to build a temple in Jerusalem, the new capital, as the central focus of religious worship. King David began gathering materials to build the sacred structure, and then passed the project over to his son, Solomon. Solomon gathered a vast army of men to cut stones from a quarry, where each block was cut into shape. According to 1 Kings 6:7:

> Only blocks dressed in the quarry were used, and no hammer, chisel or any other tool was heard at the temple site while it was being built.

Solomon also needed a vast amount of wood to complete the project, and this was where his father's friend, Hiram, the King of Tyre, came in. In the ancient world, the Lebanon (where Tyre was situated) was known as a great source of timber. King Hiram had been an ally of David's, and was happy to sign a treaty that would help David's son to complete the Temple. Hiram supplied Solomon with all the cedar and pine timber he needed, and had it hauled down to the sea, where it was sent on rafts for Solomon's army of labourers to collect.

King Hiram's greatest gift to Solomon, however, may have been to deliver his craftsmen to the King of Israel, and not just Hiram Abiff but others, too. There seems to be little doubt from both the biblical account and other traditions that the craftsmen of Tyre had a huge impact not just on providing building materials for the Temple, but in the design of the structure, too. This may seem curious for a building that became the symbol of Judaic devotion, and becomes even more so when one considers that the people of Tyre did not worship Yahweh, the god of the Israelites. Rather, they had their own deities, such as Baal and Astarte.

There is some evidence that Solomon's First Temple was indeed built along very similar lines to traditional Phoenician temples. These habitually consisted of three main elements: an outer hallway, and open inner courtyard and an inner sanctuary, the 'Holy of Holies', where God dwelt. All three elements are contained in what we know of the Temple's design. In addition, the two bronze-clad pillars, or columns, in the Temple, known as Jachin and Boaz, may well have been inspired by Phoenician design. The Greek historian Herodotus reports having visited one temple in Tyre that he was informed was already 2,300 years old. According to his account, this temple had two remarkable pillars: '...one of pure gold, the other of emerald which gleamed with a strange radiance.' Other observers have also pointed to the similarities between a temple dedicated to Baal (or Melqart, another Phonecian god) in Tyre and the one in Jerusalem. It has even been suggested (though there is little or no hard evidence to support this claim) that the Temple in Jerusalem was originally built for the Phoenicians. (This speculative view is, of course, completely at odds with what is stated in the Old Testament.)

Nonetheless, the similarities between the architecture of the First Temple and the temples built by the Phoenicians and others elsewhere in the ancient world are hard to ignore. Interestingly, the Temple was not very large. According to the Bible, inside it was just 27 m (89 ft) long, 9 m (30 ft) wide and 13.5 m (44 ft) high. However, the location and geometry of the building were just as important as its scale. According to later occult traditions, the dimensions of the Temple were in perfect harmony with nature. This is where the spiritual coincides with mathematics; the idea that geometry can express the harmony of the world. In other words, the perfect harmony of the earthly temple is supposed to reflect the spiritual harmony of the universe. Later groups such as the Knights Templar were to find in Solomon's Temple an inspiration; a representation of the universal soul forged out of stone, wood, bronze and gold.

The authors Christopher Knight and Alan Butler have an even bolder theory about the Temple, its design and its location. In *Solomon's Power Brokers* (Watkins, 2007), they argue that Solomon intended the Temple as a place in which there would be a literal communion between the kingdom of Earth and the kingdom of heaven. To support their arguments they use astronomy, claiming that every 40 years the planet Venus completes a full cycle of the zodiac, and then returns to the place it started from. They argue that this astronomical event would have been well known in the time of Solomon, when experts closely studied the movement of heavenly bodies, and that the movement of Venus was so regular that it acted like a 'wonderful clock and calendar for astronomer-priests'. Solomon, they claim, would have been well aware of the importance of such 40-year cycles, and they point out that the number 40 often appears in the Old Testament (for example, Moses stayed on Mount Sinai for 40 years).

The authors further claim that of even greater astronomical significance was the fact that every 480 years there is a conjunction of the planets Venus and Mercury, meaning that these two planets form together what looks to observers like one large star. They call this the 'Shekinah' (in Judaism this word refers to God's presence in the world). Moreover, every three cycles – that is, every 1,440 years – this event was believed to have extra special significance. One of these 'special events' was scheduled to happen in 967 BC. This event, they claim, coincided with the building of the Temple, which was designed to be a 'carefully constructed mechanism that would act as a conduit to all gods' at such an auspicious astronomical time. Knight and Butler claim, however, that Solomon and his people lacked the expert knowledge required to build a temple that precisely fulfilled this demand, which was why he needed help from the Phoenicians, whose knowledge of astronomy was considerable.

## The Ark of the Covenant

One of the key components of Solomon's Temple was the so-called 'Holy of Holies', the place that was built in order to house the Ark of the Covenant. The Ark of the Covenant is one of the most fascinating and intriguing objects described in the Bible. God told Moses to build the Ark when the Jews were wandering in the Sinai desert. The Ark was said to be a box just under 1.2 m (4 ft) long, made of acacia wood and plated with gold. On its cover were the figures of two cherubim; on its bottom it had four gold rings through which poles could be slotted, enabling the box to be carried.

According to biblical accounts, as Moses led his people through the desert the Ark was carried some distance ahead. It periodically shot out flames that destroyed any thorn bushes, scorpions and snakes that stood in the way of the Jews. But the Ark was not only dangerous to animals and plants; one story holds that when the sons of Aaron, Nadab and Abihu, brought 'unauthorized' fire to make a sacrifice, they suffered a terrible fate brought about by the powers of the Ark. According to Leviticus 10:2:

> So fire came out from the presence of the Lord and consumed them, and they died before the Lord.

Still other stories tell of how just looking at the Ark could bring death. The Ark was carried around the walls of Jericho before those defensive barricades came tumbling down. In another story, the Philistines, enemies of the Israelites, managed to capture the Ark and took it back to their city. However, after a series of misfortunes befell them, including plague and the destruction of an idol of their god, the Philistines not only returned it to the Israelites but sent it back with gifts. King David eventually brought the Ark to Jerusalem, though even this was not without incident. One of the drivers of the cart carrying the Ark was called Uzzah, and at one point he put out his hand to touch it in order to steady it after one of the oxen pulling it had stumbled. He was immediately struck down by the Ark's mysterious power. It was later brought to Jerusalem, and once Solomon had completed the construction of the Temple it was brought to its resting place in the 'Holy of Holies'.

Spiritually, the Ark had (and still has) a vital place in Judaism, as it was within the Ark that the Ten Commandments handed down by God were kept. For Jews, the Ark represents God's manifestation on the face of the Earth (when Moses spoke with God, His voice came from between the two cherubs). Yet the Ark has also excited followers of the occult and devotees of secret societies; in particular, the mysterious and deadly powers attributed to it in the Old Testament and in other traditions. There is fascination, too, with reports that the Ark was at one point not carried by people at all – it was able to carry its bearers above the ground. Yet another compelling feature of the Ark was that clouds appeared around it, accompanying the voice of God.

In any case, one thing is certain: the Ark of the Old Testament has vanished. It is said to have rested within the First Temple, in Jerusalem, until the invasion of the Babylonians under Nebuchadnezzar and the eventual destruction of the Temple in the 6th century BC. The Ark disappeared around that time, and is presumed to have been destroyed. Nonetheless, many legends and stories maintain that the Ark survived and is still waiting to be rediscovered.

## Solomon's Demise

Solomon is said to have ruled for 40 years, a period which, as we have seen, has some astronomical significance, and which is a frequently recurring time period in the Old Testament (and also the New Testament; for example, Jesus is said to have been tempted in the desert for 40 days and nights, and to have ascended to heaven 40 days after his resurrection). His reign is understandably noted for his wisdom, his wealth, his construction of the Temple and for the power held by Israel at the time.

We are led to believe that Solomon's power and influence waned, however, in the final years of his reign. The Old Testament lays much of the blame on his penchant for foreign wives and concubines, and on the different gods and religions they followed. 'His wives led him astray,' the author of 1 Kings notes laconically. In fact, the Old Testament (1 Kings 11:4–5) explicitly accuses the great king of worshipping other gods himself, in addition to the Israelites' one true God:

> As Solomon grew old his heart was not fully devoted to the Lord his God…He followed Astoreth the goddess of the Sidonians and Molech the detestable god of the Ammonites.

The decline in Solomon's powers are also reflected in the fate of his kingdom after his death. The united kingdom of Israel later split into two separate states, one called Israel (the Northern Kingdom), the other, Judah (the Southern Kingdom).

The above reference to Solomon's devotion to 'Astoreth' is interesting.

She is better known as Astarte, and was a well-known Phoenician (or Canaanite goddess) who, in various forms and under different names, was worshipped widely in the ancient world at that time. The Old Testament refers to her as the goddess of the Sidonites (the people of Sidon who lived in what is now the Lebanon), but she was worshipped, too, in Tyre and in Byblos. Some of her titles included 'Queen of Heaven' and 'Our Lady of the Sea'. There can be little doubt that even among the Israelites, Astarte was, for a period, an important figure of devotion. At one point, temples to Yahweh and Astarte were supposedly built side by side in the ancient town of Mizpah. Later, in 2 Kings 23:13, we learn that Josiah, King of Judah, ordered a wholesale destruction of all objects of devotion and altars that were dedicated to anyone other than their Lord.

> (The King)…desecrated the high places east of Jerusalem…the ones Solomon king of Israel had built for Astoreth, the vile goddess of the Sidonians.

## Undying Gods

In the Phoenician religion, Astarte was seen as the consort goddess of the great god Baal. So it is by no mean far-fetched to think that some early Israelites regarded her as the consort to Yahweh. In the ancient world, the concept of having a sun or sky god with masculine traits and a moon or fertility goddess with females traits was common. The move towards monotheism was a gradual one, as we have seen in the example of King Solomon; he is one of the great figures of Judaism (and Islam), yet he clearly worshipped other gods, too. Eventually, however, Judaism was to become resolutely monotheistic, as did its offshoot, Christianity, and in both cases the concept of a goddess was lost.

In the case of Christianity, however, we shall see that the goddess motif may not have been completely discarded, but instead survived in a disguised form. This brings us to the importance of goddesses such as Astarte in the story of secret societies and hidden knowledge. Solomon, the Temple and the Ark were all to feature strongly among later secret groups. Deeply intertwined with the traditions that were to develop in the coming centuries were the symbolic concepts of the goddess, the resurrected god, the rebirth of the soul and the cyclical pattern of life. These themes would become central for occultists and religious heretics alike, and would force them into secrecy.

The world of the ancient gods and goddesses is a bewildering one.

Names overlap, as do the attributes of the gods themselves. Gods worshipped in one area were often adopted by people in another area, but sometimes under a different name and with qualities perhaps appended to the new god from their existing deities. The Hittites (the former inhabitants of what is now Anatolia, in Turkey), for example, were notorious for adopting gods from their neighbours.

There emerge, however, some clear themes that are common to many gods and their stories. Of these the most important – and the one central to the story of what we might call the Hidden Tradition in the west – is that of the dying god who is reborn. This story was played out endlessly by many different gods (and goddesses) throughout the ancient world. An example of such a story is that of Astarte. Her counterpart in Babylonian religion was Ishtar, who had a consort named Tammuz. (As so often in these recurring stories the goddess's consort is also her son and/or brother.) In Astarte's case, she is often described as the consort of Baal, the Canaanite god, but she is also associated with Adonis, a fertility god whose story and name was later adopted by the Greeks. The story goes that Astarte fell deeply in love with Adonis, and tried to persuade him to give up the dangerous pursuit of hunting. He refused, and one day was killed by a wild boar. Astarte arrived at the scene of her lover's death and was distraught, though eventually she was able to bring Adonis back to life. Each year the blooming of the red anemone flower that grew in the region symbolized Adonis's spilt blood, and thus his death and resurrection.

The story of Adonis's death and resurrection was apparently celebrated annually at the temple dedicated to Astarte in Byblos. It is thought that effigies of the dead god, dressed in red, were symbolically buried, or thrown into the sea amid much wailing and sorrow, then the next day his rebirth would be celebrated with equal vigour. Interestingly, there is a strong association between Adonis and trees: he is said to have emerged as a baby from inside a myrrh tree, into which his mother had been turned by a vengeful god. He was also referred to as 'He on the tree'.

Adonis's association with trees is far from unique. As we will see, the dying god Attis was also associated with a tree, and we have already seen the links between Osiris and the tamarisk tree. In another story set in Phrygia (now part of modern Turkey), worshippers followed the cult of the widely revered mother goddess, Cybele (her consort was her son, Attis). There were a number of stories concerning how the young god met his end: one is that he castrated himself at the foot of a pine tree and bled to death. According to at least one version of the story, Cybele herself drove Attis to this grisly end, but was able to bring Attis back to life again. This 'event', which symbolizes the endless cycles of the season (in which 'death' is the winter and the new life is spring), was re-enacted by devotees of the cult.

We know this much about the practices of the cult revolving around Cybele because in 205 BC the worship of Cybele was brought to the now powerful city of Rome. The Romans celebrated the story of Attis's rebirth in a rather bloody way. Priests (or Galli) would castrate themselves in emulation of the god's fate, while others would simply cut themselves. An effigy of Attis was dressed in linen and tied to a pine tree. After three days of mourning, Attis was deemed brought back to life again, which was the cue for great celebrations. These celebrations became known in Roman times as the Hilaria Festival.

Some aspects of mother-goddess worship appeared to have shocked the morals of the Israelites, as well as those of other cultures. The concept of 'sacred prostitution' was particularly scandalous. This was the idea that once in a woman's life, at some point before marriage, every woman had to go to the temple of the goddess and prostitute herself. In other words, she was to have sex with a stranger in return for money. This money was then 'paid' to the goddess as an offering. The historian Sir James Frazer referred to this practice in his famous work, *The Golden Bough* (Macmillan, 1922) as 'sanctified harlotry'. He noted that: 'The sacred precinct was crowded with women waiting to observe the custom. Some of them had to wait there for years.'

Variations on this custom were applied to the goddesses Astarte, Ishtar (from Babylon) and Mylitta (known by the Greeks as Aphrodite). In the case of Astarte, it was the custom of women in Byblos to shave their heads once a year to mark the death and rebirth of Adonis, the goddess's handsome lover. Any woman who did not want to lose her hair in this way had to go to the temple and give herself to a stranger in return for money. This type of practice appears to have existed until at least the 2nd century. An engraving found in Lydia suggests that a woman called Aurelia Aemilia had been a sacred prostitute, as indeed had her mother and her other female forebears. Interestingly, no shame appears to have been attached to either herself or her parentage. Sir James Frazer also notes that it was the Roman emperor Constantine (who ruled in the early part of the 4th century AD) who abolished the practice of religious custom at Baalbec in the Middle East, destroying the temple and building a church in its place.

## Isis and Horus

Of all the gods and goddesses in the ancient world, perhaps the most important to the story of secret societies and hidden knowledge is the goddess Isis. She is a key figure in what might be termed the hidden tradition of Christianity, and subsequently among both magical societies and those mystical groups that insisted upon an alternative view of Christianity.

Isis had many names in the ancient world, including The Queen of Heaven, The One Who Is All, Mother of the Gods and Star of the Sea. In his famous work from the 2nd century, *The Golden Ass*, the Roman writer Lucius Apuleius quotes the goddess, imbuing her with words that sum up her importance and status in the ancient world:

> I am she that is the natural mother of all things, mistress and governess of all the Elements, the initial progeny of worlds, chief of powers divine, Queen of heaven! The principal of the celestial Gods, the light of the goddesses: at my will the planets of the air, the wholesome winds of the Seas, and the silences of hell be disposed; my name, my divinity is adored throughout all the world in diverse manners, in variable customs and in many names, for the Phrygians call me the mother of the Gods: the Athenians, Minerva: the Cyprians, Venus: the Candians, Diana: the Sicilians, Proserpina: the Eleusians, Ceres: some Juno, others Bellona, others Hecate: and principally the Ethiopians which dwell in the Orient, and the Egyptians which are excellent in all kind of ancient doctrine, and by their proper ceremonies are accustomed to worship me, do call me Queen Isis. *(The Golden Ass* by Lucius Apuleius, translated by William Adlington, Book 11, chapter 47)

An inscription on Isis's temple at Sais, in Egypt, is said to have read: 'I, Isis, am all that has been, that is or shall ever be; no mortal man hath ever me unveiled.'

Isis began as an Egyptian deity, probably as a local goddess in the Nile Delta. In time, the worship of her spread, and ultimately she became one of the most important goddesses not just in the Middle East but also throughout much of Europe. Just as they would do for Christianity (and for the worship of Cybele, as we have seen), so the Romans helped spread devotion of this Egyptian goddess to far-flung parts of its empire. (A temple devoted to Isis was even found in London, and she was worshipped in parts of Africa as well.)

To many Romans, Isis was simply another form of Cybele, the mother goddess from Phrygia introduced to the city at the end of the 3rd century BC. In Egypt, the goddess was often depicted with a headdress in the form of a throne (her name literally means 'seat' or 'throne'); at other times, she was shown with the horns or head of a cow (this is the case when she is identified with the goddess Hathor). Occasionally she is seen in the form of a bird.

The most important story regarding Isis – and the one reflecting the resurrection stories common to many ancient world goddesses – involved the powerful Egyptian deity known as Osiris. Osiris was the Egyptian saviour god and the god of death, and Isis was both his sister and wife. Osiris's brother, Seth (or Set), was jealous of his sibling, and set out one day to trap him. He tricked Osiris into lying inside a coffin, then shut the lid and had it thrown into the Nile. A distraught Isis hunted for her partner and eventually found his coffin embedded inside a tamarisk tree that was being used as a pillar in a palace in Byblos; she was able to bring Osiris back to life. Seth, however, found his brother again, and in a rage tore his body into pieces. Isis once more went to rescue Osiris and succeeded in putting him back together. All she lacked was his penis (which was eaten by a fish) and so, according to one tradition, she fashioned a replacement from clay. (Isis was noted for her magical powers, which accounts for her popularity among later magical traditions.) Osiris was restored to life once more, but this time he became ruler of the underworld. Meanwhile, Isis and Osiris had a son whom they named Horus, and Horus's mission in life was to avenge his father against his evil brother, Seth.

There are clearly strong parallels between this ancient tale and the resurrection myths of, for example, Cybele and Attis, or Astarte and Adonis. Equally important is the image of Isis as a loyal consort or wife in the way she looks after Osiris, and as a loving and dutiful mother to her infant, Horus. There is, for example, a rather beautiful tradition that the annual flooding of the Nile Delta is caused by the teardrop shed by Isis when weeping for her lost partner, Osiris. For her worshippers, these signs of devotion were two important traits of the goddess, while Horus, in his turn, was worshipped as a loyal and loving son. Images in the ancient world showing Isis holding Horus underlined both these qualities.

One is irresistibly drawn to make the comparison between images of Isis and Horus and those of the Virgin Mary and the infant Jesus. (In one of the many apparent paradoxes of ancient mythology, Isis was identified as virginal even though she was also revered as the wife of Osiris and the mother of Horus.) Naturally enough, few Christians would accept any link between a 'pagan' deity such as Isis and the Virgin Mary, the mother of Christ the Saviour. As we shall see, however, the symbolism of Isis as a mother and virginal goddess was to have an important impact on later beliefs.

## Hermes and Thoth

As noted, Isis was known for her magical abilities, which has since led her to become a key part of certain occult magical traditions. However, the undoubted master of magic in Egyptian mythology, and one of the key figures for occultists down the centuries, is Thoth. Thoth was an important Egyptian deity whom the Greeks later identified with their own god, Hermes. Later, a new 'character' emerged who combined the characters of both of these gods; this character became known as Hermes Trismegistus, meaning 'thrice-great Hermes'. Hermes Trismegistus is regarded as the father figure of modern magic, as well as a prolific writer, sage and prophet. His importance to the story of the occult, alchemy and magic in later centuries was to be profound.

Thoth himself was the scribe-deity of the Egyptians, who was supposed to have invented writing and law. He was also a god of time, mathematics and astronomy, as well as being the lord of magic in the Egyptian pantheon. Frequently depicted with the head of an Ibis, Thoth was often shown carrying a writing tablet on which he would record the weighing of the souls in the so-called 'judgement hall', presided over by Osiris, the lord of the underworld. Thoth was also seen as a mediator between other gods and portrayed as a trickster and messenger – qualities which the Greeks strongly identified with their own deity, Hermes (Mercury to the Romans), who was the famed messenger of the gods.

The important figure of Hermes Trismegistus is therefore seen as an amalgam of the Greek and Egyptian gods. There may also have been a third element to this character, and from a rather more surprising source: early Judaism. Some scholars claim a link between Hermes or Thoth and the Old Testament prophet Enoch; presumably an influence that would have come from the many years the Israelites supposedly spent in captivity in Egypt (though some scholars debate whether this really happened). Enoch himself is described in the Book of Genesis 5:24 as having lived to the age of 365.

His end is described thus:

Enoch walked with God; then he was no more, because God took him away.

While there is little here to indicate why Enoch should be associated with Thoth and Hermes, a different story emerges when we consider the so-called Book of Enoch, a series of apocryphal writings which are not accepted by mainstream Christianity as part of the canon of the Holy Bible, and which date from the 2nd century BC to the 1st century AD. These and other traditions give a rather more vivid picture of the character known as Enoch. Here he is described as being taken up to heaven and is positioned next to God's throne, where he learns all manner of mysteries and knowledge. He is regarded as the executor of God's wishes as well as His messenger, and is seen as the inventor of mathematics, astronomy and writing. These traits clearly share some similarity with both Thoth and Hermes, and act as an important reminder that the contents of the Judaeo-Christian belief system and those of the so-called 'pagan' traditions are not quite as separate as we have tended to assume. Indeed, it is precisely this crossover between Judaeo-Christian tradition and that of the 'pagan' beliefs upon which many secret societies have focussed their attentions.

Hermes Trismegistrus was regarded in the ancient world and by subsequent followers as the embodiment of the Universal Mind, the First Intelligence. But he left a rather more tangible legacy, too. According to tradition, he also wrote many texts and books. These included a series of texts known as *Hermetica*, which touch upon a number of themes, including philosophy, mysticism and Gnosticism. They also contain many occult references to such subjects as magic and alchemy. These surviving texts are written in Greek, and probably date from between the 1st and 3rd centuries AD. They likely reflect much of the thinking in the 'pagan' world of the time. In particular, the texts were most likely influenced by the culture of Alexandria, the Egyptian city that had been greatly influenced by Greek thought.

The body of work by Hermes Trismegistrus that has survived is likely to be copies of sections of what would have been a much larger body of work, which, sadly, no longer exists. In a sense, these writings, reflecting as they do many of the pagan themes of the time (including the important philosophy of neo-Platonism), can be regarded as the 'bible' of paganism and magic, much as the Old and New Testaments reflect the thinking of Jews and Christians of the time. They also, despite the influence of the Greeks, clearly reflect Egyptian thought. For example, one text talks about removing 'foreigners' from Egypt, a reference to a kind of nascent Egyptian nationalism at a time when the Roman Empire controlled the country.

Despite the non-Christian content of these writings, the early Christian writers who were familiar with them were not entirely hostile. As Manly P. Hall noted in his self-published tome, *The Secret Teachings of all Ages* (1928): 'One outstanding point in connection with Hermes is that he was one of the few philosopher-priests of pagandom upon whom the early Christians did not vent their spleen. Some Church Fathers went so far as to declare that Hermes exhibited many symptoms of intelligence, and that if he had only been born in a more enlightened age so that he might have benefited by *their* instructions he would have been a really great man!'

The early Christian teacher and writer, Clement of Alexandria, maintained that there were originally 42 books written by Hermes, and much of what we know of their contents come from him. According to Clement, 36 of the books contained the 'whole philosophy of the Egyptians', while the others he categorized as medical: '...treating of the structure of the body, and of diseases, and instruments, and about the eyes, and the last about women.' While we cannot be sure who the author of these texts actually was, they are commonly attributed to Hermes Trismegistrus. Furthermore, some claim that while some of the original books were destroyed, others were hidden in the desert, their location known only to a few. The whereabouts of these ancient missing books, written on papyrus, has led to much speculation and intrigue.

## Pythagoras

Secret societies thrive on arcane knowledge, hidden traditions and different interpretations of existing information. But they also need charismatic leaders to create them in the first place, and to help them flourish thereafter. We have already seen how the ancient world was positively full of ideas, secrets and religious beliefs, from the mysteries of Solomon's Temple, sacred geometry and the knowledge of its Phoenician builders, to the death and resurrection stories of goddesses and gods and the magical traditions of figures such as Hermes Trismegistrus. These ideas typically needed leaders to create these secret societies in the first place, to preserve and extend their hidden knowledge, and to help teach initiates deemed worthy of the message. One such man was Pythagoras.

Today Pythagoras is best known – indeed, practically only known – for his contribution to mathematics. The famous theorem that is attributed to him (that in a right-angled triangle the square on the hypotenuse is equal to the sum of the square on the other two sides) is familiar to many of us. Pythagoras was, however, far more than a mathematician. Born c.580-572 BC on the Greek island of Samos, near the coast of what is today Turkey, Pythagorus was also a mystic and scientist.

According to legend, before Pythagoras's birth the Oracle at Delphi in Greece told his parents that their child would surpass all others in both beauty and wisdom, and that he would make a huge contribution to humankind. It was even claimed that Pythagoras was the product of a virgin birth – a familiar quality of the gods in ancient mythology – and that he was actually a god who had become flesh and blood. His followers used to say that there were three categories of being: men, gods and men like Pythagoras. Another legend states that he had a golden thigh, a sign of divinity.

Little can be said with great certainty about Pythagoras's early life, nor indeed about his belief system, as none of his writings have survived. However, his education (if the stories are true) was extraordinary. Near Samos was the city of Miletus (on the mainland of modern Turkey), where Greek 'thought' began. It later reached its zenith in Athens with Socrates, Plato and Aristotle. Pythagoras's contemporaries were important Greek thinkers in their own right, and included men such as Anaximenes and Xenophanes.

Pythagoras was not content with the knowledge he could find at home. He thus travelled widely, studying in the temples at Sidon and Tyre (where his merchant father originally came from), then living in Egypt for many years. There he is said to have been taught by priests in the ancient capital city of Memphis, and to have been initiated into the 'Egyptian Mysteries', including those of Isis. He also supposedly travelled among the Jewish community, and even incorporated some of their ideas into his own philosophy.

In around 525 BC the Persians invaded Egypt, and Pythagoras was made a prisoner and taken to Babylon in captivity. Here, however, he was able to learn first-hand from the wise men of Babylon. He was initiated into the sacred rites and mysteries of the Magi, and learned as well about mathematics – a discipline for which the Babylonians were famed. It is also said that Pythagoras learnt secrets from Hinduism. If all of these stories about Pythagoras are true (and we will probably never know for sure if they are), then he had one of the most extraordinary educations the ancient world had ever seen.

The first man in history known to have described himself as a philosopher (a 'lover of wisdom') rather than a wise man, Pythagoras did not waste what he had learnt. In around 520 BC Pythagoras left Babylon and headed for Croton, a city that was part of what was called Magna Graecia, or Greater Greece (now in southern Italy). Here, over the course of the following years he gathered around himself a group of disciples and became both a teacher and a leader. The group became part mystery cult, part school, part secret society. The rules of the group were strict, and among the most severe concerned secrecy itself. The group, cult or sect – however one wants to describe it – had an inner and an outer circle. The outer circle did not live with the group, were allowed to own possessions and were allowed to eat meat; while the inner circle lived as a group, were vegetarians, had no possessions and were closely supervised by Pythagoras himself.

Pythagoras's group was an early form of secret society, often referred to as a 'brotherhood'. It was secret in the sense that membership was restricted, and the precise teachings and beliefs it held (many of which came from Pythagoras's travels) were kept secret. However, we do know the nature of some of the beliefs that Pythagoras and his followers held, and one was reincarnation; more accurately, the transmigration of the soul whereby a human soul can return in another life in animal form. This belief, which had not been taught in Greece previously, almost certainly derived from Pythagoras's time in Egypt. It is said that on one occasion Pythagoras ordered someone to stop beating a dog, explaining, 'From his cries I recognize the ghost of a friend.'

It must also be noted that some Greek writers at the time of (and later than) Pythagoras were doubtful about some of his claims and behaviour. In his book, *Pythagoras and the Pythagoreans* (Hackett, 2001), Charles H. Kahn states that: 'In fifth and early fourth echoes, the fame of Pythagoras is that of a fabulous sage and religious teacher, who was perhaps also a charlatan.'

Pythagoras did, however, leave a rather more enduring legacy: as a proponent of the idea that geometry and numbers are key to understanding the nature of the universe; of the harmony within numbers; and of the fundamental relationship between mathematics and music. Pythagoras ascribed a quality to each number; for example, the number ten is the number of the universe, and the number one the number of reason.

Exactly which mathematical theorems are correctly attributed to Pythagoras is hard to know, as it seems that some of his followers' achievements were posthumously credited to their leader. Even Pythagoras's famous theorem about the right-angled triangle (*see page 30*) may already have been known to the Babylonians long before Pythagoras's time, though he may have been first to prove the theorem. Wherever the truth about Pythagoras's contributions lies, there is little doubt that later Greek philosophers such as Plato and Aristotle – indisputably giants of Western philosophy – owe a debt to Pythagoras, even if scholars debate the precise importance of his teachings. It is clear, too, that Pythagoras made an impression on later generations by the way he chose to live his life (as a teacher), his ethics and his emphasis on intellect and virtue. For Pythagoras, religion and the mysteries of the universe were not separate from numbers and science; rather, they were an inseparable part of it. This belief in the sacredness of numbers and geometry, as seen previously in reference to Solomon's Temple, was to become a recurring theme amongst secret societies and the occult. Mathematics and geometry were regarded as expressions of the true, mystical and ultimately harmonious nature of the universe.

The exact circumstances of Pythagoras's death are shrouded in uncertainty. There is some suggestion that Pythagoras and his followers may have achieved an element of political power in Croton, and that he and his disciples were the victims of a revolt by factions opposed to him and his philosophies. According to one grisly tradition, Pythagoras and his followers were burned alive by their enemies. In another story, he is said to have died in exile. One of the more colourful claims is that Pythagoras escaped death at the hand of his political enemies, but soon afterwards died of despair brought on by the seeming impossibility of bringing enlightenment to the world. All of the stories seem to agree, however, that Pythagoras and his cult attracted enemies. This is a theme that has remained constant in the history of secret societies; justly or otherwise, they have usually been regarded as a threat to society and have faced persecution or elimination, or they have been forced underground.

**Greek Mysteries**

Another controversial cult that existed in the time of ancient Greece involved the followers of the so-called Dionysian mysteries. Dionysus was the Greek god of wine, but this powerful and important deity was also linked with the endless cycle of life and death. He was a capricious god whom the Greeks almost certainly adopted from other cultures – Minoan, Cretan or Phrygian. As well as being a 'conventional' god, Dionysus was also the object of rites and worship rituals that were at times wild and outrageous – even subversive. Those acting out the Dionysian rituals symbolizing the death and re-birth of their god became intoxicated under the ecstasy and intensity of their devotion. Many followers were women, known as the *maenads*, whose wildness when under the influence of their worship was legendary. The most infamous story concerned the unfortunate King Pentheus of Thebes, who tried to stop the god being worshipped. Unable to control the power of Dionysus or his followers, the *maenads*, led by the King's own mother, eventually ripped him to pieces.

This apocryphal story tells us something about how the Greek world viewed the ferocity of the worship of Dionysus. It is also illustrative of how the cult and its followers were feared by rulers. The subversive element of the rites lay not only in the abandoned way they were carried out, but also in the very nature of the people who took part in them. Given its ancient foreign origin, there was always a sense of 'foreignness' about the Dionysian rites as far as many Greeks were concerned. This unease was further exacerbated by the fact that the cult attracted foreigners, slaves and women; such a following was bound to arouse the suspicion of any ruler trying to rule within a society traditionally run by Greek men of high birth. Unsurprisingly, some Greek rulers sought to suppress, or at least control, the cult. (A more tame form of rites seems to have been encouraged in Athens, for example.)

It was in Rome that we see the most dramatic example of how the subversive rites of a secret religious society could clash with state values. In 186 BC, the city of Rome was the emerging power in the Mediterranean, and was well on its way to eclipsing other states and peoples in the region. The Romans were certainly not adverse to adopting the deities of other cultures, and the Greek Dionysus was identified with the Roman god Bacchus. (Many other Greek gods were assimilated in this way as well.) The Roman Senate was, however, constantly preoccupied with the maintenance of public order and the sometimes delicate and shifting

THE DAWN OF TIME

balance of power that kept the Republic stable. A cult that attracted slaves, women and foreigners, and that operated outside the usual state religion and rules, was not something to be welcomed. Thus, in that year, the Senate issued a law outlawing this 'dangerous' cult.

The reasons behind the criminalization of the cult were, ostensibly, the immoral (i.e. sexual) nature of the rites, along with allegations of murder involving its followers. However, it seems that the main underlying purpose of this suppression was the fear that the cult could undermine the security of the republic. It has been estimated that several thousand people died in this bloody clampdown, yet another reminder of how secret groups can be demonized by authorities – and of the grim consequences that can follow.

The Roman authorities may have been right to fear the Dionysians. If the Greek historian Plutarch is to be believed, a form of Dionysian worship was involved in the start of the great gladiator and slave revolt of 73 BC, an uprising that went on to become a major threat to the security of Rome. The leader of this revolt was the Thracian Spartacus and, according to Plutarch, the gladiator's wife (who had been in captivity with him) was a devotee of the Dionysian rites. According to Plutarch:

*'They say that when he was first taken to Rome to be sold, a snake was seen coiled round his head while he was asleep and his wife, who came from the same tribe and was a prophetess subject to possession by the frenzy of Dionysus, declared that this sign meant that he would have a great and terrible power which would end in misfortune. This woman shared in his escape and was then living with him.'* (Plutarch, *Life of Crassus*, translated by Rex Warner, London: Penguin Books Ltd, 1972)

The fact that Spartacus's wife was a devotee of Dionysus, and that she believed her husband to possess divine powers, is unlikely to have had a decisive impact on events, as the rebellion had a whole raft of social and political causes. Yet it is interesting that a Greek writer noted the existence of a link between the social rebellion and Dionysian worship.

## Mithraism

As we have seen, ancient Rome liked to control all aspects of society, including religion. Yet there was considerable religious freedom in Rome, as long as the outward forms of respect and the due forms of devotion were observed among the people – unlike among the devotees of Bacchus, for example. The city had an ever-shifting pantheon of gods, and these were incorporated into what was in effect a state religion. Emerging political figures such as Julius Caesar held important offices in the state religious apparatus, as well as more conventional political positions.

After the rule of Augustus and the start of the imperial system in Rome at the end of the last century BC, this general tolerance was extended to religion – as long as the supremacy of the emperor was accepted. As the emperor became increasingly associated with the gods and came to take on divine status, his supremacy became almost an article of faith for any Roman. As we will see, this put Rome on a collision course with some new mystery cults, including Christianity, the followers of which refused to accord divine status to the emperor. This tension was gradually worn down from the fourth century onwards, when the emperors themselves adopted Christianity. Yet this embracing of a new faith had in fact already occurred well before the advent of Christianity in the form of another fast-growing mystery cult of the time: Mithraism.

In fact, Mithraism and Christianity were to become rivals for the affection of the Roman Empire. The eventual prize for the victor would be a Europe- and Asia Minor-wide religion that would ultimately dominate the Western landscape. Indeed, at one point it looked as if this faith would not be Christianity, but rather Mithraism. As the French philosopher and writer Ernest Renan observed: 'If Christianity had been arrested in its growth by some illness, the world would have been Mithraic.' Like Christianity, Mithraism was based on an individual's personal relationship with God and the notion of salvation and immortality. And, like Christianity, it had more in common with the ecstatic faith of Dionysian worship than with the existing state religions and philosophies.

Mithraism was more secretive than Christianity, or at least less willing to share its core beliefs. We are therefore unclear about much of this faith's belief system, and we cannot even be sure where it came from. Some scholars postulate that it is an adapted form of the Persian religion of Zoroastrianism, which had its own semi-divine character known as Mithra. However, the Zoroastrian Mithra seems to have relatively little in common with the saviour god Mithras of Mithraism. For example, Mithras's depiction as a bull-slayer has no known link with the Zoroastrian Mithra. An alternative view is that Mithraism sprang up as a composite of various beliefs from Asia Minor (or possibly Phrygia), and was brought to the Roman Empire by soldiers stationed there. It was certainly a cult that remained popular with legionnaires in all parts of the Empire, from Syria to Britain, as well as with merchants and state officials.

Unlike Christianity, this secretive cult excluded women. Members met in underground churches or caves (Mithras himself was said to have been born in a rock or a cave) to carry out 'mysteries' rituals about which very little is known. It is, however, thought that its members practised some kind of sacred feast involving the symbolic slaying of a bull, thought to have represented salvation and new life. Initiates into this cult seem to have had to progress through seven different stages of initiation, passing from 'raven', 'bridegroom' and 'soldier' through to 'lion', 'Persian', 'messenger of the sun' and, finally, to 'father'. A follower who had attained the level of 'father' was apparently known as a *Pater Partum*, or 'father of fathers', who, as the Catholic Encyclopaedia points out, seems to have been '…a sort of pope, who always lived at Rome'. This graded system of initiation within Mithraism has also prompted some to describe it as 'Roman Freemasonry'.

An important factor in the survival of Mithraism within the Empire had to do with the fact that the cult became linked with a solar cult known as *Sol Invictus*, or 'Invincible Sun', which in turn was identified with the emperor. It would appear that Mithraism had little difficulty in outwardly accepting the supremacy of the Roman emperor, whatever its secret theology. As a secret religious society, therefore, it proved remarkably successful and influential.

## The Birth of Christianity

As we have seen, secret societies throughout the centuries have drawn enormous inspiration from stories involving Solomon, ancient so-called pagan mystery cults, the magical tradition of Egypt and the pantheon of gods in the ancient world. But perhaps it is the story of the birth of Christianity and its theology that have given birth to the most hidden and secret traditions, at least in the Western world.

Christianity was based on a very different message from other cults and religions of the time. Its basic premise was not that God had sent prophets and great leaders, as Judaism had taught; nor that the divine essence could enter the human soul through ecstatic worship in some symbolic re-enactment of the cycle of life and death, as the mystery cults maintained.

Instead, Christianity (at least in its traditional teachings) claimed that God was born on Earth in human form, was thereafter executed, and then came back to life again in order to save the whole of humanity. All humans had to do was to believe this story and they would be 'saved'.

In Judaism, the idea that a human being, even a Jewish leader, was the actual incarnation of God on Earth was unthinkable. For mystics and philosophers brought up on the *symbolic* act of a god dying and then being brought back to life, the notion that God had walked on Earth in human form, and had been killed and then came back to life was naïve. Indeed, many so-called 'pagan' philosophers derided the lack of sophistication of Christian theology, complaining that Christians were taking literally what was clearly supposed to be an allegorical story. Indeed, this was broadly the view that many Gnostic Christians took; Gnostics (the word *gnosis* being Greek word for knowledge) were less interested in the historical person of Jesus Christ than in the spiritual truths his story encapsulated.

It is important at this point – and crucial to the later stories of hidden and secret traditions – to appreciate that there are in effect two different stories of Jesus Christ contained in the New Testament. Each vied with the other for paramount status. The first story is what might be called the Jewish tradition. According to this version of events, Jesus was a Messiah in the form of a political and/or religious leader, a man who would help free his people at a difficult time in their history from the oppression of the Roman imperialists and their political puppets in the region. This Jesus certainly had an exalted status as a saviour figure for the Jewish people, but in no literal sense was he Son of God, even if that expression was used in Judaic writings. According to his followers, Jesus was a great man, but still a man. He was born of a man and woman, lived and died a Jew and certainly had no intention of starting a new religion, let alone one that would bear his name. (Or, rather, his title – 'Christ' comes from the Greek translation of the original Hebrew word 'Messiah', or 'Mashiah', which literally means 'anointed one'.)

The second version is what is sometimes referred to as Pauline Christianity, its name coming from St Paul. In this version of Christianity, Jesus is far more than a great political or even religious leader. He is nothing less than the Saviour God, the divine-made flesh whose mission it is to save humanity by dying and then being re-born. This was a battle not for the rights of the Jewish people, but for the very soul of humanity, a spiritual battle that could only be won if each and every follower accepted the truth that this Saviour God died so that they might be re-born.

This Pauline view clearly had some similarities with the mysticism of the mystery rites in the ancient world, and also with the stories of the dying and resurrected gods so prevalent at that time. The key difference was that Pauline Christianity was built on an historical figure; a god, yes, but a god who occupied a quantifiable time and place here on Earth. (Curiously, Paul rarely discusses Jesus's human life in his writings, while the four gospels – Matthew, Mark, Luke and John – written later, do so.)

As history has shown, it is this Pauline version of Jesus and his mission that became the dominant version of Christianity. Indeed, for many practising Christians, the very idea that Jesus is not literally the Son of God and that he did not die on the cross to save humanity is little short of blasphemy. Even many people who do not consider themselves especially devout, but who have been brought up in a Christian society, might be surprised, to say the least, to hear of anything other than the dominant Pauline view. Surely it has become an accepted historical 'fact' in Christian society that Jesus founded a new religion based on his new beliefs and on his own divine status?

In recent decades of scholarship, biblical analysis and archaeology, freed from looking through the lens of Christianity (in other words, freed from the assumption that the accepted view of Jesus is true), have started to tell another story. From these more sober studies an alternative view of Jesus has started to emerge: that of the Jewish messiah. Entwined with this story are politics, rebellion and secretive sects. In this version of the story, Jesus is a player in the all-too historical, bloody world of the Roman occupation of Palestine, rather than appearing to exist in a parallel universe to it, as he does so often in the Pauline Christian tradition. This new understanding of the events surrounding the New Testament has come about partially as a result of the discovery of the Dead Sea Scrolls, vital documents found in caves east of Jerusalem over a number of years starting in 1947.

Our views about the historical nature of Jesus are not the only ideas to have changed as a result of the discovery of the Dead Sea Scrolls and other scholarship. Indeed, perceptions of other biblical characters have been altered as well. For example, Jesus's brother, James, who is largely peripheral in the gospels, now emerges as a central character who took on the mantle of leadership after the death of Jesus, before he too was killed whilst promoting their cause. John the Baptist, who makes a relatively fleeting and subservient appearance in the New Testament, emerges as an important personality whose relationship with Jesus was rather different from that assumed in Pauline Christianity. Meanwhile, and more controversially still, there have been claims that Mary Magdalene was no fringe figure to be pitied and forgiven for her sins. Instead, some argue, she was the Apostle of Apostles, and may even have been Jesus's partner. (This belief has long been maintained by some secret traditions of Christianity.)

It appears, then, that modern scholarship might be just catching up with some traditions that have existed on the fringes of Christianity from its inception, which have spawned secret societies, and which have led to much intrigue, controversy and persecution down the centuries. When the Roman emperor Constantine – the first emperor to become a Christian – convened the ecumenical council of the Christian Church in Nicaea (what is now Turkey) in AD 325, one of his aims was to establish once and for all the beliefs and dogma of the Church. To a large extent, it and subsequent councils did just this, helping to develop the Christianity that is accepted around the world today. However, stories and traditions dating from during and just after the lifetime of Jesus and his companions were not so easily dismissed. Over the centuries, these alternative and potentially explosive stories were to become entwined with local traditions and myths, kept alive by secretive groups and individuals. Just occasionally, as we shall see, these traditions sometimes emerged out of the shadows and into the history books in some curious ways.

# 2

# Merovingians, Cathars and the Knights Templar

I N 2003 AN AMERICAN WRITER by the name of Dan Brown published a
mystery detective novel that was to become a publishing sensation.
Since hitting the bookstands, *The Da Vinci Code* (Bantam, 2003) has
sold tens of millions of copies, and has led to the making of a popular
movie in 2006 starring actors Tom Hanks, Audrey Tatou and Jean Reno.
The publication of a novel does not often create a stir, but in this case both
the book and the film provoked considerable controversy. The reason was
that the author purported to tell a secret and explosive story that, if true,
would completely change the entire basis of Christianity. And though the
book was clearly written as a work of fiction, this fact has not stopped much
speculation about the 'secrets' it contains. The controversy was in part
fuelled by a note at the start of the novel which, under the heading 'Fact',
reads: 'All descriptions of artwork, architecture, documents and secret
rituals in this novel are accurate…'

As a result, and because there had already been a number of non-fiction
books on similar themes, a significant proportion of readers considered
*The Da Vinci Code* to be telling what is essentially a real story. The novel
relates a highly improbable tale that Jesus had a child by Mary Magdalene,
and that through this child a 'Jesus bloodline' was created. Equally
improbably, Jesus's descendants came to live in France, where they were
known to history as the Merovingian dynasty – an actual royal clan of
Frankish kings who ruled part of France for three centuries from the end
of the 5th century.

### The Merovingians and the Priory of Sion
The best known and most powerful of the Merovingian kings was Clovis I,

probably the first great name in French history. In 751 the last Merovingian king, Childeric III, was deposed in a palace coup, had his traditional Merovingian long hair cut off and was packed off to a monastery. However, according to the novel, the ousting of this dynasty was not the end of the story: the secret of the Jesus bloodline was protected by a secretive group known as the Priory of Sion, which wanted to restore the Merovingian/Jesus bloodline and bring about a more spiritual world.

It's a fascinating story, and if it were to be true, it would prove the existence of the most secretive and certainly one of the most powerful secret societies imaginable. But could any of it be real? The simple answer is no. The Merovingians have been plucked out of historical obscurity, and while this may encourage some people to study what is a fascinating piece of history, there is, sadly, not a single piece of credible evidence that links them in any way to Jesus or Mary Magdalene. The Priory of Sion, exotic and mysterious as it sounds, appears to be either someone's idea of a practical joke or hoax, or, as is common with secret societies, it is simply a modern group claiming antique ancestry in order to enhance its reputation in the eyes of recruits. For as far as one can tell, the Priory of Sion was established not in the 5th century BC, but rather in the 1950s.

Furthermore, no convincing evidence has come to light to show that this mysterious priory – whose Grand Masters were supposed to have included Leonardo da Vinci and, even more improbably, Sir Isaac Newton – existed before modern times and had any role in history. On the face of it, the whole story seems an ingenious, entertaining, but wholly fictional plot – a plot that is worthy, in fact, of an entertaining mystery novel.

However, there are elements of this fictional story that merit further inspection from an historical point of view. For it seems that quite independent of the modern fascination with 'arcane' knowledge relating to Jesus and his supposed family, there are ancient stories that hint that the family of Jesus was more important than conventional Christianity allows. Some even imply he may have had a partner or even a wife. Some of this thinking has emerged from a re-evaluation of Jesus' brother, James. As we have seen, though a marginal figure in the gospels, James appears to have taken over as the leader of Jesus's organization after his execution. Most interesting of all is the idea that it was various secretive groups that preserved such arcane knowledge.

In a meticulous piece of biblical detective work, the historian James D. Tabor has pieced together the story of Jesus's extended family. The title of his book, *Jesus Dynasty: The Hidden History of Jesus, His Royal Family, and the Birth of Christianity* (Harper Element, 2007) is a clue to the nature of his discovery. Tabor claims that it is likely that Mary, the mother of Jesus, had been due to wed Joseph in an arranged marriage, but had become pregnant by another man before the ceremony, and that she went on to have six other children – four boys and two girls. (The father of these children was either Joseph or Joseph's brother, Clophas, after Joseph's death.) The historian cites the claim attributed to the 2nd century Greek philosopher, Celsus, that the true father of Jesus was not God or Joseph, but a Roman soldier by the name of Panthera. (Panthera or Pantera did exist as a surname at the time in the ancient world, including among Roman soldiers.) Other historians have pointed out that in Germany there was a gravestone of a Roman soldier called Tiberius Julius Abdes Pantera, who died in the middle of the 1st century, and who had probably been in Palestine at about the time that Jesus would have been conceived. (None of this, of course, means that this extraordinary theory is true.)

Tabor also claims that Jesus saw his relative, John the Baptist, not as a *harbinger* of the Messiah (i.e. himself), but rather as a prophet and teacher in his own right – the person who would bring about the Kingdom of God on Earth as was foretold in the Old Testament. John and Jesus – the former descended from the priestly line through Aaron, the latter through the kingly line of David – worked together and came to represent the idea that two Messiahs would come to save the Jewish people. For them, the Kingdom of God was imminent on Earth, and they had come to proclaim it. This was not, Tabor argues, the start of a new religion, but rather the fulfilment of Jewish law, or the Torah.

The preaching of John and Jesus aroused suspicion among both other Jewish groups and the authorities, and John was brutally murdered – legend claims his head was put on a platter at the wish of Salome, daughter of Herodias, the wife of Herod Antipas. After Jesus was executed, it was his brother, James, who took over the 'Messianic Movement', which was still firmly fixed within Jewish tradition. As Tabor writes, 'James and his successors represent an original version of Christianity, linked more directly to the historical Jesus, that has every claim of authenticity.' The author also makes it clear that the Pauline Christianity that became the accepted version of the Jesus story developed independently of James and his followers. 'The message that Paul began to preach in the '40s and '50s

AD...was in no way dependent on, nor derived from, the original group of Jesus's apostles led by James. It was based upon his own visionary experiences of a heavenly Christ.'

This story places greater emphasis on John the Baptist than we see in the Bible and, as we shall see, the tradition that John the Baptist was a far more important figure than conventional Christianity suggests may have lingered on through various groups, including the Knights Templar.

## An Alternative View

The Dead Sea Scrolls have helped give us a very different picture of Jesus's life, or more particularly, the background events that would have informed his life and those of his associates and followers. They suggest, for example, that the Jewish sect called the Essenes – who were apparently based at Qumran (at the northwestern edge of the Dead Sea in Jordan), where the parchments were found – were a group whose ideas seem to have had some influence on John the Baptist, Jesus and James. The once accepted notion that the Essenes were a small isolated sect who lived in the desert and had little or no say in the events of society is being replaced by a very different picture: that their membership was widely spread, including in Jerusalem. In particular, it seems that they were strong proponents of the belief that the messiah was about to come and the world was about to end.

In their book, *The Dead Sea Scrolls Deception* (Simon & Schuster, 1991), an account of how the important information contained in those documents took many years to emerge from the clutches of a small group of researchers, authors Michael Baigent and Richard Leigh claim that this new information is vital to the story of Christianity. They write: '...Christianity did not arise from a single unique event in the history of the world...[o]n the contrary, it emerged from a religious movement that already existed – a movement that produced the texts we know as the Dead Sea Scrolls.'

It is clear, then, that scholarship is beginning to show a very different interpretation of the Jesus story. The more the historical Jesus is subjected to scrutiny, the more one finds traces of a real man; a man with a mission, certainly, but a flesh and blood man who was very much a part of the society in which he lived and died. We already know that when Jesus emerges as an adult in the New Testament to begin his ministry, he is said to be aged 30 – coincidentally the age at which the Essenes believed a man reached maturity and was allowed to join the highest ranks of their group.

Furthermore, it would have been considered unusual for most men at this time not to be married at this age. But if Jesus had been married or had a partner, why did we not hear of her?

## Mary Magdalene

The answer is that we may indeed have heard of her. Mary Magdalene's appearances in the New Testament are few, but they are important ones. It is Mary Magdalene who, according to the Gospel of John, first discovers the empty tomb after Jesus's body had been put there following his execution. Then, as she is weeping outside the tomb, she is approached by a man whom she takes to be the gardener and asks him if he has taken the body away. However, when he uses her name she realizes that it is Jesus himself. Given that the central core of Christianity is that Jesus rose from the dead to save humanity, the fact that it was Mary Magdalene who first saw the resurrected god is highly significant. The Gospel of Mark is quite explicit that it was Mary and no one else – not Peter or one of the other disciples – who saw Jesus first. In another New Testament episode Mark 14:9, when an unnamed sinner – who we assume to be Mary – angers the disciples because of her actions in 'wasting' expensive perfume, Jesus does not just defend her – he heaps the highest praise on her:

> I tell you the truth, wherever the gospel is preached throughout the world, what she has done will also be told, in memory of her.

Yet despite this passage, Mary has had through the centuries what might be described as bad press. She was, and is, usually identified as the unnamed 'sinner', and also the same person as the woman called Mary of Bethany. It is this unnamed sinner who anoints Jesus with expensive perfume and who even wipes his feet with her hair. The tradition grew that Mary Magdalene was in fact a prostitute who had repented for her sins and had been forgiven. This image of a 'fallen' woman who had received forgiveness has been a powerful one in the Church – even though at no point is she referred to in the gospels as a prostitute. In fact, it was only in 1969 that the Catholic Church officially removed her status as a 'penitent'; that is, as a sinner undergoing penitence for her sins.

The importance of Mary Magdalene and the fact that she was said to have been the first person to see Jesus after he rose from the dead have prompted some to ponder whether the relationship between them was simply that of master and follower. After all, for Mary to be there on her own at Jesus's tomb suggests the behaviour of a wife. Even more tantalizing is the discovery of what is known as the Gospel of Philip, a work that was probably written some time in the 3rd century. It was discovered in the 20th century, one of the Gnostic texts found at Nag Hammadi in Egypt. According to this work, much of which deals with the sanctity of marriage, some of the disciples were unhappy about the closeness of the bond between their master and Mary. The Gospel describes Mary as Jesus's 'companion', and states that he loved her more than the other disciples. It also makes reference to Jesus kissing her frequently. The Gospel recorded the reaction of the disciples:

> They said to him, 'Why do you love her more than all of us?' The Saviour answered and said to them, 'Why do I not love you like her? When a blind man and one who sees are both together in darkness, they are no different from one another. When the light comes, then he who sees will see the light, and he who is blind will remain in darkness.'

In another gospel found at Nag Hammadi, the Gospel of Thomas, there is a further reference to Mary. Here, Peter is quoted as saying to Jesus:

> 'Make Mary leave us, for women do not deserve life.'

Even if one accepts all these words at face value, none of them prove conclusively that Jesus and Mary were partners. However, they do point to such a relationship. And were such a relationship accepted as fact, it of course would profoundly affect the way that we view Jesus and Christianity. At the very least, it would certainly make Jesus appear far more human and, perhaps at the same time, less divine.

One fascinating (though it has to be said un-provable) theory is that Mary was a devotee and possibly a priestess of one of the many different religions flourishing in the Middle East at the time. In her book, *Mary Magdalene, Christianity's Hidden Goddess* (Caroll & Graf Publishers, 2003), author Lynn Picknett points to the significance of the anointing of Jesus by the (unnamed) Mary with the expensive oil. She speculates about whether the anointing here was part of sexual/spiritual rituals practised in some cults of that time. She writes that '...there are strong suggestions ... that she was not his legal wife but rather his lover or even sexual intiatrix into the ancient pagan rite of the *hieros gamos* or sacred marriage.' Picknett also points to the fact that in one version of the story of the anointment, the woman (Mary) is described as wiping Jesus's feet with her own hair; yet it was apparently forbidden for Jewish women to show off their hair in this manner outside marriage. This could suggest that either Jesus and Mary were married, or that something else was going on; as Picknett says, some form of mystery ritual. Or, she speculates, perhaps Mary Magdalene came from Egypt or Ethiopia. In any case, it matters less whether Mary and Jesus did have a 'relationship' or not than whether some in the ancient world *believed* that they had. If there were some who did believe this potentially explosive story, then such information had to be preserved, especially given that the Christian orthodoxy frowned upon such 'blasphemous' stories.

If Mary Magdalene was as important a biblical character as has been suggested, then her fate after Jesus's death is clearly also of crucial importance. Her role in the early development of the Church would thus have been an important one. But where did she go?

The Orthodox Church has a tradition that Mary Magdalene travelled to Ephesus (in modern Turkey), an important city in the ancient world. In the ancient world, Ephesus was best known for its magnificent Temple of Artemis, which was once one of the seven wonders of the world. (It was later destroyed and, sadly, very little of it remains today.) The Orthodox Church also believed that the Virgin Mary went to Ephesus; visitors to the area today can still see a home known as the House of the Virgin Mary, which is popularly believed to be her last resting place. Ephesus was also a place very familiar to St Paul, who had lived there for a time. It is hard to resist linking the stories of the two Marys going to Ephesus with the fact that it was known throughout Asia Minor as one of the chief places of worship of the mother goddess Artemis.

Perhaps the most fascinating tradition surrounding Mary Magdalene is that she left the Holy Land and travelled to southern France, where she continued to spread the message of Jesus. There is, of course, no hard proof of this theory, and at first glance it may seem almost as fanciful as the Merovingian story. But in parts of the south of France there are remnants of a persistent local tradition that Mary Magdalene made her way there after the death of Jesus. The story is that Mary, her brother Lazarus and a group of other disciples made their way by boat across the north Mediterranean and landed at a place now called Saintes-Maries-de-la-Mer in the Camargue, west of Marseille. Saintes-Maries-de-la-Mer translates in English to 'Saint Mary's of the Sea', and refers to the three Marys: Mary Magdalene, Mary Salome and Mary Jacobe, who saw the empty tomb of Jesus. (At one time the place was apparently called Notre-Dame-de-Ratis, or 'Our Lady of the Boat'.)

Though such a journey may seem hazardous for that period, in fact it would have been a relatively routine trip. Greeks from Phocea had founded a settlement at Marseille (they called it Massalia) in around 600 BC, and there were well-established trade routes to and from the area at the time, along which Mary would have travelled. This was an era in which the Roman Empire had imposed law and order throughout much of the Mediterranean Sea (the Romans called it 'Our Sea'), and for the most part maritime trade flourished.

The legend in France is that Mary travelled to Marseille where she started preaching, eventually converting the whole of the area to Christianity. Curiously, she is said to have preached on the site of a temple dedicated to the goddess Diana (also known as Artemis). She is said to have then practised the life of a hermit, living in a cave near La Sainte-Baume (a place in what is now Provence). After her death, Mary's body was laid to rest in an oratory at Villa Lata, which became known as St Maximin after the man who had it built. Her relics came to be a major focus of devotion, and what is claimed to be her skull still attracts pilgrims and visitors to the church at Saint-Baume.

## The Black Madonnas

While researching their book, *The Templar Revelation: Secret Guardians of the True Identity of Christ* (Transworld Publishers, 1997), authors Lynn Picknett and Clive Prince travelled widely in the south of France, and examined this legend of Mary Magdalene and her local connections in some detail. They point to the widespread number of sites that are devoted to Mary Magdalene across the southern half of the country. They also point to a possible link between the worship of Mary Magdalene and the presence of sites devoted to the phenomenon of Black Madonnas.

A Black Madonna is, as its name suggests, a depiction of the Madonna or Virgin Mary as black-skinned. These statues are surprisingly common in Europe – perhaps as many as 500 dating from the Middle Ages exist (there are thought to be about 180 in France alone). These Black Madonnas are in a different category from those in Africa and some parts of the United States, where the Virgin Mary is also sometimes shown as black. The presence of Black Madonnas at European sites, however, has long puzzled experts. The colouring of some of these statues, typically made from wood, may be explained away by the materials used, or through darkening as a result of pollution. But many were undoubtedly intended to be black, even though European society at the time was overwhelmingly white and certainly most biblical characters were depicted as such. One school of thought holds that such images have their roots in pre-Christian times, perhaps influenced by the worship of ancient goddesses such as Diana, Cybele and Isis. This theory is further strengthened by the strong tradition of past pagan worship in many of the sites where Black Madonnas are found.

A study by author Ean Begg in his book, *The Cult of the Black Virgin* (Penguin, 1997), shows that there does appear to be some correlation between the Black Madonnas and Mary Magdalene; indeed, the two are found together in around 50 different sites. It is also interesting to note that in the town of Saintes-Maries-de-la-Mer, where Mary Magdalene supposedly arrived in France, there is still an annual festival that attracts Roma people, or Gypsies, in honour of Saint Sarah, or 'Sarah the black'. (Sarah is held to have been the black Egyptian maid who attended the three Marys, and who arrived in ancient Gaul with them.) Prince and Picknett, meanwhile, claim that the link between the Black Madonnas and the cult of Mary Magdalene is 'undeniable', and further suggest a link between both Marys and the worship of the goddess Isis.

The authors also draw attention to the Song of Songs, the love verse that sits rather oddly in the Old Testament. The verse, which is also known as the Song of Solomon, contains a line from the Beloved as she talks to her 'Lover': 'Dark am I, yet lovely', a clear reference to the colour of her skin. Some have claimed this verse refers to Solomon's wife, the daughter of the Egyptian pharaoh; others claim that it refers to the Queen of Sheba, who came to visit Solomon and who may have been from Ethiopia. However, there is also an early Christian tradition that links the verse with Mary Magdalene, possibly because of the erotic nature of the words and the reputation that had been ascribed to Mary. Of course, these words were written well before Mary's time, so they cannot actually be referring to her. But the fact that some early Christians linked her name with the Song of Songs and its black heroine bears comparison with the way in which her cult is linked to the Black Madonnas in France.

**Heretics and Blasphemy**

The tradition that Mary Magdalene went to France to preach the word of Jesus would not have been heretical to the early Christian Church. But while Mary Magdalene is praised by Jesus in the gospels, and was the first to see him resurrected, the idea that Mary had any kind of physical relationship with him is another matter. That would have been – and was – regarded as a blasphemy of the worst order. Anyone holding such a belief would have had to keep that belief secret or face a severe reprimand from the Church. Indeed, it would have made no difference whether there really ever *was* such a relationship. What would have mattered is whether people believed such a heresy, and the impact that this belief would have had on society and history. Historical evidence points to the fact that one, possibly two, secretive groups did indeed believe that Mary and Jesus were partners. One of them was to pay a heavy price for such heresy.

Nowadays the old and remote Cathar countries of southern France are a tourist attraction. The regions of both Languedoc-Roussillon and neighbouring Midi-Pyrénées try to entice visitors by publicizing the Cathars and their castles, many of which are surrounded by breathtaking scenery. Visitors are told about some of the events that led to the end of Catharism in the south of France, including the ultimate fall of one of their last bastions at Montségur. The result is that the story of the Cathars and how they met their end cannot help but sound a little romantic, occurring as it did so long ago and in such beautiful countryside.

The truth, however, is rather bloodier. The Crusade that tried to wipe out the Cathars was one of the more brutal and appalling episodes in Europe's admittedly long and brutal history. (Some scholars have even spoken of it as the first genocide in modern history.) The reason why the state and Church authorities were determined to obliterate the Cathars was that this secretive movement held 'Christian' beliefs that differed from those of traditional Catholicism – including the belief that Mary Magdalene was the wife of Jesus.

**The Cathars**

So who were the Cathars and where did they come from? This is actually a complex question. The first point to note is that the Cathars are not a separate race of people, but simply a group of people who came together because they shared similar beliefs, and who, as a result, formed communities based on those beliefs. The second point is that the Cathars were not just based in the south of France. There were people with Cathar-style beliefs in other parts of France, notably in the north and the centre, as well as in Germany (around Cologne) and Italy.

The name 'Cathar' seems to have been applied to these people rather than chosen by them. The word 'cathar' comes from the Greek word for 'pure', and refers to the kind of life that they endeavoured to live. Another name for them was 'Albigensians', after the French town of Albi, which was one of their strongholds. The Cathars seemed to have simply referred to themselves as *Bons Hommes* and *Bonnes Femmes* ('good men' and 'good women'), or *Bons Chrétiens* ('good Christians'). This last name is important, because it shows that they considered themselves true Christians who were being faithful to the truth of Jesus Christ as they saw it. It was the traditional Church that had corrupted the faith.

Exactly when, how and why Cathar beliefs started to develop in Europe is still unclear, yet there had always been traditions of religious disputes and dissenters within Christianity. Indeed, when the newly Christian Roman emperor Constantine called the ecumenical council in AD 325, one of its principle aims was to settle the doctrine in the Church in the face of the claims of Arianism, a doctrine that held that Jesus was not equal in status to God the Father.

By the 11th century, a new wave of dissent was growing in various parts of Christian Europe. Some of this was simply a concerted form of anti-clericalism, the familiar charge that the Church and its clergy had hijacked the faith and become corrupt as a result. However, some groups seemed to go further and rejected the hitherto accepted teachings of the Church, while substituting some of their own. For example, in AD 1025 a 'heresy' was uncovered at a castle at Monteforte near Asti, in Italy, which involved a community of 30 or more, many of them from the nobility. This group preached asceticism and rejected the corrupt pleasures of the faith – apparently believing or hoping that one day humans could, 'like bees', reproduce without the sexual act. Far more dangerous (for them) was their belief that Jesus Christ was the soul of man, *beloved* of God. This belief flatly rejected the accepted Christian doctrine that Jesus Christ *was* God – and part of the Holy Trinity. The Bishop of Milan quickly rounded this group up, and they were soon burnt on pyres, having refused a last chance to embrace the cross. A common theme of such heretics was that they rejected the image of the cross, which many dissenters saw as a symbol of pain. Curiously, this strange group of people were said to have come from 'some unknown part of the world'.

By the middle of the 12th century a rather larger group of 'heretics' had sprung up in Cologne, Germany; one of the first groups we can start to identify as Cathar in nature. These believers refused to eat any food that came as a result of sexual intercourse (for example, meat or milk, though curiously fish was allowed because people then believed that fish reproduced asexually), and even marriage was regarded as fornication. The group had three grades or levels of membership, and their ranks included women, too. Though they rejected the hierarchy of the Church, they also seem to have had their own bishop.

Again, as with the Italian group, the 'heresy' of this group appears to have had foreign roots. The members claimed that theirs was a faith that had existed for many years, and came from Byzantium – the home of the Orthodox Church that had been going its separate way from the Roman Catholic Church since the fall of the Roman Empire in the West in the 5th century. They, too, met a fiery death. Clearly, groups of people, whether working in an organized way or not, were safeguarding beliefs and traditions dating from many years before – and these beliefs and traditions were regarded as a threat to society.

By the mid to late 12th century, Cathar beliefs had taken a particular hold in the southern half of France, as far west as Agen and stretching right across a swathe of the country to and beyond Carcassonne. It is important to keep in mind the historical context of the development of Cathar ideas. This was the age of the Crusaders. In 1099 the First Crusade captured Jerusalem, and the 12th and early 13th centuries saw the mounting of more expeditions, initially after the fall of Edessa in 1144, and then following the fall of Jerusalem in 1187 to Saladin's army. This meant that many Crusaders from France and other western nations were exposed not just to a bewildering mix of cultures and beliefs in and around the Holy Land, but also to those of Constantinople (now Istanbul), the capital of the Byzantine world. In his magisterial work, *The Hidden Tradition in Europe: The Secret History of Medieval Christian Heresy* (Penguin, 1995), Yuri Stoyanov describes the explicit link that the Roman Catholic Church made at the time between the growth of heresy in southern France and the influence of foreign heresies on the returning crusaders. According to Anselm of

Alessandria, these knights had been '…led astray by Bulgars … throughout France these persons are called Bulgarian heretics.'

The use of the word 'Bulgars' here is a reference to the Bogomils. The Bogomil heresy is often seen as the forerunner to Catharism. Bogomilism appears to have developed some time in the 10th century, arising at a time and place in the Balkans of intense rivalry between the Byzantine and Bulgarian empires. The Bogomils were dualists, meaning that they believed that the world was involved in a constant tension between good and evil, a world in which the devil was a fallen angel who had actually created the material world – and man. The devil is depicted as God's eldest son, who rebelled and thus fell, leaving Christ to be raised up to the status of the eldest.

The origins of this heresy remain unclear. Some believe it to have Iranian roots; others believe it to have been influenced by Manichaeism. Manichaeism, once an important and widespread religion, originated with a man named Mani, who was born in Mesopotamia and raised as a Christian. In his youth, Mani apparently had a vision that compelled him to begin his missionary teaching. He saw himself as creating a kind of successor faith to Christianity, Buddhism and Zoroastrianism. Doubtless partly as a result of its success in attracting followers, Manichaeism was often vigorously suppressed. Its followers were, for example, persecuted within the Roman Empire both before and after Christianity took hold in Rome. (Mani himself also fell out badly with the Magi of Persia.) A strongly dualistic faith, Manichaeism's central idea was that the Father of Greatness, or God, was in conflict with the 'Prince of Darkness'. Its believers further held that the soul was trapped inside the material (i.e. dark) world, and that the 'Father of Greatness' was required to send a saviour to awaken those who were trapped.

Another intriguing theory is that Bogomilism was influenced by Mithraism (*see page 35*). If so, this would suggest a fascinating and direct link between the old secret 'pagan' world in which early Christianity developed and the relatively modern world of medieval Europe. It would show how arcane knowledge and secret doctrines can be passed on down through the generations, away from the full glare of the rest of the world in a kind of parallel history. We cannot, however, be truly sure about the origins of Bogomilism. Nor can we sure about the background of the priest, Bogomil, the 10th-century cleric from Bulgaria who is credited as the founder of the heresy. The name of the movement may have come from the priest's name, or he may have been given the name after the growth of the faith. There was even a curious tradition in Eastern Europe that stated that Bogomil and his followers were later incarnations of the Egyptian magicians who had opposed Moses as he led his people out of exile.

One thing does seem clear however: the importance of Bogomilism upon the development of the Cathar heresy in Western Europe. Bogomilism appears to have been a kind of conduit for ideas and beliefs that connected not just the ancient and modern worlds, and it also acted as a kind of ideological link between East and West. In the end, its existence can be said to have been one of the causes of a bloody showdown between conventional Christianity and the Cathars.

## Persecution and Turbulence

The southern half of France, especially Languedoc-Roussillon, was probably already fertile territory for Cathar beliefs to flourish. Manichaeism is said to have been popular in southern France by the 4th century, and the Catholic Church in France was still uncovering Manichean-style heresies in as late as the 11th century. Some have also suggested that Languedoc was particularly open to new ideas or 'heresies' because it had a strong local culture, and it was a region where learning and ideas were particularly highly valued. 'In contrast to the prevalent climate in Western Europe, Languedoc society was markedly more tolerant and cosmopolitan and had also attainted a high degree of prosperity,' writes Yuri Stoyanov. Whatever the reason, by the middle to late 12th century, Catharism had taken a strong hold in much of the region, crucially among many of its noble families.

Catharism seems to have had a particularly strong following among women in the nobility. This may be because the asceticism of Catharism and its championing of the spiritual over physical gratification chimed with the ideas of chaste, courtly love that were popular at the time, and were expressed in the songs of the travelling minstrels known as the troubadours. For example, Philippa, the wife of the Count of Foix Eaymond-Roger de Foix, became a Cathar, as did the count's sister. Catharism was thus nurtured and protected by the region's elites.

The Catholic Church eventually began to look at the proliferation of Catharism in the Languedoc with growing alarm. Its heretical views about Jesus Christ, its ascetic way of life and its bitter opposition to the Church hierarchy made Catharism a real threat to Rome's authority. As early as the middle of the 12th century, the theologian St Bernard of Clairvaux had gone on a mission to Toulouse in an effort to shake the region from the grip of heresy. His visit met with little success, though similar peaceful attempts at ending Catharism were supported by subsequent popes. The start of the 13th century was, however, a turbulent time in Christianity. Saladin had retaken Jerusalem in 1187, and the disastrous Fourth Crusade had not only failed to win it back – it had 'succeeded' in sacking Constantinople, the capital of the Byzantine Empire, and thus its supposed Christian allies. Now Pope Innocent III turned his attention nearer to home, and to a heresy that existed within Christian Europe itself.

The Pope had sent his legate, Pierre of Castelnau, to meet with Raymond VI, Count of Toulouse, the political ruler of the area, and a cultured man who was suspected of protecting the Cathars. Negotiations did not go well, however, and Raymond was excommunicated for aiding and abetting heresy. On 15 January 1208, Pierre was murdered as he returned to Rome, and the papacy naturally assumed that Raymond was behind the killing. Innocent III ordered a crusade against the area – an extraordinary occurrence when one considers that this land was part of Christendom.

The first target of the crusade was the town of Béziers (a place best known today for its rugby team and bullfighting), a centre of Cathar belief and toleration at that time, though there may only have been a couple of hundred practising Cathars among the population of 15,000 to 20,000. A Cistercian abbot by the name of Arnaud Amaury led the crusade, and was a merciless commander even by the standards of the times. Alongside the abbot were many noblemen from the north of France, who had apparently been promised land in the south upon its confiscation from the Cathar-supporting nobility. Notably, the Knights Templar and the Hospitallers played little or no active role in the crusade despite the fact that these groups had a strong tradition as crusaders. This fact was hardly surprising, however, as both groups were strongly represented in the south, and Raymond himself was patron of the Order of Hospitallers. Arnaud Amaury was undeterred, however, and his men advanced on Béziers in July 1209.

The town was soon entered and quickly taken by the abbot's men amid scenes of extraordinary slaughter. The lack of mercy displayed by the Abbot of Cîteaux is illustrated by the infamous words he is said to have uttered when asked by a fellow soldier how the crusaders were supposed to tell heretic Cathar from pious Catholic, who of course made up the majority of the population. 'Kill them all – the Lord will know his own,' came the chilling reply.

Arnaud Amaury was as good as his word. Men, women and children were dragged out of church, blinded, mutilated and killed. Others were used for target practice or dragged behind horses. It must have been a horrific scene. At the end of the attack, the abbot was able to write to the Pope: 'Your Holiness, today twenty thousand heretics were put to the sword, regardless of rank, age, or sex.' While this figure may have been an exaggeration, there's little doubt that many thousands died a horrible death, including many non-Cathar inhabitants of the town.

The degree of support shown by many ordinary Catholics for their Cathar neighbours was striking. According to reports, the Catholic townsfolk were given a chance to hand over the Cathars, or at least to leave the town themselves in order to escape the slaughter that was promised later. Perhaps the inhabitants simply refused to believe that a Catholic army would unleash the full horrors of the crusade on fellow Catholics, and thought they were safe within the city. The alternative theory is, of course, that the Catholic population sympathized so with the plight of their Cathar friends and neighbours that they were prepared to die alongside them.

There are two important details about the slaughter that give us a clue as to why such ferocity was aimed at the inhabitants of Béziers. Firstly, the church from which hundreds (if not thousands) of townsfolk were dragged to their death was called the Church of Mary Magdalene. More significant, however, is the date on which this attack was launched – 22 July, the feast day of Mary Magdalene in the Catholic Church. It seems unlikely that these factors were a mere coincidence. Furthermore, Mary Magdalene was significant to the Church because the Cathars held a belief about her that was totally anathema to conventional Catholics: that she was Jesus's wife. As we have seen, this was an idea that was expressed, or at least strongly hinted at, in early so-called Gnostic Christianity. And yet somehow it had now surfaced in a heresy in the south of France, and indeed was supposedly part of the Cathars' secret teachings, only imparted during secret meetings.

Exactly where the Cathars' belief that Mary was Jesus's wife derived from is unclear. This does not appear to have been from any Bogomil influence, even if other aspects of Cathar belief may have been influenced by the Balkan heresy. As Yuri Stoyanov states: 'The teaching of Mary Magdalene as the "wife" or "concubine" of Christ appears...as original Cathar tradition which does not have any counterpart in Bogomil doctrines.' If the belief came from the existence of this story in the Gnostic

Gospel of Philip, then it must have been from another copy of the work, as this text was only discovered in its Egyptian hiding place in the middle of the 20th century. An alternative possibility is that the belief was based on another work that was known in the 12th century but has since been lost.

In any case, we know that this belief mattered a great deal to the Cathars, just as it did (for entirely different reasons) to the Pope's crusaders. Writing a few years after the slaughter at Béziers, a Cistercian monk called Pierre des Vaux-de-Cernay was characteristically scathing about the Cathars' beliefs and the importance of the date of the attack at Béziers. 'Béziers was taken on St Mary Magdalene's Day. Oh supreme justice of Providence!' wrote the young monk. 'The heretics claimed that St Mary Magdalene was the concubine of Jesus Christ,' he said, adding that it was therefore only just that these 'disgusting dogs' be 'massacred' on the feast day of the saint they had insulted.

The tragedy of Béziers marked the beginning of a 20-year crusade against the Cathars in the region. It is often known as the Albigensian Crusade, after the alternative name given to the Cathars. Many thousands were to die in the fighting over that period. For a while the crusade was led by the ruthless Simon de Montfort, who had little hesitation in burning the heretics, or *perfecti*, as they were often called. (They were also known as 'parfait', meaning 'perfect' in French; this was a term given to the Cathar elite, whom the Catholics regarded as perfect or complete heretics.) Perhaps the most notorious single act in a campaign punctuated by violence was the punishment that de Montfort meted out to a widow called Lady Geralda from Lavaur castle. She was thrown into a well, whereupon large stones were thrown down upon her. The crusades did not meet with total success, however, and the Cathars and their nobles staged a number of revivals over the periods. De Montfort himself was killed in battle, hit on the head by a stone as he and his men besieged Toulouse.

By the time the crusade was formally ended in 1229, the Cathars had been dealt a severe blow, with many of their elite being led to the flames. However, they had not yet been wiped out. That task was now given over to the other medieval Catholic Church enforcement agency: the Inquisition. Those carrying out the Inquisition were given wide-ranging powers to hunt down and eradicate heresy in the region, a task which they began with considerable resources at their disposal. They faced a fierce backlash, however, and the progress slowed. In 1242, members of the

Montségur killed two members of the Inquisition, an act that was bound to provoke a bloody reaction.

The siege of the seemingly impregnable Cathar castle at Montségur began in 1243 and lasted for nine months. By March 1244, the situation of the remaining Cathars inside the castle was hopeless and surrender terms were finally agreed. The 200 or so Cathar *perfecti* in the castle – which included bishops – were given the option to recant their heretical beliefs or face a fiery death. They chose death and, according to legend, were burnt on a pyre at the bottom of the mountain (though in fact the bonfire may have been in a nearby town). Some accounts speak of Cathars running down from the castle and jumping into the flames. It is a curious feature of the story that, according to some reports, the Cathars often embraced their grisly ends with something approaching eagerness.

According to some sources, not everyone died in the siege. It is believed that three to four Cathars escaped from the fortress at some point, and are supposed to have taken away some Cathar 'treasures' with them, though we do not know what these treasures were. Most likely they were writings sacred to the Cathars, but if so they remain lost to us. Inevitably the story has led to much speculation about the nature of the Cathar treasure that was secreted away, with one tradition even claiming that it was the Holy Grail itself. Just possibly, the writings (if that is what these treasures were) contained some clue as to the origins of the Cathar beliefs, including their beliefs surrounding the relationship between Jesus and Mary Magdalene. The Inquisition, meanwhile, had made sure that few other Cathar writings survived, and to this day very little of their work has been found; a gap in our knowledge that only adds to the mystery that surrounds this lost group.

The end of the siege at Montségur has long loomed large in occult and mystical circles. The mystery of the Cathar treasures in particular continues to excite massive interest. However, the siege marked the effective end of Catharism in the region. Over the next few years, the Inquisition continued its work against anyone daring to espouse the Cathar beliefs, and the occasional uncovering and punishment of Cathar heretics continued for the rest of the century. Nonetheless, the Cathars were now a spent force in Languedoc, and survivors from the area fled to safer havens such as in Lombardy.

The rise and fall of this secretive sect has undoubtedly influenced history; albeit unknowingly and unintentionally, it helped change both

France and the Catholic Church. For the French state, the result of the campaign brought the Languedoc region under its control, while for the Church the campaign helped precipitate the establishment of the Dominican Order, the branch established to confront heresy. Furthermore, the success of the crusade against the Cathars illustrated the effectiveness of an institution such as the Inquisition in hunting down and rooting out those whom the Church saw as heretics. The modest devotees of Catharism had therefore left a considerable mark on history, even if it was not the one they had intended to leave.

## The Knights Templar

The Cathars may have been vanquished, but another group from that time with similar claims to secret knowledge not only survived – they flourished. Few groups in history have excited the imagination, and attracted as much speculation, as the Knights Templar. Countless books and theories have been devoted to them, their beliefs and their eventual fate. To some they were simply a group of soldiers whose purpose in life dwindled once the crusades had failed to retake the Holy Land. Others claim that they were an ancient, occult body that was – and, some claim, still is – the guardian of sacred knowledge. Few doubt, however, the impact that this remarkable organization had on history.

The Knights Templar (or the Templars) were created in 1118 in Jerusalem by French knight and veteran crusader Hugues de Payens. They were established for a specific reason: to protect the many pilgrims who were travelling from Europe and elsewhere to visit the Holy Land and, ultimately, Jerusalem. This was something of a golden age for medieval Christianity; Jerusalem had been seized in 1099, and now many Christians were eager to visit the place where Jesus Christ had died and risen again. Unfortunately, many of these pilgrims never made it to the city thanks to the bandits and outlaws on the roads heading from the coast. Thus, nine European knights, led by de Payens, volunteered their services to protect these pilgrims. In effect, they were a bit like a firm of security guards (they operated in much the same way as, for example, private security firms have been doing in Iraq to protect Western civilians).

Baldwin, the king of Jerusalem at the time, allowed the knights to base their headquarters on the Temple Mount, the site of the captured Al-Aqsa Mosque. This was also the site where King Solomon's great Temple had supposedly stood, which is why the knights called themselves the Poor Knights of Christ and the Temple of Solomon, often shortened to Templars. Ironically, given the order's later wealth, these original Knights apparently had little money and few possessions, although some of them were well connected through their families. They thus lived off donations from grateful pilgrims.

Though the original Templars appeared to be a small-scale and humble organization, it was not without influence. The nephew of one of the Knights was a Cistercian abbot by the name of Bernard of Clairvaux, an intelligent and ambitious man who, for reasons that are not entirely clear, apparently took it upon himself to promote this new order of knights. Baldwin, too, had seen the advantages of such a group of men, whose story could easily capture the imagination of people – and valuable potential allies – back in Europe. But it was St Bernard who seems to have acted rather like a one-man PR agency for the Knights, writing a set of rules for them, writing letters extolling their virtues and intervening directly with the Pope. Hugues de Payens himself also travelled to Europe to build support for the organization, and was warmly received by Pope Honorius. Their efforts were rewarded in 1128 when the Church officially recognized the Order. Just over a decade later the Order was officially exempted from all taxes and given freedom of movement within Christendom; from then on they were answerable only to the Pope.

Though the Templars owned little in their own right, there was nothing to stop them holding money and owning land collectively as an organization. It was not unusual for wealthy individuals to entrust large sums to the Templars for safekeeping; for example, while off on crusade to the Holy Land. In time, the Templars operated like a banking organization, helping pilgrims and others transfer their money. Soon the Templars owned land and buildings both in the Holy Land and across parts of Europe. At one point towards the end of the 12th century they even briefly owned the ancient and strategically vital island of Cyprus in its entirety.

Meanwhile, back in the Holy Land, the Templars had become the guardians of various holy sites, and had also begun to fight in battles alongside other crusaders. Volunteers were keen to join this glamorous organization (it had become celebrated throughout the Christian world), and their numbers swelled. As soldiers the Knights were renowned for their bravery and refusal to give in to defeat. One of their most celebrated victories was at the Battle of

Montgisard in 1177, when a small number of Knights helped their fellow European soldiers defeat a much larger force led by Saladin. According to Charles G. Addison in his 19th-century work, *The History of the Knights Templars* (1842), the Master of the Temple, one Odo de St Amand, led a group of just 80 knights on a surprise raid into the heart of Saladin's camp and right through his feared Mamluk guards, and nearly succeeded in catching Saladin himself in his tent. '...[T]he sultan escaped with great difficulty, almost naked, upon a fleet dromedary.' Saladin's men, according to Addison, were thrown into confusion and '...slaughtered or were driven into the desert, where they perished from hunger, fatigue or the inclemency of the weather.'

Despite such successes by the Templars, Saladin and his army were to triumph in the end, taking Jerusalem in 1187, and gradually the crusader states in the Holy Land were surrounded and defeated. Just as the Christians were gradually pushed out of the Holy Land, so too the Templars' purpose seemed to vanish. The last major Christian and Templar outpost was to fall in 1291 with the capture of Acre, though their presence in the region had been vastly diminished long before then. Yet despite the loss of the Holy Land, the Templars remained an immensely wealthy and powerful organization with money, contacts, land and influence throughout Europe. They have even been described as the first multi-national corporation in history, which, given their strong 'brand' and immense power in many countries, is a fair analogy.

It is not hard to see why the Templars would attract the envy and mistrust of some rulers in the West. Thanks to their exemption from tax and freedom of movement, the Templars represented what amounted to an alternative, parallel power base to conventional states. In particular, Philip IV of France (known to history as Philip the Fair), who ruled 1285–1314, had some reason to be envious and mistrustful of the Templars. He needed money for his wars against the English, and was said to be in debt to the Templars himself. Getting rid of this powerful organization would thus clear some of his own debts, as well as enable him to get his hands on the Templar wealth. The order was still under the protection of the papacy, but Philip had some influence over Pope Clement V, who was based in France.

On Friday 13 October 1307, Philip had Grand Master of the Temple Jacques de Molay and many other senior Templars in France arrested. The Templars were then tortured until they confessed to a variety of blasphemies and confessions which, when publicized, led to a public scandal and demands for the toughest action against the Order. Meanwhile, Philip had also written to other monarchs asking them to take similar action against Templars, though this request was met with a varied response. De Molay was eventually burnt alive in Paris in 1314, his last request being that he could face the Notre Dame Cathedral and pray towards it. Defiant to the last, he is said to have predicted that both Philip and Clement would soon be dead. (If he did indeed make such a prediction, he was correct.) Many other Templars were also burned for their heresy, including more than 110 in Paris and others in Reims, Carcassone, Normandy and the Lorraine. Elsewhere a number of Templars were freed provided they agreed to confess and did not subsequently revoke their confession when the torture ceased (as some did). While many former Templars went on to join other orders, the Order of the Knights Templar was no more.

The nature of the confessions forced upon the Templars has long been a subject of debate. Apparently the Knights admitted to worshipping a mysterious demon called Baphomet; to taking part in homosexual orgies; to defiling the cross; to denying Jesus Christ and the Virgin Mary; and even to revering a severed head. According to Addison, it was alleged that '...the devil often appeared [in one Templar group] in the shape of a cat and conversed with the assembled brethren and promised them a good harvest, with the possession of riches, and all kinds of temporal property.' In one confession that took place in England, a Templar claimed that the Grand Master de Molay had pointed to an image of Christ and declared that '...he was the son of a certain woman and was crucified because he called himself the Son of God and I myself have been in the place where he was born and crucified and thou must now deny him whom this image represents.' Obviously, such accusations are at odds with the Templars' proclaimed mission as defenders of the Holy Land and of Christendom. The most likely explanation for this inconsistency is that these were exotic heresies dreamt up by the inquisitors and put into the mouths of the tortured members of the Order in order to discredit them with what would have been seen as obscene blasphemies.

Yet there are some who insist that, behind the undoubted exaggerations of these tortured confessions, the Templars did hold some unorthodox beliefs – beliefs that had come from their experiences in the Holy Land and Byzantium. These beliefs were supposedly based on ancient knowledge dating back to the time of Christ and even before. For example, one Templar is said to have been shown a crucifix, whereupon he told his examiners: 'Do not put much faith in this, it is too young...' According to some observers this curious statement hints at Templar beliefs that stretch back well before the time of Christianity. The Templars were certainly always linked with Solomon, right from the time they based their head-quarters on the supposed site of the King's temple. At this place and elsewhere in the Holy Land, they are supposed to have unearthed the relics of holy men of the past. These items clearly meant a great deal to them; at one point they are said to have possessed a relic of a portion of the True Cross – the actual cross upon which Christ was crucified. (It is said that Saladin captured this relic in battle, then later auctioned it back to the Templars.) However, reverence for relics was not unusual in those times.

**Myths, Legends and Relics**
Many of the myths and legends that surround the Templars centre on the Holy Grail, the cup supposedly used by Jesus at the Last Supper (though some consider the legend of the Holy Grail to have a more spiritual meaning). The story is that the Templars somehow came across this most sacred of relics, and that one of their principle missions in life was to guard it. This idea was later reflected in the stirring tales of knights and their quest for the Holy Grail (which also later became blurred with stories about King Arthur) that began to circulate from some time in the late 12th century. There is no real evidence, however, that the Templars ever did possess such a relic. Perhaps more important is the fact that many members of subsequent esoteric and occult circles *believed* that the Templars possessed the Grail – an object which was thought to have magical powers.

Another theory regarding the mission of the Knights was that they had originally journeyed to the Holy Land with the express purpose of gaining access to Solomon's temple. According to this view, the Knights' public mission, to protect the routes to and from Jerusalem, was little more than a cover story. Supporters of this view point out that such a small band of just nine men – who allegedly did not recruit new members for some years – would hardly have been enough to protect the many travellers heading to and from Jerusalem. In their book *Solomon's Power Brokers: The Secrets of Freemasonry, the Church and the Illuminati* (Watkins Publishing, 2007), authors Christopher Knight and Alan Butler allege that the Templars formed a secret mission to 'excavate' the site of Solomon's Temple. In support of their claims they point out that in the 19th century a British military expedition dug down into the site and came across a series of tunnels, in which a number of artefacts identified as belonging to 12th-century knights were found. If the Templars really had dug down into the ruins of the site, it would seem likely that they were searching for something specific; after all, one does not usually start a major dig on the off chance of finding something. Knight and Butler think that what the nine Knights were searching for was what they described as the 'most fabulous treasure map ever created': the Copper Scroll.

The Copper Scroll is one of the Dead Sea Scrolls, and was discovered in 1952 in Qumran. As is apparent from its name, this scroll was made not from parchment or leather, but from copper. This presumably suggests that the scroll was intended to last a long time, and was therefore important itself, or contained important information. Indeed, the scroll contains an itemization of gold and silver pieces that, at today's values, would be worth hundreds of millions of dollars. Moreover, the scroll appears to describe just where those treasures are hidden – though thanks to changes in culture and landscape, the locations and instructions make little sense today.

Nonetheless, the Copper Scroll was an exciting find, and many experts (though not all) agree that the scroll refers to a real treasure. Knight and Butler argue that the Knights must have been looking for the Copper Scroll, which in turn would lead them to that real treasure. However, as far as anyone can tell the Dead Sea Scrolls remained hidden for the biggest part of two thousand years, so the Templars cannot have found the Copper Scroll nor the treasures recorded therein.

Knight and Butler, though, claim that there were in fact *two* versions of the Copper Scroll. The one found at Qumran, they argue, was a secondary or junior form of scroll that refers to the existence of another scroll. Another possibility is, of course, that the Knights had simply heard tales of buried treasure at the Temple site and had gone there to look for it. They may not have even known about the existence of any scroll.

No one is sure which treasure – assuming it existed – the Scrolls supposedly refer to, and to whom it belonged. Theories range from it being the property of the First Temple (the one built by Solomon) to it being treasure belonging to the Second Temple, or even belonging to the Essenes. In any case, Knight and Butler claim that the Templars did ultimately find a scroll and thereafter the treasure, and that this was presumably the initial source of their great wealth. In support of this theory they point to the behaviour of Hugues de Payen's former Master, one Hugues de Champagne. This wealthy landowner had previously visited the Holy Land whilst accompanied by Hugues de Payen, his vassal. Yet in 1125 Hugues de Champagne left all his lands and money to his nephew and went off to join the Templars. This meant that Hugues de Champagne had voluntarily gone from being Hugues de Payen's master to being subservient to him within the ranks of the Templars. Such an unprecedented action can only be explained by the Templars having come into huge wealth and the possession of important documents, say the authors. While no hard evidence exists to support the claim that the Templars found treasure, some suggest that they did find ancient documents that provided an important link between themselves and later secret organizations (*see Chapter 3*).

An alternative theory about the Templars' mission states that they were not looking for buried treasure at all, or even for documents or the Holy Grail. Rather, they were, according to some traditions, searching for the Ark of the Covenant. As described previously (*see page 19*), the Ark was the sacred container that accompanied the Jews out of captivity and into Israel, and was also the place from which the word of the Lord was heard. The Old Testament describes, too, its terrible powers. It has been suggested that some of the writing in the Copper Scroll refers to the possible whereabouts of the Ark (though most experts believe that it was destroyed). There are stories that the Templars went as far as Ethiopia in search of the Ark; there were even ancient legends that the Ark had been taken to Ethiopia by Solomon's and the Queen of Sheba's son.

If the Templars truly did hold unconventional beliefs and possess secret knowledge, there are perhaps other, more plausible reasons for this. In their travels throughout the Middle East and Eastern and Southern Europe, the Templars were exposed to many different beliefs and traditions. It would not have been surprising if, as a result, they adopted some kind of private belief system. We have already seen how the Catholic clergy in this period blamed the rise of heresy (for example, the belief that Mary Magdalene and Jesus were married) on the knights who had returned from the Crusades. Often, these were knights who had just gone on one visit to the Middle East or Byzantium. It is certainly not implausible to suppose that the Templars, who were permanently based in the Holy Land (at least until they were forced to leave when Islamic forces finally dislodged them), would have adopted some unorthodox views as a result of their own more profound experiences. (Some researchers have gone further and suggested that the Templars were not created in 1118 at all, but were the descendants of an ancient order that had existed long before this time. Again, it is hard to find any hard evidence to support this claim.)

## A Special Reverence

There is certainly evidence that the Templars had strong links with the south of France, where both the Mary Magdalene tradition and the Cathar heretics existed. But perhaps the most intriguing reason for supposing that the Templars held ancient, secret beliefs stems from the special reverence they held for John the Baptist. During the confessions of the tortured Knights (*see page 61*), it was claimed that the severed head the Templars allegedly worshipped was (or represented) that of John the Baptist. They are also said to have possessed a finger of the Baptist as a relic.

In one sense, reverence for John the Baptist would not seem that surprising among a group of Christian knights, for conventional Christianity teaches us that the Baptist was the person who heralded the true mission of Jesus. However, recent scholarship, supported to an extent by the Dead Sea Scrolls, has suggested that the New Testament downplays the role of John the Baptist in relation to Jesus. As we have seen, there is a view among some experts that John the Baptist was himself the leader of a messianic movement, and that it was only when he was killed that Jesus assumed the role of leader. This mantle then passed to his brother, James, when Jesus died. Another variation on this theory holds that Jesus joined John's movement, and then they led the movement jointly. The biblical scholar Professor James D. Tabor writes in *The Jesus Dynasty* (Harper Element, 2007), 'Jesus valued his kinsman John as highly as anyone could value another – as a Prophet and Teacher, and inaugurator of the Kingdom of God. Jesus joined the movement John had begun, being baptized by John, and working with him to advance the Messianic Movement.'

This unconventional view of John the Baptist is not just a modern one. In the years after the deaths of John and Jesus there developed what is called the 'Johannite' tradition. This tradition held that John was a more important prophet than Jesus, and that it was he who had come to spread the word and save the world – though he was not regarded as divine in the way in which the Christians regard Jesus Christ. There was also a religion known as Mandaeism, which stills survives to this day, whose followers believe that Jesus was a false prophet who corrupted the true message of God, and revere John the Baptist above all other prophets. It is at least possible that the Templars came across such 'heresies' in the Middle East, and came to adopt the same reverence for John the Baptist.

Another curious question is the identity of 'Baphomet', whom the Templars are said to have worshipped. By far the most likely explanation is that this name is an old French variation on the name Mahomet, or Muhammad, the prophet of Islam. Given that the Templars were in constant contact with the Islamic world, it would hardly be surprising if some of their beliefs were influenced by that faith. An alternative view put forward by the biblical scholar Dr Hugh J. Schonfield is that the word 'Bahomet' was based on an ancient code, and that the name means 'wisdom'.

**The Templar Legacy**
During their nearly two centuries of existence, the Knights Templar had a considerable impact on the world. From beginnings that can be described as, if not mysterious, then rather curious, they went on to become one of the most powerful institutions in the medieval world. As mentioned, perhaps foremost in their accomplishments was their development of a trans-European banking system that enabled travellers to journey without the need to carry valuables that could be stolen on what were often lawless routes. Ultimately, of course, they and other crusaders failed to retain the Holy Land in the face of a newly resurgent Islam, and the Templars were forced to concentrate their activities back in Europe. They thus became a crusading group without a crusade.

Perhaps it is no coincidence that shortly after the fall of the last crusader stronghold the Templars were targeted and ultimately crushed by a European monarch. Any group with the lands, wealth and the following possessed by such an organization was likely to be seen as a threat. And when it came, the backlash against the Templars was ferocious. Although many of the allegations against the Templars were clearly fabricated – and helped along by the application of torture – their suppression was probably also due to the fact that there was some genuine doubt over whether their beliefs were truly in line with mainstream Christianity. The long years spent in the Middle East had perhaps left the Templars with the taint of heresy.

The Templars left a number of legacies. The wealth, land and power they held can be seen, for example, in the names that still survive, even if their possessions were either seized by the Crown or handed to other orders of knights. In England, for example, legal chambers such as the Middle Temple take their names from the site where the Templars owned property. The Temple Meads Station and other similarly named property show the influence of the Templars in Bristol.

The suppression of the Templars was also a sign of the growing strength of nation states and state institutions during a period in which individual countries (rather than supra-national organizations such as the Church) would emerge as the real political powers in Europe. To this day there are still Knights Templar organizations, many of which are affiliated to the United Nations-recognized Knights Templar International. One of these groups, for example, is the Grand Priory of Knights Templar in England and Wales. This Priory describes its purpose as trying to maintain 'high ideals of morals, ethics and Christian principles in an ever increasingly secular world.' (Such groups claim no direct link with the original Templars.)

Another modern-day Templar organization, the Ordo Supremus Militaris Templi Hierosolymitani (The Sovereign Military Order of the Temple of Jerusalem), claims descent from a Templar organization set up in 1804 by a French physician called Bernard Raymond Fabré-Palaprat, with the backing of Napoleon Bonaparte. Fabré-Palaprat claimed to have discovered documents proving that the Templar Order had in fact survived in secret since the 14th century, and that he was now restoring it; he subsequently became known as the 45th Grand Master. (Such claims are not unique in the world of secret societies; as we shall see, it is quite common for creators of such societies to 'discover' ancient origins.)

The Templars also left behind a rather less tangible and more tantalizing legacy. It seems at least possible that, because of the time spent in the Middle East, the Templars were recipients of beliefs that had origins dating from or before the origins of Christianity. At the very least, they came to be regarded both in the popular mind and in powerful occult circles as the keepers of hidden knowledge, even as the custodians of secret treasure.

The dismantling of the Templars in the early 14th century seemed to be the end of their story despite the revival of modern day versions. But it is hard to keep a good conspiracy story down. Eventually, a new and ultimately more pervasive organization was to emerge in Europe, and in time people claimed that this new organization sprang from none other than the Templars – that order of knights that seemingly refuses to go away.

# 3

## Freemasonry

O N THE EVE OF THE great round up of Templar Knights by the French king in 1307 (*see Chapter 2, pages 60–61*), the Templar fleet had lain quietly at the harbour in La Rochelle, on the west coast of France. The Order had long kept a significant fleet of merchant vessels and warships, knowing that it needed a fleet to protect itself if it was to maintain its trade and banking empire. The day after the arrests, however, the ships were nowhere to be seen. The Templar fleet had vanished; indeed, it was as if the entire Templar Order was about to sail out of the history books and into permanent oblivion. Many believe, however, that the Templars did not completely disappear. Instead, so the theory goes, the Templars were to play a major role in the development of one of the most mysterious, secretive and controversial organizations in history: the Freemasons.

Few movements have such debated and contested origins as the Freemasons. One view is that they are indeed the true inheritors of the mantle of the Knights Templar, possessing at least some of the secrecy, rituals and beliefs that the Templars are alleged to have had. Others argue that the origins of Freemasonry go back to the time of Solomon and the Temple, and perhaps even before then, to the stonecutters and workers (the masons) who helped build that monument. Many of these craftsmen were Phoenicians who worshiped not Yahweh, the god of the Hebrews, but rather gods such as Baal and Astarte. Other researchers have claimed Egyptian origins for the movement.

The conventional and most widely accepted view amongst historians is that Freemasonry grew out of the medieval guilds of stonemasons who worked on the cathedrals and churches of Europe. Gradually, the masons developed an elaborate system of beliefs and rituals, many of which have their origins in the ancient past. In truth, however, none of the explanations for the origins of Freemasonry are wholly satisfactory. Even the most credible of these theories – that they were a 17th- or 18th-century creation – poses some puzzles.

## Modern Origins

The history of what we might call 'modern Freemasonry' can be precisely dated to 24 June 1717, the day the Grand Lodge of England was created. The fact that this day is the feast day of St John the Baptist is no coincidence, as John has always been (and remains) an important figure in Freemasonry. The first meeting of the Lodge took place in the wonderfully named Goose and Gridiron alehouse in St Paul's Cathedral Yard in London. This alehouse was home to one of the four existing lodges that were grouped together to form the Grand Lodge (the others were The Crown alehouse, the Rummer and Grapes tavern and the Apple Tree, all from central London). A man by the name of Anthony Sayer was chosen as the first Grand Master, after which all those present sat down for a convivial dinner. Out of this rather ordinary beginning developed the modern structures and hierarchies of modern Freemasonry, though there have been a number of schisms and new organizations along the way.

The fact that the first Grand Lodge was an association of lodges proves that organized groups of Masons had existed before 1717. Some Masonic commentators further claim that the fact that there were apparently only four lodges willing to join the new organization at this time suggests that the movement was going through a difficult time. Though it seems likely that many of the rituals and beliefs we now associate with Freemasonry were introduced in the early 18th century, there were in fact lodges operating in London and elsewhere in Britain. Clearly these lodges came from somewhere; the question is where, and why, had they formed?

Real stonemasons had formed guilds in the Middle Ages in England, Scotland and many other parts of Europe. During a time of large-scale building across Europe, much of it religious in nature, masons were naturally an important force. Their organizations existed to nurture and protect their trade, a sort of combination between a trade union and a professional trade body. Traditions were passed down from generation to generation, from master mason to apprentice. Stonemasons travelled a great deal, coming into contact with other masons around the continent. The head mason in charge at a building site was known as the Master Mason, while the 'office' from where the work was organized became known as the 'Lodge'. The buildings on which the masons worked were often intricate and complicated projects, and the men who built them were highly skilled in their trade and keen to guard the secrets of how they worked.

The term 'operative mason' now refers to these stone craftsmen – the actual stonemasons who built things. In contrast, the masons who founded the Grand Lodge in 1717 and others of the time are what are called 'speculative' masons; that is, they have no physical connection with the industry. Instead the tools of the masonry trade, the organization and its rituals are allegorical and symbolic in nature. It is these 'speculative' Freemasons who focus on the spiritual meaning of the 'Craft', as the organization is sometimes called. But if it seems clear that what began as practical 'operative' stone working eventually turned into esoteric 'speculative' Freemasonry, it is far less clear exactly how or why this transformation took place. How did workers' guilds, in an industry that by the 16th century was beginning to lose its importance, metamorphose into modern 'middle class' Freemasonry some hundred or more years later? The short answer is that no one can be sure. There is, however, a suggestion that the 'missing link' in the move from stonemasonry to Freemasonry is to be found in Scotland.

In 1583 a man named William Schaw was appointed by James VI of Scotland (later James I of England) as Master of the Work and Warden General. In 1599 Schaw published the second of two statutes governing the duties that individual masons held to their lodges, the working of the lodges and the roles and responsibilities of Master Masons. The second statute refers to 'the art of memory', a technique developed in the ancient world but practised at this time by contemporary 'occultists' such as the famous Italian Giordano Bruno (*see Chapter 5, page 134*). On one level this 'art of memory' was a purely practical tool, a visualization technique used, for example, to help people memorize a long speech, yet on another level it was used by some occultists for more esoteric purposes; for example, to make contact with the spirit world.

An acquaintance of Schaw's, William Fowler, is said to have met Bruno some years before, and Fowler wrote a treatise on the subject (he may even have taught the technique to James VI). This, then, is a tantalizing hint that the 'operative masons' who worked as stonemasons may have had some involvement in more speculative, esoteric matters. Perhaps further evidence lies in the fact that this was a time in Europe in which the Renaissance had helped to liberate thinking from some of its medieval shackles, and there was considerable interest in (as well as mistrust of) the occult and magic in educated circles (*see Chapter 5, page 133*). Robert L. D. Cooper, Curator of the Grand Lodge in Scotland and an acknowledged authority on the history of the Craft, believes that the stonemasons used the 'art of memory' technique for practical purposes: '...much of their esoteric knowledge would not have been committed to paper, in order to keep it secret...the art of memory would therefore have been very suited as a tool to keep certain knowledge secret from non-stonemasons and as an efficient tool to its memorization,' he writes in *Cracking the Freemason's Code: The Truth About Cracking Solomon's Key and the Brotherhood* (Rider & Co, 2006).

From the 17th century onwards there are records of what are called 'non-operative' members being allowed into the Craft. For example, the famous creator of Oxford's great Ashmolean Library, Elias Ashmole, became a Freemason in the middle of the 17th century. In a diary entry dated October 1646, he recounts that he had been made a 'Free mason' in Warrington in Lancashire. This is the first known account of an English gentleman joining a Lodge, a sign that times were changing. Ashmole, who was also a keen alchemist, appears to have kept up his Masonic membership for the rest of his life; he was certainly still attending meetings in the early 1680s. In Scotland, the first record of a 'non-operative' to join a Lodge was even earlier, with John Boswell, Laird of Auchinlech, joining a Lodge in Edinburgh in 1600.

Exactly why such well-connected men as Boswell and Ashmole felt the need to join what were essentially organizations of stonemasons is unclear. However, in his controversial account of Freemasonry, *The Brotherhood: The Explosive Exposé of the Secret World of the Freemasons* (Harpercollins Publishers, 1985), the late Stephen Knight comes up with an interesting psychological explanation: '...it appears that the original interest of the gentry in the masonic lodges stemmed from curiosity, antiquarian interest and a kind of fashionable search for an unconventional, exclusive social milieu – rather like a jet-set fad for frequenting working men's pubs.' Knight then argues, however, that the 'novelty' of joining in with the artisans began to pale, and that this led to the development of their own, more genteel lodges, and ultimately to the Grand Lodge and the birth of Freemasonry as we know it. Yet another view holds that outsiders were simply attracted to the secrecy that the stonemasons practised in their guilds.

The exact process through which masonry became Freemasonry, and precisely what lay behind this takeover of medieval working guilds by the middle and upper classes, still remains unclear. Some have even suggested a 'shadowy' group of well-connected men was behind the takeover, and whose plan it was to create a secretive organization that would have influence far beyond what one might expect from a relatively small membership. But who these men were and indeed whether they really existed is not known, and so must remain speculation. Thus, although the medieval stone-guild theory is the most conventional and widely accepted explanation for the rise of Freemasonry, it nonetheless raises questions that have not yet been answered.

Another alternative view of the origins of the modern 'speculative' form of Freemasonry also involves Scotland – but by a different route. One problem with the conventional theory expounded above is that while Scotland possessed a few stonemasons' lodges, continental Europe had many more. It would therefore be reasonable to expect speculative Freemasonry to have originated in Europe rather than in the north of Britain, yet this clearly did not happen. According to a popular, if controversial, theory, the answer to this riddle lies just a few miles south of Edinburgh in a building called Rosslyn Chapel.

## Rosslyn Chapel

Rosslyn Chapel was built in the middle of the 15th century in the village of Roslin, in Midlothian, having been commissioned by Sir William St Clair. Work began on the Chapel in around 1440, though it took some 40 years to complete. Interest in the building stems from its unusual architecture and decorations, as well as from the man who commissioned it. Sir William's family was descended from Norman knights and was well connected throughout Europe. His ancestor, another William St Clair, had fought alongside Robert the Bruce at Bannockburn in 1314, when the Scottish decisively beat the English (it has even been claimed that the battle was won with the help of a contingent of Knights Templar arriving late in the day). A later William St Clair (the name became Sinclair) was the first Grand Master Mason in Scotland.

However, it is the architecture and the objects inside the Chapel that have aroused the most curiosity. It is said, for example, that the layout of the Chapel is very similar to that of the floor plan of the Jewish temple built in Jerusalem by King Herod and subsequently destroyed by the Romans. There is also a curious carving of a blindfolded man with what appears to be a noose around his neck; the posture of the man is said to resemble that of someone about to undergo the initiation ceremony in modern Freemasonry. The problem with this claim, however, is that modern Freemasonry developed a couple of hundred years *after* this mysterious figure was carved. If that is the case, how can it depict a modern Freemasonry ritual? Supporters of the Rosslyn Temple theory of the origins of Freemasonry say that it is precisely the existence of such an image that validates their theory: that the Chapel's unusual design and decoration are proof that it was influenced by Templar designs and beliefs.

Another image in the Chapel appears to show two men riding a single horse, a symbol used by the Knights Templar on their seal, supposedly to represent the individual poverty of the Knights by indicating that they could not even afford a horse of their own. Other curious carvings in the Chapel include a figure generally referred to as the Green Man, probably a representation of the god of vegetation and fertility, a deity commonly linked with Celtic cultures.

One particularly interesting feature in the building is that of the so-called Apprentice Pillar. This pillar takes its name from a story about a Master Mason who worked on the construction of the Chapel along with his apprentice. According to the legend, the Master Mason refused to believe that his young apprentice could complete the design without having first seen the decoration which inspired it. The Master Mason decided to go and visit the inspiration for the decoration himself. Upon his return, he discovered that the young man had indeed managed to complete the job. The mason is said to have been so envious of his protégé's talent that he picked up his mallet and killed him. This story obviously bears some similarities to the legend of Hiram Abiff and his murder at the hands of fellow builders of Solomon's Temple (*see Chapter 1, pages 12–15*), a story that is now central to modern Masonic rituals.

Proponents of the theory that the Rosslyn Chapel was influenced by the Templar Order say that after the Order was routed in France and disbanded elsewhere, a number of Knights made their way to Scotland in search of a safe haven. It has even been claimed that the Templar fleet that vanished from history after the arrest of its members in France (*see page 60*) reappeared off the Scottish coast. The result, say proponents of this argument, is that an underground Templar movement began. This movement mingled with Freemasonry and ultimately led to the creation of the modern speculative Freemasonry we see today. The beliefs, rituals and love of secrecy practised by Templars are all said to have been influences on the development of Freemasonry.

The historian John J. Robinson has put forward yet another fascinating theory. He claims that the Templars did not vanish from Britain after their dissolution as an order; rather, the Templar elements went underground and formed a secret society which was, Robinson theorizes, one of the organizers of the famous Peasants' Revolt which took place in England in 1381. In *Born in Blood: Lost Secrets of Freemasonry* (M. Evans & Co, 1990), he writes: '…there is the haunting evidence of rebel leaders who confessed to being members of a Great Society which no historian has ever attempted to define. Once the origin of Masonry in the fugitive Templars' secret society is accepted it is easy to conclude that the Great Society…was the direct descendant of the Templar fugitives and the predecessor of the secret society of Freemasonry.' Another historian (and Freemason), Paul Naudon, has researched the origins of medieval guilds across Europe, and has suggested that the Templars were involved in establishing brotherhoods of builders, and that after the Order was dissolved a number of Templars were initiated into builders' guilds.

If true, then either of these theories could provide the missing link that explains how what were essentially working guilds became the esoteric organizations they are today. They are certainly more credible than some other theories about the origins of Freemasonry, which include claims that Freemasonry has direct links with the stoneworkers of the megalithic age, with ancient Egyptians or with the Phoenician masons who built Solomon's Temple. The Templars were a powerful and widespread group with well-established rituals, and it would be strange indeed to think that all remnants of their beliefs and rituals vanished in the 14th century, even if proof that they directly influenced Freemasonry is hard to find.

## Freemason Beliefs

The nature of what Freemasons believe is no less mysterious and controversial than the movement's origins. The first question to address is whether Freemasonry is a religion or not. Masons themselves insist that it is not, as do many non-Masons. However, this is a not a view shared by everyone.

Some faiths – notably the Catholic Church and other Christian groups – have objected to Freemasonry on the grounds that it puts forward a different view of God from their own, and therefore is in conflict with Christianity. For their part, Masonic Lodges say they do not have any separate god, and that they have accepted members from many different organized religions, including Christianity, Judaism, Islam and Hinduism.

Masonic Lodges are free to use a variety of sacred texts, and each one has a volume of what it calls the Sacred Law on show; this volume can be any recognized sacred text from any mainstream religion. The one used by a particular Lodge varies depending on the part of the world in which the Lodge resides and the dominant faith there (though in practice it is usually the Christian Bible). However, a prerequisite for membership in most Lodges throughout the world is that the person must believe in a supreme being, or in supreme intelligence. In Freemasonry, this deity is often referred to as the Great Architect of the Universe, or sometimes as the Great Geometrician. Indeed, there are many references to geometry within the rituals and beliefs of Freemasonry, many drawing direct inspiration from the story of Solomon's Temple and its construction. In fact, the importance accorded to geometry by the Freemasons has strong echoes of the reverence in which Pythagoras and his followers held this discipline (*see Chapter 1, page 29*).

Freemasons themselves say that their beliefs and practices focus on morality, truth, the helping of others and on self-improvement. Indeed, a great deal of emphasis within speculative masonry is on inner awareness. Through self-discovery a Mason is encouraged to grow both as an individual and as a member of society.

Many of the inner beliefs of Freemasonry are both esoteric and symbolic. For example, the square and the compass are two key Freemasonry symbols. These symbols can represent various ideas within the Freemason belief system, ranging from the more literal to the more mystical; for example, the square is said to remind Masons to 'square' their actions by the 'square of virtue', while the compass urges them to 'circum-scribe' their passions. However, a more esoteric meaning is that the square, which has its angles fixed at 90 degrees, represents the unmoving nature of matter, while the compass, which is free to move, symbolizes the spirit. (This concentration on dualism, the difference between matter and spirit, has parallels with Gnostic belief.) In Freemasonry, the compass and square are often depicted together in order to show, it is claimed, the dependence of the one upon the other.

Another key aspect of Freemasonry is secrecy. In some respects Freemasonry is not a secret society in that we know about its existence, its membership (up to a point), its buildings and many of its beliefs. Indeed, Masonic speculations on the origins and meanings of its rituals and symbols are frequently published, and many of these thoughts are freely available in pamphlets and on the Internet. However, there are aspects of Freemasonry that are kept secret from non-Masons, including the secret signs Masons use to recognize each other. Such signs are not just a special type of handshake, but can be gestures as well as words. From time to time the nature of these secret signs are revealed by outsiders, so Lodges are free to create their own signs, and they can – and do – change them.

Perhaps the most sinister-sounding Masonic ritual is the oath that a member must swear about maintaining Lodge secrecy. The prescribed penalties for revealing the secrets of Freemasonry vary according to the degree that a member has reached: an Apprentice (the First Degree) who breaks the oath faces having his tongue ripped out; the Fellow Craft Mason (the Second Degree) risks having his heart ripped out; while the Master Mason (the Third Degree) is warned that he will have his bowels burned to cinders. Such archaic punishments are, today's Freemasons assure us, merely symbolic. In practice, Freemasons who break the view of secrecy face being reprimanded, suspended or ultimately being kicked out altogether.

Apart from these broad outlines about the Freemasonic 'credo', it is remarkably difficult to be precise about just what Freemasons in general or any particular Masons believe. Indeed, as noted earlier, individual members of the Craft are positively encouraged to speculate on the possible meanings of their symbols and history. The process of becoming a Mason and rising within the organization is seen as a personal journey, with each person interpreting and understanding the steps in their own way. As in many secret organizations in history, the outward journey – the level of membership or status that a person reaches – mirrors the member's inward spiritual journey.

## Degrees of Membership

In classical Freemasonry there are just three degrees: the Apprentice, the Fellow Craft Mason and the Master Mason. It is not hard to see the origins of these names in stonemasonry guilds, possibly with an element of the story of the building of the Temple of Solomon thrown in. For initiation into the First Degree (Apprentice), the would-be Mason is first questioned as to his motives, to assess whether his reasons for joining are worthy. Once he is accepted, the initiate is led, blindfolded, into an inner room at the Lodge headquarters. Once the blindfold has been removed, the initiate is then shown what are known as the Three Lights: the compass, the square and a sacred volume (for example, the Bible). They are informed about the various passwords and handshakes, and then told about the true meaning of Boaz, one of the pillars of Solomon's Temple. Finally, they are awarded a Masonic apron.

Initiation into the Second Degree (Fellow Craft Mason) is similar to that of the First Degree, though the initiate has more questions to answer, and he is taught the true meaning of the other great pillar in the Temple: Jachin. The level of Third Degree (Master Mason) was added in the early 18th century, and it is in this ritual initiation that the legend of Hiram Abiff is used. The initiate assumes the role of the builder/architect of Solomon's Temple, who is then symbolically killed by other Masons. The candidate falls to the ground, but is then lifted to his feet by the head of the Lodge, who is known as the Worshipful Master.

For most Masons, the Third Degree (or Master Mason) is the highest they will ever reach, or aspire to reach. But the world of Freemasonry is nothing if not arcane, not to say paradoxical. For the United Grand Lodge of England proclaims that: '…pure, ancient Masonry consists of three Degrees and no more… those of the Entered Apprentice, the Fellow Craft, and the Master Mason *including the Supreme Order of the Holy Royal Arch.'* Thus a degree known as the 'Royal Arch' is seen as part of the Third Degree. Yet, curiously, the Royal Arch Degree has its own initiation ritual, and even has what are called 'preparatory' degrees that lead up to it: Mark Master Mason, Past Master and Most Excellent Master. Masons who have reached the Royal Arch Degree meet together in groups that are known not as Lodges, but rather, as 'Chapters'. As far as these Masons are concerned, the knowledge and insight that comes with this Degree is far more complete than that which comes through becoming a Master Mason. As one website dedicated to this Degree claims: 'Without the Royal Arch, the Master's Degree is like a song half sung, a tale partly told, or a promise unfulfilled.'

Indeed, even the Royal Arch is not the end of it. There is yet another strand within the movement in which the Degrees go even higher – to 33rd degree. This happens within a rite known as the Ancient and Accepted Scottish Rite of Freemasonry, or the Scottish Rite, as it is frequently called. Freemasons hailing from anywhere are free to join this Rite if they want to increase their understanding of Freemasonry. The names of the various degrees in the Scottish Rite vary slightly around the world, but many are wonderfully exotic; examples include Secret Master for 4th degree, Prince of Jerusalem at 16th degree, Grand Pontiff at 19th degree, Prince of Mercy at 26th degree, Knight Kadosh at 30th degree and Sublime Prince of the Royal Secret at 32nd degree. By contrast, the 33rd degree has the disappointingly mundane name of Inspector General. The system under which initiation takes place varies around the world, but in each area in which the 33rd degree Rite is used there is a Supreme Council that oversees it.

**Masonic Organization and Structure**

Though many view Freemasonry as a uniform movement, there is in fact no central body that controls it worldwide. As ever with Freemasonry, the organizational structure is a complex one. Generally speaking, the hierarchy of Freemasonry is organized on a country-by-country basis, and there is more than one tradition of Freemasonry in the world. One group follows the beliefs and practices adopted by the United Grand Lodge of England (UGLE), while other Lodges around the world follow the lead of the Grand Orient of France, based on a continental European strand of Freemasonry that developed in 1733, and which has generally followed a different path from that of UGLE masonry. For example, in the 18th century women were allowed to join some of the Lodges linked to the Orient movement, and in 1877 it agreed to admit people who did not believe in a Supreme Being. (This policy was in keeping with a strong tradition of laicism, or secularism, which is strong in countries such as France in which there is now no established church.)

Just to add to the confusion, the United Grand Lodge of England is so-called because it united two groups of Masonry that had split in the 18th century. In 1751 a group of Lodges rejected the Grand Lodge by forming a rival organization, which they called the Most Ancient and Honourable Society of Free and Accepted Masons. Its members claimed that their form of Masonry was more ancient and 'pure' than that followed by members of the original Grand Lodge, whom they dismissed as 'moderns'. Thus began the split between the two factions known as the Ancients (sometimes written 'Antients') and the Moderns. This sometimes bitter feud continued until 1813, when the original Grand Lodge and the Antient Grand Lodge merged to become the United Grand Lodge of England. This tale underlines just how complex the world of Freemasonry is, and the dangers of assuming that there is one single fixed, homogenous form of Masonry to which all Freemasons adhere.

## Freemason Membership

It is estimated that there are around two million active Masons in the world spread through many different countries, especially Europe, English-speaking countries and those nations that are or once were a part of the British Commonwealth. As many as half of Freemasons live in the United States, where the movement is probably the strongest in the world. However, Freemasonry has touched just about every part of the globe. There is evidence, for example, that Freemasonry reached China as early as the 18th century through the influence of European merchants. In the 19th century lodges were established in Hong Kong and in Shanghai, though the Craft remained more popular with expatriate Westerners than with local Chinese.

After Mainland China became communist in 1949, Freemasonry declined and eventually vanished on the mainland, but it continued in Hong Kong and on the island of Taiwan. In India, Freemasonry is almost as old as the age of modern Freemasonry in the West. Members of the East India Company in Calcutta formed the first lodge in the country in 1730. However, it was the 19th century before the first Indian person was to be allowed into a lodge. The first record of a Hindu becoming a member of a lodge was in 1857, with the first Sikh following four years later. In Bengal, local rules prevented an Indian from joining a lodge until 1872. The Grand Lodge of India was founded in 1961, some years after independence, and it is now estimated that there are around 15,000 Freemasons in the country.

## Persecution and Supression

Even in modern times, Freemasonry has not been practised freely in all parts of the world. Many communist regimes attacked Freemasonry and effectively outlawed it, describing it as an agent of capitalism or Western imperialism, or both. In fact, Masonry has fared badly under most totalitarian regimes. In 1938 the Japanese military dictatorship blamed its problems with China on the 'fact' that the Chinese nationalistic leader, Chiang-Kai-shek, was following in the footsteps of his 'master', the famous revolutionary figure Sun Yat-sen, whom they claimed was a Freemason. In fact, Sun Yat-sen was never a member of what might be termed a Western Masonic Lodge, though he did have close links with a movement that is sometimes known as 'Chinese Freemasonry' (*see Chapter 9, page 244*).

Mussolini's fascist Italy was another regime that cracked down on Freemasons. The dictator forced members of the Fascist Party to choose between membership in the party or membership in a Lodge. At least one prominent fascist and Mason reportedly chose the latter – and was later imprisoned for his pains. Freemasonry was formally dissolved in the country in 1925.

Under the rule of Francisco Franco in Spain, simply being a Mason earned you a jail sentence, and Freemasons were routinely persecuted. In fact, Franco had an obsession with Masonry, partly prompted by personal reasons. Franco was close to his pious Catholic mother, but was alienated from his father, a man who was sympathetic to Freemasonry and who later quit the family home to live with another woman. Meanwhile, Franco is said to have applied three times to join the Freemasonry, and to have been turned down each time. Before long, as a patriotic and Catholic young soldier, Franco came to share in the widely held belief in Spain that many of its ills, including the rise of left-wing politics and liberalism, sprang from Freemasonry.

After 1946, when the dictator had already ruled Spain for some years, he began to express his loathing for Freemasonry in a series of articles written for a Spanish newspaper under the pseudonym 'Jakim Boor'. These outpourings of hatred for Freemasonry (among other things) were later published in book format, and indicate that Franco appeared to believe that the whole of modern history had been shaped by Freemasonry, and that Spain had been especially hard done by as a result. He blamed his country's plight on a British nobleman, Philip, Duke of Wharton, who apparently introduced Masonry to Spain in 1728. Franco even claimed that the wartime leaders Winston Churchill and Franklin Roosevelt had formed a Masonic/communist plot in cahoots with Stalin's Soviet Union at the end of the Second World War.

Whilst Freemasons were among Franco's many victims in his suppression of dissent, it was in Hitler's Germany that the Freemasons suffered the most in the 20th century. Hitler and other prominent Nazis regarded Masonry as a tool of 'Jewry', and Lodges were disbanded in 1934 soon after the dictator came to power. Anyone who had been a member of a Lodge was prevented from working in public service. Nazi persecution of Freemasons continued as Germany occupied much of Europe; Lodges were closed down, their property seized and sold off at auction; documents were taken, and many Masons were sent to concentration camps. No one knows for sure just how many people were murdered at the hands of the Nazis simply for being Masons, but a conservative estimate is said to be 80,000.

Masonry was also suppressed in the Soviet Union, and appears to have died out there altogether. However, since the fall of the Berlin Wall in 1989 and the collapse of the Soviet Union, there have been some signs that Freemasonry is slowly returning to Russia.

## Criticisms of Freemasonry

As we have seen, much of the criticism of Freemasonry in different countries has been of a very generalized nature. Communist countries tended to associate it with capitalism and imperialism, while in fascist countries it was linked with the Jews and Zionism. (In the Middle East, the Iraqi dictator Saddam Hussein associated Freemasonry with Zionism; Freemason activities in that country could attract the death penalty.) In addition to these general criticisms, there have been more specific complaints about Freemasons, specifically about the ways in which they behave and what they believe.

One of the main targets of attack has been the secrecy in which the Masons indulge. The United Grand Lodge of England, in common with other Grand Lodges, insists that Freemasonry has nothing to hide – and that it does not hide anything. 'It is not a secret society since all members are free to acknowledge their membership and will do so in response to enquiries for respectable reasons,' says the UGLE. 'Its constitutions and rules are available to the public. There is no secret about any of its aims and principles. Like many other societies, it regards some of its internal affairs as private matters for its members. The secrets of Freemasonry are mainly confined to the ways in which members recognize each other.'

Critics, however, say that these sorts of comments are disingenuous. They argue that Freemasonry acts as a covert network of often-influential people, whose identities as Masons are not always known to outsiders, whatever the

UGLE says. This secrecy, say the critics, can be corrosive, especially when two or more Masons are involved in important decisions and the general public has no idea of their hidden link. In Britain and other countries, for example, there have been frequent complaints about Masons working covertly in collusion within the law, the judiciary, the police, local politics, the City, the armed forces and many other parts of society. Unless everyone knows just who is and is not a Mason, so the argument goes, the suspicion of corruption will always linger, even if there are no specific grounds for it. In this sense, Freemasonry is said to act like an 'old boys' network', though on a larger, far more organized – and some would claim sinister – scale.

Another frequent line of attack against Freemasonry is that it holds occult beliefs, and, according to some Christians, it indulges in 'devil worship'. This charge is levelled by Catholics and by some fundamentalist Protestants as well, though not by the Roman Catholic Church itself. Some of these accusations stem from the love of ritual and ancient symbolism that is at the heart of Freemasonry; for example, the Masonic apron given to candidates after admission is said to have been influenced by Egyptian dress. Far more sinister, in the view of some Christians, are the overt links made by some Masonic scholars between the origins of Freemasonry and Egyptian gods such as Thoth (Hermes in the Greek form), Isis and Osiris. Though it is hard – almost impossible – to accept that Freemasonry is in any way a direct descendent of the Egyptian mystery religions, there is little doubt that the symbols of deities such as Isis have had an influence on Masonic beliefs and rituals. For fundamentalist Christians, the very idea that an organization could have links with ancient 'pagan' gods is proof enough that it is wrong.

One of the more specific charges levelled against Freemasonry concerns the ritual of the Royal Arch (*see page 77*), with some claiming that within this ritual the true name of the Great Architect, or Supreme Being, was revealed. This name is Jahbulon (sometimes spelt Jabulon), a word whose origins and meaning are as mysterious as they are controversial. Indeed, there has been much debate about how this strange word came into the Masonic lexicon. One view is that it was first used among French Masons in the early 18th century; another is that it was used as a Masonic password in the mid-19th century. By far the most controversial view of the name is that it is a combination of both the Jewish deity and what Christians would call 'pagan' gods. According to this interpretation, the word is pronounced

Jah-Bul-On: JAH is supposed to be a form of Jahweh, or Yahweh, the god of the Hebrews, and BUL is supposed to be a reference to Baal, the Phoenician god who was worshipped in cities such as Tyre. The Phoenician masons who are said to have built the Temple of Solomon would have worshipped a deity called Baal, and indeed Solomon himself may have worshipped this god. (Over the centuries the word Baal has become associated with the Christian concept of the Devil.) The last part of the word, 'ON', is said to represent the Egyptian god Osiris, although the etymology of this word is far from clear.

If one accepts that Jahbulon is truly a composite of these three names, then it is hardly surprising that some Christians regard the use of this name as the ultimate name of the Supreme Being as not only blasphemous, but akin to devil worship. The American soldier, writer and prominent Freemason of the 19th century, Albert Pike, described his distaste at this 'mongrel' word, which he claimed was partly made up of the 'devil's' name. The supposed meaning of Jahbulon was also highlighted by author Stephen Knight in his book, *The Brotherhood* (Dial Press, 1974), and though the revelation was not new, the prominence given to it caused a stir: the Church of England labelled the use of a composite word made up of pagan deities blasphemous if used as a name for God. Knight himself writes that he had spoken to more than 50 Royal Arch Masons who had been happy to cooperate about various aspects of Masonry, yet '...all but four lost their self-assurance and composure when I said, "What about Jah-Bul-On?"'

The response of the Royal Arch Masonry to the concern over the use of the word 'Jahbulon' has been confused. On some occasions, Masons have suggested that the name was simply a password; on others, the line has been that the critics' derivation of the name is based on faulty etymology. Whatever the case, the word Jahbulon was removed from the Royal Arch ritual in 1980 following the publicity given to its use. This appears to be a tacit admission that the use of such a name laid the movement open to charges of, at the very least, 'flirting' with devil worship. However, many of the critics of Freemasonry have been confused themselves. Even if 'Bul' does mean 'Baal', most scholars now accept that this deity name was in fact more of a title or prefix meaning 'Lord', and was used in the names of a number of different gods. Moreover, it was Christianity that chose to turn 'Baal' into the devil, thereby making the name 'evil'. (The Phoenicians who worshipped their Baal gods would certainly not have thought of themselves as worshipping something evil.) Seen in this context, the Masons' apparent use of the names of old deities can hardly be seen as devil worship. It would be more accurate to say that Freemasonry, albeit in some forms and among some members, is as open to the occult and to 'paganism' as it is to Christianity.

The association of Freemasonry with evil refuses to go away, however. In his follow up to Stephen Knight's book, author and documentary maker Martin Short quotes the experience of a British man's initiation experience. In Short's book, entitled *Inside the Brotherhood* (Harpercollins Publishers, 1995), the man (who is not named) describes his initiation into the Third Degree, when he is symbolically killed and lies motionless on the floor wrapped in a black shroud. 'As I lay there I suddenly felt the overpowering presence of evil. I had never consciously thought about evil before, let alone felt it, but now my brain was pounding. I felt a piercing pain in my skull like the worst headache you can ever imagine.' According to Short, the man stayed a Freemason for a number of years, but his unease grew and so he left. Eventually he became a born-again Christian. Short writes that such 'confessions' were typical of many interviews he had carried out among former Masons who had left and become born-again Christians. From such research it is clear that some people have genuinely been scarred by their experiences as Freemasons, and have since found comfort in enthusiastically embracing Christianity. 'I believe it is of the devil, it has a Satanic origin,' says one former Mason who is now a born-again Christian.

Yet it is equally clear that some responses to Freemasonry have been absurd overreactions. A good example of this occurred in the American town of Kempsville, Virginia, in the mid-1990s. The story centred on a man called Arthur Ward, a devout family man, a Christian, a railway worker and also a Freemason. Ward died in 1979 aged 64 and, being a much-loved member of the community and a founder member of the local Baptist church, he was remembered with a special plaque in the church's memorial garden. For many years Arthur Ward and his memorial lay in peace close to the church. But by 23 April 1996, ten members of the church had become convinced that something about the memorial garden was terribly wrong. They tore up all of the cobblestones in the garden, ripped out all the plants and flowers, burned the wooden cross and then broke the stone on which the plaque was mounted. The reason they gave in explanation of these destructive actions was that they believed the garden to be full of Masonic symbols. The church members then sprinkled the entire area with holy water so as to 're-consecrate' it. 'It sounds so ridiculous. It sounds like something right out of the Dark Ages,' said the church deacon, William Forbes.

Like Forbes, many members of the congregation were appalled by this attack on the garden dedicated to the resting place of popular citizen and church member Arthur Ward. A group protested to the vicar, the Reverend Jackson, but he defended the church members' actions, pointing out that the garden had contained roses that had been planted in the form of a cross. It seems that the Reverend and the others had taken the cross and roses as a symbol of Freemasonry, when in fact they were just simple roses. (The 'rosy cross' is the old name and emblem of the Rosicrucian secret societies (*see Chapter 4, page 109*), but Ward had no connection with these societies.) The *Scottish Rites Journal*, a Masonic publication, described what happened next:

> As news of the garden's destruction spread, a near hysteria, reminiscent of the Salem witch trials of 1791, gripped the congregation. Church members reported nightmarish visions welling up from the garden's soil. Sunday School children, hearing the adults, began stories that bones or bodies were buried in the garden. These reactions following the garden's destruction only seemed to validate the actions of the perpetrators who believed a cloud of evil threatened the church's purity.

According to the *Journal*, many members of the congregation left the church as a result of this attack on the garden. Arthur Ward's widow, Donna Ward-Meekins, said: 'My family and I continue to feel the pain and live under the shadow of this incident.' She and her son later received an apology in court from church leaders. Such incidents are, of course, rare, and many Christians happily accept Freemasonry; many are indeed Freemasons themselves. However, such incidents show that the mystery and secrecy that continues to surround the Freemasons still have the capacity to attract bitter controversy.

This controversy is unlikely to go away, and is now being fuelled by a vast amount of 'debate' on the Internet about the nature of Freemasonry and what exactly its members believe. For example, there is a website called Ephesians 5:11, which describes itself as 'a counter-cult ministry which specializes in subversive religious organizations which deny being religions'.

The largest of these 'subversive groups', it says, is the Masonic Lodge. The aim of the website is not, however, merely to convince Freemasons to extricate from such dastardly groups. 'If (a member) leaves the occult organization, he is still headed to hell, unless he accepts Jesus Christ as his saviour,' says the website. (The site also regards the Catholic Church as 'subversive' because of its 'worship' of the Virgin Mary.)

Though such groups may lump Freemasonry and the Catholic Church together, the Church of Rome itself is far from indifferent when it comes to the Craft. Since the 18th century, the Church has consistently taken a tough line against Freemasonry, even if it has stopped short of associating it with devil worship. In the 18th century, three Masons were put to death after being condemned by the Portuguese version of the Inquisition. And though nowadays Masons may not have to fear for their earthly survival, a 1983 statement from the Vatican made clear what it thought of anyone joining a lodge: 'The faithful who enrol in Masonic associations are in a state of grave sin and may not receive Holy Communion,' it announced. One of the main theological reasons the Church objects to Freemasonry is that, while accepting that Masons believe in God, their view of Him is 'deist' in nature. Deism is the belief in a god that does not interfere in the affairs of humans and nature. This belief is regarded as being contrary to Catholic dogma.

## Historical Connections to the United States

Over the 300 years of the existence of modern Freemasonry, the movement has been closely associated with some major historical events and developments, even if the precise nature of its impact upon them is harder to gauge. As we have already seen, the movement has attracted a great deal of 'blame' from authoritarian regimes of both left and right for the state of the world. The left has considered Freemasonry to be a tool of capitalism and Western imperialism, while the right has characterized the group as subversive, an enemy of traditional values, and even as Zionist. But aside from these general accusations, Freemasonry has been connected with specific events and periods. In particular, Masons have been connected with two of the most pivotal events in modern history: the revolutions in America and France.

Freemasonry in the United States has a long history, stretching back almost to the beginnings of modern Masonry itself. It is said that the first native-born American to become a Mason was Jonathan Belcher, the

Governor of Massachusetts, in 1703. We certainly know that by 1730 several lodges had already been set up in Pennsylvania, and in 1731 the Grand Lodge of Pennsylvania was established – it claims to be the third oldest Grand Lodge in the world after those in England (1717) and Ireland (1729). It is hardly surprising that Freemasonry found fertile territory in the New World in which to grow. Masonry at that time was associated with progressive, new ways of thinking; with ideas of personal liberty and equality; and with the importance of science and reason in the world. The pioneers were seeking a new life away from some of the old thinking and social restrictions of mother Europe. For such persons, Freemasonry was a natural home.

By the middle of the 18th century the tension between the American colonies and the British government in London was growing, as was membership of Masonic lodges. It would, of course, be absurd to suggest that the War of Independence and the ultimate break with British rule in North America was part of a Masonic 'plot' (historians have identified numerous economic, social, political and philosophical reasons for the war). However, there is a strong correlation between membership in the Masonic lodges and the key players in the independence movement. An interesting potential link lies in Boston, where the famous Tea Party occurred in 1773. One of the main centres for agitation against the British was the Green Dragon Tavern. It may just be coincidence, but this was also the meeting place for St Andrew's Lodge in the city. (St Andrew's Lodge was founded in 1756, and had links to the Scottish Grand Lodge.) There is a theory that St Andrew's, along with other Scottish-linked lodges, attracted more radical and revolutionary members compared with the more conservative English-linked lodges in the Americas.

One member of the St Andrew's Lodge was Paul Revere, a heroic figure of the American Revolution. Revere was responsible for the celebrated 'Midnight Ride' in 1775, when he rode through the night to warn American commanders of the movements of British troops. Another member of the same lodge was Joseph Warren, an important figure in the independence movement in Massachusetts. Warren was killed in the Battle of Bunker Hill in 1775 while fighting on the front line, having turned down a request to lead the troops.

The purported link between Freemasonry and the American War of Independence (1775–1782) is an interesting one. Bob Cooper, the curator at the Grand Lodge of Scotland, in Edinburgh, says he believes there is a link between the values and aims of the American revolutionaries and the origins and background of Scottish Freemasonry, which had always been a grassroots organization. 'It was the original egalitarian society, and that's what we took to America,' he says.

However, there are other, even better known links between American independence and Freemasonry. One of the best-known key figures in the Revolution was Benjamin Franklin, one of America's founding fathers and also a diplomat, writer, politician and scientist. Franklin, who was born in Boston, was a prominent Mason who became Provincial Grand Master in Philadelphia, and who also had close ties with Masonry in Scotland, England and France, where he served as American ambassador. Indeed, for two years he was Grand Master of the Les Neuf Soeurs Lodge in Paris, a prominent lodge that helped encourage French support for the American Revolution. The Lodge attracted some of the most brilliant people of the time; as well as Franklin, the great writer and thinker Voltaire was an honorary member. John Paul Jones, an American sea captain and a hero of the war, who had been born in Scotland, was also a member of the same lodge. Indeed, it is claimed that at least 8 and as many as 19 signatories of the famous American Declaration of Independence were Freemasons.

The most famous American Freemason at this time was George Washington, the father of the nation and the first President of the United States. Washington was initiated as a Master Mason at Fredericksburg at the age of 21, and he remained a Mason for the rest of his life, though, perhaps for understandable reasons, he did not attend many Lodge meetings and never attained the status of Grand Master. Washington's status as a Mason has aroused controversy, and there have been attempts to claim that he had either renounced Freemasonry or that had never been a Mason at all. However, after he died his widow, Martha, made efforts to ensure that he was buried according to Masonic rites. In 1932 the George Washington Masonic National Memorial was erected in Alexandria, Virginia, the town where Washington was a member of Alexandria Lodge 22.

In recent years it has often been claimed that the influence of Freemasonry extended not only to key personnel in the fight for American independence, but also to some American buildings. The new capital, Washington DC, was built at the end of the 18th century, allegedly to a 'Masonic' design. Though George Washington was involved in the decision to appoint the original designer of the city, Pierre Charles L'Enfant, there is no evidence that the French-born American architect was a Mason. Nor is there evidence that Andrew Ellicott and Benjamin Banneker, two other architects involved in laying out this new, gleaming city, were Masons. Moreover, the man who had much to do with overseeing the plans for the city was Thomas Jefferson, who was not a Mason.

The theory linking the city of Washington DC and Freemasonry comes partly from the fact that the intersection of key junctions in the city appear to form a five-pointed star, or a pentagram, a symbol that has long been closely associated with the occult. This fact appears, however, to be just a coincidence. In any case, while the pentagram is used in some Freemasonry regalia, it has no special significance within the movement.

Scottish Freemason and historian Bob Cooper, however, believes that there is a link between the Masons and the building of Washington – even though it is not the esoteric link in which some conspiracy theorists believe. Cooper claims that at the time the capital's buildings were being erected, there was a shortage of skilled stonemasons. This shortage was partly due to the fact that up until this time, many of the country's buildings had been made of wood. 'So the mother lodges in Scotland were contacted, and stonemasons, who were also Freemasons, were headhunted for the job,' says Cooper. 'We know this because their absences and where they went had been logged to explain their non-payment of Lodge dues. There were scores of them from Lodges all over Scotland,' he says.

Meanwhile, in Ohio lies one American town that can definitely claim to have been designed on Masonic lines: the town of Sandusky. The surveyor who drew up the street plans for the town in 1818 (two years after it was founded) was one Hector Kilbourne, and he was the Worshipful Master at the local Lodge. The streets of Sandusky were deliberately laid out to form two of the great symbols of the Craft: the compass and the square.

Another theory alleged to prove some kind of Masonic 'plot' in the establishment of the United States of America concerns the design on the reverse side of the Great Seal of the United States, parts of which feature on the country's one-dollar bills. The most controversial part of the bill's design is the image of a pyramid with an 'all seeing eye' at its apex. Underneath this pyramid are the Latin words *Novus Ordo Seclorum*, which means 'A New Order of the Ages'; above it are the words *Annuit Coeptis*, meaning 'Providence Has Favoured Our Undertakings'. Some see this image, together with these words, as 'proof' that the founding of the United States was part of an occult plot.

While it is true that the 'all-seeing eye' does have significance in Freemasonry, this kind of image was also used in Christian imagery during the Renaissance, so it can hardly be said to be uniquely Masonic. Some theorists have also translated the words below to mean 'New World Order', signifying that a secret organization is planning to take over the government of the entire world. However, the explanation for the symbol and words on the bill is relatively straightforward, and were provided by the man in ultimate charge of its design, Charles Thomson, back in 1782. According to Thomson: 'The pyramid signifies strength and duration; the eye over it and the motto allude to the many signal interpositions of providence in favour of the American cause … the words … signify the beginning of the new American Era.'

## The Morgan Affair

Concern over Masonry and its practices and aims peaked in the United States in the first half of the 19th century, when an infamous kidnapping and possible murder occurred in which the Freemasons were implicated. The affair caused a nation-wide sensation. The victim was William Morgan, from Canandaigua, New York State. Morgan may or may not have been a Mason himself, though he does appear to have been initiated into the Royal Arch Degree in 1825 – possibly by tricking his way into a Lodge.

In 1826, Morgan was engaged in writing a book that purported to reveal certain Masonic secrets. He received threats, and then one night he was seen being bundled into a carriage by four men. It is believed that he was taken to an abandoned fort, but after this the trail runs cold. He simply vanished. Although Morgan's body was never found, it is thought likely that he was murdered.

A number of Masons were convicted in relation to Morgan's kidnapping, but were given lenient sentences, fuelling a growing public fear that the Masons were looking after their own, and that society was under threat from the movement. Amid this clamour, the Antimasonic Party was formed, and support for it soon mushroomed in New York and neighbouring states. For a brief while this party became a genuine 'third political party' in the United States, and its presence generated some long-lasting changes in American politics, including the invention of the party convention. The Party also succeeded in getting some of its members elected to the House of Representatives: a senator and three state governors, no less.

Though the party quickly fizzled out, it actually had an impact upon Masonic membership, which plummeted for a couple of decades. The concerns that had been raised by the Party against Freemasonry have become familiar ones in countries around the world since. Such concerns have not, however, stopped a number of Masons from subsequently becoming United States presidents, including Gerald Ford, Franklin D. Roosevelt and Harry S. Truman.

## Freemasonry and the French Revolution

There is little doubt that Freemasonry has played a significant role in French society and political life for centuries. It was prominent both immediately before and after the revolution of 1789, which saw the *Ancien Régime* torn down and eventually replaced with more egalitarian forms of government. In fact, Masons have perhaps had more impact on France than they have on any other European country.

It is often claimed that the Freemasons were the plotters and planners of the Revolution, and that it was essentially their plan that was put into action with the storming of the Bastille on 14 July 1789. Such claims massively overstate their influence, however. The powerful social, economical and philosophical forces that brought about change in France can easily be explained without any recourse to the Freemasons. Yet there is no doubt that French lodges and Masons did indeed have some influence on French society.

By the 1780s, there were about 40,000 Masons in France, spread through more than 1,200 different lodges. (Some respected historians even put the figure as high as 100,000.) We've already seen how influential some of these lodges – Les Neuf Soeurs Lodge, for example – were in French life (*see page 88*). Without doubt there was a great crossover between the Freemasons and the French intellectuals – the sons and daughters of the Enlightenment – who wanted change in France. Freemasonry had spread down from the noble elite (who were the first in France to embrace it) to middle class intellectuals, who found membership in the movement to be both a good way of networking among like-thinking people and a relatively safe place to discuss talk of change.

Paradoxically, many Freemasons were members of the nobility, and though they may have wanted change, they certainly did not envisage the sort of upheaval and bloody slaughter that followed the events of July 1789. Furthermore, many members of the French clergy were Freemasons, and concern over the power of the Church was one of the many grievances that fuelled the main actors in the Revolution.

The claim that the Freemasons plotted or planned the French Revolution stems largely from the work of two men who wrote shortly after the Revolution: a Scotsman named John Robison, a Freemason himself, and a Jesuit known as the Abbé Augustin de Barruel. Both men claimed that continental Freemasonry had provoked the revolution as part of a supposed plot that sought to sweep away both the monarchy and the Christian Church. They also claimed that the Illuminati were involved in this plot (*see Chapter 4, page 106*). Modern scholars, however, regard such writings as the work of counter-revolutionary propaganda, and many of their contemporaries also criticized their polemical nature.

It is true, however, that many who joined the revolutionary government were Freemasons (though most were relatively moderate in their views), and also that Freemasons were prominent members of the Jacobin clubs (French political clubs that were popular at the time) that played a key role in the revolutionary timetable. Indeed, one important figure in the Revolution was the Duc d'Orléans, the cousin of King Louis XVI. An immensely wealthy man whose desire for change may have been led as much by personal as ideological reasons, the Duc was also Grand Master of the Grand Orient Lodge.

While there is no hard evidence to support the notion that French Freemasonry was either united enough to want a revolution, or indeed wanted a revolution of the kind that unfolded, it is likely that the lodges, which were anti-monarchical by inclination, provided a breeding ground for the dissemination of revolutionary ideas and a network for people to use. In this way, the Freemasons did play a role in one of the most important events in modern history, even if not quite the crucial one that some conspiracy theorists would suggest.

Freemasonry has continued to play a role in French political life. Less than a century after the Revolution, Masons featured in the events surrounding the Paris Commune. When revolutionary forces briefly seized Paris in 1871, the Masons vainly tried to negotiate a settlement between the commune leaders and the French authorities in Versailles. As many as

10,000 Freemasons are said to have marched behind their Grand Masters through the city. Having failed to achieve peace, the Freemasons threw in their lot with the commune. Some Freemasons even shared in the bloody fate of many of the 'communards' when the city was eventually attacked and overrun.

The Nationalists and some Catholics shared the French right wing's mistrust of the Freemasons. Hostility to the movement became evident during the infamous Dreyfus Affair, the political scandal that deeply divided French society at the end of the 19th century. This scandal was one of the causes of the division between church and state that occurred at the start of the 20th century.

Today, all mainstream political parties in the country jealously guard the secular status of the French state. According to Stephen Knight's book, *The Brotherhood*, however, Freemasonry has nonetheless played a major role in modern French politics. He quotes a former Grand Master of the Grand Orient of France, Fred Zeller, who claims that the Socialists would have won the 1974 presidential election had the candidate of the right, Valéry Giscard d'Estaing, not 'colluded' with French Freemasons and agreed to become one himself.

## Freemasonry and the Latin American Revolutions

Freemasonry also features prominently in the series of revolutionary movements dating from the second decade of the 19th century that eventually saw Latin American countries declare independence from their Spanish colonial masters. One of the key figures in these wars of independence was General José de San Martín, the liberator of Argentina, Chile and Peru. San Martín had become a Freemason in Spain in as early as 1808. When he arrived in Buenos Aires in 1812, he and his collaborators established their own lodge called the Lautaro Lodge. Another important revolutionary figure, Bernardo O'Higgins, joined the Lodge in 1816.

It would appear that San Martín set up the Lodge explicitly as a tool to further the cause of South American independence, using it as a way of networking in secret away from the gaze of Spanish spies. It even had its own revolutionary credo, which stated: 'Thou shalt never recognize as the legitimate government of the country any other than that which is elected by the free and spontaneous will of the peoples, and the republican system being the most adaptable to the government of the Americas, thou shalt try by all means within thy power to have the peoples adopt it.' That San Martín took the Lodge and its oaths very seriously is suggested by the fact that years later, with independence won, it is said that he refused to discuss Lodge matters with a non-member, even though that man was a good friend. Meanwhile, the most important figure of all in South American independence, Simón Bolívar, was also a Freemason.

## Britain and the Freemasons

In the UK, Freemasonry has perhaps been less overtly politically controversial than in countries such as France. One reason for this is the fact that there was no equivalent to the French Revolution in Britain (though there was the Glorious Revolution of 1688, when James II was removed from the throne and William of Orange replaced him.) The author Stephen Knight believes it 'plausible' that Masonic lodges may have backed the cause of William and Mary, but there is no evidence to support this.

Freemasonry arguably had no need of a revolution to gain influence in England (and later Britain) because it had already gained membership at the highest levels of society. This includes many members of the royal family. Kings George IV and William IV were Freemasons, as were Edwards VII and VIII, and then the present Queen's father, George VI. The current Duke of Kent is today the Grand Master of the United Grand Lodge of England, having taken on the role in 1967. (Apparently the Queen's husband, Prince Philip, was not interested in taking up the position.)

The roll call of British politicians and establishment figures who called themselves Freemasons is equally impressive. These include Winston Churchill; the important 19th-century statesman George Canning; the explorer, adventurer and colonialist Cecil Rhodes; the historian Edward Gibbon; the explorer Robert Scott; the writer Sir Arthur Conan Doyle; and even an Archbishop of Canterbury, Geoffrey Fisher.

It is within other, less visible facets of society in which the presence of Masons has been most numerous – and most controversial. For the main accusation against Freemasonry in Britain, apart from the claim that it is akin to devil worship, is that the Craft has, over many years, formed a tight-knit, powerful and potentially dangerous network of members who have permeated many professions and institutions in the country. As suggested earlier, the Masons are said to be a kind of 'old boys' network', only on a much larger and more organized scale.

In their various books on the influence of Freemasonry in Britain, authors Stephen Knight and Martin Short have detailed cases in which Masonic influence is said to have had an impact on the City, the local government and the Church. Above all, they highlight cases involving the judiciary, the legal profession and the police. Knight quotes the words of a former senior CID officer, David Thomas, who stated in 1969: 'The insidious impact of Freemasonry among the police has to be experienced to be believed.'

In many ways, the accusations that Freemasonry can influence and ultimately corrupt such institutions as the law and the police are the most serious charges levelled at the movement. The very nature of such professions dictates that much of what goes on within their inner workings has traditionally been hidden from the public gaze. This secrecy has led to some serious allegations: that Masons have helped each other to gain promotions, covered up mistakes and errors for fellow Masons and even helped them get off criminal charges.

In his foreword to Knight's book, *The Brotherhood*, Martin Short recounts a story that he gave as evidence to the Home Affairs Select Committee. In the mid 1990s this committee, prompted by growing public and media concern, had decided to investigate the influence of Freemasonry on British police and the judiciary. The tale involves a father and son from Leicestershire who were staying in a hotel in Blackburn and were having a late-night drink at a ground floor bar. Several powerfully built men came in and told the pair they should not be drinking there. After a brief 'discussion', these men then proceeded to beat up both father and son. Mysteriously, the police didn't arrest the four assailants; rather, they arrested the father and son despite the fact that they were the ones with injuries.

At a subsequent court case it emerged that most of the group of men who had confronted the father and son were police officers and members of a lodge in Blackburn. Much of the prosecution evidence was also contra-dictory. It seems that through no fault of their own, the father and son had been drinking at a Masonic function, a mistake to which some lodge members had taken exception. The jury threw out the case and, after many years and many obstacles, the father and son were able to sue their assailants successfully for £170,000. Interestingly, it was the Lancashire police force that paid up the compensation on the grounds that the beating had taken place in their capacity as police officers. Short argues: 'In my view it is outrageous that the public should be expected to pay anything towards righting what appears to be a thoroughly Masonic wrong...'

Such accusations about Masonic interference in the judicial system are certainly not confined to Britain. For example, this author is aware of a case in Sri Lanka in which a man was turned down for a job simply because the company's doctor claimed that the man had a health problem. No other doctor who examined the man found anything wrong with him, and so he decided to take the case to tribunal – which he won. Despite a complete lack of evidence on their side, the company appealed this decision and took it to court. Just before the hearing started, the man's lawyer turned to him and said gloomily: 'I'm sorry but we've got no chance, we will lose this case.' The man was baffled, given the weight of medical evidence on his side. 'How can we lose?' he asked. 'Because the judge is a Freemason – and so is the company doctor,' said the lawyer. And indeed, coincidence or not, the supposedly un-losable case was lost.

Accusations that Freemasons protect their own in this way and behave like a kind of 'closed shop' in many professions, especially the law, continue to this day. In 2003 a Welsh barrister called Roger Everest claimed that his application to become a judge was turned down because he had not become a Freemason. Everest told the *Western Mail* newspaper that 30 years previously he had been warned that he would never get on in the legal profession after he turned down an invitation to join the Dinas Llandaff Lodge in Cardiff. 'The judiciary in South Wales is a closed shop, which I believe excludes ethnic minorities, women and men who are not part of it,' he told the newspaper. 'After over 30 years as a practising barrister on the Wales and Chester circuit with hundreds of satisfied clients – not one of whom has ever made a complaint against me – I am furious never to have been offered the opportunity to sit as a judge.'

As previously mentioned (*see page 82*), the widespread concern over Masonic activity in the professions and public institutions did provoke some government action at the end of the 1990s. After recommendations made by the Home Affairs Select Committee, the British government set up a system under which members of the criminal justice system were invited to register membership in the Freemason movement. However, many have criticized this system as ineffective because it is purely voluntary for serving members of the criminal justice system. For example, in 1999 it was reported that when Crown prosecution lawyers were asked about their membership, 41 per cent did not respond. Other Freemasons have proclaimed silence, arguing that the compulsion to reveal their membership would be a breach of their human rights.

This issue also arose when the Welsh Assembly made it compulsory for assembly members (AMs) to disclose the fact that they were Freemasons, and then made such membership a criminal offence. Representatives of Wales's estimated 18,000 Masons protested strongly, and there were even threats of legal action under human rights laws. The Freemasons pointed out that they were being discriminated against, as they were the only group whose membership had to be revealed by Assembly members. James Bevan, the Provincial Secretary of the southeast division of Freemasonry, explained what this meant in practice: 'We had the ridiculous situation that, as a Freemason, if I wanted to become an AM, I would have to declare my membership. But a member of the Ku Klux Klan…would be all right.' In 2005 the Assembly voted to make it a requirement to register membership of any 'closed membership group', though a breach of these rules was no longer a criminal offence.

The United Grand Lodge, meanwhile, says that society has no need to fear the influence of Masons in public life, and that favouritism to fellow Masons is forbidden under their code of behaviour. 'That would be a misuse of membership and subject to Masonic discipline,' claims the Lodge. 'On entry into Freemasonry each candidate states unequivocally that he expects no material gain from his membership.' Nonetheless, unease remains about the role of Freemasons in public life. In a second report on Freemasonry in 1999, the Home Affairs Select Committee noted: 'We repeat the point made in the previous Report: there is a great deal of unjustified paranoia about Freemasonry, but Freemasons, with their obsessive secrecy, are partly to blame for this.' The Committee later added. 'We are also aware that there is a widespread belief that improper Masonic influence does play a part in public life. Most of these allegations are impossible to prove. Where they can be carefully examined, they usually prove unfounded. It is clear, however, from some of the examples cited in this Report and the previous Report, that there are cases where allegations of improper Masonic influence may well be justified.'

## Conclusions

The claims made by some about the ancient heritage of Freemasonry and its direct links with older societies may be flimsy. But this does not mean that the Craft has not had a major influence in shaping the modern world. Masons may not have masterminded the American and French revolutions, but prominent members were indeed involved in both world-changing events, and helped provide the conditions in which the ideas that led to those revolutions could develop. To this extent, Masonry can be seen as a quasi-political force in history, one that helped bring about changes in society that reflected the values that Freemasons claim to believe in: those of freedom, equality and the brotherhood of man. Many see this as evidence of this secret society's positive influence on the world. 'The Masons have been the single most influential source of democratic ideals in the Western world in the last three centuries or so,' says John Michael Greer, author, member of several secret societies and initiate into all degrees of the Scottish Rite up to 32 Degrees.

On the other hand, at various times in recent history the mere existence of Freemasonry around the world has been cited as proof of a global conspiracy, whether working on behalf of Zionism, capitalism or imperialism. Such criticism is easily dismissed, coming as it usually does from groups and regimes on the far left or right of the political spectrum. It is harder, however, to shrug off the claims that in some countries and in some parts of society, Masons have abused their network of contacts to indulge in favouritism for fellow professionals, and have even, in some cases, intervened corruptly to help them out.

Doubtless Masons will claim that any organization has a few 'bad apples', and that certainly Freemasonry is now more open about both its membership and actions compared with the past. But not everyone is satisfied. To its critics, Freemasonry remains a continuing concern, a potential source of corruption and bias at the heart of many of society's most important institutions. This view is ironic given the Masons' role in promoting ideals and principles that helped sweep away some of the world's more outdated and restrictive forms of government.

# 4

## The Enlightened Ones

ACCORDING TO FORMER PROFESSIONAL SOCCER player, BBC sports presenter and Green Party activist David Icke, an elite group of 'reptilian' humanoids has controlled the planet since ancient times. To this day, he believes, some of the most prominent people in the world belong to this exclusive club: Elizabeth II, Her Majesty the Queen of the United Kingdom of Great Britain and Northern Ireland, Hillary Clinton, George W. Bush and Tony Blair, to name but a few. Icke believes that all of these people are either reptiles in human form, or are at least controlled by this group. This idea may sound a little far-fetched, best suited to an episode of *Doctor Who*, but for Icke, these lizard-humans form the oldest and most powerful secret society imaginable: the Illuminati.

Icke is not the first and nor will he be the last to invoke this name. Type the word 'Illuminati' into a major search engine and the number of web pages that come up runs into several million. In the world of secret societies, conspiracy theories and covert global agendas, 'Illuminati' is one of the most commonly used names. In a sense, this is hardly surprising, as the word is the plural of the Latin *illuminatus*, which means 'enlightened'. Thus, any group calling themselves 'illuminati' are claiming to have a special insight into the nature of life and humanity.

Throughout history various groups have immodestly claimed this title as their own, while in more recent times it has become a sinister title that critics have pinned upon alleged dark, shadowy groups they claim are trying to take over the world – or have already done so. Icke's lizard theory, then, is just one of the latest in a long succession of claims made about the Illuminati. It is eccentric to say the least, and it is fair to say that few treat such theories with anything but derision. However, a number of groups throughout history have indeed called themselves the Illuminati.

## The Alumbrados

The concept of a person being 'enlightened' is an ancient one, stretching back to early Christianity and before. In the past, the act of baptizing someone into the faith was described as a means to 'enlighten' that person. In slightly more modern times, in late 15th- and early 16th- century Spain, there was a group known as the Alumbrados; the name means 'enlightened' in Spanish, and can be translated back into Latin as 'Illuminati'. The Alumbrados weren't an organized group; rather, they were a collection of individual Catholic mystics, people who sought to reach divinity through meditation, prayer and inner contemplation. One of the leading Alumbrados was Maria de Santo Domingo, best known as La Beata de Piedrahita.

The origins of the Alumbrados 'movement' are obscure, and there appear to have been different strands of it, existing among both educated and uneducated sections of society. One theory is that its roots were in Italy, but this form of Catholic mysticism was especially strong in Spain, particularly in older cities such as Salamanca and Toledo. The fact that many Alumbrados were associated with these old cities, and that some were Catholic converts from Judaism and Islam, suggests that the mysticism at the centre of the movement may have had some non-Catholic origins, too.

Within Moorish Spain, Toledo was well known as an intellectual centre, where scholars from the West travelled in order to learn from and discuss ideas contained within books brought to Spain by Islamic scholars. Many of these books originally came from Ancient Greece. Because Church authorities had banned or even destroyed the works of many 'pagan' authors, it was not until these Islamic scholars brought these tomes to Spain and Sicily that the ancient ideas and knowledge therein were discovered (or rediscovered) in the West. In any case, whatever the origins of the Alumbrados, and despite the fact that these mystics seem to have been remarkably peaceful, the Spanish Inquisition took a dim view of them. This was, after all, a time when the rise of Lutheranism and the Reformation was posing a threat to Roman Catholicism, and thus a number of Alumbrados were burned as heretics.

## The Illuminés d'Avignon

An entirely unconnected group bearing a similar name was established many years later in southern France. The Illuminés d'Avignon was a society created by a former Dominican priest called Antoine-Joseph Pernéty and a Polish count called Thaddeus Grabianka. Pernéty, who had worked as a librarian for Frederick the Great in Berlin, was clearly a learned man who had read widely on Freemasonry and the occult, as well as about Christian mysticism. A Swedish mystic, theologian and scientist by the name of Emanuel Swedenborg, who claimed that he could converse with angels and demons, also influenced this short-lived society. Swedenborg, who was not a Freemason himself, also influenced other later Masonic groups.

Not a great deal is known about precisely what Pernéty and his followers believed, nor about the rituals they practised. However, their beliefs seem to have combined a mixture of alchemy, Freemasonry, hermetic magic and the occult in general. They also seem to have had a special devotion to the Virgin Mary. In 1789 two English visitors were apparently 'finally initiated into the mysteries of their order', but it seems that the society died out soon afterwards, as the French Revolution unfolded. It seems certain too that the Illuminés of Avignon had nothing to do with the Alumbrados, nor with the most important and certainly the most publicized Illuminati group in history: the Bavarian Illuminati.

## The Bavarian Illuminati

The Ancient Illuminated Seers of Bavaria is one of the best-known secret societies in history. It is an organization that, since its creation, has launched a thousand conspiracy theories and endless speculation. Indeed, its founder, Adam Weishaupt, would doubtless be surprised (and pleased) to know just how prominent his organization has remained in the more than two centuries since it was created.

The Bavarian Illuminati society was created on 1 May 1776, in Ingolstadt in Upper Bavaria. Its founder, Weishaupt, was an academic. Born in 1748, he had been educated by Jesuits and became the first lay-professor of Natural and Canon Law at the local university. Weishaupt was deeply influenced by the Enlightenment, and was a free-thinker, marking a distinct break with the teachings he had received as a child. However, his time with the Jesuits was far from wasted. Apart from teaching him how to think, the Jesuits had unwittingly impressed upon the young man the importance of loyalty, discipline and discretion when running an effective organization – lessons that Weishaupt was to put to good use within his new society.

When Weishaupt originally established the group, his idea had been to call it the Society of Perfectibilists, though this curious name was later changed to Illuminati. The original name is something of a clue to the nature of the group that the former Jesuit pupil wanted to create. Weishaupt wanted the members of his society to improve themselves, to strive for human perfection; they were told to read both the ancient classical writers such as Aristotle, along with newer thinkers, too. Each new member or initiate had a tutor who would help guide him on this path towards understanding and enlightenment. The ultimate aim for this group of superior beings was to one day take over political power and create the perfect society based on their wisdom. It was, indeed, a secret organization formed with the specific aim of governing society.

It would, however, be unfair to depict Weishaupt as a power-crazed individual who sought to rule the world. He seems genuinely to have believed in the ultimate goodness of humans, and wanted merely to unlock that potential. The main obstacle to human perfection, he believed, was traditional thinking that was hidebound by politics and by Church teachings. These old-fashioned ways of looking at the world had to be pushed aside.

From the start, the Bavarian Illuminati had close links with Freemasonry. Weishaupt himself was a Freemason, though he appears to have been frustrated with the rule that lodges did not get actively involved in politics (even if some of their members did so as individuals). However, for someone looking to set up a self-consciously secret society, Freemasonry provided a fantastic opportunity. Weishaupt had already learnt, from his time with the Jesuits, the benefit of running a disciplined organization.

In the Masonic lodges, Weishaupt saw an opportunity to take over an existing secretive structure and to use it to promote his own society and ideals. The academic in him also realized that for his ambitious plans to succeed he would need to have influence over the most important sections of society: people with ability, money and connections, as well as those in positions of power. The lodges were full of such people, as in 18th century Europe Freemasonry was hugely popular among the intelligentsia. So it was that Weishaupt set about creating what became a secret society within a secret society. He did this by recruiting the heads of various lodges, thus gaining control over the lodges themselves. It was a tactic of which his former teachers in the Jesuits would have been proud.

The secrecy employed by the Bavarian Illuminati was extraordinary. For example, each member of the group was given a code name. Interestingly, Weishaupt chose the name Spartacus, after the gladiator-slave turned revolutionary, whose revolt in the 1st century BC at one time threatened to bring Rome to its knees. It was a small but telling sign of the Professor's radical agenda. Adolph Knigge, a minor nobleman and writer from Hanover who had helped Weishaupt create the society, took the name Philo, after the 1st-century Jewish philosopher. Another key member, a diplomat named Xavier von Zwack, was known as Cato after the Roman statesman. Other adopted names included Lucian, Diomedes and Pythagoras. Places, too, were given codes names; the society's headquarters was in Munich, and this was known to them as 'Athens'. Messages exchanged between members were also written in code. Even the names of the months of the year were changed, as was their entire calendar; members dated their letters in relation to the year in which Yazdegerd III, a Persian king, ascended the throne. (Yazdegerd III was the last of the Sassanid and Zoroastrian rulers, and he came to the throne in June AD 632; the Parsees still date their calendar from this time.) For Weishaupt, secrecy was a vital element of the organization, and was certainly prudent given the society's revolutionary aims and the nature of politics at the time.

The membership of the Illuminati was divided into three main levels. Indeed, its organization had some similarity to that of the Masonic lodges. The first level was that of the Nursery. The Nursery had three degrees within it: Novice, Minerval and Illuminatus Minor. The second level, known as the Masonic degrees, consisted of Illuminatus Major and Illuminatus Dirigens. The third level was called the Mysteries, and this was sub-divided into Lesser Mysteries and Greater Mysteries. These were broken down further, too: the Lesser Mysteries was made up of the Presbyter and Prince degrees, while the Greater Mysteries consisted of the Magus and Rex degrees.

Though there are similarities with Freemasonry in this structure, there was one important difference when it came to membership. To be a member of a lodge, Freemasons at this time had to believe in a Supreme Being, whereas there was no such requirement for membership in the

Illuminati. The Illuminati was a secular organization that believed in changing society, freeing it from what it saw as the dead hand of tradition. The group was also against notions of private property and social institutions such as marriage. Some have even described the group's vision as being that of a new world order (this expression is often used by modern conspiracy theorists to describe the ultimate aims of secret societies).

For several years Weishaupt and his key lieutenants were successful in their attempts to spread Illuminati influence. Though its original focus had been on Bavaria, the secret society soon had members in other parts of Germany, Switzerland and sections of the Austro-Hungarian Empire. The great German writer Goethe was an initiate, as were the rulers of Weimar and Gotha. Exact figures on how many members the society had at its peak are hard to come by. Some say that perhaps 2,000 people were initiated into the Illuminati during its existence; another view is that no more than 650 persons reached the important degree of Illuminatus Minor. These figures may not seem great, especially when the society had as its aim the creation of a new form of society, yet most of these members were important people whose influence was greater than the numbers would suggest.

Though the Order of Illuminati prided itself on its secrecy, its existence and goals eventually began to leak out. By as early as 1782, a number of Freemasons who were not members of Illuminati knew about its existence and its plans to use lodges to extend its power. Then, over the next year or two, lurid stories began to circulate in sections of Bavarian society about the existence of a dangerous secret organization lurking in its midst. In 1784 and 1785, the Bavarian authorities issued edicts outlawing secret associations. The once-secret Order of Illuminati was a secret no more.

According to one colourful story, the authorities learnt of the existence of the Illuminati after one of its members was struck dead by a bolt of lightning. Officials who examined the body found incriminating letters written by Weishaupt sewn into the dead person's coat lining (whether in code or not is not known). However the breach happened, the Illuminati were unearthed and Weishaupt feared the worst. He fled Bavaria and made his way to Gotha, and to safety. Weishaupt probably thought then that he had a chance to rebuild the Order once things had calmed down. But they didn't. The secret police in Bavaria soon came across a large cache of Illuminati documentation and correspondence, and the resulting publicity and controversy effectively spelled the end of this once secretive society.

Weishaupt did not himself suffer too much as a result of the discovery of the Order. He spent the rest of his days in the relative calm of Gotha writing, mostly about the Illuminati, its philosophy and how it had been brought down. The influence that the Order had on wider European thought and events is harder to gauge. The Illuminati were part of the Enlightenment movement, and Weishaupt was strongly influenced by the works of Voltaire. The Order also had a number of important members across much of Europe, who were influenced by Illuminati ideas even if the society itself was no more.

## The French Illuminati

Indeed, once the group was unmasked, the name of the Bavarian Illuminati became publicly known across Europe, and some former members of the Order undoubtedly, if discreetly, continued to promulgate its beliefs. For example, a French journalist, writer and publisher called Nicolas de Bonneville had close links with a prominent member of the Illuminati called Christoph Bode. De Bonneville, who had become a Freemason in Britain in 1786, was a radical who played a part in the French Revolution. He was allegedly one of the first to suggest that the Bastille should be stormed, the action that became the best-remembered event of the entire Revolution.

On 13 October 1790, de Bonneville and a radical priest called Abbé Fauchet created a secret society called the Cercle Social (or Social Circle), which some believe was modelled on Illuminati structure and, to some extent, beliefs. The aim of the Circle, which had members in both Britain and the United States, was to propagate the 'doctrine of love which is the religion of happiness'. De Bonneville even published his own newspaper called *La Bouche de Fer* ('The Mouth of Iron'), a publication that became the society's own mouthpiece. Among de Bonneville's demands were freedom of the press, the sharing out of lands and the abolition of the Catholic Church. It was a radical agenda, in line with Illuminati thought.

Another secret society that sprang up during the Revolution was the Conspiracy of Equals or Conjuration des Égaux, as it was originally called in French. This society was formed by François Noël Babeuf, who became known as Gracchus Babeuf – after the politician of the Roman Republic who had worked on behalf of the common people against the aristocrats. Babeuf had known de Bonneville in the early days of the Revolution, but it was with another man, Philippe Buonarroti, that Babeuf set up the Conspiracy of Equals in 1796.

The aim of the society was to counter the more conservative direction the Revolution had taken after the Terror; indeed, the society was explicitly revolutionary, seeking to seize power through a core of dedicated activists drawn from important positions and officials. Babeuf wanted to create 'perfect equality' and 'universal happiness'. Unhappily for him, his tight-knit group of revolutionaries had a spy in its midst who was working for the authorities. Once officials learnt of the group's plans they struck, first arresting all of its leading figures. Attempts were made to spring Babeuf from jail but they failed, and in May 1797 he was guillotined. Buonarroti was deported and went on to write a book entitled *Histoire de la Conspiration pour l'Egalité* (1828), which told the story of Babeuf's plans, and went on to become a kind of handbook for later revolutionaries and secret societies.

Despite its links with a handful of revolutionary figures, it would be difficult to believe that the Illuminati had a great influence on the French Revolution had it not been for two writers: a former Jesuit called Augustin de Barruel and John Robison, a Freemason from Scotland. In separate works they both claimed that it was the Illuminati (and the Freemasons) who had plotted and executed the French Revolution. The two books appeared in 1797, eight years after the start of the Revolution, and caused a stir across Europe. Both works purported to prove that the French system had not collapsed because of abysmal government, an outmoded monarchy and appalling inequality; instead, it was all down to the machinations of revolutionary secret societies. Here was the proof that some people had been looking for.

The English-reading public already knew Abbé Barruel. In London he had published an account of what happened to the French clergy during the Revolution, a work that he dedicated to the British nation in recognition of the kindness it had shown to clergy forced to flee from across the Channel. This doubtless made people more receptive to his more controversial work, entitled *Mémoires pour Servir à l'Histoire du Jacobinisme* (1798–1799). His thesis was that the Freemasons had prepared the way for the Revolution, but it was the Illuminati who had worked as an 'inner circle' of Masonry to carry out the Revolution itself. He also memorably described Weishaupt as a 'human devil'.

It seems that Barruel either made a lucky guess, or appears to have known that the Illuminati's infiltration of Freemasonry was indeed part of a deliberate plan by Weishaupt. There is little or no evidence, however, to back up his theory that the Revolution owed its origins to the Bavarian order. Nonetheless, Robison had, in his book, independently come to similar conclusions, though he appears to have been influenced by the Abbé's writings. Robison, too, blamed both the Freemasons and the Illuminati in his lengthily titled tract, '*Proofs of a Conspiracy against all the Religions and Governments of Europe, carried on in the secret meetings of Freemasons, Illuminati and Reading Societies*'.

It's not hard to see Barruel's motives for his book: he was a monarchist and a supporter of the papacy, so the Revolution opposed everything he stood for. Robison's motives were slightly different, however; as a Scottish Freemason he wanted to put some intellectual distance between the safe, god-fearing folk of British Masonry and the exotic, subversive Freemasonry practised by continental lodges and allied groups such as the Illuminati. He claimed that he himself had been asked to join the Illuminati, but refused. Both works were widely read and found a ready audience among those who bemoaned the loss of the *Ancien Régime* in France and the overthrow of established order by a revolutionary rabble. Even so, some contemporaries criticized Barruel and Robison for producing little or no evidence to support their extravagant claims.

Weishaupt once wrote that the '…great strength of our Order lies in its concealment…let it never appear in any place in its own name…' Once the group was uncovered by the Bavarian secret police, its usefulness as a behind-the-scenes agitator for political change vanished, whatever Barruel and Robison claimed. Yet the story – or mythology, one could say – of the Illuminati lives on. While they may have had some small influence on events in their own short lifetime in their spreading of ideas and acting as a justification for repression, the real legacy of Weishaupt and his fellow Illuminati lies in the way they have become a catch-all representing all secret societies in world history.

## Origins and Legacies

Numerous theories have developed about the Illuminati, many of them suggesting that the group never really disappeared, but simply reformed and stayed hidden. Others have claimed that the Illuminati were inheritors of a much older secret society. What is clear, however, is that the true nature of the Illuminati has largely been obscured as the many theories surrounding them and their origins have mushroomed out of control.

One common theory holds that the Bavarian Illuminati were the original inspiration for communism. It is certainly true that Weishaupt foresaw an end to private property in his utopian society, but there is no economic analysis within the order, no division of society into economic classes, no discussion of a bitter class struggle – all of which were developed by Karl Marx in the following century. Instead, the Illuminati were liberal elitists whose ideas sprang from Enlightenment thinking with a sprinkling of ancient-world mysticism thrown in. Others have argued that the Illuminati were part of a secret tradition that could trace its ancestry all the way back to ancient Babylon. Still others claim that, after he went into exile, Weishaupt simply set up the Illuminati again, this time succeeding at maintaining its secrecy.

A willingness to see the Illuminati as the hidden puppet-masters of world history continues to this day in the form of scores of different conspiracy theories, including those of Icke mentioned earlier (*see page 99*). One of the most prominent advocates of this Illuminati-centred view is the John Birch Society, an organization set up in the United States in 1958. A dozen self-styled 'patriotic and public-spirited' men, the leader of which was a retired sweet manufacturer from Massachusetts called Robert Welch, founded the organization. The Society takes its name from a military intelligence officer and Baptist preacher called John Birch, who was killed by Chinese communists just after the official end of the Second World War. One of the Society's chief preoccupations has always been the threat of communism, and it claims Birch as the first American victim of the Cold War.

The John Birch Society further believes that the Bavarian Illuminati were the precursors to modern-day communism. An article published by the Society states: 'The Order of the Illuminati, created by an obscure ex-professor named Adam Weishaupt on May 1 1776, was the ancestor of the Communist movement and the model for modern subversive conspiratorial movements.' This claim, says the article, is 'documentable'. The article ends: 'In 1848, a disreputable hack journalist named Karl Marx ... published the Communist Manifesto, which digested the Illuminist program into a form suitable for mass action.'

## The New World Order

Closely allied to the Bavarian Illuminati conspiracy theory is the idea of the 'New World Order'. Indeed, it is this New World Order that the Illuminati and their secretive descendants are supposed to be trying to impose upon the world. The John Birch Society is one group that has warned about the New World Order, but it is by no means alone. In 1991, for example, the well-known American television evangelist, Pat Robertson, published a book called *The New World Order* (Word Publishing, 1991) in which he linked the Illuminati and Freemasonry with Satanism and a plot against Christianity. He further claimed that the French Revolution was part of this great plot.

New World Order theorists also point to the words on the reverse of the Great Seal of the United States and the reverse side of the one-dollar bill: *Novus Ordo Seclorum*. As we have seen, these words are usually translated as 'A New Order for the Ages', but New World Order theorists render the words as 'New World Order'. A key part of the New World Order theory is the goal of a world government, and conspiracy theorists point to the growing power of the United Nations, the European Union and even the North American Free Trade Agreement as proof that the Illuminati are inexorably pushing the world's sovereign peoples in this direction. This concern is also linked to international organizations such as the Bilderberg Group (*see Chapter 6, page 164*), which, as we shall see, is supposed to represent the Illuminati in modern form.

## The Rosicrucians

Although the Bavarian Illuminati have inspired many theories and legends, we can at least be reasonably certain about their origins and how they organized themselves. The same cannot be said, however, about one of the most truly mysterious secret societies in history: the Rosicrucians. In fact, it is not even possible to talk in terms of one Rosicrucian Order or Fraternity; for the truth is that down the centuries there have been many groups and organizations that have claimed this name, or variations of it. The name 'Rosicrucian' is derived from the Latin words for 'rose' and 'cross'. But there is little else that is simple about this mysterious movement that has long intrigued occultists and historians alike. In essence, it is an esoteric movement or tradition that probably has its roots in mystical Christianity, but which has links with alchemy, the Kabbalah and Western occult and magical traditions. Its chief preoccupation is the perfectibility of the human soul.

Rosicrucianism first appeared in the early 17th century when three pamphlets were published anonymously in short succession. The first is known as the *Fama Fraternitatis*, and appeared in 1614 in Kassel, Germany. The second, often referred to as the *Confessio Fraternitatis*, appeared a year later in the same town, while the third was called the *Chemical Wedding of Christian Rosenkreutz*, and appeared in Strasbourg in 1616. The first of these 'manifestos' tells the story of a mysterious monk known only by the initials C.R.C. (though the third pamphlet makes it clear that this refers to 'Christian Rosenkreutz'). Apparently born in around 1378 to a high-born but not very wealthy German family, the young Christian was said to have been handed over to a monastery when he was just five years old. While still a very young man, Rosenkreutz, who was well educated and intellectually curious, went on a pilgrimage to the Holy Land (a common enough practice then) in the company of an older priest. On the way, however, the priest (who is known only as 'Brother P.A.L.') died in Cyprus, the traditional staging post on the way to the Middle East in those days.

Rosenkreutz carried on alone, travelling first to Damascus, where he is said to have come into contact with many wise men and scholars from across the Mediterranean and Middle Eastern world, and where he was able to find books on all kinds of esoteric subjects, plus works on algebra and astronomy. From Damascus the young scholar made his way deep into the desert in Arabia into what is today the Yemen. Once there, Rosenkreutz is said to have studied medicine and mathematics for several years before moving on once more to Egypt, and then to Fez (in what is today Morocco), where he supposedly studied magic and astrology.

After leaving Fez, the young Rosenkreutz decided to head for home via Spain. It is noteworthy that Rosenkreutz's story thus far bears some resemblance to that of Pythagoras, who, like Rosenkreutz, had been a precociously bright youth who had travelled widely in the East to learn first-hand ancient secrets and knowledge. And, rather like Pythagoras, we are told that the travel-weary Rosenkreutz now wanted to go back home and share the secrets of what he had learnt with others. However, when he returned to Europe, Rosenkreutz found that rather than being appreciated for the knowledge he had acquired, he was laughed at. Dismayed at his reception, Rosenkreutz retired to the monastery in which he had been raised.

Now aware that the world was not yet ready for the knowledge he had acquired, the monk established a secret organization called the Fraternity of the Rose Cross, with himself as head of the Order. The rather ambitious long-term goal of the Order was to bring about a wholesale 'reformation' in the world. Rosenkreutz established a system of rules for the secret society, which included taking vows of unselfishness, chastity and the absence of pride. He even established a headquarters, which he called the House of the Holy Spirit. Rosenkreutz is said to have lived for more than a hundred years, and after his death his body was concealed within a vault. A member of the Order is said to have found the body, surrounded by esoteric books, some hundred years later.

To this day scholars cannot agree on whether Rosenkreutz was a real historical figure or whether his story was simply a symbolic tale that may consciously have drawn on examples from the ancient world, such as Pythagoras. Indeed, this may indeed be the simplest explanation. A clue lies in the monk's name, which means 'Christian of the Rosy Cross'. If Christian Rosenkreutz is a parable, not a real person, then the young monk's travels throughout the world acquiring knowledge can be seen as representative of the steps that an alchemist takes. (An alchemist is by definition someone who is on a journey, making his way along the path to creating gold out of base matter – in a spiritual sense, achieving purity.)

There are other theories, however, about the true character of Rosenkreutz. One of the more plausible is that he was modelled on a real person called Paracelsus. Born Phillip von Hohenheim in Switzerland in 1493, Paracelsus was a noted scientist and doctor with an avid interest in alchemy, astrology and the occult. Like Rosenkreutz, Paracelsus is said to have travelled widely, not just in Europe but also in the Holy Land, Arabia and Egypt. He was noted for bringing back medical theories from the East, but had a reputation for arrogance, with the result that his ideas were not always well received. The parallels with the Christian Rosenkreutz story are apparent.

Other theories about the origin of the Rosenkreutz story delve back even further in time. One story claims that the reason why Rosenkreutz was taken to a monastery at the age of five was that the rest of his family had been slaughtered for being heretics. The story goes that he had been born a Germelshausen, a German family who owned a castle deep in the Thuringian forest. This family had held Cathar beliefs, which was why they had been targeted. The story further holds that a monk who had originally come from the south of France, and who had sympathy with Cathar doctrine, rescued the young boy. The monk then took the boy to a monastery, where he knew the boy would be safe. Yet other stories claim that Rosicrucianism started long before the Middle Ages, having originated in the 1st century as a blend of Egyptian Gnosticism and early Christianity.

The 20th-century Belgian writer and Rosicrucian, Émile Dantinne, has suggested that the Order had a strong Islamic influence. In particular, he claimed, there were links with a particular a group of Islamic philosophers who had formed a secret organization in the 10th century. 'One is inclined to believe that Rosenkreutz had found his secrets amongst a society of philosophers which had formed in Basra ... which ... applied itself seriously to scientific research,' he wrote in 1951. 'Their doctrine, which had its source in the study of the ancient Greek philosophers, became more pronounced in a neo-Pythagorean direction.' This would not have been surprising, as much of Islamic scholarship was deeply influenced by Greek philosophy, and it was through such scholars that a number of Greek philosophical works came into the West.

According to Dantinne, the group of philosophers was forced to keep its views secret because they did not accord with conventional Islamic beliefs. Dantinne's description of how the group operated certainly resembles the ways in which secret societies work: they met in secret locations from which non-members were excluded, helped each other out in life and had degrees of initiation. The lowest degree, according Dantinne, was Master of Crafts, while the highest was known as the 'Royal Degree'. He notes that the group also had some similarities with the Sufi tradition (a mystical tradition within Islam).

Yet another theory comes from Frances Yates, one of the best-known and most highly respected historians of the Rosicrucians and of occultism in Elizabethan England. She suggests that the famous epic English poem, *The Faerie Queene*, written by Edmund Spenser in 1590, has a Rosicrucian theme. In particular, she points out that a central character in the poem is the Red Cross Knight (or Redcross knight), a name that could have been rendered in German as 'Christian Rosenkreutz'. Her theory is that the Spenser poem was influenced by the philosophy of the English occultist John Dee (*see Chapter 5, page 133*), who may have disseminated his occult ideas during his own travels abroad. Interestingly, the poem was written more than 20 years before the first Rosicrucian 'manifesto' was published.

Yates also regards Shakespeare's play, *The Tempest*, as 'almost a Rosicrucian' manifesto, even though it, too, appeared before the manifestos were published. She writes in *Occult Philosophy in the Elizabethan Age* (Routledge, 1999), '...the history of the occult philosophy in the Elizabethan age is really the history of Rosicrucianism, though not called by that name. It acquires that name when it is exported, when, as a result of Dee's mission, it spreads on the continent...'

Whatever the true origins of Rosicrucianism, the appearance of the three pamphlets at the start of the 17th century caused something of a stir in intellectual and occultist circles in Europe. The idea that there existed a secret society that had preserved ancient knowledge and wisdom and was now talking about changing the world – not just in the arts and science but in politics as well – was a powerful one. To some it was exhilarating; to others it was dangerously subversive. Various enthusiasts made attempts to get in touch with this mysterious society – indeed, one of the pamphlets actively called on people to do just that – though with little apparent success.

Did Rosicrucianism as a belief system even exist? In truth, we do not know. It is conceivable that this fraternal order was simply a collection of like-minded people who shared an interest in subjects such as alchemy. Likely figures in this movement include the English physicist, philosopher and astrologer Robert Fludd, who studied in continental Europe at the end of the 16th century and the start of the 17th century. While Fludd denied that he was a Rosicrucian himself, he publicly defended Rosicrucianism from some of the attacks it faced when the manifestos were published, including charges that it was essentially Satanic in nature. Another important 17th century figure who wrote about Rosicrucianism, and who has been described as Fludd's 'successor' as an English apologist for the movement, is Thomas Vaughan. In 1650 Vaughan wrote a tract that was dedicated to the 'regenerated Brethren RC'.

A link between Rosicrucianism and politics also existed in much the same way as it did between both Freemasonry and the Illuminati and politics. These movements may have discussed seemingly arcane ideas, but they did not exist in a social vacuum. Any new idea or movement could be seen as a challenge to orthodoxy, and thus as potentially subversive.

The Rosicrucians were part of the debate and spirit of the age at a time when the fledgling discipline of science was beginning to break off some of the shackles of orthodox social and religious dogma. Rosicrucian philosophy may have found a political champion in the shape of Frederick V, the so-called 'Winter King' who was ruler of the Palatinate of the Rhine from 1610-1620, and who was also briefly king of Bohemia. A Protestant, Frederick was seen as a potential contender to take over as emperor of the then Catholic-ruled Holy Roman Empire, but he and his followers were also associated with Rosicrucian ideas.

In 1613 Frederick married Elizabeth, daughter of James I of England, in London. It is interesting that Shakespeare's play, *The Tempest* – the most magical of his plays and one clearly influenced by the story of John Dee – was performed for the couple before they left the country. However, Frederick was to last barely a year as King of Bohemia, ensuring his mocking nickname of 'Winter King' stuck, and his political influence faded after he was stripped of even his Palatinate title in 1623.

**Rosicrucianism and Freemasonry**

During the 17th century, the Rosicrucian Order (assuming it was an actual secret society) was elusive, to say the least. Soon, however, Rosicrucianism was to come into contact with another secret society that was about to emerge into the public gaze: Freemasonry. As early as 1621, Scottish poet Henry Adamson mentioned the fraternity of the 'Rosie Crosse' alongside Freemasonry in a poem. Another link is provided by Elias Ashmole, the well-connected 17th-century astrologer and antiquarian who, as we saw in Chapter 3 (*see page 71*), described how he was initiated into a Masonic lodge in England. Ashmole appears to have shown a keen knowledge of the Rosicrucian manifestos that appeared in the early part of the 17th century. He even quoted from one of them in the preface to a collection of writings on alchemy, another passion of his and one that is intimately linked to Rosicrucianism. Moreover, according to Rosicrucian historian Christopher McIntosh, there is, in the Bodleian Library in Oxford, a letter written in Ashmole's hand that is addressed to the 'Brothers of the Rosy Cross', which asks if the unsigned writer can join the fraternity. It seems, therefore, that close links between Rosicrucianism and Freemasonry existed as early as the 17th century.

By the 18th century, when speculative Freemasonry had emerged, the links between it and Rosicrucianism had become explicit. The two traditions came together in continental Europe and involved the Scottish Rite, or Scottish Degrees of Masonry, that was created in the first half of the 18th century. Ironically, the Scottish Rite had little to do with Scotland; rather, it was associated with Freemasonry in France and other parts of continental Europe. Perhaps this association was part of a deliberate attempt to distinguish continental Freemasonry from orthodox British Freemasonry by using different rituals; others have suggested that it was an attempt to return to a supposedly 'pure and uncorrupted' Freemasonry of some imaginary bygone era. In any case, it is in these continental rituals that Rosicrucian influence can clearly be seen. The 18th degree of the Scottish Rite, for example, became known as the Knight of the Rose Croix. It has even been suggested that Rosicrucianism was behind the transformation from so-called operative masonry to speculative masonry discussed in the previous chapter (*see Chapter 3, pages 69–74*). There is no hard evidence to prove this theory, however, though it remains an intriguing possibility. At the very least, such a theory shows how, throughout history, many secret societies have become intertwined.

## Rosicrucianism Around the World

Apart from the original Rosicrucian Order (assuming it existed), the first concrete evidence we have of a real Rosicrucian secret society is the Order of the Golden and Rosy Cross (*Gold und Rosenkreuzer* in the original German). This Order was created in the middle of the 18th century (possibly in 1757) by an obscure German alchemist and Mason called Hermann Fictuld, about whom we know very little (the name Fictuld may have been a pseudonym). The organization appears to have been a recreation of an earlier and looser-knit group of the same name that had been established by another alchemist, Samuel Richter. Author Christopher McIntosh has suggested that there may have been an 'alchemical movement, calling itself the *Gold und Rosenkreuzer*, widely spread but operating secretly.'

Under Fictuld the organization, which flourished in many parts of Germany and also in Prague, was tightly controlled, and was part Masonic Lodge, part Rosicrucian Order. Given that the initiates were encouraged to study alchemy as part of their initiation process, it is probable that the group attracted frustrated Freemasons who wanted to get involved in esoteric practices.

The Order developed a fascinating (if highly improbable) story about its origins. It claimed to have been founded by a man called Ormus, an Egyptian magus who, at the end of the 1st century, converted to Christianity and set up a secret society. This society fused Egyptian esoteric knowledge with the new Christian faith and adopted the Red Cross as its symbol. The society later joined forces with the Essenes, the Judaic sect (*see Chapter 2, page 43*), and eventually passed its knowledge on to the Knights Templar in the 12th century. Secret societies steeped in this ancient wisdom were then established in Scotland and England. Alas, there is no evidence for any of these claims.

As we have seen, secret societies at this time were rarely divorced from society and politics, yet few societies can match the direct political experience of the Order of the Golden and Rosy Cross. Unusually for the time, the Order was politically conservative and boasted a number of high born members – eventually even a monarch. Frederick-William II, the nephew of Frederick the Great, became the fourth King of Prussia and reigned for 11 years, from 1786. Unbeknownst to many, five years earlier Frederick-William had been initiated into the Order of the Golden and Rosy Cross, taking the name Ormesus Magnus within the group.

One of the major influences on Frederick-William within the Order was Johann Christoph von Wöllner, the low-born son of a pastor. When Frederick-William became King, von Wöllner became his Finance Minister and most influential advisor. Johann Rudolph von Bischoffswerder, the man who had actually initiated the then-Prince into the Order, was also a close confidant of the monarch. Von Wöllner's economic reforms and his zeal for ensuring Protestant orthodoxy in the country proved unpopular, however, and he eventually fell out of favour even with Frederick-William. But despite von Wöllner's diminishing influence, the Rosicrucian 'circle' remained in power as long as Frederick-William lived, disappearing from the scene only when the late monarch's son, Frederick-William III, came to power.

Berlin was not the only place in which the Rosicrucians held influence in important circles during this time. Indeed, in Russia the growing influence of both Freemasonry and Rosicrucianism was beginning to alarm Empress Catherine the Great. A leading figure in esoteric circles in Moscow at this time was a man called I. G. Schwartz, who had been born in Transylvania, and who in 1779 had gone to teach German at Moscow University. Involved to some extent with the Russian Freemasons,

Schwartz's real interest was in Rosicrucianism, and during a visit to Berlin in 1781 he met with von Wöllner.

Upon returning to Russia, Schwartz reorganized the existing Freemason Harmony Lodge as a centre of Rosicrucian activity in the country. This use of a Masonic lodge to promote Rosicrucianism was probably carried out without the knowledge of most Lodge members. Indeed, out of a provincial network of up to 60 lodges across Russia, only the Lodge Masters were aware of the Rosicrucian link. The Rosicrucians also took advantage of a relaxation in publishing laws to set up their own registered publishing company to produce esoteric works (though they also covertly ran a private, unregistered one). When Schwartz died in 1784, his place was taken by Baron Schroeder, who continued to report back to the group's Rosicrucian masters in Berlin. Later, when Frederick William II became King of Prussia, von Wöllner directed his influence through Prince N. Trubetskoy.

Catherine the Great herself had never had much time for Freemasonry, though initially she regarded it more with mock-horror amusement than with genuine alarm. Gradually, however, her concern about the existence of secret societies began to grow. The unmasking of the Illuminati by Bavarian agents in 1784 heightened her concern, though it was the outbreak of the French Revolution in 1789 that finally brought home to her the potentially subversive danger of secret societies.

Though she was a child of the Enlightenment and had been a regular correspondent with Voltaire, Catherine was first and foremost an autocratic ruler. She was prepared to tolerate many things, but not a threat to her rule. Thus she ordered a close eye to be kept on Masonic activity in Moscow – which effectively meant Rosicrucian activity too, given their control of the lodges – and eventually ordered an investigation into their publishing activities.

A Freemason called N. I. Novikov, who had been a member of the Harmony Lodge since the time of Schwartz's reorganization, carried some of this work out. Novikov was later accused of holding secret meetings, swearing eternal oaths to the Rosicrucians and having conducted a secret correspondence in code with von Wöllner. Though never formally tried, in 1792 Novikov was sentenced to 15 years imprisonment in a top-security prison, which, even then, was regarded as a harsh sentence.

Catherine's tough treatment of Novikov is often cited by critics who cast doubt on her reputation as a relatively liberal, book-loving, benign ruler – an image she cultivated, especially in her early reign. However, the Empress was worried not just about her own rule, but about what would happen to Russia under her son and heir, Paul. Catherine was already convinced that Paul was not up to the job of becoming emperor, and there is evidence that the Rosicrucians/Freemasons tried to recruit him to their cause. For example, one of the charges against Novikov was that he had tried to ensnare a 'certain person' into their sect – this was code for Paul. And correspondence clearly shows that from the early 1780s, Schwartz and his Rosicrucian masters in Berlin hoped to recruit Paul.

Though Paul may never have joined the Rosicrucians/Freemasons, he certainly shared an interest in the occult and esoteric. Russian Rosicrucians even wrote hymns of greeting for Paul. One went:

In you Paul we see
A pledge of heavenly lore.
In your wonderful union
We read the sign of the angel.
When you are adorned with the crown
You will be our father.

Moreover, some of the influential people around Paul were Freemasons, while others belonged to other secret societies. For example, the influential Admiral S. Plescheyev, who was Paul's naval adjutant, had travelled to France in 1788 where he had joined a secret society based in Avignon called New Israel. Another member of this group was a nephew of the leading statesman, Nikita Panin, who had been Paul's tutor as a boy. And when Paul eventually acceded to the throne for what was to prove a short and ill-fated reign, one of his first acts was to release Novikov from prison. At the end of the 18th century, the Rosicrucians evidently had some powerful allies.

After the death of Frederick-William II and the end of the Rosicrucian 'circle' at the Prussian court, the Order of the Golden and Rosy Cross seems quickly to have faded from the scene, not just in Prussia and Russia but also from areas throughout Eastern Europe, where it had gained members. By 1800 the Order appears to have vanished altogether. Yet the 19th century was to prove a fertile time for Rosicrucian thinking. There was a revival of interest in the subject throughout the French-speaking world, with evidence of a possible Society of the Rosa Croix on the island of Mauritius at the end of the 18th century.

In the second part of the 19th century, the Marquis Stanislas de Guaita and a former bank clerk by the name of Joséphin Péladan created a society called the Ordre Kabbalistique de la Rose Croix, or the Kabbalistic Order of the Rosy Cross. Formed in 1888, the Order had a ruling council of 12 members with de Guaita as the Grand Master. The identity of six of these members was kept a closely guarded secret, so that the Order would be able to reform itself in case it came under threat. Whether these six other members really existed or whether this was simply a device to add an air of mystery we do not know.

The Order had three different degrees, which initiates reached after studying and passing exams on occultism and occult history – in some senses it was a kind of Rosicrucian university. Members are said to have included the composers Erik Satie and Claude Debussy. By 1891 Péladan, a devout Catholic, had fallen out with de Guaita and other Order members, and he set up his own explicitly Catholic Order known as l'Ordre de la Rose-Croix Catholique et esthétique du Temple et du Graal. This Order proved very popular within artistic and intellectual circles in the last decade of the 19th century. Meanwhile, de Guaita's Order continued well into the 20th century, claiming Grand Masters into the 1980s.

France was far from being alone, however, when it came to what was almost an explosion of interest in Rosicrucian ideas and societies in the 19th and early 20th centuries. New organizations came and went, often with almost bewildering regularity. One of the most important in Britain was called the Societas Rosicruciana in Anglia. This organization was founded in 1866, and appears to have derived from a similar group that had formed in Scotland. The Society had three Orders divided into nine different grades or degrees, and the head of the Society was known as the Supreme Magnus. One of its later members was the writer Rudyard Kipling.

Yet another important development in Rosicrucian history took place in the United States. The arrival of those with Rosicrucian sympathies on American shores dates back to pre-Independence times, when members of German Rosicrucian groups made their way to the New World to set up their own communities. One group, colourfully called 'the Woman in the Wilderness' after the description in the Book of Revelation 12:6, founded a community in Pennsylvania in 1694.

It was only in the middle of the 19th century, however, that Rosicrucianism really took off in the United States. In 1861 the *Fraternitas Rosae Crucis* was established, and claimed themselves as the same 'authentic Rosicrucian Fraternity' that had been set up in Germany in the second decade of the 17th century and 'the direct descendent of the original Rosicrucian Fraternity'. On its website today the Order claims that in the 18th century, before the Revolution, the ultimate ruling body of Rosicrucianism in the Americas was the Great Council of Three, and that this consisted of Benjamin Franklin, George Clymer and Thomas Paine. The website further claims that during the American Civil War the members of the Great Council were 'Paschel Beverly Randolph, General Ethan Allen Hitchcock and Abraham Lincoln'.

## Rosicrucianism in the 20th Century

The 20th century saw the establishment of various Rosicrucian orders, some of which are still with us today. One short-lived society was the Order of the Temple of the Rosy Cross, which was founded in 1912 but did not survive the First World War (1914–1918). (It was closely linked to the Theosophical Society.) Some claim that this Order will re-emerge, but with a different name, in 2012, the year of its centenary.

Another British society was formed in 1924, this one called the Rosicrucian Order Crotona Fellowship. A journalist and actor called George Alexander Sullivan, who wrote under the name Alex Mathews, founded the Order, which later established a Rosicrucian Theatre in southern England, and may have had links with the revival of modern witchcraft as an organized force.

The United States saw the birth of yet another order, the Ancient Mystical Order Rosae Crucis (often known by its initials AMORC) in 1915. The founder was illustrator and occultist Harvey Spender Lewis who, according to AMORC history, had previously gone on a trip to France, apparently to find out more about the Rosicrucian tradition and to assess his 'worthiness' to become a leader. According to the AMORC, '…in 1909 (Lewis) was directed to make his appearance before certain high officials in France. He visited Toulouse, the ancient centre of the Rosicrucian international conclave, and returned from that country in possession of further authority.'

## Modern-Day Rosicrucianism

Most, if not all, current Rosicrucian groups claim ancient ancestry for themselves, even if it's apparent that they were set up in modern times. The creation myth for AMORC, for example, is that it originated in Egyptian mystery schools in the 15th century BC. Such claims, however, probably have more of a symbolic than a literal purpose. In any case, this does not stop such groups from being thoroughly modern when it comes to their current day activities. Many of them focus on teaching the un-initiated about what they see as the true path to self-enlightenment and fulfilment through a blending of different occult paths, techniques and knowledge. For example, AMORC's website offers 'simple weekly lessons' that students can study at home. What do they study? In AMORC's case, they study what the website calls the 'Rosicrucian system':

> The Rosicrucian system is unique – it provides a foundation that ties together all of the different aspects of metaphysical study, and demonstrates their inter-connectedness. To our knowledge, it's the only system that does this. Understanding the natural laws that govern all realms – physical, mental, emotional, psychic, and spiritual – leads to true prosperity and peace of mind. This is exactly what the Rosicrucian Order provides – a systematic approach to the study of higher wisdom that empowers you to find the answers to your questions about the workings of the universe, the interconnectedness of all life, your higher purpose, and how it all fits together. (www.rosicrucian.org)

As with so many religions, sects and therapies, much of modern-day Rosicrucianism is about self-help and seeking the path to enlightenment. An example of this type of teaching can be found on the website of the Rosicrucian Order, whose headquarters are based in Las Palmas, in the Canary Islands, 'symbolically' halfway between 'the Old World and the New'. The Order's website (www.rosicrucian-order.com) states:

> In the present Information Age we know that computers can be programmed and re-programmed, producing different results. The mind works in a manner that is similar to the computer. Incorrect programming can cause serious illness and trauma leading to personal misfortune in life.
>
> We can learn how to correct a great deal of the illness from which we suffer. We can program ourselves to improve memory, to gain security and

confidence, for the improved functioning of our personality, and to enjoy better health.

So very many things are possible when we know the potential of our own Inner Mind. With this knowledge we can send the suffering to the place where it truly belongs: NOWHERE.

Though many Rosicrucians still have strong links with Christianity and Christian beliefs, they have from time to time come under attack from some Christian groups for their interest in the occult. An example of such an event occurred in the 1980s, when the Evangelical Church of West Africa tried to get the AMORC banned from Nigeria, essentially on the grounds that it was a secret society. A far more exotic claim is that AMORC was linked with Operation Gladio. This controversial and still disputed operation was an attempt to safeguard against a possible Soviet-led invasion of Western Europe after the Second World War. The idea was that certain paramilitary groups would 'stay behind' after Allied troops had left in order to support potential guerrilla, sabotage and resistance movements. It has even been suggested that AMORC and other groups were the creation of the French secret services. AMORC has dismissed any such suggestions as an 'out and out lie, pure fabrication, pure calumny and pure slander'.

Whatever the claims against it, the Rosicrucianism movement – which is probably the best way to describe it – has clearly had an impact on Western music, culture and mysticism, occupying a place somewhere between mainstream religions and more magical traditions. From its first appearance in Western culture, when society was in transition between the superstition of the Middle Ages and the movement towards science, the Enlightenment and eventually the Industrial Revolution, Rosicrucian ideas have arguably helped straddle these periods. But the tradition of magic has survived the age of reason, and has made a comeback in the 20th century. It remains with us to this day.

# 5

## Magic, Hate and the Old Gods

MAGIC HAS ALWAYS EXCITED strong emotions. In the ancient world magic was widely mistrusted because many believed it to be very powerful – and thus very dangerous. In the Middle Ages in the West it was mistrusted for similar reasons, but also because it was supposed to be the work of the devil and thus contrary to Christianity. In modern times magic is generally dismissed as pure nonsense.

While each of these assertions is a generalization, the point is that the reaction of most societies at most times to most magic has been hostile, driving those who believe in and practise it underground, into secrecy. The fact that magic and secrecy have often gone hand in hand underlines the importance of magic in the story of secret societies.

### Classical Definitions

Society's often ambivalent view of magic was exemplified by the Greeks. For them the highest level of magic was 'theurgy', which was magic connected with the gods. This concept was linked with the so-called high magic of the Egyptian tradition. For the Greeks, the Egyptian deity Thoth became synonymous with their god, Hermes. From the mixture of Greek and Egyptian traditions emerged Hermes Trismegistus, or 'Hermes the thrice-great' ('thrice-great' was an epithet traditionally applied to Thoth) (*see Chapter 1, page 27*), the legendary founder of magic in the Egyptian and Greek worlds.

For the Greeks, the aim of magic was usually ultimately religious in nature – achieving union with the divine. Pythagoras, who was to acquire semi-divine status among later followers, was reputed to be a great magician of an enlightened and high-minded kind. On the other hand, there was also what the Greeks called *mageia*, which is perhaps closer to what we might call sorcery, or practical magic. The term came from the word *magoi*, used to describe the traditional astrologers of Persia, and was later used to refer to a 'magicians' as a whole; for example, those who claimed to be able to heal people. From this word we also get the term *magus*, often used to describe the 'three wise men' who followed a star to find the infant Jesus in the New Testament. The Greeks were sometimes mistrustful of the work of these hired-for-magic *magi*, and Plato regarded them as a danger to society. (The Persians were also enemies of the Greeks, so there may have been a political reason why some Greeks came to mistrust them.) Even worse in many Greek eyes were the *goetes*, the makers of cheap potions and authors of spells to help people fall in or out of love or cure minor ailments.

The Romans were probably even more mistrustful of magic than the Greeks. Rome admired order and good governance above all else, and anything that appeared beyond the control of conventional administration was considered a threat. Just as the Romans tried to control subversive mystery cults such as the rites of Bacchus (*see Chapter 1, page 34*), so they often dealt harshly with sorcerers. Professor Jeffrey B. Russell, in his book, *A History of Witchcraft* (Thames & Hudson, 1982), points out that Roman emperors were actually worried about coming under magical attack. Sorcery was feared as the 'least detectable' and hence the 'most dangerous' of threats, and was therefore to be punished severely. Russell cites the case of a young man who was spotted in the baths touching the marble tiles and then his chest while uttering the seven Greek vowels. This spell was commonly employed to help cure stomach ailments, but this didn't stop the unfortunate bather from being tortured and executed. 'The harsh tradition of Roman law was one of the foundations upon which the medieval persecution of witchcraft was based,' writes Russell. Once again, thus, we see that fear of secrecy and secret groups can sometimes have more of an impact on society than does the secret activity itself.

Roman disapproval of magic didn't, however, stop some prominent citizens from indulging in it. Writing in the 1st century AD, Pliny the Elder describes the Armenian king Tiridates as a 'Magus', and recounts how he came to Rome at the time when Nero was emperor. 'He brought the magi with him and initiated Nero into their magic banquets,' writes Pliny. 'Yet although Tiridates had given Nero a kingdom, he was unable to teach him the art of magic.' Pliny, a keen observer of society and nature, was clearly no fan of the magi or of magic. 'This should be sufficient proof that magic is execrable, achieves nothing and is pointless,' he adds, proving that there were sceptics about the power of magic in the ancient world, too. Elsewhere he dismisses the 'tricks' of the Magi as 'ineffective' as they are unable to 'call down the gods or speak with them'. But Pliny also acknowledges that anxiety over sorcery and curses was widespread. 'Everyone fears being jinxed,' he admits.

The Romans were, indeed, an intensely superstitious people, from Julius Caesar downwards. They were also not averse to using various bizarre methods in trying to divine the future. One such method involved the observation of how eagerly chickens fed on a particular type of food; if they ate well, it was supposed to be a good omen. Rulers and military leaders didn't always like what the divinations told them, however. One Roman admiral was so displeased when the sacred chickens didn't eat well before a sea battle with the Carthaginians that he had them thrown over the side of his ship. Needless to say, he lost the battle. Indeed, as we shall see, one of the more interesting aspects of magic in relation to secret societies is that its impact is usually directly proportional to the number of people who believe in it – not just within the secret group, but in wider society, too.

## The Early Magicians

Western culture is full of stories about magicians who supposedly had great powers, Pythagoras being an early example. One of the most fascinating of these characters was Simon Magus, who appears in the New Testament as a close contemporary of Jesus. Simon is mentioned in the Acts of the Apostles where, in some translations, he is referred to as 'Simon the Sorcerer', a pretty good clue as to his reputation in mainstream Christianity. The New Testament further states that Simon had 'practised sorcery', had 'boasted that he was someone great', was known as the 'Great Power' and had a huge following (Acts 8:9–11).

Nonetheless, Simon and his followers were impressed enough with the preaching of Philip the Apostle to get themselves baptized into the new faith of Christianity. Simon, who was from Samaria, was said to be even more struck by the power of Christianity when he saw Peter and John laying their hands on people who then received the 'Holy Spirit'. In fact, Simon was so impressed that he is reported as offering the two apostles money in exchange for 'this ability' so that 'everyone on whom I lay my hands may receive the Holy Spirit'. Peter was furious with Simon for this suggestion, castigating his 'wickedness' in trying to buy the divine power and describing him as 'bitterness and full of sin'.

Simon Magus is similarly attacked in the writings of early Christians, who regarded him as the 'first heretic' of the new faith, and also as the founder of Gnosticism, the mystical, non-literal, philosophical belief system so despised among most Christians who believed literally in the story of Jesus's resurrection. At one time Simon Magus described himself as a messiah, and later referred to himself as a god or the 'word of god'. He also travelled with a female companion called Helen (later known in Christian writings as Helen the Harlot). After Simon's death, his followers – known as Simonians – worshipped Helen as an incarnation of the goddess Athena.

There are many stories about Simon Magus's powers, including one in which he turns stones into bread; he was even said to have been able to fly. Among Christian writers, from whom we know the most about Simon, he is often depicted in a magical contest with Peter to see who has greater power. In one story, Simon shows off his ability to fly in the forum in Rome. Peter then calls upon the gods to stop Simon and the latter falters and falls to the ground, breaking his legs. An unimpressed crowd then stone him to death.

One curious feature of the stories surrounding Simon is that Christians seemed to accept that both he and Jesus had great powers. However, there were two crucial distinctions between the two 'magicians'. The first was that, self-evidently as far as Christians were concerned, Jesus's powers (and even those of his followers) were far superior. Secondly those powers were of a different type than those of Simon Magus. The magic of Simon Magus was not based on his belief in God, and was thus regarded as inferior and emanating from the devil. Jesus's miracles, on the other hand, were divine in nature. Indeed, a number of observers say that the early Church felt it necessary to denigrate Simon Magus to help people distinguish clearly between the good 'miracles' of Jesus and the bad 'magic' of Simon Magus.

One fascinating, if improbable, theory is that 'Simon' was not actually his true name; that 'Simon Magus' is really Saint Paul. As we saw in Chapter One, there were two distinct traditions of early Christianity, and Paul was the leader of one group – the group that ultimately triumphed (*see Chapter 1, page 37*). According to the Simon Magus theory, the coded criticism of Paul remained, and is contained in the story of the flying magician.

If the idea that Simon Magus may really have been St Paul seems hard to credit, then most Christians would simply regard as blasphemy another radical theory about magicians from that period. The American scholar Morton Smith wrote a book called *Jesus the Magician: Charlatan or Son of God?* (Ulysses Press, 1998), the title of which gives a clue as to the book's controversial theme. Drawing on Jewish and pagan (i.e. non-Christian) stories, Smith draws parallels between the story of Jesus and those of other miracle-working healers of the time. One tradition is that Jesus went to Egypt, where he was taught the secrets of magic. It's an outlandish theory in the context of modern Christianity, and unsurprisingly, it has mostly been simply ignored. However, it would at least explain why early members of the Church were so keen to distinguish the works of Jesus from those of Simon Magus in people's minds.

Another magician of the time was a man called Apollonius of Tyana, who died in around AD 97. He, too, was an itinerant miracle worker/magician who foretold the future and healed the sick, and is said to have travelled widely – even as far as India, Ethiopia and Spain. His biography shares similarities with that of Pythagoras, whose teachings he embraced. Most of what we know about Apollonius comes from his biographer, Philostratus, whose testimony is not fully reliable. (On one occasion, Apollonius is credited with bringing the daughter of a Roman senator back from the dead.) Apollonius was to become an important figure in later pagan and occult writings and traditions, as well as in the realms of science and philosophy.

Christianity has always had an uncomfortable relationship with magic. On the one hand the miracles performed by Jesus and also those of later saints were proof of the invincible power of God and the rightness of their faith. Yet similar acts not performed in the service of their religion were viewed at best as misguided, at worst as works of the devil. The battle became one of good magic over bad magic, with Christians invoking the names of their favourite saints or the Virgin Mary to get what they wanted, or to ward off evil. Indeed, one person's prayer was not so very different from another person's magical spell.

The identification of sorcery and witchcraft with Satanism grew in medieval Christianity to the point where, by the middle of the 15th century, it exploded into what is known as the 'witch craze'. According to the agents of this widespread persecution of witches, the whole of Europe was full of secret covens and groups plotting evil deeds in dark corners. People were accused of devil worship, taking the forms of other creatures and cursing the Christian sacraments – all tell-tales signs of diabolical witchcraft – and convicted on the flimsiest of accusations. There followed a kind of collective madness across the continent (and briefly in the New World, too) in both Catholic and Protestant countries, with numerous plots and Satanic conspiracies apparently uncovered. Neighbour denounced neighbour, sometimes out of spite, other times simply to prevent him or herself from being the object of suspicion.

Few, if any, of the devil worship accusations contained any truth at all. This fact did not, however, stop thousands of innocent people from being tortured and then executed in many different countries over a period of around 200 years. Alleged witches were killed before and after this period, but this was the height of the witch craze. These innocent victims were dis-proportionately women – often women who were widowed or who, for whatever reason, had never married, and were easy targets for groundless accusations.

But men were accused and executed, too. For example, in 1628 a man named Johannes Junius, who was accused at the notorious German 'witch house' used by investigators at Bamberg, was facing certain execution. Before the sentence could be carried out, he managed to send a moving letter that he had written to his daughter, Veronica. It begins, 'Dearly beloved daughter Veronica. Innocent have I come into prison, innocent have I been tortured, innocent must I die…' Junius then describes his ordeal in the 'witch prison', including how he was tortured with thumb-screws. 'And so I made my confession … but it was all a lie,' he tells her. At the end of the letter, after urging Veronica to keep the smuggled letter secret to save him from more torture, he writes: 'Good night, for your father Johannes Junius will never see you more.'

The reasons for the witch craze are numerous and much debated by historians. A growing instability and insecurity in society, a changing climate and the impact of the Black Death have often been cited as factors, together with a rise in heresy (for example, that of the Cathars) that had created a climate of fear amongst both the populace and the authorities. Another possible factor was, ironically enough, that the beginning of this period saw a massive upsurge in what might be called highbrow magic within intellectual circles. For those unable to differentiate between 'high magic' and witchcraft, the presence of the one merely encouraged the belief in the presence of the other.

## Renaissance Magic

Magic, astrology, divination of the future and other occult and esoteric practices have always been present in European culture, especially around royal courts. However, the interest in such subjects was given major impetus thanks to the presence of Islamic scholars and their books in Europe's own backyard: Spain. From as early as the 10th century and certainly from the 12th century, Spain, which had been occupied by the Moors since the early 8th century, resembled a European intellectual swap shop. In fact, the process was mainly one way. As we have seen, scholars from across Western Europe made their way to Spanish cities such as Toledo to read and translate ancient texts – many from Greece – that had been 'lost' to Western intellectuals for centuries. These eager scholars, some of them sponsored by bishops, some by secular rulers, devoured works on subjects as diverse as the occult, astrology, astronomy and falconry. Thus Moorish Spain became an important conduit for esoteric information moving out of the East and into the West.

An example of the kind of person who visited Spain at this time was Michael Scot, a Scottish intellectual and mathematician who became astrologer to the Holy Roman Emperor Frederick II. Scot, who was born in 1175, travelled first to Palermo in Sicily, another cultural exchange centre, and then to Toledo. Having learnt Arabic, he was able to read not just translations of Aristotle, but also the important original works of Islamic scholars such as Averroes and Avicenna. Scot's greatest reputation, however, was probably as a magician/astrologer, and the kind of works available in Moorish Spain would have given him ample chance to pursue his studies in these areas.

A colourful character, Scot is credited with having foreseen the manner of his own death (though we are not sure exactly when he died). From his astrological and necromancy practices Scot had 'seen' that a small stone of a precise weight would one day fall on his head and kill him. So, as a precaution he took to wearing an iron skullcap. One day, however, he entered a church for the Feast of Corpus Domini and took off his hood.

Apparently not wanting to have people stare at his strange headgear, he then also took off his protective skullcap. Soon afterwards a small stone fell and struck him on the head, causing a minor wound. When Scot picked up the stone and weighed it, he realized that it was precisely the same weight as the stone he had 'foreseen' would kill him. Resigned to his fate – or perhaps just hopelessly impressed with his predictive ability – Scot promptly put his legal affairs in order. He died shortly thereafter.

## The Kabbalah

Spain also played a key role in the development of another part of what would become the Western magical tradition. This was the Kabbalah (or Cabala). In Judaism, the Kabbalah is a complex and mystical tradition passed down by rabbis. It is a way of interpreting and finding hidden meanings in Jewish texts, including the Old Testament, based on the use of numbers and numerology. (There is a similarity here with the Pythagoreans, who believed that the secrets of the universe were contained within mathematics.)

The Kabbalah, which began as an oral tradition, is supposed to date from the very beginnings of humanity, when an angel is said to have revealed its secrets to Adam, the first man. In fact, most scholars accept that the Kabbalah, in its written form at least, dates from the 12th and 13th centuries, from rabbis in southern France and Spain who themselves drew on ancient texts and traditions for inspiration. At the time, these countries hosted some of the most important and educated Jewish communities in Europe.

The principle text of the Jewish Kabbalah is the Zohar (meaning 'Splendour'), a series of books that first came to light in Spain in the 13th century. The publisher was Moses de Leon, and its authorship was attributed to a 2nd-century rabbi who was said to have been inspired to write it after spending years in a cave trying to escape persecution by the Romans, time he spent reading and re-reading the Torah. In fact, Moses de Leon was probably himself the author, though he may well have drawn upon much older oral traditions.

The Kabbalah did not, however, stay an exclusively Jewish phenomenon. As early as the 13th century (about the time that the Zohar appeared in Spain), a Catalan mystic and occultist by the name of Ramon Lull developed what became known as Lullian Art, a technique for understanding the nature of the world and the truth of the Christian faith. This technique was influenced by the superior intellectualism of Judaism and Islam of the time. The British historian Frances Yates has described Lullism as a 'medieval form of the Christian Cabala', even though it did not use Hebrew.

The Christian Cabala was created much later than the Jewish version – towards the end of the 15th century – and became fused with Hermetic magical tradition after two key events in Western history. The first was the fall of Constantinople (now Istanbul) in 1453 to the Ottoman Empire. This formal end of the Byzantine Empire, which had been ailing for many years, led to the exodus of many scholars to Western Europe. A number of these scholars brought ancient texts with them, which led to profound interest in the works of the legendary Hermes Trismegistus (*see Chapter 1, page 27*).

The second key event was the military triumph of the joint rulers of Spain, Ferdinand and Isabella, known as the 'Catholic Monarchs', in 1492. Their defeat of the last Moorish stronghold in the country ultimately led to the expulsion of not just Muslims but Jews, too, from the Peninsula. Many of the Jews who left Spain both before and after 1492 went to Italy, creating renewed interest in the Jewish Kabbalah.

One of the key figures in the fusion of Kabbalistic ideas with Hermetic magic – the cornerstone of modern Western occultism – was a philosopher from Florence called Giovanni Pico della Mirandola. Like his contemporary Marsilio Ficino, Pico was an important part of the development of Renaissance thought, drawing heavily on Plato and Neoplatonism. In 1486 Pico published a series of treatises known as the *Conclusions*, which outraged sections of the Catholic Church. Condemned as a heretic, he was lucky enough to have powerful allies to save him from being executed. Among these conclusions was Pico's view that the Kabbalah justified and proved the truth of Christianity. In particular, he stated that 'no Hebrew (i.e. Jewish) Kabbalist can deny that the name IESU, if we interpret it on Kabbalistic principles, signifies the Son of God.' Pico also stated: 'No science can better convince us of the divinity of Jesus Christ than magic and the Kabbalah.' This shows that though Pico was condemned as a heretic by the Catholic Church, he saw his work on the Kabbalah as being firmly in the Christian tradition.

Influenced by Pico, in 1492 a German scholar called Johannes Reuchlin published *De verbo mirifico* ('Wonder-working word'), a book on the

Christian Kabbalah that helped spread the idea to other parts of Europe. In 1517 he published a second work, *De arte cabalista*. This was followed in turn by *De occulta philosophia*, written by the occultist Henry Cornelius Agrippa, which explicitly fused Hermetic magic and the Kabbalah into one occult work. As we saw earlier, Hermetic magic stemmed from the Greek-Egyptian tradition, and holds that the material world – objects – mirrors the spiritual world, perhaps best summed up by the famous dictum 'As above, so below'. Following the fusion of the two traditions, the symbolism of Kabbalism was described as the 'toolkit' of practising Hermetic magicians.

Agrippa, who was born in Cologne, was also a magician, and it is believed that he may have established his own secret society dedicated to the study and practice of alchemy. Agrippa believed that different types of magic existed; for example, he made a distinction between 'natural' magic and 'mathematical' magic. He also saw a difference between 'bad' magic, which made use of demons, and 'good' magic, which used Kabbalah to converse with good angels.

According to British historian Frances Yates, Agrippa saw the Kabbalah as providing the highest form of magic, and also as a form of protection for magicians against demons. Thus, not only did the German scholar see a clear divide between bad or black magic and white or good magic – he was clearly on the side of Christianity and the 'good side'. Moreover, Agrippa, who travelled widely, had a broad circle of contacts across Europe, including some important figures in the Protestant movement. Yet this did not stop Agrippa from acquiring, after his death, a fearsome reputation as a black magician. In particular he is supposed to have, on his deathbed, conjured up a black dog that became his 'familiar'. Such accusations came against the background of the witch craze and show how even 'high brow' magic among self-proclaimed Christians could render people as suspect. Little wonder perhaps that Agrippa is thought to have been advised to delay his publication of *De occulta philosophia* for fear of the reaction it might produce. He certainly waited 20 years before releasing the book, which was published just two years before his death.

However, as author and academic Jeffrey Russell points out in *A History of Witchcraft* (Thames & Hudson, 1980), while such highbrow magicians tried to emphasis the difference between 'good' high magic and the 'evil' sorcery associated with witches, '…this distinction was generally lost on public opinion, so that the result was that humanistic magic itself abetted the rise of the witch craze'. Little wonder that much of the work of many magicians was carried out in conditions of secrecy and with the support of powerful patronage.

## John Dee

One of the best examples of how 'high magicians' had to walk the tightrope between so-called good and so-called evil magic was John Dee. Dee, who was born in 1527, became one of the best-known and most controversial figures of Elizabethan society. Undoubtedly an exceptionally gifted man, Dee was an excellent mathematician and astronomer, and was an expert in the art of navigation, as well as having a life-long passion for high magic, including Hermetic magic and the Kabbalah. Dee also played a role in helping to develop the mythology of Britain, being credited with coining the terms 'British Empire' and 'Britannia', and in moulding the country's mythological past to fit in with the Elizabethan plan for expansion. For a country that was no longer under papal authority, this myth-building was an important facet in creating a distinct identity for England. The fact that Dee believed that he was descended from an ancient British royal family probably helped him in this respect.

Throughout his life Dee was involved in secrecy and magic, and frequently had to defend himself against charges that he was in league with evil demons. In fact, as British historian Frances Yates has pointed out, he saw himself as a Christian Cabalist, and thus literally on the side of the angels. According to Yates, 'This conviction was at the centre of Dee's belief in his angelic guidance, and it explains his pained surprise when alarmed and angry contemporaries persisted in branding him a wicked conjuror of devils.'

Dee's commitment to secrecy did not just concern his magical activities and studies, however. It has long been claimed that Dee acted as a kind of wandering secret agent for the Elizabethan court, and though the evidence for this is unclear, he was certainly an expert in the writing and deciphering of codes. He may also have been spying for the then-princess Elizabeth, when Queen Mary was on the throne (1553–1558), a dangerous time for the Protestant-leaning Princess given Mary's ardent Catholicism. (If true, this may explain why Dee was chosen to pick the most auspicious day for Elizabeth's coronation, which took place on 15 January 1559.)

Another important aspect of Dee's life was his personal library of books on the occult and many other subjects at his home in Mortlake, southwest of London. Not only was his collection reputed to be the finest of such books in England, it was also said to be one of the best in Europe. Yet despite his undoubted brilliance and many achievements, Dee's life ended with him penniless and out of favour at the court of King James I, dogged by claims that he summoned demons. It was a sad end for such a man. Yet, as British historian Frances Yates has suggested, Dee's influence lived on, and not just in his creation of the notion of a 'British Empire' for England and as a supporter of the colonization of North America. Indeed, his work may well have led to the development of Rosicrucianism, and he also became a talismanic figure to later generations of magicians.

One of the most important factors about Dee's life was that he, like others before him, straddled both the occult and what we would today call science and mathematics. To us, an interest in science and mathematics seems unexceptionable, but in Dee's time it could be enough to get you burned as a heretic. It was not unusual for a person to combine an interest in mathematics and magic; as we have seen from Pythagoras and the Kabbalah, numbers have often been thought to contain the secrets of the universe. While the interests of such men as Agrippa and Dee (and also Sir Isaac Newton, who was fascinated by alchemy) in these esoteric subjects might seem odd, this does not detract from the fact that such men were pioneers of scientific and philosophic thought. Indeed, one could argue that the occultists of the 16th and 17th centuries were the midwives of the age of reason and science that would ultimately be embraced by Europe.

Another figure to have straddled the occult together with science and mathematics was Giordano Bruno (*see Chapter 3, page 70*). A brilliant philosopher and cosmologist, Bruno was also profoundly influenced by the Hermetic magical tradition, and may have established a secret society of his own during the late 16th century (though there is no hard evidence for this). The Catholic Church, as we have seen, looked upon such beliefs with disfavour, and Bruno was eventually charged with heresy, tortured and executed. It is thus evident that while Bruno, Dee and others may have been midwives of the age of reason and science, their offspring would take a little while to reach maturity.

**Modern Magic**
Though high magicians of the 16th and 17th centuries such as John Dee

may have left their mark on the world, the extent to which these occultists were involved in magic-based secret organizations is less clear. It would be the Rosicrucians and the Freemasons who would become the best-known secret societies over the next couple of centuries. However, a revival of interest in the occult and magic in the middle of the 19th century and in the 20th century led to the creation of many new societies. One of the most influential was the Theosophical Society, founded in 1875.

The Theosophical Society started life as a secret society with its own passwords and degrees of initiation, and created an inner circle of members concerned with practical occultism. It did not remain a magical society, but nonetheless it was to have a huge influence on occult thinking and practitioners in later years. Its founder was a woman of Russian extraction called Helena Blavatsky (usually referred to as Madame Blavatsky) who was living in New York at the time. Blavatsky wrote two influential books, *Isis Unveiled* (1877) and *The Secret Doctrine* (1888), the second of which was published after she had moved to London, and made use of Hindu philosophy. The influence of Theosophy spread beyond the magical world; Rudolf Steiner, best known for the education system and schools that bear his name, headed a branch of the society in Germany.

While the Theosophical Society had a wide impact on general occult thinking, it was another society formed in the second half of the late 19th century that was to become the best known magical secret society in the modern world: the Hermetic Order of the Golden Dawn. The Golden Dawn, as it is usually called, was formed in 1887 by three men: William Woodman, Samuel Mathers and William Westcott. These men were all Freemasons, lived in Britain, and were members of the Societias Rosicruciana in Anglia; Westcott had also been a member of the Theosophical Society. Once again, we can see the inter-connected nature of many occult secret societies.

As with many secret societies, The Golden Dawn claimed antique origins. In its case there is a picturesque story that Westcott was browsing in a bookshop when he came across an old manuscript written in code. Upon deciphering the code he discovered that the manuscript contained rituals for a magical secret society, complete with the contact details of a female member of the society in Germany. Westcott got in touch with the society and supposedly received a charter to set up a Golden Dawn temple in England. The true origins of the group were, however, much more prosaic. The order was probably based on documents that had belonged to the Masonic scholar Kenneth Mackenzie, and which had passed into the possession of William Westcott.

The Golden Dawn quickly became one of the premier magical societies not just in Britain but also in the Western world. Temples were established in such diverse places as Edinburgh, Paris, throughout the United States and in Weston-super-Mare, in the west of England. The organization attracted members from high levels of society, along with writers and artists, including the poet William Butler Yeats. There were three orders of grades, or membership, within The Golden Dawn: the First Order, the Second Order and the Third Order. The First Order grades were Neophyte, Zelator, Theoricus, Practicus and Philosophus. The grades of the Second Order were all known as Adeptus, with the divisions being Minor, Major and Exemptus. The Third Order consisted of Magister Templi, Magus and Ipsissimus.

The importance of the Kabbalah and the Hermetic magical tradition to the Order was evidenced by the fact that each grade also had a pair of numbers attached to it. The first number indicated how far up the initiate was on the Kabbalastic Tree of Life, while the second showed how far down from the top he was. Thus, as the first number rose, the second fell; the Neophyte, for example, had no position on the Tree, and so was 0=0, while the Ipsissimus, meanwhile, was 10=1.

The Golden Dawn gave its members a step-by-step induction into the occult and practical magic, including their rituals and ceremonies. The organization was spiritual in nature; in other words, it was concerned with theurgy, the process of self-improvement by making contact with the divine spirit. But unlike other groups that might simply study the subject, The Golden Dawn was focussed on actually practising magic.

From the start, The Golden Dawn was an avowedly secret society. As author R. A. Gilbert states in *Revelations of the Golden Dawn* (Quantum, 1985), initiates had to agree to '…keep secret this Order, its Name, its Members and its Proceedings, from every person outside its pale; and even from Initiates unless in actual possession of the Pass-Word for the time being…' They also had to agree to study 'with zeal' the occult sciences, and aspiring members were warned that, 'This Order is *not* established for the benefit of those who desire only a superficial knowledge of Occult Science.' Further, initiates had to believe in a Supreme Being and to take an interest in Christian symbolism. Gilbert also states that The Golden Dawn

The importance of Isis and Horus, seen here depicted on a temple at Philae on the River Nile, stretched far beyond their native Egypt. Isis in particular was worshipped in all corners of the Roman Empire and has been a key deity to a number of secret societies.

PLATE 1

Pythagoras may nowadays be best known as a mathematician, but he received one of the most remarkable educations in the ancient world, and later established a secret society based on the teachings he had learnt and developed during his extensive wanderings.

PLATE 2

This image of the Virgin Mary and the infant Jesus is one of the most iconic in world history. Yet it may be an adaptation of an even earlier traditional image from the ancient world that featured the Egyptian goddess Isis with her child, Horus, in a similar pose.

PLATE 3

This church at Segovia, in Spain, is known as the Church of Vera Cruz, which means 'true cross' in Spanish. The building, which has twelve sides and a tower to the south, was consecrated by the Knights Templar in 1208. Noted collectors of holy relics, the Templars built the church expressly to house a precious sliver of wood that they believed was a piece of the true cross upon which Christ was crucified.

PLATE 4

By the start of the 14th century, the Templars had become a wealthy and powerful organization. Some rulers saw their status as a threat, however, including King Philip IV of France, who arrested and tortured them. Many were burned at the stake.

PLATE 5

The Freemasons are traditionally associated with architecture, ceremony and charity work. All three are combined here in this image from 1808 of the impressive Freemasons' Hall in London. The picture shows a prominent Mason of the time, Chevalier Bartholomew Ruspini, with two young girls from the Royal Masonic School, which he founded in 1789. Among the guests at the ceremony are the Lord Mayor of London, the Prince of Wales and the Ottoman Ambassador to Great Britain, underlining the extent to which Freemasonry was popular within the upper echelons of both society and government.

PLATE 6

The use of the 'all seeing eye' and the Latin words *Novus Ordo Seclorum* on the American one-dollar bill have excited much interest amongst some conspiracy theorists, who see them as proof of a Masonic or Illuminati plot.

PLATE 7

George Washington is perhaps the most famous Freemason in history. Though he never became Master of a lodge, membership seems to have been important to him as his widow arranged for him to be buried in accordance with Masonic rituals.

PLATE 8

The Spanish dictator General Franco developed a hatred of Freemasonry, on which he blamed many of Spain's ills. The reasons for his dislike were political as well as personal: his father, who had abandoned his wife and the young Franco, had been a Mason.

PLATE 9

The Grand Temple, pictured here, is one of the most important buildings in British Freemasonry. It stands at the heart of Freemasons' Hall in central London, and is a key meeting place for members of the United Grand Lodge of England. Its huge bronze doors weigh well over a tonne each, and its chamber is capable of seating up to 1,700 persons at a time. Possessing fine acoustics, the Grand Temple is often used to stage concerts.

PLATE 10

Freemasonry has a long and important tradition in France, where a number of Masons took part in the great revolution of 1789. The current Grand Lodge of France – or La Grande Loge de France, as it is known in French – pictured here was formed in Paris in November 1894, and uses the Ancient and Accepted Scottish Rite. It also explicitly supports the three core principles of the French Republic: Liberty, Equality and Fraternity.

PLATE 11

This image, entitled *A Rosicrucian Crucifixion,* is by American artist J. Augustus Knapp (1853–1938). Rosicrucians believe that the crucifixion symbolizes the passing of the human spirit through the cycle of life, death and resurrection, towards purity of the soul.

PLATE 12

Adam Weishaupt, shown in this portrait, was the founder of the real, if short-lived, Bavarian Illuminati in the 18th century. Educated by Jesuits, Weishaupt rejected their teachings but employed their organizational skills to set up his famous secret society.

PLATE 13

Adventurer, imperialist and diamond magnate Cecil Rhodes (1853–1902) left a will in which he expressed the desire to establish a secret society with the goal of bringing the world under one central government – essentially that of the British Empire.

PLATE 14

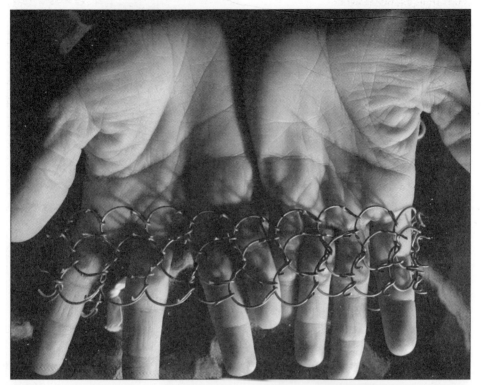

The Catholic organization Opus Dei has aroused considerable controversy since Spanish priest Josemaría Escrivá founded it in the 1920s, including over the fact that some members continue to practise the Opus Dei ritual involving mortification of the flesh. One popular mortification technique is the wearing of a cilice, pictured here. Usually worn out of sight on the upper thigh, the cilice is intended to cause the wearer some discomfort. It is typically worn for two hours a day.

PLATE 15

The Church of Scientology, founded by the late science fiction writer L. Ron Hubbard, is run internationally from its headquarters in Los Angeles, California. In the United States, as in other parts of the world, Scientology is recognized as a religion.

PLATE 16

'...appealed to esoterically-minded Freemasons...[and to]...members of the Theosophical Society who were disenchanted with the Eastern bias of the Society's teaching...' By February 1889 the organization had already attracted 60 members, including women – indeed one of the reasons for its popularity was the fact that it was open to female members.

It is a feature of many occult societies that they attract strong personalities who are then unable to agree on the direction the organization should take, and so it was with The Golden Dawn. After Woodman's death in 1891, Westcott and Mathers were left to run the Order, with Westcott apparently happy for his brilliant but somewhat unstable colleague to play the major role. However, in 1897 Westcott was forced to quit the Order. His day job was as a coroner, and when the authorities found out that he was involved in a secret magical society Westcott was forced to choose between his job and membership in The Golden Dawn. As another Golden Dawn member, Aleister Crowley, amusingly put it, the authorities had '...intimated to Dr Westcott that he was paid to sit on corpses, not to raise them.'

There was a suspicion that Mather was responsible for the authorities finding out about Westcott's occult activities. This, however, was only the start of The Golden Dawn's problems. By 1899 the highly-strung Mathers had fallen out with other members of The Golden Dawn and was eventually deposed as its leader, though some members remained loyal to him.

One reason why Mathers was deposed as leader was that he was involved in a row over a shadowy group known as the Secret Chiefs. The Secret Chiefs are supposedly 'cosmic moral guardians' whose role it is to oversee the smooth working of the universe and the workings of a magical order here on Earth. The late-18th-century Bavarian academic and occult writer, Karl von Eckartshausen, had suggested the existence of such a phenomenon in his book, *The Cloud upon the Sanctuary* (1802), and at one point he refers to a 'society of the Elect'. Von Eckartshausen also wrote: 'We must not, however, imagine this society resembles any secret society, meeting at certain times, choosing its leaders and members, united by special objects...this society knows none of the formalities of which belong to the outer rings, the works of man. In this kingdom of power all outward forms cease.' Madame Blavatsky (*see page 135*) had also claimed to be in contact with the Secret Chiefs (although she called them the Tibetan Masters, reflecting her interest in Eastern occultism), and some Rosicrucian groups had also hinted at their existence. Indeed, Westcott and Mathers claimed that they had initially set up The Golden Dawn through the Secret Chiefs, though Mathers later vehemently denied that Westcott had been in contact with them. In a letter written in 1900, Mathers insisted that '…it is I alone who have been and am in communication with the Secret Chiefs of the Order.'

The Order had other troubles besides its unstable leadership; it was also hit by bad publicity. The public first learned about the Order when the lurid details of a court case were reported at the start of the 20th century. An American couple who had set up an organization called The Order of Theocratic Unity were tried at the Old Bailey in London for conspiracy to defraud young women and for procuring three of them 'for immoral purposes'. Though there was no connection between The Golden Dawn and the Order of Theocratic Unity, the American couple had met Mathers and duped him, later using Golden Dawn rituals in their Order's own bogus ceremonies. The name of The Golden Dawn was thus revealed in court, much to the embarrassment of Mathers and other members of the Order. One member later wrote that the guilty American couple had been 'punished' by occult means, and that '…the terrible vengeance of the Secret Chiefs fell upon them.' They also received lengthy jail sentences.

The Golden Dawn members eventually split into three groups: the Alpha et Omega (led by Mathers), the Order of the Morning Star and the Holy Order of the Golden Dawn. Some temples survived until late into the 20th century, but in general they soon petered out. However, the influence of The Golden Dawn was considerable. Israel Regardie, an occult writer, member of the Order of the Morning Star and once Aleister Crowley's secretary, wrote, 'There can be little doubt that the Golden Dawn … was … the sole depository of magical knowledge, the only Occult Order of any real worth that the West in our time has known.' Indeed, The Golden Dawn and its successor groups went on to produce people such as Dion Fortune (born Violet Firth), a highly regarded author on the occult and magic, and there are still societies that exist to this day that use the name 'Golden Dawn'.

### Aleister Crowley

Probably the best-known magician and occultist of the 20th century was Aleister Crowley. Briefly a member of The Golden Dawn and an ally of Mathers (until they fell out), Crowley was later dubbed the 'Wickedest Man in the World', which only added to his colourful reputation: he was involved in sex magic and also became addicted to heroin. In 1934 he unsuccessfully sued an author over a book that had described him as a 'black magician'. The suit left him bankrupt, as well as ensuring his lasting infamy. The judge, Mr Justice Swift, claimed that he had, '…never heard such dreadful, horrible, blasphemous and abominable stuff as that which has been produced by [Crowley].'

Crowley's lurid lifestyle undoubtedly helped reinforce the link in many people's minds between magic and evil, yet he was also an important figure in occult philosophy. In 1904, while on holiday in Egypt, Crowley claimed that a messenger of the gods called Aiwass had spoken to him and informed him that a new magical Aeon, the Aeon of Horus, had begun. As a result of this event, Crowley wrote – or, as he claimed, had dictated to him – a book he called *Liber AL vel Legis*, or *The Book of the Law*. This, he claimed, was the 'scripture' for a new religion he called Thelema, from the Greek for 'will'. The core philosophy of this religion was the rule: 'Do what thou wilt shall be the whole of the law'. (Traces of this philosophy, which was not original, can be found back as far as Simon Magus, who suggested that initiates who had found god were 'free to live as they please'.) The new religion of Thelema was to underpin Crowley's approach to life and magic thereafter.

Crowley attempted to use his membership in another important magical secret society, the Ordo Templi Orientis (OTO), or Order of Oriental Templars, to further his magical ideas. The Order had been founded at the start of the 20th century, and its leading figure was a journalist and music-hall singer called Theodor Reuss. Reuss eventually invited Crowley to take over the British and Irish section of the OTO, and Crowley became a dominant and controversial figure in the Order, often warring with other members, especially after Reuss's death in 1923. Though Crowley largely failed to move the OTO in the direction of his Thelemic religion, this did happen to some extent after his death In 1947. Today, the OTO and its various offshoots claim several thousand members, and have a presence in scores of countries. It remains one of the most important magical groups in the world.

Crowley was also connected with the development of another very important movement in the world of the occult: the Wicca religion. Now popular in many parts of the world, Wicca employs witchcraft in its rituals despite attempts by fundamentalist Christians (especially those in the United States) to portray it as evil. Like so many secret organizations past and present, Wicca asserts an ancient heritage. Its 'creator', Gerald Gardner, a retired British civil servant, claimed upon its emergence in 1954 that Wicca was the continuation of ancient witchcraft cults that had somehow survived down the ages despite the slaughter of the witch craze. (There is little or no evidence for this claim.)

Whatever the truth of his movement's origins, Gardner can be said to have helped substantially with the reinvention of modern witchcraft. Gardner had known Crowley, and it was expected by some that Gardner would take over as head of the OTO in Britain. He didn't, instead creating Wicca. Exactly what role Crowley had in the formation of Wicca is unclear, but given the nature of some of the magical rituals in the *Book of Shadows*, the Wiccan magical book, it is likely that he had at least an indirect influence on Gardner.

The fact that Gardner's antique claims for Wicca are dubious does not necessarily mean that he invented them from scratch. He was involved with the Rosicrucian Theatre in southern England, and we have already seen that establishment's links with a Rosicrucian society (*see Chapter 4, page 120*). Moreover, Gardner is said to have been initiated into a witches' coven that was based in the New Forest area, though again we cannot be sure whether this coven was fact or fiction.

Gardner's creation of Wicca was born in wartime Britain, and it was during the Second World War that one of the more unusual stories of modern occultism is said to have taken place. After Nazi Germany's invasion of France in 1940, it seemed only a matter of time before Hitler's troops tried to cross the English Channel and invade Britain. It was at this dark moment in British and European history that a group of magicians and witches gathered together to help save the country. According to Gardner, the New Forest coven and others joined together in the forest to carry out what would have been the ultimate banishing ritual. They apparently raised a witches' 'cone of power', which they directed at Hitler and his troops, and which said simply: 'Do not come'. A number of the more elderly witches involved were said to be so overcome by the exertion involved in the ritual that they died some days later.

Dion Fortune (*see page 138*) and other magicians are also said to have been involved in a magical battle against Hitler, though whether this involvement was in the New Forest ritual or a different one is unclear. Such stories have echoes of similar tales about England's other famous escape from invasion: its escape from the Spanish Armada in 1588, which was apparently thwarted thanks to the intervention of magicians.

## Nazism and the Occult

It seems that the British occultists understood that Nazism had its own links with occultism. Of course, the rise of Nazi Germany can be and is completely explained by less esoteric factors; it would be absurd to suggest that Hitler's rise to power, his genocide against the Jews and the entire Second World War depended on the occult. But this does not mean that the occult did not have some role to play in shaping the ideas that underpinned Nazism and some of the emblems and motifs it employed.

A key philosophy that helped shape National Socialism, or Nazism, was what is called Ariosophy, an offshoot from Theosophy (*see page 135*). As we have seen, in Theosophical belief the whole of humankind embarks upon a form of spiritual progression, gradually evolving through time. In the Ariosophical worldview, the Aryan race – which had once been the 'master race' and sprang from the divine – had succumbed through mixing with 'lower' races and breeding with 'dark-skinned beast men'. The corruption had started when Eve had become 'involved' with a demon, the products of which were the so-called lower races. The solution was for the Aryan race to be 'purified', thus allowing it to take its 'natural' place once more as the leader of the world.

One of the main architects of Ariosophy was a man called Lanz von Liebenfels, an Austrian journalist and former monk. In 1905 Liebenfels started a magazine called *Ostara* in order to publicize his extraordinary views. Two years later he created his own secret society called the Order of the New Templars (Ordo Novi Templi), a mystical association that sought to harmonize science, art and religion on a basis of racial consciousness. Progression within this Order apparently depended on the 'purity' of the initiate's stock: the more Aryan he or she was, the more he or she rose up the degrees of membership. An order of the same name survives to this day.

It is known that Adolf Hitler was among the subscribers to *Ostara*, and may also have met Liebenfels, its founder. Dietrich Eckhart, a writer and occultist who had a powerful influence on the young Hitler and on the early development of National Socialism, was also a subscriber. In his book, *Hitler and Stalin: Parallel Lives* (Knopf, 1992), Alan Bullock, the distinguished biographer of Hitler, wrote: 'Eckhart was the man from whom Hitler learned the most in [the] early days of the movement.' Eckhart died in 1923, and Hitler paid tribute to him on the final page of his now notorious work, *Mein Kampf.*

Eckhart was also associated with another important organization of the time: the Thule Society, an offshoot of a German occult secret society called Germanenorden, or 'Order of Germans' (also known as the 'Order of Teutons'). The Society's founder was veteran occultist Rudolf von Sebottendorff. Sebottendorff set up the Society in 1912 as a magical occult organization, the purpose of which was to counter the 'Jewish conspiracy' and other such 'secret societies'. Needless to say, the organization was virulently anti-Semitic, and championed the supremacy of the Nordic peoples. The Thule Society took its name from the mythical lost continent of Thule, a place the Greeks and Romans had believed existed somewhere in the far north (some later identified this idea with that of the lost city of Atlantis). It was on Thule, claimed members and supporters of the Society, that the original Aryan race had lived.

While Hitler himself appears to have shown little or no interest in the Thule Society, there were clear links between its members and the rise of Nazism. In 1919 two Thule Society members, Karl Harrer and Anton Drexler, set up a fledgling political party called the German Workers Party (DAP), which Hitler joined. This quickly became the National Socialist German Workers Party (NSDAP), better known as the Nazi Party. It has been claimed that Rudolf Hess, a key figure in the future Nazi party, and Ernst Rohm, the head of Hitler's thuggish Brownshirts, were either members or attended meetings of the Society.

Another connection between the Thule Society and Nazism is that both adopted the swastika as one of its emblems. At the time of the rise of the Nazi Party, the swastika was already popular among various German groups, not as a symbol with an overtly political meaning but as a representation of the ancient roots of the Aryan people. The swastika symbol is in fact a very old one, with origins in ancient Aryan/Indian culture and elsewhere in the world. Indeed, examples of the symbol were found in excavations of the ancient city of Troy (in what is now Turkey), where it was, somewhat ironically, regarded as a positive symbol indicating wellbeing, life and goodwill. The racially focussed Ordo Novi Templi used the symbol as early as 1907, and then, of course, the Nazis adopted it as their symbol, forever changing its perception.

While Hitler's interest in secret societies may have been minimal, another key figure in Nazi Germany was seriously interested in the occult. Heinrich Himmler had been brought up a devout Catholic, and had been in contact with the Jesuits when he was young. As Himmler grew older he became interested in German folklore and mythology, and also in the occult philosophy of Ariosophy. Whilst head of Hitler's elite SS regiment, he is said to have consciously drawn on the Ordo Novi Templi for the organization's racial purity guidelines, and on the Thule Society for such imagery as its swastika and dagger emblem.

Himmler also drew inspiration (if that is the right word) from the theories of the Higher Armanen Order, a secret society created by Guido von List who was, along with Lanz von Liebenfels, one of the developers of Ariosophy thought. This society held that there were three castes of ancient Germanic tribes, with the highest being the Armanen or priestly-rulers. (Though a tiny minority, there are still some groups which appear to follow some of von List's ideas.)

Yet another connection between Nazism and secret societies lies in the fact that Hitler's SS regiment was modelled on the organizational structures of such societies as the Freemasons (though not on their beliefs – they were persecuted in Nazi Germany) and the Jesuits. Indeed, Hitler is said to have joked once that Himmler was 'our very own Ignatius Loyola', in reference to the 16th-century founder of the Jesuits.

## The Ku Klux Klan

One secret society that consciously used notions of racial superiority was the Ku Klux Klan (commonly known by its acronym the KKK). The name 'Ku Klux Klan' is a combination of the Scottish word 'clan' and the Greek word for circle, 'kyklos'. Six veterans of the American Civil War (1861–1865) who had fought on the Confederate side founded this notorious group in Tennessee in 1865. The first Klansmen wore ghost and goblin outfits to frighten people, but soon the organization took a rather more sinister turn and started attacking political opponents and former slaves.

Members of the KKK dressed in white outfits with hoods, a form of dress based on old Irish custom. They also had strange titles such as Titans, Wizards and Goblins. The federal government managed to curtail the original KKK's activities and by the end of the 1870s it had disappeared. However, the KKK had become a kind of racial supremacist brand name, and a successor organization started during the First World War, preaching its message of hate against blacks, Catholics and other non-white and non-Protestant groups. This message apparently struck a cord, and by 1924 the KKK's membership was close to four million. Its popularity fell in the late 1920s and plummeted in the 1930s, however, after its leaders allied themselves with pro-Nazi groups.

Since the Second World War (1939–1945) there has been some resurgence of groups claming the KKK label, and the name still carries the potential to encourage racist activity. Yet the KKK has not been without opposition from other secret societies. One such society sprang up in the 1920s specifically to oppose the Klan: the cheekily named Order of Anti-Poke Noses. Its stand was against 'any organization that attends to everyone else's business but its own'.

## The Odin Brotherhood

One secret society that has come to light in recent years is the Odin Brotherhood. Once more, as with so many such organizations, the group claims to have been in existence for many years; in its case, since 1421. The organization was apparently created to help the Old Religion – the worship of the old deities that Christians call pagan gods – during the time of the witch craze. The organization says that the Old Religion has survived, though it 'bears the teeth marks' of Christianity, a faith for which it clearly has little time. Information about this group came to light in 1992, when academic Dr Mark Mirabello published *The Odin Brotherhood* (Holmes Publishing Group, 1992), which was based on conversations and interviews that he had had with members of the group based in Britain.

Initiation into the Brotherhood involves members making three small incisions in their flesh. In the case of men, these are made on the chest; women make the marks on their right index finger. The cuts are made in the name of 'holy, necessary violence'. The Brotherhood rejects the concept that there is one god, an idea they dismiss as 'preposterous and absurd'. Instead, it says there are many gods; these include the familiar Norse deities such as Odin, Thor and Freya. Initiates believe in life after death but reject the Christian concept of 'hell', and talk about the need for people to 'seek knowledge' rather than to rely on faith, which they insist can 'paralyze the mind'. The Brotherhood also values strength over weakness and pride over humility, prizes courage highly and urges members to live well and 'die bravely'.

It is hard to know exactly where to place the Odin Brotherhood among the many secret societies in the world, or how to gauge its importance; indeed, we have little idea how many members it has or how widespread its membership is. There are many groups nowadays that seek to promote heathen/pagan religions, including the old religions of Northern Europe, but these are usually of comparatively recent origin. Like the Wicca religion, these groups try to re-interpret older beliefs and practices and adapt them for use today. The survival of a secret society from the early 15th century that was set up explicitly to protect those old religions would be extraordinary indeed.

Dr Mirabello believes that he was given information by the Brotherhood because '…they wanted me as a recruiting tool.' He says: 'There was a tacit understanding that my function was to reveal certain information. I was asked never to write anything negative about the group and to reveal no personal name; in return I would receive "fame" as a messenger.' He goes on to describe his preparations as 'quite elaborate'. 'First, a series of what appeared to be meaningful encounters in bookstores, then invitations to exotic dinners at night, then introductions to people who claimed to have met the Norse gods, then mysterious letters, written in verse, postmarked from Germany, claiming to be from the god Odin. Ultimately, in 2002, long after the work was written, a mysterious woman from Germany visited me suggesting she was (sent) from Odin. When she appeared on my small university campus, she made quite the impression.'

# 6

## Money and Influence

FOLLOW THE MONEY. THAT'S WHAT they say when it comes to crime riddles and political scandals, and it is certainly true when it comes to conspiracy theories and the secret societies that supposedly run our world. As we have seen, the Illuminati are the usual suspects behind this world plot, even if the proponents of these theories cannot always agree on exactly who its members are – or whether they are even terrestrial. But any conspiracy needs finance to make it effective. The finger of suspicion often points to bankers and Jews – and often to Jewish bankers – as the moneymen behind this world plot. Chief among the 'suspects' are the Rothschilds, the Jewish banking dynasty that moved out of the back streets of Frankfurt in the early 19th century to become one of the wealthiest and most powerful families in the world.

One of the reasons for the Rothschilds' early and lasting success in banking was that the family sent four sons of the original Mayer Rothschild to major European cities. The brothers went to London, Paris, Vienna, Austria and Naples, Italy and, once there, were instructed to establish another branch of the family network. The eldest sibling, Amschel, meanwhile, remained in Frankfurt, Germany to oversee the original family firm.

Keeping the business under tight family control was a successful strategy, though it inevitably raised suspicion and envy. The fact, too, that the Rothschild family made a large slice of its early fortune subsidizing the British in the wars against Napoleon – in other words, making money out of war – merely added to such suspicion. Furthermore, according to Stephen Knight in *The Brotherhood*, his book on Freemasonry, the Rothschilds have been Freemasons for generations. The family also maintained such close connections with the governments of Austria and

Great Britain that they were able to help bail out their central banks, and members of the family were ennobled in both countries, all of which has added further fuel to the conspiracy-theory fire.

Yet there is little or nothing that the Rothschild bankers have done that is not perfectly explicable by normal banking practices. Indeed, the family lost influence in the 20th century because it had not developed a big enough interest in the economy that was about to become the powerhouse of the world: the United States. This is hardly the behaviour of an elite family that is supposedly able to manipulate entire economies and even provoke world wars to suit its aims.

The United States has also had its share of financial giants linked with conspiracy and secret societies: John D. Rockefeller, who died in 1937, and John Pierpont Morgan (better known as J. P. Morgan), who died in 1943. These men may have been both powerful and ruthless, but again, there is no evidence that they were involved in any kind of Illuminati-inspired plot.

## Anti-Semitism and Secret Societies

The fact that the Rothschilds feature at the centre of so many conspiracy theories is perhaps no coincidence. For it is sadly the case that many claims alleging secret societies have contained more than a tinge of anti-Semitism. This state of affairs reached its nadir, of course, in the beliefs promulgated by the leaders of Nazi Germany, who claimed that there existed a world Jewish conspiracy (*see Chapter 5, page 141*). However, such views were by no means confined to Germany and its ideas of Aryan supremacy. Anti-Semitism has manifested itself over many hundreds of years, fuelled at times by a strand within Christianity that blames the Jews for the death of Jesus. This strand is based on the chilling line from the Gospel of Matthew 27:25 in the New Testament, when Pontius Pilate, the Roman Governor, disclaims all responsibility for what is about to happen to the arrested Jesus: 'Let his blood be on us and on our children,' shouts the crowd which Pilate is addressing.

Pogroms against the Jews have taken place at various times throughout history and in many places across Europe, including at York in England at the end of the 11th century. At the end of the 19th century, the anti-Semitism that already existed in much of the Western world was given a new twist: this time, the claim was that not only was there a Jewish secret society seeking world domination, but now the society actually had a written programme describing how to achieve this.

The *Protocols of the Elders of Zion* is one of the most extraordinary – and dangerous – hoaxes in history. Few pieces of writing can have caused as much misery, pain and death as this one. It is claimed that the Protocols were a covert plan drawn up by Jewish leaders, though where and when this mysterious meeting of the secret society takes place is never specified. The plan itself is nothing short of a blueprint on how to take control of the entire planet. The Protocols were first published in a Russian newspaper in around 1905, although rumours that such a text existed may have been circulating for a few years before this.

It is thought that the Protocols hoax originated some time in the 1890s, though who exactly carried it out is still a matter of debate. One suspect is a Russian aristocrat by the name of Yuliana Glinka, who had lived in Paris and had developed an interest in Theosophy. She was also said to have been a Russian spy. Another theory is that a man named Matvei Golovinski, also believed to have been working for the Russian secret service, was their author. He too had worked in Paris, and while there had met a Frenchman named Charles Joly. Charles was the son of Maurice Joly, whose satirical work from 1864, *Dialogue in Hell between Montesquieu and Machiavelli*, was clearly plagiarized for use in the Protocols. Joly's work may itself have been based on another work that criticized the Jesuits rather than the Jews, but whatever the case, neither of those works was anti-Semitic. A novel by Hermann Goedsche called *Biarritz*, written in 1868, may also have been a source of inspiration.

Whoever did compile the Protocols hoax (the one thing we can be sure of is that it was not Jewish elders), and whatever inspired its language, it was soon being put to good use by a *bona fide* secret society that had formed in Russia. The Black Hundreds was a grouping of conservative and reactionary organizations that were acting as part secret society, part political wind and part thugs and assassins. The group supported the Tsar and opposed any political reform in Russia.

The Black Hundreds became especially active after Russia's disastrous military defeat at the hands of the Japanese in 1905. This reversal prompted calls for an opening of Russia's closed and archaic political system, something the Black Hundreds members were desperate to prevent. In an attempt to undermine support for reform, the Black Hundreds published the *Protocols of Zion* as a pamphlet. Their reasoning was that if people believed that the suggested reforms were all really part of a Jewish plot to undermine Christianity and take over the world, support for the reforms would plummet. Knowledge of the Protocols spread throughout much of the country and became part of the standard armament used against the supporters of reform or revolution. It was all deeply ironic: here was a real secret society using a hoax to 'expose' the activities of a non-existent secret society.

As we know, attempts to thwart the revolution in Russia were ultimately doomed. But when the White Russians fled westwards after the Bolsheviks seized power in 1917, some of them took copies of the Protocols with them. By 1920 the work had appeared in both German and English, and had even merited a mention in London's *The Times*. Meanwhile, in the United States, the work found its way into the columns of *The Dearborn Independent*, a newspaper owned by the car manufacturer Henry Ford.

In 1921, *The Times*'s Constantinople (modern-day Istanbul, Turkey) correspondent, Philip Groves, basing some of his work on that of another journalist, Lucien West, exposed the Protocols as a piece of shameless plagiarism, showing that it had been based in large part on Maurice Joly's work. Unfortunately this did not stop the book from becoming popular in many parts of the world, especially in Germany where, after Adolf Hitler's rise to power, it predictably became a standard textbook in schools.

It is hard nowadays to believe that the Protocol could achieve such prominence and that so many people, both in Russia and in other countries, could seriously believe that it was genuine. The flavour of this most bizarre of documents can be glimpsed from the following extract, which comes from Protocol 7, on world wars:

> The intensification of armaments, the increase of police forces – are all essential for the completion of the aforementioned plans. What we have to get at is that there should be in all the States of the world, besides ourselves, only the masses of the proletariat, a few millionaires devoted to our interests, police and soldiers.
>
> Throughout all Europe, and by means of relations with Europe, in other continents also, we must create ferments, discords and hostility. Therein we gain a double advantage.

Later, in Protocol 17, on Abuse of Authority, comes the line:

The King of the Jews will be the real Pope of the Universe, the patriarch of an international Church.

And just in case the message about the Jews and their power and money isn't clear, Protocol 21, on Loans and Credit, states:

We have taken advantage of the venality of administrators and the slackness of rulers to get our moneys twice, thrice and more times over, by lending to the goy [i.e. non-Jewish] governments moneys which were not at all needed by the States. Could anyone do the like in regard to us?
(*Translation by Victor Marsden*)

Sadly, in some parts of the world, this work is still taken seriously and treated as genuine. It is also a reminder of how complex the world of secret societies can be. Indeed, it seems that a secret society that does not exist can have just as much impact on the world as one that does.

## The Elites

Just because many conspiracy theories grossly overstate the threat from elites forming secret societies, this does not mean it does not happen. In some cases, though, the secret societies are aimed at seeking pleasure rather than world domination. Such was the case of the now notorious Hell-Fire Club of the 18th century. In fact, there seems to have been not one but several such clubs that purportedly were set up to practise Satanism and mock Christianity, though in truth their main motivation appears to have been plenty of drunken and sexual fun.

The first such society was probably that which was started by Philip, Duke of Wharton, in around 1720, though this might itself have been modelled on an earlier secret society. The club organized by Wharton (who was also briefly a Freemason) appears to have been short-lived, though similar societies sprang up elsewhere, including in Ireland. It was not until the 1740s that Sir Francis Dashwood created a secret society that came to be regarded as *the* Hell-Fire Club, even though it was not called that at the time. This group was styled 'The Order of the Friars of St. Francis of Wycombe', and was based at the former Cistercian Abbey at Medmenham, west of London, which Sir Francis had renovated. Above the entrance to the Abbey were inscribed the famous words of 16th century French writer

François Rabelais: '*Fay ce que voudras*', or 'Do as you will'. This sentiment would be similarly employed a century and a half later by Aleister Crowley as the central tenet of his secret religion (*see Chapter 5, page 139*).

The Order's motto gives a clue as to what went on at the Abbey: lots of drinking, dressing up and sexual innuendo, or activity. It also appears that the ceremonies were more pagan than Satanic in nature. There has even been some suggestion that the Order, which was eventually disbanded in the 1760s, may have had some kind of political purpose. If so, it seems that this more serious purpose was probably secondary to the Order's pursuit of irreverent fun.

Around the time that Sir Francis's Order was in full swing, another club was being established across the Atlantic Ocean at Yale University in Connecticut. The Crotonia, named after the place where Pythagoras established his mystery school, was a literary society and was certainly in existence by 1750. However, it was not until eight years later at Yale that the best known – and, many would claim, perhaps most notorious – of the American college fraternities was formed. This was called the Skull and Bones Society.

An undergraduate called William Huntingdon Russell created the Skull and Bones Society in 1832 following a trip he had made to study in Germany the previous year. While there, he is said to have became friendly with a member of a secret society – they were common in Germany at that time – and was given permission to found a chapter of the society in the United States. When Russell returned to Yale he did just that, enlisting 14 fellow students to join along with him. The club was known at first as the Eulogian Club, but it soon changed its name taking it from the piratical skull and crossbones symbol on the flag it adopted: hence the Skull and Bones Society. To this day, Russell's name lives on in the form of the Russell Trust Association that runs the Society, including overseeing the property it owns: the 50-acre Deer Island on the St Lawrence River, the site of the Society's headquarters in New Haven (known in society parlance as the 'tomb').

Membership of the Skull and Bones Society is restricted to just 15 undergraduates a year, and these are selected by existing members, or 'Bonesmen'. Since 1991 women have also been allowed to join this exclusive club. The Society has a number of initiations and other rituals that have sometimes been described as 'Masonic' in form, and members are supposedly given names that relate to ancient mythology, perhaps not unlike the Illuminati in the previous century.

The Society has inevitably been the source of much controversy over the years, stemming partly from the considerable secrecy that has surrounded the Society, its rituals and its headquarters. However, the main reason for the controversy surrounding the Society is that many of its undergraduate members have gone on to become very powerful in American society. This concern is not new, having begun in the 19th century. In 1873 an anonymous article written by a student at Yale University who was not a member of the Society stated: 'Year by year the deadly evil is growing. The society was never as obnoxious to the college as it is today, and it is just this ill feeling that shuts the pockets of non-members. Never before has it shown such arrogance and self-fancied superiority ... it is Yale College against Skull and Bones! We ask all men, as a question of right, which should be allowed to live?'

This article seemed to have had little impact, however, on the Society and the success of its members. The first former Bonesman to become United States president was William Taft, who was elected to the White House a few years before the start of the First World War. Since then there have been two more: George Bush senior and his son, George W. Bush. Had Senator John Kerry won the presidential election in 2004, he would have been the fourth Bonesman to enter the White House.

In 1947, the Central Intelligence Agency (CIA), America's main espionage organization, was set up on the recommendation of a post-war committee chaired by Robert Lovett, a former member of the Society. As a result, many Bonesmen are said to have passed through the doors of the CIA's Langley, Virginia, headquarters over the years. Indeed, it has even been claimed that the old Yale name for a member of a secret society is 'spook', the same word the CIA uses to describe its spies.

Inevitably, some see the hand of conspiracy here. However, it is hardly surprising that an elite university such as Yale and an elite selection of Yale students such as the Skull and Bones Society should have members who go on to become prominent. Indeed, the Skull and Bones Society fares poorly when compared with Freemasonry, which can boast a total of 14 members who have become presidents of the United States. Even the 19th-century-drinking club, the Benevolent Protective Order of Elks (which is still very popular), can claim five presidents. The truth is that the Skull and Bones Society should be seen for what it is: an undergraduate self-consciously secret society that is not without importance and influence, but which is essentially a great place to make friends and influence people – an 'old boys' network with a twist of ritual.

## The Friendly Societies

Secret societies such as the Skull and Bones Society may be places where the rich can make new contacts, but it is not just elite groups that form secret societies in order to improve their financial status. In 18th-century Britain (and in a few cases, even earlier), many trades and craft workers established societies that were designed to provide mutual support for members. These were the forebears of what became known as the Friendly Societies, those hugely important mutual organizations that were formed to help members in need of financial help. They were a form of private welfare state within a state, and were widespread until the state-sponsored Welfare State in Britain took over most of these responsibilities in the 20th century. This phenomenon took place not just in Britain, but also in much of the English-speaking world. In the United States, for example, such groups ultimately led to the development of fraternal benefit societies.

One such society was called the Odd Fellows. No one is sure where this group got its name, or even when it began. It is assumed to have sprung out of guilds of workers and craftsmen (often known collectively as 'journeymen', who were paid by the day) sometime in the late 17th or early 18th century. One theory is that the group first developed in the English county of Yorkshire and in the Midlands just to the south. The Odd Fellows' story bears a strong similarity to that of the Freemasons, which trace their origins from the guilds of stonemasons. This is not surprising, as Freemasons, Odd Fellows and many other societies of this period shared a great deal in common. Indeed, they were a place for like-minded people from similar backgrounds to gather, help each other, discuss ideas and generally form a fellowship. Often, as was the case with Freemasonry, these societies formed rituals, rules of membership and had a tendency towards secrecy, or at least privacy.

Like the Freemasons, the Odd Fellows formed lodges. The earliest known rules of an Odd Fellow lodge shows that it met in public houses in London, as did many Masonic lodges. For example, members of the Odd Fellows' Loyal Aristarchus Lodge met alternatively in the Oakley Arms in Southwark, the Globe Tavern in Hatton Garden (known today for its jewellers) and the

Boar's Head in Smithfield (known today for its meat market).

In common with many other secret societies, the Odd Fellows have a tendency to glamorize their origins. The Odd Fellow Lodges and their members claim to be able to trace their ancestry back to the Israelites in captivity in Babylon. These Israelites were said to have survived the destruction of the Temple in Jerusalem in AD 70, and Roman legionaries are said to have later taken the lodges to Britain. Sadly, there is no evidence for this colourful history.

Though the Odd Fellows shared many similarities with the Freemasons, where they differed ultimately was over their aim and direction. Freemasonry, while still a support network, tended to concentrate on the esoteric, on ritual and on intellectual speculation. The Odd Fellows and similar groups, however, tended to focus more on practical help for its members through providing overnight accommodation, helping when its members were sick and with funeral expenses, providing financial help for widows, and so on. This process was accelerated in the early part of the 19th century when a new order of Odd Fellows from the Manchester area chose to break away from the existing structure under the Grand United Order of Odd Fellows and form an independent order. This became known as the Manchester Unity.

While its aims seem wholly laudable now – providing financial help for the needy, for example – organizations such as the Odd Fellows had to be careful how they operated in case their activities alarmed the authorities. There were two main reasons why the British establishment was nervous about such secret societies at this time. One was the still-fresh memory of the French Revolution and the alleged role of secret societies such as the Freemasons (continental ones, not British) and the Illuminati. The result of this fear was legislation at the end of the 18th century prohibiting 'unlawful' societies, including those whose members swore oaths to each other. This was known as the Unlawful Societies Act of 1799. At one point it even appeared as if Parliament might outlaw all secret societies in Britain, including the Freemasons. However, legislators were more worried about radical secret groups such as the London Corresponding Society, the Irish secret society known as the Society of United Irishmen and related groups such as the United Britons, the United Scotsmen and the United Englishmen. In the end, and after lobbying from influential Freemasons, existing Masonic lodges were exempted from the new law. But groups such as the Odd Fellows had to be careful, even if their activities were not the principal target of the legislation.

During this time period more and more workers were beginning to organize together, not just to protect themselves from poverty and sickness, but also to improve their rights. This was the time of the birth of the labour movement, and there was inevitably considerable crossover between the work of such groups as the Odd Fellows and the nascent trade unions. An example of the nervousness of the Manchester Unity over this situation came in 1834, when the Tolpuddle Martyrs – agricultural workers protesting against low wages – were prosecuted under another piece of British legislation, the Unlawful Oaths Act, for 'administering unlawful oaths'. The Grand Master and other leaders of Manchester Unity promptly met to remove their own oath of mutual support, replacing it with a less conspiratorial-sounding 'obligation' on members to help their fellows.

In the United States, the Independent Order of Odd Fellows, founded in the 19th century, helped make the Fellowship the largest secret society of its type in the world, eclipsing even the Freemasonic lodges in membership numbers.

But the Odd Fellows were not the only such groups of the time, even if they were the most popular. Other groups that came and went in Britain included the Ancient Order of Buffaloes, the Free Potters, the Rechabites, the Order of Good Templars, the Foresters, the Shepherds and the mysterious Horsemen (sometimes known as the Society of the Horseman's Word). This last group is thought to have existed in Scotland as late as the 20th century, and was a gathering of 'horse professionals' – blacksmiths and trainers, for example – who supposedly had an amazing ability to train horses by uttering just one word. (Today they would be known as horse whisperers.) Recent research claims that these people may have used powerful ointments and potions to make the animals obey them. They were also said to have had a number of strange rituals, including reading parts of the Bible backwards, and they were sometimes accused of practising magic.

According to Russell Lyon, author of *The Quest for the Original Horse Whisperers* (Luath Press, 2003), six of these Scottish horse experts were recruited into the Confederate cause in the American Civil War. In an interview with *The Scotsman* newspaper, Lyon claims that, '[These horse experts] became cavalry officers and, at the end of the war, these six young men were bored and decided to set up a secret society using their knowledge of the whisperers' traditions and oaths as the basis.' Lyon also claims that though most have died out, at least one Horseman society still exists and meets regularly at a location in the Orkney Islands.

Another fascinating secret society of this time was the Order of the Free Gardeners. As their name suggests, the Free Gardeners was a gathering of gardeners who organized themselves in lodges similar to those of the Freemasons. Scottish Freemason and historian Robert L. D. Cooper, in his book, *Cracking the Freemasons' Code* (Rider & Co, 2006), explains that the formation of the Order roughly coincided with wealthy landowners' new-found interest in landscape design, and their 'subsequent employment of a large number of working gardeners'. The first known 'constitution' of such a group, the 'Fraternitie of the Gairdners of East Lothian', in Scotland, dates from 1676. The first Free Gardeners' Grand Lodge was created much later, in 1849, leading to the formation of 60 new lodges, including three in the United States.

Other independent Gardeners' lodges existed at the same time as those of the Free Gardeners. One theory is that these independent lodges contained actual gardeners, while by this time the other united lodges tended to pursue what might be called 'speculative' Free Gardenery. Cooper cites the Free Gardeners' own definition of 'Free Gardenery' as the '…applying of the cultivation of the ground and its products as symbols expressive of the necessity of cultivating the mind in intelligence and virtue'.

As with the Freemasons, the Free Gardeners looked back to Solomon's Temple for inspiration, with their first three degrees of initiation all containing references to it. According to the Free Gardeners' rituals, Solomon was the Master Gardener because he had 'planted a garden in Balhama and had knowledge of all the trees, shrubs and other plants from the lofty Cedars of Lebanon to the lowly ivy and hyssop.' The Free Gardeners further believed that not only did their 'forebears' help build the Temple by supplying timber, they also looked after the building once it was finished by, for example, supplying the olive branches that the High Priest took into the Holy of Holies. Indeed, the olive tree seems to have held special significance for the Order. According to Cooper, the Free Gardeners 'were and are' more secretive than the Freemasons. He adds: '…it appears that they offered esoteric knowledge on a par with that offered by Freemasonry'. However, unlike Freemasonry, Free Gardenery has not survived. A Friendly Society linked to the Free Gardeners existed well into the late 20th century, but by then the Order itself had vanished, probably taking some of its secrets with it forever.

## Cecil Rhodes

One of the accusations frequently made by conspiracy theorists is that secret societies are trying to destroy nation states and impose some form of world government. Usually this charge is utterly wrong, or at best massively overstated. However, in the case of the adventurer, mining magnate and politician Cecil Rhodes, this accusation is to a large extent justified. Rhodes, who was born in 1853, and after whom Rhodesia (now Zimbabwe) was named, was an ardent supporter of the British Empire, and at one time envisaged that the whole world might be brought under its effective control. Indeed, in one of his early wills, Rhodes explicitly outlines his intent when he makes provision for:

> ...the establishment, promotion and development of a Secret Society, the true aim and object whereof shall be for the extension of British rule throughout the world, the perfecting of a system of emigration from the United Kingdom, and of colonisation by British subjects of all lands where the means of livelihood are attainable by energy, labour and enterprise.

However, by the time of Rhodes's final will, which was acted upon after his death in 1902, his methodology had been scaled down somewhat, and he contented himself with providing a series of scholarships for students to study at Oxford University, including students from the United States. A number of prominent people have benefited from Rhodes's bequest; for example, former United States President Bill Clinton was a Rhodes Scholar in the 1960s.

Though Rhodes toned down the provisions of his will, his zeal for the British Empire and his long-cherished hope that the United States be brought once again under British rule scarcely dimmed. Indeed, Rhodes is credited with establishing a secret society to promote both goals. This was known as the Society of the Elect, the very name of which gives a clue to the elite nature of this venture. It is also one of the names that Karl von Eckartshausen used to refer to the Secret Chiefs (*see Chapter 5, page 137*). We know very little about this secret society, including whether it ever amounted to anything more than a name. One view is that Rhodes had intended to set up this group, but when he failed to gain enough support for it he quietly allowed it to drop. An alternative view is that it was formally established in 1891 and worked successfully in furthering the aims of Rhodes and his close associates, and was so covert that few outsiders knew of its operation.

The respected American historian, Carroll Quigley, believed that there was indeed a 'conspiracy' to create a world government, and was convinced that the Society of the Elect was a real entity. The Society was based on inner and outer circles of membership, rather like the Illuminati and other secret or secretive groups. The inner circle were the Elect, while the outer circle was a group of supporters and backers initially called the Association of Helpers. The Elect, unsurprisingly, included Rhodes himself as 'General' of the Society, along with an executive committee of three: banker Nathan Rothschild, a journalist called William T. Stead and the then British High Commissioner in South Africa, Alfred Milner. Milner had his own influential circle of brilliant young Oxford graduates known as the 'Kindergarten', and was a powerful personality who shared many of Rhodes's views about Britain and the Empire. Alongside this committee there was also a circle of 'initiates'.

The Rhodes–Milner axis was to prove an important one, even after Rhodes's death in 1902. In 1909 a conference in Wales established the Round Table groups, also known as the Rhodes–Milner Round Table groups. Some claim that these groups were the successor organizations to the Association of Helpers, and so directly linked to the Society of the Elect. The Round Tables – which were established in various parts of the world, including the United States, India, Canada, Australia and Britain – are credited with considerable influence both before and after the First World War. They were closely associated with the establishment of the Union of South Africa, the British Commonwealth and the League of Nations. This last named entity was the ill-fated organization set up after the end of the First World War in a bid to provide a forum for solving international disputes.

Quigley also believed that Milner was the true author of the well-known Balfour Declaration. This was the declaration contained in a letter written in 1917 by British Foreign Secretary Arthur Balfour to Lord Rothschild (son of Nathan Rothschild) stating that the British Government officially backed plans for a Jewish homeland in Palestine. If this belief is correct, then there can be little doubt that the Rhodes–Milner axis and its associated groups and personalities had considerable impact on shaping the world at the very highest levels.

The Rhodes–Milner Group was also important as a blueprint for future groups with similar aims. In his book about the influence of international groups, *Transnational Classes and International Relations* (Routledge, 1998), Kees van der Pijl, Professor of International Relations at the University of Sussex, writes: 'As a structure of socialisation through which a momentary ruling class consensus is shaped, transmitted and transformed into policy, the Rhodes–Milner Group became the model for all subsequent…groups.'

Meanwhile, within South Africa itself – a land that made Rhodes rich, and where Milner wielded considerable power – a very different kind of secret society was created, one that worked emphatically against the British, and their values. Known as the Afrikaner Broederbond, or African Brotherhood, and created in 1918, this society was formed to help the Afrikaner people achieve their 'destiny' of ruling their own country on the continent. The society was anti-British in outlook, and was closely connected to the rise of Afrikaner economic and political power in South Africa after the Second World War. Some have even suggested (though the evidence seems scant) that the Broederbond, believing their system was doomed, helped bring about the end of Apartheid in return for the granting of *de facto* economic power to the Afrikaner minority.

## The Council on Foreign Relations

A key figure in the Rhodes–Milner groups, a member of Milner's Kindergarten and later allegedly a senior figure in the Society of the Elect was a man called Lionel Curtis. Curtis was a strong advocate of the British Empire (or Commonwealth, as it became), and sought to extend its influence around the world. In 1920 Curtis became involved in the creation of the Royal Institute of International Affairs, of which he became Honorary Secretary. The Institute survives today, and is now known simply as Chatham House, after its premises in London. While most people regard it as an unexceptional body devoted to analyzing international events and policy, to some conspiracy theorists the Institute is, or at least once was, a form of secret society not unlike the Society of the Elect. The Institute's chief claim to notoriety in the subject of secret societies is its close association with an American counterpart: the Council on Foreign Relations (CFR).

The CFR began life in 1921, and the idea for it sprang from the same meeting of foreign policy experts and advisers at the Paris Peace Conference in 1919 that had led to the foundation of the Royal Institute of International Affairs. Its aim was (and still is) to provide detailed and non-partisan advice on, and analysis of, American foreign policy. At the CFR's inception it was at the centre of a network of powerful businessmen (including the Rockefellers) and various politicians, government officials and academics. Since then it has been intimately involved with the major foreign policy issues of successive White House administrations. It is perhaps unsurprising, therefore, that this powerful, elite group has been the target of much speculation, controversy and conspiracy theories. According to Jim Marrs, in his popular book, *Rule by Secrecy* (HarperCollins Publishers, 2000), the CFR is the '…granddaddy of modern American secret societies.' He also adds that: 'Many writers view the CFR as a group of men set on world domination through multinational business, international treaties, and world government.' The John Birch Society (*see Chapter 4, page 108*) has also been a frequent critic of the CFR.

It is simple to dismiss much of the criticism of the CFR as both extreme and paranoid. It is equally hard to justify the claim that the CFR is in any meaningful sense a secret society; its membership is known and published, for example. However, as is often the case, many critics ignore some of the more prosaic but nonetheless real concerns that surround such organizations and the way major discussions amongst the powerful take place behind closed doors. The CFR is certainly a private organization, and discussions held at its New York headquarters are kept confidential. Naturally there are good reasons for this; such privacy allows Council members, who include former presidents Bill Clinton and Jimmy Carter, as well as the doyen of American statesmen, Henry Kissinger, to speak frankly about policy without fear of it being made public. And after all, the CFR is a private (i.e. non-governmental) organization. Yet the members of the Council are so influential, powerful and well connected with the administration in the White House that we must wonder if there is a legitimate question mark over the issue of accountability.

It may well be useful for a US administration to discuss new ideas or to hear new arguments about foreign policy in the privacy of a CFR meeting, but if this means that its ideas are adopted without having been subjected to public scrutiny then, arguably, we should be concerned. We might also be concerned about the possibility that some business interests with influence over the CFR may seek to use the organization as a kind of lobby group to get their voices heard in the White House in order to promote policies favourable to their business interests.

Indeed, the economist John Kenneth Galbraith expressed concern about the way in which the Council operated when he resigned from it in 1970. His anxiety concerned the way in which the CFR allowed government officials to hold off-the-record briefings with certain business interests. Meanwhile, the respected journalist Joseph Kraft, who was himself a member of the Council, once wrote that it '...comes close to being an organ of what [has been] called the Power Elite – a group of men, similar in interest and outlook, shaping events from invulnerable positions behind the scenes.'

A recent controversy has developed over whether the CFR is trying to push ideas for some form of North American union between Mexico, Canada and the United States in the wake of the creation of the free trade association known as NAFTA (North American Free Trade Agreement). In a 2004 article for *Foreign Affairs*, the CFR's journal, International Relations Professor and CFR Task-Force Chairman Robert Pastor wrote, 'The three governments should work to develop a North American passport, available to a larger group of citizens with each successive year.' He added: 'The US, Mexican, and Canadian governments remain zealous defenders of an outdated conception of sovereignty even though their citizens are ready for a new approach. Each nation's leadership has stressed differences rather than common interests. North America needs leaders who can articulate and pursue a broader vision.' Successive White House administrations have denied having plans for any such kind of 'union' or pooled sovereignty.

## The Trilateral Commission

The Trilateral Commission (TC) is another private organization, and has proved even more controversial than the CFR. Formed in October 1973, one of the driving forces behind the TC from the start was David Rockefeller, whose family also had close links with the CFR. Significantly, the TC's first meeting was held in Kyoto, Japan, and the first full meeting of its regional members took place in Tokyo in 1975.

From the start the TC's aim was, in its own words, to 'encourage mutual understanding and closer cooperation' between North America, Europe (in the form of the EEC, now called the EU) and Japan. This cooperation is aimed at the spheres of banking, finance, industry, economic policy and politics, and the TC has always included many prominent business people and industrialists among its membership. Since those early days the membership has expanded; the Japan group has become the Asia Pacific group, containing members from Australia to China. The European group has also enlarged as EU membership has grown, and the North American bloc now includes Mexico.

Like the CFR, the TC is a private body, but its membership reflects some of the biggest names in politics. The list has included former President George Bush; his son's Vice President, Dick Cheney; former Secretary of Defense Caspar Weinberger; former Deputy Secretary of Defense Paul Wolfowitz; former presidents Bill Clinton and Walter Mondale; as well as the ubiquitous Henry Kissinger, without whose membership no such group would be complete. The list also includes former Japanese Premier Kiichi Miyazawa, and Sergei Karaganov, a senior adviser to Russian presidents Yeltsin and Putin and some senior journalists.

In the 1970s the presence of another United States president in the TC's membership ranks caused a stir, one that has ensured that the TC remains controversial to this day, especially among conspiracy theorists. The president in question was Jimmy Carter. When Carter moved into the White House, having resigned from the TC as he was obliged to do, he chose a large number of TC members to serve in his administration; as many as 26, according to some claims (though the TC itself admits only 17 members in total). The issue caused a row, and in 1980 the Republican candidate Ronald Reagan attacked Carter and his then Republican opponent George Bush (later his vice president) on the grounds of their membership in the TC. Some critics claimed that the TC had 'selected' Carter as their presidential candidate and used him to further their own agenda; others claimed that Carter had used the TC's network to boost his image in influential circles.

Reagan's attack on the TC sparked a debate that continues even to this day, more than a quarter of a century later, and the TC constantly feels the need to defend itself against charges that it effectively operates as an (unac-countable) arm of the United States government and big business. On the 'Frequently Asked Questions' section of its website, the Commission tackles the Carter question head on. It states that when the TC was formed in 1973, its members felt that they were short of representatives from the Southern United States. 'It was decided, therefore, to consult with some individuals in Atlanta about prospective members from the South,' says the Commission. Carter, who had been Governor of Georgia, was chosen because he had been a 'very able' Governor, and because of his interest in trade issues concerning Japan and Western Europe. States the Commission, 'When he was elected President, Mr. Carter naturally turned to some of the people in the Trilateral Commission whose abilities and personalities he had come to know to ask them to join his new Administration.' It adds that many of these officials would have been 'natural choices' for a Democratic president, whether they were in the TC or not.

As with the CFA, much of the more lurid criticism of the TC, its membership and its work can be easily dismissed. The Commission has a wide-ranging group of members who come from an ever more diverse background of countries, cultures and regimes. The notion that they or even an inner core of them are involved in a secret project to impose world domination/government on the rest of us is far-fetched. TC members might be flattered to be described, as some observers have done, as the 'Architects of the New World Order', but this description simply doesn't work. As American academic Michael Barkun writes in *A Culture of Conspiracy* (University of California Press, 2003), the list of powerful names amongst TC members is 'heady stuff' for conspiracy theorists. He notes: 'People on both the left and the right who share this antipathy [towards wealth and corporate power] have found the Trilateral Commission and similar organizations attractive targets.'

Yet such overstated attacks on the TC overshadow less sensational but rather more solid concerns. Professor van der Pijl, while careful to reject any suggestion that the TC has a plan for world government, nevertheless points to its importance as a body for the ruling elites. He writes in *Transnational Classes and International Relations*: 'The Trilateral Commission [is]...a consultative ruling class forum ... in the tradition of the Rhodes–Milner group.' He also points to its role as a 'consultative body' of 'owner-managers and officers of transnational corporations.' Van der Pijl further notes that in the mid-1980s two-thirds of the biggest one hundred global companies had membership links with the TC.

As with the CFR, the problem with the TC is one of accountability. The TC correctly points out that it is not a 'secret' organization, and that it has always freely supplied both its membership and its aims and objectives (which it dryly notes do not include 'world government'). Furthermore, it states that, 'Only the discussions at the meetings are kept "off-the-record" to encourage frankness and maximize the learning process for members.' Yet given its access to privileged information, its inside knowledge and connections and the sheer high-level position of so many of its members, the suspicion remains that important policies are discussed – and perhaps decisions are even made – that escape the usual democratic scrutiny we have come to expect.

While concerns about the TC's and the CFR's lack of accountability continue, there is yet another similar organization that provokes even more criticism and controversy than both of those bodies. It is known as the Bilderberg Group.

## The Bilderberg Group

It all started amid the gently rolling hills of eastern Holland, not far from the German border. It was here that, on 29 May 1954, a fleet of shiny black limousines arrived at the gate of a pleasant if unremarkable hotel. But if the hotel was unexceptional, the same could not be said of the men inside those cars. As these guests strolled into the hotel, a casual onlooker, had he or she been allowed near the premises, would have seen some of the most powerful men on the planet coming together for an unprecedented meeting. This was no Yalta or Potsdam conference, where the world's great leaders met under public gaze to discuss how the future of Europe might look after the Second World War. Rather, this was a secretive meeting between the power brokers of the Americas and of Europe, at which there was no written agenda, no account of the discussions and no declaration afterwards about its deliberations. The following day the powerful guests packed their bags and returned to their own countries, with most of the rest of the world utterly unaware that this meeting had even taken place.

Even today this group of men still has no formal title, but it has been informally named the Bilderberg Group, after the Hotel De Bilderberg, at Oosterbeek near Arnheim, where the meeting took place. The hotel has now reverted back to what it always was: a fine place to stay amid beautiful forests and rolling countryside. The meetings that it spawned, however, continue to this day. Just about every year since 1954 the so-called Bilderberg Group have held a conference, usually in an upmarket hotel in

Europe, or more rarely in North America. The membership of the Group may change with the passage of time but their prominence remains a constant. Indeed, its list of participants includes some of the biggest names in modern history: Henry Kissinger, Bill Clinton and Tony Blair have all attended (Tony Blair first attended in 1993, before he became leader of the Labour Party and then Prime Minister of the UK).

The Bilderberg Group (or the Bilderberg Conference, as the meeting is sometimes called) has been described as an 'international who's who of the wealthy, influential and powerful'. Alongside politicians are the less well-known but arguably just as important financiers, bankers, business people and officials who play prominent roles in driving global trade and the economy. For example, at the Bilderberg Conference that took place in Germany in 2005, the attendees included the heads of the World Bank and the European Central Bank; the chairmen or chief executives from BP, Pepsi, Nokia, Unilever and DaimlerChrysler, as well as those of other prominent large corporations; editors from five major newspapers; various politicians and government officials; and even a few monarchs, including the Queen of the Netherlands and the Crown Prince of Belgium.

Curiously, as this list shows, many senior figures in the media are present at these annual congregations. However, there is no chance of their readership becoming informed of these figures' attendance, as one of the golden rules of the meetings is that what is said and done inside the four walls of the conference room stays inside. The various journalists from the *New York Times*, the *Financial Times* and the *Wall Street Journal* and other such media organizations who have been given access to the exclusive conferences have been sworn to secrecy. The meeting rooms are always swept in advance for electronic bugs and other listening devices, and the local staff are rigorously vetted and checked. At one meeting held in Canada, even local uniformed police were obliged to show their identity badges before they were allowed entry to the venue.

So what does the Bilderberg group do and what is it for? Why was it set up in 1954 and what are its current aims? The current Chairman of the 'organization' is a former European Commissioner and corporate director, Viscount Etienne Davignon, a Belgian in his mid-70s who is extremely well connected in both politics and business. In a rare interview in 2005, the former Eurocrat maintained the familiar line that the Bilderberg Conference is simply a meeting of European and American leaders that allows them to discuss the problems and challenges of the world. The fact that they meet behind closed doors – 'in private', as the group says – is to encourage people to swap and discuss ideas frankly away from the glare of publicity and the media. Davignon insists that the group has modest aims: 'Bilderberg does not try to reach conclusions; it does not try to say "what we should do". Everyone goes away with their own feeling and that allows the debate to be completely open, quite frank, and to see what the differences are,' he told the BBC. 'Business influences society and politics influence society – that's purely common sense. It's not that business contests the right of democratically elected leaders to lead.' But the notion that the Bilderberg Group takes the trouble to meet up every year in great secrecy simply to have cosy chats about world issues is not one that satisfies its many critics. They claim that the move towards greater transnational organization of the world – from the European Union to the World Trade Organisation – is one of the group's main aims. For example, the creation of the Bilderberg Group in 1954 at the initiative of senior European officials came just three years before the formation of the Common Market, the structure that in time evolved into the current closely integrated European Union. The structure was set up despite fierce opposition by figures such as General Charles de Gaulle, the leading French hero of the Second World War and a trenchant nationalist.

In fact, some Bilderberg members have admitted to a link between the Group's discussions and subsequent events. 'In some cases discussions do have an impact and become policy,' Jack Sheinkman, Chairman of the Amalgamated Bank, said in 1996. 'The idea of a European single currency was discussed several years before it became policy. We had a discussion about the US establishing formal relations with China before Nixon actually did it.' Its critics say that such discussions are proof that the un-elected Bilderberg Group has a secret agenda, and that its aim is nothing less than the eventual establishment of a world government.

Opponents of the organization also say that its senior members identify and nurture rising young stars of politics and business – people they think will help further their cause one day. This is an accusation that Viscount Davignon denies, at least in part. He admits that the group's steering committee '…does its best assessment of who are the bright new boys or girls in the beginning phase of their career who would like to get known. It's not a total accident, but it's not a forecast, and if they go places it's not because of Bilderberg, it's because of themselves.'

American journalist James P. Tucker Jr, who has pursued the Group around the world for years, disagrees. He insists that the group not only chooses rising political talent; it can also depose troublesome politicians if they oppose the Bilderberg agenda. To Tucker this transatlantic group is simply 'evil'. This view strikes a chord with some in Serbia, the heart of former Yugoslavia. In certain circles there it is believed that the Bilderberg Group was behind an international plot to get rid of their arch nationalist leader, Slobodan Milosevic, and that the Group helped spark the war that led to his eventual downfall in 2000. Indeed, many critics believe that what is discussed amongst the Bilderberg Group one year can become reality the next.

Tucker has certainly got 'up close and personal' with the Bilderbergers. Not only has he reported on the group for more than 30 years, he has also attempted to gatecrash their secretive three-day meetings held every year. Before he started tracking the Group, Tucker had already worked for many years as a journalist for what he calls the 'mainstream' press. In 1975 he went for an interview with an organization called Liberty Lobby (a right-wing organization founded by Willis Carto). '[Willis Carto] asked me what I thought about Bilderberg and I said I had never heard of them! I was sceptical,' he recalls. Tucker says that Carto then handed him a file full of cuttings about the group. 'I read it and I was shocked and outraged to think I could spend 20 happy years with daily newspapers and reading wire services and be absolutely unaware that such a group existed,' says Tucker. 'After that I became a dedicated pursuer of Bilderberg.'

Tucker, who is now in his 70s, uses an informal network of readers and journalists around the world to help him find out where the next Bilderberg meeting is being held (this is never publicized by the organization itself). The organization typically takes over the entire hotel in which it holds its conference, so the veteran reporter tries to get inside the building before its top-level guests arrive. 'Normally I get there a couple of days in advance before they seal the site off. They usually start that on a Wednesday, the barricades go up, the uniformed police are dispersed around the place, there is private security; sometimes even the military are there,' he says.

'A few times I have gotten inside before they catch me and throw me out. Security gets tighter every year,' says Tucker. To get information about the Group's agenda and what is said in the meeting, Tucker tries to enlist the help of the hotel's staff by tracking down where they drink after work.

'There is always a pace to this. On the Monday evenings I am just a curious bystander…asking about the big important meeting coming up. By Tuesday afternoon or Wednesday morning some of the staffers get the idea that something evil is going on and they become cooperative. The only payoff is that I pick up their bar tab. It's a beer bribe not a cash bribe…!'

Tucker says that in the early years, when the Bilderberg Group was little known, he was often the only reporter around the conference site. 'I was able to get in more often. I'd go up drainpipes and through hedges late at night. One time, having found out where the hotel staff drank, they gave me a brown jump suit just like they wore. The next day I had a rake in my hand and was raking the resort grounds while eavesdropping and picking up papers! I have always been successful in picking up bits of paper. Someone dropped a memo from (Henry) Kissinger to someone else. That told me part of what was going on…plus part of a guest list…something they tried to keep private then,' he recalls. Tucker also states that, perhaps predictably, he is often kept under surveillance at such meetings. 'One time the head of security in a hotel came up to me and said, "Mr Tucker, the Bilderbergers are very unhappy that you're here." I said, "Well, they've never been very gracious to me." He replied: "They are afraid that you'll pick up stuff." I said then that they *ought* to be afraid, because if I can pick up stuff, I will.'

Tucker also dismisses the suggestion that the Bilderberg meetings are not secret, merely private. 'It had been a secret meeting until we made it not a secret. The Trilateral kids can say [that their meetings are not secret, merely private] because they will say the time and place for their meetings. They will not take over the whole hotel. They do seal off two floors of the hotel, one for private lodgings and the other for meetings, and they'll have guards outside the doors to stop you going in, but the meetings are not a secret, they are disclosed,' he claims.

'The Bilderberg meetings, however, they tried to make secret. For years they said "there's no such thing as Bilderberg" and they denied their existence. They said it was right-wing conjecture … then I swiped some of their stationary and their letterhead on it … how they could say they did not exist when they had a letterhead!?'

To Tucker this emphasis on secrecy is further proof of the malevolence of the Bilderberg Group. 'Good works are performed in the sunshine and evil is performed in the darkness,' he says. 'They don't *need* that kind of security…they could be like the Trilateral kids and have a private meeting in a hotel, like, for example, the Chamber of Commerce can do,' he states. 'Every time I come out of a Bilderberg meeting I am able to write advance stories on what's going to happen later in the year.'

'For example, I was able to write an advance story on the downfall of Mrs Thatcher as Prime Minister. She had attended one meeting of the Bilderbergs, but she had nothing to say and she didn't like it. The Bilderberg boys said they had to get rid of her and they replaced her with a trapeze artist [John Major, whose father was a trapeze artist] from the same party.'

'Some years before her last stroke I had a chance to talk to her at a social function in Washington,' says Tucker. 'I asked what her reaction was to being denounced by Bilderberg, and she said, and I paraphrase closely, that she regarded it as a "tribute" to be denounced by them.'

Jim Tucker says that he was also able to write the 'advance story' on the political rise of Bill Clinton. 'He was attending his Bilderberg meeting at Baden-Baden in Germany in 1991, and a year later that obscure Governor of Arkansas was elected President of the United States.' Tucker claims that through the Group's network of members and contacts, which include David Rockefeller in the United States and the Rothschilds in Europe; various US officials, including senior members of Congress; and bankers and financiers from around the world, it can wield 'immense influence'. He adds, 'We are talking about big bucks and big influence. I'm not saying they can do it all by themselves, but they can sure help the process.'

The veteran Bilderberg observer gives yet another example of how he claims Bilderberg meetings have predicted or caused future events. This example concerns the Bilderberg meeting that took place in Ottawa, Canada, in 2006. 'I was able to report that in the year ahead many hundreds of thousands of American home owners would lose their homes because of these crazy finance systems. Someone actually laughed about that at the Bilderberg meeting. One person even said, "The stupid jerks deserve it." To their credit, another member said, "That's awful cruel",' claims Tucker. Certainly the number of home repossessions in the US was a worrying trend from 2006 to 2008 in what is called the 'sub-prime' lending market, in which certain financial organizations give loans to people on low income or with poor credit records. Such homeowners were hit by a succession of interest rate rises, and fears over the ability of the borrowers to repay their loans – and of the lenders to survive – prompted large falls in many of the world's stock markets, the so-called 'credit crunch'.

Tucker also insists that the Bilderbergers are committed to closer integration among transnational organizations, ultimately hoping for a world government. 'They are committed to a European super-state, which it almost is at this moment. They are angry at Britain for resisting the euro because the pound is a symbol of British sovereignty, like the dollar is a symbol of US sovereignty,' he claims.

'Their main intention is to create a world government – for the United Nations to evolve into a world government. That's their ultimate goal, but they are disappointed at the moment, they thought that they would have been further along this road by now. The battle plan is that the EU becomes effectively a single state while the American "union" of countries becomes a state without borders and which has a single currency – NAFTA [The North American Free Trade Agreement] is an expansion in that direction. One day [this super-state] will also include Cuba. The idea is that there will be an American parliament similar to the European Parliament, and a supreme court as well. An Asian-Pacific union will then be the third leg, with the world conveniently divided into three great regions for the administrative convenience of the world government run from the UN,' claims Tucker.

In a meeting with a senior (un-named) British politician who has also attended Bilderberg meetings, Tucker claims that such apparently outlandish plans were confirmed. 'He said that there were plans for an American Union similar to the EU and a common currency for the Western Hemisphere,' says Tucker. 'He said our children and our grandchildren would laugh at all these petty currencies that we once had. He confirmed all this directly, it confirmed what I had written before.' Tucker also predicts that one of the big issues in coming years will be that of dual citizenship involving the United States and other countries. 'Dual citizens cannot be one hundred per cent loyal to one country without being zero per cent loyal to the other country,' says Tucker. 'This is part of their public agenda, the brainwashing of the public. They regard nationalism as too provincial.'

Though Tucker's views are sincerely held and, unlike those of many conspiracy theorists, have been formed from close personal observation and reporting, they are in the end as hard to sustain as some of the more extreme criticism of the Council on Foreign Relations and the Trilateral Commission. However, this doesn't mean that the Bilderberg Group has no impact on the world, nor that we shouldn't be worried about its activities. The Bilderberg Group is also notably more secretive and closed than groups such as the Trilateral Commision. Indeed, it seems that one of the main reasons the Trilateral Commission was created was because the Bilderberg Group refused to allow the Japanese into their ranks at a time when a certain group of American politicians and businessmen felt that Asia needed to be brought into the fold.

Professor van der Pijl also raises important concerns about the Bilderberg Group. While rejecting the conspiracy-theory view of groups such as Bilderberg, the Trilateral Commission and the World Economic Forum (which meets regularly in Davos, Switzerland), he is nonetheless trenchant in his criticism of such bodies. 'I am a democrat and this, of course, is a terrible form of undemocratic behaviour. If you just look at the people who are members of government there – why don't they report on what they talk about at this high level in their respective parliaments?' he states.

'Of course not a word is spoken on it. So it's a process of opinion formation, which is not as effective in terms of power as many people think, but it is completely side-stepping the formal channels of power and the control of power. It's profoundly undemocratic and I think it's also dangerous.'

Van der Pijl believes that there are essentially two schools of thought on how societies evolve and are run. One school considers the power of 'elitism', while the other is based on 'class theory'. He subscribes to the latter. 'According to elitism the elite is everything; they have control of the world, they can manipulate everything, control the news, you name it. They can even create their own enemies to conjure up threats that allow them to have another round of governing the world, etc. So elite theory is basically conspiracy theory,' he says.

'With class theory there is a ruling class of people who structurally profit from how the world is run. But they exist always in a permanent struggle with forces opposing them. These forces may be very weak, as they are today. But that still does not give the ruling class a free hand.

'Being a ruling class it has as its number-one priority the mission of trying to neutralize those forces that resist the ruling class. That is a full-time job, so to speak,' says van der Pijl. The professor considers that the Bilderberg Group and similar bodies such as the Trilateral Commission are performing a role today that has been carried out by organizations stretching back to the 18th century; one of these past groups is none other than the Freemasons. Van der Pijl further states, 'The argument of my work is that the West emerged as a liberal space in which there was free transnational movement, at least for the upper classes. Freemasonry was the first instance of what was almost a transnational liberal party.'

The Professor does not believe that groups such as Bilderberg are trying to 'run the world', but rather that they are struggling to control the forces below them – and not always with much success. 'I tend to think of all these bodies, whether they are the Freemasons, or the Bilderberg Group or the Trilateral Commission, as surfers,' he says. 'The sea is heaving and there are waves and all kinds of things and the people on the board appear on top...but in fact they are at great pains to negotiate with the forces that they are on top of. That's how it operates.'

He says that from his experience of studying Bilderberg meetings he knows that some of them begin with the frank admission from participants that no one present will be able to control a particular group or event. 'They are more or less open about the fact that they are negotiating with forces that they cannot dominate.' He adds: 'There is no way of denying that these are among the most centrally located people ... they command vast networks of information, etc, though in the end they can't even protect the Green Zone in Baghdad. They are up against forces they cannot control.'

According to van der Pijl, the Bilderberg Group was formed to help heal a growing rift between the United States and Europe in the post-war years, and thus the heart of the organization actually stems from the Second World War. 'It's not a coincidence that Bilderberg originated in the early 1950s, when transatlantic disagreement was at its height ... over McCarthyism ... that was rejected in Europe, and a difference of opinion in the Soviet Union and the end of Stalin and what that meant and so on,' he says. 'It became so bad, there was so much mutual vilification, that they created this network that actually dated from the Second World War.'

He says that there had been a group of wartime planners in London whose job it was to help sketch out the future of a post-war Europe. In particular, says van der Pijl, they were there to 'negotiate all kinds of plans for preventing Eastern Europe falling to the Soviet Union and what to do with Germany.' Key figures included Prince Bernhard of the Netherlands and Polish-born Joseph Retinger, an adviser to the Polish government-in-exile and a keen advocate of pan-European cooperation. 'It was this network that was activated again ... to come together again in the early 1950s,' he says. 'They had all developed post-war plans on assumptions of active American involvement, so when that began to unravel in the early

1950s they more or less had a reunion.'

The Professor also believes that the 'dangers' of bodies such as Bilderberg are not just over the 'abstract' notion of being 'anti-democratic'. He explains, 'There is at least the possibility that the anti-democratic quality actually results in forms of violence or blackmailing, or whatever.' In support of this claim, he refers to the assassination of leading German banker Alfred Herrhausen in November 1989. Herrhausen was killed by a roadside bomb shortly after leaving his home at Bad Homburg on 30 November 1989. He was travelling in an armoured Mercedes with bodyguards in vehicles in front of and behind his car when a 20-kg bomb ripped through it. Herrhausen was the Chairman of the powerful Deutsche Bank, and was also a key advisor to then German Chancellor Helmet Kohl. He was also, says van der Pijl, the leading financier of President Gorbachev, then President of the Soviet Union, at a time when relations between the West and the rapidly crumbling Soviet Union were at a delicate stage.

'[Herrhausen] was assassinated at a moment that followed various earlier conferences – not just Bilderberg's,' says the Professor. 'At one of these Bilderberg conferences earlier in 1989 – a conference of which I have seen the documents – it was argued by one of the speakers that Gorbachev should be kept under pressure and that all those, especially in Germany and Austria, who were willing to give Gorbachev breathing space should be disciplined,' He adds: 'I cannot say that they ordered the assassination of Herrhausen ... but at least I make the argument.' He says that it is not hard to imagine the discussions that must have taken place when the Bilderberg members went back to their own organizations or offices, and what sort of comments trickled down the chain of command.

'When they come back into their respective environments some might say, "Well the big problem today is that there are people who are completely spoiling the game by extending credit to the Soviet Union" ... before you know it ... that sort of discussion may degenerate – depending on the environment where it lands – into a license for acts of violence and so on and so forth,' van der Pijl states.

Van der Pijl accepts that one has to be careful how far one takes this kind of suggestion. 'You have to walk a very thin line here because before you know it you are in a conspiracy theory,' he admits. 'But I think that the other extreme – as naïve as a conspiracy theory itself – is to think that if there are challenges of this type, for example those of Gorbachev, it would be naïve to think that the people who have the power to intervene in such a situation would just sit back and say, "well let's just hope for the best".' At the time of writing, no one has been convicted of murdering Alfred Herrhausen, though for a while members of the Red Army Faction, a German terrorist group, were suspected.

According to most sources on the subject, the agendas debated at Bilderberg meetings always revolve around key current or even future concerns for its members and their organizations or countries. Experts in particular subjects are often invited as guest speakers to give insight into particular issues. For example, at the Bilderberg meeting in Istanbul, Turkey, in 2007, one of the key themes was the growing public backlash against globalization, including rising popular discontent over supra-national bodies such as the European Union. (Plans for an EU constitution had just fallen apart when the voters of France and Holland voted against the idea.) The Chairman of British Petroleum and the investment bank Goldman Sachs, Peter Sutherland, is said to have told the meeting that it was an error to have allowed popular votes on the subject. 'You knew there was a rise in nationalism; you should have let your parliaments ratify the treaty, and it should (have been) done with,' he is said to have commented. Kissinger, meanwhile, is said to have made similar comments about the unification of the Americas, emphasizing the need to mobilize sections of the enlightened media behind the idea.

Another key topic at the Istanbul meeting was China. According to one claim, an item on the agenda was, 'When it will be appropriate to start talking about China as the world's next "evil empire" and the next "enemy".' It seems highly improbable that the Bilderbergs would use such language to discuss the issue, though highly probable that China would have been on their list. The question of 'what to do about China' has been growing in the minds not just of statesmen and diplomats but of business-people too. 'It's obvious that the popular base for an anti-Chinese policy is readily available, it can easily be whipped up,' says van der Pijl. 'People are fascinated but also they are frightened, and that's an ideal terrain to develop a policy,' he says. 'But that requires you knowing what your policy will be, and for you to have reflected on it and listened to specialists about what the consequences and possibilities are. That is what these networks are for. To bring together people who are not just knowledgeable in an abstract sense, but who have major stakes in however this will evolve.'

One offshoot of the Bilderberg Group had a rather different motivation. The Pinay Circle, named after the conservative former French Prime Minister, Antoine Pinay, and also known as Le Cercle Violet after the French right-wing lawyer Jean Violet, was originally a French and continental European group with strong British and American connections. The founders of this group were unhappy at what they saw as the 'lethargic' reaction of groups such as Bilderberg and national governments to the unrest and riots of 1968. These sentiments were especially acute in France, where unrest had rocked the government to its foundations.

'[Some people] felt that a more militant approach was in order,' says Professor van der Pijl. Many stories and rumours have emerged about the impact of the Pinay Circle, though hard facts about its operations are more difficult to come by. However, it seems to have had a diverse range of contacts. For example, in *Transnational Classes and International Relations*, the Professor records that at a two-day conference in Washington in 1979 organized by the Circle, among those present was a former CIA official who had been involved in Operation Gladio in Europe (*see Chapter 4, page 122*), plus representatives from the right-wing American organization, the Heritage Foundation, created in 1973. The Circle also included German politician Franz-Josef Strauss, the controversial right-winger from Bavaria who tried but failed to become Chancellor of West Germany in 1980. Van der Pijl writes, '...the envisaged use of provocative terrorism in Germany as part of a Pinay Circle campaign to bring Strauss to power in Germany reveals how violence was part of restoring class unity and discipline in the absence of hegemony.'

Another leading figure with connections to the Pinay Circle is Otto von Habsburg, the head of the Habsburg family. A strong believer in a unified Europe, von Habsburg, who was born in 1912 and has lived through many of Europe's most turbulent years, is also one of the most prominent Catholic political figures in Europe. Indeed, there was a strong Catholic background to the Pinay Circle, which saw its mission as both the strengthening of Catholic Europe and fighting against communism.

The Catholic Church has long harboured groups which have carved out their own, sometimes secretive, roles for themselves around the edges of politics and society, and who have as a result attracted considerable mistrust and criticism. It is to those groups that we now turn.

# 7

## Opus Dei

THE SOCIETY OF JESUS CROPS up frequently in the story of secret societies, but it is fair to say that it cannot today be described as a 'secret society', even if in the past its power was feared and its motives mistrusted (and not just by non-Catholics). Its members, today commonly known as 'Jesuits', are well known, and there is very little doubt about the organization's purpose: it exists to spread the word of Jesus Christ in a Catholic context. As the religious order's own website rather breathlessly states: 'We are still men on the move, ready to change place, occupation, method – whatever will advance our mission in the Church of teaching Jesus Christ and preaching his Good News…'

### The Jesuits

As we have seen, the Jesuits have had considerable if unlikely influence on other secret and covert organizations, from that of the Bavarian Illuminati to Heinrich Himmler's SS. What seems to have impressed its observers – even those among groups who were bitterly opposed to it – was the Society's organization, discipline and discretion. Moreover, in the distant past the Society itself has been implicated in some distinctly un-Christian activities, including being dispatched to England to undermine the rule of Elizabeth I in the 16th century. And while it's now clear that the leading Jesuit priest in England, Henry Garnett, was in no way a leader of the Gunpowder Plot to blow up King James I and the Houses of Parliament in London in 1605 – indeed, he apparently thought it a bad idea – he knew of the plot's existence in advance.

The founder of the Society of Jesus was Ignacio López de Loyola, later canonized as Saint Ignatius of Loyola. Born in 1491 in the Basque Country of

Spain, Ignacio was originally a soldier, who discovered inspiration for a religious life while convalescing from leg injuries inflicted during a siege. Loyola was particularly inspired by the example of St Francis of Assisi, and became fired up with enthusiasm to convert non-Christians in the Holy Land.

Having left the army and travelled to Paris to study at a university there, Ignacio gathered around him a group of six like-minded fellow students. In 1534 they set up the Company of Jesus (later called the Society of Jesus), which was formally recognized by Pope Paul III six years later. From the start, two key components of the Society's work were the provision of education and missionary work. At the same time the Protestant Reformation was sweeping across much of Europe, and the Society of Jesuits – the 'Soldiers of Christ', as they were sometimes called – played a major role in the Counter-Reformation.

The Jesuits were (and still are) known for their strict observance of Catholic doctrine as defined by the Pope and the Holy See. This was summed up in Ignatius's infamous (to modern rational minds) comment: 'I will believe that the white that I see is black if the hierarchical Church so defines it'. Ignatius, meanwhile, became the Society's first head, or Superior General (the holder of this post is also popularly known as the 'black pope' because of the plain black garb required to be worn). Ignatius also wrote the *Spiritual Exercises*, an influential set of prayers and spiritual meditations, as well as the Society's constitution, which lay down the strict discipline and self-denial expected from members. Ignatius died in 1556; by 1622 he had been canonized. This was, in Catholic Church terms, a relatively quick transition to sainthood, though, as we shall see, not nearly as fast as the canonization of the creator of a more recent Catholic organization.

Like the Knights Templar before them and other organizations since, the Jesuits attracted admiration and criticism from both outside and inside the Catholic Church. Like the Knights, they were 'warriors for Christ', travelling to new lands (notably to Asia, where some reached as far as Tibet and the New World) to win recruits, and fighting against Protestantism. But they were also educators and skilled politicians who won considerable influence at Catholic courts around Europe; this influence inevitably created tensions within the Church among those who were jealous of the Jesuits's influence within both secular courts and the Holy See.

There was also conflict between the Jesuits and certain colonial powers over the colonial policies in the New World. Venice expelled the Jesuits in

1605 during a row between the city and the papacy, for instance, and in 1759 the Portuguese expelled the Jesuits from their country and all their overseas territories, including Goa, in India, where the Society had previously flourished.

Amid mounting opposition to their operation in Spain, France and elsewhere, the Jesuits faced oblivion in 1773 when Pope Clement XIV took the drastic step of suppressing the Society in all Catholic countries. Pope Pius VII eventually restored the Society in 1814, however, and today it flourishes, with about 20,000 Jesuits worldwide, more than half of whom are priests. The Society still wields considerable influence inside the Vatican.

The Jesuits were always known as the 'shock troops' of the Catholic Church, in part because their founder, Saint Ignatius, was himself a former soldier. The 'shock troops' of today's Church, however, can be said to belong to a different group altogether, though like the Jesuits, they, too, have their origins in Spain.

## Opus Dei

In 1928 a Spanish priest called Josemaría Escrivá founded the organization Opus Dei, whose name means 'Work of God' in Latin, and which has so far attracted considerable criticism in its relatively short existence. Whilst the religious organization has been well known in the Spanish-speaking world for many years, and became even better known in English-speaking countries in the 1980s, it took Dan Brown's 2003 novel, *The Da Vinci Code* (Doubleday), and the subsequent film based on the novel to make Opus Dei a household name (*see Chapter 2, page 40*). Brown portrays the group in an unflattering light: as a sinister monkish organization that condones murder, lying and cheating in order to serve its ends. The group is also featured as taking part in the 'brainwashing' and 'aggressive recruiting' of fresh members, practising 'bloody mortification', seeking wealth and power, treating women unequally, getting a concession from the Vatican in return for bailing it out financially, and for fast-tracking the sainthood of its founder, who became Saint Josemaría in 2002.

In fact, the film prompted a pained response from Opus Dei's American branch, which, in a statement issued in late 2006, responded with a detailed point-by-point rejection of these claims. 'Opus Dei is a Catholic institution and adheres to Catholic doctrine, which clearly condemns immoral behaviour, including murder, lying, stealing, and generally injuring people. The Catholic Church teaches that one should never do evil, even for a good purpose,' said the statement from the Prelature of Opus Dei in the United States. It also noted that, 'Many people are intrigued by the claims about Christian history and theology presented in *The Da Vinci Code*. We would like to remind them that *The Da Vinci Code* is a work of fiction, and it is not a reliable source of information on these matters.' However, these and other allegations had dogged Opus Dei for many years previous to the publication of Brown's novel. Indeed, at the start of his fictional work, Brown states as 'fact' that '…Opus Dei is a deeply devout Catholic sect that has been the topic of recent controversy due to reports of brainwashing, coercion, and a dangerous practice known as "corporal mortification".'

A significant number of former Opus Dei members have complained about the way they were treated within the organization, while some prominent former members have criticized the behaviour and theological ability of its founder, St Josemaría. Rather like the Jesuits – of whom they are sometimes painted as 'rivals' – Opus Dei has attracted almost as much criticism within the Catholic Church as outside it. There have also been questions about the organization and its relations with the British Establishment after it emerged that a senior British Cabinet Minister was a member of Opus Dei. Meanwhile, an American who ended up spying for the Russians also turned out to be a member of the sect. So how did this organization start?

## Josemaría Escrivá

A close associate of Escrivá's from the early days and one-time head of Opus Dei, Alvaro Del Portillo, once said: 'To understand Opus Dei, one needs to study the Founder.' And certainly the origins of this religious group are hard to disentangle from its founder's own intriguing life story. The founder of Opus Dei was born on 9 January 1902 in the small town of Barbastro in the Aragon region of north-eastern Spain. He was christened José María Julian Mariano, and his father's surname was Escrivá. (His mother's family name was Albás.)

There is an element of controversy even at this early stage in the saint's life: José María's father's name was spelled Escribá, and it was José María who later spelled it with the now-customary 'v', and may have done so from an early age. In Spanish, both versions sound the same, and the spelling of the name may seem a trivial matter. However, the 'Escrivá' spelling is considered to be a far more distinguished version, and critics say this case highlights a liking for nobility and lofty titles that, they claim, characterizes José María's life. In such details, they suggest, we may discover that the saintly image painted of him by his devotees may not be the full story.

Indeed, the 'v' or 'b' question was not the only name change in José María's life; he later experimented with adding his mother's family name to his father's name. In the Spanish world it is not unusual for people to have two surnames, their father's and their mother's. But in José María's case he put the letter 'y' (which means 'and' in Spanish) in front, hence José María Escrivá y Albás, though he did not often use this form; some say because he was ridiculed for doing so. (The use of a 'y' between two names in this way usually occurs among the Spanish nobility.)

But even this was not the end of the name changes. In 1940 José María took the decision to add 'de Balaguer' to his surname, after a town from which his family was supposed to have originated. And in the petition for the name change – which was granted – the reason stated for the request was that 'the name Escrivá is common in the east coast and Catalonia, leading to harmful and annoying confusion.' The final change involved his given names, José and María, which at some point in his life (it is unclear exactly when), the priest decided to merge into one: Josémaria. The stated reason for this change was that he was unable to separate his love and devotion for St Joseph and Virgin Mary, the origin of the two names, and so felt obliged to combine them. Critics have, however, unkindly pointed out that, while there have been several St José's in the Catholic Church, there has never been a St Josémaria; at least not until 2002.

By the time he reached his 40s, José María Escribá was well on his way to fulfilling the vision that he had seen as a young man, an experience that had convinced him that he had a destiny to fulfil. Divine interventions had come early in Escrivá's life. When he was just two he became seriously ill, and medical experts feared he would die. His mother, Dolores, refused to give up, however, and took him to the shrine of Our Lady of Torreciudad to pray for her intervention. The boy recovered, and his mother was convinced that it was thanks to Our Lady of Torreciudad. The site is now an Opus Dei-run shrine.

As he grew up, José María showed an interest in the law and studied it while also training to become a priest, a vocation he had his sights on from an early age. He was based first in Saragossa, and then, by 1927, in Madrid.

It was here, in the following year, that Escrivá had the vision that was to change his life, as well as have a profound impact on the Catholic Church. On 2 October 1928 Escrivá was praying at a retreat on the outskirts of the city when, 'like a divine seed falling from heaven', according to one version, he 'saw' Opus Dei. The precise nature of this vision we cannot be sure about, but we do know that it propelled this charismatic, intelligent and devout priest into creating a new form of organization for the Church.

The name Opus Dei emerged over time; in the early days the members of this fledgling organization described it simply as 'the work'. But from the outset the organization was distinctive in its structure compared with, for example, the Society of Jesus. The Society is a priest-dominated organization, whereas from the start Opus Dei was to put an emphasis on lay members. Indeed, this emphasis is crucial to understanding the nature of Opus Dei's work: it is about discovering and celebrating God in everyday work and life, and not just in religious establishments. The organization's international website bears the message: 'Finding God in daily life'. It continues: 'Opus Dei['s] mission is to spread the message that work and the circumstances of everyday life are occasions for growing closer to God, for serving others, and for improving society.'

Opus Dei had its roots firmly in Catholic Spain, but from the start Escrivá always intended to make it a worldwide organization. However, in the mid 1930s, as the organization was slowly beginning to grow, this ambition was checked by certain traumatic events that were taking place in his country.

## The Spanish Civil War

The Spanish Civil War of 1936–39 was a bad time to be a Catholic priest, especially if you lived in a Republican area – it was as bad as being a suspected Republican in a nationalist era. Escrivá was fortunate to escape with his life in this most bloody of civil conflicts. Out of the hundreds of thousands who died in the War and its aftermath, a significant minority were priests. It is estimated that some 200 priests alone were killed in and around the area of Escrivá's hometown of Barbastro, while three out of every ten clerics in Madrid are said to have lost their lives. At the start of the Civil War, when Opus Dei simply had a residence for university students and a handful of devoted members, Escrivá was trapped in the Republican-held capital. For a full five months he took shelter in a psychiatric clinic, pretending that he was insane. Later he and a few close associates took refuge in a tiny, cramped room at the Honduran Consulate in Madrid. However, with the Civil War dragging on and no sign that General Franco's nationalists were about to take Madrid, Escrivá and his friends decided it was time to escape. Using a bogus letter of accreditation from the Consulate, the men slipped out of the building and headed north. After a perilous journey, the priest and his companions finally made it to the safety of Andorra by the end of 1937. By early 1938 they were at the national capital, Burgos.

The following year Franco won the war and started his campaign of vengeance against his enemies. In the same year, Opus Dei's founder published the writings that were to form his most popular work, and whose messages still remain at the core of the organization. *Camino*, or 'The Way', is a collection of 999 snippets of spiritual sayings. They have been an inspiration for millions of people; the work has been translated into 43 different languages and has sold more than four and a half million copies. The maxims are bold, almost blunt and epigrammatic in style. A flavour of their tone can be found in the opening saying: 'Don't let your life be barren. Be useful. Leave a mark. Shine forth with the torch of your faith and your love. With your apostolic life, wipe out the trail of filth and slime left by the corrupt sowers of hatred.' Despite the work's popularity and its genuine appeal to many, *Camino* has not been without its critics. Some accuse it of demanding a blind, slavish obedience that critics say can make Opus Dei appear and behave like a cult. For example, maxim 941 informs the devotee of the importance of obedience to one's superior: 'Unreserved obedience to whoever is in charge is the way of sanctity. Obedience in your apostolate, the only way: for in a work of God, the spirit must be to obey or to leave.' Another maxim insists that obedience to superiors should be carried out in the smallest detail, even if it seems 'useless' to the person. And maxim 622 tells us: 'How well you understand obedience, when you write: "To obey always is to be a martyr without dying"!'

Another more general criticism aimed at the *Camino* and other examples of Escrivá's writings is that they lack profundity. One prominent Catholic critic has suggested that they show a lack of 'discernment', implying that they are superficial and, ultimately, 'un-Christian'. In the 1960s a well-known Swiss Catholic theologian by the name of Hans Urs von Balthasar suggested that Escrivá's great work had 'insufficient spirituality' to be the main text for a religious organization. The same theologian has said that he regards *Camino* as 'a little manual for Boy Scouts at the upper level'. Indeed, some who are familiar with the maxims liken them to a mixture between Christmas card verses and the many self-help books that are now on sale; others claim the work is 'vulgar', while others say that its author is devoid of original thought.

In his book *Opus Dei: An Investigation into the Powerful, Secretive Society within the Catholic Church* (Grafton, 1989), author Michael Walsh, a former Jesuit and a Church historian, refers to Escrivá's 'vulgarity', and suggests that some parts of *Camino* fall short of the priest's 'famed good taste'. Walsh cites as an example part of maxim 367, which reads: 'The choicest morsel, if eaten by a pig, is turned [to put it bluntly]...into pigflesh! Let us be angels, so as to dignify the ideas we assimilate...let us not be beasts, like so many, so very many.' Walsh writes: 'This, I would suggest, is hardly the language or the sensitivity of a master of the spiritual life.'

Others, naturally, have taken a very different view of Escrivá's seminal work, praising it for its accessibility. Veteran Vatican observer and journalist John L. Allen, who was granted unparalleled access to the organization and its members for his book entitled *Opus Dei: The Truth about its Rituals, Secrets and Powers* (Penguin, 2003), cites the words of monk and spiritual writer, Thomas Merton, on *Camino*: 'It will certainly do a great deal of good by its simplicity, which is a true medium for the Gospel message.' As is so often the case in the story of Opus Dei and Escrivá, the latter's work tends to divide opinion into two opposing camps.

## Franco's Spain

One of the accusations levelled at Opus Dei and its founder is that both flourished under the authoritarian regime established by General Franco. The organization is effectively accused of having collaborated with a government that dealt brutally with its enemies in a country where political and other freedoms were massively curtailed. In many ways, such accusations are unfair; many practising Catholics in Spain supported Franco's victory in a country where the Church had long been closely identified with Spanish nationalism. Escrivá had also seen first-hand the appalling treatment meted out to many priests by the Republicans, and it was natural that he should have a strong antipathy towards the left and communism as a result.

Whilst Franco and Escrivá met on a few occasions, there is nothing to show that they were close friends or collaborators. Nor can it be said that

Opus Dei gave the regime any spiritual justification for its excesses, even if Escrivá believed that Franco was a 'good Christian'. (This is a debatable point; Franco lost his faith for a while as a young man, and though he later regained it – his beloved mother was very pious, his despised father was not – his attachment to the Catholic Church seems perhaps to have been pragmatic, social and cultural rather than profound.) It is also important to realize that in 1946 Escrivá left Franco's Spain and moved to a new base in Rome in order to increase the visibility of Opus Dei at the Holy See and to help spread its message around the world.

Nonetheless, Opus Dei did have an important impact in Franco's Spain, and one that went beyond the narrowly spiritual. For one thing, Franco's new Education Minister in 1939, José Ibanez Martin, worked closely with Opus Dei's José Maria Albareda. The latter was given a professorship at a university, and according to Robert Hutchison in his hostile account of the organization entitled *Their Kingdom Come* (Doubleday, 1997), '…scores more [chairs in universities] would follow during the next few years.' More important still was the setting up of the Higher Council of Scientific Research Council (the *Consejo Superior de Investigaciones Científicas* (CSIC), in Spanish). The Council's work involved handing out scholarships and controlling students' travel abroad and ranged across a wide number of disciplines. Though Ibanez Martin was Chairman of this important body, he chose Albareda as its Secretary General, a post he held until his death in 1966. One Spanish writer has described the Council as the 'matrix' of Opus Dei, with Albareda surrounding himself with more than one fellow member. Hutchison describes the Council as the 'principal cover for Opus Dei's assault on higher education and [it] also helped finance its expansion abroad.'

However, Opus Dei's influence on Spanish education and scientific training, important though it may have been, was not the sect's most visible impact on Franco's regime. In the 1950s a trio of senior Opus Dei members had a huge role not just in the economic development of Spain, but also in the nature of the Franco regime itself. Indeed, it is at least arguable that it was the intervention of key Opus Dei members, their modernization of the Spanish economy and their approach to finance, that allowed Franco's regime to stay in power as long as it did.

Franco had always had a hazy, sometimes even wacky idea of economics, and this, coupled with the country's isolation in the post-war years, meant that Spain was in pretty poor shape by 1957. This was the year

Franco abruptly changed direction and decided that the country should be led by a new and generally younger cabinet. Into the government came Mariano Navarro Rubio, a Catholic lawyer, who became Minister of Finance; and Alberto Ullastres Calvo, a university professor, was appointed Minister of Commerce. Possibly even more important was Laureano López Rodó, another lawyer who became a senior civil servant and key adviser to Admiral Carrero Blanco, the figure emerging as Franco's right-hand man. These three men were all senior figures within Opus Dei, and together they would help transform Spain's fortunes over the coming years. Paul Preston, whose *Franco: A Biography* (Basic Books, 1994) is the definitive biography of the Spanish dictator, says that the three men had an 'enormous influence' on the country, 'laying the basis for the regime's survival through its economic and political transformation.'

Inevitably, the arrival of three Opus Dei members at the heart of the regime created rumours and jealousies. Franco had always juggled competing political forces on the right, including the popular-based Falange, and it was now that dark mutterings began claiming that Opus Dei was a secret society engaged in plots to control the reins of power. 'Falangist resentment combined with a readiness to believe in sinister Masonic conspiracies, led to the emergence of the idea of Opus as a Catholic Freemasonry or mafia,' writes Preston. In fact, though the men undoubtedly worked closely together, there is little evidence of an organized Opus Dei plot at work. Yet such fears underline the influence that one small organization could have over the fate of an entire country. Indeed, this concern was enough for Escrivá to feel obliged to issue a statement insisting that Opus Dei's activities were strictly 'apostolic', and that it 'is not involved in the politics of any country'.

It is difficult to conclude that Opus Dei as an institution and Escrivá as a person were prominent cheerleaders for Franco's regime, even if members of the former did become major figures in it, and even though there was a clear overlap in socio-political outlooks. There were also a number of Opus Dei members who fell out badly with the regime. However, if Escrivá was no cheerleader for Franco, he was certainly not a dissident voice either. Supporters claim that in the climate of the time it was near impossible for anyone to show disapproval of Franco's often brutal regime. However, some sections of the Catholic Church did manage to do just that. As early as 1940 the obstinate Cardinal Pedro Segura, the Archbishop of Seville, made public his displeasure at the regime's closeness to Nazi Germany and sent a copy of his pastoral letter to this effect to Franco himself. The Cardinal also refused to pay public homage to the dictator, and when in pique Falangists came up with idea of ending their victory parade on the doorstep of his cathedral, the Archbishop threatened to excommunicate the lot of them.

In 1948 the Cardinal snubbed Franco's wife, Carmen, at a banquet over seating arrangements, but despite his anger there was little the dictator could do about the cleric. There was room for determined Church figures in Spain to oppose Franco, yet this was a course Escrivá evidently chose not to take. This decision may explain Escrivá's rather defensive posture in remarks he claimed to have made to Spanish bishops. He allegedly told the bishops that if a violent uprising broke out it would be hard for the regime to stop it, and that all elements of the Church – and not just Opus Dei – would suffer. He added: '... therefore ... don't think that a single scapegoat will be sufficient; all of you will be scapegoats. One could gather ample collections of public and excessive eulogies which the bishops have addressed to the regime, which is something that no one can do with me, although I recognize that Franco is a good Christian.'

**Status and Structure**
Opus Dei is unique in its status within the Catholic Church. Usually the area that a bishop (or prelate) represents – known as a 'prelature' – is a geographical area. In 1982, however, seven years after its founder's death, Opus Dei was given the status of a 'personal prelature'. This means that its bishop has jurisdiction over its clerics and lay members wherever they are in the world. No other Catholic organization has yet received this special status. It does not mean that Opus Dei members are independent of the Church; indeed, they are still governed by their local bishops over issues such as the annulment of a marriage. The Opus Dei prelate, however, has authority over all issues that relate to the organization.

This unique position has fuelled concerns about whether the group is a 'church within a church', a separate power base within the Church. Supporters of Escrivá insist that it is the logical outcome of the priest's vision: a largely secular organization of both men and women with a relatively small number of priests. Ever since the organization was first formally recognized by the papacy in 1950, say supporters, it has been moving towards this special legal status, one that recognizes its unique place in the Church.

There are certainly far more lay members than clerics in Opus Dei. Out of a total estimated membership of more than 80,000 there are fewer than 200 full-time Opus priests. However, there is a parallel organization known as the Priestly Society of the Holy Cross, which counts about 2,000 priests as members. These clerics work as regular priests in their own diocese, but they are also members of Opus Dei. Worldwide, by far the majority of lay and clerical members are in Spain, with Mexico, Argentina, Italy, the United States, the Philippines and Colombia hosting them as well. The organization is currently trying to expand its membership. On 26 June 2007, Escrivá's feast day, the organization announced that it was beginning its 'apostolic work' in Russia. Its membership numbers in some Western countries, though, are still quite low. According to John L. Allen's account, there are only around 500 members in Britain. Allen suggests that this is partly due to the influence of the late Cardinal Basil Hume of Westminster (the country's senior Catholic), who was concerned about the way the organization worked. Hume laid down tough guidelines about how Opus Dei was to behave if it wanted to continue to operate on his patch. In particular, the Cardinal was worried about how Opus Dei recruited young people. The first of the four guidelines read: 'No person under eighteen years of age should be allowed to take any vow or long-term commitment in association with Opus Dei.' Hume's successor, Cardinal Cormac Murphy–O'Connor, has so far taken a softer line, and has appointed an Opus Dei priest in one of his parishes.

## Corporate Works

Opus Dei runs a number of what are described as 'corporate works' around the world, many of them (like the Jesuits) in the field of education. These include fifteen universities, with a total of 80,000 students enrolled. Establishments exist in Guatemala, Rome and Pamplona, where the University of Navarre is the largest such Opus Dei operation in the world. Opus Dei also runs nearly a hundred technical or vocational schools, many in deprived areas of the world, plus 36 primary and secondary schools and 11 business schools, including establishments in Argentina, Mexico and Spain. It further runs 166 university residences housing some 6,000 students, 'the vast majority of whom are not members of Opus Dei', according to Allen. Halls of residence are important to Opus Dei; its first-ever centre was a university residence in Madrid. Other projects include involvement in seven hospitals around the world.

In addition to these 'corporate works' are institutions that Opus Dei does not run, but at which it offers 'spiritual assistance'. These include two more universities and some 200 schools, including technical and business schools. From these figures it is clear that while on a global scale Opus Dei's operation is quite small, it does play a significant role in helping to educate and train young people.

One of the most striking facts about Opus Dei's educational enterprises is its involvement in business schools, including the IESE Business School in Barcelona. On its website the IESE publishes the following mission statement: 'IESE Business School is an international business school committed to the education and development of business leaders worldwide, and the generation and communication of new business ideas with impact. [Our] mission is to create an outstanding learning context for business leaders that direct organizations that are successful in the long-term, develop people around them and contribute to the new challenges that society has to face.'

The website also gives prospective students a guide to the various courses it offers, including an MBA, an 'Executive MBA', and a PhD in management. It is only under the rather more discreet heading of 'Chaplaincy' that the prospective student can find out about the role of Opus Dei within the institution. 'The IESE Chaplaincy provides a context for the spiritual growth of all members of the IESE community based on Christian principles. It is open to everyone. The priests who serve in the Chaplaincy at IESE Barcelona and IESE Madrid are members of Opus Dei, a Personal Prelature of the Roman Catholic Church, which was founded in 1928 by Saint Josemaría Escrivá,' says the site.

The fact that Opus Dei is involved with an elite institution, the (perfectly laudable) aim of which is to produce the business leaders and captains of industry of tomorrow, has added to the suspicion of some critics about its true motives. Such statements feed the idea that Opus Dei deliberately targets recruits among the world's business and professional elites (rather as the Jesuits once had the ear of many royal courts in Europe) in an attempt to enhance its status, power and wealth. In response to such accusations, the organization points to the projects it carries out in developing countries, but which attract far less publicity.

## Membership Categories

An important feature of Opus Dei is the different categories of membership it provides. The most numerous type of member, comprising nearly 70 per cent of the total membership, are what are known as 'supernumerary' category. These are lay members, often (though not necessarily) married with families, who live in their own homes and have their own careers, but who play an active role in Opus Dei and receive 'spiritual direction' from numerary members. These members also contribute financially to Opus Dei, in accordance with their means.

The second category of membership, the 'numerary' members, accounts for a fifth of the organization. They too are lay members, but are celibate and live in Opus Dei centres. Both men and women can be numeraries, but male and female centres are segregated. Though numeraries usually have their own careers – often but by no means exclusively in the professions – the majority of their income goes to Opus Dei. According to Allen's book, the numeraries play a critical role in the organization and are '…the key to the geographical expansion of Opus Dei, since opening a centre in a new country requires the presence of at least a couple of numeraries who can find jobs, support the centre financially, learn the language if necessary and get operations off the ground.' These members are also the ones who take part in the body-harming practices that have caused considerable controversy (*see page 196*).

Another category of members is that of 'numerary assistants'. These members, who are exclusively female, work full time in Opus Dei centres, and their job is in effect to provide a kind of housekeeping service. This role is sometimes likened to that of being a full-time mother. Numerary assistants are also celibate.

Yet another category of members are called 'associates'. These members are similar to numeraries (they are celibate as well) except that, for practical or familial reasons, they live in their own homes rather than in a centre. Finally, there are what are called 'cooperators'. These people are not members as such, but they choose to support the work of Opus Dei in some way or other; with money, voluntary work or perhaps prayer. Unusually for such an organization, a cooperator can be from another faith, or indeed from no faith at all. There are, according to Opus Dei, more than 160,000 such supporters around the world, plus as many as 900,000 more who take some part in Opus Dei meetings.

**Membership Roles**

Opus Dei is insistent that the different levels of membership are simply there to reflect different lifestyles and the ways in which its members are able to participate in Opus Dei life. All members are treated similarly, and all are expected to follow Opus Dei's life plan, or its 'norms' as the organization often calls them. The key here, says Opus Dei, is that the organization is about people living a holy life, one that takes them on the path – the 'way' – to holiness. In that sense membership is less about specific acts than about how members behave in their everyday lives.

Members are, however, required to perform regular acts of devotion. These start first thing in the morning, when the member is expected to say *serviam* (Latin for 'I will serve'). Many of the other daily norms revolve around prayer, with members required to go to Mass, pray the Rosary, say three Hail Mary's before bedtime, indulge in a daily examination of conscience, read from the Scriptures, offer up spontaneous prayers and sprinkle themselves with holy water before retiring to bed. Members are also expected to have weekly sessions of what is called the 'circle', where a member gives a lesson on a particular aspect of Opus Dei life, plus have regular meetings with their spiritual director. One can see from these 'norms' that being a member of Opus Dei is a demanding and intense experience.

**Recruitment of New Members**

The recruitment of new members, or what is often termed proselytism, is a key part of the life and work of Opus Dei members. There is no doubt that Escrivá put huge emphasis on gaining new apostles; indeed, a significant number of his maxims in *Camino* are devoted to the subject, including number 810, which reads: 'That burning desire to win fellow-apostles is a sure sign that you have really "given yourself" to God.' Another maxim, number 796, tells the devotee: 'You have but little love if you are not zealous for the salvation of all souls. You have but poor love if you are not eager to inspire other apostles with your craziness.'

However, Escrivá's bluntest language on the subject was reserved for the in-house Opus Dei journal called *Cronica*. In 1963, the founder pointed out that running universities and owning publishing houses were not the ultimate aims of Opus Dei's work; its true aims were personal sanctity and 'to promote in the world the greatest possible number of souls dedicated to God in Opus Dei'. In another edition of the journal, he wrote, 'Proselytism in the work is precisely the road, the way to reach sanctity…No one can be dispensed from doing it, under any circumstances. Not even the sick can be dispensed…' Further on he adds: 'When a person does not have the zeal to win others it is because his heart is not beating. He is dead.'

Given the importance that the members attach to the Father's utterances, it is little surprise that they have adopted a variety of approaches to recruiting new apostles, and are said to form teams that develop these strategies. Members are also encouraged to have a circle of up to 15 friends – four or five of whom are being worked on at any one time – who are close to becoming members. According to reports, the process of gaining new apostles is called 'fishing' in some Opus circles.

Some critics claim that many of the sect's institutions and social and cultural events are *primarily* mechanisms to recruit new members. In particular, summer schools, hostels and youth clubs are all allegedly used as a form of bait for this purpose. As the late Cardinal Hume's guidelines show, there has been particular concern both inside and outside the Catholic Church about the way Opus Dei recruits young people. Catholic schools are a favourite place for this, say critics. Members talk to young people in such establishments and encourage them to 'whistle', the Opus term for people who decide they want to become a member. Another complaint is that new recruits are initially only told in vague terms what the demands on them will be. By the time they have joined the organization they are informed that the enthusiasm with which they embrace those strictures is a test not just of their commitment to Opus Dei, but to God. Opus Dei denies such claims, and in John Allen's book, in which the organization gave him access to its members, he cites a number of examples where recruits insist that they never felt under pressure to join. They also deny that they were ever pressured into recruiting new members.

Another criticism frequently levelled at Opus Dei is that membership can cause estrangement between members and their families, especially between young recruits and their parents. An example of such an occurrence is the story of Dianne R. DiNicola and her daughter, Tammy, who became involved with Opus Dei in 1987. Dianne DiNicola is now Executive Director of the Opus Dei Awareness Network (ODAN), a group created to provide information about Opus Dei and to help those whose lives have been adversely affected by their involvement with the group.

DiNicola, a practising Catholic, says that Tammy first came into contact with Opus Dei while studying at Boston College, and had gone on a retreat with the organization. DiNicola said the main difference that she and her husband first noticed in Tammy's behaviour was that she started to attend Mass more often. As practising Catholics, both DiNicola and her husband approved of this behaviour. But when Tammy started to spend more and more of her time with Opus Dei to the exclusion of other friends, her parents became worried. 'An aloofness we never experienced before had become her normal behaviour. We experienced a profound feeling of loss, and communications were rapidly deteriorating even at this early stage,' says DiNicola.

That, however, was just the beginning. Over the next year or so Tammy became increasingly distant with her family and was becoming more involved with Opus Dei, to the point where she wanted to join them as a numerary. Unsure about what to do, the family found out more about the organization and spoke to a local priest about it. To their dismay, he described Opus Dei as a throwback to the 15th century. Meanwhile, Tammy was becoming increasingly like a stranger to them. 'She was nervous and stilted. Her happy, bubbly self had disappeared. Our relationship was completely destroyed. I couldn't help her and worst of all, I didn't know what to do. I was beginning to feel hopeless,' recalls DiNicola.

In April 1989 Tammy informed her parents that she wasn't coming home for Easter – normally a time when the family got together – because she had 'a family in Opus Dei and they needed her'. The DiNicolas drove down to Boston to meet Tammy and an Opus Dei priest, but the meeting achieved little. Later, they took Tammy out for dinner, but it was not an easy encounter. 'After we dropped her off … a feeling of complete hopelessness permeated my now fragmented family,' recalls DiNicola. 'It was as if Tammy had died yet she was walking around in her body. The Tammy we knew was buried inside of her. We did not recognize the girl we had just dropped off.'

The family then decided they needed serious help. They consulted two experts with experience of handling cults, then spoke with Father James Lebar, a cult consultant for the archdiocese of New York. He was able to put them in touch with a family who had been estranged from two of their children, both Opus Dei members, for a number of years. The DiNicolas realized that they were not alone in their predicament. They then contacted an 'exit councillor', someone who specializes in helping individuals and their families get back together when they have been estranged through a sect or cult. This, however, was not an easy step to take. 'We didn't want to destroy her spirituality and we were worried sick about the consequences,' says DiNicola. 'We wondered how we would be able to help our daughter see that the life decisions she made while a member of Opus Dei were being manipulated, and that she was being deceived.'

The family waited patiently until Tammy came home for her graduation party (the family were told that it was unusual for Opus Dei to allow this), then arranged for Tammy to meet with the exit councillor at a family gathering. The meeting was tense at times, but Tammy agreed to look at some literature that was critical of Opus Dei. Initially, she says, her plan had been to take notes to take back to Opus Dei in order to check whether their comments had been misquoted or poorly translated. Soon, however, she says that 'pinpoints of truth' began to hit home with her.

'I started to see the inconsistencies within Opus Dei. For example, Opus Dei states that they engage in an "apostolate of friendship and confidence", and yet the reality is that it is not true friendship, and it is far from confidential!' says Tammy. 'On the contrary, members regularly divulge intimate details about their recruits to their directors, and even devise strategies for each one to get them closer to joining Opus Dei.'

Tammy also pondered the true meaning of some of the words of Escrivá in *Camino*. 'The Founder of Opus Dei wrote in *The Way*, Maxim 399: "If, to save an earthly life, it is praiseworthy to use force to keep a man from committing suicide, are we not allowed to use the same coercion – holy coercion – in order to save the Lives of so many who are stupidly bent on killing their souls?"

'This is just one example of the many inconsistencies I was beginning to see in Opus Dei. What I had thought was so beautiful about Opus Dei now seemed manipulative and deceptive to me,' says Tammy. By the middle of the second day of the gathering and exit counselling, Tammy had begun to relax and found herself feeling closer once more to her family, as she began to feel intellectually, emotionally and spiritually more free. She made the decision to quit Opus Dei.

'The primary reason I decided to leave Opus Dei was because I saw clearly the cult-like techniques they employed,' she says. For example, she explains, new members are not told the full story of what is expected of them. Once they are, the new members are put under pressure to stay within the organization – even if they object to aspects of Opus Dei life.

'The new members are typically told that if they leave Opus Dei they may be damned and will absolutely live their whole life without God's grace,' she says. Tammy also describes what she calls the members' 'surrendering of control of nearly every aspect of life'. The numeraries, for example, hand over their entire salary to Opus Dei and are then held accountable for every penny they themselves spend – money they have to ask for from Opus Dei. All incoming and outgoing mail is read and must be approved, and members are often not allowed to watch films or go to watch sport. 'Numeraries do not watch television, listen to radio or read magazines or newspapers without permission,' Tammy says. (One former Opus Dei member even claims to have seen Protestant Bibles and books on evolution being burned in the garden of one Opus Dei centre.).

After deciding to leave Opus Dei, Tammy says she found it hard to adjust to life outside the organization. At times, she was overwhelmed by the simple fact of having freedom of choice restored back in her life. 'I would sit on the bed and cry because I could not pick out an outfit to wear,' she says. Now she is a mother herself, with three sons and a career. She is also a practising Catholic and possesses 'a deep faith that guides me each day.'

Tammy believes that Opus Dei has not changed fundamentally since she left despite claims to the contrary. 'Opus Dei may have made some cosmetic changes over the years ... but the central way of dealing with members and recruits is still wrought with deception and manipulation,' she claims. Meanwhile, Dianne DiNicola's experience with her daughter and Opus Dei led her to help set up ODAN, which aims to help families and individuals who share similar problems.

Opus Dei strongly denies that its recruiting or treatment of members is in any way oppressive or underhanded. John L. Allen quotes from a variety of Opus Dei members, as well as non-members who insist that there is no coercion over recruitment or of members, though Allen himself says that 'members with a particular zeal can push too hard.' Allen also notes that, 'Among some observers there's a sense that whatever the difficulties over recruiting may have been in the past, things today seem calmer.' On the question of lack of freedom and control of members, Allen accepts that there are 'scores' of accounts from former members who testify to being cowed into submission, or to having their lives minutely controlled. But he adds, 'At the same time, another group of people, comprised of current and former members, testify to the freedom they feel inside Opus Dei.' He says it is 'impossible' for him to believe that one or the other side is lying, and puts many of the differences down to the 'different frames of reference' that people use.

Some critics and former members, however, say that Opus Dei simply cannot be relied upon to tell the truth. The organization, they claim, is so committed to its apostolic cause that it is even able to justify telling lies to protect the greater good. Dianne DiNicola claims that: 'In Opus Dei, if you are lying for God, it is permissible. One of the reasons members believe they have this right is because their organization is divinely inspired. They are programmed to think they know better.' Dennis Dubro was a member of Opus Dei for 17 years, first in the United States and later in Australia, where he was a numerary. Dubro describes an occasion when the Opus Dei centre where he was living received a routine visit from the local cardinal. At a meeting of members, the cardinal asked what degree of freedom they had over issues such as visiting friends, spending money and the sort of recreation they enjoyed. The centre's vicar replied that members were perfectly free in such matters. Dubro says, however, that he and the others were surprised at this response, because *they* had been told that they must ask permission in such matters. When the vicar left, the inconsistency was explained to the Opus members. 'The director called us all together and told us that we *still* needed to ask permission in all of these matters,' says Dubro. 'He said the vicar had explained Opus Dei to the bishop in a way that he would understand.' On the issue of lying, Dubro says today that the Opus approach is 'to state the ideal rather than the real; that is, what things should be, rather than what they are, or what should happen, not what happens.'

## The Role of Women

Women play a key role in Opus Dei at many levels, though not, of course, as priests. However, Opus Dei's treatment of women is another controversial area, and one that has prompted critics to suggest that the organization is old-fashioned, chauvinistic or downright sexist in its approach. Most of this criticism is centred on the role of the four thousand or so numerary assistants, the celibate female members whose job it is to look after the maintenance of Opus Dei centres around the world.

Former numerary and critic of Opus Dei, Alberto Moncada, has claimed that the organization's founder, Escrivá, '...shared the misogyny frequent in Catholic theology and discipline and created a structure in which the primary activity of women was to care for houses and centres of the Work.' He says that in one early version of the organization's constitution, a group of female members who came from modest homes were actually referred to as 'servants'. Moncada also claims that the founder had stricter norms for women numeraries. 'Thus, among other things, women sleep on planks and used to have to ask permission to drink water between meals, although the latter rule was recently abolished,' he says.

There is no denying that there is in general a strict division between the sexes within Opus Dei. Men and women have their own councils, with the General Council reporting to the prelature on behalf of male members, while the Central Advisory Council does the same thing for the women. Contact between these two bodies is apparently very formal. Allen asked an English woman who was a member of the Central Advisory Council whether, if the women's Council wanted to raise an issue with the men's Council, they would speak on the telephone or in person. The reply was that if the women needed to contact the men, they would do so in writing. Allen also writes of the numerary assistants: '...there is admittedly something startling about an organization in the 21st century that would have a whole class of members devoted to domestic service, and that this class would be composed exclusively of women.'

Yet Allen also quotes Opus Dei members who say that the assistants are taking care of a whole 'family', not just the men, and that in any case their work demands 'intellectual capacity and administrative skills'. He also quotes assistants who are very happy with their decision to join Opus Dei, and who are content with the role they play. One such assistant, Bernadette Pliske, from Indiana, says, 'If I weren't a numerary assistant in Opus Dei I'd be doing this sort of thing anyway. I'd be in a convent or having a big family. Here I'm able to be a mother of a really big family. I absolutely love it.'

## Corporal Mortification

Some of the more lurid criticism of Opus Dei concerns what today we would call 'self-harming', but which in Christian tradition is known as 'corporal mortification'. Varying in form and manner, in the past these practices have been followed by the Roman Catholic Church. They are supposed to be a way of holding in check the pleasures of the flesh and helping the follower identify with the physical suffering of Christ upon the cross. In most Christian communities such practices have been either stopped or reduced in number and intensity, yet they still form an important part of Opus Dei.

Critics claim that such practices can cause psychological as well as physical scars, and that they are another way in which the organization exercises control over its members. Opus Dei counters this criticism by pointing out that self-denial and penance is carried out in moderation, and that no one is encouraged to carry out such practices to excess – and certainly not to do anything that would affect a person's health.

Probably the most controversial form of 'mortification' required of numeraries is the wearing of the cilice, a small chain with spikes that is usually worn around the upper part of the devotee's thigh for two hours a day, apart from feast days. It causes some pain and can leave small pinpricks in the skin.

Another form of mortification is carried out once a week using what is known as 'the discipline'. This involves whipping oneself across the back or backside with a small whip. Escrivá himself frequently used this form of mortification, and it was often reported that the walls of his bathroom were splattered in blood because of the zeal with which he undertook the discipline. A large number of the priest's maxims in *Camino* were also devoted to mortification, including one that reads: 'No ideal becomes a reality without sacrifice. Deny yourself. It's so beautiful to be a victim!'

Other less dramatic forms of mortification include taking cold showers, sleeping on the floor on occasion, kissing the floor in the morning, skipping parts of meals or certain foods and extended periods of silence. In particular, numeraries are usually silent between their examinations of conscience in the evening until after taking part in Mass the following morning. Fasting is observed on designated days, and any other personal fasting has to be authorized.

## Money, Power and Politics

One of the most constant criticisms made of Opus Dei is that despite its relatively small membership numbers, its members and supporters tend to come disproportionately from wealthy and powerful sections of society. This, say critics, means that the organization wields far more power both inside and outside the Catholic Church than the size of the organization would suggest. We have already noted the power that a handful of Opus Dei members had in Franco's Spain, and their role in transforming that country (*see page 183*). Indeed, a former member of Opus Dei, Raimundo

Pannikar, has been quoted as saying that the organization's involvement in Spain's power struggle was not an accident; it was part of an attempt to control the country.

Another part of the world in which Opus Dei is said to have had close associations with governments and big business is Latin America. Some academics claim that Opus Dei has acted as a kind of transnational network linking Europe with Latin America, a network that includes various major banks. Opus Dei is also said to have links with the Pinay Circle (*see Chapter 6, page 175*), a right-wing conservative Catholic grouping in Europe and elsewhere that has allegedly tried to intervene directly in world affairs. Others, notably the late Penny Lernoux, an American Catholic journalist, have claimed that Opus Dei has had links in the past with right wing and military circles in Latin America, specifically in Chile and Argentina. Author Michael Walsh also cites the example of a Colombian priest turned revolutionary called Camilo Torres, who joined the National Liberation Army and was killed fighting for its cause. Walsh says the leader of the army brigade that killed the revolutionary became a General, and went on to help edit a magazine linked to Opus Dei.

It is very hard to be precise in gauging the influence of Opus Dei members in politics, even if there are clear links. In the United States, Opus Dei is often associated with sections of the Republican Party, just as it has been (and still is) with right-of-centre parties in Spain and Latin America. This does not mean, however, that Opus Dei is a political machine working for the election of particular parties; there has never been any suggestion that the leadership from Escrivá onwards has ever tried to tell members which way they should vote.

More plausible is the idea that, as it is a socially conservative religious organization, the people likely to be attracted to Opus ranks tend to be those who are closer to socially conservative political parties. Indeed, it is hard to go along with Penny Lernoux's view, stated in 1989, that 'Opus Dei is an efficient machine run to achieve world power.' This does not mean, however, that Opus Dei lacks influence in the social-political arena, even if the precise nature of that influence is harder to pin down. In that same book, Lernoux suggested that Opus Dei holds influence over 52 television and radio stations, 694 publications, 38 news and publicity agencies and a dozen or so film and distribution companies.

Questions over Opus Dei's role in the world of politics were raised in

2004 in Britain, when it was confirmed that the new Education Secretary in Prime Minister Tony Blair's cabinet, Ruth Kelly, was a member. It was also reported that her brother, Ronan, is a supernumerary. In particular, there was concern about whether someone who adhered to Opus Dei's traditional views on abortion, cloning and embryo research could be impartial as head of a department that controls a massive science research budget in Britain. According to *The Times*, Ms Kelly opposed motions on embryo research in Parliament and reportedly told Tony Blair that she could never support stem-cell research. Robin Lovell-Badge, the person in charge of developmental genetics at the National Institute of Medical Research, told *The Times Higher Education Supplement*: 'If someone as senior as Ruth Kelly is not going to favour stem-cell research, we will end up with a similarly schizophrenic system in this country. It is very worrying.' Kelly herself strongly denied that her religious convictions affected her work. 'I have a private spiritual life and I have a faith. It is a private spiritual life and I don't think it is relevant to my job,' she told journalists.

One of the organization's biggest controversies came in 2001, when a former FBI officer, Robert Hanssen, was arrested for spying for the Soviet Union and then for Russia. He admitted to 15 charges of espionage and was jailed for life. This was bad publicity both for the US government and for the FBI. It was also embarrassing for Opus Dei, as he was revealed to be a long-standing member of the organization who sent his children to Opus Dei schools. It also emerged that Hanssen had confessed some of his illicit activities to an Opus Dei priest, who had told him to give to the poor any of the money he had made from spying – but that for the sake of his family he need not turn himself in.

The case turned the spotlight both on Opus Dei's secrecy and its presence within important sections of the US government. There were rumours that other, more senior, FBI officials were (and possibly still are) members. It also emerged that there had been links between Opus Dei members and members of the Reagan administration.

Indeed, Opus Dei has certainly been keen to expand in different parts of the world. As noted earlier, in June 2007 Opus Dei formally announced the start of its 'apostolic work' in Russia (*see page 187*). Meanwhile, this author has learnt that Opus Dei has been establishing contacts with the wealthy expatriate Catholic community in Shanghai, the economic powerhouse of China.

## Saint Josémaria

Opus Dei has usually enjoyed considerable support in the upper echelons of the Vatican, most importantly from the late Pope John Paul II. The Polish Pope praised as a 'great ideal' the work of the organization in trying to encourage its members to follow the Gospel of Christ in their everyday lives. His successor, Benedict XVI, is also known to be a supporter.

The support of Pope John Paul II certainly seems to have helped some Opus Dei devotees to achieve their cherished dream: to get their leader canonized following his death in 1975. The process was a swift one, at least in comparison with others in Catholic history. Escrivá was formally beatified in 1992, a crucial step on the road to sainthood in the Catholic Church. He was finally declared a saint on 6 October 2002 at a ceremony in St Peter's Square, in Rome, in front of a huge crowd of supporters.

The many supporters of St Josémaria's sainthood say that the fact that the priest's canonization occurred so soon after his death was the result of reforms made by Pope John Paul II in the canonization process – and had nothing to do with any untoward influence. Critics, however, say that the process was fast-tracked thanks to the lobbying and influence of Opus Dei, and that corners were cut and criticism of the 'saint' was overlooked.

Maria del Carmen Tapia, a former senior Opus Dei member who left the organization after many years, and who had worked closely with Escrivá (she left after falling out badly with both the organization and Escrivá), holds such an opinion. Tapia claims that when she offered to give her views on the founder of the organization before the beatification process, her offer was firmly rebuffed. In her book, *Beyond the Threshold* (Chiron, 1997), Tapia stated her opinion on the matter: 'Such a declaration [beatification] would cause a painful confusion among millions of Roman Catholics and a sad scandal to Christians of all denominations. The simple truth is that Monsignor Escrivá's life was not an example of holiness, nor was he a model to be imitated by the women and men of our time.' Indeed, a number of people who knew the priest have pointed to his bad temper and his love of expensive trappings as an indication that he may not have been entirely saintly. His supporters, however, say that no one is perfect – not even a saint.

Criticism of the sainthood process used for Escrivá has also come from neutral observers who are experts in Church history and in canonization procedure. For example, Cambridge historian Eamon Duffy, Professor of the

History of Christianity, has said: 'The canonization of the founder of Opus Dei is the most striking example in modern times of the successful promotion of a cause by a pressure group in order to extend and legitimize the objectives of that group; here the saint becomes a mascot and a means to an end for the group who venerate him.' Kenneth Woodward, an author, former *Newsweek* religion correspondent and an expert on the canonization process, wrote four years after the beatification process: '…the only fair-minded conclusion I can reach…is that Opus Dei subverted the canonization process to get its man beatified. In a word, it was a scandal … [the fact] that *Newsweek* caught Opus Dei officials making claims that were not true is a matter of record. Escrivá may have been a saint – who am I to judge – but you could never tell from the way his cause was handled.' However, supporters point out that Mother Teresa of Calcutta was beatified much more quickly than Escrivá – six years after her death, as opposed to 17 years for Escrivá.

As we have seen, views about Opus Dei are strongly polarized, with many members and non-members alike praising it as a staunch defender of Catholic values and a noble cause that promotes spirituality in the everyday lives of its members. Even its bitterest critics concede that there are many honest and faithful Christians within the organization whose sole aim is to make the world a better place. Yet there are persisting criticisms about the organization's secrecy and its influence within the Church, political conservative circles and education.

Of particular concern are the stories about coercion in Opus Dei's recruitment of members and the pressure inflicted upon them to remain within the organization. Dianne DiNicola says: 'I believe, as a practising Catholic who cherishes my Church, that Opus Dei is a cancer spreading within the institutional Church. Opus Dei takes God and uses Him for its own good, even if it means lying, manipulating and deceiving. This does not correspond with the high ideals of being a good Christian and living an honest, truthful existence.' She further adds: 'Opus Dei has much more power than is readily seen in governments, in news media, and in the Catholic Church. I base this on my experience of 16 years as Executive Director of ODAN … [and on] my conclusions based on the information that has been sent to ODAN from around the world. When you are not honest about who you are and project an image that seems to be from God, the impact would be a profound negative on the Catholic Church and the world.'

# 8

## The Church of Scientology

THE TIME IS 75 MILLION years in the past, the place a quiet, inconspicuous planet by the name of Teegeeack, one of 76 such heavenly masses in the Galactic Confederation. Suddenly the skies fill with spacecraft, vessels that bear an uncanny resemblance to the Douglas DC-8 aircraft of the 20th century. Aboard are billions of people who, with the connivance of psychiatrists, have been drugged with alcohol and glycol, forcibly removed from their home planet and sent to Teegeeack. They land on the bases of volcanoes, while hydrogen bombs are lowered inside the volcano cones and detonated. The souls or spirits, known as *thetans*, of these hapless victims are then gathered together by the president of the Confederation and subjected to religious and technological imagery in cinema-style buildings for 36 days.

The spirits, or souls, later gather into clusters and enter the bodies of any of the people who have somehow managed to survive the terrible explosions. Once inside the bodies of these survivors, the thetans become known as 'body thetans'. These body thetans afflict humans to this day, causing us to be the way we are, suffering from illness, negative thoughts and psychological conditions. However, the evil president of the Confederation (the perpetrator of this terrible act) did not escape unpunished. A mere six years after the terrible event, a group known as the Loyal Officers overthrew the president and imprisoned him inside a mountain. He remains there to his day. His name is Xenu.

If the reader thinks that the above story is simply science fiction, then he or she would be wrong – though on the right track. For the story of Xenu, the thetans and the planet Teegeeack (which is supposedly the Earth) *was* written by a popular science fiction writer. But the story of Xenu is, according to some, not science fiction. Rather, it is one of the key stories that stand at the heart of a modern-day religion, an astonishing tale that 'explains' the nature of human beings, and also why we 'need' this religion and the techniques it offers to help us realize our full human potential.

This extraordinary story was written in the 1960s by a man called L. Ron Hubbard, a US Navy Second World War veteran, science-fiction writer and founder of the Church of Scientology, a religion that has become one of the most controversial movements in the modern world. Yet even among many Scientologists the story of Xenu remains, at least in theory, unknown. For the mysteries of Xenu and the true story of the origins of humanity are jealously guarded by the Church of Scientology. This knowledge is reserved only for those who are able – and wealthy enough – to reach the higher realms of the movement's spiritual levels.

The story of Xenu reveals some of the complexities one confronts when trying to describe and discuss Scientology. On the one hand it is a self-styled religion, and is officially registered and legally accepted as such in a number of countries, including the United States. Yet on the other it began life in the 1950s as an allegedly science-based self-help therapy. This is indeed how many people come into contact initially with Scientology – as the provider of a technique that can supposedly help with all kinds of physical, emotional and psychological ailments.

Scientology's self-help programme revolves around what Scientologists call 'Dianetics'. This programme is described on the organization's main website as: '…[resting] on basic principles that can be easily learned and applied by any reasonably intelligent person – as millions have. It is the route to a well, happy, high IQ human being.' So is it a religion, as Scientology claims? Or is it a form of therapy? Even different governments seem unsure, for while it may be regarded as a religion in the United States, it has not so far been accepted as a religion for charitable purposes in the United Kingdom (though it does enjoy VAT-exemption there as a not-for-profit body).

Another difficulty when attempting to assess Scientology and its impact on society is that it is hard to know how big its membership is and which organizations are connected to it. The word Scientology is used to describe the beliefs and practices of this self-help programme/religion, while the Church of Scientology is the main umbrella name given to the various organizations that promote the programme/religion. Within the

Scientology 'family' of organizations there are many different bodies and companies, many of whose names give no immediate clue as to their connection with Scientology. This makes it hard to be sure just how wealthy and powerful the organization actually is.

The same difficulty applies to its membership details. The Church itself claims somewhere around ten million adherents worldwide, though few observers accept this figure. Other estimates vary from between 100,000 to around 500,000 members. However, the organization's importance and profile is hugely elevated by the identities of some of its members, which include a clutch of Hollywood stars. The most notable of these are actors Tom Cruise and John Travolta.

The Church has also been embroiled in a number of high-profile legal battles and disputes around the world, sometimes with national governments, and it has also been involved in litigation over the publication of its teachings on the Internet. One matter is clear when it comes to Scientology: it polarizes opinion like few other modern movements. For its supporters, Scientology provides a proven ability to help them live better lives, while for its critics it is a dangerous, mind-bending cult based around techniques that have not been scientifically validated, and which espouses some decidedly wacky beliefs.

## The Story of L. Ron Hubbard

Though Scientology's founder, L. Ron Hubbard, died back in 1986, even a basic understanding of modern day Scientology requires a knowledge of the personal history of this most colourful and controversial of characters. Despite Hubbard's death, his extraordinary personality still dominates the movement.

Lafayette Ronald Hubbard was born in the small town of Tilden, in Nebraska, in 1911, the first child of Harry Hubbard, an officer in the United States Navy, and Ledora May, a qualified teacher. On the surface, Hubbard's childhood was a relatively normal one for the period, though because of his father's naval career the young L. Ron moved around considerably. However, few things about the life of L. Ron Hubbard are clear and straightforward. According to Scientology accounts of Hubbard's early life, when he was four years old and living with his family in Montana he was befriended by 'Old Tom', an 'old medicine man' who was part of the Blackfeet tribe of Native Americans. The youngster established a close friendship with the usually taciturn Old Tom, and soon the child was 'initiated into the various secrets of the tribe, their legends, customs and methods of survival in a harsh environment.' At the age of six, L. Ron became a 'blood brother' of the Blackfeet, which was apparently 'an honor bestowed on few white men.' According to an article that appeared in the *Los Angeles Times* in 1990, however, members of the Blackfeet peoples have been unable to find a reference in their records to 'Old Tom', a name they say would have been unusual for one of their number at that time.

Another area of confusion surrounds Hubbard's subsequent claim that he had been the 'youngest Eagle Scout in the country'. At that time, however, the organization did not keep a record of its Scouts, just an alphabetical list. Thus it remains unclear just how Hubbard would have known that he was its youngest member. It was during this time as well that Hubbard is said to have met an American medic and psychoanalyst called Commander 'Snake' Thompson, a friend of the youngster's father and who had apparently studied under Sigmund Freud in Vienna. Hubbard later claimed that it was his acquaintance with Thompson that fired his interest in the human mind, and that it was shortly thereafter that he first began his research into the subject.

Confusion also surrounds Hubbard's youthful excursions to the East when his father was posted there in the 1920s. There is no doubt that Hubbard did visit Asia at this time, but what is less clear is exactly how far he travelled, what he saw and what he experienced during his trips. As his unofficial biographer, Russell Miller, writes in *Bare-Faced Messiah: The True Story of L. Ron Hubbard* (Michael Joseph, 1987), the stories of Hubbard's teenage travels are 'fundamental to [his image] as prophet'. According to traditional Scientology accounts and his own recollections, the young Hubbard roamed the Orient picking up ancient wisdom, philosophy and knowledge along the way from various wise men. These adventures apparently took him to India, China and Tibet, his trips financed by his grandfather. In China, he claims to have met a 'thoroughly insightful Beijing magician who represented the last of the line of Chinese magicians from the court of Kubla Khan.' Another account claims that the '...world itself was his classroom, and he studied in it voraciously, recording what he saw and learned in his ever-present diaries, which he carefully preserved for future reference.'

Such comments sit oddly, however, with some of the observations that Hubbard made at the time in his journal. Having left one Chinese port, the youthful Hubbard wrote: 'A Chinaman cannot live up to a thing, he always drags it down.' He later added: 'We have left Tsingtao forever, I hope.' On another occasion he wrote of his apparent disdain for the prowess of the Chinese as rulers and soldiers. 'When it comes to the Yellow Races overrunning the world, you may laugh...one American Marine could stand off a great many yellowmen (sic) without much effort...'

In 1930 Hubbard attended the George Washington University's School of Engineering, where he majored in civil engineering. He achieved some variable grades and left after two years without receiving a degree. One of the courses he took involved the study of molecular and atomic physics. He received an F grade in the subject, yet thereafter Hubbard sometimes referred to himself as a nuclear physicist. By now, Hubbard, who had learnt to fly a glider and had led a much-trumpeted boating expedition to the Caribbean, had decided to make his living as a writer. He had also married a farmer's daughter called Margaret 'Polly' Grubb, and in May 1934 his first son, Lafayette Ron Junior, was born.

Hubbard's talent as a writer was in producing what is often described as 'pulp fiction', a genre of short stories about adventures, expeditions and other dramatic aspects of life. It was a form of escapism that the American public lapped up during the years of the Depression, and though not well paid, a prolific writer could just about scrape a living. And Hubbard was nothing if not prolific. A Scientology account of their founder's life claims that Hubbard wrote up to seven million published words from 1933 to 1941 (apparently in between travelling the world on expeditions). While this figure can be discounted, there is no doubt that Hubbard wrote quickly and with some success, with both novels and non-fiction articles adding to his repertoire.

By 1938 Hubbard was venturing into the realm of science fiction writing, at which he would eventually make a considerable name for himself. His first story, entitled 'The Dangerous Dimension', appeared in *Astounding* magazine, a publication edited by a man called Joseph W. Campbell, and for whom Isaac Asimov (who came to admire much of Hubbard's science fiction writing), Robert Heinlein and A. E. van Vogt all wrote.

Even at this relatively early stage in his career, Hubbard was thinking big. He wrote a book called *Excalibur*, which was supposedly based on his analysis of the history of mankind. The cornerstone of this work was his discovery that it was in the human instinct for survival that one could explain the nature of life. Hubbard and his followers later claimed that the first half a dozen people to read the manuscript went out of their mind, such was the amazing power of the book. One contemporary writer says that Hubbard genuinely believed that the book would revolutionize the way that people regarded the world, and that it would have a 'greater impact upon people than the Bible'. Unfortunately for Hubbard and humankind, the book was not published.

Nonetheless, the scale of Hubbard's ambition was now apparent. In a letter to his wife at this time, he wrote: 'Foolishly perhaps, but determinedly none the less, I have high hopes of smashing my name into history so violently that it will take a legendary form even if all books are destroyed. That goal is the real goal as far as I am concerned.' Later in the letter Hubbard says that God must have been feeling 'sardonic' when he created the universe, and so it was up to at least one man 'every few centuries' to 'come just as close to making Him swallow his laughter as possible'. Hubbard was already working on a cosmic scale.

In 1941, amid growing certainty that the United States would have to join the war, Hubbard was commissioned as a lieutenant in the US Naval Reserve. As with so many areas of his life, the story of Hubbard's war record has become a contentious one. After the attack on Pearl Harbor in December 1941, Hubbard was sent to the Philippines, but his ship was diverted to Australia. Within a few months he was on his way back to the United States again, though in the meantime he had managed to annoy US naval personnel in Brisbane. 'Not satisfactory for independent duty assignment,' was the verdict of the US Naval Attaché, who also described him as 'garrulous' and someone who 'tries to give impressions of his importance'.

Scientology accounts, however, state that Hubbard had not only gone to the Philippines but had been wounded there, and had returned home on the Secretary of the Navy's private plane as the 'first US-returned casualty from the Far East'. Hubbard also told another officer later that he had landed in Java while a gunnery officer on a destroyer, and that when the Japanese had arrived he had lived rough in the jungle. He stated that he had also been machine-gunned in the back, but was able to make it to safety after he and another American sailed a life raft to the seas off Australia – a voyage of some 1,126 km (700 miles). The US Navy files do not record the time that Hubbard is supposed to have spent on Java.

Back in the United States, Hubbard was placed in charge of a patrol vessel used for submarine hunting, the USS PC 815, which operated off the Pacific coast. This was the time, at least according to official Navy records, when Hubbard came closest to action during the war. In May 1943 Hubbard's ship was caught up in a battle with what he and members of his crew were convinced were one, possibly two, enemy submarines. During the drama, which lasted for just over two days, the USS PC 815 fired off its guns and used up all its depth charges, and in his subsequent report Hubbard claimed that they had put one Japanese submarine out of action and badly damaged another. His men were also convinced that they had engaged with enemy vessels. However, other US craft involved in this hunt off the coast were less certain that enemy submarines were present. Later, in a confidential report, Admiral Frank Fletcher noted that: 'An analysis of all reports convinces me that there was no submarine in the area'. The senior officer also noted, by way of possible explanation for the apparent detection of a submarine, that there were known to be magnetic deposits in the area. Hubbard and Tom Moulton, another officer on board, later claimed that the decision to deny the presence of the submarines was a political one, taken to avoid causing panic among the American public.

Later in the same year, Hubbard's ship was involved in another incident, this time when it accidentally strayed into Mexican territorial waters, anchored there, and then engaged in some gunnery practice. This not only irritated the Mexican authorities, it also ended Hubbard's brief career as a commanding officer. He was transferred to other duties after a report concluded that Hubbard lacked the 'essential qualities of judgement, leadership and cooperation'. Hubbard spent much of the rest of the war ashore, though he did attract some praise, too. One senior officer stated that the science fiction writer was a 'capable and energetic' officer, if 'temperamental', that he was an 'above-average navigator', and that he possessed 'excellent personal and military character'.

Hubbard ended the war on the sick list. He had been complaining of a variety of ailments for some time, including an ulcer, alleged eye problems – even blindness, which he claimed had been caused by his having stood next to a ship's gun when it went off prematurely. He also claimed that he had contracted malaria.

The state of Hubbard's health at this time is not just biographical colour – it is crucial to the early history of Scientology. The idea that a crippled war hero could be restored to health through his own discovery of a new form of therapy for the mind is a powerful and inspiring story. According to naval records, Hubbard was a patient at Oak Knoll Naval Hospital in Oakland, California, just before and just after the end of the Second World War (1939–1945), and was at one point declared 'unfit for service' because of an ulcer. Attempts to find out what lay behind the array of symptoms that the patient complained of, which also included stomach pains and headaches, were fruitless. According to Hubbard's own account he had been blinded with damaged optic nerves, had debilitating injuries to his hip and back, and had been 'abandoned by family and friends as a supposedly hopeless cripple'. He further claimed that he had become used to being told that there was no hope, that 'it was all impossible'. But, he added: '…I came to see and walk again…'

Accounts also differ over Hubbard's status as a war hero, especially regarding the medals that he received. The official records suggest that he received four medals, none of which were for combat duty. One of these medals was awarded to everyone serving at the time of Pearl Harbor (wherever they were), and another to all those who were in uniform when victory was declared over Japan in 1945. Hubbard and his Scientology biographers, however, claim that he was decorated 21 times in all.

Hubbard's post-war years were as colourful as those before and during the conflict. One of the most curious episodes was his involvement with a talented rocket-fuel scientist called Jack Parsons, who in his spare time was a devotee of 'black' magic, a member of the magical secret society Ordo Templi Orientis and a regular correspondent with the notorious Aleister Crowley (see Chapter 5, page 139). Hubbard got to know Parsons and spent some time living at his house in Pasadena, California, a place where artists and various types of performers came and went, where attractive young women were frequent guests and where magic rituals were carried out. In subsequent accounts, Hubbard and the Scientologists were to claim that he had been sent by the authorities to the house in order to expose and break up the 'black magic' circle, though there is no official documentation showing who sent him, or indeed that he was operating in any official capacity at all. In fact, the available evidence – including some documents later read out in a court case – show that Hubbard himself took part in rituals and was personally interested in magic. Indeed, this interest in magic continued after his friendship with Parsons broke down.

By this time Hubbard's personal life had changed. He had started a relationship with a woman called Sara Northrup (known as Betty), a young blonde who had previously been Parsons's mistress. Hubbard subsequently married Betty, despite the fact that he was still married to his first wife.

Besides committing bigamy, the science fiction writer also had financial complications. He had applied for and received a small disability allowance as a war veteran, an amount he challenged as insufficient. Hubbard found himself having to write and sell increasingly more science fiction literature in order to make ends meet. It was at this time, according to Hubbard and Scientologists, that Hubbard began carrying out his own original research into the human mind. This research was to lead to his discovery of Dianetics, and soon thereafter, to the founding of Scientology.

**Dianetics**

In late 1949, *Astounding* magazine, which had by now become one of Hubbard's regular outlets for his science fiction, published an editorial about a 'totally new science' called 'Dianetics'. Editor John W. Campbell was personally convinced that Hubbard had come up with a new, radical technique, the power of which was 'almost unbelievable', and which could not just cure physical ills such as asthma, ulcers and arthritis but 'all other psychosomatic ills' too. Campbell had witnessed Hubbard trying out his new technique and had been a trial subject himself, and was sure that the writer had come up with something both new and important.

Another person who was intrigued and impressed by some of Hubbard's early experiments was a doctor called Joseph Winter, a GP from Michigan who also wrote for the magazine. Dr Winter was even more impressed when he tried out the technique on his own six-year-old son, who had developed a fear of the dark and of ghosts, and whose phobia disappeared with the help of Dianetics. In April 1950 Hubbard duly published his first article on the subject. Dianetics was born.

The essence of Hubbard's Dianetics theory was that the brain recorded every experience and event in a person's life. Bad or painful experiences were recorded and stored in what he termed the 'reactive mind' as 'engrams'. These engrams stayed in the reactive mind and could be triggered by later events and impressions in that person's life. Dianetics dictated that the patient should search through those engrams and re-experience his or her past painful experiences. Once this has been done, the traumatic memories will disappear. Hubbard claimed that there were chains of engrams, and that the key was to go back to the original, or 'basic', engram in the chain, relive the experience, and thus expunge it. The ultimate aim was to get rid of all the chains of engrams, the causes of our unhappiness or ailments, so that a person's reactive mind would be 'clear' of them all. A 'clear' person would have a mind that functioned perfectly, with a high IQ and a good memory.

Anyone with knowledge of psychology or the theory of hypnosis will see some similarities here. Hubbard's 'reactive mind' seems remarkably close to the Freudian and Jungian notion of the 'unconscious mind', and indeed Freud himself had at one point used techniques that bear a resemblance to Dianetics – though ultimately his work took him in a different direction.

In Dianetics, the therapist – who is known as the 'auditor' – encourages the patient to go back as far as possible in his or her memory to experience their early 'engrams' – even back to birth or 'pre-birth', while the person was still in the womb. When Dr Winter tried the technique on his own son, he encouraged the boy to think back to the first time that he had seen a 'ghost' – the thing of which he was most frightened. His son described an experience in which he felt as if he was being strangled at the same time as he saw a ghost-like figure. From the description, this figure seemed to be the obstetrician who had delivered him. The youngster had apparently associated the trauma of his birth with the figure of the ghostly obstetrician. Once the Dianetics therapy began, however, the boy's fears started to subside. Campbell, Winters and, above all, Hubbard, felt that they were at the start of something special. Hubbard believed that with his new techniques even the common cold could be cured, along with a host of other complaints and illnesses. Dianetics, it was claimed, could even help a person's marriage.

A book written in 1950 by Hubbard called *Dianetics, the Modern Science of Mental Health* (Hermitage House, 1950) quickly followed the initial article on the new therapy. In the book, Hubbard was at pains to emphasize the scientific nature of the technique, and claimed that it was the product of painstaking research and experiment. The publishers lacked their author's confidence, however, and initially printed only a modest number of copies. But soon they were forced to print more as the book and the new self-help technique it described suddenly caught the public's imagination.

One of the book's appeals was the way it took the complex world of psychology and psychiatry – areas that were beginning to expand in post-war America – and made them accessible to ordinary people. Moreover, the book showed people how to work the technique on each other, with one person operating as the therapist, or 'auditor', and the patient being the 'pre-clear'. It was simple, effective, and much cheaper than conventional psychiatry. Sessions were supposed to take at least two hours, during which time the 'pre-clear' sat in a darkened room and fell into a 'reverie', or state of relaxation. (This sounds suspiciously close to the state of 'suggestibility' used in hypnosis, though Hubbard, who was a talented hypnotist himself, did not use that expression to refer to the Dianetic 'reverie'.) Dianetics was proving to be an overnight hit.

Within 12 months Hubbard's book had sold a staggering 150,000 copies. Hubbard also gave paid lectures on the subject, and the newly formed Hubbard Dianetic Research Foundations started to train auditors on courses that cost $500 (£247) each. This was the first of the many organizations and bodies pertaining to Dianetics and Scientology that would be created around the world. Money was pouring in, and Hubbard's undoubted charisma as a public speaker was helping to boost the popularity of the new self-help craze. 'You just wanted to listen to every word he had to say and listen for any pearl of wisdom,' says Jack Horner, an attendee at some of the lectures, in Russell Miller's book *Bare-faced Messiah* (Michael Joseph, 1987). 'We never discussed where he had got all his knowledge … I'd been in college studying recent discoveries in psychology and they were not worth a damn compared to what he had come up with and what it would do.'

There is no doubt that the new technique worked for some people with certain problems. Modern critics say that this can be explained by the fact that often, when they used the Dianetics technique, it was the first time such people had ever formally confronted their problems. Professor David S. Touretzky of the Computer Science Department and Center for the Neural Basis of Cognition at Carnegie Mellon University, in Pittsburgh, Pennsylvania, is an Internet free-speech activist and long-time critic of Scientology. 'Everyone has problems from time to time and can benefit from a sympathetic ear,' he says. 'For people in this situation, Scientology "therapy" is just a silly, ritualized version of a sympathetic ear.' Furthermore, Professor Touretzky states, there are many people in society with serious emotional damage, including those who were physically abused as children, who suffered emotional abuse or who are what are called ACoA's – adult children of alcoholics. 'These people could benefit from professional therapy. Scientology auditing is amateur therapy, and while untrained amateurs can sometimes do a lot of damage, sometimes they are better than nothing.' Professor Touretzky adds: 'Since Scientology talks up the successful cases and buries the failures, the result is that the therapy "seems" to work. A proper test, where you compare Scientology auditing against other forms of therapy, or against talking with a sympathetic layman, is never done.'

There was trenchant criticism of the new therapy back in the early 1950s, too. The American Psychological Association issued a statement pointing out that the new 'science of Dianetics' had not been subjected to any 'empirical evidence'. It further suggested that the Dianetics technique should initially be limited to scientific investigations in order to evaluate it. A prominent Los Angeles psychiatrist, meanwhile, suggested that Dianetics was little more than a 'clever scheme to dip into the pockets of the gullible', and that a Dianetics auditor was just another name for a 'witch doctor' exploiting 'real need with phoney methods'. One body even labelled Dianetics a 'mind-healing cult'. Others pointed out there was little or nothing original in the new techniques, and that the notion of 'engrams' was scarcely different from 'abreaction', a term used in psychiatry for the resolution of a phobia or neurosis by reliving the emotions surrounding the event that first triggered the problem.

Closer to home, Dr Winter left the Hubbard Dianetic Research Foundation in 1950. He was concerned at the lack of scientific research into the Dianetics phenomenon and worried that Dianetics could be harmful in the hands of inexperienced people; he was also now sceptical of whether the state of 'clear' could ever truly be reached.

There had already been a moment of public embarrassment for Hubbard himself during one lecture. In front of a packed audience he had introduced on stage a young woman heralded as the world's first 'clear'. She had seemed perfect: a bright young physics student and pianist whose sinus problems and allergy to paint had apparently been cured by Dianetics. Furthermore, as a 'clear', she would now obviously have enhanced mental powers and a great memory. Unfortunately, the young woman was overcome by nerves and was unable to answer even basic questions about physics. When Hubbard briefly turned his back on the woman, a member of the audience asked her to recall the colour of the tie worn by the founder of this great memory-enhancing system. She was unable to remember it.

**The Religion of Scientology**

The years following the launch of Dianetics saw the evolution in Hubbard's beliefs and techniques, the start of what would become the huge bureaucracy of Scientology, and considerable turmoil in his personal and financial life. After a bitter falling-out with Betty, Hubbard married again (for the third and final time), this time to a young woman called Mary Sue Whipp, who had worked with Hubbard as an auditor. Meanwhile, a combination of bad publicity and a squabble between Hubbard and some of his partners had led to some early financial squeezes despite the huge sums of money that had been piling in. More importantly, this was the time when Hubbard started to use the word 'Scientology' for the first time, a word he defined as the practice of 'knowing how to know'. It was also the time that Scientology started presenting itself no longer just as a healing therapy, but also as a religion.

There were several reasons why Hubbard wanted his new movement to be considered a religion. One of the reasons might be termed 'theological', and arose out of the issue of 'past lives'. During auditing, some patients appeared to relive moments not just from during the birth or conception process, but from what seemed to be past lives. In *Have You Lived Before This Life?*, published in 1960, Hubbard collected around 40 case studies from auditing that purported to show that the subjects had indeed lived before. The theory of past lives was another of the reasons why Dr Winter had parted company with Hubbard. Hubbard was undeterred by Winter's doubts and, convinced that the auditing proved the existence of these past lives, he developed a theory of reincarnation at the heart of Scientology, leading it into spiritual areas.

The notion that the human soul passes through many different incarnations is less the province of self-help therapy and more the realm of mysticism, spirituality and religious faith. Modern critics, meanwhile, claim that there is a simple explanation for the so-called past-life experiences of some audited patients, and one that is a major issue with subjects of hypnosis. Professor Touretzky says: 'It's an example of what psychologists call "False Memory Syndrome", a type of hypnotically induced delusion. But they will deny this; their canned answer is: "Hypnosis puts people to sleep; Scientology is about waking people up." Their techniques do, in fact, involve a light trance state which they call "Dianetic reverie", but experts recognize this as hypnosis.'

Another reason that Hubbard wanted Scientology to be categorized as a religion rather than a mere therapy was rather more practical: Hubbard and Scientology had been having trouble getting some of their therapeutic products past the authorities. In 1958, for example, one Scientology company fell foul of the US Food and Drug Administration (FDA) over selling a vitamin product which, it was claimed, both prevented and cured radiation sickness. This was the height of the Cold War, and to a nervous American public nuclear war seemed a real possibility one day. The FDA ultimately ordered the tablets destroyed as there was no evidence of their effectiveness.

The problem for Hubbard was that medicine and medical practices are tightly regulated in many countries, including in the United States. However, in the United States not only are churches granted tax exemptions, they also have considerable freedoms to say and believe what they like under the Constitution. Thus, as a religion, Scientology would have more freedom to make such claims on behalf of its techniques.

There was, possibly, a third reason why Hubbard was keen to move towards religious status. America in the 1950s was a boom time for religion, and church attendances were growing all over the country. Hubbard soon realized that with people comes money. According to some people who knew him, Hubbard had in the past claimed that anyone wanting to make serious money would start a new religion (though Scientologists deny that he ever said this), and, indeed, Scientology made considerable sums of money after the first Church of Scientology was incorporated in California in 1954. The Church was directed to pay a 20 per cent tithe to another of Hubbard's organizations, the Church of American Science.

Church membership was just one way in which Hubbard was to become a wealthy man during the 1950s. Other sources of income included his books and training courses. In 1956, his gross income for the previous tax year was stated as being just over $100,000 (£50,000).

Since the 1950s Scientology has lived a kind of dual life, part personal therapy and self-improvement course, part religion. The religious part includes beliefs about the extraterrestrial origins of humans and the survival of the human soul, plus the outward ritualized trappings of Scientology marriage and burial ceremonies. One academic has described it as a 'quasi-religious therapy'. Professor Touretzky says that the mystical or spiritual claims of the movement should not be overlooked. 'People don't just get into Scientology for therapy,' he says. 'Some are spiritual seekers and get sucked in by Scientology's promises to reveal the secrets of the universe. Some are people looking to have some positive impact on the world; they're attracted by Scientology's high ideals and are too naive to look sceptically at how Scientology actually behaves. And for some, the appeal of Scientology is its elitist view: that Scientologists are the only people who are truly awake and aware of how the world works; everyone else is just an automaton, wandering mindlessly through life under the control of the evil psychiatrists who drug and hypnotize us all.'

Chuck Beatty, who became a Scientologist in 1975 as a young student in Phoenix, Arizona, and who stayed inside for 27 years, was one of those attracted by Scientology's claims. He had walked into a Scientology centre in Phoenix, and soon began reading Hubbard's books. 'I learned within two months that Scientology claimed to be able to deliver an out-of-the-body experience at one of their higher stage levels; their term for it is "exterior-ization". What completely hooked me was one of Hubbard's books called *The Creation of Human Ability*, and it had a list of all these processes,' recalls Beatty. He was especially impressed when he learned that, after becoming a 'clear' and moving on to the higher levels known as 'Operating Thetan' or the 'OT' levels, he would learn to 'zoom around the universe like Flash Gordon'. He adds: 'What a perfect idea! Instead of being bound by earth and archaic religions, this was like a space-age religion,' says Beatty. 'Of course, after 27 years you find out that nobody is doing this stuff. It's a complete fucking scam – it's outrageous.'

Jon Atack, another former Scientologist and author of *A Piece of Blue Sky: Scientology, Dianetics and L. Ron Hubbard Exposed* (Lyle Stuart, 1999), describes how this contrast between therapy on the one hand and religion on the other worked in practice. To its adherents, Scientology was represented as a 'science, liberating man from all his disabilities, and freeing in him undreamt abilities'. Scientology was the 'only hope of freedom for mankind', and Hubbard himself was 'nothing short of a Messiah' whose 'word was law'. Meanwhile, to the public, Scientology was represented as a 'humanitarian, religious movement, intent upon benefiting all mankind'.

People who opposed it were enemies of freedom, communists (this was the Cold War), homosexuals or supporters of the use of drugs. (This last point is ironic in that it is likely that Hubbard himself took drugs at various times in his life.)

Scientology's zero tolerance of its opponents stemmed partly from the early days of its existence and the attacks it had received, but most of all, its source was Hubbard's own personality. His ego was such that he regarded anyone who disagreed with him as being 'against him', and thus a potential enemy. One of the first groups that Scientologists systematically attacked was that of the mental health profession, particularly psychiatrists, almost certainly because of their refusal to endorse Dianetics. (We have already seen how psychiatrists were allies of the 'evil' Xenu in Scientology's origin stories; *see page 202*).

But the Scientologists' ire at the mental health profession is not reserved for events that took place 75 million years ago. The Scientology organization known as the Citizens' Commission on Human Rights (CCHR) has been prominent in criticizing mental health organizations. 'They have lobbied hard against "mental health parity" bills that would force insurance companies to provide mental health coverage at levels comparable to other types of health coverage,' says Professor Touretsky. 'Scientology's opposition is fanatical and absolute; they don't think any human being should ever be prescribed medication for a mental disability, including depression and schizophrenia.'

**Fair Game**

Hubbard's approach to anyone who disagreed or criticized Scientology – and there have been many – could be summed up by his 'fair game' policy. This policy was aimed at those who were called Suppressive Persons (SPs). Hubbard believed that about 2.5 per cent of the world's population was an 'SP'; that is, someone who wanted to destroy whatever was good or useful in the world. In practice, this meant people actively opposed to Scientology. The 'fair game' policy dictated that it was permissible to use any legal action, deception or trickery against such persons. When this approach attracted bad publicity during the 1960s, Hubbard forbade the use of the term within Scientology. However, critics say that the policy is still in effect used by Scientology today, though spokespersons for the Church deny this.

An example of alleged 'fair game' used against those regarded as hostile to Scientology was seen in 2007, during a now notorious BBC investigation into Scientology by reporter John Sweeney. That investigation is best known for the way in which Sweeney – an experienced journalist who has reported from trouble spots throughout the world – lost his temper during an exchange with a Scientologist spokesman. Sweeney later admitted about the televised outburst: 'I look like an exploding tomato and shout like a jet engine and every time I see it it makes me cringe.' The incident only served to overshadow other aspects of the investigation, however, including Sweeney's claim that he was targeted during the making of the programme. Writing about the experience, Sweeney said on the BBC website: 'While making our BBC Panorama film "Scientology and Me" I have been shouted at, spied on, had my hotel invaded at midnight, been denounced as a "bigot" by star Scientologists and been chased round the streets of Los Angeles by sinister strangers. Back in Britain strangers have called on my neighbours and my mother-in-law, and someone spied on my wedding and fled the moment he was challenged.'

As well as allegedly using such harassment tactics, Scientology has also been accused of trying to curtail freedom of speech on the Internet. This is a key issue when discussing the impact of the movement on modern society. For its part, Scientology claims that it has simply been trying to protect the copyright and privacy of its own secret religious doctrines. A number of these cases have concerned the newsgroup alt.religion.scientology, which has published references to the higher levels of Scientology teaching: the so-called Operating Thetan, or OT levels, including mention of the hitherto largely unknown story of Xenu. According to Professor Touretzky, the Scientologists '...were pioneers in trying to threaten freedom of speech on the Internet by making service providers legally liable for their customers' speech.' This battle is sometimes portrayed as 'Scientology versus the Internet'.

The Church of Scientology has also complained to search engines, notably Google, about listing pages and websites that the organization claim are in breach of their copyright. For a period, pages from a critical website called Operation Clambake, based at www.xenu.net, had a number of its pages removed by Google. The reference to clams stems from the claim made by Hubbard in one of his books, *The History of Man* (1952), that the clam was an important link in the evolutionary chain, coupled with a warning that discussing the importance of the clam to those unfamiliar with Scientology could be dangerous. 'Once a victim, after hearing about a clam death, could not use his jaws for three days,' noted Hubbard.

However, the website, run by Andreas Heldal-Lund, in Norway, has continued to publish Scientology material on his site, claiming that in doing so he is providing an important public service. He states on his website: 'After careful consideration [I] have concluded that these materials are being kept secret in order to withhold information from the public with the sole purpose of deceiving the public as to the true nature of Scientology. I feel it is my moral duty to society to reveal this information to the public in order to alert them as to its nature.'

Critics have claimed that in protecting its secret teachings, the organization is simply trying to ensure it can continue to earn the large sums of money it gets from members who have to pay to study them. Professor Tourezky believes that the secrecy surrounding Scientologist beliefs is no accident. 'It's a deliberate marketing tactic. L. Ron Hubbard called it a "mystery sandwich": you serve up a mystery to people and it arouses their curiosity; they want to learn more, which they can only do by paying for more courses.'

Scientologists, however, point out that that it is legitimate for a religion to keep some of its teachings private, and that such information – for example, about Xenu and the story of the volcanoes (*see page 202*) – should only be given to the initiated when they are sufficiently spiritually evolved to learn from them. Former member Chuck Beatty says that the Xenu story was taken very seriously within the organization, and was officially only known to those who had reached the level of OT3. 'It's like a garlic word if you say the words Xenu or body thetans. Scientologists are not even allowed to repeat these words in public,' he says. 'They believe it would jeopardize the case progress or affect their health by stirring up thoughts about the thousands of personal body thetans each person supposedly has. That incident, the story of Xenu, is an extremely important incident theologically, because it explains why everyone is infested with body thetans here on earth. It is a serious event considered to have happened. Only at the highest spiritual levels of the whole Scientology Bridge to Total Freedom do beginner Scientologists even learn about Xenu.'

The organization is also adamant that it is not just preventing its 'stolen' secrets from copyright and trade protection. It says of its teachings on one of its websites: 'A criminal clique of apostates came by the materials unlawfully. If they were allowed to succeed, their aim would be the destruction of the spiritual future of every Scientologist – and indeed, every man, woman and child on earth. This is not an exaggeration, nor an over-statement of Scientology beliefs. It is a tenet of the religion that what is at stake here is the route to salvation *for all*.'

In preparation for a court case in 1994, the organization gathered a number of testimonies from various experts in the subjects of religion and religious practices. One such expert was David G. Bromley, Professor of Sociology at Virginia Commonwealth University, who stated: '...neither the privileging of certain portions of religious doctrine nor the association of a monetary fee for access to doctrines and associated rites is in any sense unique to the Church of Scientology. The Church may well seek to preserve the confidentiality of such material on the basis that public revelation of this material out of context will precipitate misunderstanding of the Church's nature and mission, that unrestricted access will lead to inappro-priate use or have harmful consequences for uninitiated practitioners, and that unauthorized distribution would compromise the economic foundation of the Church organization... In this case all of these concerns would appear to be justified.'

**Organization and Structure**
A key feature of Scientology is its structure. The organization operates through a variety of different bodies throughout the world. For Hubbard, the group's structure and discipline was no incidental occurrence, but an integral part of Scientology. Chuck Beatty worked in computers for many years at the organization, and says that Hubbard was fixated by the potential role that computers could play in the organization. Though Beatty never met Hubbard, he was personally aware of his fascination with an example of computer usage from the distant past – one that the founder was sure could serve as a model for the future. 'There was supposedly this character called the Duke of Chug who existed millions of years ago,' says Beatty. 'It was apparently thanks to the computer system of that day that the embezzlement that the Duke of Chug was involved in was detected. [The computer system] searched through the data banks and found a replacement for the Duke of Chug,' says Beatty. 'It then authorized the order for the galactic police to arrest and execute the Duke of Chug on the spot, because embezzlement was an executable offence.

'Hubbard was glowing about how efficient things were millions of years ago, when the whole universe had been running for millions of years on these highly efficient running computers. It was all part of the plan for the Church. It was completely goddamned hare-brained but everyone was taking it seriously and working like crazy! This was Hubbard's big thing: he envisaged that the Church's computer system would some day take over the running of the Church,' says Beatty.

Beatty also says that in his view one of the 'heartless' features of Scientology when he was a member was the way the organization treated its staff. Every job had statistics associated with it, and those statistics were routinely used to judge a person's efficiency, from phone operator to top-level trainer. He explains, 'You were judged every single week. Every day your boss would come around to check how you were getting on. If your statistics were going down you were liable to be demoted. That was one of the control aspects of the organization. A lot of good people just got ground down.'

For Beatty it was this way of treating of people and the effect this type of treatment had on them that started to make him question his place in Scientology. He explains, 'Management were just eating each other alive! It was like a revolving door, a madhouse, there was no job stability at the top! That was disconcerting for me especially because I looked up to these people and they had like OT3, OT4, OT5 and OT7 in front of their names. I thought, wow, these were the big powerful dudes of Scientology and *these* people were disappearing? It was supposed to be a lifetime commitment and so why would people leave? Why can't they be convinced to stay when there is the lure of attaining these high spiritual states?'

Chuck Beatty was a member of what is called the Sea Organization ('Sea Org'). This organization provides the staff members for the upper echelons of Scientology, and is known as its religious order, or 'the Vatican', as Beatty refers to it. According to Scientology's own description. 'Sea Org members work long hours and live communally with housing, meals, uniforms, medical and dental care provided by the Church. They participate in Scientology training and auditing during a portion of each day, but otherwise dedicate themselves to furthering the objectives of Scientology through their particular functions.'

Long-standing critics of the movement are less kind. 'Scientology actually has a lot in common with the worst excesses of the Nazis, with the Sea Org playing the role of the Gestapo,' says Professor Touretzky. 'It is the only "church" with its own intelligence branch, called the Office of Special Affairs.' According to Beatty, as well as keeping dossiers on 'enemies' of Scientology, this office (where Beatty's second wife had worked) also circulated the bad press that Hubbard and Scientology attracted in what are called 'pass arounds', with the aim of helping them counter negative publicity. Members of the Sea Org (Beatty included) sign 'billion-year contracts' as part of their commitment.

## All At Sea

The Sea Org started life in 1967, when for a period of seven years Scientology was run by Hubbard from on board a boat. According to Scientology, the main reason for the organization taking to the high seas was to allow Hubbard and his fellow Scientologists to study earlier civilizations in various parts of the globe, as well as to oversee its international organization. In reality, however, this relocation was probably due to the fact that Scientology had been running into problems with various governments around the world, and the sea was one place where the organization could operate without hindrance. (Operation from the sea could also have been a way of testing potential safe havens.)

Scientology's clashes with various governments, parliaments and legal systems go right to the heart of concerns about the influence of the movement. Following an official report in Australia, for example, the Church of Scientology was banned from operating under that name and as a religion in some states from the mid 1960s. This ban was overturned in 1983, when a court ruled that the organization was entitled to operate as a religion.

In the United Kingdom, too, Scientology has come to the notice of both the British government and the legal system. In 1966, for example, Health Minister Kenneth Robinson described Scientology as 'potentially harmful', and in 1984 a High Court judge declared Scientology to be 'corrupt, sinister and dangerous'. Mr Justice Latey, ruling in a custody case involving a father who was a Scientologist, added: 'It is dangerous because it is out to capture people, especially children and impressionable young people, and indoctrinate and brainwash them so that they become the unquestioning captive and tools of the cult, withdrawn from ordinary thought, living, and relationships with others.'

Even now Scientology continues to make waves in public life. In 2007 the British media reported how the ruling Labour Party had accepted thousands of pounds in donations from a charity called the Association for Better Living and Education (ABLE). The Conservative Party was also reported to have taken money from the same organization for a stand at one of its conferences.

Either the Labour and Conservative parties are happy to be associated with Scientology, or they failed to consult ABLE's website. Under the heading 'About ABLE International' are the following words: 'ABLE's mission is to rid the world of its most devastating social ills – drugs, crime, illiteracy and immorality – through the social betterment methods and principles of author and humanitarian L. Ron Hubbard.' Elsewhere on the site, ABLE states: 'L. Ron Hubbard is the founder of the Scientology religion and ABLE programs receive much support from Scientologists and from churches of Scientology due to the effectiveness of these programs. ABLE and its programs themselves are not part of the Church of Scientology or the Scientology religion.'

The site also clearly states that its role is in 'supporting, promoting and coordinating' the activities of four organizations 'dedicated to social betterment', one of which is called Narconon. Narconon is an organization aimed at 'eliminating drug abuse and drug addiction through drug prevention, education and rehabilitation'. The Narconon International website helpfully provides the source for what it calls the 'methodology' of the not-for-profit body: one L. Ron Hubbard. It also provides links to eight Hubbard-related websites.

Commenting on the revelations that two major parties had accepted monies from such a source, Liberal Democrat MP Norman Baker was quoted in the *London Evening Standard* as saying: 'Scientology is a dubious cult at best and it's worrying that it seems to have infiltrated both Labour and the Tories in this way. It only goes to show that some politicians are prepared to take money from anyone.' Interviewed for this book, Mr Baker added: 'I find Scientology rather creepy and do not accept that it is a bona fide religion.'

A spokesman for the Labour Party, of which Tony Blair was leader at the time, said the money was part of a business transaction and did not represent a donation to the party. 'Every year exhibitors represent a range of views and opinions. Their policies may not always reflect those of the Labour Party,' he explained. A Tory spokesman said: 'Like Labour we reserve the right to exclude an organization. In this case we allowed

Narconon to rent a stand to exhibit their work on drug rehabilitation.' Yet the British Government's Home Office says it does not back Narconon's scheme because it '...does not meet the minimum standard for drug treatment delivery. It has never been funded by the Prison Service.' Back in 2001, the Mayor of London, Ken Livingstone, banned the Scientologists from promoting Narconon at an event in Trafalgar Square, dismissing it as '...a medically unproven policy which I am advised could be dangerous,' and 'a spurious medical programme that many drugs professionals are concerned about.'

In another revelation, the *Sunday Times* newspaper claimed in 2007 that Narconon representatives had given talks on drug issues at a number of prominent British schools whose staff, pupils and parents had apparently been unaware of the links between the organization and Scientology. In its response, Narconon accepted that there were links between the two, but claimed that it is an independent secular organization for both Scientologists and non-Scientologists, and that none of the links between the organization and its founder had been deliberately concealed from the schools.

Such stories raise the question to what extent, if any, Scientology plays in British public life. In his comments after that infamous outburst, BBC reporter John Sweeney wrote in May 2007: 'Despite all the pressure – the letters from lawyers, *the letters from MPs*, the strangers knocking up my family and neighbours – if people from "disconnected" families tell me that Scientology is a cult, that will be reported.' (Author's emphasis added.) The journalist appears to be hinting that some MP's may have intervened on behalf of Scientology.

## In Search of a Country

According to Russell Miller's biography, Hubbard had been hoping that Australia would become the first 'clear' continent on earth, a hope that was subsequently dashed by the sceptical approach of Austrialian officials towards Scientology. Thus, according to Miller, in 1966 Hubbard had '...scaled down his ambitions and was looking for a country which would provide a "safe environment" for Scientology.' He initially considered Rhodesia (now Zimbabwe), in Southern Africa, where the white minority government of Ian Smith was in a bitter dispute with the British Government. Apparently Hubbard believed that he had a role to play in solving the crisis, a confidence partly fostered by his belief that in a previous life he had been Cecil Rhodes, after whom the country was named.

Hubbard's plan was to invest in a luxury hotel complex, from which he could discreetly spread the influence of Scientology. Unfortunately for him, and despite his money and his supposed illustrious links with the country, the authorities in the capital, Salisbury (now Harare), did not have such a high opinion of Hubbard and Scientology as he had hoped. An extension to his visa was turned down and the religion's founder was forced to leave, believing himself the victim of a communist-inspired plot.

It was at this point that Hubbard and his new 'Sea Org' took to the sea, though his search for a suitable host country continued. In 1971 he singled out Morocco as a possible safe haven where Scientology could even, Miller writes, 'take over control'. For a while Hubbard seemed to make progress, and Scientologists were dispatched ashore, where they trained government officials and intelligence agents in Scientology techniques. In particular, they taught the Moroccans how to use an E-meter, a simple device employed by Scientologists to measure changes in electrical resistance in a person's skin, used during auditing to test the response of the subject. (The device works similarly to a lie detector.) According to Miller, the Scientologists showed Moroccan police officers and intelligence officials how to spot political subversives using the machine.

Hubbard's love affair with Morocco soon ended, however, and he left the country abruptly in December 1972. There are differing accounts as to what ultimately led to this rapid departure. Miller claims that the E-meter courses became caught up in a turf war between pro- and anti-monarchy factions within the Moroccan secret police. Yet another reason – some say the final trigger – for Hubbard leaving was his fear of extradition to France, where the Church of Scientology was in danger of being indicted for fraud.

Author Jon Atack believes that the major reason why Scientology fell foul of Morocco was that the Scientologists had imposed the organization's strict code of conduct, or 'ethics', on the Moroccan officials whom they were training. For example, the officials were disciplined if they were late to attend a lesson. Scientology's punishment system could sound pretty harsh to the uninitiated, and according to Atack, the Moroccan Post Office officials took exception when their persistent tardiness earned them the label of 'treason' from the Scientologists. (In Morocco, 'treason' automatically meant 'execution', and the Post Office staff felt this was a high price to pay for learning the wonders of the E-meter.) The staff won a brief power struggle with their tutors, and the Scientologists were forced to pack their bags once again. According to Atack, Hubbard himself was given just 24 hours to leave the country. He adds: 'Morocco was as close as Hubbard ever came to having the ear of a government.'

In the post-Hubbard era, Scientology has had other clashes with governments. In the mid-1990s a court closed down a Scientology organization in Greece. The ruling described the Scientology mission as an 'organization with totalitarian structures and trends, which essentially despises man.' Scientology had had problems with Greece in the past; Hubbard and the crew of his ship, the Apollo, were told to get off the island of Corfu in 1969. The British Honorary Vice-consul at the time believed that Hubbard was aiming to gain a foothold on the island in order to use it as the headquarters for Scientology.

In September 2007 the Church of Scientology clashed with the Belgian authorities when a state prosecutor said it should stand trial for fraud and extortion, and would also face charges of being a 'criminal organization'. This pronouncement followed a ten-year investigation by the prosecutor Jean-Claude Van Espen. According to Federal Prosecutor's Office spokeswoman Lieve Pellens, the investigation had found that Scientology's European office, based in Brussels, had been involved in unlawful practices in medicine, had breached privacy laws, and had used illegal business contracts. The European office hit back, saying it would fight any charges, and claiming that it had been hounded by prosecutors. 'For the last 10 years the Prosecutor has been using the media, trying to damage the reputation of the Church of Scientology and not been able to put a case in court,' it said in a statement. This has caused a climate of intolerance and discrimination in Belgium, it added.

However, the bitterest relationship between Scientology and a country has involved Germany. Hubbard had a generally dim view of Germany, and blamed the country for the invention of psychiatry, a profession that, as we have seen, he loathed and held responsible for many of the world's ills. Since Hubbard's death, Scientology has come into conflict with the German authorities in a bitter war of words and legal action that has even attracted the attention of the United Nations. The Church of Scientology, through the Human Rights Office of Church of Scientology International, has accused Germany of religious discrimination in general against minority faiths, and in particular of discrimination and 'harassment' of German Scientologists. In a statement, the organization says that: 'The unfortunate fact remains that Scientologists in Germany are routinely dismissed and screened from public and private employment, screened from political parties, denied the right to contract with the government, denied the right to perform their art, denied the right to use public facilities and face boycotts and discrimination solely due to their religious affiliation, and despite numerous German court rulings upholding their rights.'

In 1996 the Church of Scientology began publishing a series of full-page advertisements in the *New York Times* and the *Washington Post* condemning Germany's treatment of Scientologists, but the German authorities hit back at the sect. Spokesmen asserted that Scientology is a 'commercial enterprise', and one with 'a history of taking advantage of vulnerable individuals and an extreme dislike of any criticism.' The government also stated that it is concerned that the 'organization's totalitarian structure and methods may pose a risk to Germany's democratic society.' The German government has justified its investigations and reports into Scientology, claiming that, '...expert reports and testimony by former members confirm again and again that membership can lead to psychological and physical dependency, financial ruin and even suicide.' The authorities pointedly add, 'Because of its experiences during the Nazi regime, Germany has a special responsibility to monitor the development of any extreme group within its borders, even when the group's members are small in number.'

Part of the battle between Scientology and Germany involved celebrities who are members or supporters of the Church. The most prominent of these is Scientologist and actor Tom Cruise, and it was the screening of his 1996 film *Mission Impossible* in Germany that added fuel to the fire. Youth members of the Christian Democratic Union (then the ruling party in Germany) called for a boycott of the film after Cruise had stated in pre-release publicity that his links to Scientology were a 'personal matter'. (Millions of Germans still went to see to see the film.)

A section of Hollywood was outraged at the boycott and a full-page advertisement appeared in both the *New York Times* and the *International Herald Tribune*, which made explicit links between Germany's treatment of Scientologists and the way in which the Nazi regime had treated the Jews in Germany. The 'oppression' was starting to sound 'like the Germany of 1936 rather than 1996', claimed the advertisement, which was signed by famous actors (and non-Scientologists) such as Dustin Hoffman, and by acclaimed director Constantin Costa-Gavras. Public opinion in Germany was outraged at the linkage made with the Nazi regime, however, and in the US many claimed that the advertisement had gone too far. Costa-Gavras later withdrew his support for it.

In July 2007, Cruise was again at the centre of a row between Germany and the Church of Scientology when the German Defence Ministry refused permission to the producers of Cruise's film, *Valkyrie*, to shoot scenes on state military property. The film is a portrayal of the real-life German military plot to assassinate Hitler in 1944. Cruise plays the plot's ringleader, Count Claus von Stauffenberg. Harald Kammerbauer, a Defence Ministry spokesman, told the media: 'The film-makers will not be allowed to film at German military sites if Count Stauffenberg is played by Tom Cruise, who has publicly professed to being a member of the Scientology cult.' He added: 'In general, the German armed forces have a special interest in the serious and authentic portrayal of the events of 20 July 1944 and Stauffenberg's person.' The late Count's son, Berthold Maria Schenk Graf von Stauffenberg, who is in his seventies, also voiced his disapproval, saying that it was 'unpleasant' for him that an 'avowed Scientologist' was playing his father. 'I had hoped for a long time that the project was just a publicity stunt on the part of Cruise,' he added.

Politicians in Germany – where authorities keep the activities of Scientology under surveillance – have been debating an outright ban on the organization. In Hamburg the local Commissioner for the Scientology Task Force, Ursula Caberta, has made it very clear what she thinks about the activities and impact of the movement. Carbeta, who in the summer of 2007 published a book called *Schwarzbuch Scientology* ('the Black Book of Scientology'), noted: 'Scientology is a dangerous, extremist organization that has declared war on Europe.' She and others believe that the main aim of Scientology, which has an office in Brussels near the European Union buildings, has been to get the organization recognized as an official religion across Europe. 'During an internal event of the organization in 2006, activists were required to pledge an oath to work towards a positive image of Scientology within the media,' Caberta writes.

Tom Cruise is by no means the only celebrity Scientologist, even if he is the best known. Other members include actor John Travolta and his actress wife, Kelly Preston, along with actress Kirstie Alley. Scientology has made a conscious attempt to attract celebrities and other high-profile people, and has even created its own Church of Scientology Celebrity Centre International in Hollywood. The organization says that it exists to help people from all backgrounds, and that it must not forget those people 'upon whom society depends the most.' The Church quotes Hubbard as saying, 'The world is carried on the backs of a desperate few'. It adds: 'It is for this reason that L. Ron Hubbard saw to the formation of a special Church of Scientology that would cater to these individuals – the artists, politicians, leaders of industry, sports figures and anyone with the power and vision to create a better world. That church is Celebrity Centre International.'

Critics are less kind about the big names who join Scientology. Professor Touretzky says: 'Hubbard wanted to recruit "artists and opinion leaders", but the only group gullible enough to fall for his con in large numbers has been actors.' He further states that big names don't suddenly just join Scientology. 'Travolta and Cruise were both recruited when they were very young and just starting out. Hollywood types saw it as a way to make professional contacts and promote their careers, sort of like a businessman joining the Rotary Club,' he says. 'And Scientology "auditing" is a sort of therapy, which a lot of messed up actors need.'

## The Future of Scientology

There seems to be little doubt that with its undoubted wealth, its celebrity supporters and its relentless willingness to tackle its critics head on, Scientology is likely to be around for a while yet. As its recent spats with Germany, its desire to achieve pan-European recognition and its dealings with the British political establishment show, it is also likely to continue to have a considerable impact on society. The organization certainly thinks long term; indeed, Hubbard wrote about the history of a universe that stretches back 'trillions' of years, a considerably longer time period than the 15 billion years that is usually given by scientists as the age of the universe. And as we have seen, Sea Org members sign 'billion-year contracts' to emphasize their commitment. As Hubbard himself said about the mission of his new religion, 'The sun never sets on Scientology...our aims are simple, if great. And we will succeed, and are succeeding at each new revolution of the Earth.'

Yet critics say that Scientology is struggling to recruit enough new members to replace those who leave. One reason for this struggle is the

Internet. Despite Scientology's legal actions against website and Internet service providers to protect copyright in its texts, there is still a massive amount of information about the movement available online, much of it hostile. In particular, there are the testimonies of former members, some of whom occupied quite senior positions in Scientology, and whose damaging comments fill many web pages.

Professor Touretzky believes this explosion of material on the worldwide web could ultimately be the death knell for Scientology under the leadership of Hubbard's successor, David Miscavige. 'As predicted by one of their former PR guys, Robert Vaughn Young, the Internet has become Scientology's Vietnam,' says Professor Touretzky. 'It's killing them. First, because all their secrets, including Xenu, are now on display before the public, making it awfully hard to sell that "mystery sandwich". Every critical book or magazine article ever written about Scientology has been digitized and republished on the web.' He adds: 'Gone are the good old days when Scientologists could suppress information by stealing critical books from libraries and cutting out magazine articles with razor blades.'

Touretzky says that the Internet has also enabled Scientologists with doubts or disagreements to make contact with others who share similar misgivings. 'So the number of defections we're seeing these days is astounding,' he says. Course rooms in Los Angeles and elsewhere are 'virtually empty', he says, and the Scientology base at Hemet, in California – where Miscavige is based for part of the time – is said to be down to a third of its former staff levels. Both high-level and 'worker bee' staff have left, he says. 'And it's impossible to recruit new members of quality because all it takes is ten minutes on Google and people realize that Scientology is a scam. So the only new members they're getting these days are either children of current members – typically entering as teenagers with no skills or education – or dregs of society types, like recovering drug addicts recruited through their Narconon front group.'

Chuck Beatty reiterates that the statistics are going down, and that the movement is built on hype. After 27 years in Scientology, his verdict is as follows: 'I would say it's an over-hyped, systemically authoritarian, totalitarian, flawed quasi-therapeutic UFO new-age religious cult.' He adds: 'It's like an old-time spiritual con. As Jon Atack says in his great book, it's selling a piece of blue sky! It's simply a piece of blue sky.'

# 9

# Criminal Societies

I N THE EARLY HOURS OF the morning of 15 August 2007, the bodies of six men were found in two vehicles near a pizza restaurant in the German city of Duisburg. All six had been shot in the head, and a total of 70 bullet rounds had been fired. It seems they had just been celebrating the 18th birthday of one of the group. The news of the brutal murders shocked German public opinion and made headlines around the world. Within hours, the authorities were convinced they knew what lay behind the killings: they were the result of an ongoing Mafia feud that started in an Italian town 15 years ago and was still leaving a trail of dead.

Criminal secret societies have probably been around for as long as any other type of secretive group. Unlike some organizations, criminal gangs are not interested in religion, esoteric knowledge, preserving old traditions or even political power – at least not for their own sake. Rather, they are primarily motivated by a lust for money and the kind of power – beyond politics – that goes with such wealth and influence; a brutal, ruthless and unquestioned authority.

The stakes are often high in such criminal secret groups, both for the leaders and any members who join. Academic and an expert on secret societies Mark Mirabello says: 'In criminal groups, the initiate has to commit a crime to join. In South American rightist groups, they had to kill a policeman or a soldier. Among the Leopard Men in West Africa, they had to provide a daughter or niece for a murder/cannibal feast. Among some outlaw American groups, it is alleged that the initiate has to have sexual relations – in front of the group – with an underage girl, an elderly woman, and a corpse. The notion here is that shared guilt creates solidarity. By committing a heinous act, the initiate is separated forever from ordinary humanity and is now bound tightly to the group,' he says.

When news of the Duisburg murders first broke and were attributed to a 'Mafia feud', many observers probably initially thought this was a reference to the Sicilian Mafia (also known as the 'Cosa Nostra'), or perhaps to an American crime family. In fact, the Germany killings were blamed on a feud between rival clans of the 'Ndrangheta Mafia from Calabria, in southern Italy. Many observers believe that the 'Ndrangheta, which is made up of more than 70 clans and up to 10,000 men, is now economically more powerful than its much better known counterparts in Sicily. It is also believed that the group controls much of the Colombian cocaine that comes into Europe, including Britain; perhaps as much as 80 per cent of the trade. Italian prosecutor Enzo Macri says: 'The Colombians prefer to deal with the Calabrians. They are much more reliable. They don't talk. And they pay on time.' It is claimed that the 'Ndrangheta Mafia has a yearly income of more than £25 billion.

**The Cosa Nostra**
Though the 'Ndrangheta are arguably the most powerful of the Italian mafia groups now, they are not the best known. That dubious honour still remains with the Cosa Nostra from Sicily, the original 'brand' of Mafia in the world. If the success of a criminal secret society can be measured by its ability to remain secret, then the Cosa Nostra on that score alone can be considered exceptionally successful. For despite – or, some say, possibly because of – the many claims, legends, stories, books and films about the Sicilian Mafia, it was not until as late as 1992 that investigators and experts were finally convinced that the Cosa Nostra really existed.

Up until 1992 many people had believed that the Cosa Nostra was simply an invention. Others had wondered whether the stories of the alleged society were based on a misunderstanding of the complexities of Sicilian society, of a secretive and suspicious island people who had endured hundreds of years of invasions and conquests. This romanticized myth was promoted by the late 19th-century opera *Cavalleria rusticana* ('Rustic chivalry'), written by Pietro Mascagni, which became an overnight hit. The story captured the public imagination with its depiction of passion, dishonour and blood feuds.

The idea of a raw, untamed Sicily lingered into the modern era, and was used to explain away the 'false' notion that a genuine Mafia existed. This, so the argument went, was simply how all Sicilians behaved. As a result, as John Dickie explains in his seminal book, *Cosa Nostra: A History of the Sicilian Mafia* (Palgrave Macmillan, 2004), '…the existence of the mafia remained no more than a suspicion, a theory, a point of view, until surprisingly recently.'

The proof that there was actually a true secret society – as opposed to a way of life – only came to light when a senior Mafia figure decided that he had seen and experienced enough. Tommaso Buscetta had witnessed the death of many of his family members in the 1980s as bitter in-feuding reached a new peak of bloodshed. He was now willing to reveal details of the secret society to which he belonged, and cooperated with the Italian investigating judge, Giovanni Falcone. Soon a dramatic picture emerged, not just of a tradition of private feuds and family ties, but of a genuine secret society, with initiation rituals and an organizational structure. The name of this organization was said to be 'Cosa Nostra', meaning 'Our Thing'. In reality, this was a kind of non-name; 'Our Thing' was a shorthand way of referring to an organization that needed no other description.

The word 'mafia' technically only refers to the Mafia of Sicily, the Cosa Nostra, though it has since taken on an extended meaning, referring to any organized crime association. The word may have Arabic origins – Sicily was for many years under Arab rule – resulting in the dialect word 'mafioso', from which we get 'mafia'. The term is hard to translate precisely, but it has the sense of 'bravado', or even 'cool', about it. It was also a word that outsiders used to describe the criminal gangs; they apparently never referred to themselves as the Mafia, simply using the expression 'Cosa Nostra' instead. The name Cosa Nostra has also been used to describe the America Mafia (*see page 236*).

The testimony of Buscetta and others finally gave the Italian authorities a chance to get a large number of Mafiosi in court and to put many of them behind bars. In 1987 more than 300 members were jailed for a total of more than 2,600 convictions that were upheld by Italy's top court in 1992. It was a major victory. But within months, the courageous judge Falcone was murdered when his car was blown up, and a similar fate soon befell leading Mafia prosecutor Paolo Borsellino. The 'cool' image that had surrounded the organization was vanishing quickly. The Cosa Nostra was now exposed as a very real, ruthless and brutal organization.

There have been a number of colourful stories about the origins of the Sicilian Mafia – some of them invented, though that did not stop them from being believed by members. Buscetta himself believed that the Mafia's origins went back to the Middle Ages, when it fought off French attacks on the island. Others say it was formed to defend Sicily against the Catalans. One strange story claims the Mafia are descendants of a medieval Sicilian secret society called the Beati Paoli. The members of this romanticized group wore black hoods to conceal their true identities, and fought on behalf of the poor oppressed people of Sicily against their feudal masters and the excesses of the Church. The existence of this group was first revealed in an early 20th-century historic novel by Luigi Natoli, and opinion is still divided over whether it truly existed or not. (The story bears similarities to the Robin Hood story in England.) Naturally, some Mafiosi found this tale appealing, as they liked to imagine that they were the inheritors of this mantle of champions of the poor, nobly fighting against the oppressive rich.

In fact, it seems likely that 'mafia' gangs in various parts of Sicily sprang up in the middle of the 19th century, before and after the unification of Italy. These groups were probably involved in protection rackets, smuggling and cattle rustling, among other illegal activities. In 1864 local nobleman and politician Nicolò Turrisi Colonna published a pamphlet in which he wrote of a 'sect of thieves' that had influence across the island and that 'protects and is protected by' all country folk. He further stated that this group feared neither the police nor the courts because of the pressure it could exert on witnesses. Turrisi Colonna thought that this 'sect' was about 20 years old. According to Dickie, Turrisi Colonna may well have known what he was talking about, because there were strong rumours that the politician himself had close links with the most powerful Mafiosi group in Palermo.

From the beginning the Sicilian Mafia had its own initiation ceremonies, something common to all types of secret societies. In the Cosa Nostra, the ceremony usually took place before a small group of other 'men of honour', as members are known. The initiate is informed of the rules and commitments involved in being a part of Cosa Nostra, and his hand is cut sufficiently to draw blood. The blood is then wiped on a sacred image, typically that of a saint or the Virgin Mary. This image is then burnt with the initiate still cupping it in his hands while acknowledging aloud that if he betrays the organization, his own flesh will burn just as the image is burning in his hands. Once the ceremony is over the initiate is accepted as *la stressa cosa*, or the 'same thing' as the other members.

It is interesting to note that this kind of initiation ceremony seems to have been borrowed from Freemasonry. As we have seen, initiate Freemasons agree upon pain of horrible death to maintain the secrecy of what they learn inside the 'Craft', even if such promises are said to be purely symbolic and are never carried out (*see Chapter 4, page 76*). Indeed, the early 19th century was a fertile time for Freemasonry in southern Italy, as elsewhere in Europe. The colourful Italian patriot and adventurer, Giuseppe Garibaldi, who landed troops in Sicily in 1860 as the start of the unification of Italy, was himself a Freemason. Moreover, the revolutionary secret society known as the Carbonari, or 'charcoal burners' – who also had rituals and degrees of membership similar to Freemasonry – were active in the first decades of the 19th century throughout both the north and south of Italy. According to Dickie, 'Becoming a single, secret association using Masonic-style rites of this kind offered many advantages to the Mafia.' This included improving trust among fellow members (because they all knew the terrible price that would be paid by anyone betraying the organization), and also as a way of keeping young ambitious members in check.

The existence and even the rituals and practices of the Sicilian secret societies were known to some officials in the late 19th century. The chief of police in Palermo, Ermanno Sangiorgi, even produced a detailed analysis of Mafia activity and organization, the first comprehensive study of its kind. Yet in 1901 his attempts to smash the Mafia's activities in a series of court cases resulted in nothing more than a series of acquittals and minor convictions. Sangiorgi was despondent. 'It was never going to turn out any other way, as long as people who denounced the Mafia in the evening then went along and defended it the following morning,' he noted sourly. His report was then allowed to gather dust.

As has often been the case with the Mafia, its influence on the authorities and on politicians has been one of the principal reasons why it has been able to flourish for so long. However, there were problems ahead. When the Italian dictator Benito Mussolini came to power, he pledged to bring order and control to a country that was notoriously difficult to govern. Among the problems Mussolini wanted to clean up was the Sicilian Mafia. After a concerted campaign under Prefect Cesari Mori, the Mafia was effectively and brutally suppressed, and a number of prominent members fled abroad. The secret society only emerged as a significant power after the liberation of Italy by the Allies in the Second World War.

Today they remain an important influence, despite being eclipsed by their neighbours across the water, the 'Ndrangheta in Calabria.

## America: A New Home

When the Sicilian Mafiosi fled the fascist regime's crackdown in the 1920s a number of them fled to the relative safety of the United States. By then the American version of the Cosa Nostra had already taken hold, as there had been a massive migration of Sicilians and other Italians to the United States during the 19th century. Among the majority who were simply seeking a better life was a number of Sicilian criminals looking for an opportunity to export their skills to the New World. In New Orleans, for example, there was a sizeable Italian immigrant community by 1890 – comprising perhaps 10 per cent of the local population. Tensions rose in the city after the murder of a police chief was blamed on the Italian Mafia. When a number of Italian immigrants were acquitted of the killing, an outraged mob of citizens lynched 11 of them.

It was not until a fresh wave of Italian immigrants came to the United States after 1900 that Mafia elements began to develop organizations in the country. This happened notably (but not exclusively) in New York, the city of immigration, where Italians became the fourth largest immigrant group after the Irish, Germans and Jews. The link between Italian immigrants and Mafia crime gangs became strong in the public imagination, encouraged by excitable newspaper reporting. As is often the case in any society, the fear of immigration quickly led to a group being singled out as a scapegoat. Indeed, in 1903 a US Secret Service official described the Mafia as 'the most secret and terrible organization in the world'.

The leading figure in the new America Mafia at the time, and probably the first true American Mafia 'boss', was Giuseppe 'Piddu' Morello. Appropriately enough, Morello, a thick set and ruthless character with a deformed right arm, had been born in the Sicilian town of Corleone, a Mafia stronghold. There were close links between the Mafia in Sicily and the Mafia in America. In 1963, one Mafiosi revealed that, like its Sicilian forebears, the American Mafia also used the name 'Cosa Nostra' to describe themselves. The name has since evolved into a proper noun, and commentators and the media often refer to the group as 'La Cosa Nostra', which, strictly speaking, is the meaningless 'The Our Thing'.

Despite the close links and the similarities between the American,

Sicilian and other Italian versions, the American Mafia soon took on its own characteristics. La Cosa Nostra was now regarded as a purely American phenomenon, though with Italian roots. The Sicilians, for example, found the Americans more relaxed and rather less randomly violent (though they were still capable of many brutal acts). This difference of culture was explained by the fact that as the years passed, the American Mafia was as much influenced by the American society in which it operated as it was by its Italian heritage. For example, one of the early leading mob bosses, 'Lucky' Luciano, was born in Sicily but had come to America before he was ten years old. Similarly, the infamous Al Capone was born in the US. Nor were the origins of these men entirely Sicilian: Capone's parents were from Naples. And it was the American-raised immigrant, 'Lucky' Luciano, who ordered the death of Salvatore Maranzano, one of the Sicilian Mafiosi who went to the US to escape the Fascist clampdown, and who had been the first self-proclaimed *capo di tutti capi* (boss of all bosses) in New York.

There is little dispute that the American Mafia has had a huge impact on American society in just over a hundred years of its history. One of its 'golden periods' was the Prohibition, where the ban on alcohol was exploited by many criminal elements in the 1920s and the early 1930s, the Mafia among them. One of the most prominent and exotic characters at this time was Al Capone. Capone operated out of Chicago, and was behind the infamous St Valentine's Day massacre of 1929, which involved the shooting of seven rival gang members. Capone was eventually indicted for tax evasion.

In New York, meanwhile, Mafia operations have been run by the 'five families' since the 1930s. The not always hidden arm of the Mafia has been seen among many different aspects of American life, including in Hollywood, among trade unions and in gambling cities such as Las Vegas. Most controversial of all have been claims about links between the American Mafia and certain senior politicians, while there have long been rumours (though no hard evidence has ever been produced) that the 'mob' may have been involved in the assassination of United States President John F. Kennedy.

According to former American police-chief-turned-author, Thomas Reppetto, in his book, *American Mafia: Its Rise to Power* (Henry Holt & Co, 2004), the Mafia is now in decline in America. Reppetto predicts that sections of the Mafia will now concentrate its efforts on financial and banking crime, typically associated with so-called hi-tech crime, involving the use of computers. The FBI, meanwhile, still regards La Cosa Nostra as the 'foremost organized criminal threat to American society.'

## The Russian Mafia

A good example of the how the word 'mafia' has spread from its original meaning to include any organized crime group can be found in Russia. The many gangs who fall under the heading of 'Russian mafia' have no geographical connection with Sicily, nor do the two groups share personnel. Yet, like the Sicilian and other Italian crime organizations, this mafia's influence has spread well beyond the borders of Russia and the former Society Union, and now constitutes one of the most important and dangerous organized crime threats in the world.

This mafia has also been closely linked with the rise of the new Russian economy after the collapse of the old Soviet model in the 1990s. Its reputation is so widespread that even the many honest Russian business-people, who have made their money quite legitimately, come under suspicion. For example, in France, notaires (state-registered lawyers) will sometimes refuse to process the purchase of a house by Russian individuals in the wealthy French Riviera because of fears that the money has been laundered, perhaps from mafia sources.

The reach of the Russian mafia – or, more accurately, mafias – is truly global. They are involved in drug trafficking around the world, and have also moved into computer and Internet crime. Typically, this means targeting the data systems of financial institutions and banks, extorting money from web-based businesses in return for not taking them offline with coordinated 'cyber attacks' and conning individuals around the world with spoof emails in techniques known as 'phishing' and 'pharming'. Some have been involved in online pornography.

In 2001 Russian- and Ukrainian-organized gangs of hackers were blamed by the FBI for the theft of a million credit card details. Such gangs have little shortage of experts keen to work for them. For example, the infamous Tambov gang, operating out of St Petersburg, saw a 'business' opportunity to move into high-tech crime because that city boasts many maths and computer-science graduates. In St Petersburg, as in other parts of the former Society Union, such experts are not always well paid, and thus are especially susceptible to being corrupted.

Yet not all of these graduates are interested in taking part in these crimes – or at least not voluntarily. One Russian hacker recently recalled an encounter that he had had with a Russian criminal gang. At first he was offered a small amount of money to work with the gang, but then it was made clear to him that his options were to cooperate or face getting beaten up – or worse. The Russian mafia, who come from many different parts of the country, is particulary noted for its brutality, even when compared with other organized crime groups. According to one former New York policeman, 'They'll shoot you just to see if their gun works.'

Though the origins of the many different Russian organized crime gangs has no direct connections with the Sicilian Mafia and other secret societies, there are nonetheless some similarities. During the time of the Soviet Union, for example, organized criminal groups developed the idea of *vory v zakone*, meaning 'thief with a code of honour'. The *vory* were a secret criminal fraternity that had a code of conduct for its members and even a ritualized initiation ceremony. The initiates swore their pledges, which involved the promise to be a 'worthy thief', and were warned of the dire consequences should they betray their fellow members. The new member was also given a nickname that was formally received during a naming ceremony, and that was said to be as important among the *vory* as a Christening is for a Christian.

Many criminal secret traditions first developed inside Soviet labour camps and prisons. According to criminologist Federico Varese in his book, *Russian Mafia: Private Protection a New Market Economy* (Oxford University Press, 2001), the new Russian mafia gangs have adopted elements of the *vory* system. 'The Russian Mafia is the sum total of the criminal leaders who went through the *vory* ritual,' he argues. 'It is a market of quality and commitment to the underworld, and evokes – in the eyes of other criminals – an honourable and distinguished tradition.' In this tradition, he argues, like the Sicilian Mafia, they have been able to develop a common identity while maintaining their independence. However, Varese also argues that there is no guarantee against competition from non-Russian mafia groups – Chechen and Cossack groups, for example – who do not share the same *vory* tradition.

## The Thuggee

Further east and further back in time there existed a secret society known as the Thuggee. This society is considered by some to be the most remarkable example of organized crime in history. At its peak in the early 19th century, the group is said to have been responsible for the murder of up to 40,000 people a year in India. The origins of this strange and deeply secretive group are obscure, and the first known reference to them dates back as far as the 13th century. They were certainly active in the 16th and 17th centuries in India, and became known to the British colonialists in the late 18th and early 19th century.

The Thugs, as its members were known, worked in groups of up to 15 at a time, and claimed to be devotees of the goddess Kali. Their ploy was to befriend groups of travellers on the country's countless quiet roads and travel with them. When they passed through a designated Thuggee killing zone (known only to Thugs), one of the Thugs would give a secret sign. At this, the Thugs would turn on the travellers, strangle them, bury their bodies and make off with all their belongings. According to some sources the sites of these macabre graves would be covered in powerful herbs to put dogs off the scent. According to academic Mark Mirabello, the Thugs would also conduct a ceremony over the graves, first placing 'goor' – a form of coarse sugar – on a cloth. 'After pouring some sugar and "holy water", those that had killed that day (in order of seniority) eat the "sugar of Kali" as a sacrament. It is said that once a man tastes goor, he will always serve the goddess of death,' explains Mirabello. Traditional punishment meted out to Thugs was no less harsh that that which they dealt their many victims; some were even entombed alive inside pillars. But local rulers sometimes turned a blind eye to their activities in return for a share of the illicit takings.

The Thugs believed that they were created by the powerful Hindu goddess Kali herself, thus giving their robbery and murder a religious dimension. The silk scarves they typically used to strangle their victims were often yellow or white, colours sacred to the goddess. Thug tradition was handed down from generation to generation, from father to son, or sometimes uncle to nephew. On occasion, the children of victims were spared and then inducted into the society. Some experts have argued that the robberies were far more mercenary in nature than 'religious'. There have even been claims that the cult of the Thuggee was largely a product of British imagination, the result of a lack of familiarity with Indian culture and fear of the unknown.

It is certainly true that tales of the Thugs provoked considerable interest and horrified fascination back in Europe, and their name has survived in the English word, 'thug'. Yet there seems enough documented evidence – for example, the graves they left behind – for us to accept that the Thugs were a real phenomenon. (After all, doubts about their existence – even when the evidence clearly shows that they are real – is a common enough phenomenon of secret societies of all types.) Following a British crackdown in the 1830s, the Thugs were all but wiped out, and they had vanished by the start of the 20th century. Perhaps inevitably there have been reports that they still exist, but no evidence has been produced to back up this unlikely claim.

## The Assassins

The Assassins were an even older secret society than the Thugs. This group was founded in the late 11th century in Persia by Hassan-I-Sabah as part of the Ismaili sect of Islam. Unlike the Thugs, the Assassins were not motivated by money (though they were influenced by the promise of eternal treasures in the afterlife). Instead, this most secretive of secret societies carried out targeted assassinations of prominent individuals, always using a dagger as their weapon.

The motivation of this group was a mixture of the religious and political. A common conception is that the Assassins mostly targeted prominent Crusaders, as the era of the Crusades had just begun. Indeed, it is true that a number of prominent Europeans were singled out for assassination. For example, Conrad of Montferrat, who was nominated as King of Jerusalem, was assassinated by two Assassins in 1192 before he could be crowned. Similarly, the future king Edward I of England survived an attempt on his life by the Assassins when he was in the Holy Land in 1272. According to historian Bernard Lewis, however, the Europeans were not the main targets of the Assassins. 'Their efforts...were primarily directed not against the Crusaders but against Muslim rulers, whom they saw as impious usurpers.'

There are many colourful, if not necessarily wholly reliable, stories told about the Assassins, including the ways in which they were persuaded to carry out their missions (which usually resulted in their own death). The story is that initiates were drugged with wine and/or drugs and then taken to a beautiful location full of trees, water and beautiful plants, where their every whim and need was catered for. Later, they were given another drug that returned them back to consciousness. They supposedly believed that their founder, Hassan, had shown them a glimpse of the true Paradise, to which they would return once they had carried out their assassination.

The Assassins had a strict and complex hierarchy. 'If our information on the Assassins is correct, they had several levels of initiation, and at each level they were told that what was learned at the previous level was false,' says Mirabello. 'Finally, when they reached the highest level, they were taught that nothing was true, only action was important.' The Assassins survived as a group until the mid-13th century, gradually dying out with the arrival of the fearsome Mongol armies, to whom some of them surrendered. Others became killers for hire.

## The Triads

The Triads are some of the best-known and most feared secret societies in the world. The operation and influence of these Chinese organizations (there are many different Triad gangs) has spread to all parts of the globe, including New Zealand, Holland, Malaysia, Australia, the United States, the United Kingdom, South Africa and Brazil, though the main Triad stronghold has been, and remains, Hong Kong. These groups have come to control much of the world's heroin trade, possibly as much as 90 per cent, according to one estimate. One unnamed UN official has even been quoted as saying that the Triads represent the 'greatest potential criminal threat the world has ever known.'

China has a long history of secret societies, many of them with colourful and evocative names. During the first century, a secretive group known as the Red Eyebrows played a significant part in the overthrow of a Chinese ruler. (They were known as the Red Eyebrows for the simple reason that they painted their eyebrows red to mimic the ways in which demons were represented; in other words, to make themselves look fierce.) This group was finally wiped out when an army commander who had been tasked to exterminate the group instructed his own troops to paint their eyebrows red as well. The real Red Eyebrows were killed in the ensuing bloody confusion.

In later centuries other secret societies came and went, with some changing their names to avoid detection. In the mid-14th century, one secret group, the White Lotus Society, even managed to help topple a government and assist in launching a new era in Chinese history: the Ming Dynasty. Later, in the 18th century, another secret society called the

Heaven and Earth Society (also known as the Hung Society) was formed. This group, together with other similar organizations, is often seen as the forerunner to the modern Triad gangs.

Opposed to the prevailing Manchu (Qing) Dynasty, these societies gradually metamorphosed from political and religious self-help groups into what were in effect largely criminal gangs, preying especially upon the rich in Chinese society. In some places, especially in overseas Chinese communities, they operated as a form of internal government, running the community on a daily basis. Often they were accepted as part of society, not just by the public but also by those whom they victimized. This was partly because of their ruthlessness, but also because of Chinese respect for the past and for tradition. '[The Triads'] victims believed, as did many, that they had an almost divine right to do what they did; they were religiously constituted, rooted in Chinese history and legend,' says Martin Booth in *The Dragon Syndicates* (Caroll & Graf Publishers, 2000), his study of the Triads.

The Western name given to these Chinese secret societies comes from the symbols and emblems they used, which often featured a triangle. For the societies' members the three-pointed triangle represents the unity of the three principal forces of the universe: heaven, Earth and humans. (Indeed, a later version of the famous White Lotus Society was called the Three United Society.) Westerners who came into contact with these Chinese societies were struck by this triangle imagery, and so the name 'triad' was coined, the term coming from the original Greek for a set of three. Chinese people or Triad members themselves do not use the name 'Triad', but rather are referred to by their individual gang name, or as 'Hak Sh'e Wui', meaning 'the Black Society'.

As with other secret societies, the Triads hold elaborate initiation ceremonies in which new members are told the hidden history of the particular Triad, and are asked to swear to uphold its secrets. They are then told the secret sign by which members recognize each other, which is sometimes a secret handshake (rather like the Freemasons). There are also different ranks and positions within the Triads, including that of the Incense Master, who presides over initiation ceremonies; the Mountain Master, who is the head of the group; and Straw Sandals, the society's messenger.

Triad societies operate independently and not as part of an overall supreme pan-Triad organization; there is no equivalent to the *capo di tutti capo* of the American mafia (*see page 237*).

When examining the impact of Chinese organized crime in the mid 1990s, an Australian parliamentary committee considered the testimony of a member of the 14K Triad, one of the many Hong Kong Triad societies. The member stated: 'I was not required to pay any percentage of profits to the 14K leadership. Triads do not work that way. Triad members do favours for each other, provide introductions and assistance to each other, engage in criminal schemes with one another, but Triads generally do not have the kind of strictly disciplined organizational structure that other criminal groups like the Italian Mafia have. For example, a Triad member would not necessarily be required to get permission from the Dragonhead of his Triad in order to engage in a particular criminal undertaking, even if the particular deal involved an outsider or even a member of another Triad. On the other hand, on the occasion of traditional Chinese holidays such as Chinese New Year, Triad members give gifts to their "big brothers" or "uncles", who often are office bearers in the Triads.'

Though Triad organizations became ever more involved in crime in the 19th and 20th centuries, they still played a prominent role in the turbulent history of Chinese politics. The Chinese revolutionary figure, Sun Yat-sen, who played a key role in the overthrow of the Qing (Manchu) Dynasty in 1911, worked closely with the Chinese secret societies, the historic origins of which lay in opposition to the Manchu dynasty. (Yat-sen was also a member of a Triad society himself.) After the success of the revolution, however, he was reluctant to talk openly about his close relationship with these groups. As Booth points out, '[Yat-sen] knew the Triads had been at best uneasy republican bedfellows...'

Nonetheless, the Triads had enormous power in China under both Yat-sen and his successor, the nationalist Chiang Kai-shek. Communist China was a different matter, however. Mao Zedong was determined never to allow the Triad societies any say in his China, and after taking power in 1949 Mao struck at the heart of the Triad power base: the opium trade. Within a few years the Triads had effectively been wiped out on the mainland. The only place where they had survived was in Hong Kong, still then under British control, and where the Triads had always been driven more by money than politics. However, the spread of Chinese populations to countries around the world ensured that even though destroyed in its heartland, the Triad culture would become an important global phenomenon.

## The Yakuza

The Triads are by no means the only organized crime groups in the Far East. Another powerful and notorious group from the region are the Yakuza of Japan. Even more so than the Triads, the Yakuza have been closely identified with politics, in their case with support for the emperor and with far-right groups.

No one is quite sure when or how the Yakuza first developed. One theory is that they are the descendants of groups of unemployed samurai warriors who, during a period of peace in Japan, had little to do. To alleviate their boredom they formed roving gangs, which became involved in crime. Understandably, the Yakuza prefer the alternative theory that they originate not from those marauding former samurai, but from the heroic citizens' groups which sprang up to defend communities from their attacks.

In more modern times the Yakuza have had a considerable impact on Japanese society. After the end of the Second World War (1939–1945) they had close links with the world of business, the military and politics. At times during the 20th century their support was regarded as important to gaining political power. Best known in the West for their extraordinary body tattoos and trademark punishment of members – involving the removal of the tip of a person's little finger – the Yakuza haven't spread as far and as fast internationally as the Triads. However, their influence is felt as far away as the United States, and a number of Koreans in Japan have become members.

The Yakuza are also said to have been implicated in one of the most mysterious and debated events of the end of the Second World War. The Yakuza and the Japanese military apparently worked together to build up a collection of wealth from all over Japanese-occupied Asia both before and during the War. This was known as Yamashita's gold, after the name of the hapless Commander who was told to hide the loot as Japan looked set to lose the war. One theory is that some or all of the wealth was hidden in the Philippines to be collected at a later date, but that the notorious Philippine president, Ferdinand Marcos, had found part of it and sold it off, secretly using Triad gangs in Hong Kong to help him do so.

# 10

# The Future

THE POTENTIAL DANGER POSED BY secret and secretive organizations
has been a source of debate and concern among observers for as
long as those societies themselves have existed. The society formed
by Pythagoras in the late 6th century BC provoked a mixture of scorn and
opposition. In ancient Rome, too, the mysterious rites and beliefs of the
followers of Bacchus led to the Senate passing laws against them, while in
medieval times Gnostic sects were condemned by the Church as heretics;
for example, the Cathars of southern France. The Templars, too, provoked
fear and envy as much as admiration for their activities, as did the
Freemasons later on. Indeed, the Freemasons and the Bavarian Illuminati
were 'blamed' by some for the French Revolution, one of the most
important events in modern Western history.

Moreover, some prominent politicians have raised concerns about
certain secret societies. For example, 19th-century British Prime Minister
Benjamin Disraeli, one of the most influential politicians of that century,
was convinced of their power. In his novel, *Lothair*, written in 1870, one of
Disraeli's characters says, 'It is the Church against the secret societies. They
are the only two strong things in Europe, and will survive Kings, Emperors
or parliaments.' This may have been a work of fiction, but many experts
accept that those words accurately reflect the concerns held by Disraeli, who
also wrote about the role of secret societies in some of his non-fiction work.

Some argue that secret societies have provided a convenient scapegoat
for those sections of society that refuse to accept that there could be other
reasons for change, discontent or revolution. In other words, politicians
and commentators blame 'malevolent' secret societies for massive social
changes that in reality were caused by social forces and discontent. As there

is nothing fundamentally wrong with the way that the existing elites ran society, so the argument runs, the real culprits had to be secret societies run by dangerous masterminds. This is one of the major themes of the late, great historian, J. M. Roberts, in his book, *The Mythology of Secret Societies* (Macmillan, 1972). Discussing the social upheavals of the late 18th and early 19th centuries and the prevalence of secret groups at the time, he wrote, 'On the whole it was people who disliked these changes who felt the greatest need of some exceptional explanation to account for them and they found to hand and eagerly took up elements already in existence since the eighteenth century.'

But the argument that secret societies were merely a figment of people's imaginations falls somewhat short. Even Roberts admits that there were real secret societies at work, notably in France and Italy, which had clear political aims. And while it may be absurd to claim that the Freemasons or the Illuminati planned and executed the French Revolution, as a couple of contemporary writers insisted, these groups clearly had a role to play. As Professor Kees van der Pijl notes (*see Chapter 6, page 171*), the Freemasons operated like an international liberal party, reflecting ideas of the new social forces that were coming to the fore at the time. To an extent, he claims, organizations such as the Bilderberg Group can be seen as their direct descendants.

Professor van der Pijl's analysis makes a great deal more sense than do the views of many conspiracy theorists, who insist there are secret groups directing human society at will, and effectively enslaving us all. As Bilderberg Chairman Viscount Etienne Davignon has said: 'When people say this is a secret government of the world, I say that if we were a secret government of the world we should be bloody ashamed of ourselves.'

Yet this argument does not allow Bilderberg and other similar groups off the hook completely. They may not be pulling our strings, but they do have great influence, and that influence is not held accountable in any democratically elected body in the world. Professor van der Pijl is not alone in finding such groups 'profoundly anti-democratic' and even 'dangerous'. A similar argument could be made against such groups as the Freemasons, whose members are often accused of allowing fellow members to win promotions, work contracts or even to escape justice.

Other informed observers argue that the media conspiracy theories have distorted the true role of secret societies. One such expert is author John

Michael Greer, who is also a member of an impressive number of secret societies, including the Independent Order of Odd Fellows (IOOF), the Ancient Free and Accepted Masons, the Ancient Order of Druids in America (AODA) – of which he was elected Grand Archdruid – and the Societas Rosicruciana in Civitatibus Foederatis (SRICF). 'The key to understanding the role of secret societies in history is that secrecy is a tactic used by those who don't have the resources or numbers to accomplish their goals through the methods of ordinary politics,' he says. 'This is true even when the goals of a secret society aren't political. The Odd Fellows and many other fraternal orders came into being to provide a social safety net to their members in the days when sick pay and public health care were unheard of. They used secret society methods to keep their benefits restricted to their members,' he says. 'Similarly, Christianity operated as a secret society in Roman times, and dropped the habit of secrecy only when the persecution ended.'

Greer believes that, on the whole, secret societies have been a positive force. 'Secrecy is one of the foundations of freedom. By creating secret societies, people have built on this foundation in many ways, and the majority of these methods have been positive and socially beneficial,' he says. 'Of the approximately 3,500 secret societies that were active in the United States around 1900, for example, the evidence suggests that only a few dozen ever engaged in criminal activity or political conspiracy; rather, the vast majority served as a means for ordinary people to establish social networks and to cooperatively secure their own economic future. If the same level of social networking via secret societies still existed in the English-speaking world today, our communities and our civil liberties would be in much better shape than they are.' He adds: 'Secrecy is an equalizer; it's one of the few tools that allow the little guy to contend with the power structures of society. What the ruling class doesn't know about is a lot harder for them to trample!'

Greer fears, however, that the general public misunderstands secret societies 'in almost every conceivable way'. He adds: 'This is all the sadder because in the English-speaking world, at least, most people alive today had at least one grandparent who belonged to a secret society. Information about the old lodges isn't hard to come by; it's simply not of interest to most people. The stuff churned out by today's conspiracy rumour mills is much more exciting, and plays to current prejudices much better than the facts.'

Like Greer, academic and secret society expert Mark Mirabello also believes that secret societies serve a real purpose. 'They satisfy an emotional need,' he says. 'Humans thrive on mystery, and membership in a secret group enhances a person's sense of worth. More importantly, however, secret societies protect heretical ideas. They insure that some ideas – no matter how reviled or inflammatory – will survive. They insure that human society doesn't have the uniformity of a beehive. Remember, "ruling elites" always assume that their way is the only way. In the medieval period the ruling classes assumed that every man should have a feudal lord, that every person should kneel to the Roman pontiff, and that all land belonged rightfully to kings.'

Of course there is no denying that in some cases secret societies have been malevolent, or have encouraged malevolent belief systems. Examples include the Ku Klux Klan and Nazism, the ideology of the latter in part based upon ideas propounded by secret societies. Mirabello says that we should not be surprised that some secret societies are dangerous. 'No weapon ever cuts or fires in one direction,' he points out. 'Secret societies can bring freedom to heretics, outcasts, and members of the sub-proletariat, but when the "powerful", the wealthy elite, combine and form secret societies such as Skull and Bones, their power is enhanced beyond imagination. One billionaire can be dangerous. Six billionaires conspiring in a conclave is frightening,' says Mirabello.

Greer agrees that secret societies can be put to a variety of purposes, but claims that in many ways secret societies are now the victims. 'To a very real extent, as I see it, secret societies are the new Jews,' he claims. 'Now that anti-Semitism has fallen out of fashion, people who want somebody to blame for everything they don't like about the world have turned the same tired rhetoric against secret societies. The claims being made about secret societies today are exactly the same as the ones that were being made about the Jews back in the 1930s: the accusations of ritual murder, the self-contradictory claims that they are plotting to take over a world that they already supposedly control, the insistence that they're not actually human beings, all of it.'

In the case of secretive groups such as the Church of Scientology, their usefulness is certainly open to doubt. They claim status as a religion even though a core part of their faith is kept a closely guarded secret, available only to those able to financially afford to reach that stage of spiritual insight. The Church also 'provides' a form of therapy for which it makes huge claims, but which has not been validated by conventional science. The group has also been accused of being like a cult in the way it recruits and retains members – claims that the group denies. Nor does Scientology seem content to sit on the sidelines; it has constantly been in conflict with national governments around the world. The Belgian and German governments are two recent examples.

The example of Opus Dei is rather different, as its core theology is almost by definition orthodox Catholicism. In its case, one of the main accusations by its critics is that it has become a 'church within a church', and has built up wealth and influence from among the upper echelons of society. Critics say that this build-up is aimed at helping the organization pursue its own religious-political-social agenda, which has sometimes meant that it has found common cause with right-wing regimes. Opus Dei also faces the accusation that it acts like a cult in its recruitment of members, in its strict behavioural expectations, and in the pressure it places upon its members to never leave its fold.

## Looking Ahead

Secret societies are constantly changing. They begin, evolve and often then disappear, sometimes without the world even noticing. Often they will change into a non-secretive kind of organization once their purposes have been fulfilled (or thwarted). The mutation of various secret societies into 'friendly' societies in Britain is one such example.

There are also undoubtedly secret societies that are currently active, but the existence of which is currently unknown to us. As John Michael Greer says: 'It's really just a few of the big successes, such as Freemasonry, and a few complete failures that happen to catch the limelight anyway, such as the Illuminati and the Priory of Sion, which get the vast majority of the attention. The vast majority of secret societies have always gone about their work in a much quieter way.'

Secret societies will undoubtedly continue to excite suspicion, and in some cases, outright fear. One American commentator and author, who has written and spoken on the subject of secret societies in the past, declined to help with the research for this book for the reason that he is worried about his safety. 'I have not talked much about anything for the past few years because I am very worried that I might be killed or taken away in the middle of the night,' he explained. 'There are dark things happening in the US now – you cannot know how fearful it is in the States for anyone who knows too much.' It is hard to know how to judge such dramatic reactions.

But will secret societies survive? Greer, for one, believes they will struggle in the years to come. 'At this point secret societies have a fraction of the power and influence they had even fifty years ago, and many of them are fighting for survival,' he says. It is certainly true that membership of classic secret societies such as the Freemasons is much lower today than it has been in the past.

In this respect new technology probably acts as a double-edged sword. On the one hand the smallest details about supposedly secret groups and their beliefs can be plastered all over the Internet and available to hundreds of millions at the press of a key, thus revealing their 'secrets'. Yet the vastness of the Internet and its anonymity may also prove fertile ground for groups that want to establish a secret network in the outer reaches of cyber space. After all, the idea that the whole of the Internet is open to public gaze is an illusion; a significant slice of it – perhaps 20 per cent or more – is not picked up by conventional search engines. To take an unhappy example, paedophiles have shown that they can exploit the Internet's anonymity for their own terrible purposes. And these are the groups that are known about and actively pursued by law enforcement agencies.

Mirabello thinks that it is hard to predict the impact of the Internet on secret societies. He believes, however, that we can draw a parallel with the introduction of new technologies in the past. 'The printing press, like the Internet, fostered the spread of ideas and was a factor for change,' he says. 'Within fifty years, however, the "authorities" determined that the press, if "properly controlled", could be a bulwark protecting the status quo. Thus, by the early 16th century, press censorship was universal.' He adds: 'The Internet, I suspect, will share the same fate. In the early stages it is helping to circulate information and is fostering secret societies. In the long run, however, the Internet will be used to monitor and disrupt such groups, so I suspect secret societies will eventually distance themselves from the technology.'

In any case, the need for secrecy and privacy is such a basic human trait that it is hard to imagine that secretive groups will not continue to exist for the foreseeable future. Groups such as Bilderberg may one day become old-fashioned, but the essential network of informal contacts and exchange of information that they provide will almost certainly be fulfilled by a new, as yet un-thought-of body. It seems certain, therefore, that a significant part of the world will continue to operate behind closed doors. Whether the impact of these secret groups will always be for the good is rather less easy to determine. As Mirabello says: 'As long as there is a human species, a secret society will be a weapon that can liberate or enslave.'

# Glossary of Terms

**Alumbrados**

The Spanish word for 'Illuminati' or 'enlightened', given to a loosely connected group of mystics in 15th and 16th century Spain. Many of these Christians were converts from Judaism or Islam, and a considerable number were persecuted by the Catholic Church as heretics.

**Assassins**

One of the most famous – and notorious – secret societies in history. Formed in the late 11th century in what is today Iran, they were founded by Hassan-i-Sabah, of the Ismaili sect of Islam, and used as a means of attacking his political and religious enemies. Followers were used to attack and assassinate Crusader warlords in the Holy Land, though over time they simply became killers for hire. They vanished during the time of the Mongol invasions of the 13th century.

**Bilderberg Group**

The formation of this political gathering of world leaders and power brokers can be dated to a meeting at a hotel in Holland in 1954, though its origins probably owe much to political alliances and networks that developed in the Second World War. Each year Bilderberg invitees meet behind closed doors to discuss the great political, economic and diplomatic issues of the day. The Group has been accused by conspiracy theorists of being a front for a world government, and by other critics of working in an anti-democratic and unaccountable manner.

## Carbonari

A 19th-century Italian secret society with overt political and nationalistic aims, which included the reunification of Italy – in which they played a part. Their rituals and secrecy were based largely on Freemasonry, though their roots may lie in a French revolutionary group whose name (like that of the Italian society) means 'charcoal burners'. Though short-lived, the Carbonari had a considerable impact on Italian history.

## Cathars

One of the best-known groups of Christian heretics in history. Cathars or people with similar beliefs existed in many parts of Christian Europe from the 11th century AD, though they are most closely identified with the south of France. Another name for them is the Albigensians, meaning people from Albi, a town near Toulouse. The Cathars were Gnostics whose beliefs, which included the assertion that Jesus' teachings had been misunderstood and corrupted by later institutions, were inevitably condemned by the Catholic Church. In the early 13th century, the Church launched a crusade against the French Cathars; by the middle of the century they had been wiped out as an organized community. Their former strongholds and castles are now popular tourist destinations in southern France.

## Conspiracy of Equals

One of a number of quaintly named secret revolutionary societies that existed in France in the aftermath of the Revolution in 1789. Created by François Babeuf and Filippo Buonarroti, its aim was to seize power by focussing on a small clique of powerful officials and individuals in the post-Revolutionary government (rather than seeking a popular mass uprising). However, this subversive group was itself subverted and betrayed, and its members either jailed or executed.

## Council on Foreign Relations

One of the elite political 'clubs' that has provoked much controversy among conspiracy theorists since its formation in New York after the end of the First World War. Like the Bilderberg Group (see above), its alleged purpose is to set up a form of world government (some believe that it has already been successful). The Council is undoubtedly a very effective, well-connected and influential source of policy and ideas.

## Freemasonry

Freemasonry can perhaps best be seen as a secret movement rather than as one society, as there have been and continue to be a number of different Masonic organizations. The traditional, not to say mythical, history of Freemasonry traces its origins back to the biblical times of King Solomon or before. In fact, most – though not all – scholars believe that Freemasonry emerged out of medieval stonemason guilds whose members built many of the cathedrals that still etch the continent's skylines. The key emphasis in Freemasonry is self-improvement and the quest for better understanding and knowledge of oneself and the world; the use of its many rituals and symbols is said to assist in this process. Its modern organization stems from early 18th century England. In continental Europe and in North America Freemasonry was linked with radical and revolutionary ideas. Nowadays, it attracts criticism from those who believe its followers use their membership to help further their own careers, as well as those of fellow Freemasons.

## Free Gardeners

The Freemasons were by no means the only group to emerge from a particular trade. The Free Gardeners have been traced back to 17th century Scotland, and lodges later appeared in the US. The Order of Free Gardeners existed until the middle of the 20th century. Like their stonemason cousins, the cFree Gardeners drew inspiration from the story of King Solomon and the building of his Temple in Jerusalem. They were regarded as even more secretive than the Freemasons.

## Golden Dawn

The Hermetic Order of the Golden Dawn, to give it its full name, is perhaps the best known of modern era magical secret societies, though in its original form it was short-lived. Founded in 1887, it fractured into different groups early in the 20th century. Its focus on high magic made it very influential in occult circles, and former members went on to form their own societies and to make their marks in the esoteric world of such groups – none more so than the notorious Aleister Crowley.

## Hell-Fire Club

There was more than one Hell-Fire Club, but the original was probably formed in England 1719 by the Duke of Wharton. The best-known branch, however, was that which was founded by Sir Francis Dashwood, and that used to meet at Medmenham Abbey. Despite its name, the club's members seem to have been more interested in having lots of lascivious, debauched fun than taking part in 'Satan worship', though some have claimed the group did have some links to politics.

## Illuminati

The Illuminati is a collective name given to a secretive group of individuals who are said by conspiracy theorists to run the world – or at the least are working to take over the running of it. In fact, there was a real Illuminati secret society: the Bavarian Illuminati founded by a university academic called Adam Weishaupt in 1776. Its members all used pseudonyms and infiltrated Masonic lodges to spread their influence; the ultimate aim was to bring about revolutionary change in society. However the Bavarian authorities learnt of their existence and broke up the organization just ten years after it was formed. Nonetheless some have claimed – with little evidence – that the Bavarian Illuminati helped start the French Revolution.

## Knights Templar

One of the most famous organizations in history, the Knights Templar were thought to have begun life as a kind of early 12th-century security company protecting pilgrims on the hazardous road to Jerusalem. It soon evolved into one of the most powerful and wealthy organizations in the medieval world, with the Knights acting as both bankers and wealthy landowners. Though they were outwardly conventional Christians, the Knights are claimed by some to have picked up unorthodox and heretical ideas from their time in the Holy Land, and were brutally suppressed in the 14th century because of this allegation. Since their demise, the Templars have inspired and influenced many secret societies. Some believe their true goal was to discover the secrets of Solomon's Temple and its associated treasures. There is also a belief that Scottish Freemasonry has its origins in the Knights Templar.

## Ku Klux Klan

This racist society has had a number of different incarnations since it first appeared in the south of the United States in the middle of the 19th century. It saw a huge revival in the 1920s, when anti-Catholicism and anti-trade unionism were among the features added to its white supremacy outlook. Remnants of KKK groups still exist, though support for them is currently low.

## Mafia

This word has become a catchall name to describe just about any organized crime group, as in, for example, the Russian mafia. Its roots, however, lie in an organized criminal secret society in Sicily that sprang up in the 19th century. The members of this group did not use the name 'mafia', or indeed any other name for themselves other than 'Cosa Nostra', which means 'Our Thing' in Italian. Final proof that the Cosa Nostra existed as a true secret society (rather than a romantic idea of criminal gangs) only finally emerged in the 1990s. In the meantime, Sicily had exported the mafia to the US, where it still exists.

## Mithraism

Mithraism is a mystery cult or religion that was once a powerful rival to Christianity in the Roman Empire. Its precise origins are a matter of academic debate, though it probably began life as a blend of local beliefs and traditions in the Near East. Popular with Roman soldiers, its many rituals were kept secret – and largely remain so to this day. Many have pointed to some similarities in beliefs and practices between Mithraism and Christianity, the latter ultimately becoming the dominant belief system within the late western Roman Empire.

## Mystery cults

The ancient world was home to a number of secretive cults that can be considered to have involved 'mystery rites'. These include the followers of Bacchus (the Roman form of Dionysus) and those who took part in the famous Eleusinian rites near Athens. Followers had to be initiated into such mysteries, whose rituals and inner beliefs were jealously guarded secrets. At the centre of many of these mystery cults was a celebration of the endless cycle of death and rebirth in the world, as witnessed in the passing of the seasons. On some occasions, for example in Ancient Rome, such secret groups were treated as subversive, and were persecuted.

## Nine Unknown Men

An elite group based in India said to date from 3rd century BC. The group's original purpose was supposedly to keep secret knowledge that could be harmful to the human race, but some claim that today its members are the hidden rulers of the world. The group is mentioned mostly in works of fiction, which is probably where it should remain.

## Odd Fellows

Odd Fellowship shares some similarities and background with Freemasonry, and is thought to have originated in the 17th century in England. From the start, Odd Fellow lodges had many working-class members, and adopted ways of helping members and their families financially in times of trouble. They were among the groups that became known as 'friendly societies'. Odd Fellow lodges were very popular in the US, and there are still Odd Fellow organizations around the world today.

## Odin Brotherhood

This fascinating secret society claims to have been around since the early 15th century AD, when it was formed to protect pagan faiths against attacks from Christianity. However, the existence of the Brotherhood only became known in the late 20th century, and their beliefs were then publicized by academic Mark Mirabello. Its members honour the old gods, including Odin, Thor and Freya, and place emphasis on virtues such as bravery, strength and knowledge.

## Opus Dei

A controversial Catholic organization created by Spanish priest Josemaría Escrivá in the late 1920s (the late priest has since been made a saint). The group has a relatively small but influential membership: many of its members have links to politics and business. Its aim is to promote traditional Catholic values and, above all, to 'find God in daily life'. The organization has been criticized for being a 'sect within a sect' inside the Catholic Church, and also for its recruitment techniques concerning young people and the demands it puts upon its members. Opus Dei was closely associated with the Franco Regime (1936-75) in Spain.

## Order of Anti-Poke Noses

A delightfully named society, the Order of Anti-Poke Noses was created in the 1920s in the US as one of a number of groups opposed to the Ku Klux Klan and its hateful teachings. The short-lived Order's basic stance was that it opposed any group that 'stuck its nose into other people's business'.

## Ordo Novi Templi

The Ordo Novi Templi dates from 1907, and was created by Austrian occultist and former monk Jörg Lanz von Liebenfels. The occult world merged with Aryan supremacist views in this society, and it was a part of the intellectual and spiritual backdrop to the rise of Nazism in Germany. The society was also said to have been one of the inspirations for Himmler's modelling of the SS as a tool of Nazi supremacist views.

## Ordo Templi Orientis

Established at the start of the 20th century, this important magical secret society was later dominated by the ideas and personality of occultist Aleister Crowley. It still exists today – as do some splinter groups – and continues to be important in occult circles.

## Pythagorean Brotherhood

A secret society founded by the Greek mathematician Pythagoras in the 6th century BC, the Brotherhood was based in Crotona, in southern Italy, in what was then a Greek colony. At the heart of its teachings was the sacred nature of geometry and numbers. There was an outer and an inner circle of members, the latter being subject to a number of strict rules of behaviour. Though the Brotherhood did not long survive its founder's death, it was well known in the ancient world, and became a kind of blueprint for future secret societies.

## Rosicrucianism

There is no single Rosicrucian secret society, but rather a series of them that have existed through the centuries and up to the present day. As is so often the case with secret societies, the origins of the Rosicrucian movement is shrouded in mystery and legend. It first emerged in the world in the early 17th century in the form of a series of pamphlets, which suggested that a group known as the 'Rosy Cross' had been founded by a 15th-century monk who had travelled widely through the East, collecting ancient wisdom and traditions. Many different societies have since claimed the Rosicrucian name. The Rosicrucian movement remains an important part of the occult tradition, and its aim today is personal self-improvement and enlightenment. It has often been closely linked with alchemy in that the turning of base metal into gold is symbolic of the spiritual development of the individual.

## Church of Scientology

This organization began life in the 1950s as the vehicle for a self-help therapy devised by American pulp-fiction and science-fiction writer L Ron Hubbard. It has since developed an elaborate 'theology', and Scientology today claims to be a religion. Its stated aim is to help remove all the psychological 'obstacles and clutter' that prevent human beings from fulfilling their true mental and spiritual potential. Critics claim that the Church uses cult-like techniques to attract and keep its members.

## Skull and Bones Society

One of the oldest and best-known American secret societies, the Skull and Bones Society is credited with enormous power and influence by critics because of the high standing and power of many of its members. Membership in this Yale University society has included American presidents George Bush and his son, George W Bush, as well as President William Taft.

## Society of the Elect

This was a secret society set up by the imperialist and diamond magnate Cecil Rhodes in the late 19th century, and is sometimes seen as the 'grandfather' of such organizations as the Bilderberg Group. No one is sure how long the society lasted or how influential it actually was, but some serious commentators have suggested that in various later incarnations it has wielded enormous influence. Its aim was to create a form of federal world government, with the British Empire (as it was) at the heart of it.

## Theosophical Society

The Theosophical Society was started by Helena Blatvatsky in New York in the 1870s. It began life as a secret society before evolving into a more public organization that promoted occult philosophy. It drew on both Western occult tradition and Eastern mysticism, and was highly influential. The Society still exists today.

**Thuggees**
Members of this Indian secret society (from which the modern word 'thug' derives) used to befriend travellers on the road and then, at a pre-arranged time and place, would rob and strangle them. The Thugs, who were active as far back as the 16th century CE, claimed to be servants of the goddess Kali. They were eradicated by the British in the middle of the 19th century.

**Thule Society**
A secret society that believed in and promulgated Aryan supremacy in Germany in the second and third decades of the 20th century. Hitler himself was never a member, but he did join and dominate a political splinter group associated with the Society. The group eventually became the Nazi Party.

**Triads**
This is the generic name given to various Chinese secret societies. Such societies originally grew out of Chinese politics and national identity, but have for some time been associated more with criminal activity than with politics. Their influence has spread beyond Chinese borders to many other parts of the world.

**Trilateral Commission**
The Trilateral Commission was created in 1973 by a group of politicians, bankers and business persons from North America, Europe and Japan. One prominent member of the Commission was Jimmy Carter, who later became US president. The stated purpose of the Commission is to discuss common ideas and aims among groups of politicians, bankers and businesspersons from all over the world. The group has attracted criticism from some, who claim that its covert agenda is the formation of a single world government.

# Bibliography and Further Reading

Addison, Charles G., *The History of the Knights Templars* (original edition 1842, this edition Adventures Unlimited Press, 2001)

Allen, John L., *Opus Dei: The Truth About its Rituals, Secrets and Power* (Penguin, 2006)

Atack, Jon, *A Piece of Blue Sky: Scientology, Dianetics and L. Ron Hubbard Exposed* (Carol Publishing, 1990)

Baigent, Michael, et al, *The Messianic Legacy* (Arrow, 2006)

Baigent, Michael and Leigh, Richard, *The Dead Sea Scrolls Deception* (Arrow, 2006)

Barkum, Michael, *A Culture of Conspiracy* (University of California, 2003)

Booth, Martin, *The Dragon Syndicates: The Global Phenomenon of the Triads* (Carroll & Graf, 2000)

Butler, Alan, *The Virgin and the Pentacle: The Freemasonic Plot to Destroy the Church* (O Books, 2005)

Cicero, Chic and Cicero, Sandra Tabatha, *The Essential Golden Dawn* (Llewellyn, 2004)

Cooper, Robert L.D., *The Rosslyn Hoax? Viewing Rosslyn Chapel from a New Perspective* (Lewis, 2006)

Cooper, Robert L.D., *Cracking the Freemason's Code* (Rider, 2006)

Davies, Owen, *Witchcraft, Magic and Culture 1736-1951* (Manchester University Press, 1999)

Dickie, John, *Cosa Nostra: A History of the Sicilian Mafia* (Hodder, 2007)

Eckartshausen, Karl Von, *The Cloud upon the Sanctuary* (George Redway 1896; The Book Tree 2006)

Escrivá, Josemaría, *The Way* (Doubleday, 2006)

Frazer, J.G., *The Golden Bough* (Canongate Classics, 2004 edition)

Freke, Timothy and Gandy, Peter, *The Jesus Mysteries* (HarperElement, 2002)

Gardiner, Laurence, *The Magdalene Legacy* (Harper Element, 2005)

Gardiner, Philip, *Gnosis: The Secret of Solomon's Temple Revealed* (Radikal Phase, 2006)

Gardiner, Philip, and Osborn, Gary, *The Shining Ones* (Watkins, 2006)

Gilbert, R.A., *Revelations of the Golden Dawn* (Quantum, 1997)

Greer, John Michael, *The Element Encyclopedia of Secret Societies* (Harper Element, 2006)

Greer, John Michael, *Inside a Magical Lodge* (Llewellyn, 1998)

Hall, Manly P., *The Secret Destiny of America* (Philosophical Research Society, 1944)

Hall, Manly P., *The Secret Teachings of All Ages* (Philosophical Research Society, 1928)

Harwood, Jeremy, *The Secret History of Freemasonry* (Lorenz, 2006)

Howard, Michael, *The Occult Conspiracy* (Destiny, 1989)

Hutchison, Robert, *Their Kingdom Come: Inside the Secret World of Opus Dei* (Corgi, 1998)

Kamen, Henry, *The Spanish Inquisition: An Historical Revision* (Weidenfeld, 1997)

Knight, Christopher and Butler, Alan, *Solomon's Power Brokers* (Watkins, 2007)

Knight, Stephen, *The Brotherhood: The Explosive Exposé of the Secret World of the Freemasons* (Harper Perennial, 2007 edition)

Lyon, Russell, *The Quest for the Original Horse Whisperers* (Luath, 2003)

MacMullen, Ramsay, *Paganism in the Roman Empire* (Yale, 1981)

McIntosh, Christopher, *The Rosicrucians* (Samuel Weiser, 1998)

Madariaga, Isabel de, *Russia in the Age of Catherine the Great* (Weidenfeld, 1981)

Marrs, Jim, *Rule by Secrecy* (HarperCollins, 2000)

Miller, Russell, *Bare-faced Messiah: The True Story of L. Ron Hubbard* (Michael Joseph, 1987)

Naudon, Paul, *The Secret History of Freemasonry* (Inner Traditions, 2001)

Picknett, Lynn and Prince, Clive, *The Templar Revelation* (Bantam, 1997)

Picknett, Lynn, *Mary Magdalene* (Robinson, 2003)

Putnam, Robert D., *Bowling Alone* (Simon & Schuster, 1999)
Read, Piers Paul, *The Templars* (Weidenfeld, 1999)

Reppetto, Thomas, *American Mafia* (Henry Holt, 2004)

Roberts, J.M., *Mythology of the Secret Societies* (Macmillan, 1972)

Robinson, John J., *Born in Blood: The Lost Secrets of Freemasonry* (M. Evans, 1989)

Ross, Robert Gaylon Sr., *Who's Who of the Elite* (RIE, 1995)

Russell, Jeffery B., *A History of Witchcraft: Sorcerers, Heretics and Pagans* (Thames & Hudson, 1981)

Short, Martin, *Inside the Brotherhood: Further Secrets of the Freemasons* (HarperCollins, 1989)

Smart, Ninian, *The World's Religions* (Cambridge, 1998)

Stoyanov, Yuri, *The Hidden Tradition in Europe: The Secret History of Medieval Christian Heresy* (Penguin, 1995)

Streeter, Michael, *Witchcraft: A Secret History* (Barron's, 2002)

Streeter, Michael, *Franco* (Haus, 2005)

Tabor, James D., *The Jesus Dynasty* (HarperElement, 2006)

Tapia, Maria del Carmen, *Beyond the Threshold: A Life in Opus Dei* (Continuum, 1999)

Van der Pijl, Kees, *Transnational Classes and International Relations* (Routledge, 1998)

Van der Pijl, Kees, *Global Rivalries: From the Cold War to Iraq* (Pluto, 2006)

Varese, Federico, *The Russian Mafia* (OUP, 2001)

Walsh, Michael, *Opus Dei: An Investigation Into the Powerful, Secretive Society Within the Catholic Church* (Harper, 1989)

Williams, Paul L., *The Vatican Exposed: Money, Murder and the Mafia* (Prometheus, 2003)

Yates, Frances, *The Rosicrucian Enlightenment* (Routledge, 1972)

Yates, Frances, *The Occult Philosophy in the Elizabethan Age* (Routledge, 1979)

# Index

# Credits

Photographic credits are as follows:
Front cover: © Malek Racho/Fotolia
Plate 1: © Tibor Bognar/Corbis
Plate 2: © Blue Lantern Studio/Corbis
Plate 3: © Krause, Johansen/Archivo Iconografico, SA/Corbis
Plate 4: © Alinari Archives/Corbis
Plate 5: © Bettmann/Corbis
Plate 6: © Historical Picture Archive/Corbis
Plate 7, top and back cover: © Stefano Bianchetti/Corbis;
        bottom: © Joseph Sohm; Visions of America/Corbis
Plate 8: © Bettmann/Corbis
Plate 9: © Bettmann/Corbis
Plate 10: © Peter Aprahamian/Corbis
Plate 11: © Tatiana Markow/Sygma/Corbis
Plate 12: © Blue Lantern Studio/Corbis
Plate 13: © Archivo Iconografico, SA/Corbis
Plate 14: © Bettmann/Corbis
Plate 15: © Orjan F. Ellingvag/Corbis
Plate 16: © Jerzy Dabrowski/dpa/Corbis

# Acknowledgements

THE AUTHOR WOULD LIKE to thank the many people who have helped in the research for this book, a number of whom cannot be or prefer not to be named. Among those who can be publicly thanked, gratitude is due to Dr Mark Mirabello for his patience and skill in answering a series of questions; to John Michael Greer for his insightful comments and to Professor David S. Touretzky for his valuable assistance. Professor Kees van der Pijl also provided many interesting ideas and material, while journalist Jim Tucker was generous with his time, as was Dianne DiNicola. Thanks also to Chuck Beatty for sharing his experiences, and gratitude to Robert L. D. Cooper, who provided original information on the history of Freemasonry. Last but not least, thanks to Chelsey Fox of Fox & Howard and to Kate Parker, Giselle Osborne and Steffanie Brown at New Holland for all of their encouragement and support.

To buy books in quantity for corporate use
or incentives, call **(800) 962–0973**
or e-mail **premiums@GlobePequot.com**.

The Lyons Press is an imprint of The Globe Pequot Press
10  9  8  7  6  5  4  3  2  1
Printed in United States of America
ISBN 978-1-59921-160-2
Library of Congress Cataloging-in-Publication Data is available on file.

# strike dog

## A WOODS COP MYSTERY

## joseph heywood

THE LYONS PRESS
Guilford, Connecticut
An imprint of The Globe Pequot Press

*To Shanny, who can spell but can't read,*
*and seems to prefer it that way.*

**Also by Joseph Heywood**

**Fiction:**
*Taxi Dancer* (1985)
*The Berkut* (1987)
*The Domino Conspiracy* (1992)
*The Snowfly* (2000)

**Woods Cop Mysteries:**
*Ice Hunter* (2001)
*Blue Wolf in Green Fire* (2002)
*Chasing a Blond Moon* (2003)
*Running Dark* (2005)

**Non-Fiction:**
*Covered Waters: Diary of a Nomadic Trouter* (2003)

# Part I: Madstones and Devil's Smiles

*Commune periculum concordiam discors parit.*

Common danger brings forth discordant harmony.

# 1

# Marquette, Michigan
## April 28, 2004

Grady Service stared down at the large white metal drawers, his mind cluttered by unconnected thoughts, mostly fragments: spring, the season of change, breakup and runoff, a time of sloppy excess; his old man, whom he'd never gotten along with; more than two erratic decades as a conservation officer, mostly alone; the divorce from his late first wife; and finding Nantz, and learning he was a father—all of this rolling around in his aching head as he stared at the drawers. He felt blood rushing to his head, then racing away, his insides in chaos, at the edge of an abyss—one he knew he could not back away from.

"Grady," Captain Ware Grant said from beside him. "You don't have to do this." The captain grasped his detective's arm.

Service pushed the hand away. "Open them," he ordered the hospital orderly.

"Which one first?"

The captain pointed.

It seemed like the man took forever to pull out the drawer and unzip the black plastic bag. There was a bright yellow biohazard label on it. *The plastic didn't look strong enough to contain a human being,* he thought, his mind grasping for details to cling to, something to process that would make sense. Anything but this.

He stared down, saw Maridly Nantz's face, unmarked, like she was asleep. "The other one," Service whispered, his legs reducing to gelatin.

It was the same in the second drawer, Walter asleep, his son, his only son, the only one he was ever likely to have, his dead son, at eighteen.

"No," Grady Service said. It was not a word born of thought, but a defensive thing, a verbal arm instinctively raised to ward off an assailant.

Captain Grant stood nearby, saying nothing. The orderly left them alone in the small, chilled room.

"But she was a pilot," Service said after a long time.

"Accidents happen, Grady."

"Not to her, not to Maridly Nantz. Safety was in her blood."

The captain kept quiet.

A sign in the room said NO SMOKING. Grady Service lit a cigarette and inhaled deeply.

He smoked the cigarette down to embers, GI'd the butt, and put it in his pocket. He stood between the drawers, with one hand on the love of his life and the other hand on his son, both killed in an accident on the way back from Houghton.

Grady Service wanted reasons, tears, anything to take the ice out of his blood, but nothing came. Inside all he could feel was a cold rage, at chance, at God, at anything, everything. He had spent his life around death in all forms, but this was different.

Eventually he felt the captain move his hands away from the bodies and he watched as his superior zipped the bags and slid the drawers into the wall. The drawers squeaked, needed oil. Nantz would hate a noisy drawer, would take it as a personal affront. Walter would not pay attention. Nothing bothered the boy.

In the corridor outside the orderly stepped in front of Service. "You can't smoke in there, dude."

The blow sent the man backward, sliding down the waxed floor like a human stone in a curling match.

The captain ignored the man with the bleeding face, took a tight hold on Service's arm, and kept him walking away from the morgue, up the stairs, toward the light.

# 2

# Schweitzer Creek, Michigan
## April 28, 2004

M-35 was curvy where it crossed Schweitzer Creek about four miles south of Palmer, but the hardtop was dry, the shoulder wide, and the county road commission had brushhogged it, providing plenty of room for a sliding vehicle. Grady Service stomped up and down the road, studying the marks left by Nantz's pickup truck, trying desperately to make sense of them.

"She was a pilot," he said, as if this alone explained why Maridly Nantz could not be dead.

Captain Grant said, "Even the best pilots have accidents."

"Not this pilot—not her," Service growled. "Look, she skidded to the right here," he said, walking along the rubber marks, "fought out of it, and rolled the other way. Not that tough to get out of. We all do it in the snow every winter, and in summer on washboard roads that will rip the steering wheel out of your hands. She's done it a million times. We all have." It had been a dry day in early May. There was no excuse.

"Sometimes there's no explanation," the captain said. "It just happens."

"Not to Nantz, not to Walter. Where's her truck?"

"U.P. Autobody and Collision in Negaunee Township," the captain said.

"They should have left it here so I could see."

"You're not a trained accident investigator."

Bullshit, Service said. "They took it away before I could look it over."

"They took it away because it's standard procedure. The removal had nothing to do with you."

"I want to see it."

"The Troops are looking at it."

"I want to *see* it," Service demanded.

Marquette deputy sheriff "Weasel" Linsenman drove up, parked, got out of his cruiser, and approached sheepishly, his head bowed. "I just heard, man. Jesus, Grady. I'm so sorry."

Linsenman started to step closer, but stopped.

"U.P. Autobody," Service said.

"You want me to show you where it is?" the deputy asked.

Service and Linsenman had been friends for a long time, and had shared some tense professional moments together, but both men tended to lead solitary lives, Service with his girlfriend and son, and the deputy with his dogs. They were friends who barely knew each other, yet willingly covered each other's backs.

"I'm so sorry, Grady."

Service looked up and seemed only then to recognize his friend. "She was a pilot."

Linsenman glanced at the captain, who shook his head almost imperceptibly, a signal for the deputy to keep silent.

U.P. Autobody & Collision was in Negaunee Township, not far from the state police post. There were two main buildings, basic pole barns, painted taupe, a metal fence around the property, and rows of wrecked vehicles strewn around. Service looked at the buildings and said "Taupe," to the captain, who raised an eyebrow. Service had never heard the word *taupe* until Nantz taught him. He was the old dog, nearly twenty years older than she, yet it seemed he learned more from her than the other way around.

They went inside a door marked OFFICE and asked about Nantz's truck. A woman at reception sent them to the back building where they found a large man with a potbelly and muttonchops that hung down the side of his face like feathers.

Neither the captain nor Service was in uniform. "Hey," the man said. "Sorry, but youse can't just waltz in here."

Service grabbed the man by the throat, backed him over to a metal wall, and slammed him against it. The metal reverberated like a reluctant steel drum. "Red Ford, just came in," Service said.

The man shook his shoulders, took a step away, and pointed. "The state's not done with it yet," he stammered.

Service walked over to the wreck, which was in the back of the shop, partially covered with a black plastic tarp. The roof was flat, but had been cut open with the Jaws of Life. Both sides of the truck were caved in, the grill shattered. Two deflated air bags lay on the floor near the wreck. Powder residue from the bags spackled the floor and hood of the truck like gray pollen.

"When will the accident investigation team be back?" the captain asked.

"AIT's business, their time," the man said.

Service turned toward the man, felt fire rippling along his spine.

"His girlfriend and son were in it," the captain said.

The man's demeanor immediately changed. "I'm sorry. They said they'd be back tonight; they got called out to another accident all the way down by Traunik."

Service stared at the man. "Who're you?"

"Ptacek."

"You the honcho?"

The man shook his head. "I just drive the wrecker."

"You tow it in?"

The man nodded.

"How long you done this for a living?"

"Seventeen, eighteen years."

"You see anything that catches your attention?"

The man held up his hands. "I just haul them."

"You've got eyes and a brain," Service said.

"Nobody wants to hear what the wrecker driver has to say."

"I want to hear."

"The AIT will kick my ass."

"The Troops want to get to the truth," the captain said, intervening. "Anything that helps will be welcomed."

"I heard them talk when they come in. They think it's a rollover, pure and simple."

"You have a different view?" the captain asked.

"Over twenty years you see a heckuva lot of wrecks. You didn't look, you'd be bored outta your bloody mind, eh?"

Service lurched, his face flushing, "You think wrecks are for your *entertainment*?"

The man quickly raised his arms. "No. I'm just saying, when you see so many, you get to looking at them pretty closely."

"Have you seen something to suggest it's not a simple rollover?" the captain asked.

The man shook his head. "I could lose my job. The boss has contracts with the state in four counties."

The captain was adept at interviewing reluctant witnesses. "You won't lose your job for telling the truth. We're conservation officers . . . cops."

"Youse're game wardens, no fake?"

"The Troops will draw their own conclusions," Captain Grant said.

The man looked conflicted, crossed his arms, and approached the wreckage. "Maybe it *was* just an accident," he began.

"But?" Grady Service interjected gruffly.

"I don't have 'er all worked out in my head yet," the man said, "but as I looked it over, it seemed to me that something else might have happened."

"Work it out now," Service said.

"Here," the man said, leaning over the rear of the truck. "There's paint here, just a few flecks."

Service and the captain flanked the man, leaned over, looked down. "Green paint," Service said.

"Or blue," the man countered. "Can't tell for sure unless you actually lift a sample and analyze it."

"That paint wasn't there before," Service said.

"She might have backed into something over in Houghton," the captain offered.

"This didn't come from backing into something," the wrecker driver said. "I'd say it came from her being hit."

"Rammed?" the captain asked.

"Not rammed . . . not exactly. The bumper don't show it; in fact, nothing shows it, but look at the left rear taillight."

"Gone," Service said.

The man nodded. "Left one's gone, right one isn't. And where's the foreign paint?"

"Near the left rear light," Service said. Nantz took good care of her vehicles, would not abide even marginal damage. If she'd dinged her truck, she would have gotten it fixed immediately. It was a matter of pride for her, almost a fetish. The plane she owned, her vehicles, her house, everything had to be in working order and cosmetically shipshape. *Why had she cut him slack?* he wondered. He'd never worked that out: Her the neat freak, him the slob. It made no sense.

The man suddenly seemed to withdraw from his observations. "All these years I seen me a heap of wrecks, and after a while you get to recognize some things. I'm not saying this is how it went down, but it's possible."

"Say what it is you have to say," Grady Service said.

"Ask me, it looks like somebody put a PIT against this truck." PIT was short for precision immobilization technique, a maneuver used by police officers to spin a vehicle and end the chase.

"The state police agree?" the captain asked.

"I didn't say nothing about it to them. I didn't really see it until I got back here and started looking."

"But they'll see it," the captain said.

"Maybe, maybe not. Most cops have to PIT somebody, they're so jacked up over what they done and the fact they survived it, they don't really look at the damage. You know, if you get through it, who cares about dings in your patrol car? And why look for PIT damage on a civilian truck off the cement by its lonesome?"

"PIT," Service said.

Ptacek said, "Not just a PIT, but a PIT by a smaller vehicle against a bigger one, say a big pickup like this Ford, and probably the PIT driver in the smaller car wasn't so good at the maneuver. When you get a mismatch in vehicle size, the smaller one ain't gonna drive away without damage."

Service said, "Walk me through it."

"Walk *us* through it," the captain said, correcting his detective.

The man grabbed some bricks, set them on the shop floor, and reconstructed the accident as he thought it could have happened. When he was done, he stood up and fumbled with a pack of cigarettes. "Okay if I smoke?"

The captain nodded. "You work here."

Grady Service looked at Nantz's Ford, the dark flecks, the missing taillight, and closed his eyes, trying to match what the man had just shown him with the bricks with what he had seen out on the highway. He worked his way through the events several times and felt a wave of dizziness begin to envelop him.

"Not an accident, Cap'n." Service put his hand on the back of Nantz's truck to hold himself up. "Not an accident," he repeated.

Without remembering why or how, Grady Service had his .38 snub out of the holster in the back of his belt and was staring at it in his hand.

"Detective!" the captain said in his sharpest command voice. He looked at the wrecker driver and waved for him to get out.

The man backpedaled out the door.

"Grady, give me your piece."

"Murder, Captain. Not an accident. They were murdered."

"The gun, Grady. *Now.*"

Service pondered the captain's request and finally held out the small pistol, grip toward the captain.

"I got more guns, Captain."

"Grady."

"Captain, I am going to hunt down the cocksucker who did this and I am going to blow his fucking brains out."

The captain grabbed Service's arm, but the bigger man swept him away and barged outside.

Ware Grant found him sitting in his Tahoe and got in beside him.

"You're off duty until further notice, Detective."

"I'll find who did this—one way or another," Grady Service said, grinding his teeth. His mind was in overdrive. If Nantz had been deliberately forced off the road, there could be only two reasons, and one of them—the most likely in his mind—was revenge *against him.*

"I'll talk to the Troops. Let the process work, Grady."

Service's face twisted in a rictus of pain and anger. "Yeah, do that—but I promise you this: Whoever did this is never going to make it to trial. This is personal."

Only then did tears come, and he wasn't sure if they flowed from grief or the need for vengeance.

On his way home he called Nantz's cell phone and landline providers to request the bills from her phones. Maybe there was something there. Anything.

"I'm sorry, sir, are you related to the lady?" the cell phone company woman asked.

"I live with her."

"I'm sorry, sir, but the phone is not in your name."

"I'm with the DNR," he said, his temper spiking.

"I'm sorry, sir, but you'll need to get a warrant from the regular police."

*Regular* police! He broke off the call and pounded the steering wheel with his fists. He inhaled to settle himself, and considered calling the captain to see what he could do, but decided against it. Why the fuck didn't you marry her? he asked himself.

He then called the Marquette County Sheriff's Department and learned that Linsenman was off duty and called him at home.

"It's Grady."

"How're you doing?"

"I need a favor."

There was a pause on the other end of the line. "Like what?"

"I need to get Nantz's current phone records, but the company won't give them to me because we weren't married, the house phone is in her name, and I'm not *regular* police. Can you get them for me?"

"No problem," Linsenman said. "What do you want?"

"Home phone and her personal cell phone." He gave his friend the numbers.

"I can do this by fax. What's the rationale for the affadavit?"

"Needed for an ongoing investigation."

"The accident investigation is still open?"

"Just do it, okay?"

"Okay, drop them at your house or your office?"

"Slippery Creek."

"Your house is in Gladstone."

"I'm relocating."

"Huh," the deputy said. "I'll drop them out at the camp. Anything else?"

"I appreciate this," Grady Service said.

# 3

# Gladstone, Michigan
## April 28, 2004

It was dark and Korea-born Candace McCants was inside Nantz's house on the Bluff overlooking Gladstone, rubbing the ears of Newf, Service's 154-pound Canary Island mastiff, a breed the Spaniards called *Presa Canario*. The dog had been given to him by his former girlfriend, veterinarian Kira Lehto. Before Newf, he had been deathly afraid of all dogs, any size, breed, or shape, but over time he and Newf had bonded in ways he never would have predicted.

McCants was a damn good CO, and a close friend. She got up, came over to Service, and put her arms around him. He was more than a foot taller. No words passed between them.

He pushed her away. He went up to the bedroom and came back minutes later with a bulging canvas hockey bag he often used as a suitcase.

"Grady?"

He turned and faced her. "Either help or get the fuck out of my way," he said.

McCants didn't move. "You intimidate a lot of people, Grady, but I'm not one of them. What the hell do you think you're doing?"

"Going back."

"Going back to what?"

"Who I was before."

"—Nantz civilized you."

"Yeah, that worked out," he said bitterly.

"Put down the freaking bag."

He stared at her.

She took a deep breath. "You're not thinking. You're doing—hell, I don't know what's going through that twisted mind of yours, but you're not thinking. The Grady Service I respect thinks before he acts. He thinks about everyone and then he does the right thing."

"I *am* doing the right thing," he countered.

"Packing your stuff and running away?"

"Not running away," he said. "I'm going to get it back."

"It?"

"It," he repeated.

"And who's keeping *it* from you?"

"Me," he said. "But not anymore."

"What about the funeral. Have you made arrangements?"

"No funeral," he said. "No memorial, no words at the grave, no nothing."

"You haven't answered the question."

"Cremation," he said.

"Is that what she wanted, or what you decided?"

"What Nantz wanted," he said. "Walter was too young to have an opinion."

"Cremation and no memorial, no effort to come to grips with this, let us all grieve?"

He looked at her and showed a half-grin. "Oh, I am most definitely going to come to grips with it."

"I?" McCants said. "You. What about the rest of us—all their friends, all of us who cared about Nantz and Walter."

"You mourn your way and I'll mourn mine."

"I thought you were growing up," she snapped.

"I am," he shot back.

"You are not making any sense, Service."

He saw that McCants was on the verge of an emotional outburst and put his hands on her shoulders. "It wasn't an accident, Candi. Somebody ran them off the road and killed them."

The younger officer's jaw hung open and she blinked.

"We all got a voice message from Chief O'Driscoll this morning. He said it was an accident."

Service said, "It wasn't."

McCants began to chew her bottom lip. "The whole world thinks it's an accident, but the great Grady Service knows better."

He tapped his stomach. "Gut first, then evidence. When your gut twists into a braid you can't ignore it. I won't," he added with a glare. "Call the captain, ask him."

McCants went to her truck, got her cell phone, and punched in the number as Service looked on.

"Captain, McCants here. I'm with Grady and he says it wasn't an accident. What's going on?"

Service watched as she nodded, her face impassive. She then flipped the phone shut. "He says you've been relieved of duty for now and that you are being irrational."

He studied her eyes. "He said more, didn't he?"

"Yeah. He said you may be right, but that the Troops have to make that determination."

He quickly talked her through what he knew, and when he had finished, she said, "Okay, you want to move back to your camp, you've got it. But if the investigation comes back as an accident, all this bullshit is done and you will sit down and do the things you are supposed to do in a way that will honor your woman and your son. Am I clear?"

"You always are," he said, heading back to the house for another load.

They carried loads to his truck in silence until the bed of his personal pickup was nearly full. "What is this going to prove?" she finally asked.

"Somebody killed them," he said.

"Maybe," she corrected him.

"Maybe," he echoed. "But if it was homicide, I plan to be in shape to do something about it, and I can't do that here."

"You mean living in luxury," she said, filling in the blank.

"Right. I got soft here—I lost my edge—and if somebody killed them, I'm sure it was to get at me."

"Why do things always have to be about *you*?"

"They don't, but when they are and I don't focus, I'm asking for it."

"Your logic scares me," she said.

"It's not logic," he said. "It's all gut."

"So it's back to sleeping on footlockers in an unfinished camp in the woods."

"It's finished," he said in his own defense.

"Jesus, you big dumb bastard, it has four walls and some doors stacked around a toilet and a shower in the corner. It's not much more than a wall tent made of plywood and half-logs."

"It works for me," he said.

She followed him into the garage, where he began moving his free weights out to the truck, and she began to help.

"Maridly would want you to slow down and think," she said again, trying to reason with him.

"What Mar would want is for me to find out who did this to her and Walter and to settle it."

"Who hates you so much they'd kill your girlfriend and son? Allerdyce?"

Limpy Allerdyce was one of the state's most notorious poachers, and Service had once put him in jail for seven years for attempted murder. Allerdyce was the leader of a tribe of lawbreakers, mostly his relations, who lived like animals in the far southwestern reaches of Marquette County.

The clan killed bears and sold the galls and footpads to Korean brokers in Los Angeles for shipment to Korea and Taiwan. They killed dozens of deer each year, took thousands of fish, and got substantial money for their take from buyers in Chicago and Detroit. Despite a probable huge income, the tribe lived like savages. Since his release from Southern Michigan Prison in Jackson, Limpy had pretty much followed the law, and even claimed to have been a snitch for Service's father, who had been a CO of the old school. Since getting out of prison Limpy had begun feeding information to Service. Allerdyce was a lot of things, most of them too vile to contemplate, but this wasn't his style. Limpy did things Yooper-style, head-on and toe to toe, and whatever the challenge, he fought his own battles.

"Not Limpy," he said. "But whoever it is, they knew that Nantz and Walter were my vulnerabilities. Now they'll come after me."

"Maybe they know they can't get you and they're settling for Nantz and Walter," McCants offered.

"They'll come," he said. "They'll come."

"Tree called," she said. "He's on his way north."

Luticious Treebone and Service had finished college the same year, Service graduating from Northern Michigan University where he had been only a fair student and a competent hockey player. Treebone had played football and baseball at Wayne State and graduated cum laude. They both had been on the verge of being drafted when they volunteered for the marines, met at Parris Island, and served together in the same unit in Vietnam. They had been through hell and rarely spoke of the war since. When they got out of the marines they both joined the Michigan State Police, went through the academy in East Lansing with honors. When the opportunity came to transfer to Department of Natural Resources (DNR) law enforcement, both had made the move, but within a year, Treebone left the DNR for the Detroit Metropolitan Police, where he was now a much-decorated lieutenant in charge of vice. They had remained close friends since boot; each thought of the other as his brother.

Service grinned. "Good. Tree knows how payback works."

"Listen to yourself! Payback? What kind of shit is that? You're a cop."

"Somebody does your partner, you go after *them*."

Later, while McCant's was outside with the dog, he went through last month's house telephone bills to see if there had been any unusual activity, but he saw nothing out of the ordinary. He also checked Nantz's personal cell phone bills. Apparently she called Walter's cell phone almost every day, which surprised him. He talked to his son perhaps once a week. There was also a number he didn't recognize that came up repeatedly and out of desperation he dialed it.

"Hello?" a familiar voice answered. His son's girlfriend? Why the hell was Nantz calling her?

"Karylanne? I saw your number on Nantz's cell phone record and just thought I'd see who it was," he explained clumsily.

"It's me," she sighed. "Ah, when's the funeral?" she asked with a weak voice.

"I don't know yet," he said. Not her goddamn business. "Nantz called you often," he said.

"We were friends," the girl said.

When the hell did they become friends? Jesus Christ, was he blind to everything?

"OK, thanks," he said, and abruptly hung up.

He threw the records back in a drawer in Nantz's desk with disgust. What else could he check? He couldn't think of anything and felt even worse. You're supposed to be a detective, asshole, but you couldn't find a turd in a toilet. When the fuck would Linsenman bring the current records? He thought about going through Nantz's checkbook, but he wasn't sure where it was.

When McCants came back he was sitting alone in the kitchen looking out at the gray water of Little Bay de Noc, and trying to force his brain to give him something to work with, a place to start. Anything.

# 4

# Slippery Creek, Michigan
## May 1, 2004

Luticious Treebone and Service sat on the porch of the cabin. "The whole woods cop clan is going to close ranks around you," Tree told him.

Service took him through the facts as he knew them, and Treebone listened without interrupting until his friend had finished.

"I've seen your gut in action," Tree said. "What do you need from me?"

"Just keep people off my tail while I get myself ready."

"Kalina will be up tomorrow," Treebone said. Tree had brought his duffel and a sleeping bag, declaring he'd be staying for two weeks, like it or not. He was under Kalina's orders, and no one defied his wife.

Kalina Treebone had been named for the great Detroit Tiger Al Kaline, but where Kaline had been humble throughout his Hall of Fame career, she was outspoken, resolute in her beliefs, and intimidating to her husband and most of his friends.

Three days had passed since Service had seen the wreck. The captain drove out from Marquette and said that the state felt 70 percent certain it had been an accident, but they were not going to declare it so until they had ruled out other possibilities. Service was not happy with the news, but it didn't change his mind about what he had to do, which was to get himself into top shape by living a Spartan existence, with as few distractions as possible.

Each morning and afternoon he lifted weights. In between he ran six miles down Slippery Creek and into the Mosquito Wilderness Area, which he considered to be one of the state's natural jewels. Before Nantz, the Mosquito had been his one true love, and he had guarded it with the tenacity of his father before him. An unexpected promotion to detective in the Wildlife Resources Protection unit removed him from the Mosquito, and it had become Candi's. So far she had been as fierce in protecting it as he had been.

Two hours after the captain left, Kalina Treebone arrived toting an enormous cooler filled with food and sent Tree to her van for two more coolers.

"You two aren't going to be eating cold beans from a can if I can help it."

Tree and Service hoisted the coolers into the cabin. Kalina confronted Service, one hand on her hip and the other waving like a flick-knife. "You've always been a selfish, self-absorbed man," she said. "Just like my Tree. Why any woman would want either of you is beyond me. What you need to be doing is getting your woman and your son properly buried and prayed over. Until then there ain't nothing else matters."

"They're dead," he said coldly, "and nothing can change that. What I have to do is deal with the things I can deal with. The state has ordered autopsies and I can't do a damn thing until they release them, so if you don't mind, put your finger back in its holster and let me get on with what I've got to do." He was sick of being hugged, advised, and lectured about what he ought to be doing, and he was fed up with hangdog faces and pathetic sighs. He didn't need sympathy; he needed space. Why couldn't they understand that? Couldn't they see or sense that whatever this was—and he wasn't in any position yet to describe it—it was just starting, not ending.

He knew she didn't buy it, but Kalina was like her husband, the sort who would do what a friend needed, even when they didn't agree.

Kalina manned the phone, which kept ringing with sympathy calls. Ever since he'd arrived, the cabin had been overflowing with a stream of friends, bearing food and cringing sympathy, most of them at a loss for exactly what to say. His friends and fellow woods cops came one after the other. Gus Turnage, CO from Houghton County, and a fly-fishing friend, arrived just after Treebone. Gus hugged him but had little to say. He had lost his own wife many years back, raised three sons on his own. He had never remarried.

Their friend Yalmer "Shark" Wetelainen and his wife Limey Pyykkonen came in the next morning, followed by Simon del Olmo, the Cuba-born army vet and his girlfriend and conservation officer, Elza "Sheena" Grinda. Lars and Joan Hjalmquist came over from Ironwood; Wink Rector, the resident FBI agent for the U.P., drove down from Marquette; and DaWayne Kota, the tribal game warden from Bay Mills, also showed up. Last to arrive were the giant CO Bryan Jefferies from Luce County, and Gutpile Moody, and his young girlfriend, Kate, also an officer and close friend of Nantz's. Moody and Nordquist lived together in nearby Schoolcraft County.

Vince Vilardo and Rose came up from Escanaba. Vince was the retired medical examiner for Delta County, and a longtime friend.

Linsenman showed up with an envelope and handed it to him and Service took it to the side and opened it and scanned May's phone records. They looked like last month's, mostly calls to him, Walter, and Karylanne. She had called Walter the day before the accident, but not Karylanne. Nothing there.

Shit! He stuffed the records back in the envelope and threw it in a cardboard box in a corner.

Lieutenant Lisette McKower and her husband drove in from Newberry. McKower was five-five, 120, with short brown hair, a long neck, and the tiny hands of a doll. Service met her for the first time when she had been sent to him as a rookie to train. He thought they had sent him a cheerleader, but she had been twenty-four, had three summers under her belt as a smokejumper out of Montana, and turned out to be as tough as moosehide. She'd risen through the ranks and Service was proud of her, though he'd never have admitted it.

"I'm sorry for our loss, Grady. Hear that? Ours, not just yours."

Nantz was to have entered the DNR academy this fall.

"I talked to the captain," McKower said. "He told me what you found at the auto-body shop."

Service nodded.

"The evidence doesn't prove anything," she said. "Are you prepared to deal with it if it's ruled an accident?"

"It wasn't an accident," he said.

She sighed. "You always see the world in black and white, Grady. Remember, the Chinese say black has five colors and the Ojibwa have fourteen words for snow, including several colors other than white."

He didn't respond. She was one of those people who was pathologically rational, a woman who overrode intuition with pure intellectual power and had risen because of it. But she had also been a smokejumper and had considerable fire inside. Even if she wouldn't admit it, she understood the call to vengeance.

"I know you, Grady; you only *think* you know me," she said. "You classify me according to what's convenient for you. If this is not an accident, that does not mean it is automatically a homicide. There are shades, Grady, and there is a system and a process, and we are sworn to uphold both. We both know that the system and the process are no more than social algorithms, not final arbiters of right and wrong; they are only methods we use to determine guilty or not guilty, which has nothing to do with morality. Vengeance is not part of the system or the process," she concluded, looking directly into his eyes. "I know you will do the right thing," she said. "The captain says we are to assume this is an accident until the Troops issue a formal report to the contrary."

"Nice speech. It won't be me talking about it," he said.

"Not you talking, period," she said.

"Never been much good at it," he said.

"Nantz made you better," McKower said. "We don't want any backsliding."

"Is that the departmental 'we'?"

"That's the personal we, you big hardhead—me, and all your friends."

It seemed like half of Michigan Tech's hockey team trooped in the second morning, led by Walter's girlfriend, Karylanne Pengelly. Her eyes and nose were red and swollen, but she walked with her head up in a gesture of pride and resolve that caught Service's attention and choked him up for a moment.

His son had been in his first year at Michigan Tech and was working out and practicing with the team. Next year he would have been on scholarship. Not now. The Tech players mumbled as they shook his hand, and he understood. Elite young hockey players were like all young jocks. They hated dealing with injuries and death. Athletics was about feeling invincible, and when one of their own went down, it caused most of them to pull away so that they didn't have to face the reality or their own potential vulnerability. He couldn't blame them. He had been there once, had been a player who could have signed a pro contract if he'd wanted, but he had chosen the marines and gone to Vietnam instead of the NHL. It was a decision he'd never regretted, though it had been a hard, often nasty road from then to now.

He held Karylanne and felt her sob, but he had no words to soothe himself, much less her. All he could do was prepare to act. Why couldn't they all understand this?

That morning he had gotten a visit from the past.

The silver-haired man who walked into his cabin was tall and straight-backed with a weather-beaten face, accompanied by a small, gray-haired woman who was stunningly beautiful. "Grady, Bowie Rhodes," the man said.

Service said, "We're all getting gray."

Rhodes smiled. Service had met him when Rhodes was a UPI reporter in Vietnam. He and Tree had watched him trying to fish in a rice paddy that was actually a minefield and they had helped get him safely out. They had known each other for decades, though they seldom got to see each other. Rhodes had a job that was the envy of fishermen: he wrote a column for an outdoor magazine and traveled around the country doing nothing but fishing.

Tree came over and embraced Rhodes. "What it is, bro." They dapped in the elaborate Vietnam style and laughed, like the kids they had once been.

Service went outside with Rhodes. "I'm not much for giving advice," the old reporter said, "but I've been through this one."

"Ingrid," Service said. Ingrid Cashdollar had been Bowie's first wife. She had been a deputy in Luce County and Service had known her. She had been beautiful, funny, and an effective cop, and when she died it had affected a whole county, not just her husband. Since then Bowie had remarried and seemed happy with Janey.

"What you have to do is keep your mouth shut and let people do and say whatever they need to get out their feelings. The funny thing is that when a wife dies, everyone is concerned about everything except the husband."

"We weren't married."

Rhodes smiled. "Yeah, like paper matters." He fished in his pocket and held out a key. "When all the company clears away, you need to go off somewhere and be totally alone for a while. That key opens the door to a camp I have in west Chippewa County. You have to come in through Fiborn and drive ten miles up a two-track. There's a coded lock on the gate. What was your last day in Vietnam?"

"December 19," Service said. "1969."

"Okay, the lock will be coded 1219, and you have the key to the camp. There's no well or running water, and no electricity. There's heat from propane and kerosene lamps—very old-style, unheated outhouse included. The camp sits at the end of a finger in a huge swamp. Go when you want, stay as long as you need, and take in your own water. You remember Iron-head Beaudoin?"

Beaudoin had been a contemporary of his father's, also a conservation officer. "Out of Trout Lake, right?"

Rhodes nodded. "He was a pistol. He tracked a poacher named Carvolino for years. The camp is built where the old poacher's stand sat. Carvolino used Indian pulpies to haul in timber and built a cabin on state land in the swamp. Beaudoin didn't find it until after Carvolino died, and when it got logged and came up for sale, he bought it. After Ironhead passed, I bought it from his daughter."

The name Carvolino seemed familiar. "He the one—"

Rhodes interrupted him by nodding, opening his mouth and pointing a finger inside. "Carvolino used to sell buck racks to downstate sports in bars in Moran and Brevort and Trout Lake and Ozark and St. Ignace. He was a major lush, but he knew his way in the woods. Ran traplines. Come deer season he'd park his car somewhere for two weeks, walk into his hunting ground in a roundabout way, and stay until the season was over. He'd ship out the meat and racks using a sidecar that the Indians used to go back and forth to town. Beaudoin never could catch him. Just after deer season, Beaudoin's last before he retired, Carvolino and his wife had separated and he was drinking like a fish. He called her at the phone company in Iggy one morning and begged her to come back and give him another chance, but she was fed up and refused, and he said, 'Okay, then listen to this.' He put the shotgun in his mouth and squeezed it off. I think it broke Beaudoin's heart that he never pinched the guy."

Rhodes told a good yarn, and had a conservation officer's appreciation for stories.

"I'm serious, Grady—use the camp. And trust me: Over time, the pain will be replaced by scar tissue, which will thicken. It will never completely cover the wound, but it will make life tolerable."

That night there were twenty or thirty officers and friends in the cabin, but Grady Service was alone in the dark, several hundred yards away on a ridge, and when he began firing his pistol at a paper target he had tacked to a tree, several woods cops appeared, their 40-caliber SIG Sauers in hand, ready to rock and roll.

Treebone was winded from the run through the woods to the site of the gunfire. "What the hell are you *doing*, man?"

"Getting ready," Grady Service said.

"There it is," Treebone said quietly.

Service was certain that all of them understood exactly what he meant.

# 5

# Slippery Creek, Michigan
## May 3, 2004

Grady Service and Tree sat on the porch of his cabin. Newf and Cat stayed close. The sky was the color of sun-baked slate. He had found the cat years ago in a cloth bag with seven kittens someone had dumped in the creek. Why the one had survived was beyond him, but she had lived and turned into a feline misanthrope that he never got around to naming. Newf's color was brindle, an unappealing mix of brown, gray, and ocher, all slopped to-gether like cheap cake mix in a bowl. She had intelligent brown eyes and a wide black snout.

The crowds of well-wishers had dwindled. There was just the two of them, alone finally.

His watch said 2:40 P.M., but time had lost all meaning. The only num-bers registering now: Five reduced to three, death in a flash, sudden, unex-pected, too familiar, too permanent, the way he knew it best, had experienced it too many times before.

Intellectually he understood they were dead, but he was still trying to process the reality. Somebody had tried to drown Cat and she had survived. Nantz and Walter wanted only to live, but had died. It made no sense. Was God a jokester, or just an asshole?

Sadness had changed to anger. What the hell had Nantz been doing on M-35 south of Palmer, and why the hell was Walter with her when he was supposed to be at school? Something inside him kept telling him that if she had not gone down that road they would still be alive, but he knew the truth. Death came in its own time and in its own way. Nantz had wanted to be a conservation officer and had already adopted a game warden's habits. Like him, she never came home the same way. His fault! She had tried to copy a lot of his behaviors. Jesus.

For three years he had lived with Maridly Nantz as friends, lovers; they were a couple. In three years with Nantz he had almost become civilized—and even soft—but he had also been deeply and undeniably in love. Now she was gone and not coming back, and he had returned to sleeping on a thin mattress on military footlockers set end to end.

The autopsy results were still pending, and there had been no funeral service and no memorial. He refused to hear of it. When it was time, he would have them both cremated.

"You remember Erbelli?" Tree asked, and answered his own question. "One day in country, base camp, sniper round to the head. Wouldn't know him if he walked up on the porch right now. How many we lose from the company?"

"Fourteen dead."

"There it is," Treebone said. "We are born to die."

"God's will, that junk?" Service asked, feeling uncomfortable. Of all his friends, Tree was closest. They had been through the most together, including Vietnam, and Tree would be the one to try to reach out to him, toss him a net if he thought he needed it.

"Awhile back Kalina tries to get me down to the AMC, the Reverend Thelonious Jones, proprietor—Thelonious Jones of Howard, Harvard, and Jackson. He did fifteen for a plethora of transgressions, now reformed, his life an open book, all sins pronounced and denounced, can I hear an amen, *brother?*"

"You went to church?" This was a revelation. Neither he nor Tree put much stock in organized religion, but Kalina was undisputed queen of Treebone's kingdom.

"Ain't no quit in the sister. The reverend and me circled and sniffed each other and we both saw the truth of the other: two pit bulls with a philosophical fence between us, him wanting to redeem lost souls in order to redeem his own, and me wanting to go up the side of bad-ass motherfucking heads— his included."

"This story have a point?"

"Are who we are, is what it is," Tree said.

"Meaning?"

"We choose to walk through the Valley of Death, Grady. We don't have to like it but we got to keep on keepin' on."

"Trucking until we retire."

"After all the shit we've been through, a retirement ain't something to throw away, man."

"You telling me to rein it in?"

"No, man. There's got to be payback. All I'm sayin' is that payback can be in degrees—hear what I'm sayin'?"

"I hear." Grady Service had enough years of service, between the marines, state police, and DNR law enforcement to pack it in now, but he had begun to conceive of retirement in the context of Nantz and his son— not alone. Now they were gone.

"I never married her," Service said, his voice cracking.

# Slippery Creek, Michigan
## May 4, 2004

Service came back from a run and found Tree tying flies on the porch of the cabin. He was sitting next to a small man with a ruddy complexion and white hair in a buzz cut, smoking a cigar and rubbing Newf's ears.

"This is Father O'Brien," Tree announced.

"I'm not a mackerel snapper," Service greeted the man caustically.

"Call me OB," the man said. "Technically we don't have the Friday fish rule anymore, and in any event, I'm not here as a Catholic. I'm here as an informal grief counselor. Your captain suggested we talk."

Newf came over to Service and poked at his hand with her drooly snout. "So talk."

"As you reenter the melee, you're apt to carry a bit of anger, and maybe your judgment will be frayed. It helps to talk things through with somebody neutral, bounce feelings off."

Service started to object, but he held back, understood O'Brien's presence was the captain's way of gauging and monitoring his readiness. He had no choice but to go along with it. He could hear Nantz whispering, "Back off, you lummox."

"Whatever floats your boat, OB," Service said, going into the cabin. *If everyone would just leave him alone he would be fine*, he thought. Like Tree had said, no choice but to keep on keepin' on.

"Okay then," the priest said, following him. "I guess that's a good introduction. I'll leave my card with you. Feel free to call me every couple of days."

"One time better than another for you?"

"It's your choice. I'm mostly retired and my time is open."

Service turned around to face the man. "What sort of work did you do?"

"I taught psychology at Marquette University for thirty years. Also I was in the Marine Reserve as a chaplain, and served in the first Gulf War."

"Retirement a tough adjustment?"

"*All* of life's adjustments are difficult, son. Semper Fi."

"You're not gonna call him," Tree said after the man was gone.

"Back off," Grady Service said. "I don't need help."

"You mean you don't *want* help, man. We all *need* it."

"I called the funeral home today. I have to stop and sign papers tomorrow. They'll be cremated tomorrow or the next day."

"And the memorial?"

"Not yet."

"What does that mean?"

"It means not yet."

Two days later the two of them drove to the funeral home in Gladstone and picked up the ashes. They were in sturdy cardboard containers made to look like marble. They brought the ashes back to Slippery Creek and Service set them on the counter in his kitchen and broke open a bottle of Jack Daniel's. Tree would be heading back to Detroit in the morning.

Treebone held out his glass and touched Service's. "She was a fine woman, your Nantz, and Walter was a fine kid. It don't mean nothing."

This was what they had said in Vietnam every time something bad or inexplicable occurred. A drunk marine second lieutenant named Ploegstra once explained, "Think of a huge honker of a log floating down the Colorado River and on that log there's billions of pissants and each one of the little assholes thinks he's steering. It don't mean nothing."

But it did, Grady Service knew. It meant he was alone and would never again feel the soft touch of Maridly Nantz or smell her hair after she got out of the tub. And he would never again hear his son shout in triumph as he hooked a big brook trout with a fly. What it meant was that he had lost not just a lot, but everything, and that meant something. It meant that he would not rest until he figured out what the hell had happened and settled accounts. He looked over at his friend and Tree nodded. He understood.

# 7

# Marquette, Michigan
## May 19, 2004

Service sat in his captain's office.

"But she was a pilot," Grady Service insisted. "Don't you people *get* it?"

Captain Ware Grant looked across the table at him. "You *people*? Grady, pilots are not invincible," his captain said gently. "Have you got something to say to me?"

"I've been on the shelf three weeks," Service said.

"Take as long as you need," the captain said. "There's no hurry to come back."

"If I don't get back to the field, I'll go out of my mind," Service said. "You have to let me come back to work."

"You don't seem ready."

"I can't sit around. I need focus. I need my boots in the dirt, dealing with what I know best."

"We can't afford to have a loose cannon out there," his supervising officer said.

"You know me. You know that's not what I am."

"Sudden loss can induce a form of PTSD," the captain said. "Mourning can bring a severe form of the disorder."

"I lost my father suddenly. I've lost men in combat suddenly. I've lost friends suddenly—this is not something new. And, dammit, it wasn't *me* in the accident!" It was difficult to keep his voice at a reasonable level.

The captain studied him.

"We each mourn in our own way and in our own time. The aftermath of some situations is nearly as traumatic as the situation itself."

"Please, Cap'n." This was as close to pleading as Grady Service could bring himself.

The Upper Peninsula's DNR law boss took a long time to reply. "Okay, you can come back, but if you need downtime, take it. Just let me know. I won't ask questions."

"You won't be sorry," Service said.

"The night this happened, you said, 'But she's a pilot.' And you said it again today."

"She wasn't *just* a pilot, Cap'n. She was a damn good pilot, experienced. She was born to vehicles, didn't panic, kept emotional control when all hell was breaking loose. How does somebody like that lose control of a truck and hit a tree on a dry road? I haven't seen the report."

Grant reached into a neat pile of folders, extracted a stapled document, and slid it across the table. "Straight off the road, down the embankment and into the tree. The cab roof absorbed the main impact, buckled flat. The case is closed—official ruling is that it was an accident."

Grady Service had expected as much. He took the folder out to his Tahoe and drove from the pagoda-like Marquette Regional DNR building called "The Roof," over to an abandoned gravel pit on the Carp River behind Marquette Mountain. He parked in the shade and spent an hour smoking and reading and thinking, and when he was done, he decided he needed to see photographs—but not now. He didn't want to wallow in their deaths. He wanted to move on and find out *why* they were dead, and he knew that if he went back to the captain, Grant would be suspicious of his focus. Right now he was glad to have the green light to work.

One thing was for sure: He was no longer a family man. Now he had only the clan of conservation officers in gray shirts and green pants, a gigantic dog, and a bad-tempered cat. He had been left with less previously. He would make do with what remained.

# 8

# Slippery Creek, Michigan
## May 20, 2004

Today he was finally going back to work. Grady Service woke up thinking not about Maridly and Walter, but about this past Easter night when he had gotten disoriented in the dark and rain as he pursued three people illegally spearing pike at the bottom of the Stonington Peninusula. It had been raining hard, dark, air at thirty-seven degrees, and for reasons he had still not figured out, he had fallen into Wilsey Bay Creek, which was swollen with winter runoff; he had fought, but the current had swept him through a culvert. He had managed to struggle out of the water seventy-five yards downstream, his teeth broken, his pride and body bruised.

Ten days later he was sitting in an ergonomic tilt-a-chair in an oral surgeon's office in Green Bay trying to focus on a pair of blue jays feeding on a platform feeder a few feet away. There had been multiple injections of anesthetic into his gums and the roof of his mouth; his tongue felt like a burrito on steroids.

"We'll give it a few minutes," the surgeon said. Service had met him two days before, to "create an extraction plan." The male blue jay pushed the female aside and pecked her on the head.

The surgeon and his assistant returned. A tray was rotated under his chin. The doctor poked a metal instrument in his mouth: Service felt nothing. The doctor slid a mask over his nose, jacked open his jaws with clamps, and hung hissing tubes in his mouth.

"Feel anything?" the doctor asked.

His mind sorted possible answers: angst, shame over a stupid accident, the curse of poor dental genetics, gravity? What he said was, "Uh-uh."

"The gas will take you to the edge of consciousness," the oral surgeon said. "You'll be here, but not here."

Did that mean the doctor and his assistant were likewise here, but not here? Long ago he and Tree had been on a mission in Laos, watching hundreds of North Vietnamese black ants moving war materiel south along the Ho Chi Minh Trail. Publicly both countries were saying they had no troops in Laos, and Tree had whispered, "They here, but not here." That night they had sprung a brief but deadly ambush, leaving enemy bodies there that weren't there, and bugging out for their extraction point ten clicks west.

His mind would not settle into that zone where his thoughts would turn off. His girlfriend Maridly Nantz was a lot younger and had all her teeth. How would she handle a toothless boyfriend? If he was here but not here, did that mean that the teeth being pulled were not really being pulled?

"Okay," the surgeon said enthusiastically, "here we go."

We: Did the man have a mouse in his pocket?

Thirty minutes later his cheeks were distorted with cotton wads and he was biting down on sterile gauze pads as the assistant led him from the surgeon's office through the waiting room of the prosthodontist, blood on his chin, pink drool cascading. He saw Nantz watching him wide-eyed.

After another forty minutes he walked out to the truck with Nantz trying to steady him by holding his arm. He kept pulling away. The surgeon had extracted twenty-two teeth, upstairs and downstairs, and the prosthodontist had installed new false teeth, insisting as he gagged almost continuously that he would "over time" adjust to them.

"Don't smoke, and use your pain meds liberally," the prosthodontist concluded.

"You're handling this pretty well, hon," Nantz said as they got into the truck.

"Smoke," he said, staring out at the late April rain, the word feeling like a foreign object in a mouth full of foreign objects. He could not feel his tongue, lips, cheeks, jaw, most of his lower face.

"You won't be able to hold a cigarette," Nantz said. "You'll drop it and burn yourself."

"Smoke," he repeated, adding, "*Goddammit.*"

She handed him a pack, which he looked at. It was too hard, something not right.

"Candy smokes," she said. "They'll take care of your oral fixation and they can't burn you. The upside is that you don't have any teeth for the sugar to rot."

He flung the candy into the back. "Could use sympathy," he said, the multisyllabic word causing him to drool.

"That's what pain pills are for," she said.

"No pills!" he said. "*Embrace* pain."

"You *would* say that," she said, starting the engine.

*Embrace pain.* That was the thought in his mind as he climbed into his truck and started the engine, feeling here but not here. This is all you have, he told himself. Get your boots in the dirt, get it done.

# 9

# Mormon Creek, Michigan
## May 20, 2004

Nantz's last words just about every morning had been to ask if he had his teeth in. The things still felt like alien invaders in his mouth and already had drastically altered what and how he ate.

This morning he had gotten to the truck and realized the teeth were back in the cabin. He went back, fetched them, and drove off into the unknown, back at work after more than three weeks.

Grady Service parked his truck in a gap in a grove of aspens, grabbed his ruck, silently closed the doors, locked them, and started hiking west. He considered leaving the false teeth in the truck, but on the long shot that he might encounter someone, he left the diabolical pieces of shit in. The public might be unhinged by the visage of a toothless game warden. The sky was gray and threatening, the air heavy. As he crossed through a cedar swamp he detected movement. It was a deer, a ribby buck, one-inch nubbins of antlers in coppery green velvet, its hide still winter-gray when it ought to be reddening for summer.

A two-year-old, he guessed, standing beside a puddle of black swamp water, its legs splayed apart, ears droopy, muzzle in the water. Service passed within ten feet of the animal, which ignored him and continued to drink. Come spring and early summer, deer were often bold, their interest in food after a tough winter overriding any inborn fear of humans.

There had been neither an unusually deep snowpack over winter, nor abundant spring rain, and what snowpack they did have had melted off slowly, leaving no floods. Even with a workable water level in Mormon Creek, a lot of the local trout-takers and most old-timers wouldn't venture out to dunk red worms and crawlers until after Independence Day. Rivers were usually fishable before the Memorial Day weekend, but locals waited to fish until blackflies were on the wane. Never mind that trout fishing with flies was far better in May and June when hendricksons, brown drakes, and giant hexagenia were hatching. There were few Yooper fly fishers and even fewer catch-and-release types. Up here it was catch-and-release into grease, and once a tradition took hold, it was difficult to change the mindset, especially for na-tives who believed all fish and game that inhabited the peninsula were their personal birthright. At best, Service knew, he might encounter some hardy down- or out-stater after brookies. Most dedicated fly fishers in the U.P. were elderly males, twenty to thirty years his senior. For some reason flies had not caught on with his generation, and he had never understood why.

It still amazed him the lengths to which some brook trout chasers would go in search of a species of fish where eighteen inches was a lifetime trophy in Michigan. It amazed him, but it didn't surprise him, because serious brook trout fishers knew that the further you hiked off the grid, the better the fishing was likely to be. Chasing trout, he had decided a long time ago, was a lot like being a game warden. If you kept too close to the easy marks, you missed the good cases, and the bigger fish. The worst poachers, like the best trout, had to be hunted in their natural habitat, which was neither easy to get to, nor particularly hospitable after you reached it. Good game wardens and successful trouters learned how to ignore pain and discomfort to do the job, no matter what.

Because of the state's law enforcement manpower shortage, he had, since the first of the year, continued to double as a detective for Wildlife Re-sources Protection, the Department of Natural Resource's statewide investi-gatory unit, as well as handling slices of Marquette, Delta, Schoolcraft, and Alger counties in a more-traditional game warden role. It felt good to be back doing what he knew best, but all winter his gut had churned with foreboding, a feeling that something terrible was looming. Even in the wake of the deaths of Maridly and Walter, the feeling persisted. What could be worse than los-ing the two people who mattered most to you? *Don't think about it*, he told himself. *Keep your mind in the game.*

It had been several years since he had been into the Mormon Creek mead-ows area where the old Civilian Conservation Corps camp had once stood. As he passed it he thought about the Creekateers, a jug band made up of CCC men back in the late thirties. Why had he thought of this? He had never actu-ally seen or even heard the band, only of them—and only from his father and his hard-drinking cronies. It struck him as odd to think of something his father liked. For the most part he rarely thought about his old man, had no reason to. *Don't let your mind wander, asshole*, he lectured himself again.

The old camp was only a few miles north of Nahma Junction and US 2. Mormon Creek originated in a swampy marsh south of Lost Lake and flowed south for a mile or so before sharply turning east to dump into the Sturgeon River. All that remained of the camp was a crumbling stone foundation, spackled by patches of scratchy gray-green lichen. There were no vehicles parked along the way, and this allowed him to concentrate less on violators and more on fishing possibilities.

He liked what he saw, and cut southwest on foot down to the creek and made his way across squishy, bouncy, sphagnum moss meadows toward the headwaters, more interested in what bugs might be hatching than in any major expectation of encountering fishermen. He used a small digital thermometer to check the water temperature: fifty-seven degrees, just about perfect for brook trout. And it was unseasonably clear if you ignored the tannin that stained the water the color of liquid rust year-round.

Most trees had some new leaves, but serious foliage was still to come. The sticky May air was in the low seventies, and the humidity brought forth blackflies that landed on his hands and neck looking for places to nail him. Unless the area got significant rain soon, the fire danger was going to soar, and with the state's severely pinched budget, there were fewer fire officers to manage the blazes. Service wondered if this summer would be spent more on fire lines than regular law enforcement duties. Nantz had been a fire officer when he met her. "Stop it!" he said out loud.

When it began to drizzle he hoped it would continue, and when he heard thunder rattling to the west he smiled and returned his attention to the water. This time of year fish were starved from the long winter, and thunderstorms seemed to turn them on—until the storm got overhead. If the wind stayed down after the storm passed, the fish would start eating again. He took comfort in knowing the cycles and moods of fish and other creatures. Knowing such things helped him to find violators and poachers, who often also knew the same things.

He stopped below a riffle in the narrow, meandering creek, hunkered down, lit a cigarette, and watched and listened to the softly chuckling water. The rain was light, the thunder distant, and he guessed the cell would pass north of him, which would be good for fishing. Caddisflies began to emerge and frantically pop through the surface film. A few flies were soon followed by a steady flow of bugs, and as some of the insects got trapped in the surface film, trout began to rise and slurp cripples for quick meals. Because caddis tended to emerge from the nymphal stage to dun, and hatch more energetically than mayflies, trout tended to go after them aggressively. It was like mealtime in a boardinghouse: Grab fast or go hungry. More than once he had seen trout come entirely out of the water, taking such bugs in splashy somersaults.

Squatting beside Mormon Creek watching trout feeding on small black caddis, he reminded himself he could be content doing this for the rest of his life. He loved being a conservation officer, and after his unexpected and unwanted promotion to detective, he felt he was adjusting to the new job and learning to enjoy it, but he didn't need work to define himself. He knew that if the job ended tomorrow he'd be content wandering the Upper Peninsula's hundreds of miles of beaver ponds, pothole lakes, streams, and rivers, searching for brook trout. Being alone in the middle of nowhere was one of the greatest gifts of both his vocation and avocation, and he appreciated the solace and the silence. He could heal out here.

Tree had once told him he'd been born two hundred years late. They had been on a fifteen-day recon in the tri-border area at the time, a place cluttered with triple canopy jungle, plastic-wrap humidity, swarms of carnivorous insects, bad water, poisonous snakes, smells only maggots could embrace, and trigger-happy Pathet Lao and North Vietnamese Army regulars.

"You get off on this shit," Tree had said. "And that ain't normal."

It was not so much that he got off on it as he knew what his job was, and had the freedom to do it. Service smiled at the memory. Tree had grown up in the city, but he was a natural outdoors, and if not for keeping peace on the home front, he'd still be humping the woods as a CO and complaining about how much he hated it. The two of them shared a passion for fly fishing and brook trout.

When the caddis hatch began to wane, Service continued downstream, careful to watch where he put his feet lest he drop into a sinkhole or through one of the quivering, porous humps of muskeg tussocks that covered the meadows and lined the banks. The footing only looked solid, a potentially lethal illusion; it was strictly veneer over bottomless, frigid black loon shit.

A half-hour after the caddis petered out, a few dark hendrickson mayflies began to rise and the fish, which took a while to catch on to what was happening, eventually noticed and began to rise steadily along the length of a long, curving dark slick with dense logjams and thick tag alder cover on both sides. Because of the state's budget crisis, all conservation offices were working 80 hours every two-week pay period, but being paid only for 76. And, like every state employee, every so often they were taking unpaid furlough days off, accumulating 104 unpaid hours over the year, which could be taken as vacation, or banked for retirement when it would then be reimbursed. *If* the state could afford to pay then, a big *if* in the minds of many state employees, who dutifully took orders from elected politicians, but rarely trusted them.

Like social security, the state's future fiscal health was anything but secure. The budget crisis had been brought on by recently departed governor Samuel Adams Bozian, who had decimated the state, hit term limits, and moved on to greener, higher-paying private-sector pastures. Few people other than hard-core Republicans regretted Bozian's departure, and although

Democrat Lorelei Timms had been easily elected over a Bozian protégé, she remained unproven and was starting deep in a hole, with a helluva steep hill facing her.

Service's next furlough period would be on the weekend, and with two regular pass days tacked on, he would have four days to spend with Nantz and not think about anything except fishing and each other. He corrected himself. He would be *alone* for the furlough. He could no longer allow himself to think in terms of *they*. Life was reduced to him and the job. Still, this was a very sweet-looking spot, and probably tomorrow night there would be a spinner fall at dusk—if the wind didn't come up or the temperature drop precipitously. Most mayflies lived only forty-eight to seventy-two hours, and if they didn't mate and the females deposit their eggs, the whole purpose of their short lives was wasted. He could understand their desire to get on with their biological imperative. He sometimes thought his own drive to defend natural resources was biologically driven. Certainly he was no less zealous than his old man, who had been a CO before him. The difference was that the old man was rarely sober, and it had cost him his life. *Jesus!* Nantz and Walter. Why? Goddammit, why had she gone to Houghton and come back through Palmer? And why the hell had Walter been with her?

He was tempted to contemplate life from the perspective of an insect, but decided against it. Life was life: You got what you were born into. If there was a God, did he choose which spirits would be bugs or humans? The Indians believed that all things, animate and inanimate, had spirits, which he thought probably meant souls. Certainly, all living things were part of the cycle of life and death—but rocks? This was the problem with codified religions. When you began to try to dissect them in detail, they didn't quite work, and invariably that's when the most fervent types went to their fallback: You just have to believe—to take things on faith. He wasn't one to blindly accept anything on hope alone. He conceded that he could be deceiving himself, but he had also concluded over more than fifty years of life that a man made his own opportunities and luck, and if not, it helped to think so. Was this faith or hubris? He didn't know. Had Nantz made her own bad luck? He could not, would not believe this. No way. She was the *best*.

Why was he thinking about such things? After his divorce from his first wife, Bathsheba, he had gone through a series of girlfriends and had never felt a particular urge to remarry, much less to father children—until Maridly Nantz. She had been scheduled to enter the DNR academy in October with the goal of becoming a conservation officer. Last year's session had been cancelled because of the state budget crisis, and Nantz had gone through the roof. Her raw emotional outbursts made him wonder how she—*they*—would handle it if the academy got cancelled again. Worrying about others was *not* the sort of thing he had given much thought to in the past. Now it didn't matter.

The mercurial Nantz's interests and aspirations had become as compelling as his own. She was the major change and force in his life, even more than finding out he had a son. For the first time in his life he learned what it meant to put someone else's needs before his own. He didn't think much about love or what it meant: It just felt right, and this had sufficed. Love persisted; objects of that love did not.

He checked his watch. Time to move down the creek, cross out to the road, and get back to his truck. There was almost continuous thunder to the north, and he could see shafts of sunlight piercing the dark clouds, what his old man had called "devil's smiles." The rain was beginning to pick up, which suggested the storm cell was closing.

After fifty yards of stumbling, he decided he'd followed the meandering stream long enough. He looked for the nearest high ground and started directly for it. As he got close to the cedars he thought he saw a flash of light to his left and above. He flinched, thought his heart skipped a beat, nearly threw himself on his face, waiting for the inevitable thunder, but heard only the steady patter of soft rain and saw no more light. What the hell had it been? He sniffed the air. No ozone, which meant the strike, if there had been one, had not been that close. Still, the light had the suddenness and intensity of a close strike, and he was virtually exposed in the open, a perfect target. There was no point bending over to lower his profile. He did not move for nearly a minute, then eased up his binoculars and scanned the tree line for nearly five more minutes. Maybe there had been a light flash, maybe not. It could have been a play of light from the instable sky, or an animal's movement. Why had he overreacted? Weird. Whatever had been there was gone, and he had a long walk back to the truck. A black bear possibly, more likely a deer. Young bears were out scavenging and does were throwing fawns, the whitetails not that long out of their winter yards and still dispersing, some of them en route to their summer ranges up to fifty miles away. Come fall they would reverse course and seek denser winter thermal cover and the sparse food of cedar and spruce swamps.

He smiled as he moved. The backcountry: There was always something new to be experienced, and often it was inexplicable. The forest was an unnerving venue for people with fecund imaginations. The rain was softer now, something between a drizzle and mist. The main cell, he saw, was moving north of him. *Good fishing,* he told himself.

All officers were taught and encouraged to hide their trucks a good distance from where they intended to go, but Service tended to dump his vehicle further away than most, believing that the further away you were, the less chance you had of being detected by shitballs. Some violators used scouts to patrol roads and search for game wardens' vehicles, and with the advent of CBs, cell phones, and other radio systems, instantaneous communications was becoming the rule rather than the exception for habitual violators. A good game warden had to be willing to walk, and put his boots in dirt, mud, ice, and snow, and Service took pride in being a damn good game warden. *Maybe too much pride*, he chastised himself.

He diverted toward the area where he thought he had seen the light and began playing with the ear mike, which was irritating his ear. He was still skeptical about the devices Michigan conservation officers had recently been ordered to use, and more than anything he was constantly picking at his ear, trying to make the damn thing comfortable. Between false teeth and the ear mike, he felt anything but comfortable. He was becoming a damned android, more technology than human. He had heard that some downstate districts had told their officers to forget the new devices, but he wasn't ready to give up on it quite yet. Naturally, younger officers—Generation X or Y or whatever the hell they were being called now, those from the Nintendo generation— embraced any and all new technology, but Service thought it made game wardens look like they were playing at being Secret Service agents or James Bond wannabes. He had the microphone rigged under his shirt, and in order to transmit, he had only to press his hand to his heart. It seemed silly, but he knew there would be times when having silent radio contact and two free hands would be a good thing—*if* he could make it less annoying, Or he could stuff it in his ruck. But he had kept his teeth in and they were uncomfortable. Better to gut it out, try to adjust.

"Twenty Five Fourteen, do you have TX?" a voice asked over the 800-megahertz radio. He had it turned down and didn't catch the caller's code. He glanced at the digital display on top of the 800 stuck in its belt holster and saw he was on the district's channel.

"Twenty Five Fourteen is out of vehicle, TX in fifteen minutes," he said, touching his chest, adding, "Twenty Five Fourteen clear." He had left his cell phone in the truck. Even there he'd be lucky to get a signal. There were vast reaches of the U.P. where cell phones refused to operate with any regularity, and other places where they would not work at all.

He heard the cell phone buzzing as he unlocked the Tahoe, unclipped the tiny phone from the sun visor, and flipped it open to activate it.

"Grady? Lorne O'Driscoll."

"Chief." O'Driscoll led the Law Enforcement Division for the Michigan Department of Natural Resources Law Enforcement Division in Lansing.

Why the hell was the chief calling *him*? He had already called several times to express condolences and check on him. Enough was enough.

"Where are you?" O'Driscoll asked.

Service toyed with a smart-ass answer and rejected it; the chief was a good man, but a stickler for professional communications etiquette. "Uh, eastern Delta County—more or less." Hell, if the chief had the Automatic Vehicle Locator up on his computer screen, he could damn well *see* where he was—to within 25 meters of accuracy.

"We need for you to get over to Florence, Wisconsin. Check in with Special Agent T. R. Monica at the Florence Natural Resources and Wild Rivers Interpretation Center. It's a half-mile west of town at the intersection of US 2 and Highways 70/101; got it?"

The term *special agent* usually added up to one thing. "Feebs, sir?"

"That's affirmative. You'll be there in a consulting role. The order comes directly from the governor's office. Your mission is to remain with them until they kick you loose."

*Just great*, Service thought. "When?" he asked. A consultant to the FBI? *It sounded like a goat rodeo in the making*, he told himself. It figured that the governor was interfering in his life, but he kept this to himself. Governor Timms had been a good friend of Nantz's. He'd already received the expected condolence call from her. He had been through Florence before and knew where the center was. CO Simon del Olmo in Crystal Falls often worked closely with a Wisconsin warden from Florence County. Service had met the man several times, once at the center, where he maintained a satellite office. Florence was about ten miles due south of Crystal Falls. He had a Wisconsin map book somewhere in his truck, and he eyeballed the backseat, but couldn't see it.

"Get there ASAP. I assume you're rolling," the chief said. "Check in as you can. Any questions?"

"Nine thousand and hundred and twenty-two," Service quipped, aiming his vehicle south toward US 2.

"Join the club," the chief said.

"Sir, I've got two furlough days this weekend."

"Negative. You're working and the feds are paying for your time."

The state budget was in bad shape. If there was a chance to pick up reimbursement from the feds, O'Driscoll would jump on it. The order to join the FBI was mostly about money, he concluded.

He was about to pull away when he thought about the deer he had seen earlier. Something had registered vaguely as not being right with the animal, but he had been anxious to get to the creek and had shrugged it off. He got out of the truck and went back to where he had seen the deer and found it in the same place, still drinking—and urinating at the same time.

"Oh boy," he said out loud. The department and the state's 800,000 licensed hunters were worried about Chronic Wasting Disease moving into the state from Wisconsin and devastating Michigan's herd. So far CWD had not been detected here, but all officers had been briefed on symptoms, and this animal was showing some of the classics: spread legs, droopy ears, no fear, constant thirst, and urination. He trotted back to the truck and got on the cell phone.

It was answered after two rings. "Wildlife, Beal."

Buster Beal was a biologist in the Escanaba office, a man who loved white-tailed deer, took care of the herd as a sacred responsibility, and killed them with equal fervor during rifle and archery seasons. Beal was well over six foot, burly and hairy and known throughout the DNR as Chewy, after the hirsute *Star Wars* character.

"Chewy, it's Grady."

"You find me a big boy?" Beal expected calls from COs who saw large bucks and most of them complied. "I'm up near Mormon Creek. I've got a buck here, spread legs, droopy ears, doesn't seem the least bit bothered by me, and he's drinking and pissing at the same time."

"Oh, man," Buster Beal keened. "Shit, fuck, shit."

"Hey, I'm not giving it a label; I'm just reporting what I see. How do you want me to play it?"

"Wait for me," Beal said. "I'll be in my truck in thirty seconds, there in thirty minutes."

Service explained his current location. "I'll move my truck, meet you where Mormon is cut by the forest service road, but you've got to step on it, Chewy. I just had a call from my command and I have to get somewhere posthaste."

"Sit tight," the biologist said. "Neither of us wants the first case of you-know-what in the state to be on our watch." Last year Michigan had sold 800,000 hunting licenses, and this money, and that spent by hunters, remained a major plus in the state's crippled economy. Even so, there were fewer hunters every year. Not long ago the state was selling more than 1.5 million licenses every year.

The biologist was there in less than thirty minutes, his face red with excitement and nerves. Service led him back to where he had parked earlier and walked him to the deer, which had not moved. They stood six feet away and Beal observed for a couple of minutes until he shook his head and said, "Still in its winter coat."

"What do you want to do?" Service asked.

"Well, if it's you-know-what, the animal hasn't started to waste. He's thin, but coming out of winter, that's not abnormal. But we need to play this safe. You want to put it down?"

Service took out his 40-caliber SIG Sauer and walked over to the deer. Beal told him to wait, ran back to his truck, and returned quickly with a blue plastic tarp and a box of disposable latex gloves.

"Not the brain," Beal said. "Pop the heart. I want the brain and spinal column tissue in good shape. And don't put him down in the water. Let's limit blood loss just to be safe."

Beal waded into the water beside the deer and poked it with a stick, but the animal refused to move. Finally he had to put both hands on its back haunches and shove. Only then did it reluctantly stumble up to higher ground, its ears finally perking up, its movement still clumsy and uncoordinated.

Service took aim and fired. The animal collapsed, kicked once, lay still.

The biologist handed him latex gloves and the two of them pulled the animal onto the tarp and dragged it back to the biologist's truck, where they loaded it in the bed.

"You gonna send it to a lab?" Service asked. The state wildlife laboratory was in Rose Lake, just north of Lansing.

"After I take a good look for myself. Let's don't get too many bowels in an uproar over this," the biologist said. "There are several diseases that present similar symptoms, and coming out of winter yards, most deer are not at their best."

Service knew the biologist was trying to think positively.

"Well, if it turns out to be bad news, we've at least got a governor who won't sit on her ass," the biologist added. "Lori's got the best interests of sportsmen and resources at the center of things."

Service shared the biologist's opinion. Despite Republicans calling her Limousine Lori, the governor was a lifelong hunter and sportswoman. Shortly after taking office Governor Timms had transferred responsibility for the inspection of commercial put-and-take game farms with captive elk, deer, and more exotic animal populations from the department of agriculture to the DNR. It previously had been the DNR's responsibility until Governor Sam Bozian suddenly reassigned part of it to Ag, a move which had upset sportsmen and conservationists alike. Now it fell to conservation officers to inspect the state's nearly eight hundred game farms and operations, and being so short of people, this was pulling officers away from other law enforcement duties. Time management issues aside, the governor's decision had been the right one, and he was hearing from other officers that at least half of the game operations were out of compliance with the most essential regulations.

Service knew a necropsy had to be done—and fast. The outbreak in Wisconsin was thought by some to have originated with animals, probably elk on a cheesehead commercial game farm—animals allegedly imported from Colorado, which reportedly had been infected by Canadian imports. The whole thing with fenced-in hunt clubs and game farms bugged Service. They were playgrounds for the lazy and well heeled—a quick way to bag a trophy if you had the cash, but no time for a real hunt outside the enclosures.

The two men discarded their rubber gloves in a white plastic pail in the rear of the biologist's truck and headed their separate ways. Service had a hard time shaking the image of the strange-acting deer. He did not enjoy putting any animal down, but this was necessary. The first one he'd had to dispatch had been during his first year near Newberry. An elderly man had called during the summer to report that a deer had been hit by a car. Service's sergeant suggested the man shoot the animal to put it out of its misery, but the man wasn't a hunter, didn't own a gun, and said he couldn't kill anything. Service was sent to handle it.

The old man came out of the house to greet him and led him to the big doe, which had two broken forelegs and was entangled in an old wire fence. Service told the man he didn't have to watch, but the man insisted on staying. Service took aim with his .44 and tried to neatly clip the animal's spinal column just behind the head. Result: It began to thrash.

The old man, who was wearing white slacks and a long-tailed white shirt said, "Oh my."

Service took aim a second time, and fired into the deer's skull. Suddenly the air was awash with fine pink mist and the old man was gasping and saying, "Oh dear God . . . oh God!"

Both of them were covered with blood. Apparently the first shot had caused extensive bleeding into the ears of the animal, which had filled like cups. When Service fired the second round, the animal's head had snapped sideways, showering both of them. Since then he had learned to be more efficient, and over the years he had killed so many animals with potential and actual problems that he normally didn't even think about them afterwards. It still irked him, however, when someone brought up the story of his "red raindeer." COs were fond of repeating stories about other COs' screwups.

# 10

# Florence County, Wisconsin
## May 20, 2004

Grady Service kept most of his equipment in his unmarked Tahoe, including a couple of changes of work clothes. As a detective he operated mostly in the western half, but sometimes across the entire Upper Peninsula, which was the size of Vermont and New Hampshire combined, and larger than Delaware. Despite making it home most nights, there had been times when he had to sleep in his vehicle somewhere in the woods.

The chief had made it clear that he was to get over to Wisconsin PDQ, but no way was he going until he stopped at home in Gladstone to see Nantz. He punched in the speed dial on the cell phone, caught the mistake, and flipped the phone closed. He deleted the speed-dial numbers for Maridly and Walter and lectured himself to stay focused. *Stop feeling so damn sorry for yourself*, he thought as he drove out to US 41 and headed south toward Escanaba.

A gray-black Humvee coated with red-gray dust was parked in the lot behind the interpretive center, which was jointly run by the U.S. Forest Service, the Wisconsin DNR, and Florence County, a three-way marriage that sounded to him like a bureaucratic management stretch. There were two men in the vehicle. Service eased alongside the Humvee, got out, stretched, and showed his credentials to one of them. "Special Agent Monica?"

The man studied the credentials and pointed. "Go seven miles west on Wisconsin Seventy, turn south across the ditch at Lilah Oliver Grade Road. There's a gate there. Check in with the agents. I'll let them know you're calling."

Service thanked the man, pulled onto highway W-70, and headed west, passing a billboard, black type on a white background: IF YOU'RE AGAINST LOGGING, TRY WIPING WITH PLASTIC. There was a yellow steel tube gate across the road and behind it, a dusty gray Crown Victoria with two men in it. They let him pull up to the gate, got out, looked at his credentials, and manually swung open the yellow gate. "Command Post's a couple miles in," one of the men said. "They're expecting you."

The road was deeply rutted, the area recently logged, with twenty-foot-high stacks of maple and assorted hardwoods piled neatly along the two-track, bark chips scattered all over the road like confetti. Discarded beer and pop cans twinkled with reflected light on the edges of the road. The forest in the area was thick. Along the way he saw two red logging rigs nosed into the tree lines.

There could be only one reason the FBI would be set up so far out in the boonies: They had a crime on their hands, and no doubt a crime scene nearby as well. An unmarked navy blue panel truck was snugged close to a copse of birch trees where a camouflaged plastic tarp had been strung to create shade. Service parked and walked toward a group of people under the tarp. A crude, hand-painted slab of quarter-inch plywood nailed to a nearby tree read BEER, WEED, GAS, OR ASS — NO ONE RIDES FREE. *Life at its most basic*, he thought. The sign wasn't new, and suggested that the logging company's gate was ineffectual in deterring visitors, especially kids who obviously used the area as a party spot. As any soldier, border guard, and game warden knew, outdoor security was impossible unless you had the rare perfect terrain and a lot of bodies in the security detail.

A dark-haired woman with a prominent nose got up. She had short black hair and dense black hair on her arms. She wore khaki pants and sleeveless black body armor over an open-collar, short-sleeved polo shirt. A badge dangled from a navy blue cord around her neck. "Detective Service?" she asked.

"Special Agent T. R. Monica?"

"Tatie," she said, adding, "Follow me." She led him to the panel truck, slid open the massive door, and nodded for him to step inside. He could hear a generator humming softly. The cramped interior was filled with banks of communications equipment; the air was cool. "Take a seat," the agent said, nudging a wheeled stool over to him with her boot.

She opened a blue-and-white cooler and took out two bottles of beer. "It's sticky out there," she said, pushing a longneck Pabst Blue Ribbon at him.

"No thanks. I'm working," he said. "Tatie?"

She smiled. "When I was a kid, all I wanted to eat were potatoes: fried, boiled, baked, you name it—like that Bubba dude and his shrimp in *Forrest Gump*? You don't drink when you work, or is it my brand?"

He shook his head and wondered what this was about. She had a soft air to her, but a commanding, slightly imposing voice. She was also slender and obviously long shed of her childhood starch fixation.

"At ease," the agent said, opening her beer and taking a long pull.

Service ignored his beer.

"Is it because of your father?" she asked.

"Is *what* because of my father?"

"Your not drinking on duty."

"It's because that's the rule." What the hell did she know about his father, and why? He felt his blood pressure rise, took a deep breath, and tried to adjust his breathing.

"It's my understanding that you're sort of a cookbook Catholic when it comes to rules," she said.

"Whatever," he said, not wanting a confrontation, but if she kept this up she might get one. This gig was starting off oddly and he sensed it was not going to improve.

Special Agent Monica leaned back. "I heard you can be pretty tight-lipped," she said. "This isn't a deposition. We're on the same team."

"I don't know what *this* is. My chief told me to report and here I am," he said.

She tilted her head, sizing him up. "I take it you've had some less-than-satisfactory experiences with the Bureau?"

"Mixed," he answered, adding, "at best."

She smiled. "I'd hate to depose you," she said.

"So don't," he said. "What's this about?"

"I say again, we—you and I, all the people here—are on the same team, Detective. You are a federal deputy, correct?"

She was well briefed. "All of our officers who work state or international border counties are deputized," he said. This had taken place just more than a year ago. Anyone committing a game violation in one state and crossing the border of another state in possession of illegal game was in violation of the Federal Lacey Act. Being deputized as feds gave COs the authority to pursue them. Deputization was also supposed to enhance cooperation with the U.S. Fish and Wildlife Service, the federal agency Michigan's DNR was most likely to interface with. The implication for cooperation with and by the USFS, FBI, BATF, and an alphabet soup of other federal agencies, remained a question mark. From experience he knew that major policy farts of this kind often required glacially calibrated clocks to gauge results, by which time the rules would no doubt change again.

Special Agent Monica reached into a black leather portfolio, pulled out a Temporary FBI ID card on a black lanyard, and set it on the table. "Wear this at all times around here. If you see somebody without one, make them show one to you, or put their face in the dirt—and yell for help. The only leaks out of this outfit will be the ones we choose to make for tactical reasons," she declared.

He looked at the identification badge. It was his photo. How did she get it so fast? The chief had left him with the impression that this was a chop-chop deal, but her having his photo suggested something very different, and he was suspicious.

"I'm sure you've got a lot of questions," she said, "but bear with me for a while, and for God's sake, drink a beer." She snapped off the cap for him and pushed the bottle closer. "Your father was a game warden," she said. "He was killed in the line of duty."

"He was a game warden who died while he was drunk on duty," Service said.

"But the state honored him as a hero," she countered.

He nodded. "He liked to stop and schmooze violets," he said. "The state didn't talk about that part."

"Violets?" she said with a puzzled look.

"Violators."

She smiled. "That's what all effective cops do," she said. "You don't drink with your . . . violets?" She seemed amused by the term.

"No," he said.

Agent Monica cocked her head slightly. "What did you think of your father?"

Service stiffened. "I didn't come here to have my head shrunk." First the shrinky-dink priest, now her. *Jesus.*

"I promise not to shrink it," she said. "But I do want to dig around in there—if you don't mind."

"I do mind," he said.

"In your place, I would too," she said sympathetically. "You've worked with Wisconsin warden Wayno Ficorelli."

Wayno. "Once."

"Your opinion of him?"

"Is he up for a federal job or something?"

"Just answer the question, okay?" Like most feds, Agent Monica was an adept interviewer, accomplished at deflecting and maintaining control.

"Wayno is smart, dedicated, and determined."

She raised an eyebrow. "When did you work with him?"

"Last fall." Time tended to lose meaning for game wardens, and the older he got, the worse the time dislocation seemed to get.

"Just that once?"

"Right."

"Contact since?"

"Now and then."

"About other cases?" she asked.

"It's none of your business," he said. There was a smugness—or something—in her attitude that was beginning to really rub him the wrong way.

*Hmmm,* her lips said.

He sensed she wouldn't let up. "He wanted a job in Michigan."

"Why?" she asked.

"Wisconsin wardens aren't fully empowered peace officers."

"Have you encouraged him?"

"No, and I haven't discouraged him either."

"Why not?"

"I don't take positions in hiring decisions unless I'm tasked to do background checks."

"What was your opinion of him?"

"Smart, dedicated, and determined," he said.

"You already told me that. Is there something else?"

"No."

"Let me add something," Monica said. "He's a pathological ass-man."

"If you say so." *What the hell was going on?* Service could feel the hairs standing up on his arms.

"I do say so, and by all reports, marital status hasn't ever been an issue for him."

"Why ask me?"

"Have you ever gotten mixed up with married women?"

"Only my wife," he said, "and that's none of your goddamn business." Why all these questions? She was beginning to really piss him off.

"That would be your ex, who died on 9/11 in Pennsylvania," she said. "I'm sorry for your loss."

"I bet," he said. Jesus, did she know his entire life history? *Then she must know about Nantz and Walter,* he thought. He felt his face flush and started to stand, but she reached out and grasped his arm.

"Wayno Ficorelli is dead," she said.

Service stared at her, trying to comprehend. "When?"

"A little more than forty eight hours ago."

All the questions she had been asking were driving at something. "You think I know something about it?"

"Do you?"

"Don't be an asshole!" he snapped, standing up and telling himself if she shot off her mouth one more time, he was going to bury a fist in it.

"Have you ever lied to your violets?" Agent Monica asked.

What the hell was she trying to get at?

"When necessary," he said.

"Sit down," she said. "Please."

He sat. "How did Wayno die?"

She pondered this for a moment. "He was executed."

Service stared at her. Executed? "What the fuck does that mean?"

She said, "You have the reputation of being an extraordinarily skilled and aggressive officer."

"Do I?"

"Don't jerk me around. You're a loaded gun on bad guys. You've been wounded in the line of duty, both in the marines and as a game warden. Did Ficorelli mistreat prisoners and suspects?"

"Not that I saw," Service said.

"You and Ficorelli are a lot alike—except for a predilection for married women."

"Look," he said, trying to tamp down his rage, "I was ordered to come over here and cooperate. I didn't come here to get mind-fucked."

"Good," the agent said. "Just calm down and cooperate. I sense that you're not surprised someone killed him."

"I'm not happy about it, but I guess I'm not all that surprised. Wayno could push pretty hard."

"He stretched the envelope and made some enemies," she said.

"I worked with him just once, but I suspected he pissed off a whole lot of people."

"Which he surely did," she said. "Did you know that his second cousin is Wisconsin's attorney general?"

"No."

"Apparently Wayno talked to his cousin about you a lot. He said you were the best officer he'd ever worked with. He held you in the highest regard, Detective Service."

Service wasn't sure what to say.

"I want you to see something," she said. There was a video monitor on a table next to them, and she turned it on.

Service watched a series of digital photos, walked over to the door, and stepped outside, gasping for air. He had never seen anything so grotesque. The FBI agent was right on his heels as he fumbled to light a cigarette.

"You okay?" she asked.

"Fine."

"Have you ever seen anybody killed that way?"

He shook his head.

"Ever *hear* of anybody killed like that? In Vietnam, maybe?"

"No." Although the Viet Cong and North Vietnamese had done heinous things to people they got their hands on. He had seen too many instances of that, and had worked to erase the memories.

"You've got a reputation for locating hard-to-find people," she said.

"Most of the ones I find are dead by the time I get to them," he said.

"The nature of the search-and-rescue beast," she said softly. "Why don't you come back inside and sit down?"

"Are you going to tell me what this is all about?"

"I said I would."

Service took a slug of beer while she turned on a laptop computer and swiveled it toward him. "PowerPoint," she said. "Watch it all the way through and then we'll talk."

There was no narration. On many of the slides there were no photos, only names, dates, and locations. The first sequence ran from 1950 to 1970, followed by a gap of twelve years, then a new batch replete with crime scene photos, dates, names, and causes of death. The bodies in the second group since 2000 were mutilated like Ficorelli's. Until then the cause of death varied. The program ended with Wayno's death photo.

"What is this?" Service asked, looking away from the laptop with the photos of mutilated bodies.

"It's called a blood eagle. The Vikings used it on some of their . . . favored captives."

"Vikings."

"Yeah, Norsemen—Skandahoovians with attitude. They'd split open a captive's back to expose the spine. Then they'd hack through the back ribs, pull the lungs through, and drape them over his back. Some historians vehemently insist Vikings never did such things, that such reports were the creative inventions of Christian-centric chroniclers with political agendas, but the term 'blood eagle' exists in all the old Norse languages, and there are descriptions and drawings by Viking writers," said Agent Monica. "Some contend that exposing the lungs let the dead man's air flow out to be inhaled by those standing close to him, and if he had been especially valiant, his bravery would flow to them. Sometimes the exposed lungs flapped as they expelled air, and that's where the eagle part comes from. As far as we know, the Vikings didn't remove the eyes the way our guy has. Comments?"

"This is . . ." he started to say, but didn't finish.

"It's worse," she said. "It's said they usually did this while the victim was still alive, and sometimes they poured salt into the open wounds. Shall I proceed?"

Grady Service sucked in a deep breath and closed his eyes. Had Wayno been alive? He didn't want to think about it, and he didn't ask.

"The toll in the first go-round was twenty-seven game wardens in twenty-five states over twenty years—better than one a year."

"But it started again?" he said.

"After a hiatus of a dozen years, which we don't understand; but it's been steady since then, one a year, one in 2000, one in 2001, but two in '02, two in '03, and Wayno so far this year. The blood eagle has been the MO since 2000."

Service thought about the photos. "What about the eyes?"

"The killer started taking them in 2001—another change."

Two different killers—two separate groups of killings? "Copycat?" Service asked.

"That's one school of thought," Agent Monica answered, with a tone suggesting it wasn't her view. "Could be the killer was out of circulation during that time, out of the country, in a lockup or loony bin, or maybe he gave it up for Lent, but fell off the wagon. We just don't know," she said. "All we do know is that somebody has been killing game wardens all around the United States since 1950."

He couldn't believe what she was telling him. "I've never heard anything about this. How can game wardens be murdered around the country and nobody know about it? How can *game wardens* not know?"

"Because nobody detected a connection or saw the pattern until three years ago. Think about it. You kill one warden in a state at a rate of less than one a year, and each in a different way, and who would put it all together? Cops, like politicians, tend to think locally, and federal and state computers still don't talk to each other very effectively. Before 9/11 they didn't talk at all.

"In the latter part of the second group we had a common and spectacular MO, but the vicks in the first group were all done differently. The common denominator is that the victims are all game wardens, and it's been one per state, all of them found by water in relatively obscure, but open areas," said the agent. "Obviously we recognized we had a serial with the second batch. An analyst was first to see the pattern and bring it forward. The same analyst then went back in time and found the first group. The method was different in most of the early murders, and the way they were spread out, there were no statistical or geographic clusters to work with. If the killer hadn't started up again, we never would have known about the first group."

"But now they're all the blood eagle," Service said. He did a quick mental calculation. "Twenty-seven in group one, twenty-one in the second batch."

"We thought it might be a copycat, but we've decided the blood eagle is just his latest method. Why? Who knows? Maybe he wants to make sure he gets credit. So many dead and nobody knowing about the first batch, and maybe now he wants everybody to know, so he changes his MO to provide an unmistakable signature for his work. There was no signature or consistent MO until 2000. Why a sudden need for recognition? Again, who knows?

The key fact turns out to be that there has been one game warden killed in forty-eight states, and all that remains after Wayno Ficorelli are Missouri and Michigan."

"Are you thinking fifty is the magic number?" he asked, jumping to the obvious conclusion.

"Have you got a better take on it?"

He didn't. "A serial killer whacking game wardens," he said in disbelief.

"We prefer the term serial murderer. All the early murders were different, but we've learned that the crime sites were always by water, isolated, and probably the kills took place at night. We weren't sure about the last part until now because we never found a body that would enable forensics to unquestionably pinpoint time of death," the agent said. "The other constant is that all the vicks were professional hard-chargers, hard cases like your friend. Most were declared homicides, but not one of them in either group has ever been solved. In both sets the killer is highly organized, he's never communicated with law enforcement, clearly does his homework, understands how you people work, and finally, he seems to understand our weaknesses by changing venues and stringing out his killings over time, making it hard for a pattern to emerge."

"Suspects?" he asked.

"None," she said. "And getting the number of people we need to ratchet up the investigation has been a bitch since 9/11. Homeland Security and antiterrorism take priority and eat up a lot of resources. Add to this that state and local police units are all in terrible financial shape," she added. "We're lucky to be this far."

"Why am I here?" he asked. He could understand an unbalanced or pissed-off violet going after a game warden who'd bumped heads with him—but methodically killing game wardens all over the country? Never mind believability; it made no sense.

"You're a tracker; you're good at finding people, and you operate in the environment where all this goes down. The woods are your thing."

He shook his head. "I find known missing persons, not unknown, unidentified killers. That's for you people." He had inadvertently gotten involved in a number of homicides over the past three years and had been told repeatedly by his supervisers to keep to his own turf.

"Wisconsin's attorney general wants his cousin's killer caught, and he thought you might be able to assist. He called your governor, and here you are."

He cringed. Lorelei Timms: He blamed her for being bumped out of the Mosquito Wilderness to a detective job he neither wanted, nor sought.

"I hear your governor's a big fan," Special Agent Monica said.

Service grimaced and wondered how many changes of clothes he had in his truck.

"It's not all bad news," she said.

"No?"

"I have to apologize," she said. "I'm sorry about your colleague, but this is the first body we've recovered in the golden window," she added. "I'm also sorry about your son and girlfriend. It's difficult to deal with so many losses so close together."

He shook his head. He was beginning to distinctly dislike Special Agent Monica. She seemed pretty straightforward, but there was something missing, something not quite right about her or the situation and it was making him extremely uncomfortable. The golden window, he knew, was cop speak for the first forty-eight hours after death.

"Ficorelli was off duty and in this area to fish with a man named Thorkaldsson, who happens to be sheriff of Florence County. Thorkaldsson was supposed to meet Ficorelli, but he was late, and when he showed up, he found the body near their meeting place. He immediately secured the crime scene," she explained.

"Florence is small," she continued, "and the department is just Thorkaldsson and three deputies. The county doesn't even have its own lockup. They have to farm prisoners out to other counties. The sheriff may run a small-time cop shop, but he did one helluva job here, and we think his arrival was really close to the time of Wayno's death. Usually we find cold bodies dropped at locations different than the kill sites, so this case potentially gives us a leg up on gathering evidence and leads. We've never been able to locate an actual kill site, which means this could be the break we need. The body was still warm. It couldn't have been moved that far or that long before the sheriff arrived."

Service grunted acknowledgment, but he was still trying to process it all, and his gut was churning, never a good sign. "You think this dump site here is also the kill site?"

"No," she said, "but this is the soonest we've ever gotten to a victim. Want to take a look?"

# 11

# Florence County, Wisconsin
## May 20, 2004

They got into her Crown Victoria and headed down a slight grade. It took ten minutes to reach a place where a federal crime lab panel truck was parked, and a crime scene ribboned off. The area looked like a vehicle turnaround, and ahead Service saw four large, pale gray boulders set back in white cedar trees beyond where a berm had been piled up by a dozer. Small yellow evidence pennants were stuck in the ground throughout the area. Service got out and Agent Monica showed him a gray plastic tub filled with green rubber swampers. She also held out a box of latex gloves.

"Soft ground?" he asked.

"We're just making sure that all of us wear a boot with the same tread. Any tracks that are different won't be from us."

They both tugged on boots and blue latex gloves. He noticed that while the old road seemed to end at the berm, a new trail had been created by four-wheeler traffic a few feet east of the boulders.

The FBI agent saw him looking and said, "There used to be a bridge, but it's long gone. The river's shallow here, with a hard bottom. People ride four-wheelers across."

She led him along the four-wheeler trail to a steadily moving stream.

"Pine River," she said, pointing. "You'd think people could've found something more original for a name."

A tarp had been constructed over an area along the north bank, and the area taped off. "The sheriff did a bang-up job here," Monica said. She showed him where to walk and pointed to the boulders, which had been marked to show where the body had been displayed. "There was blood, but not enough," she added. "Usually there isn't much at all where a body is found."

"Is that significant?" he asked, adding, "That he was laid out on the rocks?" If there wasn't much blood here, it probably wasn't the kill site. You didn't do the things this slimeball did without making a mess.

She said, "Certain kinds of serial murderers display their kills to send a message."

Certain *kinds*? "The body was right next to the four-wheeler trail, so he wanted it found, right?"

"Maybe," she said. "We can talk about that later."

Service began a methodical walk-around but saw nothing significant. The pictures of Wayno had left him shaken, but what bothered him more was the fact that the FBI was aware game wardens were being killed, and as far as he knew, the Bureau apparently had made no effort to warn anyone. This realization made it difficult to think clearly.

An hour later they were back at the command post on the hill.

"Anything pique your interest back there?" Agent Monica asked.

"What strikes me is what there *isn't*. This site looks like it was pretty well sanitized. Are you thinking the perp got disrupted?"

"We can't rule that out. We're thinking he hadn't been gone that long when Thorkaldsson arrived. The body was still warm, and that's a first."

"This is work for science types—crime scene techs," Service said.

"They're all over it," she said.

"Have you done DNA?"

"It's in process," she said. "The samples are in the lab now. In any case, vick DNA is redundant. Thorkaldsson was the man's friend, and he identified him."

Service was thinking that details counted in every line of police work. It was fine to have an ID, but until you had dentals *and* DNA, you were not done. "When will you release this to the public?"

She rolled her eyes and Service held up his hands. Special Agent Monica appeared to have very thin skin. "I'm not trying to do your job. Wayno lived with his mother," he added, "not far from Madison."

"We know," she said. "Do me a favor?"

"If I can."

"Someone from NCAVC is coming in tomorrow."

"Which is?" He loathed the acronym stew of the federal government.

"The National Center for the Analysis of Violent Crime."

He thought about it for a second. "The people who do the profiles?"

"Right. Do you know much about the process?"

"Only what I've seen in movies," he said.

"Yeah, like that's real," she said sarcastically. "Movies are mostly bullshit."

"You don't believe in it?" he countered.

"Profiling can be a useful tool when it's done right—not by itself, but coordinated with all the other specialties and tools. It's definitely not a crystal ball, and done wrong, it can take you down roads that can take you a long way from where you want to be," she said. "The media and Hollywood have made profiling out to be the magic crime-solving bullet, and in the public's mind, the greatest serial killer of all is probably Hannibal Lecter. Did you know that Lecter is loosely based on an actual killer named Albert Fish, who killed and ate children back in the twenties and thirties?"

"No," he said. He couldn't care less. He thought about Ficorelli and felt bad for him, maybe worse for his mother. "I don't think I'll be much use here," Service said grimly. "I'm just a woods cop, and fiction or not, this asshole's methods seem to approach Hannibal's."

"Understood," Monica said. "But just hang in here with the team for now and let us decide your role. Cool?"

"I guess," he said without enthusiasm. Orders were orders.

There were at least eight agents on site at all times, and sometimes as many as a dozen, plus various technicians and Wisconsin state troopers. No county personnel. The county didn't have people to share, even on a major case like this. Special agents Bobbi Temple and Larry Gasparino looked no older than Walter, and seemed too young for this kind of heavy duty. Special Agent Monica explained that normally they would set up a command post at the county sheriff's office in town, but Thorkaldsson's shop was too small, and they didn't want news of the Ficorelli killing getting out to the public yet. Until it got announced and they had milked the crime scene, they would remain in the woods. The land was state-owned, the timber concession leased to a paper company, which had installed the gate to prevent interference with their logging operations. Tatie Monica thought the isolated location and gate made this as secure a site as they could wish for. Service didn't argue, but he knew that the key feature of most isolated locations was the virtual impossibility of effective security, and in the North Country, most secrets didn't stay that way for long. Did the FBI not understand this? The woods were not a blanket to hide under.

Several large canvas wall tents were being erected as Service looked at a white bag of McDonald's burgers and Chicken McNuggets and turned up his nose. He also thought about the sign near the CP, a reminder that thoroughly securing this site was not going to happen.

"Mickey D's not up to your standards?" Special Agent Monica asked.

"Just not hungry," he lied.

She raised an eyebrow. "You're what, six-four, two twenty?"

"Close enough," he said.

"Eat," she said, sounding like a mother. He reluctantly took a piece of chicken and bit into it. It was like rubber, and just as bland.

"We've got sauces," Agent Temple said.

"I'm good," Service said.

Just before dark, he told the lead agent he wanted to look at the crime scene again.

Agent Monica looked at him. "Want company?"

"Alone," he said. She irked him. She bounced between officious and obsequious and seemed to almost hang on him.

"I can drive you," she offered.

"Rather walk," he said.

He took a penlight, stuck it in his shirt pocket, and headed out. He started making a mental list of questions to ask the FBI agent as he walked in the darkness.

Why did the killer leave bodies where they could be found? It would make more sense to leave them where he killed them. Also, were the missing eyes significant, and had any been recovered? Wasn't leaving the bodies where they could be found a form of communication—a kind of message? If so, what was the creep trying to say?

Below, through the trees, he could hear a generator and see the pink-orange glow of klieg lights at the crime scene.

Where had Wayno parked, and where was his vehicle now? Had he driven down here, or left his truck somewhere in the woods?

He skirted the crime scene, waded into the river, and moved upstream to look at the banks, moving slowly and turning on his penlight as he needed it. The military had discovered that green light was less disruptive than red to night vision. Many COs in the U.P. now carried the green lights.

The Pine River had the look and smell of good trout water. It felt cool on his legs, and several hundred yards west a feeder creek dumped in more cold water. The riffles in the main river would be saturated with oxygen in deep summer and serve as collecting points for fish that didn't flee up colder tributaries. Sweepers along the banks served as fish hotels as hydraulics forced current downward, excavating holes beneath the downed trees. He had taken only a cursory look at the water near the crime scene earlier and decided it was too shallow and not an area where Wayno would have lingered. He was more likely to fish further downstream, or upstream where there might be deeper water and more fish cover. So what had gotten him out of the water? And where? He wasn't a homicide expert, but he had seen countless animal kill sites and knew the difference between a butcher site, a resting place, and a cache. He had followed such trails thousands of times.

If Wayno had not been killed here, where did it happen? He assumed the feds had carefully covered the woods for blood and other signs, but did they understand that the river itself was a natural travel and transportation corridor? Europeans had discovered most Indians living along rivers for good reasons. Water could also wash away evidence.

After a couple of hours he decided it was pointless to continue scouting in the darkness and started back to the camp. Tomorrow at first light he would return and take a more careful look. The FBI had the crime scene covered; he would concentrate on the river and surrounding area. Someone might sanitize a crime scene, but it was unlikely they would be able to entirely eliminate all traces of their approach with the ground still relatively soft from spring rains and winter thaw, which made hiding tracks a lot more difficult. He was increasingly uneasy about the whole situation, especially his role.

He was deep in thought on the upslope when a voice startled him from the darkness. "Find anything?" It was Special Agent Monica.

"Jesus Christ!" he shouted. "Don't jump out at people like that."

The FBI agent stared at him. "I thought you people were used to being snuck up on."

He growled his displeasure, but said nothing more. He was unnerved that he hadn't heard or sensed her presence. Got to get your edge back, he chastised himself.

She was immediately on the defensive. "Okay, sorry. What did you see?"

"I'm thinking he was in the water and something got him out of the water and onto land."

"Why?" she asked.

"Maybe because he came to fish for trout and had the focus of a pit bull. Where's his vehicle?" What would have gotten Wayno out of the water?

"Across the river."

"Not on this side?"

"Nope, south side."

"Why?"

"We don't know."

"Where was the sheriff supposed to meet him?"

"About where we found the body," she said. "I think."

"Hmmm," Service said. Why the hell didn't she know, and why had the two men come in from different directions? Fishing pals usually rode together in one vehicle. Fewer vehicles left less impact on parking areas and less evidence for the uninitiated that an area was good fishing. Some secretive Yoopers would park a mile away from where they intended to fish or hunt, and walk in the direction opposite of their destination, before doubling back on ground where their trail would be difficult to follow. Why the two men came from different directions was an obvious question, and he started to get on her case, but decided from her voice that she was dragging. *Her case, not yours,* he reminded himself. *Reel in before you get too much line out.*

"How long since you slept?" he asked.

"What year is it?" the agent said wearily.

"I looked around upstream. If I was going to fish and got here early, I'd go in upstream and fish my way back down to the meeting place—the water up that way looks pretty promising. Or I'd walk down and fish back up. If his partner was late or he was early, he probably wouldn't wait. He'd fish past and keep returning to the rendezvous point." That's what he and his friends would have done. "Get anything off his vehicle?"

"Not yet. It's being worked on. We haven't moved it yet."

There were swarms of mosquitoes in the air and the FBI agent swatted at them continuously. "Are you impervious?" she asked, slapping the side of her face.

"Oblivious," he said.

"I'm glad you could get over here so quickly," she said.

"I'm not a homicide detective."

"No," she said, "but you hunt people. You and other woods cops regularly capture perps in the act of breaking laws. Most of us in law enforcement tend to be called in after the fact. Right?"

"I guess." He'd never considered his job in this light, but decided Agent Monica had a point, even though the significance of the distinction was not immediately apparent. In fact, nothing in this deal was apparent other than the fact the feds had not told the states what was happening. How many lives had this cost?

"You've already looked at the scene differently than any of us might have," she said. "The more perspectives we can get, the better off we are. Diversity gives us the multiple-view intellectual edge."

What the fuck was she babbling about? This was murder and she was spouting politically correct management theory? It still bothered him that the FBI had so much information on him, and he wanted to ask why, but once again decided to hold off.

Tatie Monica showed him to a tent. "Your crash pad," she said.

"Are you out of Chicago or Minneapolis?" Service asked.

"Milwaukee," she said. "I got a BS in psychology from Marquette, and then I did most of the work for a PhD in abnormal psychology. I still have to write my dissertation. Then I went to law school in Madison. Ficorelli's cousin and I were classmates at UW. I finished higher than he did," she added. "Then I worked in Milwaukee as an assistant prosecuting attorney for three years and found it pretty unsatisfying. It always felt like the prosecution was after all the real action, so I applied to the FBI and they took me. After the academy I did four years in LA. I liked it there, but I wanted to get back to the Midwest, so I asked for a transfer to Milwaukee. Some of my friends said it was a dumb move to a career backwater, but Wisconsin has had a couple of major serial murderers, and I liked the idea of being able to study records close to the scenes. This profiling thing gets overplayed and misrepresented in the media," she said.

"Okay," Service said. He had asked only if she was out of Chicago or Minneapolis and had gotten a professional life saga. Cops were taught active listening skills and to signal receipt of every statement without prejudice. The word "okay" was the most often employed. Service and Nantz had sometimes watched *Cops* on TV, and they would bet on the number of times the word would be used during a show. Monica had supplied so much information that he wondered if she was trying to sell herself, and if so, why? She was the team leader. What more authority did she need?

"Down the road I'd like to see profile training be mandatory for all law enforcement personnel, and for all of us to understand all the components," she went on. "We spend a lot of time trying to profile the killers, but geographic and victim profiling are equally important—all part of the total picture—and both underutilized."

Service didn't interrupt her. He was trying to size her up and not having a lot of success. She had an ego and seemed ambitious, but how competent was she? His make-talk question about her office had gotten him a detailed autobiography. Something was screwy here.

After a while he said good night, went into his tent, and eased onto a cot. He had just dozed off when he awoke to find her sitting on a cot across from him, a mug of hot coffee in hand. "Have you got something against sleep?" he asked.

"Talk to me about hunting," she said.

"It's a big subject."

"Hunting violets," she amended.

He rubbed the corners of his eyes, and tried to clear his head. "Game is attracted to certain kinds of habitat at different times of year. Habitat equals food and cover: Where you find the most game, you find legal hunters—and violators. Some locations have better potential than others." He thought for a minute. "Bears, for example. In the fall when hunting them is legal, they're pigging out to put on weight for the winter sleep."

"You just camp out near their food," Special Agent Monica said.

"In the old days hunters would find their trails, put threads across runs to determine if they were in active use, and when they found one, they would track the animal. Nowadays a lot of hunters are too lazy or unknowledgeable to know what they're doing, so they put out piles of sweet baits and sit above them in tree stands. Other hunters use dogs to chase the bear up a tree."

"Dogs are *legal?*" she asked. "Is that fair?"

It never failed to surprise him how few people knew anything about hunting or the outdoors. "It's legal and there's nothing wrong with it. Hunting for most of our history has been about eating, not sport or fairness. If you go back in time, most hunting was done with dogs. In any event, some hunters have specially bred dogs for bears. Every night they drive the dirt and gravel roads and drag them clean with a metal bar or a mesh screen. First thing in the morning they load their dogs and cruise the roads looking for fresh tracks. The dog with the best nose sits outside in a basket welded to the grill. This is their strike dog. When the hunters find a track, they let the strike dog sniff it, and if it's hot, he'll take off. If he keeps going, the hunters release the pack to follow. Then they drive all over hell using radios to try to follow the dogs until the animal is treed."

"Interesting," she said. "The strike dog leads the parade?"

He stopped talking. "It was my understanding that my being here is a result of a pop-up request from the Wisconsin state attorney general, but you know too much about me for it to be that simple."

"Computers enable us to do a lot of things fast," she said.

"I thought the FBI was computer-challenged," he fired back.

"Since 9/11 we've been clawing our way into the new century. You were a sniper in Vietnam."

He wondered exactly how much she knew about what he had done during the war. "Actually the mission was long-range recon, but on occasion we did other things." He didn't want to get into details.

"Enemy military personnel?"

"Right. Sometimes we tried to decapitate certain units to disrupt and harass them."

"How did you find your targets?"

"It was all about the quality of our intelligence. Sometimes we got lucky and stumbled onto someone we wanted, but most often we sent out Kit Carson scouts—enemy soldiers who came over to our side and volunteered to work against the North Vietnamese. Most of them were reliable and good at what they did. The scout would be given a name and he'd slide off into the mountains for a week or two, and sometimes when he came back he'd have located the target and followed him long enough to discern a routine. Then we'd follow the scout and do our job."

"Any ethical concerns?"

He shook his head. "We targeted soldiers, not civilians."

"That's where you developed your tracking skills?"

"Honed them," he said, and guessing where she was going, he added, "but we always had a name and an identity, and usually a general location. We didn't just go out and wander around looking for someone. Hope is worthless in tracking." He listened to himself. Wouldn't this apply to this killer too? How did he find game wardens to kill?

She chuckled. "You're not very trusting."

"I prefer to think of it as an acute sense of situational awareness."

"I appreciate your candor," she said. "We have tried like hell to look at the victims to develop a suspect list, but the only suspects we've identified were local types who might have held a grudge against a particular murdered officer. Our perp is a bigger thinker, working on a much wider plane. You ever run into anyone like that among your violets?"

He didn't need to think long. "Not really," he said, leaving it at that.

"Bullshit," she snapped at him. "You helped take down an international poaching group last fall. You're like every other cop," she added.

She knew too much about him, and again he wondered why. "How's that?"

"It's called key fact hold-back, and that's not the name of a poker game, though cops act like it is. Cops don't willingly share with outsiders."

"What I ran into last year wasn't like this in any way," he countered.

She glared at him. "The person we're looking for has the ability and wherewithal to travel freely, and move around unimpeded. He's either independent, unemployed, or has a job that gives him the freedom he needs. The fact that he displays the bodies has us scratching our heads. Usually killers who display and arrange their victims are sexual predators, but there's no evidence of sex in these killings."

"But the guy *is* communicating," Service said.

"It's more like he's waving the medicus," she said.

"Medicus?"

"An antiquated English word for the middle finger."

The way she said it made it almost funny, but the memory of Wayno's mutilated body wiped away any humor.

# 12

## Florence County, Wisconsin
### May 21, 2004

Service's internal clock had him awake before first light. His first thought was of Newf. How could he have forgotten his animals? He was definitely not fully aware. Not a good condition to be in with a serial killer stalking the woods. He pulled on his wet boots and shirt and slipped outside the tent. He called and woke Candi McCants and asked her to check in on and feed Newf and Cat. He told her he wasn't sure when he'd be home.

He walked back into the tent and poked Monica's shoulder. "You coming?" he asked.

She snapped up and swung her feet off the cot. "Is the sun up?" she asked in a sandpapery voice.

"Soon," he said. He went outside, found an urn with fresh hot coffee, and filled two Styrofoam cups.

The FBI agent walked stiff-legged out of the tent, stretched, and dug a stick of gum out of her pocket. Her hair was molded to her head.

"You ready?" he asked, handing her a cup.

"Like the white chick said in *Dances with Wolves*, 'I go where you go.' "

"They were married," Service said.

"Don't nitpick," she shot back, sipping her coffee. "Do I need hip boots?" she asked.

"Only if you're afraid you'll melt," he said.

She shook her head and said, "Lead on, Natty Bumppo."

"Wouldn't it make more sense for the killer to leave the bodies where he killed them?"

"Most serials do. They kill, do their thing, and boogie."

"This guy wants you to find them."

"But not too easily or too fast," she said.

"What about the eyes?"

"We're clueless on that," she said. "One shrink talked to us about *mal occhio*, the evil eye, but that line of inquiry went nowhere. We had a serial in

Texas who cut the eyes out of three victims. In some Arab countries they remove eyes as punishment for certain crimes. Because of the blood eagle we had a hard look at Viking practices and beliefs and drew a blank."

It occurred to him that maybe the eyes were irrelevant, but he was locked into another question. "Why did the Texas killer take the eyes?"

"So the victims wouldn't remember him."

He looked at her. "How could they if they were dead?"

"Exactly. He said he only intended to rape and release, but he ended up killing them. Then he gave us a line of bullshit about taking the eyes to confuse us."

He pondered this. Misdirection? In the natural world misdirection was something prey did, not predators. Or did they?

They crossed the river. The four-wheeler trail continued on the other side of the river, and to his right he saw the cement pilings of the old bridge.

"How far back is Wayno's truck?" Service asked as they splashed quietly across the cobble bottom.

"Maybe three hundred yards. The road's bermed on the south terminus to keep out civilian vehicles. He parked east along a two-track that sort of parallels the river over there," she said, pointing.

Tire marks showed that four-wheelers worked both sides of the river, and Service knew that Ficorelli, like any competent game warden, would never leave his vehicle where it would be obvious or easily found, even when he wasn't on duty.

"Thorkaldsson and Ficorelli were friends?"

"Long time, I gather. The sheriff says they came here to fish three times a year, spring, summer, and late September."

Service grimaced. Routine could be fatal to a game warden, even off duty. Ficorelli seemed to have possessed the self-protective paranoia that all good game wardens needed, but how many people knew about the fishing trips, and why did the two men park on opposite sides of the river?

Thick tag alders and cedar bordered the narrow road cut by four wheelers. Tatie Monica triggered her handheld. "Julie, I'm coming up with a colleague."

"You're in our optics," a male voice squawked back over the radio.

"Julie?" Service said.

The agent smiled. "Julius White."

Another nondescript dark Crown Vick was parked sideways just behind the berm. Two agents met them. They were wearing blaze orange vests over navy blue polo shirts, with FBI in large black letters across the backs of the vests. "Anything?" she asked one of the men.

"We had a couple down here on a four-wheeler about midnight," he answered. "They drove down to the berm, stopped, stripped off their gear, and went at it on the seat." He pointed. "Right there."

"You talked to them?" she asked.

"Nope."

"What about Nelson?"

"He was makin' mud when they came racing by, but he radioed to us that they were coming."

"Did Nelson talk to them on the way out?" The annoyance in her voice was palpable.

"Yeah, he got their names and checked IDs. They told him they had a few too many. They live a few miles south. He said the woman was in tears. The guy she was with wasn't her husband."

"Who was he?"

"A playmate," the agent said, tongue in cheek. "Also a neighbor. She lives in Milwaukee and summers up here. Her old man only comes up weekends."

"They summered hard last night," the agent called Julie chirped.

Monica said menacingly, "Somebody needs to talk to them again. I want full statements. How often do they come down here? Did they see anything the night of the killing? We need to be thorough, milk every lead."

"Nelson's got their names, addresses, phone numbers. He took licenses and ran them. No wants or warrants. They both came back clean."

Service left her talking to the agents, and walked down the two-track, where he found Ficorelli's pickup backed into some white pines. It was roped off with crime scene tape, but no FBI personnel were around. Shouldn't there be security here?

Special Agent Monica caught up. "I think your guys enjoyed the show last night," he said.

"Julie's an FOA—First Office Agent," she snapped back. "Which is no excuse. He shouldn't have let the couple head back to Nelson once they got past him. They should have been detained and interviewed right there."

He agreed, and wondered if 9/11 was causing the FBI to ramp up manpower, and lower standards in the process. "This is where the truck was found?"

"As you see it."

The sun was beginning to illuminate the eastern sky with a band of low lavender and pink light.

"Your people check for foot tracks on the four-wheeler trail?"

"There are some matches with those on the other side, but that doesn't tell us much. We haven't found any that might be Ficorelli's by their size."

"Felt soles," Service said. "They keep you from slipping on rocky bottoms and leave a flat print like Bigfoot, but not distinct. Was Ficorelli wearing waders, and did his boots have calks?"

"He was naked. Calks . . . you mean, like metal spikes?"

"Not necessarily metal. Where are his boots, waders, vest?"

"We haven't found anything."

"Anything found from the previous victims?"

"Them either. Probably at the kill sites, but we haven't found one yet. What about calks?" She asked.

"They leave distinctive prints if they're not worn down." His own needed replacing, which he kept putting off. "We'll assume he moved directly downstream and fished back up to the meeting place. We ought to be able to find some sign of where he went down to the river and got out." It always amazed him that people with no outdoor interests had so little curiosity about it. In the U.P. even the least outdoorsy person knew a lot because the outdoor environment was everywhere around them and affected everyone who lived in it or near to it.

He moved slowly, using the increasing light to augment his penlight. He picked up on a trail not far from the black truck, but it looked more like a game trail than a fisherman's path. Still, he saw the muted prints of felt soles, and they were small enough to be Ficorelli's. No calks for sure. He marked two tracks with sticks, and thirty yards on, he found a pile of bear dung. The FBI agent didn't seem to notice and he didn't call it to her attention. It was a small pile, not particularly fresh.

The bank on the south side of the river was low, the water in front of it slow and skinny, not likely to hold fish. He saw no tracks or impressions in the gravel, and stood, looking across the river where the current was closer to the bank, where large rocks protruded and a lot of downed timber hung down in the water "Let's angle down and across," he said.

They waded downstream until the bottom began to tail away, the water deepening into rapids with some energy. "The soft edges of this heavy water would be best for fish," Service said, thinking out loud. "But if he had to meet Thorkaldsson, he'd probably stop short and loop back upstream to meet him."

"Soft edges?" she asked.

He tugged some hairs on the back of his arm. "Prickly water looks like that," he said, showing her the arm.

"You can look at the river and tell what people would do?"

"I can guess what an experienced fisherman would be most likely to do. With an inexperienced one, all bets are off. With an experienced fisherman, every movement in the water is about finding and positioning to cast to fish."

They crossed seventy-five feet over to the north bank. "We'll stick close to the bank," he said. "Look for anything that seems out of place."

"People are out of place here," Special Agent Monica quipped, looking around.

"They are," he acknowledged.

She didn't complain about the slowness of his movement. Neither did she offer much in the way of observations, other than to volunteer that the current could tire somebody pretty quickly.

"It's more strenuous, but safer going upstream," he said. "Downstream the water piles up behind your legs, and if you hit loose cobble, you'll lose your footing and float your hat. By the way, don't cross your legs when you wade. Move one foot, then the other."

"Float your hat: Does that mean, like, fall in?"

"Right."

"But we're going downstream."

"Be careful," he said.

He moved no more than ten feet at a time, scanning the shore. They waded for nearly forty minutes.

After a while he saw the silhouette of a straight line angled off a log. Morning light was beginning to form shafts in the trees. "See that?" he asked.

"See what?"

"Something that doesn't belong."

"No," she answered.

"Over there, a straight line," he said, pointing.

"That doesn't belong?"

"Nature rarely creates clean straight lines."

As he got closer he saw that a fly rod had been washed against a log and wedged in by the hydraulic pressure, the rod tip vibrating slightly.

He went over to it, but didn't pick it up. He could see the distinctive deep green color of the graphite and guessed it was an expensive Winston rod. He leaned his face down to the water. The reel was a pricey English-made Hardy.

"Ficorelli's?" the special agent asked, standing beside him.

"I don't know. Did you ask Thorkaldsson about Wayno's gear?"

"Not yet," she said.

Not yet? "That rod and reel are worth about fifteen hundred bucks new. A fly fisherman is more likely to risk breaking his leg or head than a good rod." Especially on a game warden's salary.

"But anyone could have dropped it."

"Right."

"You want me to get help?"

"Not yet. It could be the current carried it downstream."

"We keep moving downstream?" she said.

"Upstream. If the rod lodged here, it came down, not up, and he wouldn't be far from his rod if he had a choice."

He slowed, examining every log and rock along the shore until he looked past an overhanging tag alder and saw a metal Wheatley fly box on a log, its top open.

"I see it too," the agent said from behind him.

He moved up and studied the nearby shore, which was no more than three feet behind the log pile.

"Good place to sit and change a fly," he said, trying to visualize.

"And lose a rod?"

"Not necessarily; but if he dropped it, or it fell in, he'd go get it," Service said. "Immediately."

"If he was able," she said.

"Uh-huh."

He saw a scrape on the log beside the fly box, fresh nicks in the bark where a few flakes had broken away. In the water below the log he saw a fancy lanyard with forceps, a pocketknife, safety pins, floatant, and dessicant in special holders. The gear had sunk in soft water and was too heavy to be moved downstream by the current.

The branch beyond the fly box had more scrapes. Service moved to the end of the log, closer to the bank. He could see where the stalks of wildflowers and thistle had been broken. "I'm climbing out," he said.

"You want help?"

"Just me."

He used a tag alder to pull himself up the grassy rise. Even from a distance of several feet he immediately saw dark spots on some blades of grass. He found a stick and probed the ground. The end came out dark. Flies rose and buzzed

"You got something?" she said.

"Looks like," was all he said.

He saw signs of something heavy dragged west. He followed, and in an opening just behind the tag alders, among crushed yellow birch saplings and grass, he found the ground saturated with more blood and flies.

From there a drag trail led back to the water about twenty paces upstream of where Ficorelli had come ashore. He slid back into the river near Special Agent Monica. "How far from here to where the body was found?" he asked her.

"About three-quarters of a mile, maybe a mile," she said. "Why?"

"Did your people search down this far?"

"Not yet," she said, in a tone that suggested they had not planned to come this far.

The distance was about what he had guesstimated. He turned to face her. "I think this is your kill site. He got out for some reason and was killed up there. The body was then dragged up the river to where it was found. Dragging it through water dispersed evidence, helped drain the blood. The killer probably gambled you would be more likely to concentrate upstream because it would be easier to move the body down the river."

"Which means?"

"Our perp is strong to be able to move a body so far upstream."

"Not easy to drag dead weight against this current," she said.

"Exactly. It's not easy, but it's easier than you might think in the shallows, where the current isn't as persistent. Whoever did this is probably in pretty good shape." Ficorelli had not been a large man, but dead weight was dead weight.

"Did you find evidence of the body being dragged near where it was found?"

"Nothing; but as you saw, the site looked like it had been swept and cleaned."

"Makes sense. Ask your people to meet us at the dump site and we'll direct them down here. I think they can come in from landside." If the site had been sanitized, why had the perp left the rod, reel, and fly box here? And where were Wayno's vest and wading boots?

Service took one of the men downstream and told the others to parallel them inland. When they reached the new site he showed the items in the water to the technician who had accompanied him, and talked the others down to the blood spots.

"Luminol?" Tatie Monica called out to one of the techs.

"Needs to be darker for good results," a female technician said.

"It's plenty dark under the trees," Service pointed out. Luminol was a chemical that glowed greenish-blue when it came in contact with blood, and it didn't take much to get a reading. He had seen it used a couple of times.

The crime scene techs and agents worked methodically while he remained in the river with Monica, watching them spray the two sites he had found.

"Luminol can react with some plant matter," she said while they waited. "But our people are trained to sort out and interpret what they find."

*Asinine comment*, Service thought. Was she trying to impress him, or the others? If so, it wasn't working for him.

Service saw a camera flash illuminate the woods under the trees. The flashes went off every few minutes, and he found himself flinching, not sure why.

"Drops indicate the body was dragged up to here, over to there, and back down to the river," a tech above said, pointing.

Service asked. "Footprints? There are no drag marks where I followed him up from the river, which means he crawled out under his own power. What about human blood?"

"What other kind of blood would be here?" the tech asked.

"There's old bear scat on the far bank and there are wolves in Wisconsin. The blood could be a fawn kill, or an adult deer."

"Scat? You mean bear shit?" Tatie Monica asked.

"It was between Ficorelli's truck and the river," he said.

"You didn't say anything."

"Didn't matter."

"I'd bet this is human," the tech said after conferring with colleagues. "There's a lot of it."

Tatie Monica announced, "Ficorelli was killed here, butchered, and dragged up to the other site by the old bridge."

*No shit.* "Somebody wanted to make sure the body was found," Service said. "Right by the four-wheeler track and all. Have all of them been left in open places?"

"I'd call them more obvious than open—if we discount the fact that they've all been off the grid, more or less. Let's go back and grab some more coffee and breakfast," she added. "The techs will call us if they need us."

"More Mickey D's?"

"We tried to get Emeril, but he charges too much for backwoods culinary camp calls."

This was a long cry from the backwoods. He called out to a technician, "Look for a vest, boots, shorts, maybe waders. He wasn't fishing in the buff."

They were within fifty yards of the command post when somebody yelled, "Crapoleon on the squawk box!"

Tatie Monica rubbed her eyes and walked over to the coffee urn. "Ninety seconds," she told the other agent. She rolled her eyes when Service gave her an inquisitive look. The next thing he knew they were standing under the tarp in the birch grove and a disembodied voice was saying, "Tatie?"

"Present—or accounted for," Special Agent Monica said sleepily into a black speaker phone.

"Get your team to Missouri," the voice said. "We have another prize."

"Where?" the FBI agent asked, pen and notebook in hand. She looked at Service and mouthed *Body*.

"South central part of the state in the Irish Wilderness Area, on the Eleven Point River. A bureau bird will pick you up in Iron Mountain and take you to the old Blytheville Air Force Base in Arkansas. There's more clutter and less visibility there. You could be dropped in Springfield, but you'll have better cover at the old base. It's all general aviation now, and also a major depot for picking up and delivering Guard and Reserve troops. You won't be noticed. I suggest you move with the utmost dispatch, Special Agent. We've got another golden window."

"On our way," Tatie Monica said, punching a button to break the telephone connection. She looked at the other FBI personnel. "You heard the man, people. Let's shake and bake."

"What about this site?" Agent Bobbi Temple asked.

"I'll talk to Thorkaldsson and his people can keep it secure. You're now the site commander."

"Is it possible that this guy has struck twice so soon?" Service asked.

"It doesn't fit the pattern for our guy, or for most serials. Usually there's a resting period between kills," Monica said. "But none of these blood eagle things match the earlier group of killings, so who knows?" The other agents stood blinking until Agent Monica clapped her hands and said, "We're burning daylight, people." This sent them scrambling, and she immediately turned to Service. "First we call Thorkaldsson. We'll grab breakfast on the way to Iron Mountain. You got fresh clothes?"

"For how long?" he asked.

"Never mind," she said dismissively. "You can draw from our stuff if you need it." She turned to walk away, and Service caught her by the arm. "Whoa," he said. "This train's moving a little fast for me. Care to fill me in?"

"That was Cranbrook P. Bonaparte on the speaker. He's the BAU—Behavioral Analysis Unit—acting ay-dick who was supposed to come here. We apparently have another body—in Missouri—and we're going down there now. You're coming along, and I'll explain more en route."

"Ay-dick?"

"Acting assistant director. I'll explain later."

*Later?* It seemed to Service that explanations from the FBI agent were always in abeyance, and when and if they came, tended to be pretty thin. But he also noticed that when she gave an order the others jumped into action.

"He said, 'you,' " Service said. "Not me."

"This is my decision." She put the back of her fist on his chest. "Have you got a problem with it?"

He shrugged. "I've got some fresh stuff in my truck."

"Larry and I will ride with you," she said. "Bobbi, you keep our vehicle."

The female agent nodded and trotted away.

Service got into his Tahoe, Gasparino got into the backseat, and Special Agent Monica jumped up into the passenger seat, buckled her seat belt, triggered her handheld radio, and told the Florence County sheriff to meet her at the interpretive center.

Sheriff Thorkaldsson was a bearded six-foot-nine giant with lavender-tinted wraparound sunglasses and a field of red moles on his forehead shaped like gumdrops. "Arnie," she said as they met between the vehicles, "this is Grady Service."

Thorkaldsson nodded. "Wayno told me about you," the sheriff said.

"We're leaving, Arnie," she said. "Agent Temple is in charge of the site; Bobbi has people to cover the gate and the roads. I have no idea when we'll get back. Soon, I hope. Meanwhile, I want to continue the embargo on the announcement of Ficorelli's death."

"People around here are already yammering," Thorkaldsson said. "The county rumor mill is churning. We're getting media calls."

"Just tell them there's no fucking story here!" she snapped, and quickly softened her voice. "Just keep the lid on it, and if things go funny, you have my cell phone number. Work with Bobbi."

"Yes, ma'am," the towering sheriff said.

Service asked, "How come Wayno parked on the other side of the river?"

"Always did," Thorkaldsson said. "Superstitious, maybe. We always did pretty good in that part of the river."

"You find his rod with the body?"

"No."

"What's he use?"

"Four-weight Winnie with a Hardy reel."

"We have it," Service said.

"And a probable kill site," Special Agent Monica added. "It's downstream about three-quarters of a mile from where you found him. The tech team is there now. They'll stay but we'll have to widen the perimeter. That's why we need the Wispies." Members of the Wisconsin State Patrol were called Wispies.

The sheriff said, "Rather have people I know than strangers in on this. I've got an auxiliary."

She said. "It's Bobbi's call, but whatever she decides, keep it quiet."

Service thought the sheriff seemed a little possessive, which was not an uncommon reaction to the FBI's swooping in.

"Was Wayno's body wet when you found it?" Service asked.

"Yeah."

◉

Service and the agents ate sticky cinnamon bear claws from a gas station on their way south. Tatie Monica inhaled three of them while Service was still working on his first one. "This is what you call breakfast?" he asked.

"You prefer the golden arches?" she countered.

"Crapoleon?"

She grinned. "FBI humor. His name is Cranbrook P. Bonaparte. Bonaparte equals Napoleon. Cranbrook P. gives us Crapoleon." She looked over at him. "Don't worry, it's an affectionate name. Cranbrook is about the most charming sonuvabitch you'll ever meet, a truly nice man, and very sincere."

Her words and tone didn't quite match. "Your boss?"

"No, he's *acting* head ay-dick of the Behavioral Analysis Unit in NCVAC, which for him is a temporary gig. He's been there forever. My boss is the special agent in charge of the Milwaukee field office, but I'm the lead investigator for the case. The analyst who put all this together called me to talk about what he'd found. I went to my boss, and he grabbed onto the case and got the Bureau to give me the lead."

"A career moment," he said.

"Yeah," she said. "Up or down. If I don't bring this one home it'll be a big belly flop into Bumfuck." Her voice was matter-of-fact, resigned.

"Isn't that in Wisconsin?" Service asked with a straight face.

"Shove it," she said, grinning. "The Bureau is merciless about failure these days," she added.

"I keep wondering if it's possible that there could be two killings so close together."

"Certainly it's not what our boy's done in the past, but if Cranbrook says we have another, we have another."

She was respectful of the BAU man, Service thought, but he sensed an undercurrent of something else, a certain edge when she talked about him.

"Bonaparte's an expert on profiling?" Service asked as he drove.

"One of the pioneers," she said, looking over at him, "which puts him in a cast of dozens. Since profiling became popular with fiction writers and Hollywood, dozens of agents have stepped forward to claim they invented the concept."

"Him too?"

"No. Bonaparte's too nice and too smart to blatantly self-promote. His style is to quietly insinuate himself into those places and with those people he thinks can help him. He's got some theories that don't quite fit profiling coda."

"Is he good at what he does?"

"That's a loaded question. The naked fact is that no profiler has ever provided work product that allowed a field agent to capture a serial murderer.

We think there are about one hundred of these killers active around the country at any given time, and the only way we ever get any of them is through a back door, or their fuckup—usually the latter. In practice, profiling helps us verify what we've got *after* we have a suspect or somebody in custody, and usually for reasons that don't relate to our primary interest. Historically, profiling hasn't enabled us to intervene."

"If Bonaparte's so good at the job and a pioneer, how come he's not director or permanent assistant director for BAU?"

"Fair question," she said. "When Louis Freeh left, there was an interim director before Mueller was named, and he quickly named his own people. Cranbrook didn't have time to suck up to Mueller, so he got passed over. Right now there's an opening, so he's filling in until the current powers can find their own man."

"Sore point with him?"

She paused to mull this over. "He probably wanted the job, but he seems more interested in his theories than in running the show."

"Theories?"

"I'll let him explain," she said. "Right, Larry?"

"Uh-huh," the child agent in the backseat mumbled. Gasparino was from the Bronx, less than nine months out of the academy.

There it was again, explanations lobbed into the future like fungoes. "You're a cop, right?" she said.

"Yeah."

"Then *drive* like one, for Christ's sake. Let's light up this jalopy and haul ass! Every minute we spend on the road is a minute we don't have at the next site."

# 13

# Irish Wilderness Area, Missouri
## May 22, 2004

They dozed on the plane and were taken in a dented, unmarked twelve-passenger van from the one-time military base in Arkansas north into Missouri and the Irish Wilderness Area in the southeastern part of the state. Their destination was the Eleven Point River, named either because it was eleven-point-some miles from something, or labeled tongue-in-cheek by early surveying crews who legend said had to stop eleven times in the first mile to change and record readings. Their driver said no one could recall the exact point of reference or the precise fraction; his own theory was that the name was an Anglicization of *Leve Pont,* which appeared on early French maps of the area.

The van hurtled along narrow, high-crested roads, up Highway 19, crossing numerous razorback ridges, and eventually descending into a deep, verdant valley. They drove into a crudely paved parking lot where four Missouri game wardens waited with canoes and johnboats at a cement step-down boat launch that looked like it had seen a lot of use. A wooden sign said GREER SPRINGS.

Tatie Monica had been extremely quiet during most of the drive, but en route made a point of explaining that Missouri's game wardens were called conservation agents, and properly addressed as agents.

One of the four men was sparsely bearded with wild gray eyes. He wore a gray shirt and green pants, the same as Michigan conservation officers. "Eddie Waco," the man said with a slight nod.

"Grady Service."

"Where's Bonaparte?" Special Agent Monica asked.

"Died a while back out on some island in the Atlantic, I heard," Eddie Waco said, deadpan, giving Service the once-over. "You handle a paddle?" he asked.

Service immediately felt a kinship in that they were both thrown in with feds and Waco seemed neither impressed nor intimidated. "Fat part or skinny part?" Service answered, earning a grin.

Agent Monica got into a johnboat with one of the other conservation agents. "Move out," she barked, her shoulders hunched forward.

Service's escort tapped a pack in the bottom of the canoe. "Got you'n's kit?" the man asked.

Service said, "Somewhere in the van."

"Best fetch hit right-quick an' jes git on in, sit up front, and let me do most of the work. Level's up some from spring rains, and the current's pert steady most of the way, so we don't have to grow us no wings," he added. Service grabbed his ruck and left the remainder of his gear in the van, assuming it would be brought downriver behind them, or be waiting in the vehicle when they came out tonight or tomorrow morning.

Larry Gasparino sat motionless in his craft, as if he had been nailed in place and was about to undertake the Bataan death float. Service wondered why some native New Yorkers seemed to disconnect when they were away from their concrete canyons.

The river was deep and slow as they pulled out of the narrow side channel where the launch was situated, and wide and slow for a while before suddenly narrowing, deepening, and speeding up, the water so clear Service could see huge rainbow trout suspended ten feet down in the deeper runs. Eddie Waco stroked almost casually, using his paddle over the left side both for propulsion and as a rudder. "There an overland way into where we're headed?" Service asked.

"More ways ta kill a dog thin chokin' 'im with buttern," the man said cryptically. "We been told no fuss and ta keep the button on this."

"Have you met Bonaparte?" Service asked.

Waco shot back, "What part you got in this bug-tussle?"

"I follow orders," Service said. He started to explain, but decided against it. The Feebs seemed obsessed with security, and like it or not, he was part of the federal team for now. Keeping quiet seemed the prudent course.

The Eleven Point River snaked around small wooded islands with thick stands of Ozark cane, and later split a multihued limestone and dolomite canyon, two hundred feet high, the sides clotted with dense stands of white oak, elm, hickory, sycamore, sassafras, and clumps of shortleaf pine and spruce. There was a heavy understory beneath the trees, almost black in the early afternoon sun. Towering rocky outcrops were yellow, black, and green in places, splotched by age and erosion. Service could see numerous small caves and openings in the rocks overhead, as well as the holes of bank swallows. Lily pads dotted side coves of gray-green frog water.

The four craft eventually reached a heavier riffle with protruding rocks. Eddie Waco guided their canoe expertly into the longest "V" and deftly slid them through the pinch-point. Service wasn't sure whether the man's silence was due to shyness or from his concentration on maneuvering.

When they floated into the head of another long eddy of quiet water, Service's guide said, "No easy way to hoof inta where we're a-goin', but hit's bin done."

Service thought more information might follow. It didn't.

Service and Waco had pushed off behind the other three craft, and Eddie Waco showed no urgency to catch up.

The Missouri conservation agent nosed the canoe onto a gravel bar with softball-size yellow and gray cobble and stepped out. "Got to see a man about a dawg," he said, stepping under the canopy of some sycamores that acted as an umbrella over the edge of the gravel. Service decided to avail himself of the stop, and when he'd finished and returned, Eddie Waco was sitting with one leg draped over a gunwale.

"You'n a part of this thing?"

"Michigan conversation officer," Service said. "I'm here to consult."

"Consult, eh?" Eddie Waco parroted. "What might that be?"

Service shrugged. "Beats me. You got any idea what we're doing?"

"A man's always got idees, but we been ordered ta walk the chalk," Waco said, offering a tin of Redman.

The man's words seemed a vague complaint, but Service shook his head, said "No thanks," and lit a cigarette. He had no idea what the man was talking about.

"Hear-tell you'n make a passel of cars up Michigan way." He wondered if the man's accent was real or put-on. The man seemed serious.

"That would be in Detroit," Service said, adding, "which many of us don't consider part of the state."

"Like St. Looey hereabouts," Eddie Waco said with a grin. "You not a city feller?"

"From the Upper Peninsula," Service said.

"Do tell," Waco said. "Heard you got some bears up thataway."

"Quite a few."

"We get us some mosey up from Arkansas time to time," the man said. "Couple years back I think a farmer up north a' here shot one a' them wolves a' your'n."

This was true. A young collared Michigan wolf had rambled more than five hundred miles from the Upper Peninsula into north central Missouri where it had been shot by a farmboy, who had mistaken the animal for a coyote stalking his family's livestock. It had made the news throughout the Midwest. "I remember," Service said.

"Long walk ta go a-clicketing," Eddie Waco said, smirking.

A-clicketing? Strange word, but the meaning seemed clear and Service laughed. "Never say never." The young wolf probably had been seeking a mate to establish his own pack.

"I reckon."

"Shouldn't we be moving on?" Service asked. They had been sitting on the gravel bar for close to half an hour.

"Whatever them feds got downriver, I'm thinkin' the weathern's gon' turn a tetch bad."

Service looked at the man. "Meaning?"

"Storms comin' in—big ole front. Expect 'em in two . . . three hours, if'n we're lucky. Could bring some black-stem twisters, I reckon."

Tornadoes? Service wondered if Bonaparte and Tatie Monica knew this, and, if so, why they were all headed into a wilderness in canoes and john-boats, or headed there at all?

"I'm sure the feds have a plan," Service said.

" 'Speck folks up New York–way couple years back might opine differ'nt."

Eddie Waco spit a bullet of tobacco juice, straddled the stern, nodded for Service to get in, pushed the canoe away from the gravel, and hop-stepped into the stern, digging his paddle into the bottom to ease them into the current.

Special Agent Monica was already waiting on a small gravel beach and prancing anxiously at the mouth of a steep trail. She motioned for him to follow her. Service nodded at his boat mate. "You coming?"

"Feds ain't give us the secret handshake," Eddie Waco said, shaking his head.

Service looked at the swirling yellow-gray sky and started up the steep, sandy trail. He could feel the pressure change in his ears and wondered what it meant.

Tatie Monica glared over her shoulder at him. "What the hell took you and Pa Kettle so long?"

The air was heavy, thick, making sweat pop. "Pit stop," Service explained. "People down here seem to move at their own pace." A lot like people in the U.P., he thought, which he had always considered a good thing.

She muttered, "Bonaparte can be a dickhead about being late."

"Have you heard a weather forecast?" he asked. He didn't realize they had an ETA to meet.

She nodded. "Some rain. Bonaparte will have it covered. He's the detail man." Did she mean to imply that she wasn't? In his experience being an investigator was almost entirely about details.

"Agent Waco says there could be tornadoes."

She looked up and chewed her bottom lip. "Shit happens," she said.

There were sycamores and shortleaf pine, sassafras and other trees reaching over the narrow trail. "Not the greatest place to get caught in toothy weather," he said.

She said over her shoulder, "I thought you outdoor types thrived on this shit."

"You ever been in a twister?" he asked.

She shook her head. "You?"

"Once was enough." He'd been in a cyclone in Southeast Asia. It had wrecked a base camp and killed two marines and a Kit Carson scout named Minh. The only difference between there and here would be direction of cyclonic rotation.

When they finally reached the top of the bluff they found an eight-person FBI crime scene team out of the St. Louis field office, and a four-wall, olive-drab green shelter with a generator humming outside. The FBI crime team members were dressed in white biohazard coveralls with hoods and face masks and looked like a NASA team getting ready for a launch. It struck him how a person could be alive and healthy one minute and dead and a health threat the next and this made him think of Nantz and Walter and made his stomach flip. The team's gear was scattered around helter-skelter. Service studied the area, thought it might have been a campground at one time. There were scars and scorched stones where there probably had been fire-pit rings.

Monica introduced herself and Service to the lead tech. "Where's Bonaparte?"

"Split," the crime scene tech said.

"When?"

"Three hours ago, maybe less. He said the weather was turning and he couldn't afford to get trapped out here. He said to tell you you're in command—you'd know what to do."

"*Did* he?" she said, her response clipped, her voice low and oily. "What do we have?"

The man led her to the shelter. "Refrigeration unit," he said. "Bonaparte said he wanted the site left untouched until you got here."

Untouched? How had they set up the shelter without fouling the site? Service wondered. The sheriff in Wisconsin had done a professional job—but this?

The man said, "Walk the green tape."

Service saw tape held to the limestone surface with small rocks.

The air inside the shelter was almost frigid, and while Service welcomed the cold at first, he quickly wished he had a jacket or a sweater. Dumb to leave his extra clothes in the van.

There was nude male body on the ground, mutilated in exactly the same manner as Wayno Ficorelli. The man was huge, with red hair and a flaming red beard.

"What have we got?" Special Agent Monica asked.

"One very sick puppy," the tech said quietly.

"How long has the body been here?" she asked.

"By ambient air and body temperature, thirty-six hours, give or take. We can't be more accurate until we get the remains back to the lab."

She looked at the man. "How'd you get here?"

"Down the river, same as you."

"Did Bonaparte take a boat out?"

"Chopper," the man said with a disapproving grunt. "He seemed to be in a hurry."

"Who found the body?" Service asked.

"Don't know," the man said.

"You hear there's severe weather coming in?" Service asked.

"We heard, and if the winds pick up, this place will be toast. You got a plan?"

"Just keep doing what you're doing," Agent Monica said. "But do it fast."

"Mostly we've been waiting on you. We've done most everything we can do here. Bonaparte insisted we leave everything as is until you got a look."

"Not much blood," she said, leaning over the corpse. "Kill site?"

"Doubtful," the technician said, shaking his head.

The plastic walls began to snap and shake as the air turned blustery.

"Shit," the tech said. "That wind gets worse, it'll turn this thing into a parasail."

"You looked for alternate shelter?"

"No, ma'am. Our orders were to stand by, wait, and not talk to the locals."

Tatie Monica turned to Service. "We need a safe place to store the body — and us," she said.

"I'll tell the Missouri agents," he said, stepping out into the wind. He squinted as sand blasted his face. The storm was coming in fast. He felt a tug on his arm and found Larry Gasparino. "Weather's heading south; am I right, or what?"

"Way south," Service agreed, glancing at the swirling, dark clouds.

He bounced his way down the trail, found the watercraft tethered to chains at the end of nylon ropes on the beach. There was nobody with them. He sniffed smoke, looked at the pea gravel, saw impressions leading around a huge boulder on the downstream side, and followed them.

The prints and path led to an overhang six feet deep and high, and ten feet wide.

The four Missouri agents were squatting around a small Sterno fire. Eddie Waco looked up at him.

Service said, "Feels like the twisters are ahead of schedule."

"Always got they own minds," Waco said.

"We have a body up top and we need to get it under cover before the storm hits full force."

The conservation agents followed him at a jog to the top, without comment. Crime scene techs had already transferred the corpse into a black rubber bag. Service and the Missouri men labored down the steep trail as the wind suddenly stopped and everything became still.

Not even birds sang.

Service had one corner of the bag as it began to sprinkle. Eddie Waco said, "She be upon us, boys."

They dragged the bag under the overhang cave just as the rain started. It came down like marbles, a giant spigot opened wide, the rain coming in a steady roar. The eight techs, four Missouri agents, Larry Gasparino, and Tatie Monica pressed in with them, fifteen people and a corpse in a bag crammed into a tight space.

"What direction are we facing?" Service asked Waco. The trip down the twisting river with heavy overcast had pretty much obliterated his sense of direction. There was no sun to orient him.

"Southwest," Eddie Waco said. "More or less."

"Figures," Service said. A tornado would blow directly in on them. "We should find another place."

"Thet dog hain't a-gonna hunt," the conservation agent said. "Have to ride 'er out here."

Special Agent Monica got out her handheld radio and tried to get a chopper to evacuate the body, but was told through massive static there would be no flying until the storms passed.

Service thought she looked outwardly calm. He wondered what her real emotions were. He was on edge. Did she not realize what could happen? Could she be *that* clueless?

The steady rain turned to huge, loud drops that sounded like stones.

The drops changed to golf ball–size hailstones that clicked and ticked and ricocheted like bullets.

The temperature plummeted.

The wind started changing directions, intensified, and began to blast them with chips of chert, dust, and shards of bark. Everyone in the stone shelter covered their heads with their arms and turned their backs to the opening.

Service heard a roar he first thought was a helicopter, a thought he amended to a train a moment before his brain put it all together: *Tornado!* The afternoon sky was as night.

Large things began crashing and thumping against the side of the cliff. "I'll be go to hell!" one of the techs cursed from his crouch.

"We all just might," another shaky voice said.

Wind suddenly ripped into the cave, toppling Service onto his side.

He immediately reached for the wall of the cave, looking for something to hold on to as the man beside him disappeared.

"Service!" Tatie Monica shrieked.

Service saw her arms splayed as she was yanked and spun outside by the wind. He jumped on her legs, trying to pin her with his weight, but they both kept sliding and skidded off a slippery ledge, and all he could think was, *Shit.*

The water was a shock, much colder than he expected.

He kicked his way to the surface, saw a boulder looming, and managed to use a hand to straight-arm it as he was propelled downstream, spinning. *Where was Tatie Monica?*

No idea how much time had passed, aware only that it was lighter, the rain still coming down in sheets, but there seemed to be more light and a little less wind. A tree crashed into the water ahead of him and raised a spout like a depth charge as objects began to splash all around him. At one point he saw a spotted fawn floating by, its neck bent at ninety degrees. He looked around, saw several people bobbing and splashing in the water, stretched out and swam to get speed, and when he had his stroke going, looked up, saw a gravel bar ahead, and swam onto it, scraping his chin as he beached himself.

A tech came by holding out a hand and Service got a wrist-lock and yanked him ashore. The man was bleeding from the mouth and nose. He helped a second man ashore and looked upstream but saw no more people. He assumed the others had found a way to safety or were somewhere downstream. The dead fawn was wedged between some rocks just below him.

He heard shouting, the rain drowning out most of the words.

"Body bag," a voice screamed. Service thought it was Tatie Monica, but he had no idea where she was.

Eddie Waco was soon crouched beside him. "I seen where hit went," he told Service, who nodded and said simply, "Let's go."

They eased into the water together and began to swim side by side.

The rising river carried them fifty yards through a narrow neck with a riffle before dumping them into a long frothy eddy. Service saw the bag floating ahead of him and got to it first. Eddie Waco joined him, and the two of them guided it, kicking their way into flatter water, pushing and pulling it toward the cliff wall with the most shoreline.

"I need a smoke," Service said, his chest heaving.

The Missouri man held out his snuff tin. "Why I carry this," he said.

Service shook his head. "We need to secure the body."

"Not down here," the man said. "This rain still a-goin', they'll be a crest rollin' downstream."

"How high?"

"Don't take much ta push 'er up six ta eight feet. I seen as much as twelve a couple times, and back in the nineties she once come way up over thirty."

Service scanned the rocks above them. "Another cave?" he asked.

"Plinty ta choose from, but we need ta get ta one up high enough."

The heavy rain reminded him of monsoons in Vietnam, but Waco had nylon rope and carabiners in his waist pack, and located a cubbyhole above them. Service climbed up while Waco secured the line to the body bag. With Service pulling and the other man climbing, and pushing and guiding, they got the body fifteen feet above the waterline and wedged into a space that was more scallop than cave.

"We ought to check on the others," Service said.

"They hain't safe, nothin' ta be done about hit."

Service stripped off his vest and turned it inside out. He always carried two packs of cigarettes sewn into a waterproof pouch inside the back of his bulletproof vest. He peeled off the vest cover and dug out a pack.

He reached into his pants pocket and fished out a sealed plastic container of wooden matches. "How long until it crests?"

"Cain't say, but she's a-risin' pert fast."

Service looked down and saw that it was true.

"The body's gonna be in bad shape," Service said.

"Dead's dead," Eddie Waco said.

Rain continued to fall unrelentingly, and an hour after they had snugged into their perch, they heard a voice shouting along the canyon wall. It was impossible to make out any words. Eddie Waco got outside and inched his way toward the sound, came back, and grabbed his pack.

"What?" Service asked.

"Got us a snakebite," the man said. "Water drives serpents ta cover, same as us."

Service lurched and looked around. He was not crazy about snakes. "*Poisonous* snakes?"

Eddie Waco said. "Like most folks, snakes don't bite less'n they's feelin' cornered."

"Great," Service said sardonically. One of the comforting things about the Upper Peninsula was the rarity of poisonous snakes.

The conservation agent put on his small pack and started along the rock wall. Service looked around, began imagining snakes in all the little crevices in the cave, and decided to go with Waco, invited or not.

It was a long, slippery, and clumsy crawl along the rock face through sheets of cold rain and powerful wind gusts before they reached another conservation agent. "Lady fed got herself bit," the man told them.

Service noted they were a little higher than where they had the body stashed.

Special Agent Tatie Monica was sitting in a hole sculpted from the limestone by nature and time. Her dark hair was mashed to her head like a helmet. Her eyes were rheumy, more from irritation than fear. A crime scene tech was sitting next to her. Every time he reached for her, she swatted his hand away.

"Tatie!" Service barked.

She glowered at him.

"What happened?"

"Snake," the tech beside her said.

"You get 'im?" Eddie Waco asked.

"She mashed its head with her pistol grip," the tech said, pointing.

The reddish-brown earth-tone serpent was piled up between some stones. Eddie Waco found a stick and prodded the reptile, which moved.

"Jesus, it's still alive!" the tech yipped, scrambling away from the FBI field agent.

Eddie Waco probed with the stick again and the snake pulled away. He kept poking it until he uncovered its tail, grabbed it, and snapped the snake backward like a whip. It cracked sharply in the heavy air and he dropped it on the ground, unsheathed a small knife, and cut off its head. "Copperhead," he announced. "Just a little feller. You'n got heart problems?" he asked Agent Monica.

"Field agents aren't authorized in the field if they have heart problems," she said defiantly.

"That's real good to know," Eddie Waco said. "How ya'll feelin'?"

"Stupid," the woman said.

"You got pain?"

"It burns."

"Where?" the conservation agent asked.

"Buttock," the tech said. "She won't let us look."

"Let's git thim trousers off," Eddie Waco said, but he found himself staring at the barrel of a 9-millimeter.

"You got antivenin?" Tatie Monica asked.

"No, ma'am."

"Snakebite kit?"

"No, ma'am."

"I don't want my ass carved," she said, her eyes rolling.

"The way it is," Eddie Waco said quietly, "copperheads don't kill many people except'n young 'uns and ole folks with heart problems. This 'un's not too big, which means not a lot of pizen, but even little fellers got enough ta kill flesh and muscle at the bite site. I reckon we need to get what pizen's in there out right quick afore it spreads."

She brandished the weapon. "*Nobody* touches my ass," she repeated.

Grady Service raised his left hand to deflect the barrel of her weapon up, and struck her hard on the chin with the heel of his right hand. The pistol came loose and she slumped to her left. He picked up the weapon, popped out the clip, and handed the weapon and magazine to Gasparino, who had joined them, his eyes bulging like jumbo egg yolks.

Eddie Waco rolled the stunned woman onto her stomach, cut her belt with his knife, and sliced open the fabric of her pants and underpants, skimpy black French cuts, which made Service think of Nantz and gulp.

The fang marks in her right buttock were small but distinct. The skin was already red, shiny, and swollen.

"You going to cut and suck?" Service asked.

"Cuttin' causes more damage less'n you'n a doctor man," the Missouri man said, "which I hain't." He put down his pack, reached into it, and took out a red bandanna, which he unfolded to reveal a flat, oval rock, white with brown speckles. He set the stone aside and took out a small, single-burner camp stove, connected the fuel canister, and handed a metal container to Gasparino. "Fill 'er with watern, quickety split." Eddie Waco lit the burner, which hissed.

Gasparino crawled clumsily down to the raging river, filled the cup, and passed it up. Waco took out another cup and filled it from a flask. He put the second cup on the burner, took some antibacterial soap out of his pack, washed the wound, and blotted away excess moisture.

Tatie Monica tried to roll over, but Service pressed her shoulder down. "Keep still," he said.

"Don't cut me," she muttered, with the side of her face pressed to the ground.

"Be no cuttin'," Eddie Waco said calmly.

When the liquid boiled he put the stone in it and let it bubble for a while. He took his Leatherman tool off his belt, opened it to form pliers, and extracted the rock, which had turned pure white from heat. Eddie Waco looked at Service, saying, "Bes' hold 'er down." Then to her, "This might could smart some."

He took the stone in his glove and pressed it to the wound, where it seared the flesh. Tatie Monica bucked and cursed, "Fuckers!"And passed out.

Service turned his head to avoid the smell. "What now?" Service asked. It was still pouring, but the wind had slackened.

"We wait," the Missouri agent said.

Service had no idea what was going on. "Is this for real?"

"I seen it done afore," he said. "You got a better idee, Michigan Man?"

Service didn't.

Waco turned off the heat under the boiling liquid, picked up the flask, and handed it to Service. "For what ails you'n."

Service took a sip, swallowed, felt the fire bloom in his stomach. Eddie Waco also took a sip. "White mule yella corn," he said. "Best there is, aged some eight years." He held the flask out to Service again, who held up a hand.

"I'm good."

Service pointed to the stone on the FBI agent's right buttock. "What *is* that?"

"My great-granddaddy done shot him a white deer, found hit in the animal's belly, done passed hit down to my daddy, and Pa done passed hit on ta me. People down this way use such stones for the rabies."

"It works?"

"Sometimes, but hit's plenty good for snakebite, you git ta hit soon enough and there hain't too much pizen."

"What's it called?" Service asked.

"Madstone," the man said.

"You believe in witchcraft?" Service asked.

"I don't, but if'n I was in a pinch, I'd ask a witch for help, wouldn't you'n?"

Service nodded, knowing desperation was more the mother of invention than pedestrian need.

The tech left Service and Eddie Waco alone with Monica. "She'll live," Waco said. "Who be in the bag back yonder?" he asked.

"Don't know," Service said. "I just got a quick look when the storm blew in."

They sat for two hours, and when the stone fell off the agent's bare flesh, Eddie Waco reheated the stone in the alcohol, which turned green, and applied the madstone again.

"Maybe the stone cauterizes?" Service offered.

"I hain't much on science," Eddie Waco said.

After forty minutes, the stone came loose again. This time Eddie Waco repeated the process, but the alcohol remained clear and the stone wouldn't stick. He wiped it dry with the faded red bandanna, meticulously refolded it, and carefully put it in his pack. "Snake didn't get much inta her," he said. "She'll be fine, but we best git her outside to the hospital."

Service looked up at the sky, which was still roiling, but there were devil's smiles beginning to slice into the canyon, turning the water below them to quicksilver.

"How far to the get-out by boat?" Service asked.

"I reckon six mile," Eddie Waco said, "but with the watern up, they'll be a heap a' trees pilin' up in the narrers."

"The poison works on the heart, right?"

The Missouri man nodded.

"We gotta keep her still, limit exertion."

"Weather clears, we might can get a chopper in," Eddie Waco said. "Have ta mule her up top, but we got enough men for thet."

"No boats?"

"Too risky," the conservation agent said. "Would take too long."

The water looked like it had come up five feet and was still rising.

"She'll peak in two, three more hours, drop pert fast after thet."

Service found Monica's radio and gave it to the man. "Can you arrange pickup through your own contacts?"

"Not thim feds?"

"A fed left us here," Grady Service reminded him. "We can get the body and her out at the same time."

Eddie Waco nodded and started trying to radio for help.

Tatie Monica stirred beside them. "No cuts," she mumbled.

"No cuts," Service said. "Just a little brand for a keepsake."

She whined. "My ass."

"Think how good it'll feel when it stops," Service said. "Let's get some trousers from the others," he said to Eddie Waco.

"Just gon' cut 'em off when they get her inta the whirlybird," the man said.

"Looks like you get to moon the world," Service told her.

"My mother would just die," she mumbled.

"P'int is, ya'll don't," Eddie Waco said.

It took two hours to get the agent and the body bag on top of the bluff, and by then a Missouri Highway Patrol Huey was waiting with a medical team. Gasparino looked disoriented and Service couldn't blame him. The past few hours had been tough. Service sent two techs with the body. Tatie Monica was mostly awake, but far from alert, and offered no resistance.

They watched the helicopter rev its rotors, lift a swirl of debris, and lumber away.

"Missouri emblem on the chopper shows two bears," Service noted.

"They musta snuck up from Arkansas," the conservation agent said with a grin.

Service called over to the lead tech. "You recover photos?"

"Cameras are with our gear," he said, "if the wind didn't carry it all off to Kansas."

"Wind comin' from t'other direction," Eddie Waco pointed out.

The refrigerated shelter had been shredded. Pieces were pasted like confetti in trees, the metal frame posts twisted and bent. There was no sign of the generator. The crime scene techs' gear was scattered, but most of it had been blown inland. The tops of some trees upriver had been severed by wind shear. Eddie Waco surveyed the trees, said, "Twister jes sorta skipped over top like a flat rock."

The chopper had gotten in and out, but the leaden sky continued to threaten, and from time to time they heard thunder and saw flashes of lightning. It took the lead crime scene tech thirty minutes to find the plastic lockbox with the camera and digital crime scene photos. Why hadn't Tatie Monica brought the camera with her when they hauled the body down from the top of the bluff? Panic? Service and Eddie Waco sat on a downed tree and opened the box. The Missouri conservation agent studied the photographs and handed them back to Service without comment, his tanned skin looking a lot lighter.

"Somebody you know?"

"Agent Elray Spargo," Waco said with a sigh. "Elray was a card-carrying comminist lib'ral atheist, a by-God, down-to-the-bone secular humanist, which hereabouts is akin to bein' the devil. All that mattered to Elray was the law. That was his only religion, and he wrought legal hell on lawbreakers."

"He made enemies?"

"Most a' which he sent off to jail. After more'n twinny year, he purty well had control, an' ever-body knew it. Loan me one a thim cig'rettes a' your'n?"

Service held out a pack.

"I got me this feelin' they's more ta this thin just Elray," Eddie Waco said.

"Yeah?"

"You gonna say different, Michigan Man?"

Service shook his head. "It's a federal show."

"Way we see hit, kill one a' our kind makes hit *our* show."

Service understood and sympathized, but did not tell the man what he knew. "I hear you," he said.

"We best mosey," the Missouri game warden said.

"I thought we had to wait for the water to recede."

"I thought we'd take us a walk. Thim others can wait an' take the boats out."

Service called Gasparino over. "Agent Waco and I are walking out. Special Agent Gasparino, I guess that makes you in charge."

"Me?"

"Wait until the water level goes down and take the boats downstream." Service gave him Tatie Monica's handheld radio. "You'll probably have to wait for more boats to help haul everything out."

Gasparino nodded solemnly. "Where are you two going?"

"Things ta tend to," Eddie Waco said, standing up, putting on his pack, and offering no further explanation.

"What about more tornadoes?" the young FBI agent asked.

"Might be, might not," Waco said. "They come, you best find cover."

"What if somebody gets snakebit again?"

The Missouri game warden scratched his head. "Best hope hit ain't a big 'un."

# 14

# Fourteen, Missouri
## May 23, 2004

They had been walking in the darkness almost four hours, following military crests, occasionally dipping down to the uneven floors of steep ravines before climbing back up. The humidity was overwhelming in the valleys, but there was an occasional swirling breeze on top, and Grady Service found himself falling into the mindless trance that came with long-distance hiking.

Eddie Waco rarely stopped, and when he did it was usually for less than a minute before pushing on.

During one of their pauses in a canyon bottom Waco said, "Y'all stay put," and moved into some stunted yellow-bark trees with intertwined trunks.

Service waited five minutes and looked for shade. He had taken a couple of steps when the bark of a hickory tree in front of him exploded by his head, clipping his shirt and face. He dropped to his belly as a second round took a chunk off a tree just behind him, the reports echoing through the canyon, their source impossible to pinpoint.

He had his hand on his SIG Sauer when he looked up and saw Eddie Waco grinning. "Stand down, Michigan Man," the Missouri warden said. "Thet's jes' thim ole Mahan boys a-barkin' on you'n."

Service got to his feet and brushed himself off.

"Whiii I say stay you best heed," Eddie Waco chastised him.

"Barking?" Service said.

"Thim Mahans got a still halfway up yonder ridge," he said, pointing ahead. "Anybody they don't know gits too close, they plink a few rounds inta the trees to discourage 'em. They don't shoot to hit nobody."

Waco cupped his hands and shouted, "Ikey, you and your brother put down them long guns. This here's Eddie Waco an' I'm just passin' through."

"We seen you hain't alone," a voice shouted down from some trees on the hill.

"He's the law, same as me. We hain't comin' yore way, boys, but you squeeze off another round, I reckon we gonna come up yonder, all ya'll hear?"

"We hear," the voice called back.

Waco looked at Service, nodded, and started walking.

"A still?" Service said.

"Don't got 'em up where you'n hail from?"

"Meth labs," Service said. "And marijuana plots in the state and national forests."

"We got us a dandy weed crop down this away too," Eddie Waco said. "I'd rather tussle with moonshiners."

Seven hours after they struck away from the Eleven Point River, they descended to a shallow, shale-bottom stream running down a steep canyon and walked into a clearing with a half-dozen dark stone buildings that looked like they had grown out of the ground. The dwellings were narrow, one-floor affairs, each with an oversize wooden porch under a steep roof. All of the wood needed paint. The roofs were covered with rich, yellow-green moss. The houses looked like sturdier versions of old mining company houses in the Upper Peninsula's Copper Country.

"Where are we?" Service asked.

"Fourteen," Eddie Waco said.

"Fourteen what?"

"Jes Fourteen's how hit's called."

Service stopped, knelt, and splashed cool water on his neck and face. It had misted off and on during the hike, but the longer they walked the more the sun stayed out. Tendrils of steam rose off the rocks and ground. He stood up and looked: buildings but no people. "Ghost town?"

Eddie Waco grinned. "They's likely fifty sets a' eyes on us hain't ghosts, I 'speck. Long guns neither. The Spargo clan's partial ta goin'about armed."

"Elray Spargo lived here?"

"Lived up top, but he was a-born and reared down here. These here is his people and they need to know what's gone on."

"We should be moving," Service said, thinking of the FBI and his own ambiguous role in the undertaking.

"People got their own pace back this way," Waco said. "Do you good, stand down a bit, pay attention, listen, mebbe learn some."

A man in a rumpled brown suit appeared from the tree line and walked slowly toward them. He had a shotgun slung over his shoulder, the sling made of soiled gray rope. He wore a thin black tie, distressed high-top logging boots turned gray from use, and a dusty black porkpie hat cocked rakishly to the side and back of his head. Service realized the man had the hat pushed back to keep his eyes clear for possible shooting. He had done the same thing too many times to not recognize it for what it was.

"How do, Agent Waco," the man said, staring at Service. "Your'n partner be sippin' thet crick watern, he'll soon be havin' runs a-spurtin' outen 'is backside."

"You drink the watern?" Waco asked.

Service shook his head.

"Not too much trouble, we could use some sweetwater, Cotton," Waco said.

A young girl came out of the woods with a couple of quart jars and gave one to each of the two game wardens. Service noted that she kept her eyes down. She wore new white Asics tennis shoes with gaudy red and gold trim.

The water was cold and pure. Service looked at the girl and thanked her as she slunk back toward the trees.

"Sir, I done come ta talk," Waco told the old man.

The man in the brown suit walked over to them, gave Service the once-over, and squatted. Waco and Service squatted with him. "Cotton, I'm powerful sorry to tell you'n Elray got hisseff kilt."

With no emotion in his voice or face, the man said, "That what the ruckus over to the Leven Point was about?"

"Yessir, hit was."

"Did the boy die brave?" the man asked.

"He lived plenty brave; I expect he died the same," Eddie Waco said.

The man reached down and scooped up a handful of white dust, which he let play through his fingers. "Was a Jimsonweed Christian," the man said. "The Lord never took hold with the boy."

"He was a lawman," Eddie Waco said.

"I reckon. You on your way to tell Fiannula?"

"Yessir."

The man nodded solemnly. "Reckon I'll jes mosey along with all y'all. You'n know how Fi kin git."

"Suit yerseff."

It occurred to Service that Waco was overly deferential to the old man.

"Fiannula packs 'at scattergun whin Elray's away," Cotton Spargo said.

"She knows me," Eddie Waco said.

"She frees thet wildcat, thet won't matter," Cotton said. "They gon' fetch my boy home?" the man asked.

"Thought I'd use the radio at Elray's to take care of it."

"Be good, we get the boy on his way to the Lord. How long since he done went?"

Waco looked at Service, who said, "About forty-eight hours."

"We ain't got much time left, this weather'n all," Cotton Spargo said.

The men stood up. No other people appeared. The man in the brown suit led the way with Waco and Service following. The man walked with re- markable grace at a brisk pace. Service guessed he was in his eighties.

"The body's legal evidence," Service whispered to the Missouri agent as they marched up a steep hill surrounded by a thick forest of gnarled pines.

"Things is differ'nt in these here hills," Eddie Waco said.

"Jimsonweed Christian?" Service whispered.

"Hush," Eddie Waco said softly. "Save your questions."

The house on the hill was built in a clearing with no trees closer than two hundred yards. The building was one story with rooms protruding at different angles. Something about it reminded Service of base camps in Vietnam, de- signed so that anyone approaching would have to cross a long stretch of open ground. Open space and the way rooms jutted out at ninety-degree angles suggested the place had been designed to create shooting lanes. It looked like a tidy fortress. Unlike the houses in the valley, this one was all wood and freshly painted, but in a brownish-gray color that made it difficult to see until you were actually in the clearing.

"Was Spargo ex-military?" he asked as they started across the clearing.

"Taught survival skills ta flyboys out ta Washington State," Eddie Waco said with a frown. "No more questions."

There was a small woman waiting on the porch. She had a sawed-off side-by-side shotgun in the crook of her right arm and a baby in the crook of her left. She had auburn hair in a severe bun and looked to be in her late thir- ties, her skin leathery from too much sun. She wore oversize bib overalls em- broidered with colorful flowers, and yellow flip-flops. Service saw small faces in several windows. The woman's eyes were dark coals in red beds. She had been crying.

"Fiannula," the elder Spargo said.

Her eyes were locked on Eddie Waco and Service.

As they got closer Service smelled something sweet. The woman looked over her shoulder. "You young 'uns git away from them winders or I'll be cut- tin' me a switch!" The faces disappeared instantly.

"Word done come about Elray," she said, turning back to her visitors. "I was jes about ta put on the black."

Service wondered how she knew, but Yoopers also had a grapevine that often surprised him in its speed and accuracy.

"They gon' fetch him home?" she asked

Cotton Spargo said, "Agent Waco here will see ta Elray, Fi."

"Obliged," the woman said with a faint nod to the conservation agent.

"Okay ta use the base radio?" Waco asked.

The woman nodded toward the house and made eye contact with Service. "Furriner," she said.

"Game warden from Michigan," Waco said. "Good man."

The woman sighed, said, "All y'all c'mon in the house," and shouted, "You kids fetch tea!" She had the bearing and demeanor of a drill instructor, Service thought.

The interior was neat and clean. There were bouquets of forget-me-nots in mason jars on every surface.

The woman led them into a large room with a long table and ten chairs around it. Everything appeared to be handmade, but there was nothing amateur about the work.

A boy of nine or ten brought a pitcher of tea and glasses.

They all sat down. "They best be gettin' my husband home right quick," she said. Service considered telling her that the authorities were slow to release bodies in cases of homicide, but this was Missouri, not Michigan, and he was a game warden, not a homicide detective. Curiously, the woman did not ask any of the normal questions about Elray's death, and he wondered how much she knew.

A couple of younger girls came into the room and crawled into Cotton Spargo's lap. Service drank his sweetened tea and kept quiet.

Eddie Waco came back and poured tea for himself. "Doug Hakes will make sure Elray gets brung up by helicopter, have him here at dayspring,"

The woman nodded. "Them feds gon' raise a fuss?" she asked.

Service wondered how she knew about the feds.

"Sheriff's a-takin' care of hit," Eddie Waco said.

The woman's fingers tapped the trigger guard of the shotgun, which lay on the table. "Elray tell about his dream to you'n?" she asked her father-in-law.

The elder Spargo nodded. "I told him not to go see the man if'n he had the dream two nights in a row."

*What dream? What man?* Service wondered.

"I told 'im the Lord works in mysterious ways," the woman said. "But Elray, he laughed at me and said hit was my job in the family ta talk ta the Lord." She shook her head and flashed a wistful smile. "No way ta change thet man," she added. "You *Spargos*."

The old man said, "My Liddy used to say stubbornness takes more men 'n pride."

The widow clucked her approval. "My Elray was a stubborn one."

Service wanted to ask questions, but Eddie Waco pressed a knee against him and Service got the message.

"You seen Cake?" Eddie Waco asked.

The woman stared at Waco, got up, and took the baby and shotgun away.

While the woman and her kids made dinner, Service and Waco sat on the porch in handmade wooden chairs. "What's going on?" Service asked.

Waco said, "I wanted to get over here and hear what got said. People hereabouts got they own ways."

"Nobody seems overly broken up about this," Service said. "What was Spargo's dream, how come his wife's not asking for details and knows about the feds, and how are you going to get the FBI to release the body?"

Waco grinned. "You'n listening real good, Michigan man. I done asked the sheriff and he'll take care of it. These people need to git Elray inta the ground. Feds want to exhume later, they can go through the courts. Old Doug Hakes will get 'im up here and the fun'ral will be tomorrow afternoon. You'll see plenty of sad then. Right now they's blinded by the git-evens."

"Like the start of a feud?" Service asked.

Eddie Waco chuckled. "You git thet from some ole Hatfield-McCoy movin' pitcher?"

Service felt like a fool, but the other man interrupted his embarrassment. "The real old days was sure 'nuff like thet, but it always got kept betwixt hill people. If an outsider done this, they got other ways. Widder will ask for a champeen."

Service didn't ask what this meant. "What's this about a cake?"

"Why we're here," Eddie Waco said. "Elray hardly went ta the privy without Cake Culkin skulkin' nearby."

"Culkin was an enemy?"

"More like a partner, though he don't wear a badge. Elray sent 'im off to jail a long time back and looked after his kin while he was away. Cake come out and they bin fast friends ever since. I'm thinkin' that whatever happened to Elray, Cake will know something."

"The wife already knew," Service said.

"Word moves fast in these hills," the Missouri game warden said. "The old man knew too, and I'm thinkin' hit was Cake brung word."

"Jimsonweed Christian?" Service asked.

Waco smiled. "Not a true believer," he said.

"There's a radio here?" Service asked.

Eddie Waco said, "Yup, but you don't need to be a talkin' at thet FBI woman. Word is she's in hospital down ta Wes Plains an' all drugged up."

"What happens now?" Service asked.

"We red up for supper," Eddie Waco said. "Then we eat, but don't be eatin' big on account we gon' be eatin' a whole heap till we git done here."

*Red up?* The local dialect and terms had Service befuddled, and suddenly he thought he knew what it was like to be a troll wandering into a village in the black spruce swamps of the Upper Peninsula for the first time. The people here, he decided, were a lot like Yoopers, and he found the thought comforting.

Service and Waco got a couple of sleeping bags out of the room in the house where the dead conservation agent kept his gear cache, took them out in the field, made a fire ring of stones, took wood from a pile near the house, kindled a fire, and settled into their bags to catch some sleep. Kids from the house brought them biscuits and ham and some kind of beans in runny red gravy.

Service was physically tired and sore, but couldn't sleep. Whenever the breeze let up, mosquitoes dropped on him en masse. He paid no attention to them. It seemed to him that people continuously filtered in and out of the house, most of them carrying food and other things the family might need. Two carpenters set up sawhorses just off the porch and hammered and sawed all night, making a simple coffin of white oak planks.

There were no stars and not much light from the house. Service could smell more rain in the air and wondered how long until it moved in. Sometimes the wind seemed to pick up, but then it would die away, which told him they were on the edge of a front rather than in the bull's-eye. If it stiffened and held, he knew the rain would quickly ride in on it.

His own cases back home sometimes had taken odd twists, but this was in a class of its own. How could somebody have been killing game wardens for so many years with impunity? As far as he was concerned, a bulletin should be sent immediately to all state fish and game agencies, wardens doubled up on patrols for safety, and all of them alerted to what was going on. But this had not happened, and probably wouldn't. One thing was certain: When he got back to Michigan he would make damn sure that Chief O'Driscoll heard what he had to say, even if he had to go over the chief's head to Governor Timms. Hell, *she* was the one who'd put him into this damn mess.

In his short time as a detective he had learned that making a case required intense and continual attention to detail—and some luck. The greater the focus on details, the more likely you'd catch a break. So far he'd seen little in Tatie Monica's approach to create confidence. She was like an inexperienced angler in a major hatch, frantically chasing from fish to fish rather than focusing on one until it was caught, or stopped rising. Jumping around created movement, not direction, and movement for its own sake was not progress. He was beginning to have serious doubts about the special agent's abilities to manage this case. Or maybe it was inexperience and he just couldn't see. But it seemed to him that the team should have remained in Wisconsin at the kill site to investigate it, rather than running down to Missouri to start all over. Something in the sequence and priorities just didn't set right.

The number of visitors seemed to increase well before sunrise. Eddie Waco led Service into the woods and downhill to a spring where they stripped off their shirts, rinsed with freezing spring water, and used their fingers to straighten their hair. They spent some time trying to knock the dust and dirt off their clothes and boots in order to achieve some semblance of presentability.

Cotton Spargo met them with a pot of coffee and two cups.

"Elray had a dream?" Eddie Waco asked.

"Said he done dreamt of this white light which he thought was the Lord Himself, but the Devil come out of it and grinned at him. Bothered the boy," Spargo said. "Would me too. Elray ain't been sharp since Sister Rosa went over to the Lord."

Cotton Spargo nodded politely, and stopped talking. Service followed Waco into the wood line.

They had heard the whine of a helicopter's turbines while they were at the spring, and by the time they got back to the house, the body had been carried inside and the chopper was sitting in the field, its rotors wobbling like a vulture's flight feathers in the variable breeze.

Waco introduced Oregon County sheriff Doug Hakes, who wore a chocolate-brown and blue-gray uniform shirt and a sweat-stained brown baseball cap. "Any trouble with the feds?" Waco asked.

"Snakebit fed's not able to make a fuss, and the young 'un's feelin' so much pressure he seems a bit tongue-tied," the sheriff said.

"What about Bonaparte?" Service asked.

The sheriff took off his hat and stroked his brush cut. "One which come out by whirlybird afore the storm? He's long gone."

Service wanted to ask where and when, but bit his tongue.

"They's fixin' ta clean Elray up," the sheriff said, leading them into the house. A young man came out of a room looking green and spewed vomit as he dashed for the outside.

Eddie Waco offered Service a small container of Vicks and Service dabbed a little under each nostril.

"No call for thet," the sheriff growled. "He was 'frigerated and we brung him home in ice." He pushed open a door and held out his hand for them.

The room was white and stark. Service saw nail holes in the walls and knew that the room had been cleared. There was a table in the center. The dead man was unclothed, stretched out on his back, his skin gray. Damp white cloths lay on his hands. There were quarters where his eyes should have been. Service flinched at a *whump*, marking an explosion not that far from the house.

"Dirt up this way's thinner'n Maggie's drawers," Eddie Waco explained. "Hardpan and rock right up to a man's boot soles. Dynamite's quicker'n shovels."

Service understood. During the winter in the U.P., bodies were kept in storehouses until spring when the ground frost melted and holes could be dug for graves. What had to be done for and with the dead was not something most people gave much thought to until it was staring them in the face. Once he had arrested a poaching crew out of Champion. They used a body-storage facility to stash their take over winter. Standing among boxes of frozen human corpses and hanging deer carcasses, the lead poacher had looked at him and said, "Hell, dese folks don't mind, eh?"

Service studied the body. Elray Spargo looked even larger all spread out on his back than he had looked in the refrigerated tent on the Eleven Point River. Spargo had long red-gray hair, a thick neck, and broad shoulders. His beard had the texture of steel wool. His hands had protruding knuckles, and long thick fingers. What clothes had the man been wearing? More importantly, had Spargo intended to fish the night he'd been killed? There had been no mention of that so far. If fishing wasn't involved, did this mean another shift in pattern, another mistake, or had he misunderstood the pattern?

Service made a twisting motion with his hand and Eddie Waco said to one of the men washing the body, "You don't mind, you fellers want ta help me roll ole Elray over on his belly?"

They did as they were asked. It was obvious they had handled bodies before.

The lungs had been removed, or put back into the body. The wounds that remained were horrific, and had been crudely stitched with what looked like coarse, braided black fishing line. Service was certain Tatie Monica and the FBI would go ballistic when they found out they no longer had the body. *Why did the killer remove the victims' eyes?* His mind kept going back to this and he wasn't sure why.

The law officers helped the men roll Elray Spargo onto his back again and went outside. Service lit a cigarette, Waco put a pinch in his cheek, and Doug Hakes took a cigar stump out of his shirt pocket and stuck it in his mouth without lighting it.

Thunder was buzzing intermittently to the southwest.

"Should hold off," the sheriff said, looking up. "What you make a' all this?" he added, glancing at Waco.

"Ain't no ord'nary man could git the edge on Elray."

"You hear anythin'?" the sheriff asked.

"You?" Eddie Waco answered, countering the question with a question, the sign of an experienced cop. Service hadn't known Waco long, but he was comfortable with him, and though Waco played the hick, and was a bit stingy with words, he seemed to have a sharp mind and a reason for the things he did.

"Think Cake was around?" Hakes asked.

"Have to see," Eddie Waco said, noncommittally.

At 10 A.M. people began to queue to view the body and pay their respects.

Hakes wandered off to talk to a plain woman in a navy blue frock. "Okay to ask questions yet?" Service asked.

"Not yet," Waco answered.

Service heard a lot of crying and wailing and caterwauling inside, but when people came out, they seemed composed, and joined in normal conversations with others.

During the night sawhorses, doors, and planks had been used to make temporary tables outside the house. Around noon people began filtering to the tables and standing behind their chairs until Fiannula Spargo came out of the house with her eight children, all of them dressed in black. A small veil of black lace hung over her face. After the family was seated, the others sat down.

Platters of food were served: hams, turkeys, roasts, tubs of mashed potatoes, corn on the cob, string beans and black-eyed peas, huge pans of corn bread, endless pots of black coffee, and sweating pitchers of iced tea.

Eddie Waco snatched a cob of corn and began gnawing. Between bites he said, "This here's a real offmagandy. Local crop won't be in for two month. Somebody done toted this in from outside." Waco ate the corn without salt, pepper, or butter, shoveling ears into his mouth like logs on a conveyor belt. Because of his false teeth Service couldn't eat corn without cutting it off the cob, so he contented himself with other things, like the corn bread, which had onions and green peppers in it, and more than a dash of sugar to sweeten it.

People laughed and talked and gently scolded their kids like it was a church social. Service saw a man take two heaping plates, walk out to the wood line, and come back empty-handed a short while later. He nudged Eddie Waco, who said, "I seen," as he attacked another ear of corn.

After the meal was finished and table cleared, Service watched a sleek black horse pull a small trailer with rubber tires across the field toward the house. The horse was tall and wore a headdress of gaudy, tall, black plumes, which undulated as it moved. The air remained close and heavy. The open coffin was carried out by six men and slid onto the trailer. Elray Spargo was beginning to ripen. Service touched his upper lip and Waco gave him another dollop of Vicks.

The dead man's wife and children walked directly behind the horse-drawn trailer. Cotton Spargo and other relatives followed the widow. The rest of the mourners filed along behind. The shoes of two hundred people raised dust, leaving an opaque cloud hanging in the humid air. Thunder continued to rattle softly in the southwest like someone shaking cookie crumbs off a baking pan.

The grave had been blown out of a more or less flat spot by some boulders and several spiky white oak trees. The widow and her children gathered around as the coffin was placed on short logs beside the gaping hole. The six men worked ropes under the casket and stepped back.

The minister who stepped forward had a withered arm, and the twisted countenance of a demented chipmunk, but the crowd responded almost immediately, and in no time the preacher was slapping the sides of the casket and railing against sin and evil and demanding everyone live a righteous, God-fearing life.

Service tuned him out. The sermon, if that's what it was, went on interminably, but didn't dull the responsiveness of the mourners.

Cotton Spargo spoke. "Y'all know Elray done his duty twinny-four years. He done loved Fiannula and his kids and all his kin. Police respected him, lawbreakers a'feared him. Anybody needed help, Elray was there. All y'all know how he was. Couldn't bear to see people in bad times. . . . Bin a heap a' Spargos called home ta the Lord, but this time Lord—and preacher, I apologize for a-sayin' this—hit's too dadgum soon. I cain't explain God's ways, and neither can you'n, so we just accept and keep on livin', but I tell all y'all this . . ." He gulped, paused, and sobbed. "I loved that big ole boy a' mine, an' I'm gon' miss 'im ever day."

Grady Service choked up, remembering two boxes of ashes sitting in his cabin.

The crowd, led by the children, sang, "Will the Circle Be Unbroken." The young voices touched something inside Grady Service. He kept thinking about Walter, the son he had known nothing about until a year ago. At seventeen, Walter had left California alone to find his biological father. The boy had courage and determination beyond words. Service thought, *My life is out of order. Fathers should go before their kids.*

He remembered standing numbly at his own father's grave. There had been no children singing the day they buried his old man, only a bugle and rifle shots as snow wafted across the gray November landscape. There had been shock more than sadness, a sudden void where a partial void had been before, his father working most of the time and rising to legendary status.

The six men used the ropes to lower Elray Spargo's coffin into the grave. One of the men helped Cotton Spargo climb down, and handed him a screwdriver as he slid the lid in place and tightened the screws. When the dead man's father had finished, the men helped him out of the hole, and the preacher went into his ashes-to-ashes, dust-to-dust routine, and the crowd began to sing "Good-bye Until We Meet Again."

There was nothing rehearsed about any of this, nothing fake or forced, and Service felt himself enveloped in real community and family, and he found himself fighting back sobs with people he doubted he'd even recognize six hours from now. A steel-eyed Eddie Waco squeezed Service's arm.

The mourners dropped rocks and soil into the six-foot-deep hole until it was full. A wheelbarrow full of black dirt was dumped on top, and a dozen small children began tamping the dirt with their bare feet. Service looked at the pattern of footprints and saw young life walking on new death. He couldn't watch and turned away.

Fiannula Spargo watched her father-in-law hammer a small oak cross into a dirt mound and pile stones around it for support. She bent down, placed Elray's sweat-stained service cap on top, joined her hands, and straightened up. "All y'all come on back ta the house an' eat afore ev'thin' spoils."

What did a game warden's career reduce to? A lifetime of unending responsibity and duty, Service thought, then ashes to ashes, dirt to dirt, and all that remained was an old baseball cap perched on a rough-hewn cross, pounded into hard ground. He told himself he would rather be left where he fell to feed the wolves and coyotes and ravens and crows. It was too damned hard to put the living through this. His old man's funeral had been a circus, mourning a drunk run down by a drunk. But this was different. It had quiet, simple dignity, an acceptance of death as part of the cycle of life, even if it was sudden and from the hand of an animal. Maybe he had been selfish in not holding services for Maridly and Walter. It was an unsettling thought.

"Ready to work, Michigan Man?" Eddie Waco asked, interrupting Service's thoughts.

Service nodded and followed the Missouri conservation agent.

The man seated on the rock ten yards from the grave had a plaster cast on his lower left leg and a sling holding up his left arm. From a distance he was youthful-looking, with windblown, corn-colored hair. Up close he looked ancient and battered, with a ruddy complexion and crooked teeth that jutted out from lips grooved like licorice twists. There were two empty plates on the ground by the rock.

"We knew you'n was feelin' poorly, some of the boys woulda hepped draw you up closer, Cake," Eddie Waco said.

"I heared what got said," the man said. "Cain't face the widder and them young 'uns. You know was a time I took the fever, and Elray carried me home, and he and Fi and them kids done ministered ta me. They even got the Cherokee ta drive his buggy up and have a look. They had me in thet house goin' on a month—just like I was kin."

"You and Elray was close," Eddie Waco said supportively.

The man sighed. "I got the shame upon me."

Service heard the patter of raindrops on the oak leaves overhead and knew that if the rain came hard enough, it would leak through once the leaves were soaked.

"How's that, Cake?"

"What happened to Elray."

"Ya'll thinkin' hit's yore fault?"

The man nodded. "Shou'n'ta happened."

"You were with 'im, was you?"

"Made me stay back, but I seen what was done."

"You seen it happen?"

"I seen afterwards."

"After he met someone," Eddie Waco said.

"Yessir."

"You know who he met or what it was about?"

"I never seen the man and he wouldn't say. Jes said hit was official."

"Thim his words?"

" 'Zackly how he done said."

"Did you hear anything?"

"Nossir. He done tole me stand tight for an hour less'n I heard a ruckus."

"And you waited."

"I always done what Elray asked."

"I know you did, Cake. Did you find him where you thought he'd be?"

"Said he'd be by the old bat cave camp, but he weren't."

"You found him at the abandoned Hurricane Creek Camp."

Waco pronounced the word *hur-a-cun*, and it took a second for Service to interpret.

"He was gone," Cake Culkin said, looking off in the distance. He took a deep breath. "I peeked quick and run," he said.

"Did you see anyone?"

"I just lit out and hit me a tree and whanged my shoulder and fell down a drop-off an' busted a bone in mah leg. Cracked it like a dry stick. Had to wait till first light to make me a splint and find a stick to hold on to, and then I come direckly here."

"When was this?"

Culkin looked up, like he was trying to recall. "Four days ago?"

"You hain't sure, Cake?"

"Like I said, I done hiked on over to Cotton's thet next day, an' me an' him done told Fi, and Cotton a'hauled me on over to the Cherokee's in his wagon, and the Cherokee popped my shoulder back in an' put that dang plaster on my leg. Ask Cotton when it was I come."

"You walked all that way on a broke bone?" Eddie Waco asked.

The man looked up at them. "Thet day I got out a jail, I went right out to my pap's and got me my twinny-two and went out and shot me a turkey to take over to my gal. I called a big ole Tom right in and put 'im down neat and quick. When I got over to thet bird, old Elray stepped out and grabbed a'holt a' my arm. He sit me down and lit up 'is pipe. Elray done said he was mighty perplexed about what to do with the likes a' me. He said he didn't want to send me back to jail since I'd just been gone six months. But he didn't feel like he could trust me, he said."

Cake Culkin paused. "Ole Elray finally says, 'Let's us do this with honor. Right here, right now, man to man. You c'n whup me, you go right on shootin' and fishin' whenever you a-want. I whup you and you'n never break the law again.' " Cake paused again, obviously reliving the moment. "Elray was a big ole boy with considerable grit, but I was on the wiry side myself and I had me some nasty scraps and allus handled what got throwed my way. So I said, 'It's a deal.' We spit on our hands and shaked, fair and square. Then my head done exploded and I could feel I was goin' out and all I could see was Elray's eyes. I swear, he was *enjoyin'* whuppin' me near to death. Next thing I knew the Cherokee was a-tendin ta my face. He done sewed me up and Elray took me to my kin and give 'em thet turkey, too. For that man, I'd a' crawled to his kin with my head cut off."

"You become his pine shadow."

Cake Culkin nodded. "I never broke the law once, all them years—not that I weren't tempted time to time—but when I seen him dead like that, I run like a yella dog."

Eddie Waco patted the man's back. "You're no coward, Cake. You backed up ole Elray for twinny years, and the two of you'n barely got through some of them times. He was here now, he'd say you done right by 'im. You'n done what he asked and you'n cain't ask a shadow more'n thet."

"I cain't face the widder," Cake said.

"Sure you can," Eddie Waco said. "And soon as thet laig gets healed up, you gon' be my shadow; that sound okay by you, Cake?"

"I'll jes let you down," the man whispered, studying the ground.

"You'n do and I'll put a whuppin' on y'all make you'n think what Elray done give you'n was a schoolmarm's slap. You with me?"

"Sir, I reckon," the man said, nodding unenthusiastically.

The two game wardens helped the man walk to the house and set him down with the widow, who hugged him. They left them talking, with the kids gathered round. Service saw that the kids had great affection for Cake Culkin.

"State's never got money for enough agents," Waco explained. "Was Elray come up with the idee of shadows—unofficial helpers. Cake there was a young man when Elray took 'im on, poachin' since he was tin. Not a better man in the woods, and he never did break the law again—leastways not that Elray or any of the rest of us knew."

Michigan had used unarmed volunteer conservation officers—VCOs—for many years. They had twenty or so hours of training and worked for free. Last fall Chief Lorne O'Driscoll had cancelled the program because the state's lawyers felt there were substantial liability issues. A lot of officers were still complaining about the decision. Two sets of eyes always beat one set, and two bodies at night served as a deterrent when violets turned frisky or vicious.

"The state knows about shadows?"

"Not officially, and ain't nothin' writ down on paper," Waco said, "but a body don't rise to top dog less'n he works his way up. It just don't get talked about . . . officially or unofficially. I believe Elray even done give some of his pay to Cake, but I hain't sure on thet. Wouldn't surprise me none, though."

The widow came over to them. It had been raining off and on since the funeral and the field was muddy. She carried two cups of coffee and handed them to the men.

"You'n not a G-man?" the woman said to Service.

"No, ma'am. I'm just along to see if I can help."

"You want to hep, find him which murdered my husband," she said. She held up a large cloth sack and Service looked inside. It was the horse head-dress with the tall black plumes.

"Each a' them feathers rep'sents a Spargo done fell in service to his country. Most of 'em was durin' the wars—One, Two, Korea, Vietnam. Elray's the first lawman in the clan, and he deserves his feather, but I cain't put it in till we know justice's been done. You get things took care of, you bring 'em back, and I'll know."

Grady Service tried to return the bag to her, but she pushed it back at him. "Let it remind you what it is you got to do," she said.

Her sweet scent overwhelmed him, and all he could do was nod as she marched away to talk to others.

"What is that perfume?" Service asked.

"Plumgranny, not perfume," Eddie Waco said after a theatrical sniff. "Bin around as a sweet scent since the time a' Shakespeare, I hear."

"Does she actually think I can do something about finding her husband's killer?"

"Seems to me, you'n the one holdin' the bag," Eddie Waco said, grinning and looking down. "You done been made Elray Spargo's champeen, and thet hain't no little thing in these here parts."

Service rolled his eyes and muttered, "Just great."

# 15

# West Plains, Missouri
## May 26, 2004

The glassed-in lobby of the hospital in West Plains had the sharp angle of a ship's bow. Service found Special Agent Tatie Monica in a single room, in bed, flat on her stomach.

She craned to look over her shoulder and glared. "They stole our body."

"They?"

"Them, they, somebody. Our evidence is *gone*."

She was a very unhappy fed. He said, "You mean the man's family? They didn't steal him, they buried him."

"Some damn hillbilly sheriff carried it away in a helicopter," she said. "Without authorization, which is tampering with, and impeding a federal investigation."

She wasn't listening. "He did it for the family, and relax—I know where he is."

"You know? You *know!* Jesus, why didn't you stop them?" she asked.

Service got a chair, pulled it around so she could see him, and sat down with the back of the chair against his chest. "They have some pretty firm convictions about how and when they bury their dead." He didn't reveal Agent Eddie Waco's role in what had happened.

She rolled her eyes and clenched her fists.

"You'll heal faster if you stay calm," Service said.

"I'm trying to find a murderer, some hillbilly sheriff garbs my evidence and . . . and *now* I'm getting health advice from a man who makes his living chasing people who chase *animals!*"

"Add fish, and that's a pretty good job description," he said.

The agent let loose a hiss of anguish. "I want *out* of this fucking place!"

"Who's stopping you?"

"They had to do surgery."

"I thought you said no cutting."

"Bite me," she shot at him.

"You brought it up."

She looked at him through tight eyes. "No bull, you *really* know where the body is?"

"I was at the funeral."

"I can't believe you didn't stop them," she keened.

"I also met a man who saw the body right after the killing."

Special Agent Monica sucked in a breath. "Don't shit me," she whispered, propping herself up on her elbows.

"Truth," he said. "He was the dead man's pine shadow."

She rolled her eyes again. "English, Service. What the *fuck* is a pine shadow?"

"Down here it's an unpaid volunteer partner to a conservation agent. Other places it's probably the darkness behind and below a tree when the sun shines on it."

She grimaced and switched on a professional tone. "This guy told you something?"

"Not yet." Cake Culkin had been in no shape for cogent thought, much less a penetrating interview.

"But he will?"

"That's the plan."

"Jesus," she complained. "Does the lead agent get to know this plan?"

"That's why I'm here," he said.

"Visitors are supposed to boost a patient's spirits and confidence."

"Real confidence comes from within," he said.

"Are you pathologically objective?"

"When I need to be."

"I don't like how this is playing out," Agent Monica said. "Two kills so close in time—that's never happened before."

"Maybe he's in a hurry."

"This guy doesn't make mistakes: He's unbelievable. We're taught that the average murderer makes at least two dozen mistakes. This guy hasn't made any so far . . . but it could be his psychosis is deepening," she said, almost to herself.

"We've got a potential witness here and the kill site in Wisconsin. Those're mistakes, and maybe there are more."

"And?" she said impatiently.

"Wayno's body was warm and wet. Thorkaldsson could have walked up on the killer, which means his timing was off, his source of information and calculations not what they've been, right? And he didn't bother to collect the fishing gear, which led us to the kill site. There's bound to be more if we look in the right place, and ask the right questions."

She looked at him for a long time before covering her eyes with a forearm and moaning loud enough to concern him. "You want me to call a nurse?"

Tatie Monica struggled to sit up and hissed, "I want *out* of here. I've been after this asshole for three years, and now that he's accelerating I am *not* going to lay here like of leg of ham."

"Lamb," Service said. "Leg of lamb, not ham."

"Lamb, Spam," she grumbled.

"Is that what happens in these cases—the killers speed up?"

"This one defies generalization," she said. "I've insisted all along that man is an imperfect animal. Locard's exchange principle tells us that when two things come in contact, each will leave something behind. There has to be *something* this guy is missing, *has* to be." She looked at him. "What's the plan?"

"Agent Waco is with the witness. When you're ready to leave, we'll go see them."

She pointed at a wall locker. "My clothes are in there."

"You were sorta short on clothes last time I saw you."

"My people brought more stuff."

He took out slacks, a blouse, and boots, and set them on the chair.

She managed to swing her legs down to the floor and sit up, but not without a lot of puffing and contorted faces. He pushed the chair down the side of the bed so that it was in front of her.

"You sure you want to do this?"

She said, "Stop gawking and get out."

He stepped outside the room to find Special Agent Larry Gasparino carrying two Styrofoam cups. Service blocked the door. "She's getting dressed."

"They're kicking her loose?" the young agent asked.

"In a manner of speaking. You got off the river okay?

"We had to use chain saws and axes all the way down. How is she?"

"Testy," Service said.

"Normal, then."

"She thinks things are falling apart."

Gasparino stared at him. "Optimism isn't part of her genetic wiring."

"Perfectionist?"

"Tendencies, but usually she knows when she goes too far."

"Pressure's getting to her," Service said.

"The list is her safety valve," the agent said.

List? "We all gotta believe in something," Service said, "and a list is as good as anything." What was Gasparino inadvertently disclosing?

"So far," Gasparino said. "Not that it's put us ahead of the game."

*A list of what?* He knew he couldn't ask directly. Gasparino had let something slip and didn't seem to realize it. "Been with her long?"

"January," the man said. "Fucking Wisconsin winters. We got people in our office who pray for thirty below for Packer games, and I'm talking, like, *out-fucking-doors!* They paint their man-boobs in Packer green and go to the frigging games *shirtless.* Is that supposed to be normal, or what?" The man shook his head.

"Monica good to work for?"

"Better than I thought she'd be," Gasparino said.

Service saw a flash of panic in the man's eyes. Rule one for feds: Never talk outside school.

He backed off and told himself he needed to know more about the list but didn't want to spook the young agent.

"You talk to the agent holding down the site in Wisconsin?"

"Bobbi?" He shook his head again. "I've been too busy securing what we brought down the river. Then I slept like a dead man. I thought chain saws were supposed to make wood cutting fast and easy."

Service nodded sympathetically. Were any of the agents focused on the big picture in this case? "That storm was bad."

"I was in the city on 9/11," Gasparino said. "Not near Ground Zero, but it was scary enough. This was worse."

The disaster in New York City had become the standard for measuring the magnitude and meaning of all disasters and atrocities, Service thought. People who survived natural disasters had similar respect in the aftermath. Gasparino was young and seemed earnest, but he was also green. He had mentioned the list on the unwarranted assumption that Service was in the loop, and his gut told him he'd better quickly find a way into it.

Tatie Monica limped gingerly out of her room and started down the hall with the two men flanking her. "This turns out to be bullshit . . . ," she muttered, not finishing her statement.

# 16

## Left Shoulder Ridge, Missouri
### May 26, 2004

Gasparino had a fairly new black Ford Expedition, and he helped Monica into the backseat so she could stretch out her legs. Service sat up front to navigate. Eddie Waco had shown him the road to Cake Culkin's place during the trip to West Plains to drop him off. He told Gasparino to turn north along the border between Oregon and Ripley counties.

"Jesus, are we there yet?" Monica asked repeatedly, the first time less than two minutes outside the West Plains city limits.

"Chill," Service said the first time she complained. "It's about forty miles—and there's no interstate."

Gasparino reacted by speeding up, but when he fishtailed around a curve, Service told him to slow down. "We don't want to end up in a ditch with the snakes," he said. This reminded him that Nantz would have easily negotiated these roads, which were a lot more difficult than M-35. *Not an accident*, he told himself for the umpteenth time. What did he need to move the Troops off their conclusion and to reopen the investigation? More importantly, who would want to run her off the road?

"Goddammit, Larry, *listen* to the man!" Tatie Monica squawked from the backseat.

Cake Culkin lived about five miles from the Spargos' place, in the rocky saddle and shadow of a razorback ridge called Left Shoulder. They parked on the main gravel road and Service led them on foot down the edge of a rutted dirt-and-gravel track that served as the man's driveway. The cabin was small and tidy, with a rickety carport and an older-model black Chevy pickup in front, the truck Eddie Waco had used to take him to West Plains. Service left the agents in the woods while he went to the house. The hood of the truck was cold. He stood to the side of the door, knocked, waited.

Eddie Waco answered the door, looked up, and nodded. "Back quicker'n I figgered," he said, opening it. "Them feds lurkin' out yonder?"

"Two of them."

"Best fetch 'em on in."

Service looked back and waved.

Waco led them into a small kitchen. Cake Culkin was sitting at a small round table, his hands folded in front of him, his leg up on a chair.

"Cake, these folks want ta talk at ya'll some," Waco said.

The man didn't look up. "They feds?"

"Two of 'em," Eddie Waco said.

"You can wait outside," Tatie Monica said dismissively to the Missouri conservation agent.

"We both stay," Service said.

The FBI agent glared.

"Waco saved your ass," Service said. "Literally."

Monica shrugged with resignation and rolled her eyes. She couldn't communicate without facial punctuation, a lousy habit for a cop or a poker player. The more he saw, the greater his concern about her competence. He couldn't put his finger on it, but there were moments when she seemed almost desperate.

"You found Agent Spargo," she began, a statement, not a question. Right to the point, no empathy for the man's potential discomfort or anxieties.

"I reckon I seen 'im," Cake said. "And run." His voice cracked as he sucked in a breath.

The FBI agent seemed to realize something was wrong and she suddenly switched gears. "Your name's Cake, right? I'm Tatie." Off a beat and too late, Service thought. The man was going to turtle. Was it lack of skills on her part, or impatience?

Cake Culkin gave a pleading look to Eddie Waco, whose face remained impassive.

"Let's start again," Tatie Monica said. "I'm Tatie, Cake. You want anything?"

Too late, Service thought. Her initial directness had put the man on his heels, left him tight and withdrawn.

"I hain't sick," Culkin said.

"Cake," Eddie Waco said, "these folks want to find who done Elray like thet."

"I'll talk ta you'n," the man said. "And him," he added with a nod to Service, "but I already done took all y'all through this afore."

Service brushed Monica's sleeve to let her know she should keep quiet. Apparently she got the hint.

"Memories kin be a might slippery sometimes," Eddie Waco said. "'Member back whin you'n an' Elray an' me done chased thet ole boy kilt his wife over ta White Briar? Me an' Elray was sure it were a blue truck, but it weren't. Was black, jes like you said."

"Had dirt all over it," Cake Culkin said. "Coulda bin blue."

"But it weren't, and been just Elray and me, we'd a' missed that ole boy, but havin' you along made the case. That's what we got here, Cake. More heads we got, better off we are, okay? We need to go over what you seen again."

"Shoot," Culkin said with a grin. "You been ta college and you got you a steel-trap mind."

"The trap sometimes gets a mite rusty," Waco said with a smile.

Service could feel Tatie Monica fidgeting and bumped her to settle her down.

"Seein' Elray that way spooked us all," Waco added.

"You boys din't run," Culkin said, running his hands through his hair and sucking in a deep breath. "Who you think wanna do somethin' like that ta Elray?"

"Don't know yet," Waco said. "But you can help us ta help Fi and them young 'uns."

Cake Culkin nodded emphatically. "I done said what I seen."

"He had a meeting?" Waco asked.

Culkin nodded.

"Who did he meet, Cake?"

"Elray didn't say."

"You and him went way back. You *knew* him."

"Nobody knew Elray. Well, mebbe Fi. He was differ'nt to differ'nt folks. Always told me he was a *thespeen*. What's that mean?"

"Actor," Service said.

Culkin grinned. "That was ole Elray."

"You cain't work all them years with a man and not know him," Eddie Waco said,

"You agents is all the same. Nobody knows all y'all."

Eddie Waco said, "I take yore pint, Cake, but the way it is, you don't give us somethin', we gon' be plumb outta luck."

"You mind if I ask a question, Cake?" Service asked.

" 'Speck not."

"You got good trout fishing around here?"

"Passable, I reckon."

"You fish?"

The man said, "Whin I git the chance."

"How do you know when the bite's on?" Service asked.

Cake Culkin rolled his tongue inside his cheek. "I jes keep my eyes open."

"Weather, maybe?"

"Wind tells a man a lot. Warm rain fallin'. An' I kick the grass with my boots, see what might skitter about."

"Spiderwebs under bridges?" Service asked.

Culkin grinned and raised an eyebrow. "I reckon you done some fishin' yoreseff."

"Some," Service allowed. "What we have here, Cake, is an empty web, and we're not kickin anything up in the grass. Did you and Elray plan to fish that night?"

"Nossir."

A *change*, Service thought. Had the other dead officers been fishing, or were they just found near water? This wasn't clear and it bothered him not to know. "Was Agent Spargo's meeting with a man?"

Culkin's face darkened. "Not proper a married-up man meet private-like with a womarn not his'n."

"Unless he had official business with her and needed to keep it private," Eddie Waco interjected, picking up on Service's comment.

"Thet's so," Culkin said. "But were a man got met."

"You're certain?" Service asked softly.

Culkin chewed his lip and spoke haltingly. "I ast, all ya'll 'll tell Fi and them young 'uns it were a man?"

"We'd do that," Eddie Waco said. "Sometimes ole Elray, he asked you to keep things in confidence."

"Was how it were."

"And if that was the case here, you'd keep that confidence no matter what. You'd not be able to say it."

"A man's word's his word," Culkin said.

"You understand how important this is," Eddie Waco said.

"Yessir, I truly do."

"It's good you keep your word, Cake. How about we bend this saplin' another direction?"

Culkin looked skeptical, but shrugged and said, "I reckon."

"Just for now, let's jes say a man is a one and a womarn is a two. You with me?"

Culkin nodded.

"If a man's one and a womarn's two, what was the sum of the people at thet meetin' ole Elray had?"

"Four," Culkin said without hesitation.

"Now, Cake, it cain't be four," Eddie Waco said. "Gotta be two or three."

"Were four," Culkin insisted through clenched teeth.

Service intervened: "One plus one, *plus* two?"

Culkin nodded. "Thet's four."

"At the same time?" Service added.

"Reckon not," Culkin said.

"You saw one of them, Cake?"

"Could be."

Waco took over again. "Let me guess. You seen a two, but not a one, on account Elray done made you think the meeting was with a one, only you seen a two and mebbe now you're a'wonderin if'n there was a one a'tall."

Tatie Monica moaned and Service dug his heel into her instep, making her recoil.

Cake Culkin was sweaty and deathly still.

"You'n recognized the two," Eddie Waco said.

"Reckon you'n would, too," Culkin said quickly, "her wearin' a badge an' all."

"Y'all seen a badge?"

"Not thet day."

"But you know who this two is, am I right?"

"Rigmutton, I 'speck, not the sort you see at weekly meetin's."

"This be a badge a body might see round the courthouse?" Waco asked.

"Could be," Culkin said. "Hear tell there's a place on the Warm Fork, west end of Millstone Holler."

"West of Koshkonong?"

"I just heard they's a place over thet way is all."

"How long after you saw the two did you find Elray?" Service asked.

"Not long after the lightnin' done spit."

"Lightnin' spit?" Waco asked.

"Seen the flash, never heard the boom."

"When?"

"A while after Elray done went on by hisself," the man said, his hands shifting to palms up. Service suspected they'd heard all they were going to hear.

Service asked, "You didn't find Elray where he said he was going to meet?"

"Nossir. Found him over to the Hurricane."

"How?" Eddie Waco asked.

"Blood trail," Culkin said, hanging his head.

Service said, "You said the sum was four, but Elray and the woman make three. Are you counting yourself?"

Culkin shook his head. "I reckon they was another."

"You saw another man?" Waco asked.

"Jes a peek."

"When?"

"Jes afore I come upon Elray at the Hurricane."

"Did you see the two?" Waco asked.

"Nossir, but Elray said he was meetin' her."

Service intervened. "You actually saw just the man."

"I reckon she was there somewheres."

Eddie Waco walked Service and the feds outside. "A setup. I'm thinking she arranged for Elray ta meet someone."

"Jesus," Tatie Monica said. "Who the fuck are we talking about? Ones and twos? *Hello!* Jesus, is this *Earth?*"

"Laglenda Owens, deputy with Oregon County. Hired from Jeff City 'bout a year back. She calls us both with stuff she sees out on road patrol."

Deputies in the U.P. did the same for Service. "They were friends, Deputy Owens and Spargo?"

"I reckon thet's all they was. Once Elray met Fi, that was hit for other womern."

"How can you be sure she's the right woman?" Service asked.

"Only one female totin' a badge in the county, and I know where she lives, 'zackly the place Cake was talkin' on. Want, we can run on over there."

Tatie Monica said, "Okay, Opie and Gomer, can we fucking do this now, or do we have to have a chaw and spee-it fest first?"

Eddie Waco held out a tin of Redman. " 'Backy?"

Even Tatie Monica laughed.

Service found it odd that they had just learned the location of another possible kill site and she wasn't asking questions. How far was it to the Hurricane camp from where Spargo was supposed to meet the deputy—*if* he met her? He thought about Elray Spargo. It was one thing to drag the diminutive Wayno Ficorelli up a river. It was a whole different challenge for one man to drag a giant like Spargo over rough ground through brush tangles. And if Spargo had no intention of fishing that night, wasn't that a break in the pattern? Where were his clothes? Grady Service had endless questions, but Tatie Monica seemed to have none. He didn't know if her lack of interest made him angry or worried.

# 17

## Warm Fork, Missouri
### May 26, 2004

As soon as they got into the Expedition, Tatie Monica again demanded to know how long the drive would take.

Service said, "Let's wait for Agent Waco."

The conservation agent drove his truck out to the gravel road, parked in front of them, and walked back. "I jes talked at Sheriff Hakes. Owens has herself four days off and Doug thinks she mighta run up to Jeff City ta see kin. I called out ta her place, but all I got was a dadblame machine."

"We need to take a look," Tatie Monica said. "How far is it?"

"Good sixty mile from where we sit now," Eddie Waco said, "Twinny mile t'other side of Alton."

Special Agent Monica leaned her head back and muttered, "Shit."

Eddie Waco nodded Service toward his truck. "Join me?"

Service told Gasparino he was going to ride with Waco, and the two vehicles pulled out.

Waco drove at a steady, almost leisurely pace and Service wondered if it was intentional. He looked back and imagined he could see Monica fidgeting in the backseat. "Who actually reported findin' Elray?" Eddie Waco asked.

Service said, "You don't *know?* I assume it was Cotton Spargo. Cake Culkin went to him first, right?"

"Nope. I done talked to 'im, and he only tol' family. But Cotton hain't one to spit it all out. Could be he called Doug Hakes and Doug called the state."

"Which agency got the official notification? We got our call from Bonaparte."

"Where'd that ole boy get off to, anyways?" Eddie Waco asked.

"Beats me. You met him at the river site."

"Never set eyes on the man," Waco said. "Heard from the boys he's a nice-enough feller, not strung tight like your typical fed. You gettin' a feel for what's a-goin' on?"

On the contrary; it seemed like every few hours the case seemed to tumble into a flat spin. "I wish."

"I can tell you this: Somebody got the jump on Elray, they's somethin' special."

"Or they had help," Service said. He'd seen Spargo's size. Even he would have a hard time in a scrap with a man that large. Maybe there was more than one attacker? No evidence for this, just a thought—but it took hold.

Eddie Waco looked over at Service. "Hit don't play, Laglenda Owens bein' in the middle of this. She's a solid deputy. She mixed up in this, I'm thinkin' she got herseff blutterbunged."

"Blutterbunged?" Service repeated. "What language is this down here?"

"Means tricked, some say. The language ya'll hear some claim is close ta what got spoke in Shakespeare's day." Eddie Waco winked. "It prolly done changed a tetch . . ."

"There or here?" Service said.

Both men laughed. "Both," Eddie Waco said.

Service said, "If the Owens woman is out of town, we can still call her, right?"

"Doug's people don't leave town without leavin' a contact number," Eddie Waco said. "Doug Hakes may be a country boy, but he runs his ship tight as a tick on a blade a' long June grass."

"What's the Owens woman's background?"

"People in these parts don't put much stock in the past what was somewhere else. What matters is what a body does now."

"Cake implied the deputy was . . ."

"Cake's a prude," Waco said. "But she's a young 'un with fire in 'er belly."

"You and Elray share Oregon County?"

"Mostly his. I got Ripley, and sometimes we worked together."

Waco looked in the rearview mirror and smiled. "They close 'nuff to lick our bumper."

Service looked back, saw Gasparino tailgating only a few feet behind them. Tatie Monica was gesticulating wildly from the backseat.

"The thing about breakin' in a mule," Eddie Waco said, maintaining his speed, "you jes gotta baffound 'im."

The Warm Fork of the Spring River, like the Eleven Point, flowed in a southeasterly direction, starting as Howell Creek in the town of West Plains. The water was cloudy with a grayish-green cast to it, and a rocky bottom. More limestone, Service thought, or clay. The flow was steady, down small steps into skinny-water pools, the banks heavily wooded near the deputy's small house.

They left the vehicles two hundred yards up the road from the house and moved down through scrub brush, tall Ozark cane, and small, tightly packed trees. The one-story house was small and narrow, facing the river, which flowed less than thirty feet from the back stoop. The main entrance was on the south side. Eddie Waco volunteered to go up to the house because he knew the deputy. Service watched the back of the place. Monica and Gasparino each took a side.

A grim-faced Eddie Waco stepped onto the back porch and waved Service in. Service smelled the odor before he got to the door, and accepted Vicks from the Missouri agent.

The woman was unclothed on the bed, a large hole in the peak of her head, the pillow, sheets, and backboard stained with brain tissue and blood. No defensive wounds. The only entry wound was under the chin. Had she known the killer? Her clothes were ripped and scattered around the room. Eddie Waco showed Service the body and shook his head. There were flies in the room, and a computer in the corner.

"Gunshot," Service said. No weapon in sight. "Homicide."

Waco nodded, and Service went out and summoned the FBI agents.

Tatie Monica took a deep breath and said, "Okay, first we isolate the house. Call the county to provide perimeter security—but *only* the FBI comes down the road this far. Second, get the crime scene team back from St. Louis." She looked at the computer in the dining room. "Third, tell them to send someone from cyberforensics, Larry. Got it?" Gasparino nodded and dashed outside.

"Not my business," Eddie Waco said, "but Doug Hakes ain't gonna sit second banana with one a' his deputies a-layin' here dead. This here's *his* deputy and hit's *his* county."

"You're right," Tatie Monica said. "It's *not* your business, and who the fuck is Doug Hakes?"

"Sheriff."

"This connects to a federal case," she said. "You send this Hakes to me when he gets here."

"Won't have to send 'im," Waco said. When Monica went outside to find out if Gasparino had gotten through to the St. Louis field office, Eddie Waco said, "Don't you jes love jurisdictional harmony."

Sheriff Hakes arrived on the scene twenty minutes after the word went out. He came in talking and puffing, his face red with an adrenaline surge. "Okay, I got people settin' up a perimeter, and the state's got a crime scene team rolling," he announced.

"That won't be necessary," Tatie Monica said.

"I guess I'll be decidin' what's necessary," the sheriff shot back.

They were nose to nose, their voices low, words clipped.

Service said, "Comforts one to see how 9/11's got law enforcement agencies operating as one team."

"Sound as sweet as buzznack," Eddie Waco said under his breath.

Tatie Monica attacked. "There's no debate here, Sheriff! The death of Deputy Owens is related to the Spargo case."

"Says who?"

"A witness places her at the crime scene at or about the TOD."

"Mebbe I ain't buyin' what you'n sellin', and we'll jes see what the county prosecutor has to say 'bout this."

She brandished her forefinger like a sword. "You tampered with a federal investigation, you sonuvabitch, and you removed evidence without authorization. When you talk to the county prosecutor, make sure he knows there'll be a federal warrant coming down with *your* name on it. He can file it under 'A' for asshole."

Service watched Hakes take a half-step backward. His jaw was still rigid, but he had just retreated and given up ground. "You hain't heard the last word on this," the sheriff said.

"I have from you, Ernest T. Bass. Just make sure your people keep the goddamned road closed off." She turned to Gasparino. "St. Louis?"

"Chopper in the air in thirty," he said. "Cyberforensics is sending Pappas."

Tatie Monica stepped outside and looked up the road and pointed. "The chopper can put down over there. Tell them." Gasparino took his handheld and stepped away. Monica muttered, "Glory Drophat, that airhead bimbo."

Why was Tatie Monica directing the helicopter landing site and not examining the crime scene? "Where's Bonaparte?" Service asked.

Tatie Monica looked at him and tilted her head. "Don't tell me how to do my job," she said, turning away.

Service caught her by the arm. "I'm not trying to tell you *anything*. I'm trying to figure out what *I'm* supposed to be doing here."

Her attitude softened. "You're doing fine. Just stay close to me, and if you see something you think I should know, tell me."

"What about Bonaparte?" he repeated.

"*My* case," she said. "Not his."

When she tried to turn away again, Service stepped in her path. "Who reported Spargo's body? Bonaparte called us and we came, but who told him and put all this into action?" He wasn't sure when the thought implanted, but his mind kept swinging back to Bonaparte, his role, his movement, his absence.

She looked at him and smiled. "Now *that's* the kind of question I like to hear asked." Statement made, she walked away and, as usual, no answer was forthcoming.

Service studied the dead woman's body and wondered if there had been consensual sex, a rape, or no sex at all.

"Somethin' weighin' y'all down?" Eddie Waco asked.

Grady Service walked to Waco's truck and pulled latex gloves out of a box he has seen there. He returned to the house and leaned over the body. "You got a magnifying glass?" he asked.

"Got some cheaters I use ta tie on itsy-bitsy flies."

"Mind if I borrow them?"

Waco brought them back and Service hovered over the dead woman's face for nearly two minutes, stood up, and handed the magnifiers back to Waco. "Did Cake actually see the woman that day, or did Elray just tell him about her?"

"Thet still hain't real clear in my mind neither," the game warden said. "You see somethin'?"

"Not sure," Service said. In fact, her eyes looked normal, an observation that strangely disappointed him. Why did the blood eagle killer take his victims' eyes?

They found the sheriff sulking up the road.

"Who gave you the word on Spargo?" Service asked.

"The highway patrol got a call from the feds and they called me."

"You didn't talk to Cotton Spargo or Cake Culkin?"

"Jes at the fun'ral."

Service and Waco looked at each other, but said nothing. *What feds?* How had the FBI learned about the body before local law enforcement? In previous cases, had anyone called the FBI directly, or had information about new killings come up through other law enforcement agencies? The longer this thing went on, the more questions he had, the less direction there seemed to be, and the more irritated he was getting.

# 18

## Warm Fork, Missouri
### May 26, 2004

The cyberforensics expert arrived with the crime scene team, floated into the house without greeting or acknowledging anyone, sat down at the wooden chair in front of the dead deputy's computer, and tapped a key to turn it on. She looked up at Gasparino and said, "I need the full name, place, and date of birth, names of vick's parents and siblings, and a photo album."

Glory Drophat was well over six feet with a thick mane of corn-yellow hair and a figure that would make men gape and women roll their eyes. Service thought she also had the slightly distant stare of someone in need of a new contact lens prescription. Her fingernails were chewed to the quick.

Gasparino looked at Tatie Monica, who nodded assent and approached the computer expert. "You're supposed to check in with the lead agent, Glory."

"Don't start," the blonde said wearily, "and *don't* call me that. LA is history. I'd say bury the hatchet, but this is the twenty-first century. You ought to think about joining it."

A less-than-harmonious history between the women, Service surmised.

Ten minutes after Gasparino gave her the things she asked for, the statuesque agent reported, "I'm in," adding, "E-mail's through AOL, same passwords for everything." She clucked disapproval and mumbled, "People are so predictably stupid." Having invaded the dead woman's electronic domain, she turned to Special Agent Monica. "What am I looking for?"

"We're not sure; maybe a string of notes, an invitation to meet, something."

"Hoping for luck to strike again?" the woman said, turning her back to Monica and tapping keys.

"Just do your job," Tatie Monica said.

"Not a problem when you're competent," the woman countered.

Service nudged Gasparino. "What's all this about?"

The two men stepped into the next room. "Word has it that Pappas and Monica were part of a high-profile investigation out of the LA field office. They have a history."

"Pappas?"

"Glory Drophat is what Tatie calls her. Her name's Alona Pappas. The way I heard it, Pappas boffed somebody above Monica to get the team lead on that case, but after she got it, the investigation went into free fall. Monica never bought what Pappas was selling and went her own way and broke the case. Pappas moved over to cyber and Monica ended up in Milwaukee. Last we heard Pappas was in New York, on loan to Homeland Security. We didn't know she was in St. Louis."

Service inferred that both women had been disciplined. "What kind of case in LA?" Special Agent Monica had told him Milwaukee was her choice.

"Multiple homicide: four people sliced and diced the same night in an upscale Brentwood apartment building. Pappas was sure it was an inside job, but Monica thought it was too much like an unsolved in Houston. Pappas pushed for the arrest of a simp, the twenty-something-year-old son of one of the vicks. Monica insisted the simp might do one out of passion, but not four. There was no apparent motive or weapon, and nothing in the man's background to indicate serial murder personality traits, like sadistic tendencies. Monica learned that one of the suspects from the Houston case had moved to LA, and she hunted him down and found the weapon stashed at a house where he worked as a gardener."

It sounded to Service like good police work. "Why Drophat?"

"Tatie claims Pappas will boink anybody, anytime, anywhere, to get ahead—like, at the drop of a hat?"

"Okay," Service said. Not only did he not understand yet why he was here or what exactly they expected from him, but now it appeared he would also have to contend with internecine warfare. Of all the agencies he had worked with over the years, the FBI was, hands down, the most uncooperative, secretive, and parochial, and, from what he was hearing, 9/11 hadn't improved either their attitudes or their performance. If anything, the FBI was imperious, looking at itself as the penultimate professionals of law enforcement and all other agencies as rank amateurs. Wink Kedur, the FBI man who covered the U.P. out of Marquette, was a good guy, but even Wink pretty much towed the agency's line, and Service had learned the hard way to be wary.

Service walked outside and found Eddie Waco perched on a rock by the river. "How all y'all doin' in 'ere?"

"Whole lot of thunder and no lightning," Service said.

"Any word from thet Bonaparte feller?"

"I'd be the last to know," Service said. He still hadn't even met the man.

Eddie Waco propelled a stream of tobacco juice onto the ground. "Make y'all wonder a-why they done brung you to the hoedown?"

"It's crossed my mind," Service admitted, knowing it was time to nail Special Agent Monica's ass to a record. How many days had he been gone? It seemed like a month, and he had not called the captain, the chief, or O'Brien. The captain and chief would both understand. Grant would explain to the priest he was out of state and on a case and didn't have time. "Your man Cake be okay?" Service asked.

"Cake's Cake. He be lookin' like a sick dawg with a thorn in his foot fer now, but he'll get on, I reckon."

# 19

# Alton, Missouri
## May 27, 2004

Service waited until they had checked into a sleep-cheap in Alton for the night before calling Tatie Monica out to the parking lot. "Pappas get anything?"

"Not yet. She'll take the hard drive to St. Louis, see what she can recover. Don't bother crossing your fingers."

"Then what?"

"St. Louis will send more agents and we'll canvas friends and associates of both vics and see what we get. It would've been too easy if the computer gave us a trail," she lamented.

"As slick as this guy seems to be, you'd think he'd be stupid enough to use a computer?" he asked.

"We'll have to check it out to rule it out."

Slogans made Service cringe.

"You can do without me. I think I'm going to head for home," Service announced. He doubted that talking to hill people would give the FBI much more than they had. It was a tight society not open to outsiders unless they got vouched in by someone like Eddie Waco. He had work to do back home. Nantz's killer was on the loose. He was wasting his time here. Also, if a serial killer planned to knock off a Michigan CO to fill his scorecard, Service had no business being out here. People needed to be warned.

The FBI agent looked at him through squinty eyes. "Leaving on whose authority?"

"My own," he said. "I'm not in the homicide business."

"I already explained your value to the team and effort," she countered, looking like she wanted to scream at him. After a pause and a glance at the night sky, she added, "How about waiting for Bonaparte? Will you do that?" She sounded like she was choking on her words.

"When?" Service asked.

"Soon," she said.

"Not good enough," he shot back. "I ask questions and the check is always in the mail. When will he be here?"

"Not here," she said. "Wisconsin."

"When?" Service pressed.

"First, we have to get things squared away here," she said, clumsily negotiating for time."

"Dammit, Tatie, *when?*"

"He's supposed to be there tomorrow."

"Good. Get me on a plane tonight."

"I don't have that kind of muscle."

"I'm out of here, one way or another."

He thought she was on the verge of a tantrum, but she toggled her handheld and said calmly, "Larry, call Wes and tell him we need a bird to transport Detective Service back to Iron Mountain."

Gasparino asked, "Now?"

"*Right* now," she said emphatically.

"Wes?" Service asked.

"My boss in Milwaukee."

The two of them stood in the parking lot not saying anything. A red Jeep Liberty pulled into a parking spot and a couple got out, laughing. When they started groping each other Tatie Monica growled, "Take that shit inside!" The startled couple fled.

"Drives me crazy," she said to Service, "us up to our asses in gore and people carrying on like the world is normal."

"It is normal," Service said. "At least, it's our job to make it seem that way."

Gasparino came outside. "Bonaparte's here," he said breathlessly.

"Here?" Monica asked, unable to hide her surprise.

"He walked into the hotel ten minutes ago and wants a sit-down, ASAP."

Tatie Monica looked confused, then concerned. She turned to Service. "I guess you won't need that plane."

"We'll see," he said.

Cranbrook P. Bonaparte was a nondescript man with a receding hairline, pasty skin, and the benign, almost grandfatherly countenance of the legendary basketball coach, John Wooden. His eyes were pale green and he had a number-three pencil poised in his right hand. A half-dozen more pencils were on the coffee table atop a pocket protector, making it look like a raft. He also had a notepad, a cell phone, and a handheld radio in front of him. His squint suggested contacts or weak eyes. Service guessed his age as late fifties, give or take. A cane was hooked on the edge of the desk.

When Service walked in with Monica and Gasparino, Bonaparte brightened and, looking at Service, stood, extended his hand, and said, "I don't believe we've been introduced."

The man's voice was friendly and welcoming, his handshake neither too soft, nor too emphatic. Nothing about him suggested FBI. His shirt was wrinkled and he had a smudge above his shirt pocket.

Tatie Monica said, "Detective Grady Service, Michigan Department of Natural Resources."

Bonaparte studied him. "Yes, of course."

"I thought he might add a unique perspective to the investigation, and he has already helped locate the kill site in Wisconsin by thinking like a trout fisherman."

Service picked up on her words. *She* thought? Hadn't his involvement been the Wisconsin AG's idea?

"Excellent," Bonaparte said. "Creative initiative, Special Agent Monica, invariably yields results."

They all sat down and Tatie Monica took Bonaparte through the Wisconsin killing, then the Missouri murder, adding, "Detective Service identified a witness who accompanied the dead man. The witness saw a woman he knew near the kill site. We later found her body. She was murdered in her home. She was a local deputy county sheriff."

"*May* have accompanied the vick," Service corrected her. "And we haven't found the actual kill site, but Culkin told us approximately where to look."

Tatie Monica looked over at him. "Culkin said Spargo met the woman, and with the storm coming in, we can't be sure of the kill site, though the body was found not that far from where the witness thought the meeting took place."

When did she learn this? Service said, "That's not what I heard Culkin say. Deputy Owens may have been at that scene, or she may have just set up a meet for Spargo—or neither."

"I heard what the man said," Special Agent Monica said too forcefully.

"We should wait for the autopsy to determine her TOD," Service said.

"Is that your *professional* opinion?" the FBI woman shot back.

"Common sense."

Service expected Bonaparte to intervene, but he continued to scribble notes.

"Sorry to interrupt," Service said.

Tatie Monica resumed her report, explaining the theft and subsequent burial of the dead conservation agent's body. Service thought he detected a twinkle in Bonaparte's eye. Either he was enjoying Monica's anguish, or he was just an agreeable sort, which seemed to fit his demeanor.

When Tatie Monica finished, Bonaparte looked at Service. "Any other observations or constructive criticism you would care to share, Detective?"

Jesus Christ, was the man inviting him to pile on? Was Bonaparte trying to irritate Monica? Service considered questioning his own role in the boondoggle, but decided this wasn't the right time. He wanted clarification and direction, not more conflict and confusion. Monica allegedly had responded to the Wisconsin attorney general's request to bring him into this, and he still didn't fully understand why. Had she lied? "I've seen some things, but it would be useful to see all the case reports and wait for the autopsy on the Owens woman."

"All before these last two are in the computer," Tatie Monica said. "We'll get you a password."

"I'm not comfortable with the electronic world," Service said. "I like the feel of paper in my hands."

"A man of traditional values," Bonaparte said pleasantly, "a view I wholeheartedly share."

Service smiled and tried to get back to the point. "When can I get hard copies?"

Monica looked at Gasparino, who left the room. Service quickly excused himself and followed the man out, leaving Tatie Monica and Bonaparte alone. "Larry, the case reports will include the list, right?" He tried to keep it light, a friendly afterthought.

"Tatie's the only one who issues copies of the list. It's her baby."

"I lost mine," Service lied. "Any chance to get another copy?"

Gasparino paused before answering. "Sorry, it's her rule; only she makes copies," the young agent insisted.

*Shit,* Service thought. "How about a quick look at yours? I just need to refresh my memory on something before I dig into the case reports."

Gasparino paused again, but shrugged and said, "Okay, man. When I get the other stuff—cool?"

"Thanks," Service said, and let himself back into the meeting room where a tight-lipped Tatie Monica passed him on her way out.

"Ah," Bonaparte said as Service sat down. "Your timing is propitious. I wanted some time alone with you, and let me say at the outset that I must apologize for Special Agent Monica's impetuosity. She sometimes lets enthusiasm turn to zeal, which tends to overpower all reason. For example, I had no idea she would call in a favor from Wisconsin's attorney general."

"What favor?"

"To have you seconded to the investigative team."

"I'm not following this," Service said, but he was. *Seconded?*

"Your governor was asked to send you here so that Agent Monica could look after you. Your governor, of course, was not fully informed, and it's a questionable judgment—albeit grounded in the best of intentions. This sort of knee-jerk reaction has marked her career."

*What the hell was going on?* Bonaparte had just taken a crap on the case's lead agent.

"Why would she want to 'look after' me?" He didn't know whether to laugh out loud or let Bonaparte keep talking.

"I have tried to convince her that we are in pursuit of the perfect killer," Bonaparte said, "a killer who makes no mistakes—or if he does, cleanses them, the net result being perfection."

"Nobody's perfect," Service said.

Bonaparte said enthusiastically, "It comes down to faith, you see? Mankind accepts perfection in God by whatever name, and we are taught we are all made in the image of a creator, and while the vast majority fall short, statistical probability alone tells us there will be the occasional perfect human being."

Mother Teresa, Service could buy—maybe—but not a murderer. "What does any of this have to do with my being looked after?"

"Precisely," Bonaparte said, fluttering his eyebrows. "It's not at all clear to me that a professional of your caliber needs protection, but she has developed the list, and that seems to be driving all of her decisions and tactics."

"List?" he asked.

"Yes," Bonaparte said wearily. "I'm surprised she hasn't filled you in. When our analyst informed us of his findings, she immediately queried the states and asked them to rate their top officers in terms of effectiveness, aggressiveness, and so forth. God knows why, much less what all she threw into the stew," Bonaparte said. "It's ludicrous and presumptuous to think she could so easily develop a predictive instrument—or even attempt it—but that's our Tatie, both decisive and intuitive, even when she's wrong."

Ranking game wardens? Service nearly laughed until it suddenly dawned on him that his name must be on her list. Why else would she have singled him out? Cuo Turnage was the best CO he knew, and he could think of at least ten men and women in the state who deserved to be on such a list, and why the hell was Lansing even giving out such bullshit information?

"The point is," Bonaparte continued, "the killer simply switches targets, which folds opportunity cost into the equation. If Special Agent Monica mobilizes to protect A, he strikes B. This flexibility is part of his brilliance."

"B?"

"Look at the situation in Missouri. The top-rated man on her list is an Agent Waco, but it was number two who got killed."

"Elray Spargo," Service said, feeling his pulse quicken. "Are you telling me that my being here puts somebody else at risk back in my state?"

"I'm speculating, but I would think there is an extremely high probability," Bonaparte said solemnly. "The killer seems to have well-established goals."

"Are you suggesting that the best course for me is to retreat to my own turf and wait?"

"I wouldn't call it a retreat."

Service felt a bolt of ice in his heart. "Has he attacked families?"

"Not yet; but given his adaptability, we can't rule it out, can we? He's creative, and if the analysis is correct, Michigan appears to be the final task in his mission."

"Monica brought me here to protect me," Service said, still not taking the thought fully on board.

"Good intentions, but poorly thought out," Bonaparte said. "He could go after you anywhere. But on your own territory, presumably you would have the advantage."

"Has he killed a warden outside the warden's state?"

"No, but he's both dedicated and creative. Most serial murderers are psychotic and essentially unstable. This one appears to be neither. A sociopath perhaps, but for whatever reason he seems to have set this mission for himself, and when it's completed by the rules he's set for himself, he'll stop."

"That's what your profile predicts?"

"A profile is a work in progress until the killer is captured or killed."

"But he's already gone off his pattern," Service said, "with two kills so close together, and perhaps the Owens woman as well. That's a change. Tatie thinks he's feeling pressure."

Bonaparte countered. "Special Agent Monica has a tendency to engage in wishful thinking. It's more likely that this has been part of his plan from the start."

"The guy's got to be a wacko," Service said.

"Why?" Bonaparte asked, leaning forward.

"Look what he does to the bodies, how he tears them up."

Bonaparte studied him for several seconds. "Is what he does to a body any worse than what a bomb does?"

"Bombs aren't aimed at individuals."

"No? As I seem to recall, it was exactly such intent that got the the most recent war rolling in Iraq, and if the bomb doesn't hit the intended target, is the destruction of others less gruesome?"

Before Service could respond, Bonaparte said, "May I call you Grady?"

Service nodded. Bonaparte was one of the strangest people he had ever met, yet he felt comfortable with the man.

"Tell me, Grady, do you really think that the ability to kill requires one to be insane; for example, a mother defending her child in self-defense, or an executioner following a sentence prescribed by law? Ah," he said. "What enables any soldier to kill in combat?"

Again before Service could answer, the FBI man added, "Thanks to Special Agent Monica, we're aware of your record: You've killed."

"In a war."

"Do you remember the faces of the men you killed?"

"No." He remembered the emotions needed for killing, the intensity and desperate rage, but not the individuals.

"Do you think you're the *only* person who can kill and not be affected? Here you are, a contributing member of society, an effective law enforcement professional in a difficult and underappreciated field. Individuals are individuals, Grady. Some serials remember faces, others do not. Everything we think we know about these people we have to unlearn and start over. Some people can kill as easily as they urinate. Some can't do it at all, no matter the stakes. Judeo-Christian morality proclaims, 'Thou Shalt Not Murder,' and cultures built on this turn right around and support their soldiers in war, imploring God to assist them by making a distinction between murder and killing for society's benefit. Some states and nations have capital punishment, others don't. We're a fragmented and splintered world, Grady. We can't really decide *what* we think about the taking of human life. And as for those who carry out government policy, they kill because they possess the necessary aptitude. Some people can jump four feet straight up. Some can't get their soles off the ground. Each of us is born with certain capabilities and potential. Did it ever occur to you that what you did as a marine with your country's blessing was sanctioned serial murder?"

The man was making outrageous statements, yet they seemed almost rational. One thing seemed certain: the man believed what he was saying. It was time to cut this off.

Service stood up and stared down at the Behavioral Analysis Unit veteran, who announced, "I think we shall review the Wisconsin once in more detail and as a team."

"You can inform Special Agent Monica that I'm returning to where I belong."

"A sound decision, Grady," Bonaparte proclaimed. "I'll tender your regrets, but I wish we had more time to get to know each other better."

Service made eye contact with the man for several seconds before turning away. He fetched his gear from his room and found Eddie Waco in the lobby. "I'm going back to Michigan," he told Waco.

"How?"

"Closest commercial airport?"

"Springfield," Waco said, answering the question about an airport. "I've got my rig," he added.

Special Agent Larry Gasparino caught up to them in the parking lot and handed a large envelope to Service. "The reports you wanted."

"The list too?"

"I made you a copy. Don't tell Tatie."

"No problem—and thanks, Larry."

"You bugging out?"

"Taking care of some loose threads," Service lied.

Service felt duped by Tatie Monica, but he wasn't angry at her. He could sense her desperation to catch the killer, and in her shoes he might have made the same choices, but one thing was for sure: with only Michigan remaining, the COs at home were entitled to know what was going on. He told Eddie Waco the whole story about the killings and the list. They were twenty miles down the road when Service's cell phone rang.

"Good news," biologist Buster Beal greeted him. "It's definitely not what we feared."

"Is that the lab's conclusion?"

"Nope, mine," Beal said, "but I sent slides and tissue samples to confirm. I found the deer's problem. The poor bastard had pneumonia and was blind."

"You're sure?"

"Certain to four nines." Service knew this was techie talk for 99.99 percent. "I sent both eyes to the lab to confirm, but I'm telling you I'm sure."

"Blind," Service said. This would explain some of the animal's bizarre behavior.

"It happens. It also looks like his nose was injured, which compounded things—no sight, no smell, all he had were his ears, and they aren't much good for finding food. Think what that would do to you."

Service felt relieved. Buster was a damn good biologist, and if he was certain this wasn't CWD, chances were it wasn't. "Okay, thanks. Anything else?"

"Yeah, it looks to me like the deer's eyes were burned."

"How does an animal burn its eyes?"

"That's an answer I *don't* have, but if I had to characterize it, I'd say the animal was exposed to some source of concentrated heat or light. Maybe he got mixed up with a downed power line or something. Deer aren't the brightest bulbs in the woods."

"That's pretty hard to swallow."

"So is a deer eating fish," Beal said.

The biologist had once observed a small buck walking the shallows of a river, its snout in the water. Beal took several photographs of minnows hanging out of the animal's mouth. Nobody could explain it, but it had happened, just as Service had once watched a thirteen-stripe chipmunk eating another of its kind, which had been struck by a vehicle. According to biologists, such creatures fed exclusively on seeds, nuts, and the occasional insect, not the flesh of other mammals, especially their own kind. "I hear you," Service said. "Thanks, Chewy."

"I'm just glad it was a false alarm," the biologist said.

Service closed the cell phone and lay it on the dash.

It immediately rang again. "Grady, Gus. Where the hell are you?"

"On assignment."

Gus Turnage chuckled. "The shadowy world of secret squirrels." This was what COs sometimes called their detectives. "Listen, I thought you'd want to know that the word is out that Honeypat Allerdyce was seen in L'Anse."

"When?"

"About a month ago."

Service made a quick calculation. Honeypat was Limpy's daughter-in-law, and she had once tried to usurp power in the clan and nearly killed Limpy in the effort. Limpy was the sort to tackle problems head-on. Honeypat was something entirely different, and dangerous. "Source?"

"I heard it from the magistrate here in Houghton. He heard it from a Baraga County judge named Kryder."

"The judge saw her?"

"That I can't say for sure."

"Can you pin it down for me?"

"Can try, if it's important."

"It could be." Honeypat Allerdyce had cleared out, no doubt with a serious grudge against him. He knew she was capable of attacking Nantz and Walter for revenge. His heart began to race.

"Everything going okay?" Gus asked.

"Jury's out on that," Service said, hanging up,

"Home front?" Eddie Waco asked.

"Yeah." He no longer had a home front, but he kept this to himself.

"Whin families and wardens find out what has gone on, they all gon' be one unhappy bunch," Eddie Waco said. "I can't believe game wardens bin gettin' kilt and nobody got told," Waco added as they drove along.

"I had a hard time believing it too, but you saw Elray's body, and he's not the first one. There are all those others."

Service had shared Bonaparte's theory of the killer. Waco looked over and said, "You'n ever meet a perfect lawbreaker?"

"Excluding politicians?" Service responded, which got them both laughing.

Waco grimaced. "What thet ole boy tole you'n, how I was the big dawg here, thet ain't true."

"Bonaparte said Special Agent Monica got your name from your department."

"Our honchos are a secretive bunch. You git on thet Internet thing just to get the name a' yer local agent, and you won't be a-findin' hit there. They hain't no way the feds gonna get a list worth coon pie from our people. I'm tellin' you'n, Elray Spargo was *the* man and has been for years."

Which meant the killer had not killed anyone except the top person on the list, Service concluded. Why did Bonaparte tell him differently, and why was he suddenly in a rush to get home if he was the target and not Gus or another officer? He found himself lost in his thoughts as the truck's headlights bored a hole in the darkness. *Honeypat back in the U.P.?* This needed to be confirmed. If true, maybe it would provide the leverage he needed to get the Troops to go back and take another look at Nantz's accident scene. His mind was swimming with images, but the one that kept coming back was the freaky light he had seen at Mormon Creek; at the time he didn't think much about it. There also was a blind deer with burnt eyes, and maybe there was sort of a thread, but he couldn't see it. Cake Culkin also claimed to have seen something he seemed to think was lightning without thunder, and the killer who inflicted his victims with the blood eagle had removed their eyes. Service looked over at Eddie Waco. "Is there a television station near here?"

"Closest is West Plains."

"Let's talk to Cake again and go visit the weatherman," Service said.

Eddie Waco said, "I hear grit in 'at voice," he said. "I believe you'n and Elray would've got along good."

# 20

# Left Shoulder Ridge, Missouri
## May 28, 2004

Cake Culkin came to the door looking antsy. "Where's them feds at?" he asked, craning to look into the night past the two game wardens.

"Hit's jes us, Cake," Eddie Waco said. "We found Laglenda Owens dead."

The blood ran out of Culkin's face.

Service jumped in. "Cake, did you actually see Deputy Owens that night?"

"Nossir. I told all y'all I didn't see her badge thet night."

"And not her without the badge, out of uniform?"

"Nope; Elray done tole me he was gonna meet her and another feller."

"He say what about?" Waco asked.

"Nossir."

"Remember telling us you saw a flash of light?" Service asked.

"Lightnin'"

"But you never heard thunder."

"Right."

"You sure it was lightnin', Cake?"

"Was bright enough, I reckon. What else might it be?"

Service asked, "Was Elray acting normal before this happened?" He knew from experience that even when you thought your mood was hidden, others could often read it — especially a partner or a lover.

Cake chewed his lip. "He weren't quite right since his baby sister Rosa done got called ta her reward. They was close, them two."

"When was that, Cake?" Service asked.

"Couple fortnights back, I reckon, give or take."

"How'd she die?"

"Her car rolled over," Agent Waco said.

"Anything unusual about the crash?"

Waco said, "Only that she was a good driver and the weather was good."

He had seen no cars in Fourteen, and no roads. "She didn't live with the family?"

"She lived over ta West Plains with her husband and young 'uns."

"Huh," Grady Service said. Spargo's sister and Nantz and Walter had died about the same time and in a similar manner. It was a weird coincidence.

Service looked at Cake Culkin. "You followed a blood trail and found Elray's body?"

"I said."

"Big blood trail?"

"Like a deer got drug."

"Can you show Agent Waco where you picked up the trail?"

"Rained since then, won't be no p'int."

"Still like ta," Waco chimed in. "Kin we get us a four-wheeler back thet far?"

"I reckon," Culkin said.

"Back tomorrow, Cake," Eddie Waco said.

Service wanted to be sure what he had heard. "Elray said he was meeting Deputy Owens and another man. You never saw her, but you got a glimpse of a man, is that right, Cake?"

Culkin nodded. "That's how it were."

# 21

## West Plains, Missouri
### May 28, 2004

The meteorologist at the television station was middle-aged and overweight with gray-blond hair in a pompadour.

"You got records for the weather goin' back a spell?" Eddie Waco asked.

"That depends on how one defines spell," the man said. "A spell of love can last seconds or a lifetime, a spell of weather somewhere in between."

Service gave him the date.

"Clear night," the weatherman said. "Could see smiles in the stars."

"You can remember what the weather was back then?"

"What they pay me for. We've also got records to corroborate."

"No lightning?" Service asked.

"Nothin' closer than western Kansas, and if you boys are seeking Oz, you don't have to travel that far afield."

Back in Waco's truck Service said, "What lightning was Cake talking about?"

"He's a bit addled. Is it important?"

"I don't know." He was having trouble sorting out the things he had seen and heard, and he was tired.

# 22

# Cabool, Missouri
## May 29, 2004

Service didn't want to answer his vibrating cell phone. It was Special Agent Tatie Monica. "Service, you are *not* leaving until we talk."

"I've had enough talk," Service said.

"Please," the special agent said. "Where are you?"

Service looked over at Eddie Waco. "Where are we?"

"Short spit down the road from Cabool," Waco said.

"Near Cabool," Service told the FBI agent.

"Afghanistan?" she asked.

Service looked at Waco. "She wants to know where that is."

"Texas County," the Missouri man said. "North a' her."

Service passed the word.

"They got an airport?" she asked.

"Airport?" Service said.

"Size of a three-cent stamp," Waco said.

"Little one," Service told her.

"I'll meet you at airport security in two hours," she said. "And I'll arrange for a plane to take you to where you want to go. Just wait for me, okay?"

"Don't waste my time," Service said.

"I'll be there."

He closed the cell phone and cut her off.

"Change in plans?" Eddie Waco asked.

"The feds want a meet."

"And you agreed?"

"She said please."

"I reckon that changes everything," Waco said.

They drove past darkened fields and, on the outskirts of town, farm-implement dealer lots filled with huge, brightly colored machines illuminated by garish neon lights. They pulled into the parking lot of an orange building called The Fish-Walker. The interior was dark, with a century-old stand-up bar, vases filled with peacock feathers, and dusty stuffed fish on the walls, mostly trout.

The waitress had long straight hair and a gaunt face. She stood with her legs apart like a linebacker waiting to make a tackle.

"How'd this place get its name?" Service asked.

"Town's posed to be named for some Indian. The place is named for the owner. Why is anybody's guess. He's a lawyer over St. Looey way, a bit in his own world, all twisty-headed about trout. They ain't no fish on the menu today, gents. What'll it be?"

Waco ordered fried pork steaks for both of them, and Service settled in with the reports.

While Service tried to read, patrons tentatively approached Agent Waco, each of them using the same opener: "Hey, got a question for you." Every game warden in the world had heard this so many times that it was an inside joke.

The commonalities in the cases were few: Every victim had been a game warden; no collateral fatalities had been discovered, unless Deputy Owens counted; the most recent victims had been killed and displayed in the same way, their eyes removed. All the bodies had been found unclothed near water. No kill sites had been discovered until Ficorelli's. Culkin would show Waco another possible kill site, but in the wake of the storm, it was unlikely there would be much evidence there. But these were only the second batch. What about records for the first set of killings?

He saved Monica's list until last. His name was listed for Michigan, Eddie Waco for Missouri, and Wayno Ficorelli for Wisconsin. His name didn't freak him out as much as make his face turn red with anger.

A waitress brought the steaks, said to Waco, "You need anything more, you give a wave okay, hon?"

"You're top of the list," Service said.

Eddie Waco glanced at him. "Thet list hain't right."

"Any way to find out who sent the information from your higher-ups to the feds, and to whom?"

"I reckon, but I'm thinking weren't nothin' sent."

"How long have you been a warden?" Service asked.

"Twenty year."

"You been ta college," Service said, mimicking Cake Culkin.

Waco nodded. "Mizzou."

Service raised an eyebrow: University of Missouri. "Studying what?"

"Biology and forestry."

Service said, "I thought you said you don't know science."

"Learned enough ta slide through. All I ever wanted was to be a game warden."

"I guess you turned out to be a pretty good one."

Waco's eyes narrowed. "Elray was the best I seen. You think the feds are going to waste your time again?"

"Our time," Service said. "The way I figure it, we both have a stake in this fiasco, and if I'm in, you're in. The feds have had this thing closed up in a box for too damn long. It needs air and light."

After eating, they waited in darkness at the airport. The unlit field was tiny, with only three small planes parked in the open air.

"Where's Security?" Monica asked when she pulled up.

"I reckon we're it," Waco said.

"Let's go inside," she said.

"We're outdoor guys," Service said. "And there isn't an inside unless you want to sit in the truck."

Eddie Waco grinned.

Monica handed him a large envelope. "Larry only gave you the records from the second group. I thought you might want these."

"You lied to me," Service said. "You put the bite on your old classmate. It wasn't his idea to contact Governor Timms. It was yours."

She held up her hands. "*Nolo contendere*," she said. "I wanted you close."

"To protect me," Service said.

"The killer hasn't struck an officer outside his home state. If you were with us, I figured you'd be clear until we could get this damn thing figured out. I swear it was in your interest."

"Bonaparte says you're a zealot."

She said, "I'm also damn good."

"Which is why you got dumped in Milwaukee."

"That's bullshit. I broke the case in LA and I *asked* for Milwaukee."

"Your colleagues say differently."

"Gasparino?" she said. "Larry's green, still susceptible to the most outrageous gossip. There's always gossip when a woman gets the job done. You want, call my boss in Milwaukee. He'll confirm it."

Service looked over at Eddie Waco, who shrugged.

"You have had a chance to look at the reports?" she asked.

"We looked."

"And?"

"Not much there."

"That's the truth."

Service said, "But it seems to me we have a few things. Bonaparte insists this guy is the perfect serial murderer, but he hit Elray Spargo, when Agent Waco is the top man on the list for Missouri. He also may have killed Deputy Owens, and the fact that he may have brought her in as a third party to arrange a meeting suggests he's changed his ways, or is unsure of himself. Something is changing. He was also close to getting confronted in Wisconsin by the sheriff. This guy may be good, but he's not flawless—if your list means a damn thing. The real key is what do all the victims on the list have in common—other than the obvious?"

She scratched the corner of her mouth. "That's one of the things I wanted to talk to you about—the list."

"We're listening," Service said.

"The analyst who discovered the pattern also suggested the list. I mean, who were the victims? Were they targets of opportunity, the best guys, or unlucky foul-ups? The list was intended to help us pinpoint more of a pattern."

"Which it did."

"It became pretty clear that only the top people were being targeted."

"But Spargo died, not Waco."

"You have to understand, we were getting a little desperate. We have to fight like hell for resources nowadays and we were getting big pressure to produce. We thought the list would be a way of assessing patterns, and then it started to have predictive value, so I decided to rig a control, hoping I could speed up things."

Service thought he misheard. "You *switched* Spargo for Waco?"

"It was strictly an alphabetical choice. They were both on the Missouri list."

"Which got Elray killed," a tense Eddie Waco said. Service wondered if he should move the federal agent away from him.

Tatie Monica shook her head and sucked in a deep breath. "Maybe, but the fact that the killer went for Agent Spargo tells us a couple of things."

Service said, "One, he makes mistakes."

"Hit also says he's wired into the dadblame list," Eddie Waco interjected.

"Which has very limited distribution," Monica said.

"I managed to get a copy," Service said, "which doesn't say much for your security."

"I know, I know, but I wanted you to have the list, and you would have gotten it, but you duped Larry before I could get to it."

"It wasn't difficult."

"He came to me and told me what he'd done. His instincts are good."

"The killer has thet list," Eddie Waco repeated.

"Only he fucked up," Service said.

"Not in *his* mind," Monica said. "As far as the killer's concerned, and according to the control, he took out the top man in Missouri. In his mind, he's still perfect, and it's what's in *his* mind that matters to us."

"Bonaparte said the man's flexible and creative."

"Both of which may be true, but he still took the wrong man. Bonaparte says I'm a zealot, but he won't give up his bullshit perfect-killer theory."

"Who called the FBI about Spargo?" Service asked.

"The call came into the St. Louis office," she said.

"Recorded?"

"Yes, but the audio people say the caller used a pay phone and a masking device. They haven't been able to filter it yet, and they probably won't."

"Pay phone where?"

"St. Louis," she said.

"How did Bonaparte get involved?"

"He was in St. Louis when the call came in. I had talked to him about joining us in Wisconsin, but this broke before he could get there."

"And he went to the site here and left before we came in?" Service asked.
She nodded.

"Does he go to all the crime scenes?"

"Not all, but it's fairly standard procedure for BAU people, especially in a major case."

"Even for an acting assistant director?"

"He's been a profiler for a long time, and his management gig is short-term."

"He really believes his theory?"

"Absolutely," she said.

"Supporters?" Service asked.

"These killings are certainly earning him some. Look," she said, "if you want to go home, it's your call. I'm sorry I pulled you into this the way I did."

"We might have met with my lungs pulled through my ribs."

"I know," she said. "I was desperate, and I'm sorry."

"Officers have a right to know all about this," Service said, looking to Eddie Waco who nodded. "Do the states' fish and game division law enforcement people know this is going on?"

"No," she said.

"*Unacceptable!*" Service said, nearly shouting.

"We thought we could get the guy without making a big public case."

"All ya'll were wrong," Eddie Waco said. "That puts some of the body count on all ya'll's heads."

"I hear what you guys're saying, and in your position I might be feeling the same thing, but we can't call back the past. There's no do-overs in this, so all we can do is move on."

"How many people are privy to the list?" Service asked.

"Two dozen max."

"Two dozen like Larry?" Service shot back.

"I hope not," Tatie Monica said.

"This don't give a soul a heap of confidence," Eddie Waco chimed in.

"Look, I admit I've made mistakes. But now you know, and it's up to you to decide where you go from here."

Service studied her. "You remember when you asked me about hunting?"

"I remember."

"I forgot to say it's not a group activity," he said. "I'm thinking Agent Waco and I need to talk, and then we'll get back to you."

"Are you going to stay?" she asked.

"Did you order a plane?"

"Be here soon."

"Good. I'm going to go back to Michigan."

"Home?"

"I haven't decided that yet," Service said.

Special Agent Monica looked at Eddie Waco. "You?"

"Like the man says, we'll get back at you'n," the conservation agent said.

"Any chance the killer has both the original list and the control?"

"Looks that way, but I don't see how," Tatie Monica said. "Only the analyst and I had the list with the control."

"Did the killings that took place before the list, conform to the list?"

"Yes," she said.

"But those states that already had lost a man wouldn't be on the list."

"We went only to the states that had not lost someone."

"What about the states that had already lost people?"

"We had names of victims, and went directly to each state to get a sense of the victim's value."

"They all valuable," Eddie Waco growled.

"I didn't mean it like that," the federal agent said. "Some of the states said the victim was their top performer, or a top performer."

"But the killer has focused on the top warden in each state."

"What are you getting at?" she asked.

"How did the killer identify victims before the list?"

She looked at Service for a long moment. "We don't know."

Service said, "You can't just wander into the woods and hope to bump into the top warden—or any warden, for that matter. Most of us aren't predictable in our patterns. And, if you want to target the top people, it takes time to find them in order to do what you're gonna do. Who supplied evaluations to you?"

"The top law enforcement official in each state."

"How long to get back to you?"

"A day or two at the most."

"States don't keep such lists," Eddie Waco said, "an' the top law dog is the attorney general."

Service said, "Safari Club gives an award every year to the outstanding law enforcement officer in Michigan. Probably other states, too. The turkey federation also gives an award. Probably Ducks Unlimited too."

"You ever win any of those?" Tatie Monica asked.

Service shook his head.

"Then they're irrelevant," she said.

"This list thing isn't helping," Service said. "The killer has to have a way of picking targets, a connection between the violets other than their jobs. We just have to figure out what it is. Where's that plane?" he asked.

"I said I ordered it."

Service looked at her and frowned. "It's coming here?"

"Destination?" she asked.

"Iron Mountain. I need my truck."

She went to her vehicle, got on the radio, scribbled some notes, and came back. "Here's fine. One hour."

"You'd better call someone and get the lights on here." Obviously she had not ordered the plane, or was holding it back, hoping she could convince him to stay.

"I really think it would be better if you remained with the team," she said.

"No chance," he answered. He still couldn't figure her out, but he had too many doubts about her motivation and competence to keep doing what she wanted.

"You'll be in touch?" she asked.

"If I have reason."

When she was gone Service looked over at the Missouri agent. "You can go too. I've got plenty of reading to keep me occupied."

"Pass me some a' them files, partner."

"Don't you have something to do?"

"I *am* doing it," the man said.

After reading by flashlight for a while, Waco said, "If the same feller did all these folks, he musta got started whin he was the size of a popcorn fart."

Service looked over at the man. "I've had similar thoughts."

"Hard as it is ta find the likes of us, could be more'n one perp, I 'speck." Waco added, "I'm thinking you want a well, you best be willin' to dig all the way down ta water, and if this ole boy's the perfectionist them feds claim and he's never got hisself caught, how come he'd switch to a new way? Way I read history, ole Babe Ruth never stopped swingin' for fences even if he struck out more times thin he smacked homers. And Old Ty Cobb never stopped slidin' with 'is spikes up."

The plane arrived and pulled in, Service walked across the apron, verified his credentials, loaded his gear, and walked back to the Missouri agent.

"Good huntin'," Waco said, extending his hand.

"What makes you think I'm going to hunt?"

Waco grinned. "You got the look. You think you get you a scent, call me and we'll make it a pack hunt." Waco handed him a card with several phone numbers and an e-mail address. "Me'n Cake will look at the site in the morning."

Service watched the conservation agent standing expressionless in front of his pickup as the plane taxied into position for takeoff.

# Part II: Michissippi

*Prendre le chemin des écoliers*

To take the schoolboy's route

# 23

## Wisconsin Redux
### May 30, 2004

Grady Service found himself beset with jumbled thoughts. The killer had not struck every year in either group. Why? Waco had suggested there was a group at work, and although possible, this didn't seem likely. Still, a group would better explain how the killer might track his targets. More than one killer could explain how someone could get the better of the imposing Elray Spargo, much less drag his huge body alone. Most COs didn't have easy or predictable routines for an outsider to key in on, and often they didn't know from one moment to the next where they would be or what they would be doing.

He knew that successful long-term fish and game violators tended to be fairly well organized, and often the shooters were not the same ones who located the targets. It could also apply to humans. That's what their Kit Carson scouts had done for them in Vietnam.

But if a crew had been operating over so many years, the odds were that one of them, or somebody who knew one of them, would have snitched. And why had there been a gap of a dozen years between the groups? Had "helpers" outlived their usefulness? The death of the Missouri deputy was definitely something the FBI ought to be taking a long, hard look at, but would they? They had known about the killings for three years and not informed game wardens around the country. Jesus. They were running around with a lot of people, and what seemed to him more velocity than direction. What the hell was Special Agent T. R. Monica really thinking? There were moments when she seemed to be on top of things, and others when she seemed almost clueless. Whatever she was, his gut said not to trust her. As he thought about it, he even wondered if she was somehow involved. Why else would the investigation seem so cockamamie and have so many holes? He wondered if he could check her whereabouts against the killings and timing to see if there was a pattern, but decided this was a reach. Sometimes in an investigation you could have some strange notions. It paid to recognize them for what they were and move on. It would take one imposing person or two to take down Spargo, and Monica had been with him in Wisconsin, which eliminated her from involvement. Right?

Early on she had seemed most interested in his tracking abilities. Why? What trail was he supposed to follow? He was on the list. Okay, but what else? He didn't know if he was tracking a chimpanzee or a chickadee. He had a record of finding people who were *known* to be lost. And he had a good record of intervening in outdoor crime because he had experience and pretty good instincts about where things might happen. Wanting to protect him seemed ludicrous, but she had used political connections to pull him in, and she had admitted it to him. Maybe she believed having him close was the right thing to do.

Whatever her reasoning, he decided there was only one trail, and that was in Wisconsin. He knew from experience that when you lost a trail, you often had to double back to where you'd lost it—all the way to the beginning, if necessary.

He was still in the parking lot of Ford Airport in Iron Mountain when he decided he would not head home. He drove toward Florence, deep in thought.

Why would the man who had killed so invisibly in so many different ways in the first group, and most of the second, suddenly switch to the blood eagle, which was impossible to hide? He had tried not to think about the gruesome details of the most recent killings, but he had a curious thought that such butchering required a fair amount of knowledge about the human anatomy, and some cutting skill. How the hell could someone just jump into killing like that unless they'd first tried it out? Could forensics see a difference in the technique of the mutilations from killing to killing? Was the killer getting better, or worse; was he changing his cutting methods . . . anything? There was no analysis of techniques in the reports. He knew from experience that gutting and butchering a large animal was not something you did perfectly the first time. The more you did it, the more efficient you got.

The fact that he'd never heard of the blood eagle didn't mean it had not been used somewhere; maybe not the whole thing, but part of it. If the killer was truly a perfectionist, as Bonaparte insisted, and he wanted to get it right, he'd do all kinds of homework about game warden habits and movement patterns. Wouldn't he also do the same in creating the blood eagle? So why had his timing been off in Wisconsin?

Only Monica and her analyst knew about the control. Significance? He wasn't sure. Why didn't Bonaparte know? Had she intentionally withheld it from him and other agents? And if so, why?

And what was it that Bonaparte had said to him that struck an odd chord? He couldn't remember the specific thing, only that it had jarred him momentarily.

Something Eddie Waco said had stayed with him: "Babe Ruth never stopped swinging for the fences." In hockey when you tried to score a goal on every shot, you were bound to score some, miss some, and have some blocked or saved. So why didn't this killer ever miss?

This thing was way out of his league, he decided, but he had to do something, and he knew he needed help.

Special Agent Temple met him when he parked at the command post on the hill above the Pine River. Her hair was mussed, her clothes dusty, her shirt soaked with sweat. The temperature was in the low nineties, the humidity unbearable, especially for those who lived this far north. Yoopers would walk about on a sunny thirty-below-zero day talking about the nice weather, and carp incessantly when the temperature got above eighty in summer.

She said. "Tatie called me about what you found in Missouri."

He nodded. "Anything new here?"

"Not a lot. The techs don't think the vick got it in the water. No drag marks up to the kill site, just down that other bank. Something or someone got him to get out."

The techs *thought?* "That's it?" Service said, mulling over the information. This wasn't new. Dammit, he'd read the signs himself, pointed them out to Tatie Monica.

"I swear this asshole could clean my apartment," Temple added. "He's a neat freak."

If so, why hadn't the neat freak picked up Ficorelli's fishing gear in order to mask the kill site? He felt like blowing up, but took a deep breath. This wasn't Temple's fault. "Where's the vick's vehicle now?"

"Impounded in town."

"Has it been announced yet?"

"If it had, I'm sure you would have heard about it," she said. "We've been able to sit on it so far."

Given where he'd been the last few days, he might have missed the opening of World War III. "Does his mother know?"

"She died last month."

Service sucked in a breath. "She died?"

"Car wreck."

*Another car wreck?* Service said, "This needs to be announced. If the media finds out you've been sitting on this for so long, they may jump on you and play the story in a bigger way than they might have."

"You're singing to the choir. Special Agent Monica has her own mind and ways of doing things. Her orders are to sit on it."

Service said, "If it's made public, we might get some people coming forward, maybe find someone who saw something that could help us." This tactic had worked with fish and game violations and had led to the conviction of illegal wolf and bear killers.

"More likely to pull in cranks and nutcases," she said.

"Some of the things cranks and nut jobs see are real," he reminded her. What had Bonaparte said—that the perp had never tried to communicate with law enforcement? Would an announcement stimulate that? Maybe, maybe not. "What else have you got?" he asked. "Did those people seen down by the river that night get interviewed?"

"Transcripts for you," she said, pulling a clipboard out of her vehicle and handing him some stapled pages.

"You mind if I look around the site?" Service asked.

"You know the drill," she said.

The only change he saw at the kill site was an orange-string grid and several marker flags inside a yellow-ribbon perimeter. Other pennants had been placed where he had found the rod and fly box. Service thought himself through what he'd seen previously, and retraced the discovery of the kill site. After an hour he moved over to the riverbank and sat on a cedar blowdown to read the transcripts. The man and woman both had been interviewed. Neither had been shown a photograph of Ficorelli. All the questions had been about movements on the road on the other side of the river, and questions about any suspicious activity they might have observed. What the hell was the FBI thinking? They'd missed the point.

Service tapped the pages. They had not just missed a potential trail, but also ignored the possibility of another angle. He corrected himself: They had no way of knowing firsthand about Wayno's predilections, so he couldn't fairly hang an oversight on them. But not announcing the killing to the public could have played into the law of unintended consequences, and he had a hunch. Not exactly a hunch; more like elevated curiosity. Monica knew Wayno couldn't keep it in his pants, but it was doubtful she knew the extent of his philandering.

Service didn't let Special Agent Temple know his real intentions, but asked permission to take his truck through the river at the four-wheeler ford. When he asked her for a photograph of Ficorelli, she hemmed and hawed before providing one.

According to transcripts, the woman's name was Sondra Andreesen, married fifteen years to Monte, who owned Super-Saver Appliances & Electronics, a chain headquartered in Milwaukee, with stores stretching from northern Illinois up to St. Paul, Minnesota. She was forty-four, her husband, forty. The man the FBI had caught her with was Jinks Schwarz, thirty-nine, a house painter and year-round resident of the area; no criminal record, not even a traffic citation.

He saw no point in talking to Schwarz until he met the woman.

The Andreesen house was five miles south of the river. It looked new and out of place, a three-story glass-and-steel-beam monstrosity that towered over a grove of five-year-old aspens like a botanical goiter. A driveway curved about a hundred yards from the road to the house. The road to the river was invisible from the house.

When he arrived, a woman was standing on the porch. She wore a yellow sundress draped to her ankles, and stringy gold sandals with soles as thin as vellum. She had a deep, unseasonal tan, no jewelry or makeup, but reddish polish on several fingernails. It looked like she had been interrupted. He could smell fresh nail polish.

"Mrs. Sondra Andreesen?" He showed his FBI ID. "Do you have an electronic security system?" Service asked.

"Why do you ask?"

"It looks to me like you were out on the porch waiting for me."

"I was just on my way out to run some errands."

Service said, "I thought maybe your system alerted you I was coming in."

"It's an eye or something," she said, blinking furiously. "I don't really pay attention to it."

"You didn't finish your nails."

She instinctively curled her fingertips to hide them.

"Can I have a few minutes of your time?" Service asked.

"I have some errands," she said. "Really."

"This won't take long," Service said. She was uptight.

"I already talked to the other agents," she said, adding, "and I'm ashamed. Are you people ever going to leave me alone? I don't even know what the point of this is."

He could sense she wanted to let loose her indignation, but was holding back. Her eyes were wide, her posture tense. She was nervous as hell about something.

"If you give me a few minutes, maybe I can clarify the situation," Service said.

She reluctantly opened the door and led him into a great room with one wall of windows and half a roof of sloping skylights. The place was shades of white, totally sterile, no sign of children. "Plenty of room," Service said, looking around.

"This house was Monte's idea," she said. "I wanted a little cabin in the woods and of course he wanted an investment. With Monte everything is about money."

A less-than-blissful union, Service observed.

She didn't offer a seat or refreshments. "What's this about?" she wanted to know.

Service handed her a five-by-seven photograph of Wayno Ficorelli.

She lurched visibly, but tried to recover her poise.

"Do you know this man?"

She answered, "With Monte's business we meet so many people."

"His name is Wayno Ficorelli," Service said.

"I just don't remember," she said, avoiding his eyes. "Is it important?"

Service considered his options. The woman had been caught in *flagrante dilecto* with one man, and there had to be a reason other than fishing for Ficorelli to keep coming back to this area. It was a long shot that felt right. "He's been murdered, Mrs. Andreesen."

Blood ran out of the woman's face and she started to wobble. Service caught her by the arm and guided her down into a chair. She shook her head listlessly and stared at the floor, her breath coming fast. "When?" she asked.

Service told her the date and she began to gasp for air.

"Nothing . . . in . . . news," she mumbled, her voice cracking.

"There are reasons for that," Service said, not amplifying. "I'm sorry to be the one to tell you, but we need help finding his killer."

She responded with an almost imperceptible nod.

"You knew him," Service said, a declarative statement, not a question.

"Yes."

"When did you see him last?"

"That same day," she said. "He got here late morning and left to meet Arnie Thorkaldsson to fish."

"You know the sheriff?"

"For a long time."

"Did Wayno act different in any way on that day?"

She rolled her eyes and managed a smile. "God, he was the poster boy for different."

"But that day specifically?"

"He wasn't himself," she said with resignation. "He was really hurting over his mom's death. He never talked about work. I want work talk, Monte has more than enough."

"What time did Wayno leave here?"

"Four, maybe a little after. He usually left about the same time. He and Arnie always bet a beer on the most fish and he liked to get there first. But that day he was reluctant to leave, said he wasn't in the mood, and I told him to go," she said, stifling a sob.

"This is not your fault," he said, trying to keep her calm and talking. "Did you see Wayno often?"

"Whenever he came to see Arnie."

"Three times a year?"

"Yes," she mumbled, her eyes wide with disbelief, obviously disturbed that he knew the frequency.

"Does Arnie know about you and Wayno?"

"Nobody knows," she said. "*Knew.*"

"Where'd you two meet?"

"Monte's company sponsors youth outdoor education programs, and sometimes we have Wisconsin wardens come in to talk to the kids. Wayno was a guest speaker at a meeting near Fond du Lac."

"How long ago was this?"

"Seven years."

"And you've been seeing him ever since?"

"It was flingy," she said. "You know, not serious. Wayno had a wild, bad-boy side and Monte has none, and doesn't know anything about having fun unless he's making money."

"Seven years seems like a long fling," he said.

"Like I already said, Wayno was Wayno, and what it was, was all it ever was going to be," she said.

"How'd you arrange your meetings and times?"

"We set them a year ahead," she said.

"And he never missed?"

"He said he controlled his own schedule," she said. "Did he suffer?"

"No," Service said, knowing this was what she wanted to hear. "Did you vary the dates?" he asked.

"No, it was pretty much the same three days every year. You know, because of the fishing, something to do with certain insects."

"I appreciate your cooperation," Service said, knowing now that fishing was not Wayno's only reason for coming to Florence County.

"Who told you about us?" she asked.

"That's confidential, and you also need to keep this quiet. We won't be talking to your husband."

She rolled her eyes. "Like *I'm* going to talk about it?" she said. "I feel stupid and I feel bad about all of this. Wayno was . . ." Tears were welling in her eyes.

"I can let myself out," Service told her. He turned around at the door. "You said Wayno was really bothered by his mom's death?"

"Devastated. He couldn't understand how it happened."

When he got to the truck he sat for a while. Wayno's mother, Elray Spargo's sister, Maridly Nantz. Two murdered game wardens and another on the alleged target list, and all with sudden losses of people they were close to. This defied coincidence. He had seen Wayno in action. He had been an aggressive warden. And because of his mother's death Wayno may not have been on his game.

Now he also knew that Wayno wasn't as unpredictable as he should have been. Three times a year, same place, parking in the same spot—these were things a killer could work with, and they probably had cost him his life. What it didn't do was explain why Ficorelli was chosen by the killer, or how. Killer or killers, he reminded himself. The list? Maybe, maybe not. *Keep an open mind,* he cautioned himself, as he drove back down to the river, showed his temporary ID to the security agents on duty. He parked where Wayno's vehicle had been, got out his waders, and walked down the path into the river and up toward the kill site, trying to sort out his thoughts.

The killer had missed Ficorelli's gear. Had he planned to dump the body and come back? Had Thorkdalsson's arrival been too close a call and spooked him? What else had he missed?

# 24

# Florence County, Wisconsin
## May 30, 2004

What would get a fisherman out of the water? Correction: not just a fisherman, but a game warden. If he had been on duty, it might have been to help someone, or to watch or stop something, but Wayno had been off duty, and fishing. Service sat on the log where he had found the rod and the fly box, which had been submerged, but open. Had Wayno been changing flies? If so, was it because he wanted a new pattern, or because he'd lost one in the trees or foliage? The greenery was certainly dense enough along the bank to eat flies.

Service tried to read the water. There was a pool with smooth water about thirty yards upstream, and a riffle nearer to him—less a riffle than pocket water. The best run was close to the bank, and that's where the trout were most likely to be—unless a hatch was happening in low light, in which case the trout would be inclined to move more toward the middle to feed, which could have put Ficorelli's backcast in jeopardy. But if the rises had been along the seam by the bank, Wayno would have been in the middle casting toward shore, with little chance of getting hung up high behind him. The old rule was that if you weren't occasionally getting hung in the low wood, you weren't fishing aggressively enough. Rising trout stuck close to cover, which meant casts had to be no more than an inch or two off the target. His attention kept shifting from the coincidental deaths to Wayno's fishing. He needed to focus. He sat down, lit a cigarette, and let his eyes begin to sweep the foliage along the banks. Looking for a fly in a tree was worse than looking for a needle in haystack.

Grady Service was studying the trees when Special Agent Temple showed up.

"Bird-watching?" she joked from above him.

"Something like that."

What would be hatching now? Not sulfurs at night, and it was too early for hex. Drakes probably, brown or gray. Drakes would mate and spin down over the riffle. Drakes were good-size flies, 10s or 12s. If Ficorelli had lost a fly, was it because he snagged a leaf or a woodpile, or because of a bad knot? Bad knots combined with poor casts took more flies than anything else. He guessed Ficorelli was a pretty good caster, but everyone tied bad knots, either because they were in a hurry, or because the tippet was old or frayed.

"Geez," he said out loud.

"What?" Temple asked.

"Where's the evidence recovered from the river—the victim's rod and the fly box?"

"Locked up back at camp."

"Let's go take a look."

"Are you going to tell me what this is about?" she wanted to know.

"Tree fish," he said, not bothering to expand.

When they got to the evidence locker, he put on latex gloves and got out the rod with the reel still attached. He looked at the tippet, the end-portion of the leader, and saw a telltale curlicue, which suggested a bad knot or weak tippet. The leader was segmented with different diameters of monofilament, hand-tied. The closest knot to the end of the tippet was about four inches up. Obviously some tippet had come off with the fly. "Okay then," he said.

"Okay what?" the federal agent asked.

"I'm pretty sure it's a tree fish," he said. He handed her the rod, peeled off the gloves, and started back to the river.

He tried to use the late sun to his advantage. If tippet was still attached to the fly, the monofilament might catch and reflect some light. He eased slowly along the bank, using a long stick to part leaves and branches. It took fifteen minutes to find what he was looking for: about six inches of mono wrapped around a tag alder branch, impossible to reach unless you got onto land and came down the other side of the trees.

The body had been found just above here. If this is when the attack came, he reasoned, Wayno would never have reached the fly, and considering that other evidence had not been picked up by the killer, the fly might still be there.

He considered getting onto land, but studied the mono for several minutes. Years of fishing had taught him that the sorts of angles and tangles that could beset a line would confound all known laws of physics. The key to recovering a fly on a light tippet was to work the line slowly and gently, not to jerk it. There was sunken timber in front of him, just below the broken tippet. He moved over close, bent down, and began to run his hand along the back of a small log behind a larger one. It didn't take long to feel the fly stuck in the wood. He put on another pair of latex gloves, knelt on the larger of the logs, leaned close, and wiggled the fly loose. There was a curlicue of monofilament hanging off the fly. He now thought he understood. A fish had been rising near the wood, and Wayne's cast had gone into the tags and hooked the wood, but when he tried to pull it loose, it had broken. Not being able to see anything but the monofilament, Ficorelli probably had gotten out of the water to see if he could retrieve it from landside.

Why the hell would he retrieve a fly if he had fish rising? Most fishermen would just tie on another fly, cast again, and hope the fish kept coming up. But by getting out and coming in from the land, he would not have had to wade through the run and put down rising trout. This made sense. When you fished for trout, you did everything in your power not to disturb what was happening. It was in your own self-interest.

Okay, he thought. The scenario makes sense. Rising fish, stuck fly, retrieve it, don't disturb the risers. Service stared at the fly. It looked vaguely like a brown drake, but in a dressing and style he had never seen before. As he handled it, the hook itself fell apart and dropped into the water, leaving him with only the upper part of the fly.

He put the evidence in his pocket, sat down, and lit another cigarette. The scene was forming in his mind. Wayno had gotten out of the water to recover a lost fly and was attacked. Was it the only one of that kind that he had? Possibly. He probably never saw the attack coming, which suggested the assailant had been shadowing him along the bank. Because he had a pretty good idea where Ficorelli had gotten into the river and crossed to this side, he had a pretty good idea where the shadowing began. He got out of the river and walked downstream along the bank, keeping the same distance from the water as the attack site had been.

Eventually he came to a downed oak, one that had rotted and probably come down under the weight of winter snow. There was a partial track in between some branches near the ground. The track was treadless. Felt soles? Service guessed that the assailant had stopped here and watched Ficorelli come across the river and begin fishing upstream. Eventually the hung fly offered opportunity.

Service took some tissue paper out of his pocket, broke off a stick, pushed it in the ground, and attached the tissue to it like a small flag. He continued backtracking across a cedar swamp, past an old bear-bait site, and up a gentle slope to a two-track turnaround. The whole area was covered with thigh-deep ferns, but he moved cautiously and used a stick to part the ferns until he saw something near where some vehicles had turned around. Wading boots, shorts, a vest, and a nylon shirt were on the ground beneath the ferns, and from what he could see, there was no obvious blood. He used sticks to mark the spot and tried to estimate how far from the kill site he was. Maybe another half-mile, which meant he was close to a mile and a half from the dump site, and close to two miles from the FBI camp. Had the feds checked the two-track in front of him, and if not, *why* not?

He hiked back through the lengthening shadows of the cedar swamp and started toward the camp, and along the way met Bobbi Temple coming toward him. Service nodded for her to follow, led her to the print and explained his theory, and then took her through the swamp and showed her the clothing.

"Did your people check out this road?"

"Have to ask Tatie," she said. "I spent most of my time at the dump site."

She was on the radio as he approached the old bear bait.

He heard Agent Temple's voice behind him, asking, "Where do you think you're going?"

He didn't bother to answer her. The FBI reeked of incompetence. He had no time or desire to slow down and pull the feds along with him.

Sheriff Arnie Thorkaldsson was in his cramped office with his long legs and huge boots propped up on a desk glider. "Monica back too?" the sheriff asked.

"Just me."

"We ought to be announcing this thing," the sheriff said. "This delay is outrageous."

"It's the FBI's case," Service said.

"You must have your own opinion . . . or have they brainwashed you?"

"I've got one, but it carries the same weight as yours."

"The feds make us locals feel like tits on a boar."

"They do the same to state types," Service said. "Do you mind if we run through the timelines of that night?"

"Be my guest," Thorkaldsson said. "I can't get it out of my mind."

"What time were you supposed to meet?"

"Nineish. The hatches don't get started till closer to dark, but I got held up on a traffic deal and I was a little late."

"How late?"

"Forty-five minutes or so."

"Were you always late and him always early?"

"No, he was usually the late one." Service made a mental note.

"Why'd you go to the old bridge ford?"

"We always met there," Thorkaldsson said. "Like I told you earlier, he always came up from the south and parked across the river. Probably superstitious. We always had good luck there, and you know how luck and fishing get joined at the hip."

*No doubt*, Service thought. If Thorkaldsson suspected anything about Ficorelli's dalliances with the Andreesen woman, he wasn't letting on.

"Good a reason to park there as any," Service said.

"Only reason, ask me. Easier to get to the river from my side, and we could close the gate behind us." The sheriff stared at Service. "This thing's bigger'n Wayno, isn't it?"

"I can't say," Service said, feeling guilty. It was wrong to hide information from other police agencies.

"How long are you gonna hang with this boondoggle?"

"That's what I'm trying to figure out," Service said.

"You need anything, just sing out. We don't have much manpower here—and not much need for it—but I swear I'd personally give Madison an enema with a fire hose to help find Wayno's killer."

"Okay if I tie up one of your phones?"

Thorkaldsson stood up and stretched. "Use mine. Dial eight to get an outside line," he said from the doorway. "I'm gonna go up the street and grab supper at the Puddin-Et-Pi. My sister-in-law owns the place."

The phone in a Detroit law office was answered on the first ring. "Grady Service calling. Is Shamekia available?"

"I'll see if she is, sir."

Shamekia Cilyopus-Woofswshecom was an ex-FBI special agent turned attorney, her last name so strange as to be unpronounceable by earthlings. Why the hell she didn't change it, Service didn't know, but people were kind of strange about their names, and what did it really matter? Most people who knew her didn't attempt her last name, simply calling her Shamekia. His friend Tree had introduced him to her, and she had helped him solve a couple of complex cases.

"Ah, the intrepid woods cop," she greeted him. "How's life in Michissippi, Grady?"

A black Detroit politician had labeled the U.P. this way because of its sparse population and heavy unemployment. "Been better."

"What have you got going this time?"

He took her through the case, ending with the possibility of some sort of trial-run killings.

"Lord Almighty," the attorney said. "VICAP didn't spit out anything?"

VICAP was the FBI's Violent Criminal Apprehension Program. All police agencies were supposed to enter their local violent-crime data so all the information could be searched by any police officer anywhere. He wondered if the DNR filed its data in the system, and if so, who handled it.

"I don't know, and I don't know exactly what they did or how or when; I'm just wondering if there's something that was missed."

"You know," she said, "some cops call it VICRAP for a reason."

"Really?"

"Yeah, it's a monster, and it's easy to miss something; or are you coming at this from a different angle than the Bureau?"

"Case myopia," he said.

She clucked. "Uh-huh. Linkage blindness happens to all of us at one time or another. You let yourself get going on certain leads or angles and you can't let loose even when it's obvious you're not getting anywhere."

"Something like that," he said.

"What exactly are you looking for?"

"If I knew exactly, this wouldn't be so hard. Several questions come to mind: Has this blood eagle thing been used anywhere at any time? Or have there been killings with edged weapons that are sort of bizarre and ritualistic? And not just game warden victims, any cases."

"Anywhere in the whole country?"

"Hell, anywhere in the solar system."

"Some sort of geographic starting point, at least; location of the first killing or something along that line?"

He tried to remember the state where the first murder had taken place, but he couldn't. "Let me call you back on that."

"Never mind," she said. "There's enough in the way of unique factors here to get me rolling. I'll be back at you if I find something. You got your cell phone with you?" She paused and added, "You understand that the system has flaws? Some local agencies, especially in cities, don't enter all their current cases, and a lot of them don't have the funding or enough trained people to go back and log the old cases. The program started up in 1985, and most agencies have lagged behind since the beginning. VICAP is a great tool when it works, but win or lose, it's always a crapshoot."

"Thanks, Shamekia."

She laughed and said, "Stay safe," before breaking the connection.

Service called Chief Lorne O'Driscoll, who answered his own phone.

"Service."

"Are you still in Wisconsin?"

"Just back from Missouri," Service said.

"What the heck is going on?"

Service described the cases and imagined he could hear the chief's blood pressure rising.

"Forty-nine officers?"

"Yessir."

"Grady, I don't know what crap they're shoveling at you, but no such list came out of here, certainly not without my knowing. I'm telling you I would *never* release such a list unless the FBI director himself was standing here in my office holding a gun to my head—and even then the chances would be fifty-fifty."

"My name is on the list, Chief."

"*Dammit!*" Lorne O'Driscoll exploded.

"Sir, I'm thinking we ought to at least alert our people."

"You let me worry about that," the chief said.

"And sir, it was the FBI who asked the Wisconsin secretary of state to request me from Governor Timms. You want me to stay?"

"Why did the FBI do this?"

"Partly to protect me, but beyond that I'm not sure." There was something else, his gut told him, but so far he couldn't get a nail into it.

"Do what you think you have to do, Detective. List, my ass," O'Driscoll muttered with disgust before hanging up.

Service walked over to the main drag to join the sheriff at the Puddin-Et-Pi.

Thorkaldsson greeted him as he sat down, "You've got the look of a man with fresh dog shit on the soles of his brand-new church shoes."

"Did you call the FBI when you found Wayno?"

"No reason to call the feds out of the gate," Thorkaldsson said. "I got my people in to secure the site and called the Wispies. We rarely get homicides in this county, but when we do, I call the state first."

"You don't know who contacted the feds?" Service asked.

"Not me is all I know. I assume it was the state," said Thorkaldsson.

"When did the feds come in?"

"Monica was about an hour behind the Wispies, and her people swooped in an hour after that and took over," said Thorkaldsson. "The Wispies musta known the FBI was coming because they just stood around and waited with their thumbs up their keesters."

Service asked, "Special Agent Monica strike you as competent?"

The sheriff shook his head slowly and said, "Define competent."

Service drove back to the encampment near the crime scene, hoping Shamekia would come up with some answers. Had the feds missed something? This was more than possible, he knew; the Bureau was the same outfit that knew some jerkwads from the Middle East were taking flight lessons with more interest in takeoffs than in landings, and did nothing about it. Shit happened in bureaucracyland; investigators blinded themselves with their own assumptions, and it didn't hurt to question everything, even with an agency with more assets than God.

In his experience the FBI and other government agencies tended to reach for an ICBM when a bottle rocket might better do the job. Maybe they had handled this just fine, but he needed to know, and so far what he was seeing was way below his own standards. Back at the camp he walked into a clearing, opened his cell phone, got three bars, and punched in Father O'Brien's number.

"OB here," the priest answered.

"Service."

"I gather you're okay," O'Brien said.

"I guess I deserve that," Service said. "But I got called out of state on a case and I haven't been back yet. Call my captain."

"I already did," the priest said. "I wasn't being sarcastic."

"Do you remember a psychology student from your days at Marquette?"

"Does she have a name?"

"Last name is Monica."

"Ah," the priest said. "The indomitable Tatie. Sure, I knew her."

"What can you tell me about her?"

"Why do you ask?"

"I can't say."

"Pretty good student, hardworking, strictly out for herself, which is normal for students seeking higher degrees. What's she doing now?"

"She's an FBI agent."

"That doesn't surprise me," O'Brien said. "She had a strong interest in abnormal psychology and did a couple of insightful papers on serial killers." There was a pause. "Is *this* about a serial killer?"

"I can't say."

O'Brien remembered her. Good student. He felt disappointed, wanted to hear something else, only he wasn't sure what. "Aren't most students in PhD programs supposed to be more than pretty good?"

Long pause. "She was superb at memorizing facts but less strong at analysis."

"In what way?"

"She'd get a notion into her head and not let go, even when her approach was clearly wrong."

"Yet she got her doctorate."

"She qualified. I was sure she'd never make it in a practice, but in the context of the FBI or a large organization, she'd do okay."

"She did papers on serial killers?"

"Borderline obsession for her."

"You remember which ones?"

"Sorry; it's been a long time, and I had a lot of students. My memory isn't so good anymore."

"Anything else you can tell me about her?"

"I remember that she had a tendency to rely more on instinct than empirical data, and sometimes she tried to stretch miminal data beyond its inherent value to support her position."

"That's it?"

"Martin Grolosch," O'Brien said. "He was a killer in Wisconsin in the 1920s. He got caught by some people up near Hurley and they hung him before the authorities could intervene."

"She was interested in Grolosch?"

"Like I said, it was close to an obsession."

"Any idea why?"

"Sorry. Something about a minister in Rhinelander who hung himself."

"I don't get it," Service said.

"Me either," the priest said.

"So . . . ," Tatie Monica said from the trees. "The prodigal son."

Service stepped toward her. "I talked to my chief. He says there's never been a Michigan list and he sure as hell didn't talk to you."

"Semantics," she said. "There are lots of roads to the same destination."

"You want me here for something more than protecting me," he said.

"We'll talk about it."

"When—after my lungs are pulled out my back?"

He was not surprised when she didn't follow him.

The eastern sky was hinting azure when Service stepped into Tatie Monica's tent with two cups of coffee from the camp urn. She was asleep, an arm draped over her face, snoring a steady buzz.

He sat down beside her. "Wake up."

She answered with a snort.

"Coffee," he said.

She removed her arm and looked up at him. "I hate this outdoor shit," she said.

"You're not outdoors. You're in a tent."

Tatie Monica winced as she swung her legs off the cot and pushed herself up. She was wearing running shorts and rumpled gray T-shirt. Service held out a cup.

"What?" she asked.

"Too many question marks," he said. "The only constant in this thing has been inconsistency."

"You see what I've been living with for three years," she said. "Consistency is the hobgoblin of small minds. I don't remember who said that."

"From where I stand you look like the vector of inconsistency."

"I said I've made mistakes. You haven't?"

"I try to fix mine."

"Must be nice to have a job that lets you," she countered.

"Where did the list come from?"

"I had our field agents talk to game wardens."

"That's not exactly a scientific sample."

"Fuck science," she said. "It's vastly overrated."

"Did you even try to approach state agencies?"

"A few, but they stonewalled me."

"So you gathered the names based on gossip."

"Don't give me any shit," she said. "How many of you in Michigan?"

"One eighty or so in the field, two forty overall."

"In an operation that size, everybody knows who the go-to guy is. All cops keep track, you know that: who's good, who's a liability. Walk into a New York or Detroit police precinct and every officer can tell you who their top cop is, so don't preach to me about science. The point is that the killer has validated the list by his actions. He's hitting only the top people."

"Except in Missouri."

"Spargo was the control. The conclusion stands."

"You let a man die."

"Your long-term 'violets' don't know how to use the system against you? This guy sure seems to know ours. He crosses jurisdictions and uses time and geography to his advantage. The fact that we even found the first group is close to a miracle. The biggest problem we have sometimes is getting local agencies to cooperate with us. They want to hold on to their cases, can't see beyond what they've got. I suppose you've never held things back from other agencies?"

"It's a two-lane road. You're not telling them more, so they go with what they know."

"Bullshit. The real problem is elected law enforcement personnel. They all want merit badges for their next election."

He agreed, but this was off the point. He needed for her to focus. "How did you find the pattern in the first group?"

"VICAP," she said.

"You mean VICRAP?" he countered. "I'm told it's not particularly useful in cases before 1985, and the older the case, the greater the crapshoot."

Monica paused before responding. "That's partially true," she said. "But rural areas are pretty good about loading their cases. It's mostly the cities that seem to lag, and where have our killings taken place? Not in cities. VICAP has its weaknesses and its critics, but it did the job this time."

"Who actually found the first group?"

She took a sip of coffee before answering. "Micah Yoder."

"A Milwaukee buddy?"

"Why are you asking this? You going to redo all of our work, check on us twice, like Santy Claus?"

"Your idea for me to ask questions."

"Micah's not just a computer geek, he's an analyst, and VICAP was only one source. There are half a dozen other national databases. Do you think I made this up?" Her voice was rising.

"I'm trying to focus and get up to speed. You brought me in blind and the light hasn't been fast in coming."

"Okay," she said. "Let me back up. Micah *is* a computer nerd, but he's also more than that . . . a lot more. I've known him for ten years, and he can always find what I can't."

"Like tying your Houston killer to LA?"

"Know how we learned he was in LA?"

Service didn't answer.

"The Houston killer took credit cards, but never used them. We assumed he threw them away. But a Houston vick's card popped up in LA, and Micah was the only one who caught it. We checked all the suspects for the date and all but one had an alibi, and that one couldn't be found in Houston anymore. He'd blown town. I took the suspect's photo to the store that processed the card, the clerk made a positive ID, and the LAPD helped us take it from there."

"Quite a story," Service said. He didn't point out that if Houston agents had been keeping close tabs on all their serious suspects, they would have known the man was gone. Still, it was pretty good police work.

"In our business, networking supports luck," she said. "You find good people and maintain relationships. They help you, you help them."

"Any chance I can talk to Yoder?"

"Why?"

"Maybe I can use him for my network," he said sarcastically.

"You really can be an asshole when you set your mind to it."

"I haven't even tried yet," he said. "I just want to understand how he did this."

"Micah's pretty hard to see."

"He works, right?"

"Not regular hours."

"The FBI allows this for its staff people?"

"I never said he worked *for* the Bureau. I said he's an analyst and he's out of Detroit."

"Has Yoder worked with Bonaparte?"

"Micah works alone."

"You mean he freelances for you. The Bureau allows agents to use outside analysts?"

"You're suddenly an expert on Bureau culture and procedures?"

"The woman your boys talked to about being with the guy on the four-wheeler by the river that night?"

"What about her?"

"She and Ficorelli had a thing."

"A thing?"

"A seven-year thing."

"Jesus," she said, "how did you learn that?"

"I talked to her, showed her Ficorelli's photo."

"And she just spit it out?"

"More or less. Your people talked to her, but it was just about seeing strangers on the road or in the area. Ficorelli wasn't a stranger. He left her place at 4 P.M. the day he was killed. She didn't want to talk, but I convinced her, and I told her that her husband didn't need to know."

"How did you suspect?"

"You said it the night I got here—that Ficorelli was a pathological ass-man with a penchant for married women. He's been coming here for years, same time every year, parking in the same spot. There was a chance there was more to it than fishing. The real question is why you didn't think of the possible connection and see to it that your people showed the woman his photograph."

"That's damn impressive investigative work," she said.

"Martin Grolosch," he said.

Tatie Monica looked at him and blinked. "What did you say?"

"Martin Grolosch and Rhinelander."

"What about him?"

"You tell me."

She drained her coffee, obviously trying to collect her thoughts. "Grolosch was from Rhinelander. My grandfather went off to the war in 1941. My grandmother hung herself while he was gone. He didn't know until after the war because he was a POW. When he came back and found out, he hung himself in the same tree."

"Sad story," Service said. "Why did your grandmother kill herself?"

"Martin Grolosch was her son by her first husband. She and my grandfather never believed Martin was a killer. But Grandmother started to do some renovations in their house and discovered a cache of papers—things Martin had written about what he had done. He killed fourteen women before he got caught. Grandmother couldn't live with what her son had done."

"Your interest in Grolosch is personal."

"Personal and professional," she said quickly. "My brother Lance hung himself at fifteen, and afterward my parents discovered he had been torturing small animals. This is a typical finding in the background of a serial. It was really sick, and I started wondering if there's a genetic component to serial murder; you know, if it runs in families."

"You wondered if your brother would have become a monster."

"Yes," she said.

This cinched it for him: Tatie Monica was damaged goods and had no business running the team. "I've done about everything I can do here," Service said. "I'm heading home."

"There's a target on your back," she said as he started to get up.

He turned and looked down at her. "No, I'm the strike dog," he said.

"Who's the pack backing you?" she asked.

"I wonder the same thing," he said. "But don't bother coming to the U.P. to protect me."

"There are forty-nine dead game wardens," she said, "some of them the best in their state, and they couldn't avoid it. What makes you different?"

"I know the asshole's out there," he said. "And if some of those dead men had known, this might have put an end to this shit a long time ago."

He walked out. He was done listening to her. He had a high quotient for bullshit, but some of what she said was right. Networking was key, and he had his own to tap into.

It was time to go home, sort things out there, and get ready. Tatie Monica was chasing personal demons. He was going to hunt a killer who did not yet know he was the prey.

# 25

# Foster City, Michigan
## May 31, 2004

For one of the few times in his life Grady Service found himself at a loss for exactly what to do—both professionally and personally. How many times had he reached for the cell phone to talk to Nantz, only to remember she was no longer there? Where was home, and *what* was it? Him, a giant dog, and a surly cat?

He pulled into the lot of the Mill Town Inn. He needed caffeine and time to think. The inn was a converted house about forty-five miles west of Escanaba. Swedish pancakes were the specialty, the atmosphere quiet, and it was run by an ex-marine and retired Saginaw homicide detective named Barratt, who was called Toe Tag by most of his cop friends.

Gaudy white and yellow flowers bloomed in beds below the front porch; others climbed vines on a green trellis. The scents of lilac and Russian olive perfumed the small yard.

There were two narrow dining rooms in the old house, single white flowers in small red bud vases, and the work of local landscape painters framed on the walls. Barratt Adams saw him and immediately brought coffee. "Haven't seen much of you recently."

"I've been here and there," Service said.

"Got a big brown last night at dusk on a brown drake. You gonna ask where?"

"A man needs to keep from wroto," Service said.

"Semper Fi. Yell when you're ready for chow."

Service was staring at his cup when he felt someone watching and looked up to see a small, wiry man in a blue blazer, white shirt, and narrow red tie. He stared at the man for a moment before it dawned on him. "Allerdyce?"

"I seen youse sittin' dere makin' eye-holes in dat coffee. Youse got tea leaves or chicken guts in dere, sonny?"

Limpy eased his scrawny frame into a chair and grinned.

Service had never seen him with teeth before. "Suit, teeth, clean-shaven, no ponytail. Very spiffy."

The old poacher cackled. "Hunt turkey, youse gotta wear camo, am I right, sonny?"

Allerdyce was prone to strange pronouncements that seemed like bizarre non sequiturs, but the old man rarely spoke without intending to convey a message. His crude ways made him seem stupid and ignorant to a lot of people, but Service knew better.

Allerdyce nodded toward the cash register. Service saw an attractive woman, fortyish, in shorts, platform sandals, and a turquoise tank top. "I'm poppin' dat," the old poacher croaked, making a fist.

She looked well groomed and light years away from Limpy's class. "Is she blind?" Service asked, making the old man scowl. Limpy's prodigious sexual appetite and reputation were legendary, but this woman? Not possible.

"I got what she wants," Allerdyce said. "Youse an' me got no more bull-shit between us, eh."

"Where are you living?"

"Where I always been," the man said.

The woman came over to the table and stood beside the poacher with her hand on his shoulder. "Introductions, Andrew?"

"Dis here's DNR Detective Service."

*Andrew?* Service stifled a grin. Even the man's rap sheet listed him as Limpy.

The woman extended her hand. "*You're* the one. I'm Joan Pillars." She had a soft voice and a firm handshake. "Andrew has told me a lot about you."

"She's a schoolteacher up da college," Limpy added.

"Visiting professor from North Carolina–Wilmington," she said by way of amplification. "I've been at Northern since the first of May. It's a one-year appointment." Her accent was from the Northeast, maybe Maine, Service thought.

"Writin' her a book," Limpy said with a toothy grin that unnerved Service.

"About over-the-hill poachers or broke-down paroled felons?" Service said.

Limpy protested. "I'm retired, not over no bloody hill."

"But still a paroled felon," Service said.

"Actually, the subject is rural crime and the public's widespread lack of recognition," the woman interjected. "Perhaps you would have some time to talk to me," she added. She slid a business card onto the table, took out a ballpoint pen, and wrote something on the back.

Service ignored it. "I'm kind of busy," he said.

"Told youse," Allerdyce said. "Da boy ain't much on makin' social da way 'is ole man was."

The woman started for the door and Limpy got up and leaned over. "She's a screamer, dat one. Be seein' youse, sonny."

"Whatever you say, *Andrew*. You hear Honeypat's back in the U.P.?" Gus had not yet confirmed this for him, but Service wanted to see the old man's reaction.

Allerdyce stared at him. "Where?"

Service shrugged. "Just a rumor. If I confirm it, I'll get in touch."

Allerdyce frowned as he followed the woman out the door, turned around, and came back. "I'm real sorry about your gal."

Barratt came over to the table. "You decided?"

"Stack of Swedes. Keweenaw lingonberry jam?"

"You bet, but Dottie put back some chokecherry jelly last fall."

"Make it Dottie's," Service said. Dottie was Toe Tag's wife, a local girl, the chef for the restaurant, and manager of the two-room guesthouse. Toe Tag provided the capital and did odd jobs for her between fishing trips.

"I'll tell 'er."

"Grab a cup and join me."

The retired cop came back with a cup and two giant apple fritters. "Some habits don't break easy," he said sheepishly, offering the plate to Service, who held up a hand.

"Who's the woman with Limpy?"

"Professor of some kind. They've been in a couple of times. He tell you he's getting that?"

"He says that about every woman," Service said.

"I don't buy it with this one. Gotta say, though, she sure cleaned him up good." Allerdyce was well known for his less than enthusiastic or consistent personal hygiene.

"He says he's living back at the compound."

"Maybe he rebuilt," Barratt said. "His bunch isn't exactly the sort to broadcast their news."

"The clan scattered after the compound burned."

"Not that far, I'd think. That old man's got an eerie hold on them, like a black hole always pulling the rest of his universe toward him."

"His hold on Honeypat didn't seem too firm," Service said. Honeypat was the daughter-in-law who had tried to take over the clan.

Barratt grinned. "Exceptions to every rule. The hell of it is, I kind of like old Limpy. I imagine you might have a different take."

Service didn't reply. The truth was that with all of Allerdyce's disgusting ways, he sometimes got a perverse kick out of the old man. He just didn't understand or trust him. "How long were you in homicide?"

"Fourteen years," Barratt said. "It took about fifteen minutes to adjust to retirement. I saw enough dead bodies for several people, let alone one worn-out old cop."

"Did your department use VICAP?"

"Ate from it more than we fed it. The entry process wasn't that easy, and we never had enough people or money to spend the time."

"But a good tool?"

"Better now than then. They've simplified data entry over the years. Nowadays if you have a hot case, they have the staff at NCAVC jump on it quick. It will get better, but it works now."

"Did you ever catch any serial murder cases?"

Barratt smirked. "Hey, we had druggies whacking homeboy competitors like they were cockroaches on their mama's birthday cake, but these weren't the sort of serials the Feebs got off on. Most of our body count was domestic or drug-related. Our dealers were small fish on the fantail of the Chicago-Detroit-Flint supply ship. Why the interest?"

"We're never too old to learn."

Barratt laughed. "You and Allerdyce: Neither of you ask questions without purpose. You hear the President's coming?"

"Which one?"

"Dubya," the retired cop said. "Marquette, next month. He'll be the first sitting President in the U.P. since Taft in 1911."

The President coming to Marquette? So what? It wouldn't have any effect on him.

After breakfast he dropped the woman's card in the trash by the register but found another one under his windshield wiper. The woman had scribbled, "I'm very persistent!" She had added a smiley face. He loathed smiley faces.

He looked at the card. It read: Joan Pillars, PhD, Professor of Criminology, University of North Carolina at Wilmington. He stuck the card under the sun visor, opened his cell phone, and called the Marquette office.

Captain Grant's formidable door guard, Fern LeBlanc, answered. "It's Grady. Is he in?"

"One moment, please."

"Detective," the captain greeted him. "The chief has briefed me."

"Has the word gone out?"

"Not yet. The chief and I want to meet with you."

"The word needs to get out yesterday, Cap'n. What this guy does to people is not pretty."

"Tomorrow afternoon in my office, sixteen hundred hours?"

"The chief will be *here* tomorrow?"

"He'll be here for a security meeting at noon."

"The Bush visit?"

Heavy silence from Grant. "Where did you hear that? It's not been announced yet, and the trip is only tentative."

"Toe Tag Barratt."

The captain said in his faint southern drawl, "The Secret Service is going to have its hands full up here."

U.P. residents didn't like being fenced in or herded by the government, even one they had elected.

"Tomorrow at four, Cap'n."

He started driving east on M-69 toward Escanaba, checked his cell phone for a signal, and called Gus Turnage.

"Were you able to confirm that thing with Honeypat?"

"The judge saw her at the casino in Baraga. She was wearing a wig, but he's sure it was her. He had her in his court a couple of times. He tried to talk to her but she pretended to be someone else. I talked to the captain right after he got off the phone with you, and he's going to put out a BOLO to all of our people."

"Thanks, Gus."

"Where are you?"

"Heading for home."

"You got something working?"

"I'll talk to you later."

Honeypat would have a reason to hurt him through Nantz and Walter, but Ficorelli and Spargo also had close relatives killed in auto accidents not long before they died. Was Honeypat Allerdyce the only possibility? If it was her, it had nothing to do with the serial killings. Or did it? Her reappearance only complicated things.

# 26

## Slippery Creek, Michigan
## May 31, 2004

He dropped his gear and bags inside the front door, surveyed his cabin, and saw it for what it was: a wooden shell, not a house—and certainly not a home. But he couldn't think how he could change it, or why he should bother. It had always been adequate, and would be again.

He gathered his clothes and took them to the laundry in a small room off the back porch and mudroom. He loaded the washer, poured in some detergent, set the dials, and started the load. He looked around for Cat and Newf but couldn't find them. Eventually he found a note on his refrigerator from McCants, saying she had taken them to her place. He had been gone longer than he had expected. He hadn't really thought about the logistics of Mc-Cants coming by each day, twice a day, to let Newf out. He should have suggested she take them in the first place. He wasn't thinking things through.

He considered calling McCants and picking up his animals but decided not to. The animals were safe and that's all that mattered. What else was he overlooking?

A serial killer was out there, and he was the next victim on the list. For a fleeting moment he thought of locking the cabin door. It would have been ridiculous. He never had before and he wouldn't begin now. The killer would be waiting for him in the woods. That's how he worked. And Service would be ready for him.

# 27

## Marquette, Michigan
### June 1, 2004

If the best part of being a detective was not wearing a uniform every day, the worst was spending time in a cookie-cutter cubicle in the DNR's regional office. Most Wildlife Resources Protection unit detectives operated out of home offices, but Captain Grant insisted on Service putting in a regular appearance in Marquette, probably because the captain wanted to keep track of him. As a CO, Service had for years operated out of his truck and Slippery Creek Camp, and had been accountable primarily to sergeants, who largely had left him alone. He had never been one to need or welcome a lot of direction and supervision.

He waved at Fern LeBlanc on the way to his cubicle, stopped, and pulled his mail out of his box. He went to the copier room, made copies of the FBI reports, and went back to his office and turned on his computer. While it was booting up, he checked his voice-mail messages. One was from Joan Pillars. *Who the hell?* Then he remembered: Limpy's alleged squeeze. She had left a card and note in the restaurant, stuck another under his windshield wiper, and now, here was a phone call. She said she was persistent and it appeared she was true to her word. He decided he'd call her back if he had time — just to get her off his back.

Fern LeBlanc appeared in his cubicle. "They're ready for you."

Service checked his watch: 3 P.M. "The meeting's not until four."

"Things change," she said, "They're waiting."

"Sounds like I'm in trouble," he joked.

"Familiar terrain for you," she said, but her tone suggested she was joking. *Weird*, he thought. The woman had never liked him. But even Fern was treating him differently since the accident. *Not an accident!* He quickly corrected himself.

"On my way," he said, gathering his folders.

Captain Ware Grant and Chief Lorne O'Driscoll were sitting in the captain's office, which looked out on distant Lake Superior. The lake was lit by the sun, and a gentle breeze made it look like it was pocked with diamonds.

The captain pointed to a chair at the table with the chief and remained behind his desk. Service gave one set of records to the chief and the other to the captain. "Coffee?"

"Buzz Fern," the captain said, opening his folder.

"I'll get it," Service said.

"I could have done that," Fern said as he filled three cups in the canteen. "You don't need to do my job for me."

"Sorry," he said. So much for joking. Nothing he did, it seemed, met with Fern's approval. She scowled and walked away.

The chief looked up when he returned. "Ficorelli's death was announced last night," he said. "No details, no date, and only an approximate location. It's being called a homicide. Why such a long delay?"

"The Feebs found their first kill site there. They wanted to protect it. I argued for a release to encourage tips." He didn't tell the captain or chief he had been the one to find the kill site.

Captain Grant said, "The bureau loathes media attention unless they want to tell a story that will benefit them."

The chief glared at one of the photos of the mutilated wardens, tapped it on the table, and shook his head. No words came out and Service understood. The photos were enough to turn the stomach of the most callous lawman.

The three men sat in lugubrious silence. Service sensed they were as much at a loss of where to start as he was. Finally, Chief O'Driscoll spoke. "Do you believe the FBI arranged to have you in Wisconsin to shield you?"

"They admitted as much," Service said.

The captain asked, "If you had been the victim, would they have brought Ficorelli or the other man in to protect them?"

Service hadn't considered this angle, and wondered why the captain had asked it, and if he was trying to make a point. "I don't know," he said. Elray Spargo was their control, which had doomed him. "It's down to one state now." Why Spargo and not him or Ficorelli as the control? Pure luck, he guessed.

"I called Director Mueller in Washington," Chief O'Driscoll said. "He is somewhat familiar with the case, but I believe he knows nothing about the list or the Missouri control angle. I told him we'll request assistance if we need it to protect our own, but it's our intent to handle this ourselves."

"He agreed?"

"He said they have to bring a team here as an adjunct of the presidential security detail, so they'll be available. I think that's his way of telling us to expect them to be around."

*Great*, Service thought.

"The Bureau has resources we don't," the captain said, playing devil's advocate.

"Which have gotten them nowhere," the chief said. "This is our problem." O'Driscoll looked into Service's eyes. "We have to assume you're the target, but I intend to brief all officers. Captains will brief lieutenants and sergeants, and together they will meet with all personnel in each district."

"What about leaks?" Service asked.

"There will be no leaks," the chief said. "I will tell our people about the killings and what we know, but you will not be identified as the possible target. We want all officers on their toes, and all officers up here will be asked to exercise extreme caution in riverine environments. We'll continue solo patrols, but backup is to be called in if any officer encounters *anything* that seems unusually suspicious or out of place."

Service wondered how many officers would take the chief's advice to heart. Most of them tended to be self-reliant, stubborn, and not easily intimidated. "Will you show them a photo? Asking for caution is one thing; seeing the reality is a whole other thing."

The chief looked over at the captain, who nodded agreement.

"How do you propose to handle your situation?" the chief asked. "Are you pulling yourself off the FBI team?"

Did he have that option? "I haven't thought it through yet. I called a contact in Detroit. She's using her sources to go through the VICAP data. Agent Waco, the warden I worked with in Missouri, thinks it's possible that there's more than one perp—that even in targeting specific individuals, wardens are difficult to track. Considerable preparation would be essential."

"Why VICAP?"

"Two groups of killings. The MO varies throughout the first group. But the blood eagle is a constant in only the most recent killings in the second group, and the location near water is the same for both groups. There was a method change in the last few, and the feds don't understand why, or what it means. Given the complexity of the blood eagle, I think it's possible the perp gave the method a test run—maybe on civilians. The Feebs claim VICAP led them to both groups. I thought I should go back and see exactly what it gave them." He said nothing about Tatie Monica's non-FBI analyst.

"VICAP should have turned up something," the chief said.

"You'd think," Service said. "I didn't know much about VICAP before this, and what I've learned so far is that it has more wrinkles than a cheap suit. It's not unreasonable to expect that something has been missed, something small but significant."

"We're not going to lecture you on caution," the chief said.

"I hear you," Service replied. "Everybody's going to be uptight about this. I want to keep working my sources. This guy is methodical, and method implies routine, which suggests predictability. There's got to be something we're not seeing."

Service thought about sharing information about the fly he had found, and the coincidental deaths that might or might not be linked to the killings, but he decided he didn't have enough information to make sense and kept quiet. Besides, he had stuck the fly in his pocket and forgotten to turn it over to the FBI for evidence.

After O'Driscoll departed for Lansing, Captain Grant said, "The FBI pulled you under their wings for more than protection. They were buying time to get their act together. Understood?"

"It's occurred to me that they want me to be their bait," Service said.

"Where's the ideal spot to place bait?"

"Where the predator expects to find it."

"Does such a place come to mind?" the captain asked.

"Several."

"Good. When you're ready, let me know."

"I'm thinking the more sources I reach out to, the better off we are."

"I agree," the captain said. "I'll do the same."

"Do you want me to check in with O'Brien?"

"Not necessary," the captain said. "He's a good man and will help you only if you need it. You *are* all right, yes?"

"I'm good to go, Captain." But he wasn't convinced, himself. "Cap'n," he added, "You talked to Gus about Honeypat Allerdyce?"

The captain nodded. "I put out a BOLO. Are you thinking there is a connection between the woman's return and Nantz's death?"

"You know her background. We can't rule it out, and there's another reason for revisiting the accident." He explained about Ficorelli's mother, Spargo's sister, and the timing.

The captain made notes, looked up, and pointed with his pen. "I'll follow up with the Troops. You make sure to keep your mind on *you*."

# 28

## Jefferson, Wisconsin
### June 8, 2004

Wayno Ficorelli's memorial was held in an old firehouse-turned-community-meeting-room in Jefferson, the town where he'd lived with his mother. While the service had involved mostly family members, Service and three Wisconsin wardens were included.

The way Wayno died had left everyone pensive. It was one thing to be killed in the performance of duty and another to be slaughtered like a pig. The public had not been told about the mutilations, but the family of the victim and his fellow wardens knew.

There was a reception at the Ficorelli house, a mile north of Jefferson, after the burial. Marge Ciucci, Ficorelli's aunt, was in charge. She had obviously been cooking for several days. She was effusive and friendly, circulating like a dervish, making sure her guests were overfed and comfortable. At one point she came over to Grady Service: "You're staying tonight, yes?"

"Thought I'd head back to Michigan."

"Nonsense," she said. "You're staying. We need to talk, you and me."

Service thought she had the voice of an angel and the eyes of hangman.

When the last guests were gone, Marge Ciucci took him to a small outbuilding. It was filled with fly-fishing equipment and tying materials. The walls held more than a dozen impressive brook trout mounts.

"It was Wayno's plan when he retired to open a fly shop up north," she said. Over the years he and my sister bought several fine properties on good rivers." She paused and took a deep breath. "He would have wanted you to have some of his gear," she said. "He'd want the sheriff to have his rods. I'm giving you all his flies; there are boxes and boxes of them."

"I can't do that," Service said.

"Plus the gear the FBI has," she added. "When they release that, I'll send it to you. He thought you were the best," the dead man's aunt said, "and he had a high opinion of himself, that boy."

Service sensed the woman fighting to hold back her emotions.

"So you take all this stuff and load it in your truck; use it in good health and enjoy. Life is too short."

"I don't know what to say," Grady Service said.

"Say you'll get who did this," the old woman said.

It was more than clear in the woman's tone that she was not referring to simply bringing the killer to justice, but something more final.

"The justice system will take care of it," he said.

"The system?" Marge Ciucci said. "*Non me rompere le palle!* In the old country they have other ways to take care of animals like this." Her face tightened into a mask and she hissed, "*Nessuno me lo ficca in culo!*"

Service understood her anger, but not her specific words "I'll do my best."

The old woman reached up, pinched his face, and nodded. "Compari to settle the stomach before we go to bed?"

It was not a question.

In the morning she had coffee waiting and fried three eggs for him. "I'm sorry about last night," she said. "You don't speak Italian and I lost my temper, but you and Wayno are men of the world, and you have a right to know what I said. First, I told you not to break my balls. Then I said *nobody* fucks me up the ass! You catch the *animale* who did this to my nephew and you cut off his balls, *si?*" She made a violent slicing gesture with the side of her hand.

*Definitely not someone he would want to cross,* he thought as he loaded Wayno's boxes of flies into his vehicle.

# 29

# Allerdyce Compound, Southwest Marquette County, Michigan
## June 9, 2004

On the way back to Michigan, Service called the cell phone number that Joan Pillars had left for him. The phone rang interminably and he was about to hang up when she finally answered. "Hello?"

"This is Grady Service."

"*Yes*," she said, her voice brightening. "The detective. Andrew's friend."

Limpy's friend? He almost laughed out loud. "You said you wanted to talk."

"Not over the phone," she said.

"I'm free this afternoon."

"Oh," she said. "Well, I'm at Andrew's camp today, and tomorrow I'm leaving for North Carolina for a few days."

It was difficult to picture the chic professor in Allerdyce's crude camp in southwest Marquette County. "I'll be there in about three hours, give or take."

There was a two-track off a U.S. Forest Service road down to the compound's parking area, then a half-mile walk along a twisting trail from there into the camp itself. The surrounding area was dense with black spruce, cedars, hemlocks, and tamaracks. He parked and began to make his way along the dark trail on foot.

It was normal to not see a soul en route to or in the compound, but today there were people everywhere in the camp, and Allerdyce himself was seated at a picnic table, freshly shaved, teeth in, grinning. It irked him that neither he nor the old poacher had their real teeth.

"Sonny," he said, "Joanie told me youse was dropping by, but I din't believe her, eh." The old man winked. "She got the gift for sure."

Service had no idea what gift Allerdyce was referring to and didn't care.

Pillars walked out of the old man's cabin, drying her hands on a dishtowel. "Good afternoon, Detective."

Pillars invited him to sit at the table, turned to Allerdyce, and said, "Shoo, Andrew! This is business." Allerdyce laughed his wheezing laugh, got up, and walked through the camp as people came up to him and engulfed him with questions.

The cabin was new, identical to the old one that had burned, though this version had a new metal roof. Other buildings in the compound were under construction, but there were no construction company trucks.

"Andrew's family is doing all the work," Pillars said. "They can do anything."

She was obviously impressed. Service wasn't. "You wanted to talk."

"Yes. I'm writing a book about woods crime. It started out as rural crime, but as I got into the subject I realized that what goes on in the deep woods is a lot more interesting and complex, and I shifted my focus. My publisher doesn't understand how I can find enough to fill a book on the subject, but I could write several if I wanted to. At this point I've talked to a lot of people around the country, but now I want to start shifting gears and get the views of law enforcement."

One of Limpy's grandchildren brought iced tea in tall glasses. The boy wore a Packer chook pulled down over his ears, and a Pistons jersey and shorts that reached almost to his beat-up high-top sneakers, a rural thug in training.

The professor took a sip. "I've interviewed many criminals around the country, but I have to tell you, Andrew is by far the most interesting of them . . . and near as I can tell, he's also been one of the most successful."

"If you don't count his stint in Jackson," Service said.

"Yes, Andrew told me about that. He said it was an accident that you got shot. He still feels bad about that."

Service knew better. Limpy Allerdyce had no conscience.

"Andrew genuinely cares about you," the woman said. "You'll never hear it from him, but it's true. He's very old school about not emoting."

Service wanted to say that this was because the only emotions the man had were evil, but he kept this to himself.

"I believe Andrew has changed," Pillars said. "He readily admits to his violent past and says that since he nearly died, he has reevaluated and changed his ways."

Service wanted to laugh out loud. Among his many skills, Limpy was at heart a world-class con man.

"Ah," the professor said. "I can see in your eyes you don't agree. When we undertake to change ourselves drastically from what we once were, people are understandably skeptical.

"Words are cheap and only actions speak, but the truth is that he and his family are no longer poaching or breaking laws," she added. "He has seen the light, and has inculcated the others."

*Bullshit.* Limpy hated the light. He was a creature of darkness, secretive in nature, evil in intent. He and his tribe were cedar swamp savages. "Right," Service said, his voice dripping sarcasm.

"The interesting thing about Andrew is that although he's not formally educated, he is extremely intelligent, and even more than that, he's very clever. He has made a great deal of money in his endeavors, but he has spent only what he's needed for his operations. He chooses to live quite frugally. Do you know that he owns a warehouse in Marquette that's being converted to condos with a view of the city harbor? He's the majority shareholder in the development, and the condos are a thousand square feet and going at a million dollars each. The project was fully subscribed before construction even began," Pillars said.

*Allerdyce in real estate?* Nantz had shown him the development overlooking the old iron dock in Marquette, insisting that the city would be the state's next Traverse City. She claimed that people would flock to the area from California and Texas to buy lake properties, and that in ten years Marquette would be a far different place than it had been. Her prediction had turned his stomach, but she had wealth she never talked about and seemed to understand money at a level he couldn't imagine.

"He owns a great deal of prime property," the professor added.

"He claims."

"Yes, of course, but he authorized me to talk to his accountant, and I have seen proof. Andrew is a man of considerable wealth, which is likely to keep increasing as he moves deeper into development."

There was a picture: Poacher turned developer! Service tried not to laugh. It was just a different facet of the same business, driven by the same values. "What can I do for you?" he asked. The last thing he wanted to do was listen to some professor sing the praises of the worst poacher in the state.

"He really has changed," Pillars repeated. "In fact, if you check with your RAP people, you will find that they have gotten a number of anonymous tips over the past sixty days, and all of them have led to arrests and convictions." RAP (Report All Poaching) was the 800 line to Lansing where people called in infractions. She put a piece of notebook paper on the table. "All the times of the calls are there. Check them out and you'll see. Instead of breaking laws, Andrew's people are helping you and your colleagues enforce them. Who better to help than someone who is an expert on the other end of the process?"

Service shoved the paper into his pocket.

"Crimes vary in their severity," she said. "And criminals vary in the degrees and extents to which they are involved. How do you see the criminals you engage?"

He couldn't believe he was having this conversation, but he was here and he wanted to get it over with. "Most fish and game violations grow out of unchecked common emotions, not evil intent," Service began.

"That's a remarkably enlightened view," the professor said.

"All I can tell you about is my own experience. Some churchgoing, Boy Scout–leading wrench-twister from Flat Rock sees not one, but two eight-point bucks, and before he can sort out his emotions, *bang-bang*, two dead deer and only one permit. Accidental violator."

He plowed on, "Or a woman from Oscoda gets a weekend pass from her old man. She's on the East Branch of the Black River catching trout, nice ones, big ones, eager ones. One, three, five, limit reached—but God, are they ever biting. Geez, I can't quit now. Might never ever have another day like this in my life, and the hubby won't believe me if he doesn't see the evidence. Just this once, I'll take them home, all twenty-two of them, when the limit is five and no more than three over fifteen inches. Out steps the game warden and uh-oh, accidental violator. The fine will be ten bucks for every fish over the limit, and she has a big fine to remind her to follow the law in the future. Most folks are sorry about it and won't do it again. Sometimes we warn them, and sometimes we cite them, but these people are not the ones that cause the real problems."

"But Andrew is different," said Pillars.

"Limpy and his people are in it for one thing—money—and the way to that is wholesale slaughter by whatever method works best. They take jobs for people who want trophies, or they take huge quantities of meat and fish for black-market sales. They will do whatever it takes to get what they want, and they won't stop on their own."

"You're saying they're professionals," she said.

"Right, but there's also another class: the career violators who do it because they like the game between us and them, and like the feeling of getting away with something. Sometimes these people turn violent, but mostly it's just a game, and they take their tickets and pay their fines or do their time and eventually go back to doing what they did before. They're like those folks who pirate cable lines from the neighbor's house, or break the speed limit with radar detectors. They like to see how far they can push the envelope."

"What about subsistence poaching?"

"That goes on," Service said. "But we usually know which people are in need--even the proud ones who won't admit to it. If I catch one of these folks, I usually warn him and let him keep what he has, but I also tell him not to do it again. Later I make sure that when we confiscate game from violators, I deliver it to people who need it."

"But some people would starve without such things."

"Some yes, and some I'm not sure about. A lot of people who need the meat also have the most modern weapons, new trucks, snowmobiles, boats and motors, ATVs, all the toys. The fact is that their per-pound cost is higher for the game they take without licenses or without regard to limits than if they bought it at the local IGA. A lot of people try to pass themselves off as subsistence poachers when really they're in that see-what-we-can-get-away-with group."

The professor was making occasional notes in a small notebook, but mostly checking a small tape recorder sitting on the table. "Are you seeing changes in the kinds and frequency of crimes?"

"It used to be the woods were full of jacklighters and people shooting deer out of season. We don't see as much of that anymore. We see more drugs and timber theft than we used to—probably because lumber costs so much now. The patterns change, but there's usually some fairly apparent reason for it. One of the reasons for decreasing frequencies is that fewer people are hunting and fishing. Not as many kids grow up in the woods anymore, and they never learn how to do it legally, much less consider illegal methods. If they can't do it on a couch with a remote, they aren't interested." His son Walter had loved the outdoors.

"Are you saying the woods are getting more peaceful?" Pillars asked.

"No, the patterns are just changing. Now we see more boozers and druggies lugging around weapons, some legal, some not. More domestic abuse, assault, the same stuff other cops see."

"Do you really believe that people don't change, or that they can't?"

"I hear people claiming to change, but I don't see the actual changes. People will tell a cop what they think a cop wants to hear."

"That's an exceptionally pessimistic view of the human condition," she said.

"Pessimism for a college professor is reality for a woods cop."

"On that uplifting note," she said, turning off the tape recorder.

As he talked to Pillars, Service carefully watched what was going on in the camp. Interview completed, he stood up and stretched. "You claim Limpy has changed," he said, pointing to one of the cabins. "But there's a rifle leaning against that cabin wall, and he's on parole and cannot possess or be around anyone with a firearm. And that red Honda four-wheeler over here doesn't have a registration. If I walked through this camp I could write at least a dozen violations. Limpy claims he's changing? Great. That would be good, but I deal with evidence, not hot air, and maybe you shouldn't either."

Allerdyce came back as they were preparing to leave. "You stayin' for supper, sonny?"

"Gotta move on," Service said.

"Fresh brook trout," the old poacher said, smacking his lips

"And if I looked in your freezer, all you'd have is the daily possession limit, right?"

"Cross my heart," Allerdyce said with a cackle. "Changed my ways, boy."

Service nodded for Limpy to follow, and as they walked away from Pillars he said to the old man, "Honeypat was in Baraga at the casino awhile back."

"She's gone," Allerdyce said, his eyes gleaming.

"Gone?" Service asked.

"Moved on; won't never be back."

"You saw her?"

Allerdyce said, "Tell me dis, sonny. How a woman who can fly an airplane crack up a pickup down below Palmer on dry road, eh?"

"The state ruled it an accident."

Allerdyce shook his head.

Service left Limpy and turned back to Pillars. "Tell him the things I pointed out."

Service was certain the poacher would always be out for himself. You could paint a skunk red and call it a fox, but it was still a skunk under the paint job, and he did not like Limpy's tone when he said Honeypat was never coming back, or his question abut Nantz's death.

# 30

# Negaunee, Michigan
## June 9, 2004

**Back at his car,** Service turned his attention to his own concerns. He read the accident report. Then he drove to the regional state police post in Negaunee and talked to a sergeant named Chastain. He had known Chastain casually for many years, but had never worked with the man, who had the reputation of a laid-back straight shooter. "Hey, Chas," Service greeted him after he showed his credentials and was admitted to the operations area.

"Geez, Grady, everybody feels really bad."

"Thanks." Service placed the accident report on the sergeant's desk. "The Troop who handled this, his name is Villemure?"

"Yeah, Fritz. He grew up in Herman."

"He on road patrol today?"

Chastain stood up and looked down into another cubicle. "Hey, Tonia, is Villemure on?"

A female voice said, "Yeah; we show him out by Diorite."

Chastain looked down at Service. "You heard?"

"I'd like to talk to him. Can you ask him to meet me at the Circle in Humboldt?"

"What's your call sign?"

"Twenty Five Fourteen. Say, thirty minutes, if that works for him."

"Tonia, ask Villemure to meet DNR Twenty Five Fourteen at the Circle in Humboldt in thirty minutes."

The Circle was a local stop-and-rob that sold live bait, snacks, deli sandwiches, ammunition, and camping gear. The state police cruiser was already parked in the lot when Service pulled up and went inside.

"Villemure?"

"Twenty Five Fourteen?"

"Grady Service." The two men shook hands. Service bought two coffees from the owner's twenty-something daughter.

"Service," Villemure said. "Geez, that wreck was terrible. I'm sorry."

"Thanks. I wanted to talk to you about it."

"Is there a problem?"

No defensiveness. The kid was straight and all-business, and Service liked him immediately. "Nope; curiosity, mostly. You were first on the scene."

"Yeah. A passerby called the station and Dispatch sent me. I was ten minutes away."

"A passerby; did he stop at the wreck?"

"No. All he said was that a vehicle might be in the ditch."

"It was a man?"

"Yeah."

"Did Dispatch get a tape?"

"I think they tape everything, but I don't know how long they keep the stuff. You'd have to ask. What's up?"

"What was your first impression when you pulled up?"

"It looked bad, and I took my handheld and called for help as I went down the embankment to the truck—is that what you mean?"

"I'm not sure. At some point did you just stand and take in the scene and try to picture what happened in your mind?"

"Yeah, later, after the EMS come."

"And?"

"I don't know."

"This isn't a test, Officer."

"Call me Fritz. Yeah, I don't know. I mean, I looked, and I thought, How the heck did she lose control there? The road was dry and it's banked and it's been resurfaced and it's smooth. I mean, it's not a place generally where people might lose control."

"Did you take that impression and go with it?"

The young Troop looked perplexed. "No witnesses, no survivors; where could I take it?"

"Did you ask about the call-in?"

"Yeah—anonymous, no name."

"Who took the call?"

"Tonia Tonte. She's on Dispatch right now, the one who called me to meet you."

"Thanks, Fritz."

"Is there a problem?"

Most young Troops worried about mistakes and the repercussions of follow-ups.

"No, no problem. Thanks for indulging me."

Service looked over the counter at Tonia Tonte. She had ebony hair with streaks of gray, wore little makeup and small dangling earrings that sparkled in the artificial lighting of the control center. "I'm Service," he said. "About a month back you dispatched Officer Villemure to a wreck down by Palmer. You got a call from a passerby."

"I'm on break in ten minutes," she said. "It's kind of crazy right now. Meet in the break room?"

He agreed, and passed the time by talking to a couple of Troops he knew in the back room, one of them a female undercover from the integrated county drug team.

Tonia Tonte came into the room and poured a cup of coffee from the urn. "You smoke?" she asked. "I can't seem to quit, and by the time breaks roll around, I'm climbing the walls."

They stepped outside. She opened her small purse and took out a pack of Salems. He lit her cigarette for her.

"That night," she began, "I never said the caller was a passerby, and he never said it, but you know how things get started."

"You have caller ID?"

"Right; the ID showed Colorado, which means it was probably a prepaid telephone card."

"It was a man?"

"Yeah, definitely a guy."

"Anything special about the voice?"

"Young; you know, the dude type. He said, 'Hey dude. I think there's a red pickup truck in the ditch.' "

"He said dude and red pickup?"

"Yes, Most people don't notice details like that."

"Do you still have the tape?"

"No. Case closed, tape gets erased. But I kept a transcript. I always keep transcripts of anonymous call-ins—just in case."

"How long have you been on the job?"

"Six years. My husband died of leukemia seven years ago, and I had to go back to work. I moved here from the Soo to live with my sister and I got this job. Lucky for me. You want a copy of the transcript?"

"Is it more extensive than what you told me?"

"No. It was short and to the point." She looked at him. "Service? It was your girlfriend and son in the truck that night, right?"

He nodded.

"That's rough," she said. "I've been there."

# 31

# Marquette, Michigan
## July 13, 2004

There had been an off-and-on rain all morning under a fuliginous sky. "Goya on acid," a college girl standing near Grady Service said as she looked up. She had long hair, purple and electric green, and wore a white T-shirt with a solid black triangle on it, and the words THE ONLY BUSH I TRUST IS MY OWN.

Grady Service was amused and tried not to smile. He was in uniform outside the Yooperdome in Marquette, waiting for President Bush to arrive; around him were dozens of demonstrators, each with a personal ax to grind. Three beer-guts in frayed camo hats wore new red T-shirts that pronounced LABORERS FOR KERRY. A man wore a blue T-shirt that read ILLINOIS IS A WAR ZONE. What the hell? Two men in camos and old jungle boots carried identical signs: HOT DAMN VIETNAM — DEJA VU. Another of them carried a huge sign that said DUBYA DUCKED: OTHERS GOT FUCKED.

As he observed, he mulled over Nantz's accident. The cop Villemure couldn't understand how it had happened. The dispatcher, Tonia Tonte, had had an anonymous caller, a male. Did that rule out Honeypat? Was he confusing two things? Not an accident. That was all he knew for sure. *Let the captain do his job and you do yours*, he told himself. *Whatever the fuck it is.* Why am I here at this circus?

The parade of signs was endless: KEEP DA U.P. WILD, EH! was followed by a bearded man carrying one that read NATIVE AMERICANS' RIGHTS ARE WAY TO THE LEFT. Another wore a T-shirt that proclaimed U.P. DUBYA DIGIT UNEMPLOYMENT. A dumpy woman in earth shoes and an ankle-length dress carried a sign: JUMP YOUR BONES FOR FOOD (OR DOPE). Service recognized her as an undercover from Escanaba.

Decades of causes, hurts, and policy non sequiturs were bubbling out, but for the most part, the demonstrators were quiet and nearly lethargic in humidity dense enough to slice like cudighi. A skinny woman in short-shorts wore a shirt that said MY BODY IS NOT PUBLIC PROPERTY. Service knew her, and if her body wasn't exactly public, it was frequently and freely shared at closing times in several local watering holes.

A college girl in a sweatshirt (representing Wildcat Women for Kerry) was telling a group of friends how she had dutifully waited in line three hours for a ticket to get inside the Yooperdome, only to be refused because she was a registered Democrat. "They're, like, *totally* fascist?" the girl said. "Too bad some of the young dudes are so hot, eh?"

"You can get a tax deduction for fucking Republicans," a girl in her entourage said. "But you can't dance with them, eh."

"Shuuut up . . ." the first girl said, giggling.

Historically the U.P. had voted Democrat and pro union, and though this was changing, it still tended toward its historical inclinations, and the Bush people were doing their best to pack the hall with vetted true believers. With Democrat Lori Timms as the state's new governor, Michigan was being viewed as a swing state, and Bush's minders were determined not to cede to the Democrats a single electoral vote. Thus, Republican legions had descended upon Marquette and a lot of locals, while honored by the leader of the land being there, were equally pissed off at the costs being imposed by the presidential visit.

It was a fine circus, and Service was there with several other officers from various agencies, all in uniform with no particular role to play other than to stand around and look official. Captain Grant had been in several meetings with the Secret Service, but in the end, DNR law enforcement personnel were deployed primarily along the twenty-mile motorcade route from Sawyer to Marquette. Service told himself he would have been happy standing out in the boonies watching the presidential vehicles fly by at seventy-five miles per hour, but the captain had asked him to join him in Marquette, so here he was among the other outsiders. He had been in Vietnam during the antiwar demonstrations in the U.S., and he figured this was about as close to such displays as he would ever get. More than a few of the protesters were of his generation, graying pence-bangers desperately fishing for another cause.

The people headed into the Yooperdome were well dressed, slicked down, and orderly, carrying red, white, and blue balloons, and wearing patriotic party hats. There were even a few signs: JUGULATE A TERRORIST FOR JESUS and AMMO SPECIAL FOR BIN LADEN: DUBYA-OUGHT BUCK! The town's year round population was about 20,000, but the crowd at the dome was expected to be more than half of that, the vast majority from places other than Marquette, buses coming in from all over the U.P., Wisconsin, and from below the bridge to pack the house with conservative pedigrees and cheering voices for George Bush.

The captain caught Service's attention and motioned for him to follow him.

They went to a parking lot away from the protesters. " 'Buckshot' is going to arrive here," the captain said as a Secret Service agent in a black suit approached them. The agent wasn't tall, but he was built like an iron-pumper, and wore dark shades despite the total absence of sun.

The captain shook hands with the man. "This is Detective Service."

The agent gave him the once-over and said, "Follow me, please."

Grady Service looked at his captain's impassive face. *Now what the hell was this?* He followed the agent to a loading dock and stopped when the man put out his arm like a railway crossing. "We'll wait here."

"For what?"

No explanation was offered.

Soon he heard sirens and saw a shiny black Cadillac limo come racing into the lot toward the dock. It was followed by several black SUVs, which stopped and unloaded Secret Service agents before anyone opened the limo doors.

The President got out and lifted his chin to stretch his neck.

Several people were talking to him and he was nodding, but appeared not to be paying a whole lot of attention to any of the voices. After a few moments, the President of the United States started walking toward the loading dock entrance. He was wearing a black suit that looked like it had cost a fortune, shiny black oxfords, a blue button-down shirt, and a pale blue tie that gave off a sort of lavender sheen in the low light.

As the President neared, the Secret Service agent stepped out and George Bush stopped, looked at Service, and as if prompted, reached out his hand. "This is Michigan Department of Natural Resources Detective Service," the Secret Service agent announced.

The President's hair was mussed some and it was much grayer than Service had expected. He was tall, maybe six feet.

"Gordy, I been hearin' good things about you," the President said with a one-sided smile that looked like a smirk.

Service blinked. *What the hell?* Before he knew it, he was saying, "It's Grady, Mr. President, not Gordy."

Flashlights were popping and Bush laughed. "Heh-heh, I meet a lot of folks, and names sort of run off on me like untamed colts, big guy. From what I hear, you got the big *cojones*, son. Your country needs men a' your caliber, so keep up the good work, and maybe there'll be a role for you in Homeland Security. Ya gotta unnerstand, that's important work, big fella."

Service looked into the President's eyes, but they were dancing around, searching for other visual stimulation. "Sir, I don't think our shaking hands out here in public is such a good idea."

Bush looked confused and giggled again. "You ain't one-a them Dem'crats, are ya, big guy?"

"Sir, have you been briefed that somebody is gunning for me, and that at this moment you could be in extreme danger?" Service couldn't help himself.

George Bush's hand dropped and he said, "Uh, heh-heh, uh . . ." and looked around with the wide eyes of a deer caught in the headlights of an oncoming eighteen-wheeler. "Uh, well, ah gotta git on inside and dew mah speech, son. Kin I count on yore vote come November?" And then he was gone inside with Service's escort and an entourage of stern-faced men.

Minutes later Service rejoined the captain. "Sir, *what* is going on?"

"Don't know for sure," Captain Ware Grant said with a grin. "The request came directly from the director of the FBI."

Service was at a loss for words.

"What was the point?"

"He likes being photographed with law enforcement and first-responder types. His handlers think it makes him look like a man of the people."

"Seeing him shaking hands with a game warden won't win him a lot of votes up here," Service said.

"Maybe that's why the chief agreed to the FBI's request," the captain said, breaking a rare smile.

Service watched a woman walk by with a sign: HOW DO YOU CONFUSE A TEXAS POLITICIAN? PUT THREE SHOVELS AGAINST A WALL AND ASK HIM TO TAKE HIS PICK.

He went downtown to Snowbound Books after the rally, looking for something to read. He saw a woman with a sweatshirt that said MOTHER EARTH PRAYS FOR YOU. He was about to turn back to a bookshelf when he recognized the woman in the sweatshirt as one of Tatie Monica's agents.

"Bobbi?" he said, stepping toward her.

The woman tried to twist away, but he caught her sleeve. "Tell Special Agent Monica I don't need a bunch of amateur babysitters." The woman fled the store.

He was pissed beyond words, threw up his hands, and walked out of the store.

Service found the captain in his office at the regional office. "There's Feeb surveillance all over me," he griped.

The captain looked at him, saying only, "A good game warden knows how to throw people off his trail."

# 32

## Slippery Creek, Michigan
### July 15, 2004

**Service had called** Shark on his way to Limpy's to tell him about Wayno Ficorelli's fly collection. Shark had called back and announced that he and Limey would be bringing dinner over that night. Grady Service didn't want company. McCants had dropped off his animals that day, and they were about all the companionship he could handle.

He had maps and charts pinned up all around the main room of the cabin. He had taken locations of killings from FBI reports and tried to convert them to points on the maps so that he could see what sort of patterns might appear. He didn't want to be interrupted, but Shark was a force, and would be there soon.

The results of his efforts so far seemed negligible. Most of the bodies had been found near rivers and streams—water. But those in Rhode Island, Louisiana, and Florida were on the ocean or one of its brackish bays. Given the disparity, how the hell had Monica's analyst found a pattern? He sure as hell didn't see it. All by water. Big deal.

Newf tipped her water bowl, a signal that it was empty and she was thirsty. As he filled the bowl, some of it slopped over the side and soaked his bare foot. It struck him: moving water. Rivers and streams moved, and oceans moved; they had tides. The link wasn't simply water, but *moving* water, and the way the killer moved Ficorelli's body suggested why. But what about Spargo? He had been killed two hundred feet *above* the Eleven Point.

It was an alarming realization. How many other obvious things was he missing?

He wanted to keep working, but suddenly the cabin door flew open, Newf started barking, and charged Shark, who collided with the dog. Limey came in behind her husband, caught Service's eye, and shook her head. Yalmer Wetelainen was an old friend from Houghton who managed a motel and worked only to finance his hunting and fishing obsessions. He was bald, thin, short, and partial to beer, especially homemade, which he made and drank in copious quantities, mostly because it was cheap. Service and Gus

Turnage had once administered a preliminary breathalyzer test to their friend during an all-night nickel-and-dime poker game. The unique Finn drank a case of beer and shots of straight vodka in a fairly short time, but never registered legally drunk. Neither CO could figure it out. Yalmer drank like a fish and ate like a pig, yet there was not even a hint of fat on his body.

They decided that their friend didn't fit any known human physiological profile, and because of his unique metabolism, they nicknamed him Shark, and the name stuck. Limey Pyykkonen was a homicide detective for Houghton County. A strapping, angular woman with a small round face, Limey had close-cropped blonde hair and thin lips. She had once had a brief fling with Wayno Ficorelli, but for some time now, she and Shark had been married and were a rock-solid couple.

Limey hugged Service while Newf and Shark wrestled. "I was really sorry to hear about Wayno," she said. "The feds got any leads?"

"Don't know," Service said as Shark came bouncing over with a gallon jug of bright red wine. "Last year's chokecherries," Shark announced, plopping it down on the kitchen table. "Kicks like a ten-gauge. Where the heck are the new flies?"

They went over to the area in the main room where Service kept his fishing gear. Wetelainen was like a kid at Christmas, ripping through the fly boxes. He shouted, "Hey woman, fetch your man some wine!"

Pyykkonen yelled back, "You break a leg?"

Service said, "I'll get it," and heard Pyykkonen mumble, "Why do men revert to adolescence when they get new toys?"

"That hurts," Service said, pouring three glasses of wine and putting one in front of her. Limey rolled her eyes.

When Service got back to Shark, he found his friend holding a fly and looking perplexed. "Somebody steal one of your patterns?"

"You know what this is?" Shark asked, holding up a fly.

Service looked at it. "Some kind of brown drake?"

Shark shook his head. "Right, brown drake, but what *kind* of brown drake?"

"Dun?"

"Holy Wah! You gotta stop working so bloody much and fish more. It's a booger brown drake."

"Is that supposed to mean something to me?"

"Booger flies," Shark said. "*Look* at it."

Service took the fly and examined it. "It's got a rubber body. Should float good, right?"

"Float *good?* Hell, they float the *best*, and they aren't made of rubber."

"Some kind of plastic?"

"Nobody knows *what* it is. A guy from Curran ties these things, or he used to. I don't know if he's still alive. Crazy old fart; he always claimed they were made from nasal mucus."

Service dropped the fly on his desk and grimaced.

Wetelainen picked it up and touched the tip of his tongue to it. "Got a faint flavor. This is the real deal, not a knockoff."

"Boogers?" Service said disgustedly.

"Could be," Shark said obliviously. "Man, you do *not* see booger flies in the boxes of weekend warriors. Only serious trout-chasers know about them, much less use them. Hell, they were three bucks a copy back when I bought them—and that's a good fifteen years ago."

"*You* bought flies tied by somebody else?"

Shark got defensive. "Just a couple. I wanted to see if I could replicate the body material, but I couldn't. The way these flies are made, they ride right in the film. Sweet! And they'll float all night. Only drawback: one good bite and they're usually shot. I thought I could come up with something more durable. I managed the durable part, but I couldn't get mine to float low like the originals."

Wetelainen suddenly looked around the room. "You putting together a national compendium of trout spots?"

"Right," Service said. "Trout in the ocean," he said sarcastically.

Shark looked at his friend. "Sure."

"Bullshit."

"Not bullshit, science."

"Trout in Florida and Louisiana?" asked Service.

"*Cynoscion nebulosus*," Wetelainen said. "Spotted sea trout."

"An actual trout?"

"The rednecks are a little loose in their definitions. They look a lot like trout, though, and they eat good. Sometimes they even call them specks, like Funnelheads call brookies. Only their specks got a couple of big fangs, like this," his friend said, using his fingers to simulate protruding fangs.

Wetelainen walked over to the maps and tapped the northeastern states where there were marks along the oceans. "I don't think *Cynoscion nebulosus* is that far north. When they talk about sea trout up there, they'd probably mean salmonids that migrate into the oceans and return to rivers to spawn. You get up into Maine and eastern Canada, and they have both rainbows and brookies that do this. In the other states, it's pretty much browns."

"I've never heard of such a thing."

"Because you live in your own world. In New England the boys who chase sea-run browns are more secretive than morel-chasers up here. Hell, the Fish and Game departments in those states can't even get an accurate estimate on the populations because the guys who catch the most fish never report them, and some people think because there's no data, there're no fish."

Service sipped his wine. In his current state of mind, drinking too much invited disaster, and Shark's chokecherry wine was known for its potency—far above commercially available wine in alcohol content. "You're telling me that all of those marks on the maps are places where trout are caught?"

"What's the question?" Wetelainen countered. " 'Course you can catch trout in all those locations."

Service pointed at the other maps. "What about the other states?"

"Hell, it's like Michigan. Some will be warm-water fisheries, some cold-water. Each state's DNR would have to tell you what's what."

*Great*, Service thought. *More information to chase.* He nudged the fly on his desk with a pencil. "Booger fly, huh?"

"You betcha. The old guy's name, I think it was Main. The old man, he was a strange duck, always going on about astronomy and physics. His shop was like something out of a Hollywood back lot, shit everywhere. But the man was a genius when it came to inventing flies. Had him a whole line of booger flies: brown drakes, gray drakes, green drakes, hexagenia, even a white-gloved howdy."

"In Curran—south of Alpena?"

"Yeah, that general area."

"You've been there?"

"Once. I'd been striper fishing down in Kentucky, and I was on my way back to the U.P. I'd heard about this guy, so I stopped in. He and I had one helluva discussion about flies and their histories."

"You bought the flies then?"

"Nah, I needed what dough I had for gas to get back to Houghton. He gave me a cheap mimeographed catalog, and when I got back I wrote him a letter and placed my order. See, his shop isn't listed officially as a shop. It's in his house. There's nothing about it in the Yellow Pages. If you asked around Curran, everybody would play dumb because he was a foul-tempered old coot and he let his neighbors know the only way people could find out about the place was through word of mouth from other trout fanatics. To know about the place, you had to hear about it and get directions from somebody who had been there. Talk about brilliant marketing! The old man didn't even have a phone. I've heard about guys who drove a thousand miles to see him, and when they got there he was gone fishing. I doubt the old bastard cared about missed sales. The flies were just something he did when he wasn't chasing trout."

"Have you still got the catalog?"

"Somewhere, but it's, like, ancient."

Shark's place was a virtual graveyard for old fishing supplies, but he was generally organized.

"Give a call when you get home and give me the address, okay?"

Shark Wetelainen shrugged. "Yah, sure."

"Let's eat, boys," Limey announced.

Shark said with a grunt, "Man, it's about time! You know, if I remember right, New Mexico tried to plant sea trout in mountain streams about fifteen years back."

"Ocean-runs or spotted?" Service said.

"Holy Wah!" Shark snorted. "What's wrong with your head? Ain't no place to run *from* into New Mexico, boy. It was spotteds, I think."

The thing about Shark was that once somebody flipped his switch, it was hard to shut off. As they sat down to eat, he said, "Zane Grey claimed ocean-run browns were the kings of the trout world, toughest fighters by far."

Limey Pyykkonen said, *"Yalmer,"* and he was immediately silent.

Service looked at his friends and knew that Shark Wetelainen was head-over-heels for the cop who stood a good six inches taller than him.

He also realized that it had been a booger fly he had recovered from the Fi-corelli kill site, and his gut was telling him this was important. If it was as rare and valuable as Shark said, it helped explain why Wayno got out of the river to try to recover it. There was one other realization: The bodies were found not just near water, but moving water, and according to Shark, it was probably all trout water. This was the funny thing about investigations. They could stall for eons and suddenly vault forward on some seemingly insignificant fact that all at once became significant. Nantz would really appreciate this. She'd be running around the room right now, pumping her arms in triumph.

"Grady," Limey Pykkonnen said. "Are you coming back soon?"

He looked at the woman and said, "I'm back," picked up his fork, and began eating. All the while he ate, he saw Nantz sitting next to Limey, the two women yakking away at each other. He knew she wasn't really there, but it felt right to imagine she was.

# 33

# Marquette, Michigan
## July 16, 2004

"I might have something for you to work with," Shamekia said. The former FBI agent tended to get right to the point. Service was sitting in his cubicle, planning to spend the morning contacting state fishery agencies to verify if the places where murdered game wardens had been found held trout. Looking at a map wasn't enough, because over many generations, most state agencies had finagled with natural orders, planting all sorts of species in places where nature had never put them, and they couldn't and didn't survive, including Shark's odd story about sea trout being planted in New Mexico. In many states fishery people were torn between planting rubber fish from hatcheries and managing the rivers to create naturally reproducing wild stocks. Michigan was moving steadily toward the latter strategy.

Shamekia added, "I'm sending everything I have via messenger, there tonight. Want it at your house or office?"

"House," he said, gave her the Slippery Rock address, and told her the messenger should leave the package and not wait for him to be there to sign for it.

She said, "Okay, it's going out the door now, but here's the short version."

She continued, "June 1970, the Mexican federal police arrested a U.S. citizen in Ciudad Juárez—that's across the river from El Paso. A woman reported her husband being assaulted by an Americano in a black El Dorado. About the same time, a couple of local cops stopped the same guy in town, probably to shake him down, and he resisted. There was a fight and they put the cuffs on him. Turns out he was driving a black Cadillac. Had a woman and a boy with him. The locals found blood all over the trunk of the Cadillac, and the assaulted man identified the adult male as his assailant. The locals called the *federales* to brag themselves up some, and the *federales* immediately swooped in and intervened. They took the vehicle and the prisoner. Turns out that there had been three brutal killings in Nogales, Mexicali, and Matamoros, all male victims with mutilations along their spines. A black Cadillac had been reported near two of the killings."

"This was 1970? Near El Paso?"

"Mid-June."

Service immediately checked the list of killings he had gotten from the FBI. The body of a New Mexico game warden had been found in late June 1970. He looked quickly at the atlas he kept on his desk and saw that El Paso, Texas, was not that far from New Mexico. Geographic coincidence? "What did the federal police do?"

"My sources say they interrogated the man with great vigor."

"Car batteries and wires?" Service interjected.

"The Mexicans believe in going right at the bad guys—unless, of course, they have some political clout and can get back at them. But this was just some asshole gringo, so they probably did a number on him. Only he wouldn't crack. He insisted he'd done nothing and, according to the reports, remained silent, no matter what they did. They tried him in 1972, found him guilty of three homicides and one attempted, sentenced him to death, and packed him off to some shithole prison in the south of the country to await execution. But before they could carry out the sentence, the American was murdered by a prison guard. This was just before Christmas 1974," said Shamekia.

"There a name for this guy?"

"Wellington Ney from Pigeon River, Indiana."

He'd never heard of a town called Pigeon River. There was a river by that name in northern Indiana, close to the Michigan border, but not a town. "What about his wife and kid?" asked Service.

"It's not clear it was his wife or his kid. The reports say simply a woman in her thirties, and a boy of fifteen or sixteen. The locals kicked them after they pinched the guy. They split after the arrest and were never seen again. The *federales* called in the Bureau, but the town name was bogus, and there was nobody named Ney anywhere in Indiana."

"False name?"

"Maybe. The Mexicans weren't that competent in those days, and it was easy enough to hide your identity, even in this country," said Shamekia.

"Did you get the names of the Bureau agents who worked the case on this side of the border?"

"Lead man was Special Agent Philip L. Orbet. He retired in 1976 and died ten years later."

"Others on the case?"

"Just Orbet after awhile. Apparently he was obsessed with the case, thought there was something more to it, and kept looking into it after he retired, but he died before he got anywhere with it. You know how cold cases go," she added.

He did. "But this wasn't a U.S. case," Service said.

"Right, but Orbet was one of those old-time G-men who felt that if this guy had been a serial killer in Mexico, he probably did it up here too."

"Where did Orbet live?" Service heard the lawyer leafing through paperwork.

"Toledo, Ohio."

"You think this fits?" he asked.

"You tell me: The victims had an ax taken to their ribs along the spine," she said.

"Hmmm," Service said. "Photos in the paperwork you're sending?"

"There are. Photos of the victims and of the man Ney."

"Can you get me an address for Orbet in Toledo, names of his survivors, all that?"

"It's in the package. You thinking he left behind his case notes?"

"Could be," Service thought.

"Okay," Shamekia said, "write this down."

# 34

# Cliff's Ridge, South of Marquette, Michigan
## July 16, 2004

He was still deeply troubled about Nantz's accident being something else, but the list of follow-up items in the federal case was mounting, and Service had begun to assemble notes to himself about things that needed to be checked out. He had not seen any further surveillance since Bobbi Temple had ducked out of Snowbound Books, but he had not moved around that much, and despite his mind being preoccupied with Nantz and Walter, he had come to the realization that he needed to reach some sort of accommodation with Special Agent T. R. Monica.

Wink Rector was the lone FBI agent in the Upper Peninsula and a pretty good guy, but also savvy enough to toe the bureau line when he needed to. Rector was rarely in his office in Marquette, and Service was surprised when he answered his phone.

"Federal Bureau of Investigation, Marquette Regional Office, Special Agent Rector."

"It's Grady Service, Wink."

"Hey, was that you I saw on the tube with the President?" Rector greeted him.

"Did you know about that beforehand?"

Rector laughed. "Hey, I'm only the resident agent up here. That sort of crap is way above my pay grade."

Bitterness or resignation? "You got time to talk?"

"Phone or in person?"

"Not on the phone," Service said. "Cliff's Ridge. The old gravel pit. About an hour?"

"Sounds mysterious. I'll be there with coffee."

The Carp River was a narrow bedrock river that squeezed through a spot the locals referred to as the Gorge, which was only about forty feet deep. Marquette Mountain ski hill rose immediately to the southwest of the area, and in summer the ski lifts looked like flensed bones sticking out of the land-scape. Decades before, the ski area had been known as Cliff's Ridge, but the name had changed, and only those with a long history in the area would re-member it by the old name.

Rector was there before Service. A huge thermos and two cups sat on the hood of his Crown Victoria.

"Black like your heart?" Rector said, holding up the thermos.

Service nodded and got to the point. "You know a special agent out of Milwaukee named T. R. Monica?"

"Heard about her, and I might have met her once somewhere along the road."

"She a pretty good agent?"

Rector took a breath to buy time to think. "Kinda depends on who you talk to. I think she's probably competent enough, but a real pain in the ass. Why?"

"Are you aware that she and her people are running surveillance on me?"

The FBI agent blinked. "On *you?*"

"You heard about the game warden murdered in Wisconsin?"

"It was on the news and I got a bulletin, but there wasn't much detail."

"I knew the guy."

"No shit?"

"He's not the only game warden to die." Service went back to his truck, got out an envelope, and gave it to Rector, who opened it and gawked at the photographs.

"Holy cow," was all he managed to say.

"Twenty-seven game wardens in twenty-five states, killed between 1950 and 1970. No common MO and no suspect."

"Suspect, singular?"

"Until three years ago, nobody saw a connection. The kills were spread out over twenty years. In 1982 the killings started again. Most recently Fi-corelli was killed in Wisconsin, and a few days later another warden bought it in Missouri. The kills in the second group were by an assortment of methods until 2000. Then they all took the same MO." Service tapped the photo-graphs. "All just like that. Monica is the one who identified the pattern, and she's lead agent on the case."

"Onward and upward," Rector said.

"Not if she fails."

Rector nodded. "True; the Bureau's got a low tolerance for public failure nowadays."

"Your people think the perp is targeting me," Service said, pausing to let the information sink in.

Rector grinned. "This is a put-on, right?"

"It's real, Wink."

"You don't seem all that broken up. If Special Agent Monica has a team up here dogging you, she must think it's credible."

"Bingo. Give the man a Kewpie doll."

"Give me cash instead," the agent said. "I've got a basement full of crappy gewgaws."

"Aren't you surprised to be out of the loop on any of this?"

"I guess not," Wink Rector said. "Since 9/11 everyone's gotten more secretive than before. We've got more compartments than a printer's table these days."

"Now you know," Service said. "Monica's got to be here somewhere, and I want to have a sit-down with her."

"Pick up the telephone."

"No. I want this on my terms, on my turf."

"I suppose you want me to arrange it."

"I figure you've got a stake in this too."

"Like that would matter," Rector said bitterly. "When and where?"

"End of the Mulligan Creek road, where it crosses the creek."

"North of Ishpeming?"

"There's only one road in from the south, which means it will be fairly secure."

"Okay, when?"

"Soon as. She can pick the time."

Rector took a sip of coffee. "I'll get on it today and give you a call when it's set."

"Thanks, Wink."

"You realize that bringing me into this is going to piss her off, and some others above her as well."

"Never had a doubt, but I also felt pretty sure you'd want to know what was going down in your own backyard. I would." This was an allusion to a wolf-killing case Service had been involved in three years before, a time when Rector had held back information from him, and the FBI had impeded his investigation.

"You were right to tell me," Rector said. "I've put in my papers, and I'm hanging it up December 31. Everything's set. I'm waiting now for my replacement to show so I can bring them up to speed on what's going on up here."

"This fits the category of what's going on up here," Service said.

Rector's reply was a muffled grunt as he picked up his thermos and cups and got into his vehicle.

# 35

# Mulligan Plains, North of Ishpeming, Michigan
## July 19, 2004

Service loaded his Honda ATV into the bed of his personal truck, stowed the portable ramp beneath the four-wheeler, and started north on County Road 550 toward Big Bay. He thought he spotted a tail near the Northern Michigan Campus, cut north, and lost the follower by going off-road to the west up a power line where only a high-centered four-wheel-drive vehicle could get through. He continued west, until he hit County Road 510 and turned north, for the Triple A Road, more than twenty miles north.

He had received the package of information from Shamekia. The photos of the victims were nothing like those of the blood eagle killings, but they were gruesome all the same.

Halfway across the Yellow Dog Plains on the Triple A, he hid the truck, offloaded his Honda, and rode the ATV south across the Yellow Dog River into the southern fringe of the Huron Mountains. Eventually the trail connected to the road that ended at Mulligan Creek. This route required a great deal of extra time, but he wanted to make a point with the FBI. The meeting was set for first light and he was in place nearly an hour early. He hid the Honda a quarter-mile away, on the north side of the creek, crossed the makeshift one-lane snowmobile bridge the DNR had built a few years back, and found a place to wait in the popples on the lip of a rise just above where the road from the south dead-ended in the shadows of steep rock bluffs.

On the sandy two-track to the west he saw a gray wolf trot northwest, nervously glancing over its shoulder in his direction as it passed. Then he heard vehicle tires swishing through soft sand on the two-track above the creek. The wolf had been spooked by the vehicle, not him.

Wink Rector drove his own vehicle to the edge of the creek, backed up twenty yards, parked, and got out. It was getting lighter, but the sun itself remained hidden by ridges to the east.

"Where the hell is he?" Tatie Monica asked when she got out.

Rector got out his thermos and poured coffee. "Game wardens don't announce themselves."

"What's that supposed to mean?"

"You see fresh tire tracks on the way in?"

"No. So he's behind us?"

"My guess is that he's already here."

"Games," she said.

"It's not a game," Wink Rector corrected her. "This is how these people live. If he asked us to meet him here fifty times, he wouldn't come in the same way twice."

"We're not the enemy," Tatie Monica said.

Wink Rector remained silent.

"I don't know why the hell he got you involved," she complained.

"Things work differently up here," Rector said. "The Bureau is just one more law enforcement outfit and we all have to cooperate to graduate."

"You've never had to keep things close?"

"I was ordered to stonewall him once, but never again. Once you earn trust up here, you do *not* want to lose it."

Service saw the woman check her watch impatiently, pick up her radio, and make a call. He couldn't make out what was being said, but he was pretty sure she had left a rear guard south on the two-track.

"Trust me, he won't come in from behind us," Rector said.

Service eased out of the tags to the side of Rector's Crown Vic and waited until Special Agent Monica turned away to step out beside Rector, who immediately spilled his coffee. "For Pete's sake!"

Tatie Monica turned around and glared at him.

Service said, "Special Agent Rector knows all about what's going on, so there's no need to play cute this morning."

"You had no right," she said. "*Either* of you."

"I've got my retirement date," Rector said. "I plan to live here. That give you a hint where my priorities are?"

She ignored Rector and stared at Service. "What the hell is this about?"

"To bring you up to speed," he said. He then laid out the situation in Mexico and watched for a reaction to see if any of it was familiar to her. It didn't appear to be.

"Why didn't you call me with this as soon as you had it?"

"I knew you were here somewhere. I saw Bobbi the day Bush was here, and that's when it dawned on me that you had a team dogging my ass."

She didn't deny it. "You're wasting my time. I could have been following up on Special Agent Orbet."

"You could have, and whatever you learned would still leave me in the dark." He did not mention what he had learned about the sites where the bodies had been found, or Shark's identification of the booger fly. One thing he had learned as a detective was that you had to keep a few cards back, not play them until they mattered most.

"What are you suggesting?" Monica asked.

"We do some of this my way."

"You have no experience with this sort of thing. You told me that yourself."

Service said, "Don't underestimate the value of someone who doesn't share your experiences and prejudices."

Wink Rector kept out of it.

"Okay," Tatie Monica said, "spell out what you want."

"First, I think we should go together to find Orbet's survivors and see if he left any records."

"Everything would have been turned over to the Bureau," she countered.

Service nodded to Wink Rector. "Is that how it is?"

"Officially he would have turned over all his paperwork when he retired, but if the case stuck in his craw, he'd have copies at home, and if he continued to investigate, there'd be paper for that too, I guess," Rector added.

"Which means there could be notes, or something."

"If his family didn't pitch the whole lot," Rector said.

"Okay," Tatie Monica said. "What else?"

"Call off your surveillance."

"It's for *your* protection," she said.

"It's also an arrow pointing right at me, not to mention a waste of time and manpower," he said. "If I want to become invisible, I can, and there's no way you can follow me."

"You're pretty sure of yourself," she said.

"There's a whole lot I'm not so good at," he said, "but finding my way around in the woods without being detected isn't one of them. *This* is where I live, who I am."

"Is that it?"

"I need to revisit Elray Spargo's widow."

"Why?"

"I'll explain later."

"How about now?"

"Later. That's how you usually answer me, only later never seems to arrive. I also want to meet your analyst."

"You're asking for the whole ball of wax," Monica said.

"If your theory's right, that I'm the final target, the whole ball of wax reduces to me. Either you get this guy this time, or—"

"Point taken," she said, cutting him off.

"Are we agreed on this or not?"

"We'll get in touch with Orbet's family to see what they have, and if they have something, and if they're agreeable, you and I can go visit them. I'll also go with you to Missouri. As for surveillance, I don't want to call it off, but I'll agree to it—with the stipulation I can turn it on again if I think we need it."

Service said, "What about your analyst?"

"He may not want to talk to you," she said.

"If we go to Toledo, Detroit is right on the way."

"I never said Micah Yoder lived in Detroit. I said he operated out of there."

"What the hell does that mean?"

"This is the electronic age, Service. With a computer, cell phone, and modem, you can work from anywhere."

"Meaning he doesn't live in Detroit?"

"I don't really know where he lives."

*Holy Christ*, he thought. "That doesn't bother you?"

"It's the twenty-first century," she said.

"Either you and I meet him, or I go my own way and you go yours, and we'll see if we intersect somewhere down the line."

"How did you find out about Orbet and Mexico?"

Service grinned. "That information came right out of the Bureau." This was not technically correct, but he knew Shamekia retained sources in Washington, D.C., which she seemed to be able to use at her pleasure.

"Bullshit," Tatie Monica said. "If the Bureau had this information, I would have known."

"Not if you didn't ask the right questions," Service said.

"What else?"

Service said, "If I think of something, I'll let you know."

"All right," she said. "I'll get my team moving on the Orbet thing, and I'll talk to my guy and see if the family's amenable to a sit-down."

"And you'll call off the minders?"

"For now," she said, offering her hand.

"And Wink here joins your team," he added, causing her to drop her hand momentarily.

She looked at Rector. "You sure you want to do this?"

"Hey," he said, "what can they do to me? Pack me off to the Upper Peninsula of Michigan and forget about me? Oh, wait—they already did that. Yeah, I'm sure."

Monica asked "Your source sent you records?"

"They're in the mail," he said, lying. "You know how the post office can be."

"I'll get back to you," she said.

"Wink, did you see the wolf tracks up the road?"

Rector shook his head.

"Crossed two minutes before you guys drove in."

"Wolf?" Tatie Monica said, her eyes wide.

"Don't worry," Grady Service said. "Little Red Riding Hood was just a fairy tale."

# 36

## Baboquivari Wells, Arizona
## July 23, 2004

Grady Service found the gate unlocked, lifted it, drove through, got out of his rental, and closed the gate behind him. He wiped the dust off his sweaty forehead, took a long pull from a $5.00 bottle of water, and lit a cigarette. The thermometer in the rental car said 108. The ground through his shoes felt fifty degrees hotter. His shirt and trousers were soaked with sweat and stuck to him, and he was tired from traveling. He had spent the previous day on commercial flights, Marquette to Green Bay to Minneapolis, where he had spent the night sleeping in an airport lounge, and this morning from Minneapolis to Phoenix to Tucson, where he rented the vehicle.

He had not asked for approval of the trip from his captain, and had not told Special Agent Tatie Monica he was leaving town.

Another call from Shamekia had put him on the move. "Grady, I've found another source for you. His name is Eduardo Perez. He was with the *federales* during the Ney investigation. He's since moved to the States and become a U.S. citizen. He works for the Border Patrol as an undercover agent, moving back and forth across the border in the Sonoran Desert. It was a fluke that I found him. He's due to go undercover again in three days, but if you can get down to Arizona, he'll talk to you. I get the feeling he is not all that anxious to talk about the Ney case." She gave him instructions for finding the place, which was near Fresnal Canyon in the south central Baboquivari Mountains, about eighty miles southwest of Tucson.

He had quickly weighed his options and decided to go. There was no time to touch base with anyone, and as he and Tree had learned in the marines, it was often easier to ask for forgiveness than permission.

A rough sand road led from a macadam state highway toward Fresnal Canyon to the east; eight miles after the turnoff he found the gate on the south side of the powdery dirt road.

He finished his cigarette, mashed the butt into the ground, got in, and drove another nine miles south to where the road ended. There was a World War II jeep parked near a stand of saguaro cacti, which cast almost human shadows.

The colors of the landscape ranged from black to orange and ochre. He got out and walked over to the jeep. There were no prints. Around him there were creosote bushes, and more saguaros, these with multiple bullet holes, and several stunted Joshua trees.

The ground was caliche, baked sand that seemed to absorb and radiate the sun. Service sat with his legs out of the car, kicked off his shoes, and switched to his boots. He got his pack, water supply, his compass, and started walking. To the northeast he saw a shimmering line of mountains and in the middle, a peak that looked like a large white nipple. Immediately ahead of him there was a small rise with pale yellow boulders and between two of them, what appeared to be a game trail. What sort of animals could endure such heat? On a rock near the boulders he saw the tail of a snake flick as it escaped into the shadows of a small crevice. The game trail continued eastward and, reaching the crest of the second steep hill, he looked down into a valley with hundreds of saguaro.

The trail led into the middle of the giant plants where he saw a structure of crude slats with a flat thatched roof. The slats looked like gray bones; the structure was vaguely reminiscent of a rib cage. A man sat cross-legged on a blanket in the shade of the shelter and looked up at him.

Service batted dust off his clothes.

The man was thin, with a reddish-mahogany complexion, smooth skin, and ragged black salt-and-pepper hair. He looked freshly shaved.

"Perez?" he greeted the man. "Service."

The man looked up, pointed to a blanket across a small cook fire. There was a pot hanging over the fire, which made almost no smoke. The man lifted the red earthenware vessel beside him and poured its contents into clay mugs

"You got your bona fides?" the man asked in a sonorous voice.

Service showed his state badge and ID. "You?"

The man took a gold shield out of his pocket and hung it around his neck. It read CBP BORDER PATROL, PATROL AGENT PEREZ.

Service wanted to start asking questions, but decided they needed to sit for a few minutes, get used to each other. The worst thing you could do with a reluctant interviewee was to push too hard too soon, especially when the heat was beyond belief. "Been with the border patrol long?"

"Drink," the man said. He had delicate hands and moved slowly.

Service sipped the reddish liquid. It was slightly sweet, slightly fermented. "Ten years," the man said. "This is called *nuwait*. You?"

"Twenty plus," Service said. "You talked to Shamekia?"

"Yes, the lady lawyer from Detroit with the impossible last name. She said you want to talk about the Ney case."

"Affirmative. She also said you seemed reluctant."

The man smiled. "Occupational lockjaw. This job, it sometimes pulls our lips tight, yes? Too much time alone, perhaps."

Service understood.

The man said. "Silence is often a better weapon than a gun."

Perez had no accent. "You were with the Mexican Federal Police."

"Yes. I grew up in Nogales. My father was a judge. I came to the States for college, law enforcement administration at Arizona State in Tempe. After I graduated I went home. My father was a wise and moral man who hoped that U.S.-style training for *federales* would lead to a less corrupt, more effective force, but what difference can one man make?" the man said with a shrug. "I spent three years on the Yucatán and rose to the rank of special inspector. This earned me a transfer to the north and a unit called Special Crimes, those involving foreign nationals."

"That's how you got on to Ney."

"I was visiting my parents in Nogales when Ney was detained in Juárez. It was I who picked out the detail of the Cadillac and convinced my superior to take the team there to investigate. The locals, of course, resisted, but the boss called in authority from above and we took custody of the suspect."

"Ney never talked," Service said.

"He talked quite a lot and he was pleasant, but he never admitted to the crime. All he would say was that his work was complete."

"Meaning?"

Perez shrugged and held out his hands. "We had no idea, but he was convicted and sentenced to die."

"And killed while in custody.'

"Not in the way you may think. He convinced a guard at the prison to kill him, in exchange for ten thousand U.S. dollars, for which he provided a letter of credit at a bank in the Cayman Islands. When the guard contacted the bank, they denied his letter."

"Ney was dead by then."

"Of course. To a naive, simple man, ten thousand American dollars is a treasure. There was a great deal of anger over the death. The FBI sent a scathing and critical letter to the head of our national police, but there was nothing to be done. Ney was dead, the case finished. We tried to clean up the aftermath, did an autopsy, and punished the guard, who admitted his foolishness."

"An autopsy?"

"The rules are the same there as here for any violent or unexpected death. The pathologist found the man filled with cancer, which had metastasized. He had only weeks or months to live, and the death would certainly have been agonizing. The care in our prisons was less than humane. Faced with such an end, any man might consider a similar solution."

"But you could not positively identify him."

"It was the FBI who had that responsibility and no, they failed."

"The reports said a woman and a boy were with him."

"Indeed, when he was stopped in Juárez, but of course he was stopped there because the locals wished only *mordida*, you understand?" Perez rubbed his fingers together. "The man resisted and they arrested him. They let the woman and the boy go before we arrived. We never saw them."

Service tried to process the information, which didn't seem to amount to much.

"I have told you what I know," Perez said. "May I ask your interest?"

Service explained about the murders of game wardens, and the blood eagle MO. "We thought that the man might have tested the method. Shamekia found the Ney cases in Mexico. Interestingly, a game warden was killed in New Mexico about ten days after Ney was arrested."

"I see," Perez said. "But of course, this Ney could not have killed the man in New Mexico."

"I realize that," Service said.

"Was this killing in New Mexico one of mutilation?" Perez asked.

"No, the man there was strangled."

"Do you have other questions for me?"

"Not right now."

Perez got two bowls from a soft pack beside him and scooped something from the pot over the fire. "Mesquite beans, barley, corn, cholla buds, and hot peppers," he said. "The peppers heat you inside to reduce the difference with the heat outside."

The soup was thick and distinctive. Nantz and Walter would have loved it.

When their soup was gone the man gave him a pancake-like thing, which had been sitting on a rock in the sun. Onto this he poured a viscous orange substance. "I don't know the name of this food in English," he said. "It is something I have made and enjoyed since I was a child. The syrup is taken from the fruit of the saguaro."

The syrup was a vague blend of fig and strawberry flavors, sweet but not overpowering.

"You are here at a propitious time," Perez said. "The saguaro are giving us their fruit and my people are making foods from them, including the wine."

The man took another pull on his wine and refilled his glass. "The idea is to fill our bodies with wine so that God will fill the earth with rain and everything that depends on it can live another year."

"Your people?" Service asked, taking another drink of wine.

"Tohono O'odham—Papagos," the man said. "Desert People. We are among the few native tribes to never have been removed from our reservations. Long ago the Apache were our traditional enemies and we helped the American army bring Geronimo to justice."

Service was confused. "I thought you were Mexican."

"We were once called Pima, and we lived on both sides of the line which divided Mexico from America under the Gadsden Purchase. In Mexico they call us *Frijolero*—bean people. Traditionally we have lived among ourselves in the Sonora, but my father was unique. He was educated in Mexico City, Spain, and the United States. Being a *Frijolero* among *federales* was a position of low odds. I decided to come to America. Now I am employed to look for and interdict coyotes; you understand?"

Coyotes were illegal immigrants. Service nodded.

"I spend weeks alone in the field and return to my home in Tucson from time to time. Before I go back into the field, I come here to harden myself for life the old way and to readjust to the air, the heat, and the hardships of the caliche. My people have never mixed well with whites, and the Sonora is a prime area for coyotes, so I can move among them freely and not arouse suspicion."

The solitude of the man's job reminded Service of his own.

"When I was first hired, the Border Service believed that my people were involved in coyote trafficking. I knew this to be untrue, so I agreed to take the position. It is well established now that their premise was wrong. I never thought I would come to love such a way of life, but I have. I am happiest here, alone, and dependent solely upon myself. I have friends who are game wardens. We live a similar life, you and I."

Service nodded.

"This man, Ney. I talked to him many times. He was a pleasant and gentle fellow."

"And a killer."

Perez shrugged. "Perhaps."

"You think he was innocent?"

"The man is dead. We will never know."

"But you suspect something."

"It is only that he repeatedly asked only about his son. He showed no interest in the woman."

"He called him his son?"

"Yes, but never by name. Always it was 'my boy, my creation.'"

"My *creation*?" Odd.

"Yes, his exact words."

"And the woman?"

"He never mentioned her, never once inquired about her fate."

"Maybe she wasn't his wife," Service said.

"I would agree with that," Perez said, refilling their mugs. "Take off your shoes, my friend."

Service stared at the man. "Why?"

"I will show you something special."

Service took off his shoes and socks and wiggled his toes. There was no breeze, but the thatched roof gave shade and made the temperature almost manageable.

Perez went off into the rocks and came back with a bowl of red powder, which he mixed with water until it was a deep vermillion paste. He handed the bowl to Service. "Paint the bottom of your feet with this."

Service laughed, but did as the man asked.

The substance dried almost immediately.

"We get drunk to appease God," Perez said, "but we paint our feet for our women."

Service shook his head. "Listen . . ."

"Do not be alarmed, my friend. I am not *berdache*—a man who sleeps with other men. You have left a woman behind?"

"No." Service could hardly get the word out.

"It doesn't matter. We will paint our feet to honor the women who gave us life, and we will fill our bodies with *nuwait* for I'itoi, the creator of all souls. If we drink enough, our women will dream of us tonight. I'itoi lives on the mountain behind us," Perez said. "I think he is too busy to come to visit tonight, so we will sleep drunk and tomorrow we will rise with thick heads and leave for our missions: you to find the killer of men who protect animals, I to find those who would steal the souls of the desperate."

The two men went at the wine with serious intent.

In the morning Eduardo Perez looked fresh and was already shaved. Service felt like hell and could hardly stand up. The man gave him two of the red earthenware jugs. "These vessels are called *olla*. The large one holds *nuwait*. The smaller one contains powder. If you want a particular woman to love you, paint your feet and drink *nuwait* with her and she will be engulfed by great desire for you."

Service laughed. "Isn't that date rape?"

Perez held up a finger. "Don't wait too long to use the power of *nuwait*, my friend or it will turn to vinegar, just as love sours when it is not nurtured."

The man put on his pack. He wore long black trousers, a loose, light-colored shirt, and ankle-high moccasins. He took a step out of the shelter and turned back. "Hunt with your brain, *compadre*, not your heart."

Service watched him lope away into the cool morning air and lay back with a pounding head.

When he got back to his rental he found the doors unlocked and two mason jars of *nuwait* on the front seat with a note: *Service, one of these is for you and a woman you choose. The other I would ask that you deliver for me. When you get on the hard road north to Sells, go two miles and you will see a cemetery off to the east. Park and go through the fence. Look for the grave with purple flowers and leave the other jar there. Via con dios, compadre. Eduardo.*

The cemetery was in a white sand area. There were hundreds of markers and crosses, all of the graves decorated with gaudy flowers and plastic statues of everyone from Jesus Christ to Darth Vader. The grave with purple flowers was in the back, closest to the purple mountains in the distance. Service looked at the name carved into a crude wooden cross: ROSALITA PEREZ, 1950–2003.

Perez was a widower and alone.

They had more than their jobs in common.

# 37

# Fourteen, Missouri
## July 24, 2004

He could not get Eduardo Perez out of his mind. The man had lost his wife a year ago and was burying himself in work. Had this contributed to his wife's death? Or was it a result of it? As soon as he got to the airport in Tucson he changed his ticket to Missouri.

When he had left Michigan he had begun to feel the distance, which made his sense of loss heavier, and he chastised himself for allowing his feelings to disturb his concentration.

He got some questions in security about his mason jars and *olla*, but when he showed his identification and surrendered his sidearm, they allowed him to board.

It was afternoon by the time he reached Springfield, rented a vehicle, called Eddie Waco's cell phone, and got his voice mail. "It's Service. I'm just leaving Springfield, heading for Elray Spargo's house. Meet me there if you can."

When he reached the house there were three kids on the front porch, and as he got out of the rental he heard one of them yell, "Mama, that Michigan man done just pulled up."

Fiannula Spargo stepped onto the porch wearing an apron and dripping flour. "Agent Waco called, said he'll be along soon. You'n bring me news, Michigan Man?"

"No ma'am, not yet."

"What brings ye?"

"Was your husband a trout fisherman?"

She cracked a smile. "I reckon thet and the law was the only religions my man ever took to: trout on the fly. I guess we all done took to hit. Or *by* hit, I hain't sure which."

"I know it sounds strange, but would you mind if I took a look at his flies?"

She raised an eyebrow. "I reckon they's better times ta fish the hill cricks thin now."

"I didn't come to fish."

She nodded and pushed open the door for him.

Spargo kept his flies in the room that served as his home office. Fiannula stood beside Service as he surveyed the room and saw a Renzetti fly-tying vise. "Elray tied his own?"

"Was a disease," she said. "That man would hardly go to town, exceptin' ta drag me inta craft stores and the Wal-Mart, lookin' for beads and feathers and such. Said trout get used ta somethin', got to change up offerin's ta catch 'em by surprise." She opened a corner cabinet. "Hits all in thim drawers," she said, pointing.

"What about his fly boxes?"

She opened a closet. The boxes were stacked on a shelf above and on the floor in cardboard cartons. "You need anything, or can I get back at my bakin'?"

"Thanks, I'm good." He pulled a chair over to the closet, sat down, and began going through the fly boxes one by one. They weren't labeled and they weren't organized like his boxes, which he put together by month, based on the hatches that would be coming off. Elray's were organized by type: mayflies in one box, caddis in another, stoneflies in yet another, nymphs, streamers. He made a mental note, estimated fifty boxes to go through, and settled back.

"You'n got us a good lead?" a familiar voice asked.

Eddie Waco slid into the room and handed him a glass of iced tea.

"More like a real thin hunch," Service said.

"Hunches work," Waco said. "They bubble up from thet part a' the brain where we don't think. Acts like a computer, sendin' along an unexpected e-mail from time to time."

"I hope this one's not spam," Service said. Both men laughed. "Elray have a system for his fly boxes?"

"Had a differ'nt system ever time we fished," Waco said. "Only thing in his life he couldn't never make up his mind on."

Service understood. The monthly boxes were only the latest iteration of his own system, which changed frequently. "He tie all his own?"

"Thing was, ole Elray was of a frugal nature, couldn't abide buyin' what he could make for himseff."

Service pushed a carton over to Waco. "We're looking for brown drakes," he said.

"Little late for them," the Missouri agent quipped.

It took them more than thirty minutes to go through the inventory. They found brown drakes and hex, but not the pattern he had hoped for.

"You'n not findin' somethin'?" Waco asked.

"Are these all of his flies?"

"All save them which bin retired."

"Retired?"

"Elray caught him a hawg, he released the fish, and retired the fly."

"What's a hawg around here?"

"Tin pound at least."

"You've got ten-pound browns here?"

"Mosey cross the border to the White River 'round Mountain Home and they catch 'em a heap bigger, fish for 'em outen inner tubes at night."

"Where are his retired flies?"

"Have to ask Fi thet."

She was in the kitchen taking pies out of the oven, the aroma overwhelming the room. "Fi," Waco said, "Sorry to git in yore way, but where'd ole Elray keep them flies he bragged on so much?"

The woman turned and looked at the men, her face contorted. "Lord, I know I done seen them things. He kept 'em in a red tin box." After a moment she stepped into the hallway and shouted, "You kids git on down here this minute."

The children trooped into the hall beside the kitchen. "Which one a' you floor monkeys seen yore daddy's red box?"

"Wasn't my idea," a little girl said. "Was hers." She pointed to another child who looked like a twin.

"Now y-you d-done got me in trouble," the second girl whined with indignation.

"Did not. Was you'n took Daddy's red box."

"Hush," Fiannula said gently. "Just fetch it now, hear?"

"We in trouble, Mama?" the first girl asked.

Spargo's widow patted the girl's head affectionately. "I don't blame you for looking at Daddy's special things, but you'n got to put 'em back so's the others can look too."

The girl looked relieved when the second girl produced the red box and handed it to Grady Service.

"Thanks," he told the girl, who giggled and nudged her sister.

"You men want pie?" Fiannula asked. "I got a couple coolin' down on the winder ledge and still warm."

"Yes, ma'am," Waco said.

One of the twins said, "Can we have pie, Mama?"

Fiannula Spargo smiled. " 'Course you can, you and your sister. Others will have ta wait for supper."

The five of them sat in the dining area. Service opened the box. Each fly was hooked to a piece of paper with a Polaroid photo of the fish, its size, the date, and location where it had been caught. Each paper also gave the time, wind, light, and water conditions.

Service found what he was looking for near the bottom of the pile and held it up for Waco to see. "You recognize this?"

Waco said, "Yep, thet's his booger fly. Never seen him use it, but that's what hit is, I reckon."

"He didn't tie this himself."

"Nope. He done heard about booger flies from some old boy he done met down on the Eleven Point. Man was from Illinois, if memory serves me right, and Elray give 'im a warning for too many fish, and the fella give 'im the address of the man what tied them booger flies—up your way, I think."

Service looked at the date below the photo: 2003—last year.

Fiannula put large pieces of pie in front of each of them. Service held up the paper with the fly and photo. "You remember when Elray ordered this fly?"

The widow laughed. "I told him he was crazy orderin' such expensive things—especially them made a' boogers."

The little girls giggled.

"You girls hush," their mother warned them. "You come in here ta eat pie or make a show of yourseffs?"

"Eat pie," the girls said in unison.

Service asked, "You wouldn't happen to know how he paid for this, would you?"

"I reckon they's records about. The man couldn't throw away anything." She looked over at Service. "This important?"

Service nodded.

"I'll find it. He didn't send away for much, and whin he did, he paid by check."

While she was gone, Service said to Waco, "There were game wardens killed in Kansas and Illinois. When I get back, I'll send you their names and personal information. Think you could call their families and find out if they were fly fishermen, and if so, did they use flies like this, bought from Michigan?"

"You send the information, I'll take care of 'er," Waco said.

"How's Cake?" Service asked.

"Up and stumpin' aroun' on crutches. Cain't wait ta get started as my pine shadow. You think this fly thing gonna take us somewhere?"

"I hope," Service said.

The widow came back, looking perplexed. "I cain't seem ta find thim boxes with the taxes and checks," she said. "You reckon I could send 'em along whin I find 'em?"

"Give them to Eddie and he'll get in touch," Service said.

"All y'all better get at thim pies afore they cool too much," she said.

"Mama," one of the twins said, "I think she got a bigger piece thin me."

"Did not," the other girl snapped with a big grin.

"Kids," Fiannula Spargo said with a big grin. "Little kids, little problems; big kids, big problems. I expect hit never ends for parents."

Service thought: *Something I'll never know.*

# 38

# Slippery Creek, Michigan
## July 25, 2004

It was just before 11 P.M. when the flight landed at the Marquette County Airport, twenty miles south of town. The airfield had once been K. I. Sawyer Air Force Base, a combined Strategic and Air Defense Command base. The B-52s from Sawyer had dropped thousands of bombs on Vietnam when he and Tree were there. Service found Tatie Monica waiting near his truck.

"How were Arizona and Missouri?" she greeted him, adding, "Maybe we can't follow you out in the damn woods, but the rest of the goddamn country is *our* turf."

"It was okay," he said.

"I've made arrangements for the Toledo trip."

"Now?"

"If not now, when?" she said.

"What about your analyst?"

"I'm working on it."

"No deal," Service said.

"I'm keeping my end of the bargain," she argued.

"Selectively," he said.

"You are operating without authorization," she said.

"You talked to Orbet's family?"

"His son and widow. They say he left a couple of boxes of papers and we can make copies, but they want to keep the originals."

"Did he get anywhere in his investigation?"

"The wife says no. The son says his father hinted at having something," Monica said.

"Maybe you'd better check it out."

"Not you?"

"I need to get home and take care of my animals." McCants had come to the rescue again. He was going to owe her.

She said, "Don't go running off on me."

"Wouldn't think of it," he said.

"Bullshit."

Newf greeted him with huge slurps and followed him to where he looked up the site names of the dead game wardens in Illinois and Kansas, and called Eddie Waco to pass along the information.

"Fi found thet cancelled check. Hit's made out to Booger Baits, Curran, Michigan."

"Date?"

"March a' this year."

"I had the impression it was older."

"Fi's thinkin' Elray reordered."

"There an address on the check?"

Waco gave him the number on DeJarlais Road.

Newf sat with her massive head on Service's leg while he toggled his 800 megahertz radio. "Station Twenty, Twenty Five Fourteen. Who's the officer in Curran?"

"Denninger," the dispatcher in Lansing reported. "Seven, Two Twenty Two."

"Denninger on tonight?"

"Affirmative, Station Twenty clear."

Service switched to District Seven's channel on the 800. "Seven, Two Twenty Two, Twenty Five Fourteen."

"Go, Twenty Five Fourteen."

"You know an outfit called Booger Baits?"

"That's affirmative."

"An old man named Main still run the business?"

"Son's in charge now. The old man's still around though."

"They have a history with the department?"

"Negative, but they aren't real friendly."

"If I drive down there, can we meet?"

"Affirmative; where and when?"

"Tomorrow, early afternoon. How much longer you on?"

"Couple hours. I'm really sorry about Nantz. She and I knew each other."

"Thanks. I'll bump you when I get close tomorrow."

"Seven, Two Twenty Two clear."

# 39

## Curran, Michigan
### July 26, 2004

Newf had paced all night and gotten into a scrap with Cat. Service had not slept well and called McCants in the morning. She agreed to watch the animals until he got back, and said she would pick them up around noon.

"You made good time," Denninger said. She was about five-eight or -nine and slender, with long brown hair knotted in a thick French braid, long legs. "Heard a lot about you," she said, extending her hand.

He left his truck and rode with Denninger.

"Booger Baits," he said quickly, trying to get them focused on the job.

"It was started by the old man, Charley Main Jr. He moved up here fifty years ago. Now his son Charley Main the third runs the show. Locally he's known as Charley the Turd."

"You get along with him?"

"I've made a lot of people unhappy since I got here," the young officer confessed. "My FTO told me the locals were going to piss and moan, complain and hate me no matter what I did, so I might as well bring the hammer down early and let them know how it was going to be.

"The Mains don't like anybody. People in parts of this county think they make their own laws. It's either rich dicks in their fancy clubs, or mulletheads who can't read cereal boxes."

Service thought the woman sounded pretty negative for so early in her career.

"Charley the Turd?"

"Treats everyone like shit. Their house looks like a garbage dump, but don't be fooled. They've made a bunch of dough off their business. How, I have no idea. What's this about?" she asked, looking over at Service.

"Got a case where we've found booger flies and we're thinking they might connect to something important. We need to get them to let us look at their mailing lists."

Denninger laughed out loud. "Never happen."

Service said, "If I have to I can bring in the Feebs with subpoenas."

"Must be something big," Denninger said.

"Important," Service said. "Any suggestions how to play this?"

"Get in his face. The man's a bully and he's got clout in the county, and in Lansing. You've got to get him back on his heels."

Booger Baits was a few miles south of Curran. There was no sign identifying a commercial operation of any kind. The grass was overgrown and there were boats and trailers all over the yard, sawhorses with small motors, several dogs on chains, and a six-by-six elk rack over an open garage, which was packed with so much junk it looked like there was no opening inside. The whole area reeked of refuse and dog shit.

Denninger walked up to the house with him. Service tried ringing the bell, but it didn't work. Several dogs in the yard began to bark. He knocked on the door several times, but there was no answer. "No car in the driveway," he said. "Maybe they're not here."

"They park behind the house," Denninger said. "They're here."

The young officer stood in front of the door, boots spread apart, and pounded the doorjamb loud enough to get all the dogs going.

The door swung open to reveal a man who towered over Service and the other officer, and had to weigh close to four hundred pounds. He was wearing a sleeveless mesh Detroit Lions jersey and shorts.

"Open the door, Main."

"You," he said to Denninger.

"I'm not going to ask again," she said.

"Dad's taking a nap." The man looked at Service, ignoring Denninger.

She said, "You've got no licenses for all those dogs, Main, and you're running a business on property zoned residential. You want trouble, I can arrange *beaucoup*."

The man exhaled and shook his head. "Don't let your mouth make threats your body can't back up, little girl," he said, looking amused.

Service felt Denninger tense, but her voice remained calm. "Open the door *now*, Charley."

The man opened the door. "See how sugar gets you more than vinegar," he said.

"We want to talk to you about your business," Service said.

The man's face turned red. "The county zoning commission give us an exception. Dickless Tracy there *knows* that."

"Call her that again and I'll put your head through the drywall," Service said with a menacing growl. "It's not about zoning," he added. "It's about your mail-order business."

"That's between me, the postal service, and the IRS."

Service was beginning to understand why Main was known as Charley the Turd. Service said, "We need help, and like it or not, you're it."

"You want flies, we got 'em. But we ain't no help desk for fish dicks."

Service made sure he got direct eye contact. "We're here to ask politely. You cop an attitude, I'll pass this to the FBI, and let them handle it their way."

This got the man's attention, causing him to step back. "I guess we can work something out," he said, moving aside.

The living room was stacked with old newspapers and candy wrappers. Clots of dog hair were everywhere, there were layers of dust on the furniture, and the carpet was soiled and smelled of dog urine. The man stopped them in the living room and crossed his arms. "So what's this about?"

"Your customers. We need to look at your catalog mailing lists."

"There ain't no catalog," the man said. "Dad used to send one, but it cost too much. We do all our business by word of mouth."

"Your customer list, not your catalog list," Service said.

"No fucking chance," the man snapped. "You don't got no legal right to our books."

"I'm not interested in your accounting practices," Service said. "We just want names going back as far as you have them."

"IRS says we only gotta keep records seven years."

"We're not trying to jack you around, Mr. Main. We need help with an important case and we're hoping you can provide us with information to let us take the case forward."

"You want me to narc?"

"No," Service said. "You're not under suspicion of anything." Before the man could answer, Service added, "Is there something here we *should* be suspicious of?"

"No," the man said. "We run a clean business."

"That's what we've been told. And as a legitimate businessman we're hoping you can help us."

"What do I get out of it?"

Denninger said, "The satisfaction of helping law enforcement."

"Like I give a whoop-shit," he said.

Service was annoyed. "Okay, here's the deal. We want to see your customer list. We've asked politely, but here's the bottom line: If we need to get subpoenas, we'll get them, and sit right here until the FBI shows up with the paper. Might be a few hours, might be all night, so it's your call. We're not leaving without that list."

"Lists are confidential," the man said, stammering. "It's like the federal government monitoring books people check out of the public library."

"Are you sending out something you shouldn't, Mr. Main?"

"No."

The answer suggested to Service the man was telling the truth, and his resistance was not a matter of hiding something, but being a jerk in the face of authority. It was a familiar attitude in the Upper Peninsula.

Denninger said, "If the FBI comes into this thing they're also gonna bring the IRS. They'll rip the house apart and take *everything* they think could possibly help the case. We're just asking for a list. The FBI will get subpoenas that will let them cast a much wider net, and you won't get your stuff back for a long, long time. Once the FBI comes in, all your local contacts will back off because they won't want the entanglement with the feds. You're on your own, Charley."

"They can't jack around a businessman like that," the man protested.

"They can," Service said. "And they will. I guarantee it."

"You got any idea how many customers we have?"

"No," Service said.

"Over seven years, gotta be close to twenty thousand people—all over the world."

"Just burn the list onto a disk," Denninger offered.

"We aren't into computers," the man said. "We do everything by hand. We like doing business the old way."

"So what *do* you have?"

"Files," he said. "Fifty boxes, maybe sixty; hell, I ain't never counted them."

"Then we'll take the boxes, make copies, and bring them back."

The man's eyes darkened and his cheeks puffed out. "Them files ain't leaving this house," he said. "What happens if you have an accident or something?"

"Okay," Service said, "how about we try this: You show us your files and we'll sit down and make a list from them—the old way."

"My dad won't like it," the man said.

"I thought you were running the business now," Denninger challenged him.

"I do, but I got feelings for my dad, you know."

"Main, we can take those boxes if we call in the FBI. We understand your concern about losing them, but we've offered a compromise. So how do you want to play this? The options are on the table. Pick one."

The man covered his mouth with his hand, mumbled, "You can make your list, but you gotta be done by tonight."

Grady Service was tired and beyond annoyed. "Main, we'll take as long as we need. Now show us to the damn boxes—all of them."

The number of boxes was more than a hundred, and they were dusty, falling apart, and stacked all over a musty basement with no overhead light.

"You going to tell me what this is about?" Denninger asked as they settled in.

"Have you been briefed on the game warden murders?"

Her eyes widened and she nodded. "This is about that?"

"Let's hope," he said.

Charley the Turd brought a couple of battery-powered lanterns and left without comment.

Service looked at his watch. It was going on 11 P.M. when he sensed there was someone standing in the doorway. "You folks get something to eat?"

The man was ancient, with white hair and a wrinkled face. There were veins showing in his nose and cheeks and he looked like the mere act of standing exhausted him. "You Charley Junior?" Service asked.

"I am."

"Your booger flies work great," Service said.

"You've used 'em?"

"Friends have."

"The secret is, you gotta let the snot dry," the man said.

Denninger looked up with her mouth agape.

"Don't give me that look," the old man said. "You wanted to know the secret, right?"

"Not really," Service said. "But how'd you get the idea?"

"Come to me one day when I was fishing—came to me like a gift from God. Finally got around to making a fly. Showed it to my daddy and he beat my butt red, called it disgusting. But it caught fish, right from the start."

"Dad," Charley the Turd said from behind the old man. "You're not supposed to be up."

"Man's gotta have bowel movements," the old man said, turning and wobbling past his son.

"He tell you how he come up with the booger fly," Charley the Turd asked. "The 'gift from God' crap?"

"Said he was out fishing."

"He's told that lie so long he believes it. He didn't invent anything. Was his uncle give him the idea, back in Pigeon River."

Service perked up. "The town of Pigeon River?"

"Name's Mongo now, but it used to be Pigeon River. The old man started making and selling the flies. His uncle wanted credit and royalties, but the old man, he don't know the meaning of share, so he moved up here and has been here ever since."

Service knew Mongo. He had a case a couple of years back involving a fishing camp on the river, near an Indiana state fish hatchery. "You ever hear of a man named Ney?"

"Can't say I have," Charley the Turd said.

"What about your old man?"

"Have to ask him yourself."

Just as Service walked into the other room, the old man entered the bathroom and closed the door behind him. "Mr. Main?"

"I'd say I'd be out in a minute, but at my age the bowels move at their own speed, which ain't much to speak of. Best talk at me right through the door."

"You grew up in Pigeon River?"

"Changed the name since then," the old man answered. Service heard him wheezing and grunting.

"Did you ever hear of a man or a family named Ney?"

"Nope," the old man said.

Service went back to the boxes and returned to work.

It was nearly 3 A.M. before the list was complete.

Charley the Turd was snoring in an easy chair in the living room.

They were at the front door when they heard the old man shuffling behind them. "Weren't no Neys in town," he said. "Was a whole mob of Peys, though. My uncle married one of 'em who later run off with an Army Air Corps flight engineer during the big war. Them Peys bred like rabbits, maybe 'cause they was Frogs."

"Any of them have trouble with the law?"

The old man chuckled. "Hell, they all had troubles with the law, when the law had nerve enough to bring it up, which mostly they didn't."

"What kind of troubles?"

"You name it. Anybody pissed one of 'em off, the whole clan would be on 'em."

"Any of them disappear?"

"Lots of 'em. They'd beat it out of town until the heat let up some."

"You think they're still there?"

"They ain't the kind to do much movin' around. I expect there's still plenty of Peys down there, but I ain't been back since I left, and I ain't had no interest in doin' so."

"You ever sell any of your booger flies to the Peys?"

"Had one steal some from me once, but they weren't the sporting folk the Mains was. The Peys was strictly out for meat."

"Thanks for your help," Service said. "Tell your son we appreciate his cooperation."

"My son don't know sunshine from a shoe shine," the old man said disgustedly.

"What was that all about?" Denninger asked when he got out to the truck.

"The old man told me about growing up in Indiana."

She rolled her eyes as she turned the key and started the engine.

As she dropped him off at his truck, she offered, "You want, you can bunk at my place tonight," she offered. "I live near Glennie."

"I'll sleep here, but thanks."

"You sure?" Denninger asked Service.

"I've got to get an early start."

The young woman shrugged. "You want me to type up what we have?" During the night they had realized it was too difficult to look for CO names and had instead written down all Michigan customers. Service had seen Shark's name, but that was the only one he recognized.

"Yep, that would be good, and thanks again."

He took two blankets out of the truck and spread them on the grass. He had a hard time getting to sleep. Indiana, Pey, Ney. Maybe he finally had something to grab onto. In the morning he would head south.

# 40

# Mongo, Indiana
## July 27, 2004

Service dug around in his emergency food pack but all he could find was a crumbled Moon Pie of indeterminate age. Normally he took pride in eating good food, but since the loss of Nantz and Walter, he found little pleasure in food. He ate only for sustenance, mainly junk food, and after a determined start, he was not getting the workouts he needed. He could feel a little paunch forming. *You're falling apart*, he told himself.

Just north of St. Johns he looked up the Woodpecker's cell phone number and wrote it down. Murphy Shanahan, aka the Woodpecker, was a long-time officer with bright red hair that came to a dramatic point over his forehead, and a prominent, thin nose. He had once served in the U.P. in Keweenaw County but had married a woman from Below The Bridge, and had transferred to St. Joseph County on the Indiana border. Murph was also a federal deputy, and he'd know his Indiana counterpart.

He called Shanahan on the cell but got no answer, and switched to Channel 12 on his 800 megahertz as he approached Marshall. "Twelve, Three Ten, you got TX? This is Twenty Five Fourteen."

"Affirmative TX. I had it off."

"I'm in Marshall and headed your way. I need your help with something."

"Where do you want to meet?"

"You pick."

"Sturgis at the cop house. See you when you get here."

"I need to go down to Mongo to meet the CO down there."

"I'll set it up," the Woodpecker said.

Murphy Shanahan was in top shape. He grinned when he shook hands. "What's going down?"

"You get briefed on the game warden murders?"

"Creeped us all out. This about that?"

"I'm helping the Feebs with some background interviews."

"I bumped Westy Karkowski down in LaGrange County. He'll meet us there. Indiana hasn't told their people about the killings, but I passed it on to Westy. He's a good warden, been around twenty-five years and still charging."

Westy Karkowski looked like he'd have a hard time getting off a couch, much less charging forward in his job, but he was interested, and had a quick mind. He wore the dark green short-sleeved shirt and dark green pants of an Indiana game warden, the shirt covered with gaudy state patches. The three trucks were snugged into a turnoff, next to the Pigeon River, just west of the village of Mongo.

"Indeed, there's a heap of Peys in the county, and I've had contact with more than a few of them, but the guy who knows 'em best is Arlo Danielson. He spent forty years as the warden here, and retired after I took over. Getting on now, but he's still sharp and in pretty good shape. He lives about five miles east of here on the river and spends most of his time fishing."

It seemed to Service that being a detective was more about patience and stamina than anything else. He seemed to spend all of his time trying to find somebody who knew somebody, who had heard something about somebody, and sometimes persistence paid off. It could also be a waste of time, but he knew that every lead not followed could be the one that would have paid off. As an old hockey player, he knew the essence of that game was to keep your feet moving, finish your checks, push the puck up to the guy in a better position, take every shot chance you got, and always, always follow the puck until there was a whistle. Being a detective was similar.

They found Danielson sitting on a patio, under a striped awning on a wooden deck, overlooking the river. He was a small man with a flat face and scars near his left ear that left a gap in his hair.

Karkowski made the introductions and the retired game warden said, "So many badges in one place, I thought mebbe you all thought I was pinching state fish."

Service asked about the Pey family and Danielson made a sour face. "Pips, that bunch. Worst was Big Ben. He's ninety-two now and still got his hair, his hearing, and his eyesight. I arrested him so many times that even when he *was* behaving, which he did from time to time, he'd drop by and tell me about some other family member who was running afoul of the law. Wasn't that Ben got a shot of righteousness from doing it; he just didn't like the others out on the harvest when he couldn't be."

Grady Service wasn't sure how much to reveal, but it seemed to him there was a whole lot of history on hand here, and if he failed to take advantage, he might be sorry later. He laid out the killings of the game wardens, the Mexican incident, booger flies, the whole thing.

"The man arrested in Mexico had a woman and a boy with him. The local police cut them loose and they disappeared. The man gave his name as Ney, but the FBI couldn't find any Neys in Pigeon River, or even in Indiana."

"Big Ben might could know something," Danielson said. "Let's walk over and talk to him."

"He lives nearby?"

"Right smack across the river. We got to be friends and our kids built us a footbridge so we could visit back and forth. He's bit as hard for trout as me and he isn't the wild thing he once was." Danielson chuckled and added, "None of us are."

Big Ben Pey was no more than five feet tall, with a full head of only slightly gray hair, mottled skin, and black moles all over his hands. He was wearing overalls, no shirt, and workboots that looked to be as old as him.

Danielson said, "Ben, this is Grady Service. He's a game warden up in the Upper Peninsula, down here trying to get some information."

The old man stared at Service. "Used ta hunt up that way with my boys some, but game wardens up there didn't seem too partial to outsiders. Had an old chum up there, name of Allerdyce."

"Limpy," Service said. It figured. The big poachers all seemed to know each other.

I heard he took bad-sick awhile back."

"He recovered." The thought of the Indiana poacher and retired warden being buddy-buddy stuck in his craw. It would not happen with Limpy and him.

"Never met a man knew the woods like Allerdyce," Big Ben Pey said.

"Or game wardens," Service added.

Pey laughed. "Sure enough. He used ta tell me only one of you boys ever got the best of him, but he died a long time ago."

Service was sure that this had been his father, but said nothing.

"So what's this question you're burnin' to ask?" the old man said.

He told the story again and concluded, "I just learned that Pigeon River is Mongo, and that there are a lot of your kin around here. Did you know a Frankie Ney or Pey?"

"Prob'ly Francois Ney Pey. His people come down from Québec a long time back, and they was always hung up over that French stuff. Name was François, but he went by Frankie."

"He had a son?"

"Not that I heard. Unlike the rest of the family, Frankie went off to college, got him a dandy job. Lived in Detroit a spell, I think, but he was all over tarnation and made good dough."

"He come back here often?"

"Used to be sweet on a woman named Greenleaf, lived on the river in town. Folks used to say he slipped back in to town from time to time to slip it to her, if you know what I mean, but I never seen him. I don't think he cared much for his kin."

"This woman still around?"

"Name's Esther, but ev'body called her Essie. She was peculiar, that's for sure. She lives with her daughter up in Sturgis now, in one of them Polack neighborhoods. She's got to be in her seventies now, maybe even eighty. My mind ain't so good anymore."

"What's her daughter's name?"

The old man thought for a minute. "Let me call my son." He went back into the house and came back five minutes later. "Daughter's name is Ruth Zalinske, with an "e" not an "i." Zalinskes claim to be Ukrainians, but Ukes're just another flavor of Polack."

Service asked, "Do you remember who Frankie worked for?"

Big Ben lifted his eyes toward the sky. "I think it was Sears Roebuck, or maybe Monkey Ward, one a' them big outfits. His job was to go into stores and check their bookkeeping or some such numbers thing. Frankie was real smart."

"What did Frankie look like?"

"I think I got a pitcher somewhere in the house. You want me to look?"

"If you wouldn't mind."

"Exercise do me good." Big Ben looked over at Danielson. "Got two dandy trout after you went in last night."

"I hope they were legal," the retired game warden said.

The old man laughed and disappeared into the house again. He came out carrying a faded photograph in small square format, like something from an old Brownie Hawkeye. There were marks on the corner of the photo where it had obviously been affixed to an album.

Service studied the photo. There was a vague resemblance to the Mexican photo, but he couldn't be sure if it was real or wishful thinking. "How old was he in this?"

"Oh, he woulda been eighteen or nineteen, just before he went off ta college."

"Where was that?"

"Up your way in Marquette."

Northern? "When?"

"I'd say 1932. Moved to Detroit after college and signed up for the navy after Pearl Harbor, spent the war out in the Pacific somewheres, and never come back to Pigeon River."

Eighteen or nineteen in 1932 would have made Pey thirty-eight years older when the Mexicans arrested him. Service made a mental note.

"What kind of a boy was he?"

"Just a boy, I guess, 'cept he liked school, which most Peys didn't. Hunted and fished a lot, and he run a trapline in winter. Sold furs to buy him a Chevy. That boy liked to move around."

"Liked to move around?"

"Used to drive over to Montréal every summer. Relatives there, I guess."

"What relation to you is he?"

Big Ben stared at the ceiling. "They all sort of run together. I guess I'd be a nephew. His mother was Pauline, who was my half sister."

"Is Pauline still alive?"

"Died the year Frankie went off to college."

"Died how?"

"Got murdered."

"Did they catch the killer?"

"Nossir. Somebody cut her throat. She was married, but she and her husband, Jacques, both run around on each other. Some say it was one of her boyfriends did her in, but it never got solved."

"Can I borrow this photo?" Service asked.

"If it'll help, sure," said Big Ben.

Service thanked the man and was silent as he followed Shanahan back to Sturgis. Frankie Pey was a trapper and a hunter, which meant he knew how to skin animals. And his mother had been found with her throat cut, the murder never solved. He went to college and never came back. Up in Marquette? Was this possible? This was beginning to have the feel of something almost solid, but there remained plenty of holes and gaps.

# 41

## Sturgis, Michigan
### July 27, 2004

By late afternoon they were in Sturgis in a neighborhood of small houses well past their prime and only marginally kept up. Someone had put a hand-painted sign in a yard that read POLISH ACRES. Service knocked on the door and a woman answered. "I'm looking for Esther Greenleaf."

"I'm her daughter," the woman said.

Service explained who he was and showed his badge. "Is she here?"

"She's not well," the woman said.

"It's important that we talk," Service said.

"Can you keep it brief?" the woman asked. She opened the door tentatively and let him in.

The old woman was watching television. "I always watch *Jeopardy*," she announced. "This one's a rerun, but tonight the reg'lar show's on."

The daughter said, "Mom, this police officer would like to talk to you."

"There's no category for police on *Jeopardy*," the woman said. "There was, I'd know. I seen every show ever made."

Service sat down on a couch beside the recliner where the old woman sat. The daughter stood beside her mother. "Mrs. Greenleaf, I'd like to ask you some questions about Frankie Pey."

The old woman looked up at her daughter and dismissed her with a wave of the hand. "Ruthie, you just scoot on out of here now."

The daughter obeyed without protest.

"I don't want to bring up any bad things from your past," Service began. "But you knew Frankie Pey."

The woman looked at him for the first time and scowled. "What is the definition of 'knew'?"

Service said, "You know—a friend or something like that?"

"No, it's the game! You must put it in question form, 'What was the name of the man who used to be sweet on Essie Greenleaf?'"

*Oh boy*, Service thought. The circuits in the old lady's brain were a little frayed and she was seeing the world through the prism of *Jeopardy*. "What was the name of the man who used to be sweet on Essie Greenleaf?"

"Who is Frankie Pey?" the old woman said, pressing her hands together.

Service had only taken a cursory glance at *Jeopardy* over the years, in fact, rarely watched television, and had to rack his brain for the right words.

"Okay," he said. "The category is Frankie Pey."

"I never seen that on the show," she said.

"It's coming up on a future one," he said.

"Oh good, I'll be ready."

"First answer," Service said. "Mexico."

"What is Frankie's final resting place?"

"Right," Service said. "Essie."

"What is his last lover's name?" the woman said.

"Their son's name?" Service asked.

The woman looked agitated. "Can't answer no trick question. They didn't have no son."

"The name of the boy who traveled with them?"

"Who is Marcel?" she said.

"Where is Marcel now?" he asked.

The woman lurched in her chair. "Improper question. I have to confer with the judges." She looked at the wall, whispered animatedly, and turned back to him.

"What Frankie was doing in Mexico when he was arrested?" Service said.

"What is completing his life's work?" she said, clapping her hands together. "Did I get the Daily Double?"

What the fuck was a daily double? "Sure," he said.

"No," she said, her eyes narrowing. "You're not Alex and this isn't *Jeopardy*. You don't even know the rules. I won't play with nobody who don't know the rules. It ruins everything. Ruthie!" she screamed. "Ruthie! *Ruthie!*"

The daughter rushed into the room.

"He's a fake. I need my medicine. I don't play with no fakes."

The daughter walked outside with Service, her lips quivering.

"Look," he said. "I had no intention of upsetting your mother. She's difficult to talk to, but it's clear that she may possess some information that will be important to the authorities. I'm leaving, but you can expect the FBI to come to see her."

"Oh my God. The FBI! She doesn't know what she's talking about," the daughter said. "She's trapped inside the television."

"Maybe so," Service said, but he suspected she wasn't in there alone.

# 42

## Slippery Creek, Michigan
### July 28, 2004

Service checked his e-mail and phone messages as he drove north. His in-box was empty except for routine notices from division HQ in Lansing. It was getting late.

Captain Grant had called, wondering where he was, and, as usual, the captain's voice was controlled, neutral, and impossible to read.

Special Agent Monica left a one-word voice-mail message: "Asshole."

Service stopped at the Windmill truck stop south of Lansing, ordered coffee, got out a pad of paper, and tried to make notes about the case. It wasn't long before his mind was consumed and he paid no attention to anything going on around him.

1) First batch of killings: 1950–1970 [27 dead]. Killer inactive, 1970–1982. Second batch: 1982–present (2004) [22 dead]. Ney murdered in prison just before Xmas, 1974. Never confessed.
2) Suspect in Mexico gave name as Ney; FBI had failed to identify Pigeon River as Mongo, unable to find any Neys anywhere in state of Indiana. Per Big Ben, Pey; François Pey, aka Frankie Ney. Was this the Mexico Ney? Former girlfriend Essie Greenleaf says he is/was.
3) Boy involved, named Marcel, relationship and last name unknown. Estimated age 15–16 in 1970, which would make him approx. 48–49 now.
4) A New Mexico game warden killed two weeks after Ney arrested in Mexico. The killer's work, someone else, coincidence? Definitely not Ney. (Pey?)
5) Ney cut Mexican victims along the spine. Precursor of blood eagle? Frankie Pey was trapper as a kid—has skinning knowledge, comfortable with a cutting edge. Also liked to move around. Montreal, relatives?
6) Ficorelli and Spargo both used booger flies mail-ordered from Booger Baits in Curran. What about the other victims? [Waco checking Illinois, Kansas] The list has to be carefully analyzed. FACT: List only goes back seven years; no apparent way to connect flies to the first batch of killings. If Mains use no computers, how could killer access list? Need F/U by Denninger? C. Main III

nervous about government oversight. Why? All of this seems to point to something, but what?

7) Give photo from Big Ben Pey to FBI to compare with the Mexican photo.

8) Per Big Ben: Frankie Pey may have gone to college "up in Marquette"; from same source, Frankie served in the navy in the Pacific during World War II. Did he graduate? Are there college and/or navy records on the man? Check NMU, DOD.

9) Pey might have worked for Sears or Monkey Ward. [FBI F/U] According to Big Ben: Frankie Pey a sort of roving bookkeeper or auditor. [NOTE: Seems to fit the kind of job and freedom Monica theorizes for the serial murderer.] Way to track his movements over the years and coordinate those with killings? Expense, trip, or sales reports? Anything? How long do companies keep such records, if at all?

10) Frankie's mother murdered the year he went to college, estim. 1932. Throat cut. Speculation: probably a boyfriend. No arrests. Frankie comfortable with cutting edges. Who investigated the case? Were there suspects? Was Frankie ever one of them? [FBI F/U]

11) When will Monica have notes of deceased agent in Toledo? If so, any new leads, information in the dead agent's files and notes?

12) Where is Monica's analyst? Why so difficult to arrange a meeting? What's her reluctance? Is she holding back, and if so, why?

13) Can forensic pathologist / medical examiner look at wounds in Mexico vicks, and those in the blood eagle killings, see a connection or a progression? Something?

14) Initial victims in the second group = no blood eagle. Why the sudden shift in MO. Why change? Something different in killer's state of mind?

15) Nantz, Mama Ficorelli, Spargo's sister: all killed in freak auto accidents: Coincidence, or what? How do these fit, if at all? Ptacek from U.P. Autobody says paint flecks on bumper lining should not be there, indicative of PIT? Need second opinion on evidence. [NOTE. Nantz not an accident. Others misread in WI, MO?]

16) FACT: I'm not on Booger Baits list. Never used the flies, never even heard of them until now. If killer finds victims via fly orders, how would he use list to find me? As of last night, no MI COs on Booger Baits lists—only Shark. Denninger will type Michigan list, double-check.

Most predators in the animal kingdom, he knew, were born efficient, and tended to single out a specific victim, either because it was outside the group, or perceived to be weaker than the others. Then it slow-hunted, narrowing the victim's options until it was either trapped or panicked. Prey panic? The phrase stuck in his mind. Were human predators different?

"You writin' a juicy love letter, hon?"

Service looked up, felt confused. *Nantz?* A waitress with huge eyes was bending down over him. He immediately turned over the pad and she stepped back.

"Dude," she said icily, "I wasn't snooping. You want a refill or not?"

He gave the girl his thermos and asked her to fill it with the leaded stuff.

He paid for his coffee and continued north. At eighty miles an hour it would take him roughly three-and-a-half hours to reach the bridge and another ninety minutes to get back to the cabin. *Watch for deer*, he warned himself, as he went around Lansing on the I-69 bypass and headed north. He tightened his seat belt and tried to put the case out of his mind. Stay in the moment, watch for deer, and don't forget elk after Gaylord. *Damn, it's dark.*

Vince Vilardo's Chrysler minivan was parked at the cabin. Service got out stiff-legged, and found the retired medical examiner for Delta County asleep on the footlocker bed; a stranger was asleep in his old upholstered chair. Both of them were snoring.

"Vince," Service said gruffly.

Vilardo stirred. "Two minutes, Rose."

"It's Grady, not your wife. What the hell are you doing here, Vince?"

Vilardo sat up like a spring had been unwound. "Huh . . . What?" He rubbed his eyes and shook his head. "Grady?"

"What are you doing here, Vince? Do you know what time it is?"

"What time it is?"

"It's midnight. Stop repeating what I say and wake up."

Vilardo shuffled over to the sink and splashed water on his face.

"Boy, I was zonked." He looked at Service who was looking at the stranger. "That's Charles Marschke, Esquire. He went to the Gladstone house and nobody was there. He asked the county for help and they called me and I brought him out. He claims he's one of Maridly's lawyers."

*One* of them?

"Hey," Service said, nudging the sleeping man's foot. "Wake up."

The man opened his eyes and stared up, the sleep falling off like a coverlet. He reached into his shirt pocket and took out a business card. "Charles Marschke—Maridly was my client. I'm sorry for your loss."

"You were her lawyer?"

"She had several, but I was her personal affairs lawyer, family friend, and financial manager. I'll miss her. She never mentioned my name?"

"She didn't talk about money."

The man smiled. "That was Maridly. May I ask why you never married her?"

Service kept asking himself the same question. "That's none of your business."

The man held up his hands. "You're absolutely right, and it's irrelevant. Married or not, she named you her sole heir. It will take a while to transfer everything, but it will be done in six to ten months. Do you have a financial consultant I can confer with?"

Service was confused and tired. "Hell, I haven't balanced my checkbook in I don't know how long."

The man smiled. "If you need a consultant, I'd be pleased to be of assistance."

"I don't need a consultant. I work for the state."

"But you do," the man said. "You do."

"I don't want to inherit anything from Nantz," Grady Service said.

"You're getting everything: all her assets, the house in Gladstone, her aircraft, her investments. Those alone come to about eighty, eighty-five."

"Eighty thousand?"

The man laughed. "*Million*, Mr. Service, and growing daily. She was a very, very wealthy woman, and now you are going to be a wealthy man."

Service felt his legs go soft.

Marschke took papers out of his briefcase and took them to a table, spreading them out. "There's a sticky tag in each place where you need to sign."

"What if I don't sign?"

"You'll still get it all. It will just take longer. This is what you call a done deal. Go with the flow."

"Sign," Vince Vilardo yipped. "*Sign!*"

"Shut up, Vince."

Service signed the papers and watched the man fold them and put them back into his briefcase. He walked out to Vince's car with the men and told Vince, "You keep your mouth shut about this."

When they were gone he sat down on his steps and stared into the darkness. What the fuck was he going to do with eighty million dollars? *If Nantz was here now, he'd strangle her*, he told himself. Go ahead and laugh, Mar. This is *not* funny!

At 6 A.M. and with virtually no sleep, he telephoned Special Agent Monica. "Tatie, this is Service. Just wake up and listen. When I was in Arizona I talked to a CBP agent who was part of the *federales* team that arrested Ney.

He said Ney's murder in prison was not what it seemed. Ney scammed a guard to kill him because he was dying of cancer and he had only weeks or months to live. He also said that all Ney would tell the *federales* was that he had completed his life's work. Nobody knew what that meant."

He kept talking, couldn't stop. "After Ficorelli's funeral, his aunt gave me his fishing gear, including his fly collection. A friend of mine came down from Houghton to look at the flies and he found a unique one called a booger fly. It's made in only one place, by an old guy down in Curran, Michigan, which is about thirty miles south of Alpena," he said. "I found the same kind of fly at the kill site. I think Ficorelli got out of the river to retrieve the fly and was killed."

Tatie Monica perked up. "You *found* evidence and didn't tell me?"

"Shut up, Tatie. I also went back to Elray Spargo's place. He had booger flies in his collection. I drove down to Curran and talked to the man who makes the flies. The old guy grew up in Mongo, in northern Indiana, and invented the fly there, but he moved up to Michigan and has been here fifty years. I plotted all the body sites on maps to see if I could pick up a trend. What threw me is that some were by the ocean. It took a while to remember tides—moving water. Your analyst understood that. I began to wonder if what our victims had in common was that they were all trout fishermen and they used flies—specifically booger flies. The business up in Curran has records only for seven years, but we convinced them to let us compile a list. It's run by a man called Charles Main Jr., and his son, Charles Main the third. The locals call the younger one Charley the Turd." Service picked up his notepad and looked at it. "I know it's a long shot," he concluded.

"What have you been smoking, Service?" the FBI agent asked.

"You need to listen, and we need to get on the same page. You need to get your people to go through the list, to find out how many of our victims bought booger flies by mail," he said. "I've got an agent in Missouri checking on the Illinois and Kansas victims."

"One of my agents?"

"No, Missouri conservation agent Eddie Waco—the guy with the beard? We can't look at the first batch of victims, but we can sure as hell compare the customer list to the second group and see what comes up. If it turns out they were all using booger flies, then we have a potential intersect, a way for the killer to identify certain game wardens. Maybe this is how he picked them, I don't know. Maybe it was a coincidence that victims were also some of the best in each state. You have the resources to do this; I don't," he said.

"How would the killer get their list?" she asked.

This stopped him momentarily. "I don't know yet. Now listen to this: Mongo was once called Pigeon River. It's built on the Pigeon River. The name was changed. The fly tier, whose name is Main, never heard of a family named Ney, but he said there was a large family named Pey in Pigeon River."

Service let her digest the information. "I went to Mongo where I met the current game warden, and a retired warden. The retired warden introduced us to an old man named Big Ben Pey. The old man told us he had a distant relative named Francois *Ney* Pey, and that this man went by the name of Frankie. Frankie Pey worked for Sears or Montgomery Ward out of Chicago. He went to college in Marquette, and served in the navy during World War Two. No idea if he graduated, but it's a starting place, *and* he was some sort of traveling auditor for his employer and moved all over the country. Apparently he came back to Mongo only to see a girlfriend, who was married to somebody else," said Service.

"The woman now lives with her daughter just up the road in Sturgis, Michigan," Service continued. "Her name is Greenleaf, Essie Greenleaf. I talked to her and she's batty, but she also let me know in a strange and roundabout way that she had a thing with Frankie Pey. She said Pey died in Mexico. When I asked her what he was doing down there, she told me, 'Completing his life's work.' She also confirmed there was a boy with them, but said he was neither his son—nor hers. She said the kid's name was Marcel. He was about fifteen or sixteen at the time. It can't be a coincidence that she used the same words the border agent used. Big Ben Pey gave me a photo. He says it's Frankie just before he left for college, which made him eighteen or nineteen in 1932. I think I can see some similarity to the photo I got from the *federales*, but you people have specialists and software to take this and age it and see if there's a potential match, right?"

The FBI agent said, "Jesus . . . This is unbelievable."

"I know," he said. "Where is your asshole consultant? We need to talk to him."

He heard her scratching on paper. "Eighteen or nineteen in 1932; that makes this guy in his mid fifties by 1970."

"Is that significant?"

"Ballpark age for a lot of serial murderers."

There was a long pause before she spoke again. "It can't be this easy," she lamented.

"It's not, but it's beginning to look like we've got some meat to grab, and we need to move on it. Are you awake?"

"Okay, okay," was all she could say. "I'll get dressed and head out to your shack."

"I want to talk to your analyst."

"Why?" she asked, her voice rising.

"I want to find out how he picked up on this whole deal, what his think-ing was, how he got one plus one to equal a shitpot more. I'm also wondering why the hell this second batch begins with a variety of MOs and suddenly shifts to the blood eagle? Does this signify some sort of psychological shift? Or do we have a different killer?"

Tatie Monica said, "Why in hell is somebody with your ability wasting himself in the backwoods?"

Service said, "When do I meet your analyst?"

"You won't," she said.

He waited for an explanation.

Finally, in exasperation, she said, "I can't find him, and he won't respond to my messages."

Service could hardly contain his rage. "You have got to be *shitting* me! You'd better get your people dogging his sorry ass, and I mean *right now*. Maybe this is nothing, but I don't like this guy pointing us at all this and then taking a sudden hike into Neverland."

"I've already got people on it," she said. "I'll be there with Larry and Bobbi in an hour. I take it you're not off the case."

"Let me put something else on the table: Ficorelli's mother and Spargo's sister died in car wrecks within a month of their killings. My girlfriend and son died in the same way not long ago, dry pavement, no apparent reason. I talked to a guy up here who found something that suggests my girlfriend got run off the road, and the more I think about it, the more it makes sense. The state police ruled it an accident, despite evidence to the contrary. She was a great pilot. There had to be a reason for the wreck. You ever hear of prey-induced panic?"

"No," she said.

"I'll explain it when you get here. Also, Frankie Pey was a trapper as a kid, and the year he left for college his mother was found murdered, with her throat cut. The case was never solved. I'm in this sonuvabitch to the end," he said.

"I'm running out the door now," Monica said.

Service lay on his footlocker bed and tried to sleep. The case was no longer in his mind. He had exorcised that. Now all he could think about was what the hell he should do with eighty million dollars that he had no right to. Couldn't he somehow trade it all back for Nantz and Walter?

# **Part III:** Green Bear Island

*Omnes una manet nox*

The same night awaits us all. —*Horace*

# 43

## Slippery Creek, Michigan
### July 28, 2004

While he waited for Tatie Monica, Service made fresh coffee and started making more notes, mostly questions. If the killer had access to Main's customer list, how had he gotten it, and when? Was it possible that Charley the Turd and/or his father were involved? Had the list been used for both groups of killings? Pey died in 1974 in prison in Mexico. Where did Marcel go? Was Marcel a killer? *The* killer?

"Too many holes," he said out loud, crumpling the notes and bouncing them off the wall.

He awoke on the floor to find Tatie Monica standing over him. She had the crumpled notes in hand and was trying to read them. "How long since you've slept?" she asked.

"Not sure."

"An exhausted investigator fucks up. Go to bed."

"I don't have a bed," he said.

She gave him a quizzical look and he pointed to the footlockers. "Sweet Jesus," she said. "Give me all your notes and I'll take them back to Marquette with us. You sleep. That's an order."

"I don't report to you."

"Think of me as your mother."

"She died in childbirth."

"Probably lucky for her." Special Agent Monica stormed out the door and Service lay down to try and sleep.

His mind refused to shut off. He got up and grabbed his handheld and called Officer Denninger. "I need your help again."

"Whatever you need," she said.

"If the Mains aren't computerized, how could somebody get their list? Did they ever report a theft? Talk to the county and the state, and then talk to the old man alone. Charley the Turd will just try to stonewall you again."

"I'll get back to you."

Service called Eddie Waco. "Anything on the men in Kansas and Illinois?"

"I'm in Illinois now. The officer's name here was Retucci. He was a fly-fishing nut and he had booger flies. I'm headed to Kansas next. I'd call ahead to the family, but it's better to show up in person. Gives it more weight."

"I agree. Thanks."

"I'll be back to you'n quick as I can. You gettin' close?"

"Maybe."

"Count me in for the finish."

"Your supervision will approve that?"

"You let me worry about that, Michigan Man. You'n call, I'll haul. Heck, I might even get to see me a bear."

Grady Service liked Eddie Waco. But were they really beginning to get close to something? He wasn't sure. This was like hunting blind. He dozed off thinking about hunting and bears, and he slept through the rest of the day and night.

# 44

## Marquette, Michigan
### July 29, 2004

Most of the regional HQ was dark when Service parked in the lot south of the building, but there was a light on in the captain's office. The fog this morning had been thick, the driving slow.

The captain had already made coffee. Service poured a cup for himself and made his way to Grant's office.

"You look perplexed."

Service took him through the case, omitting nothing and emphasizing the accidents of Ficorelli's and Spargo's relatives. As was his way, the captain listened and made notes before asking questions.

"The analyst aspect is disturbing," the captain said.

"It's a major loose end," Service said.

"You know the preferred tactic for weathering a shit storm?"

Service looked up. His captain never used such language.

"You sit under a good strong roof until it's done falling," Grant said.

"Are you telling me you're going to chain me to my desk?"

"You know better than that. If Nantz and Walter were killed intentionally, the killer is trying to rattle you. I'm going to insist that the state lab people go over the wreck again. What you do is keep pushing and prodding."

"Eventually there's going to be a collision," Service said.

"I have no doubt," the captain said, "but when it happens, let it be you who determines the location and rules of engagement."

"I've already had that thought."

"I was certain you had," Captain Grant said with a nod.

When Service got back to his cubicle there was tapping on his outside window. He looked out to see Limpy Allerdyce standing there. Service knew Allerdyce would not come into the building. He got a cup of coffee for the old poacher, and went outside to meet him.

"Proud of you," Service joked. "You actually touched the building."

Allerdyce squinted. "Youse tink more about youse's gal?"

Service suddenly picked up on the old man's rage, which he was struggling to contain. He pointed a finger at Allerdyce. "I don't need *your* help, thank you very much."

"Up here we take care of each udder, sonny."

"What're you gonna do, take my back?"

The old man grinned and said nothing.

"You get caught with anything that even faintly can be construed as a weapon and you'll be in violation of your parole, and you *will* go back inside. You want to ruin your image with your girlfriend?"

Allerdyce drank his coffee, scowled, and looked out toward Lake Superior, which was beginning to lighten in the rising sun. "My day," he said, "I never t'ought twice 'bout shootin' dogs, runnin' deers an' such. Dere's some t'ings a man don't turn 'is cheek to."

"Stay out of it, Allerdyce. Go blow more smoke up your professor's behind."

The old poacher cackled. "Not a joke, sonny. I changed, and my people, they changin' too. How it was ain't how it gonna be. Go ahead, youse make fun of me, but youse'll see."

"Stay out of my business," Service said emphatically, splashing his coffee on the grass as he went back inside. Being around the old man always gave him the creeps, and right now he didn't need any more distractions. Limpy was capable of just about anything. What had the professor said—to check with the RAP people? Where was that goddamn list she'd given him? He found it in a folder and picked up his phone.

"Station Twenty, Twenty Five Fourteen. I've got a list of times alleged RAP tips from informants came in to the RAP line. Can you verify receipt and disposal?" He read off the dates and times.

The RAP dispatcher in Lansing came back on the radio after ten minutes. "They all check out, Twenty Five Fourteen. There were sixteen calls, and all of them resulted in citations. All callers were anonymous."

"Twenty Five Fourteen clear." Jesus Christ, what was going on? There was no way Limpy could change. The only possible explanation was that he was up to something.

Fern LeBlanc passed his cubicle, looked in, and said, "Nice to see you could grace us with your presence." She came back five minutes later with a handful of pink callback slips. "Your adoring public," she said, dropping them on his desk.

He had just started looking through the notes when LeBlanc came back and said, "I'm going to transfer a call to you." This usually meant there was someone or something she didn't want to handle, because she was experienced and talented enough to deal with just about anything that came through the door or over the phone.

He saw the line light blink and picked up the phone. "Detective Service."

"I ast for DNR, not reg'lar cops," a male voice complained.

"This is the DNR," Service reassured him. In the minds of Yoopers, game wardens were not cops.

"When youse get deteckatives?"

"It's been awhile," Service said. He hated calls like this.

"No kiddin' . . . Well, I got me a dead calf out here. Wolf come in and kilt 'im. Somebody gonna come out and take a look? I wanta file me one of dem claims."

Service rocked back in his chair. An alleged wolf depredation call was one of the most contentious complaints to deal with.

"You're sure it was a wolf?"

"Yeah, sure, and I coulda shot da bot' a' dem, but I figgered youse guys would get yore skivvies all in a yank, so's I din't shoot, and now I'm callin' youse. Youse comin' or not?"

"Give me your address," Service said and wrote it down.

McFarland was about forty miles south, and there was no direct route. "I'll be there in thirty, forty minutes."

"What I do, them bloody wolfs come skulkin' back?"

"Secure the carcass and don't shoot them."

"Damn tings all over da place nowadays," the man said, and hung up. Service had not even gotten his name.

He told LeBlanc where he was headed and drove south on US 41.

# 45

# McFarland, Michigan
## July 29, 2004

The farm was typical of many that lay on the plateau south of Marquette, toward Rapid River: Several ancient apple trees, a few acres of potatoes, a small field of stunted corn, some multicolored chickens running loose to provide free-range snacks for local coyotes, three sway-back dairy cows, a half-dozen beefs, and a small flock of dusty sheep; all in all, a virtual walk-up café for wolves and other predators. The house was low with multiple roofs to help reduce winter snow loads, the fences hadn't been painted since soldiers wore brown boots, and there were two rusted-out tractors in a rock-strewn field serving as hotels for various birds and rodents.

The farmer was sixtyish, gaunt, dressed in all his agrestic glory: a flannel shirt with missing buttons, unlaced muddy, green, high-top Converse All Stars, a Budweiser can in hand.

"Took youse long enough," the man greeted him.

Service looked at his watch: thirty-two minutes had elapsed since he'd left the regional office lot. When you were part of the DNR in the U.P., there were myriad ways to disappoint locals, and few ways to make them happy. This was not going to be a happy interaction. Many Yoopers welcomed the return of wolves to the area, but there were few farmers in the pro-wolf forces, and Service was fairly certain that more than a few wolves were being quietly shot and disposed of. The state had a reparations program for animals lost to wolves, but in most instances the predation was done by wild dogs or coyotes, not wolves. No matter; some farmers blamed wolves for virtually all the ills of the northern part of the state, including seasonal cycles in deer populations.

The man led him to a ramshackle shed tilted precariously to the east, and showed him the dead calf. Service looked at two sets of footprints in the mud and dust in the area around the building. They were too small for wolves: coyotes or wild dogs, he guessed. He could see where they had approached, not in single file like wolves, but apart.

"Not wolves," Service told the man.

"Youse telling me I don't know a bloody wolf when it come sniffing around?"

"I'm just telling you that these tracks and signs indicate coyotes or dogs, not wolves."

"You buckos always got answers," the man complained. "Tink the rest of us a buncha emptyheads?"

There was no point arguing. "Tell me what you saw."

"Da she-wolf, she was up to da side a' da shed over dere, and she looked back, and a smaller one come up behind her."

"You saw them go inside?"

"Seen 'em on da doorstep. Din't see no coyotes."

"But you didn't actually see wolves on the kill?"

"Din't have to."

Service looked at the carcass. "How do you know it was a *female* wolf?" he asked.

"Big one and a little one."

"Twenty pounds—fifty, eighty?"

"I din't weigh 'em, eh."

"What position was the tail?"

The man looked confused. "I wasn't watchin' no damn tails!"

Service asked the man to look at the carcass. He explained, "Wolves have a fairly regular pattern of eating. They start by stripping the rump and organs. They don't hit the legs and other musculature until the bigger portions are consumed. This calf's legs have barely been chewed. Two wolves would have done a lot more damage."

"I don't know why 'n hell dey tell us ta call da state when all youse do is stonewall us."

"If you call the biologist from Marquette, he'll tell you the same thing I'm telling you."

"Bloody DNR, da whole worthless bunchayas."

"I'll call for you." Service gave the man one of his business cards and wrote down the name of a biologist in the Marquette regional office. "His name is Herndon. I'll try to get him out here today."

"I see dem critters again, I'm gonna shoot first," the farmer said.

"I wouldn't advise that," Service said, trying to retain his composure and be polite. There were so many crank calls about wolves and other things that it was easy to write callers off, but his job was to find out what happened, not discourage citizens.

As far as he knew, confirmed U.P.-wide wolf predation over the past two years had amounted to a dozen dogs, eighteen cows, a dozen chickens, and a few sheep. Since the 1990s the state had paid less than $20,000 in reparations to farmers, who claimed the DNR was purposely misidentifying predators in order to not pay them for their losses.

Leaving the farm, he had no interest in going back to the office. He called Paulie Herndon, told him what to expect, and headed south into northern Delta County to look around and think. Parking near the Escanaba River, he called Buster Beal. The visit to the farmer had started some unformed notions rolling around in his head.

"Chewy, Grady. You know much about wolf behavior?"

"Some. When you manage deer, you learn about wolves. Deer herd is like Mickey D's to a wolf pack."

"The adults in the packs bring food to the pups, right?"

"While they're in the denning area. When the pups get to about twenty pounds, the pack moves to a rendezvous area for the summer and remains fairly stationary as the pack teaches the young ones to hunt. By September pups are thirty to forty pounds and strong enough to get in on the chase, but in summer the wolves are more likely to be eating beaver than deer. They'd rather wait until deep snow in winter for their venison. Kills come a lot easier then."

"The mothers teach the pups to hunt?"

"Roles aren't that clearly delineated. Adult males and females all take part in the hunt, and the pups follow along and mimic what they see the other pack members doing. Hey, it's not a lot different than the men in the family taking a kid out to deer camp and his dad, grandpa, uncles, and older brothers all teaching him how it's done."

"Do wolves ever kill individually?"

"Beaver sometimes, but not larger ungulates. Too risky. With wolves, eating and killing are group activities."

"Single wolf and a pup kill a calf?"

"Could," the biologist said, "but usually it's only the adults doing the killing and the pups just jumping in for their share of the grub."

"Thanks, Chewy."

"That help you?"

"Maybe," Service said. The wolf incident got him thinking about Frankie Pey, Essie Greenleaf, and the boy called Marcel. He wasn't sure why. The border patrol agent said that the prisoner Ney had called the boy his *creation*.

He was beginning to formulate a thought, but it remained vague and he couldn't quite pull it together. Not yet.

# 46

## Slippery Creek, Michigan
### July 29, 2004

It was dark when Grady Service got home. McCants still had Newf and Cat and he thought about fetching them, but decided to wait until the next day.

Two Crown Vics were parked at the cabin. It looked like Gasparino beside one of the vehicles. Tatie Monica was on the porch. He invited her in and made a fresh pot of coffee. Her face was splotched with something that looked like hives, and there was a vein sticking out of her temple. She wore a black business pantsuit, black pumps with low heels, her hair in a bun, her face masked with heavy makeup. She looked like she was dressed for a vampire's coming-out party.

"What's the deal?

"I've been summoned to the Bureau to eat a shit sandwich," she said.

"Ketchup or mustard?"

"It's not a joke! I may soon be off the case, in which case they'll send a yessiroid to replace me."

She looked and sounded broken, but he couldn't summon much sympathy.

"I'm ex officio, not part of the team," he reminded her.

"If they pull me out, you're probably not going to have a choice, and you've gotten to places alone that we never got to."

"Meaning?"

"I can make sure they pull you in and sit on you."

"Control to the end," he said.

"You don't know what you're dealing with," she said.

"And you do?"

Tatie Monica held up her hands. "I'm not here to fight or threaten," she said quietly. "My analyst was not authorized by the Bureau. My career was in the incognito Batwoman mode, like going nowhere, and Check Six popped up and set the case on my platter. I hadn't heard anything from him since LA, and he was righteous that time. What would you have done?"

"Check Six?"

"Shut up and listen. You need to understand the context. The Bureau has been trying for years to claw its way out of the interregnum of Hoover and bring computers into the main culture. Freeh started a project called Trilogy, which was supposed to provide us with online connectivity and shareware built around something called the Virtual Case File. But Freeh retired after the debacle in New York. Pickard came in as interim director, and then Mueller was named to be Freeh's permanent replacement. Mueller has balls: He served in Vietnam with distinction, but now he's caught dodging political hacky sacks filled with C4. With the creation of Homeland Security, he's been dealt out of the top power loop. The bottom line is that Trilogy doesn't work and it's not going to work. The Bureau's spent close to six hundred mil and we have bupkiss. I'm guessing that within a year you'll hear that the custom-designed program will be junked for off-the-shelf technology. Meanwhile, those of us who need to share and search information haven't had shit to work with. This guy came to me and I jumped on it."

"Which your bosses didn't approve."

"Right. Do you know any computer geeks?" She didn't wait for a response. "This guy is your classic prototypical hactivist, believes the Bureau's inker mindset threatens national security. How he got into our records, I have no idea, but he did, and he found this and I took it and away we went."

"And bodies kept piling up."

She nodded almost imperceptibly. "I don't even know his real name. I lied to you about that. Check Six is one of his handles. Another is Rud Hud, and our relationship is what geeks in Electronland call h4xxOr, which means illegal. He's not supposed to be in the data he's in, and I'm not supposed to employ anyone who hasn't been vetted through Bureau security."

There was a tone in her voice that suggested an undecipherable smugness. "My out is that I haven't actually employed him in the sense of paying for his services. Officially he's like an unpaid informant, a patriotic citizen willing to help."

"You think your bosses will buy that," asked Service.

"You don't understand how they can circle the wagons to protect the Bureau's rep. I've seen some major fuckups and messes swept quietly away because the Bureau decided the guilty ones didn't intend to do anything technically illegal or immoral, and were simply trying to work their cases. The Bureau likes initiative. If I can give them a reason to let me keep going, I'm hoping they'll take it. With all the criticisms after 9/11, they don't want more, especially in the area of domestic law enforcement. The meta-logic is: Okay, we kinda, sorta, maybe fucked up a skosh on 9/11, but we're still the country's top cops, and since the seventies the crown jewel in the agency's reputation has been our record with serial murderers. Never mind that most of them were caught by accident, by local agencies, or in the backwash of their own fuckups; the Bureau has used serial murder and profiling as a sexy publicity engine for showing the public how great we are. They've milked it in ways you cannot even begin to imagine," said Monica.

"What does this have to do with me?"

"You remember the shit with Hanssen?"

"The agent who sold information to the Russians?"

"He was like a total head case. What most people don't understand is just how badly the agency screwed the pooch. They had been tipped about him by another agent four years *before* Hanssen was arrested, and it was only after the fact that they learned he was mucking around in databases where he didn't belong, asking questions he wasn't authorized to ask, not to mention leading a private life with more red flags than a Chinese picnic. Nobody had bothered to look at his electronic trail, or his personal life. You think any of us in the trenches were surprised by the 9/11 meltdown? You can't ever acknowledge a potential personal mistake or weakness because it could point upward. Hell, we are all selected for the Bureau. If we fail, the Bureau fails, and the Bureau won't allow that. That's the culture Hoover nurtured," she said. "What I'm telling you is that your sources may be able to quietly take a look and see if they can find a trail for Rud Hud. I don't begin to understand the minutiae of the cyberworld, but the truth is, I can't find him, and the only possible way is through his tracks in our files."

"This is way outside my expertise," he said. "Are you thinking this guy is more than a public-minded bird dog?"

"I don't know what I'm thinking, but you want to talk to him, and I want to talk to him, and I can't find him, and I know you have some sort of back door into the Bureau. I've seen the results."

"Your people will stay off my ass?"

"That's *our* deal, but if they replace me, that deal is off."

"How much contact did you have with this Check Six, Rud Hud?"

She reached into a portfolio and pulled out a neat stack of papers under a clip. "I printed this for you. I'm gonna be incomputerado for awhile."

When she drove away from the cabin, Gasparino came to the porch, begged a cigarette, and lit it clumsily. "She's freaking out, am I right?" the young agent asked.

"She thinks she's gonna be pulled off the case," Service said. "She's headed back to Washington."

"Oh shit. Professional Instant Death Syndrome."

*Whatever that was.* More and more he was finding that people around him were using vocabularies that eluded him.

"Fuck," Gasparino said. "If she goes down, that could mean East Jesus for me."

"East Jesus?"

"Yeah, sixty miles past Bumfuck. Nobody comes back from East Jesus, hear what I'm sayin'?"

Service invited the young agent inside for coffee. It was disconcerting how important careers were to federal officers.

"For real, you think she's out?" Gasparino said.

"She said it's possible."

"Squared shit."

"Does it matter?" Service asked.

"Hey, she's got tunnel vision and she pisses off a lot of people, but she's a pretty good leader, ya know? I trust her with my six," the young agent said.

To trust someone with your six was to entrust your life to them. This was the first positive thing Service had heard about Tatie Monica. But Gasparino was green and didn't have enough experience to understand how few people you could truly trust.

Her sudden contrition had no currency. His gut said she was a game-playing screwup with major personal issues who would never have been able to lead an investigation had it not been for the luck/courtesy of Check Six / Rud Hud. The major question now was, Who is he, and what the hell is his angle?

Gasparino departed with a sad face and Service wrote down the name *Rud Hud* several times, underlining each iteration.

He thought about sleeping, but there was too much loose detail in his mind. Even with the list, how did the killer actually *find* game wardens in the field, much less get the better of one? This case had all sorts of threads of varying lengths, like wires someone had randomly chopped. How did you re-assemble spaghetti?

The phone rang several times before the sound registered, and when he picked it up, there was nobody there. *What the hell?*

He lit a cigarette, stripped to his undershorts, and called Candi Mc-Cants. "It's Grady. I'm sorry to call so late."

"They're fine," she said. "Don't worry."

"I don't know when I can pick them up."

"Really, Grady, they're just fine. Newf loves everyone and Cat—well, she's Cat."

Service was groping for words when headlights flashed in front of the cabin. *Jesus*, he thought. "Candi, I gotta go."

Karylanne Pengelly, his late son's girlfriend, stormed into the cabin without knocking. Service scrambled for his trousers but she walked over to him, put her arms around him, put her head on his chest, held tight, and began to sob. He tried to pry her loose but couldn't break her grip; he had to stand helpless, feeling her body convulse.

Eventually the sobs relented. He led her to a chair at the card table, sat her down, gave her a box of tissues and a glass of water, tugged on his trousers, and joined her at the table.

She wiped her nose and glared at him, saying nothing. One minute she was clinging to him and now her eyes looked like they could kill.

After a long pause she said, "How *could* you? What kind of monster are you?"

Before he could say anything she shouted, "You didn't even bury them, you selfish bastard!"

He decided to keep quiet and weather the storm.

"Do you have any herbal tea?" she asked, wiping her nose again.

"Coffee."

"I can't have caffeine."

"A little won't hurt," he offered.

He lit a cigarette and she slapped the table angrily and screamed, "Put that out!"

"It's my house."

"Secondhand smoke is dangerous for the baby!"

Grady Service looked across the table at her. *Baby?*

She glared at him. "That's right," she said slowly. "I'm pregnant, and you're gonna be the grandpa, but there isn't going to be a father." The sobbing started all over again.

He had no idea what to say. And so it went: periods of sobbing followed by increasingly longer periods of rationality, and bit by bit she told him how she had been on the pill, but it wasn't 100 percent, and Walter died not even knowing. She had learned a few days before he died and never got to tell him. She had her heart set on finishing school, but she wanted the baby more than anything. She did not want to go home to her parents in Canada.

Service had learned from Maridly Nantz that women sometimes simply wanted to vent to a sympathetic ear. They were not looking for male problem solving, and this seemed like one of those times. *Grandfather?* Geez . . . He'd barely had time to adjust to being a father. But a grandfather? Christ, he was too damn young to be a grandfather!

"I wasn't going to tell anybody about this," she said, "but when I saw you I couldn't keep it inside. Do you ever get the feeling that God is a mean sonuvabitch?"

"Sometimes."

She looked up at the ceiling and shook a fist. "You can kick my ass, but you can't break me." She looked back at Service. "I guess I'll have a little coffee. Have you got cream?"

He nodded dumbly, poured coffee for her, added powdered cream, and stepped outside to have a smoke.

"Hey," she called out, "come back inside. I was out of line. This is your house. You can smoke in here—it's okay. Really," she added, "I just panicked a little. I mean, it's only been two months; it could be a false alarm."

Two months?

"Have you been to a doctor?"

"No. I used an over-the-counter test and it was positive, but I also know they have false positives. Nothing is ever a hundred percent, right?"

He flicked the cigarette away, stepped back into the cabin, sat down, and looked at her. She reached out a hand. "Can I have a cigarette?"

Grady Service pushed her hand away. "Not a chance."

She shrugged and looked at one of the notepads on the table.

"Are you into Gaelic punk?" she called out.

She had pulled him into a vortex of non sequiturs and illogic, and he was having a hard time keeping up. "Huh?"

"Rud," she said, pointing to his notepad. "Are you interested in Mill a h-Uile Rud?"

He said, "I have no idea what you're talking about."

"It's a punk band from the Seattle area. I think the name means something like 'destroy everything,' or something like that."

"Gaelic?"

"Yeah, Scotland, Ireland, even Wales, I guess. It all derives from Celtic," said Karylanne.

"How do you know that?"

"Some of Walter's teammates were big into punk. There's a retired prof in Houghton who knows all about Gaelic punk. He taught at U of M in Ann Arbor I think."

"What's his name?"

"Flaherty. He was an English professor and he's a computer nerd, but most of all he's a hockey freak. He skates with the boys sometimes, eh. He's in his sixties, but he moves around pretty good, and Walter said he's slick with the puck. He has an over-thirty team called the Galloping Gothinks."

"Gothics?"

"Go-*thinks*. It's a play on words."

"Flaherty?"

"Yeah, but all the boys call him Knickknack. He has team dinners at his house once a month during the season, and the place is filled with all sorts of weird and cool stuff—suits of armor, things like that. He's got one of Tony Esposito's old Tech sweaters in a frame on the wall."

Esposito was a Michigan Tech alum and an NHL Hall of Fame goalie. "What do you mean he's a computer nerd?"

"One of the guys on the team told Walter that Flaherty's a big-time hacker. His specialty is getting into closed university collections."

"To do what?'

"Read and learn, what else?"

"I thought hackers screwed around with things."

"Mr. Service, you really ought to find a way into this century. Hackers exploit holes in software to help make it better. Crackers are the ones who inflict damage."

"Flaherty, a hacker who knows Gaelic," he said.

"I'm not supposed to know about his computer life. See, by accessing closed collections, he saves money and time he'd have to spend traveling, and after he's seen what he needs, he lets the collection keepers know he was in and how he got there. He's like ancient, but a way-cool dude."

"Do you know him?"

"Sure, I used to go to the dinners with Walter and the team."

"Where are you staying?" he asked Karylanne.

"I had a place in Houghton with Walter."

*With* Walter. "You two were living together?"

"Yeah," she said. "Maridly knew."

"She did, did she?"

Walter had been living with this girl and he hadn't known. What else had he missed in his son's life, and why hadn't he paid more attention?

"She used to drive over and have dinner with us." Nantz hadn't told him.

"Do you know where Walter and Nantz were going when they crashed?" he asked her, already knowing what she'd say.

"I wish I did," she said. "Maybe she was taking him shopping. She sometimes did that for us." There was a lot Nantz hadn't told him. But if he'd been less thickheaded, he might have seen things himself.

"You drove here tonight from Houghton?"

"Yeah, I have to go back to Canada. I sort of ran out of money, and the landlord sort of kicked me out."

She was acting tough, but he saw fear in her eyes. "You're not going to Canada tonight," he said.

"I don't want to impose."

"If you're pregnant, Karylanne, I'd say that makes us related, and I don't turn family away." Not that he'd ever had any family before Nantz and Walter. For the longest time there had been just him and the old man. He didn't count his ex-wife.

He pointed to the footlockers. "The only bed I have."

"No offense, but that's *not* a bed, eh. I've got my sleeping bag in my car. The floor and my air mattress will be fine."

While she was getting her sleeping bag, Grady Service sat down and tried to focus on something, *anything*. Grandfather? Holy shit! Nantz would have been sky-high. He wasn't sure *how* he felt about it. He felt oddly grateful to Karylanne for being pregnant with Walter's child. This baby would be his only link to Walter, however tenuous.

Denninger called at 6 A.M.

"Where are you?" he asked.

"Home. What a day and night. Charley the Turd lost his cool yesterday and jumped me. I had to whack him behind the leg with my baton. I swear the earth shook when he hit the ground, and then he started complaining of chest pains so I had to call EMS and haul his worthless ass to the hospital. I took his father with me and it turns out he's eccentric, but pretty decent. He said they were computerized until this summer, but somebody got into their program and poached their lists."

"Did they report the theft?" Service asked.

"No. Charley the Turd just dumped the program and went back to the old way."

"Any idea who it was?"

"No clue, but the old man thinks it had to be one of their customers. They had a rudimentary website, and the guy must've come in through e-mail."

"What about Charley the Turd?"

"Not a heart attack. Turned out to be gallstones. The doctor says he may wish it was his heart in the long run."

"Can you write this up for me?"

"Planned to."

"Don't send it electronically."

"Why not?"

"I don't know," he said. "Maybe I'm old-fashioned like the Mains." Or he was suddenly feeling very insecure about the security of the cyberworld. He gave her his Slippery Creek address and she promised to send the report. He knew his apprehension about computers was turning into paranoia.

"Great job, Denninger."

"My name's Dani."

"Great job, Dani."

# 47

# Houghton, Michigan
## July 30, 2004

Karylanne called the retired professor in the morning and rode to Houghton with Service. The house on Seventh Avenue was multi-gabled and painted several shades of black and blue. A sign on the lawn said HOUSE OF DARK LIGHT.

"Did I mention he's Goth?" Karylanne asked.

Service had to think for a few seconds. "You mean, the name of his hockey team?"

"No, his lifestyle."

Another pause. "The freak-jobs who dress in black and paint their faces white?"

"Pretty much."

They parked in the street in front of the house and went up to the porch where they were greeted by a young woman in a tight, slinky black outfit and black Mary Janes. Stiff red ribbons stuck out of her glistening black hair like stalagmites. She wore a see-through black blouse and some sort of vinyl gismo underneath.

"Ice-jock girl," she greeted Karylanne. "S'up with the turkey bacon?"

"A friend."

The girl smiled at him, said, "S'up," in a cutesy voice, and slithered past them.

"You know her?"

"She's an instructor in computer engineering."

"Turkey bacon?" Service asked.

"Technically it means security guard, but more generally, any police officer."

"I'm not in uniform," he said.

She laughed. "Yeah, like *that* fools anyone."

Flaherty looked almost normal. He was average height with white hair in a buzz cut, and one tiny gold stud in his right nostril. "Service?"

"Grady."

"I'm sorry about your son. He was a great kid, and he was going to be an outstanding player. Heard you were a player too."

"Pleistocene age," Service said.

They were seated in an old-fashioned parlor. There was a suit of armor on a pedestal in one corner and a broad-blade ax with a six-foot handle on one wall.

"Is that real?" Service asked, pointing to the weapon.

"It's a replica of a Viking battle-ax," Flaherty said.

"How could anybody use that thing?" Service wondered out loud.

"Teamwork," Flaherty said. "Something to drink? Beer, soda—name your poison."

Service wasn't thirsty, and by the looks of the place, he didn't have a lot of faith in what might be served. "I'm sorry to drop in like this," he began, "but I'm working on an investigation of a hacker who calls himself Rud Hud, or Check Six. We're trying to identify him."

Flaherty said, "I thought the police had unlimited cyber assets."

"Not the DNR," Service said, not bothering to amplify. "Is it possible to find someone's real name based on a screen name?"

Flaherty smiled. "Handle is what it's called, and sure it's possible . . . depending on how the guy operates."

"Karylanne thinks the name is Gaelic."

"No doubt," Flaherty said. "I'll have to play around with it some. How quick do you need the information?"

"Yesterday," Service said.

"I'm good, not God," the retired professor said with a grin.

A boy came through a door wearing a black T-shirt emblazoned with BAD COP! NO DONUT!

Service blinked as he read the shirt.

Flaherty waved to the boy, who moved on through the house. "Atmosphere getting to you?" he asked Service.

"Some."

"Don't let their getups throw you. They're normal kids—if you ignore their IQs. I assume you already considered the obvious with Rud Hud?" Flaherty said.

"The obvious what?"

"Rud Hud Hudibras, which in Welsh is *Run baladr bras*."

"You call that obvious?"

"For some old English professors it is. You familiar with Geoffrey of Monmouth?"

Service shook his head.

"He wrote a history of Celtic kings, basically those from the period when there was no written language."

"If there was no written language, how did he get his information?"

Flaherty grinned. "There's a big debate about that, but it's probably a product of oral history. Others say it's a hoax, that he fabricated the whole thing. But in recent years scholars have found correlations in various sources like grave registers. In any event, Geoffrey's work gave a face to the unknown history of Britain and King Arthur, and the Round Table probably grew out of it. Kind of like *Lonesome Dove* for us, you know—we'd like to think that's how we were. No archaeological substantiation, of course, but hell, most Britons think Arthur was real."

What the hell did cowboys in *Lonesome Dove* have to do with King Arthur? "And Rud Hud?" He was having a terrible time keeping up with the professor.

"Troy fell, Aeneas and his son Ascanius split to Italy. Long story short, Ascanius had a son named Brut whose mother died in childbirth. Later the kid accidentally killed his father in a hunting accident, and he was banished from Italy and eventually ended up in Britain as Brut the Trojan, aka Brutus, who started a line of Celtic royalty that lasted two thousand years. A few steps down the generational ladder you find one Brutus Greenfield, whose son Leil followed him as king, but toward the end of his reign, Leil went sort of dotty, and his son, Rud Hud Hudibras, had to step in and get the kingdom under control. This would be at about the time Solomon was operating in Israel to give you some sense of time frame. Ninnyevent, time marches on, and later we get a Celtic king named Uther Pendragon, who may or may not be the Arthur of legend," said the Flaherty.

"This is for real?"

"It all stems largely from oral traditions, same as the Bible. Is *that* real? A lot of people think so. Tell me what you know about your Rud Hud."

"He thinks the feds aren't doing their jobs right."

"*Really*," Flaherty said. "That sort of fits."

"Fits what?" Service was lost in a lot of historic mumbo jumbo.

"Rud Hud more or less reformed his enfeebled old man's kingdom and ruled it for almost four decades. Centuries later, an English poet named Butler wrote a burlesque, a comic satire about the roundheads and Puritans and how they turned British society upside down. Using Rud Hud Hudibras as his model, he called the hero of his poem Hudibras, who was a sort of religious colonel who went out to clean up society in the way the Puritans wanted to, only he pretty much screwed up everything he touched, which made the

Puritans into a sort of joke, which they were in many ways, except to those who died at their hands or for their bizarre reasons. It was a damn brutal satire, somewhat along the lines of *Don Quixote*. Based on this, I'd guess your Rud Hud took his name to express his interest in reform, and I'd also guess he's exquisitely and classically educated. Most English students, even those with doctorates, don't know diddly-squat about Rud Hud Hudibras."

"Anything else?"

"You know anything about hackers and crackers?"

"Only what Karylanne told me," said Service.

"Interesting crowd. They usually don't play well with others and have poor coping skills in terms of face-to-face interpersonal communications, but put them in the privacy of their own hidey-holes with a computer, and they are unbelievably competent communicators. They've evolved their own language, mores, rules, you name it. If your Rud Hud is as educated as I'm thinking he is, I'm guessing he's also pretty sophisticated in the cyberworld, which means he could be difficult to find."

"Whatever you can do," Service said. "I appreciate this."

"Don't thank me until you see what I come up with," the retired professor said with obvious excitement at the prospect.

Service couldn't get the ax on the wall out of his mind. "You're interested in Vikings?"

"Yeah."

"You said something about teamwork."

"The Vikings liked to close en masse with their enemy, shields joined, and once joined, they broke into separate individual combats. But the warriors carrying the big battle-axes couldn't swing them *and* protect themselves with a shield, so the shield guys moved ahead of the big ax guys, who would step up and attack from behind their shields—your basic two-v-one in hockey."

"You know about the blood eagle?"

The English professor chuckled. "You mean the legendary and alleged blood eagle?"

"You don't believe it was real?"

"Certainly not with an ax like the honker on the wall," the retired professor said. "That was for rending people into chunks, not opening wounds for postmortem monkey business." Flaherty studied him. "Are *you* interested in Vikings?"

"Some," Service said.

A woman appeared from somewhere on the lower level of the house. She looked to be in her thirties. Long, obsidian hair, a leather bodice, short leather skirt with fishnet stockings, and four-inch platform shoes. "Elder Goth Dude," she said. "Time for unh-unh."

Flaherty laughed out loud and clapped his hands together. "I gotta go." He took the woman's arm and they started upstairs. Halfway up, he looked down and said, "Leave your card and I'll call you."

Service walked out to the truck with Karylanne. He lit a cigarette and started the engine. "Unh-unh?"

"The sound people make when they're really getting down; you know, kicking the gear stick? Like, grind-your-teeth animal sex?"

Grady Service shook his head and closed his eyes.

"You don't understand sex?" Karylanne asked. "That's not what Maridly said."

"Hey, hey, *hey!*" Service said. "You are *way* out of bounds!"

On the way home he pulled into the Walgreens in Marquette and killed the motor. He took out his wallet and handed her two crisp twenties. "Go inside and buy another pregnancy test. Two months is not a false alarm, and if you're not pregnant, the other possibilities aren't good."

"You don't believe me?"

"I believe you, but since the accident I've had to work like hell to control my emotions, and I think you're in the same boat. We've both been trying not to face reality. Pregnant or not, you need to see a doctor. Now, tell me the truth: Why don't you want to go home?"

Her lip quivered. "My folks are good people, simple people. They wanted me to stay home, get a job, get married, have kids. I worked hard to earn my scholarship to Tech. If I go home now, I'll lose everything, and I'll never get out of there. I want to be a mom, but I also want more than that."

He believed her, and more importantly, Nantz had believed the girl and Walter were meant to be together. He made a quick decision, one from the heart, one he was sure Nantz would approve of: "Here's the deal. If you're pregnant, we get you to a doctor. Then you go home. When you come back for fall semester, I'll pay for an apartment in Houghton. You will go to school and take care of yourself."

"You don't have to do this," she said.

"That's why I'm doing it," he answered. "I had a son for only a year, and if I'm gonna be a grandfather, I want to make sure it lasts a helluva lot longer. Deal?"

"Deal," she said, "but I don't want to go back to Canada."

"You owe it to your folks to go and tell them what's going on and what your plans are. Since we're just starting out, let's get something straight. I'll always level with you and you do the same for me. No bullshit between us."

She reached out for his hand, shook it, and went into the drugstore.

Grady Service lit a cigarette. He was taking on obligations, but they felt right. He needed to get this sorted out and get his focus back to where it needed to be.

On the way back to Slippery Creek, his cell phone rang. It was Eddie Waco.

"Booger flies confirmed in Kansas."

"Thanks, man."

"You got the scent?"

"Not yet."

"You'n call when hit's time, Michigan Man."

Minutes later it was Denninger on the phone.

"I'm almost done with the list, and guess what—your name is on it, with a Gladstone address."

He was speechless, and by the time he recovered his voice he had lost the signal and the call.

# 48

# Marquette, Michigan
## August 2, 2004

Karylanne Pengelly had left for Canada three days ago, her pregnancy confirmed, the baby due sometime in December.

Fern LeBlanc stood in the opening of his cubicle. "You seem to be in here a lot. Is everything all right?"

"Fine," he said. "Just a lot of work to do."

"That's never kept you in the barn before," she said.

When he looked up at her she was smiling.

He called Wink Rector. "Hear anything on Monica?"

"Nothing on her, and nothing on my replacement."

Fern LeBlanc came in and put a *Detroit Free Press* news clipping on his desk. The headline read HOMELAND SECURITY RESCUES LOCAL DNR OFFICER.

The story said that CO Miller French of Port Huron had confronted a group of intoxicated fishermen at a campground, and that six of them had jumped him and beaten him. Homeland Security personnel from the Blue Water Bridge detachment had shown up, and disarmed and arrested the assailants. French was treated at Mercy Hospital for a broken arm and facial lacerations, and later released. The assailants were lodged in the St. Clair County Jail.

He walked out to Fern's desk with the clipping. "Why'd you give this to me?"

She nodded at Captain Grant's office.

The captain was alone, his face to his computer. "Cap'n."

Grant swiveled around.

"Sounds like Frenchy got lucky." Miller French had trained under Gus Turnage several years back. Gus thought he was a good officer.

"Very lucky," the captain said.

"How did Homeland Security know to come to his aid?"

"Excellent question," Captain Grant said, and turned back to his computer.

Service stopped at Fern's desk. "Can you get Miller French's phone number for me?"

She came into his cubicle moments later and handed him a piece of paper. He dialed the number and the officer answered.

"Frenchy, it's Grady Service. I just heard. You okay?"

"Just dinged up. I'm in a cast for awhile, no biggie."

"Six on one isn't your normal wrestling match." Conservation officers seldom referred to even the most violent physical confrontations as anything other than wrestling.

"Thing is, I got two down, but another one of them blindsided me with a piece of firewood, and once I was one-armed, I was done."

"You hit your panic button?" The panic button was a remote signal device an officer could activate during an emergency outside his vehicle. The button activated a silent alarm in the Automatic Vehicle Locator transmitter, which alerted Lansing and the rest of the state that an officer was in deep trouble and needed help.

"Soon as the pukes turned on me."

"How long till Homeland Security got there?"

"Ten minutes, maybe less. Mouse was fifteen minutes behind them." Mouse Frissen was French's sergeant.

"You surprised to see the Homeland Security people?"

"Hell, I would've welcomed help from the Sisters of the Poor at that moment, but yeah, I never expected them."

"Take care."

"Thanks for the call."

Service called out to Fern LeBlanc. "Can you get me Sergeant Mike Frissen's cell phone number?"

"Reaching for it now," she said. She brought him another piece of paper.

He rang the cell phone, got no answer, and didn't want to leave a message.

He activated his 800 megahertz and changed the channel to District 10. "Ten, One Oh Three, this is Twenty Five Fourteen. Have you got TX?"

"Affirmative TX; it was off, Twenty Five Fourteen. Turning it on now."

"Twenty Five Fourteen clear."

He dialed the number and Frissen answered. Mouse Frissen was a long-time CO who had spent most of his career in Cheboygan County before being promoted and moving down to St. Clair County. He was a small man in stature, but big in performance, and word was that he was an excellent sergeant, who knew how to lead people without interfering with their ability to do their jobs. Service had been in many training sessions with him. "Mouse, it's Grady. I just heard about Frenchy."

"He's okay," Frissen said. "Bad luck that those asswipes broke his arm."

"Were you surprised to find Homeland Security ahead of you?"

"And how. I asked them how the hell they got the alarm, and they said they were just passing by."

Service detected a tone. "You buy that?"

"Hell no. The Port Huron paper tried to write a story and Homeland Security killed it. But a wire service kid filed and the *Free Press* picked it up. I guess the wire service kid also got bullied by Homeland Security; you know, the usual federal national security baloney, but his boss backed him, and he filed."

"The *Free Press* ran it."

"And *The News* didn't. Political leanings in our state's largest newspapers? Wow, who woulda thunk it."

Service made small talk, hung up, and went to see the captain. "I talked to Frenchy and Mouse Frissen. Mouse said Homeland Security claimed they were just passing by."

"You're skeptical?"

"I didn't just fall off the potato truck. The odds against just passing by are too damn high, and they got to the scene before Mouse. Frenchy activated his alarm. Is it possible that Homeland Security is wired into our AVL?"

"Not legally," was all the captain said.

Service went outside for a smoke and took a cup of coffee with him. If Homeland Security was wired into their AVL, who else had access?

"Fuck," he said, halfway through the cigarette. If you were wired into the AVL you could pinpoint an officer's location at all times, as long as the GPS system was up, or the officer didn't disengage it. He mashed the cigarette and went back to the captain's office.

"How could they get our software?" he asked. The DNR AVL software, as far as he knew, was tailored solely for Michigan's DNR law enforcement division.

"In the wake of 9/11, the president authorized a lot of new initiatives," the captain said.

Service had only vaguely followed news reports of wiretaps and other methods of tracking terrorists, methods the public had not been told about until journalists broke the stories.

"Would the governor have to approve such a thing?" he asked his captain.

"Not necessarily. It could come through the attorney general and, depending on the power granted to the federal government, the AG might be obliged to keep it quiet."

"But the director would know."

"Not necessarily," the captain repeated.

"Do the Wisconsin, Missouri, Illinois, and Kansas DNRs have AVLs?"

"I think almost all states have their own systems now. Some share with highway patrols, but it's pretty common."

"Captain, what if the killer has access to our AVL? He could track us with no problem."

"What if he did have access?" the captain asked, turning the question back.

Service thought for a minute. "He's a federal employee?"

"A reasonable assumption. Or he's somehow hacked his way in."

Grady Service immediately considered disabling the AVL in his Tahoe, but the captain read his mind. "Think this through, Grady. If you know you're being watched on the AVL, that gives *you* the advantage."

As he almost always was, the captain was right. The captain thought like a chess master, and regrettably, Service thought like a half-ass checkers player. He had tried to tell the captain several times he wasn't smart enough to be a good detective, but the captain refused to hear it. *Calm down,* he told himself.

Every August he drove up to an isolated spot on the Fence River to fish for brook trout. August was a time when most U.P. water was warm and low, but in this one spot there were some seeps and springs, and the water seldom climbed above fifty-two degrees all summer long. The frigid water was a magnet for brook trout from up and down the river, and he had caught so many fifteen-inch fish here over the years, he had lost count.

He went back to see the captain. "I'm gonna take my fishing vacation."

The captain looked at him and nodded. "Send me an e-mail and copy the chief."

Service understood. If someone was in the AVL, they were probably also poaching e-mails.

Was it the killer or was it Check Six? Or were they one and the same?

He called Eddie Waco on his cell phone. "How long will it take you to get up here?"

"Where's here?" the Missouri conservation agent asked.

"Crystal Falls in Iron County."

"Three days' work?"

"Drive your personal vehicle," Service added.

He called Simon del Olmo on his cell phone. "I'm going to need your help."

"Si, *Jeffe.*"

The Booger Baits list bothered him. Why was his name was on it? He had never seen a booger fly until he found Ficorelli's, and even then, he hadn't known what it was. But Nantz was always ordering flies from catalogs and other mail-order services. It had to have been her, and it was possible Shark might know something. She was always calling him and talking about flies.

He called his friend. "Did you know Nantz ordered booger flies?"

"She did? News to me."

"You're sure?"

"Hell yes. I never even told her about them."

*Damn*, Service thought.

# 49

## Marquette, Michigan
### Augst 3, 2004

He stopped by the office, called Treebone in Detroit, and talked to him about the case. The call was cut short when Tatie Monica and Wink Rector walked into his cubicle.

"You're back," Service said.

Rector stood back with a look Service couldn't quite read. "She's my replacement," Rector said, "the new resident agent for the Upper Peninsula."

"You're good with this?" he asked Tatie Monica.

"They pulled me off the team, but they're leaving me here. I can still get the guy."

"Working outside the team."

"No biggie. They gave the team to Pappas."

"I thought she was cyber."

Tatie Monica shrugged. "The powers that be have decided that this has morphed into a cyber case, that Check Six's activities make it so. What have you learned since I've been gone?"

"Nothing; I've pretty much stuck to my own business."

"Bullshit," she said. "You aren't easy to read, but I'm starting to get wise to you. You're like me. Neither of us can let go. Neither of us *will* let go."

"I don't think so," he said, "I'm headed out for a few days' vacation."

"*What?*"

"Vacation—you've heard of it, right?"

"You're up to something."

"I go every year about this time." Not quite true, but close enough.

"Where?"

"My vacation is none of your business, Tatie."

Wink Rector grinned throughout the conversation. "I think you guys are going to have an interesting working relationship."

"My stay here is strictly temporary," Tatie Monica said. "One of our psychiatrists talked to that old lady in Sturgis while I was in Washington. He says the woman is certifiable and would be unreliable as a witness. He says she's bottled up a lot of stuff and the more we press her, the deeper she retreats into *Jeopardy*. Man, that's gotta suck."

"What about the list from Booger Baits?"

"Everything's been turned over to Pappas."

"How does Bonaparte feel about her appointment?"

"Who knows. He's in his own world, that one."

"You saw him in Washington?"

"No, he was here yesterday, but he left again. He's on the road almost all the time."

"Several cases?"

"I have no idea. He pretty much goes and does what he wants, when and where he wants."

"Must be tough."

"Why?"

"I saw his cane and assumed he's got some sort of physical problem."

"Just part of his shtick. The pencil smudges are to make him look like a hard worker and a common man, not one of the suits. He thinks the cane creates sympathy, and causes people to underestimate him. I never got any details, but somebody in his group once told me that he hikes all over hell by himself. He's a fitness freak."

As soon as they left the office, he called Treebone back and finalized plans.

# 50

## Iron River, Michigan
### August 6, 2004

Service left his Tahoe at the Cedar Inn in Crystal Falls and rode with Eddie Waco in his truck. Waco wore an old pair of blue jeans and beat-up boots. The meeting place he had arranged was a small farmhouse out M-72, just a few miles north of the Wisconsin border, where Checkers Schwikert lived with his wife and her five ferrets.

Schwikert had spent his career with some megacorporation downstate and moved to the U.P. after he retired. He tied his own flies and exclusively fished the Brule River, which demarcated Michigan and Wisconsin. He was active in numerous conservation organizations and movements, and for years had headed up the Brule River Watershed Consortium. He was a quiet man in his seventies who smiled a lot and maintained a positive attitude in all things he did. He was also a great friend to conservation officers and regularly passed along information gleaned from various sources. Simon del Olmo had made several good cases because of him.

Schwikert gave them his small kitchen and went out to his garage workshop to tie flies and give them privacy. Del Olmo arrived in his personal truck as planned.

Service outlined the plan to the two men.

"He can monitor our AVL?" del Olmo asked incredulously. "Jesus."

"I think we have to assume that," Service said.

"When do you put the show on the road?" del Olmo asked.

"There are some things still up in the air, and I want to let those play out. Couple of days, I think. Not more."

He then talked them through the details, withholding only one significant part from del Olmo, who frowned all the way through. "What if this asshole sees us together?" the young officer asked.

"We're assuming he monitors AVL. He's not going to chance us seeing him." Service looked at Eddie Waco. "You got any concerns?"

"This'n's a big fish. Got ta use big bait ta catch a big fish."

Service turned back to del Olmo. "Once we're in place, you have to stay away, no matter what."

"I don't like it. You'll be out in the ass-end of hell with no close backup."

Eddie Waco grinned. "He's the strike dog. I'm the pack."

"I feel less than comforted," del Olmo grumbled.

Captain Grant called on the cell phone as Service and Waco were driving back to Crystal Falls.

"I just talked to the state lab and you were right about Nantz's truck. It seems certain she was knocked off the road."

"You mean murdered." Service felt his heart start to race.

"Wall off your feelings, Grady."

"I'm trying, Cap'n. Do we have a make on the other vehicle?"

"Better. We have the vehicle. It was rented at Detroit Metro and never returned. The county found it abandoned at an Empire Mine lot off M-94 in Palmer. There is a broken headlight, and the paint matches the paint on Nantz's bumper. The car rental agency had a video of the transaction, and we have a photo from the video. There are a lot of prints in the vehicle, but it will take time to collect and process them all through AFIS."

"Does the photo show anyone we know?"

"White male, late twenties or early thirties, big hair and a beard, probably fake. The FBI has the photo in a software program looking for matches. I'll fax the photo to District Three's office in Crystal." *Not Honeypat*, was his first thought, unless this guy was a boyfriend. That would be her style.

Something was changing for the killers. They were starting to leave traces, make mistakes. Service suddenly imagined Nantz's face and choked.

Shark called as they drove past First Lake on US 2. "Limey ordered booger flies for my birthday. She had them sent to Nantz under your name and Limey just told me about it. That help?"

*Maybe.* "Thanks." It at least explained how his name got on the list. He looked at Eddie Waco and explained that another cop would be joining them in the woods.

"Name's Treebone," Service told him.

"Ain't real common."

"That's a fact," Service said.

# 51

## Crystal Falls, Michigan
### August 6, 2004

The Cedar Inn was an old motel with updated siding and an interior decorated with an elk-head mount and prints from the Old West. They had two rooms at the end of the building next to the exit door. They spent the evening going through the case.

Service couldn't rule out that Tatie Monica's analyst was very possibly the killer—or at least one of them. Why had the man come forward to her with the two groups of victims? And why had the perp or perps suddenly started killing people close to the targeted victims? Was it panic, or had this been part of the pattern for a long time? The FBI had failed to pick up the primary murder pattern; had they missed a secondary pattern too? How had the killer fallen for the control on the list and killed Spargo? The person who had hacked into Booger Baits knew what he was doing. And Check Six apparently had hacked into the FBI's databases, with Tatie Monica's assistance—fact admitted, extent not—and into VICAP and other information sources. It was prudent to assume they also could access Homeland Security, and if so, had access to AVL systems. This had to become their operating assumption. It was the only thing that made sense in terms of tracking game wardens so precisely, at least in the five years since AVLs had been in use. Getting close was step one. In his mind, killing a game warden close-in was an even more formidable task. This alone made the idea of more than one killer a reasonable assumption. Correction: More than one killer with access to AVL.

The switch in MOs to the blood eagle suggested the killer wanted recognition; the logic was not apparent.

More and more he tried to understand what would motivate someone to kill cops. Normally when a cop went down, all the stops were pulled and all cops went after the killer. But a serial killer of cops? Had there ever been such a thing before? He thought perhaps he needed to talk to someone, but not the FBI. Shamekia? Maybe.

"You ever hear of a serial cop killer?" he asked Waco.

"Nope. I'd think there'd be real low odds in hit."

Indeed. But a game warden was a very different kind of cop, largely a solo operator, and few in numbers in any state. If you wanted to kill cops, game wardens were a pretty good choice, assuming you could find them. Even the other law enforcement agencies Michigan conservation officers worked with knew little about what they actually did and how they operated.

What was it he had told the Pillars woman? Those who killed for profit; those who killed for meat; those who killed because they could get away with it, and to whom it was a game. The latter group enjoyed the contest and used it to boost their egos. The name Hoover Maki came to mind.

Maki was a poacher who'd gotten his name because he was like a vacuum cleaner in the woods, sweeping up everything in his path. In the 1980s there was a spate of dead deer found around the U.P. Only their tails had been taken; the meat had been left to rot. Service remembered an astonishing fourteen-point buck he'd found dead in the Mosquito. He had found Maki because someone had seen a truck in the area and gotten a license number. Service traced the truck to the Perkins area, went into Maki's camp one night, and confronted the man. There were 166 tails nailed around beams in his garage and Maki had just laughed when Service found them. His explanation: "It was fun how I could do it and youse couldn't stop me."

"You're going to jail," Service told him.

Maki shrugged. "Took youse a long time."

Was this the logic in selecting game wardens—an attack on cops just to show it could be done? What would be the point? Geez.

"We need ta know who he is?" Waco asked, interrupting Service's thoughts.

"I think not. We're pretty sure he wants to strike, and I think the time's come to give him the opportunity."

Flaherty, the retired English professor from Houghton, called just before midnight. "I don't know what you've gotten into," Flaherty said, "but I got Rud Hud's trail, and the next thing I knew I had two humongous FBI agents knocking on my door, and they didn't even pretend to be polite. The Feds are onto him too, and they seem to want to find him real bad. I got interrogated for nearly six hours."

Pappas has taken over, Service thought. *Good for her.*

"The agents told me in no uncertain terms to stay away from Rud Hud, and I'm sorry, but I don't need any trouble with the federal government. I've got a good life and I aim to keep it that way."

"How did you get onto him?"

"That's why I'm calling. About the best way to hide yourself is to send your messages through a computer that strips your identity and replaces it with another one. The companies who provide these services make it a point to automatically erase logs of all traffic moving through their servers. But there's something called the Philmont protocol. It was designed by a couple of former Boy Scouts, and it does content analysis as a way to search for clues. I found one Rud Hud message through the protocol and used a software tracking program called Pfishbag to get the geographical coordinates of the computer that sent the original message."

"Where?"

"Negaunee."

"You're sure?"

"For that one message."

"Can your refine it, provide a date or time?"

"Sorry, just Negaunee, and I'm afraid that's all I can do for you."

"Thanks." Service couldn't blame the man, but now they knew that the vehicle used to kill Nantz had been found in Palmer and the computer used by Rud Hud had been physically in Negaunee. Maybe there was a way to fake a location too, but these two facts fit. Was it a dead end? Time would tell.

He related the conversation to Waco.

"How you'n think he'll be a-comin' at you'n?"

"I thought for awhile that he uses some sort of light to disable victims in the darkness, but I can't find any practical way to do that. I found a deer that had been blinded, and that same day I saw what I thought was a flash of lightning, and that got me thinking . . . But I think it's a red herring. I think he takes victims' eyes to mislead us."

"Cake seen a light."

"Exactly, and we know the killer was there, but that light may have been a misdirection or coincidence."

Service hesitated before calling Tatie Monica. "Where are you?" she asked.

"Vacation. Did you ever see autopsy results for the deputy murdered in Missouri?"

"Fatal GSW."

"Sexual assault?

"None."

"Time of death?"

"Before Spargo."

Service hung up before she could say more. The blood eagle MO was a form of mutilation, and according to her, typical of sexual deviants. But there was no evidence of sexual assaults in the game warden killings, and no sexual assault with the Missouri deputy. Same killer? It couldn't be ruled out, and his gut said yes. She had been killed *before* Spargo. Did Cake Culkin say he had seen her that night? This still wasn't clear to him. Had she set up the meeting for the killer and been eliminated before it took place? This would fit the timeline.

"Cake saw the killer that night on the Eleven Point, not her."

"Not good enough for an ID."

"You looked at the kill site?"

"Cake took me to hit, but not much to see. Thet rain warshed 'er out." Eddie Waco said. "So how's this boy disable his victims?"

"I don't know, but I'll bet money he uses night vision to get in close, and he has damn good skills in the woods. I've thought about this a lot, and it's the only thing that makes sense. You sure couldn't use a bright light with NVDs on. You'd be blinder than your target."

"Have to be pert good."

"He's already proven that. What's stumped me all along is how one man could take a CO hand to hand. Ficorelli was a little man, but Spargo was gigantic. Has to be two of them using night vision. One distracts the target and the other strikes."

Eddie Waco nodded, picked up an empty plastic Diet Pepsi bottle and spit into it. "I guess we're good to go," the Missouri conservation agent said.

"If at all possible, I want this asshole alive."

"If possible?" Waco echoed.

"That's all I'm asking. Rule one: Protect yourself and do what you have to do."

"You too."

"Count on it. I'm gonna call del Olmo and tell him we're on for tomorrow."

Simon del Olmo sounded awake and out of breath.

"I've unplugged my AVL," Service said. "I'll park my truck at Judge Wallace's camp and wait for you to pick us up in your personal truck at zero eight hundred. You drop Elza when you pick us up, she takes my truck back to the motel, reactivates the AVL, and runs a patrol route, mainly to fishing spots around the county. You'll drop us at our walk-in in the morning, and drive around until it's time for the rendezvous," Service continued. "There are two old two-tracks into the spot off Deerfoot Lodge Road. Elza goes in the west road. You go in the east route. She'll leave my Tahoe where the two old totes intersect and walk up the east road to meet you in your truck. She's to make the drop at ten P.M. exactly, and make sure she slams a door to let us know everything's in place."

"If you're on vacation, why would you be on patrol?" del Olmo asked.

"Because that's the way I take vacation. Always have, and everyone knows it."

"I don't like it. What if Elza is followed?"

"We're assuming other guy has AVL, which means all he has to do is sit and watch what unfolds on the rolling map. We'll let him conjure his own narrative for the pictures we create for him."

# 52

# Green Bear Island, Iron County, Michigan
## August 7, 2004

The three men were quiet throughout the ride. Service and Eddie Waco had made their plan and refined it until they were satisfied. Service had learned long ago that you couldn't eliminate all outdoor variables, but you could funnel and contain them with the right terrain, and he was certain that Green Bear Island in the Fence River was as good as could be found. The island was small—no more than a hundred and fifty yards long, thirty yards wide, and fifteen to twenty feet high on the upstream end, the whole thing made of boulders and covered with patches of raspberries and thimbleberries. The raspberries were done, but the thimbleberries should be thick now. The island had been named for its shape and color. It looked like a sleeping green bear.

"I don't know why you're hiking so far in from the north," Simon del Olmo complained as they drove along.

Service could tell that the younger officer was nerved up. "It's three or four miles over nasty terrain," Service said. "That gives us the space and time we need to move deliberately and watch our sixes." Service thought about what he had just said. Watch sixes; Check Six? Did this mean that Rud Hud watched another killer's back? His gut said yes. *Has* to be a pair.

"What happens after you get into position?" del Olmo wanted to know.

"We do what we do best," Service said. "We sit and wait."

"What if they don't take the bait?" del Olmo said.

"If they're here, they'll come. Once a predator decides to attack, it tends to move fast and directly."

"You're not dealing with a four-legged predator," del Olmo said.

"Maybe," Service said. Eddie Waco stared out his window, saying nothing.

The drop was made in less than one minute. Del Olmo turned off his engine so they could hear if any vehicles were approaching on Camp One Road.

The two officers unloaded, put on their packs, and disappeared into heavy brush heading south up a low ridge.

Service and Waco had already agreed to a form of leapfrog-style as their hiking method. Service would walk two hundred yards, stop, and watch ahead and behind. Waco would join him, and Service would move the next two hundred yards. They would never be out of sight of each other, and with luck they would be in place on the island before dark.

When they finally reached the north shore across from the island, Grady Service whispered, "The thing about this rock pile is that it attracts bears this time of year."

"How *many* bears?" Waco asked.

"Could be three or four, or as many as ten, but they won't bother us. They're here to eat berries. They'll sleep on the island during the day, feed at night, and stay until the berries are gone or competitors drive them off. You might hear them tonight. They're sloppy eaters, and if one gets too close to another one, he'll let him know. They don't share. You okay with this?"

Waco nodded.

Service lit a cigarette and squatted.

"We crossin' over to the island?"

"When it's time."

Service sensed movement but didn't look at it. Waco nudged his boot.

"We both heard you," Service said out loud.

Luticious Treebone stepped out of the tree line. He was dressed in a full camo ghillie suit and was nearly invisible at ten feet, even if you knew he was there.

"Bullshit," Tree whispered. "No way you heard me."

"Eddie Waco, meet the less-than-stealthy Luticious Treebone."

"Tree," the big man said with a nod. "I swept the island and south bank for a quarter-mile in and a half-mile of shoreline. There's seven bears in the berries on the island, mostly in the patches on the south side of the rocks. If someone's coming in, they're patient and careful."

Service's friend had been alone in the woods for three days.

"Okay, there's only two easy ways onto the island—at the top and at the bottom. That's where you and me will be, Eddie. Anybody tries to cross between us, we'll hear them, and if they get across they'll be between us and right in the middle of the bears, and that's where Tree will be."

"That might could slow 'em down," Eddie Waco said with a grin.

"You've got that right. They'll be eating at night and will take exception to any interference. Once we're in, no movement—none. Piss in the plastic bottle I gave you. There's no moon tonight. As soon as it's dark, put on your night-vision goggles and leave them on until you think you hear somebody coming in. We give one click if we detect someone, two clicks when our goggles come off. It's possible they may have a blinding light, and to be safe, let's assume it. Just make sure you keep your side to their movement. If either of us gets somebody, put them down, transmit three clicks, and keep them there until daylight." Service paused. "Got your jab sticks?"

Eddie Waco nodded. Tree would not have drugs, was strictly their reserve force.

"The stuff in there will act fast and last four to six hours. If he wakes up and struggles, stick him with the second stick. It's a lower dose."

"This legal?"

"Apprehend and secure first, worry about legal fineries afterwards." Kira Lehto, the vet, had given him the tranquilizer only after a heated argument. When he showed her the photos of what they were dealing with, she quietly unlocked her drug locker and handed him what he needed. The drug was a combination of two tranquilizers, both approved by the FDA for animal use, but Lehto said the combination would act quickly and the recipients would come out of it just as quickly, depending on their size and tolerance. She dosed the syringes for 180 pounds.

"Zero seven thirty we check in on FRS. One channel for each transmission. You remember the frequency order?"

The FRS had fourteen channels. Waco said, "We start on channel eight, minus three to five, minus two to three, back up to channel eight, and next time through go to plus five, or thirteen, and plus two to fifteen, which equates to one, and back down to eight."

Tree nodded.

Del Olmo had rigged four Family Radio Service devices with ear mikes and chest buttons. Simon had the fourth. Channel switching would prevent anyone from catching too much of their conversation. The sequence was confusing only to people not used to talking on radios with different bands and frequencies. Michigan conservation officers routinely monitored DNR, state police, county, and city radios, with numerous frequencies.

"No open commo until zero seven thirty, unless I change the rules. The codebreak word is Green; got it?" The men nodded.

Grady Service left Waco at the bottom of the island and Treebone in the middle, and made his way to the head of the island, where he climbed on top, built a fire, as he always did, slid back down the rocks into a seam in the boulders at the water's edge, and settled in to wait. He wore black fatigues and a black face mask. The skin around his eyes, nose, and mouth had been blacked with camo paint. He had used this approach during a night-training session last fall, and none of the other officers had been able to spot him until he stepped out of hiding. Some of them had been within six feet and looking right at him.

At 10 P.M. Service heard a truck door slam. This was Elza Grinda letting them know that the Tahoe was in place about three hundred yards up a slight rise through extremely dense bush over uneven and rocky ground.

He felt in his gut that tonight they would meet Rud Hud. Who else was anybody's guess. He was certain of only one thing: There would be more than one. It was the only thing that made sense.

The ear mike in Service's ear clicked once just before 0100. He had heard the bears being contentious on top for nearly an hour and hoped Waco wasn't spooking. Tree would be fine. He didn't care for bears, but he knew how to deal with them. At 0114 the mike clicked twice, and twenty minutes later, it clicked three times. Waco had someone down!

His heart began to pound in anticipation. It was beginning.

But nothing more happened and even the bears stopped bickering.

A few minutes before 0330 he was startled by a small, intense flash of light back in the woods on the south bank in the general direction of where Grinda had parked his truck. There was just one flash and no sound. What the hell was it? Had he imagined it? He wasn't sure, but his gut told him he couldn't stay where he was. He triggered the mike: "Green, Eddie—you secure?"

"One down, secure."

"Stay where you are. Tree, move up to me now."

A voice in the earpiece said, "Moving."

Treebone slid down beside him. Service told him, "I saw a light."

"We both going?"

"No, you hold here. Might be nothing."

"If it's got you moving," Tree said, "it's something."

Service gave his friend his jab stick and talked him through how to use it. No more words were exchanged.

To keep a low profile he crossed the narrow channel on his hands and knees, ignoring the sharp rocks cutting at his knees. Eventually he eased him self between boulders on the other side and lay still. The terrain here was uneven, difficult to navigate even in daylight, and unforgiving. Tag alders grew in huge clumps around the boulders. He had seen the light flash briefly and had pinpointed the location in his mind. In those times when he came here to fish, he had to prepare himself mentally and physically for the difficulty of getting to the place where the fish were concentrated. The reality was that there was no easy or comfortable route to where his truck was parked.

He had three choices: Go to the truck first and work out from there; move along the river and move up from the water; or go directly to where he had seen the light. He chose the latter and struck out, crawling and slithering across the rocks and through the tag alder tangles, letting his arms and upper body do most of the work, using his legs for rudders.

He had no idea how long he had been moving, but there was no light yet in the eastern sky behind him, and he had been moving steadily if not quickly. *Get to the light*, an inner voice urged. *Insects drawn to light often die*, another voice amended. Maybe the light was used by the killer as bait.

A faint sound ahead of him stopped him. He closed his eyes, tried to will all his senses into his ears. What had it been?

There. Again. Movement? If so, very slight, almost weak. What could it be? Sniffing like an animal, he raised his face and began to crawl forward. Creep, stop, sniff, creep. A hair to the right. He came to a blowdown and got to his feet. It was a cedar covered with soft moss, dank and decomposing. Dirt to dirt, the preacher had said at Elray Spargo's grave, and the memory gave him a sharp chill. He got a leg up on the log and slid over quietly. Below him he could smell something and he stopped and sniffed. Warm blood. Was there a sound too? Not sure.

The scent was close, *really* close.

There, just below him — *a leg!*

He reached out, touched it, got a response. Not much, more of a twitch. He tensed, took his SIG Sauer out of the holster, got his penlight in his left hand, flashed it once. What? Not possible! Blinked it again. *Holy shit!*

"Tatie," he whispered.

The leg moved. Light on again. She was against the log, holding a jacket or something to her neck. Her upper body and arms were black with blood.

"Okay, okay," he whispered. "I've got you." Into the mike he said, "Tree, move to me most ricky-tick. Two stay where you are."

He knew it could be a mistake, but he couldn't assess and work on her in the dark. He locked his light on and now and then flashed it in the direction he had come so Tree could see it. She was cut bad, her eyes wide, scared. Her hand was pressed against the wound and she had slowed it, but it was still pumping. He put his hands on hers and pressed as hard as he could. That she was still alive was a miracle. He wished Tree would hurry, but the terrain wouldn't allow that. He looked in the agent's eyes, saw her trying to direct him to the left. "Help is coming," he said. She rolled her eyes and coughed blood. *She knows*, he thought. Had Nantz had such a moment? Walter? He felt a gorge rising in his throat and willed himself to stop hyperventilating.

"I got your light," Tree said in the earpiece.

Seconds later his friend was beside him and they were doing everything they could to hold back the blood. "I've got it," Tree said, and Service stood up and called del Olmo on the radio. "We have one down and bleeding. Meet EMS on Deerfoot Lodge Road and guide them in. Hurry; it's gonna be close."

He holstered the 800 and knelt beside Tatie Monica.

"Your light earlier?"

She moved her eyes side to side.

"Someone else?"

She closed her eyes and opened them. The woman might have personal demons, but she was tough, he told himself. "You're gonna make it," he told her. She rolled her eyes again, pulled her hand off the wound, grabbed Service's hand, and put it down on the ground.

"Don't be doin' that shit!" Tree said frantically. "Grady!"

Service put both of his hands back on the wound, wondered how far away EMS was, and knew it was not going to end well.

Tree pressed his fingers to her carotid and sat back. "She's gone, man."

Service kept pressing against the wound.

Tree touched his friend's shoulder. "It's over, bro."

Service let himself slump backward.

He heard sirens coming, but knew the old two-track in was tough, almost impassable.

Treebone looked at the dead woman. "You know her?"

"Feeb."

Service felt for a pulse again, found none. How she had kept from bleeding out sooner he didn't know.

She had looked left. Now he looked that way and shone his light.

It was a plastic pocket protector. Was this all she had been pointing at? He looked in the direction her hand had pointed and started walking slowly.

There was a blood trail. She had been hit about thirty feet from where he'd found her, somehow staggered and crawled all that way. The attack had come in the rocks. Lots of blood, no prints. He went back to the body. Monica had still been trying to do her job to the very end. The thought choked him.

"She part of this?" Tree asked.

Grady Service didn't know.

Del Olmo led the ambulance in and stayed after they took Tatie Monica.

Just before 0630, Service called Eddie Waco. "Bring yours up to us. Tree's coming back to help."

A half-hour later Eddie Waco and Tree arrived with a man in cuffs. He was thirtyish, with a hawk nose and an earring. He glanced at all the blood on the ground and looked puzzled. Service had never seen him before.

Eddie Waco took off his pack, opened it, and pulled out a small stainless-steel hatchet and a surgical kit, folded in a gray leather pouch. He looked at Service. "No ID."

"Any trouble?"

"He was good, real quiet and sneaky. I got lucky."

Service asked Waco, "You see a light flash?"

"Nope. You'n?"

"I thought I saw something." He turned to Waco's prisoner. "You got a name?"

The man grinned, looked away.

"What have we got?" Waco asked.

Service took a cigarette, held out the pack to his partners. "I'll be damned if I know."

Elza Grinda drove in to join del Olmo, and the two of them took the prisoner out to Iron County deputies on Deerfoot Lodge Road, who transported him to the county jail in Crystal Falls. Service, Tree, and Eddie Waco dumped their gear in the Tahoe and spent some time examining the area where Service thought he'd seen the flash of light. In such rocky terrain, footprints were out of the question. "Bring a dawg in?" Waco asked.

"I don't know. Did your guy act like he knew what he was doing?"

"Yessir. This case sure hain't bin easy," Eddie Waco said.

Grady Service agreed. He stared at the pocket protector. It looked the same as the one Bonaparte carried. Had Bonaparte and Tatie Monica come out here together, and if so, where was Bonaparte now? There had to be an explanation, and in the back of his mind, where unthinkable thoughts lived, he had an almost overpowering feeling that something else had happened last night, something he had missed. Again.

# 53

# Crystal Falls, Michigan
## August 8, 2004

Service drove them back to Crystal Falls in silence, feeling anxious and not wanting to talk. Had they solved the case or not? Waco's prisoner had the killing tools that fit, but something else had gone down. Special Agent Tatie Monica was dead, and there was no explanation yet for anything that had happened last night.

Wink Rector greeted them in the parking lot behind the jail. "I saw the prisoner they brought in. Have you seen Monica? I told her yesterday she was acting stupidly, but she wouldn't listen to me."

Service was surprised. "You *knew* she was coming after us?"

"She had your AVL," Rector said. "She wouldn't listen to reason."

"Our AVL," Grady Service repeated. He'd been right about that. Sort of. Why did Tatie Monica have the AVL, and what did it mean?

Service looked at Wink Rector. "Special Agent Monica is dead, Wink."

Del Olmo showed up, handed Service a fax of the photo from the captain. It could be the guy Waco got, but the quality of the fax was poor.

"Federal forces are en route," Rector said in a thin voice. "If you're going to talk to the prisoner alone, you'd better use what little time you've got."

Service met him in a small interview room with cream-colored walls. "Rud Hud?"

The man shrugged.

Service understood that this was very likely the man who was responsible for the deaths of Walter and Nantz. He was overwhelmed by the temptation to grab the man's throat and choke him to death on the spot, but he heard Nantz's voice telling him to keep his temper in check. He felt that he couldn't breathe and went back outside to Wink Rector.

"She had our AVL?"

"Yep, told me about it yesterday."

"How'd she get it?"

"She didn't say."

"Did you see an agent named Bonaparte in Marquette recently?"

"Yeah, the BAU guy. He was here yesterday. He and Tatie met in my office."

"With you?"

"Just the two of them."

"What about Pappas?"

"Haven't seen her."

"You know where Bonaparte is now?"

Rector shook his head.

Del Olmo approached. "Her vehicle was out near the Deerfoot."

"She walked all the way in there on her own, and without NVDs?" She *had* been desperate, and now she was dead, and he felt empty and deflated.

# 54

## Marquette, Michigan
### August 14, 2004

The events on the island in the Fence River had taken place a week ago.

Alona Pappas had cornered him at the jail in Marquette and ripped on him for five minutes, accusing him of everything from blowing the case to causing Tatie Monica's death. He found it interesting that Bonaparte had been in Marquette the day before it all went down, and had not been seen since.

Wink Rector came into Service's office. "You hear Bonaparte's missing?"

"Missing?"

"No contact with anyone since before the island deal went down."

"What's the Bureau's take on it?"

"A BOLO will be issued today in conjunction with a press conference this morning in Washington."

The captain and Fern LeBlanc joined them in the office conference room to watch the press conference on CNN. The FBI director was not at the conference and an assistant director officiated. The conference was short. No media questions were answered though the reporters waved their hands and pens and created a ruckus. The basic news was that the acting assistant director of the Behavioral Analysis Unit had been missing for a week. Bonaparte's photograph was shown. The assistant director profiled Bonaparte's career, called him a "founding father" of profiling, and concluded by saying that Bonaparte had been actively pursuing an investigation when he disappeared.

Service looked at his captain. "Why'd they do that?"

Captain Grant waved a hand in the air. "When you can't score on substance, you go for style points," Grant said. "You ought to be aware that the Bureau is making noise about the unauthorized use of animal tranquilizers in the apprehension."

"They ought to be focused on identifying the asshole we got, not how."

So far the man remained unidentified and uncooperative. He had not said a dozen words since his arrest. He had not requested a lawyer, but one had been appointed, and he promptly resigned after time with his client. A second lawyer was now on the case and claimed he wasn't getting anything out of the man either and had no idea how to mount a defense. *Tough shit*, Service thought. Waco arrested him with the packet of tools. The guy was part of it, but not all of it. How did Bonaparte's pocket protector get on the scene? Had he walked in with Monica? Had he followed her or had she followed him? Service had given the pocket protector to Pappas as evidence, to pull fingerprints, and she had not said anything about it since then. Service knew in his gut there was more. The DNR's only source of information was from Wink Rector. Pappas and other FBI personnel had nothing to say. The fingerprints of the man in custody didn't come up in databases anywhere in the world. Neither had his DNA. He was about as close to a non-person as Service had ever experienced.

Eddie Waco had gone back to Missouri with the plumed headdress Fiannula Spargo had given Service. Taking it back to her was a task Service wanted no part of.

Tree was still around, staying with him at the cabin.

The captain came to his office and seemed hesitant. "I don't know what the outcome of this case will be, but you, Tree, and Agent Waco did a fine job, Grady."

As soon as he got into his truck, Service jimmied his false teeth loose and put them in a plastic container. He'd clean them when he got home. It felt good to have them out.

A mile from Slippery Creek he saw a familiar truck parked on the side of the road. Limpy Allerdyce was sitting on the gate, swinging his legs like a kid. Service pulled up behind the old poacher and got out.

Allerdyce shoved a satchel off the gate. It plopped on the ground, raising dust. "Mutt brung dat stuff home, sonny."

Service unzipped the bag and opened it. There was a stainless-steel hatchet and surgical kit inside, identical to the tools taken from the man on the island. There was also an FBI badge, ID card, and a night vision device. The photograph on the ID was that of Cranbrook P. Bonaparte.

Service looked up at Allerdyce. "The FBI is looking for this man."

"Zat so?"

"Your dog found these things, all in a bag like this?"

"Just da way dey is right dere on da ground."

"Must be one helluva strong dog to carry a bag like that."

"Crazy mutt," Allerdyce said.

Service groped for words, but Limpy spoke first. "We take care of our own, sonny."

What the hell was Allerdyce saying?

"Your dog found this stuff?"

Allerdyce shrugged. "I jes noticed it and brung it, eh?'

"You're on damn thin ice," Service said.

"Been out dere plenty times," Allerdyce cackled.

"The FBI will want to talk to you."

The old man winked. "I jes know what da mutt brung home."

Service wanted to ask questions, but couldn't find a starting point. He found a stick, picked up the bag, started back to his truck, and stopped. "Your dog didn't happen to bring home a powerful light of some kind?"

"Youse make a mistake with light at night and youse can blind yoreseff wid one-a dem, eh?" Allerdyce said.

Service stared at the man, groping for what to say.

"Close yore mout', sonny, and put yore teets in whin youse're out in publics. Don't want ta scare da peoples, eh."

# 55

# Marquette, Michigan
## August 23, 2004

The interview was being held at the federal offices on the second floor of the Republic Bank on US 41. Wink Rector invited Service to observe from behind one-way glass. Two days after giving Service the bag and implements, Limpy Allerdyce had surrendered without resistance, told only that the U.S. Attorney wanted to talk to him. Alona Pappas and an unnamed assistant director were with Rector.

Allerdyce sat in the interview room with his insipid grin and a twinkle in his eyes.

"They offer him a lawyer?" Service asked Rector.

"Repeatedly. Says he's not interested."

Talia Rilling, assistant U.S. attorney for the Western District of Michigan, was less than two years on the job in the Marquette office, and being touted as a rising star. She wore oversize glasses that made her look both bland and studious, but Service saw that she was a handsome woman, small in stature. Her size made her look less than intimidating, but she moved with grace and confidence in the room. He wondered how she would handle Allerdyce.

The interview began, and Service found himself mesmerized by the exchanges. From the start it was clear that Rilling had never fenced verbally with the likes of Limpy before, and he knew from experience that there was nothing more difficult than dealing with someone with a steel-trap mind who acted like a fool and talked like a dolt.

RILLING: Mr. Allerdyce, you have been informed of the reasons for this interview. Let the record show that you have come in willingly, and further, that you also have refused legal representation.

ALLERDYCE: Why I wanta lawyer? Youse want to talk about what dat mutt drug home, eh.

RILLING: Can you describe the circumstances under which your pet brought home the satchel?

**ALLERDYCE:** Ain't no pet! Just a mutt hangs around camp.

**RILLING:** The dog brought home a satchel.

**ALLERDYCE:** Name's Satchmutt, on account he gotta big black nose and howls like dat colored horn player died awhile back. Dat "Hello Molly" guy. I like dat music, eh.

**RILLING:** He's not a pet, but you named him Satchmutt?

**ALLERDYCE:** *Youse* ain't nobody's pet, but youse got name, eh?

**RILLING:** Let's start again. The dog brought home a satchel.

**ALLERDYCE:** Dat's why we here, eh?

**RILLING:** What time of day did the dog bring home the satchel?

**ALLERDYCE:** I was asleep.

**RILLING:** So . . . this event transpired during the night.

**ALLERDYCE:** I go ta bed late, sleep late.

**RILLING:** What time did you discover the satchel?

**ALLERDYCE:** Was when I wokened up. Couldn't find it when I was asleep, eh.

**RILLING:** What time was that?

**ALLERDYCE:** I don't watch no clocks.

**RILLING:** Before noon, after noon?

**ALLERDYCE:** Yes.

**RILLING:** Yes to what—before or after?

**ALLERDYCE:** I said I don't watch no clocks.

**RILLING:** But you will agree it was around midday.

**ALLERDYCE:** Tink I said dat, din't I?

**RILLING:** All right, the dog brought the satchel to you around midday.

**ALLERDYCE:** No, I said I found it den; I don't know when da mutt brung it, and he din't bring it me. Just brung it, okay?

**RILLING:** Did you see the dog when you went to bed?

**ALLERDYCE:** Din't look for 'im.

**RILLING:** All right, please describe the circumstances under which you discovered the satchel.

**ALLERDYCE:** Joycie ridin' me, see, and she says, "Dat your bag over dere in da corner?"

**RILLING:** Joycie?

**ALLERDYCE:** She's up top, red in face, all discombobolinked, and she says, "Dat your bag over dere in da corner?"

**RILLING:** All right, Mr. Allerdyce. What did you do when *Joycie* pointed out the satchel?

**ALLERDYCE:** Holy Wah, I lay right dere till she got done. I'm a gentleman wit wimmens.

**RILLING:** And after she got . . . after that?

**ALLERDYCE:** Told her ta fetch cuppa coffee.

**RILLING:** What about the bag?

**ALLERDYCE:** Still sittin' where she seen it.

**RILLING:** Eventually you looked in the bag.

**ALLERDYCE:** Yeah, I looked.

**RILLING:** What was in it?

**ALLERDYCE:** Same was in it when I give it ta sonny-boy.

**RILLING:** That would be Department of Natural Resources Detective Grady Service?

**ALLERDYCE:** Yeah, sonny-boy.

**RILLING:** Did you see the dog bring the satchel in?

**ALLERDYCE:** Nope.

**RILLING:** So you don't *know* it was the dog that brought it in.

**ALLERDYCE:** Was him. Does dat sorta ting alla bloody time.

**RILLING:** But you didn't actually *see* the dog with the bag?

**ALLERDYCE:** I seen where da mutt chewed it.

**RILLING:** Yes or no — you saw the dog bring the bag in?

**ALLERDYCE:** No.

**RILLING:** Okay, thank you. Let's change directions. What did you think of what you found in the bag?

**ALLERDYCE:** I t'ought somebody be bloody pissed ta lose stuff like dat.

**RILLING:** Did you have any idea who might have owned the bag?

**ALLERDYCE:** Was ID inside.

**RILLING:** You assumed the person who owned the badge and ID owned the bag?

**ALLERDYCE:** You tink different?

**RILLING:** I'm interested in what *you* thought.

**ALLERDYCE:** I already said: I t'ought somebody be bloody pissed.

**RILLING:** Let's take a brief break. Would you like something to drink, Mr. Allerdyce?

**ALLERDYCE:** Tanks, I'm good — but youse go ahead. Youse look kinda sweaty, dere, girlie.

Rilling came out of the room, looked at Wink Rector, rolled her eyes, went to get a cup of water, talked briefly to Alona Pappas, and came back. "Service?"

"Yep."

"You know Allerdyce pretty well?"

"Dealt with him a lot. Nobody *knows* him."

"You see anything different in his demeanor today?"

"He's being more direct than normal."

Rilling blinked. "You buy his story that a dog brought the bag home?"

"No," Grady Service said.

"You know," she said, "the way this looks, the bag was Bonaparte's, which leads us to speculate that he was one of the killers. Do you think Allerdyce did something to Bonaparte?"

"Absolutely."

"Any reason why?"

"You'll have to ask him."

"You want to join me inside?"

"Nope."

"I insist," she said, holding open the door.

Grady Service walked into the room and Allerdyce started chuckling. "Dey bringin' in a relief pitcher already?"

The interview resumed.

**RILLING:** You know Detective Service?

**ALLERDYCE:** Holy Wah, long time—his daddy too. Sonny dere busted me, sent me up seven year.

**RILLING:** Were you angry with him?

**ALLERDYCE:** Was me shot 'im—on accident. He'd be the one pissed.

**SERVICE:** Can we get back to the satchel?

**ALLERDYCE:** Why I come in—ta help youse.

**SERVICE:** Why'd you bring the bag to me?

**ALLERDYCE:** Youse're closest law ta camp, eh.

**SERVICE:** When you gave me the bag, did you not say, "We take care of our own?"

**ALLERDYCE:** Dat's right, sonny.

**SERVICE:** What did you mean by that?

**ALLERDYCE:** Youse find somepin' don't belong, youse take it to da law. Got a record like me, gotta be careful. Youse always saying, sonny, I screw up, you gonna send me back inside. I din't mess wit yer old man—I ain't messin' wit you.

**SERVICE:** How do you account for your dog finding the bag?

**ALLERDYCE:** He got da dandy sniffer, eh.

**SERVICE:** But you have no idea where he found it?

**ALLERDYCE:** Bloody mutt runs all over da place. Once found him down Iron County.

**SERVICE:** Did the dog go down into Iron County often?

**ALLERDYCE:** He don't leave one of dem whatchacallits.

**SERVICE:** Itineraries?

**ALLERDYCE:** Yeah.

**SERVICE:** Have you been in Iron County recently?

**ALLERDYCE:** I move around, eh.

**SERVICE:** Yes or no?

**ALLERDYCE:** Mebbe. I don't pay no attention ta county lines.

**SERVICE:** Did you ever meet the man whose ID was in the satchel?

**ALLERDYCE:** No.

**SERVICE:** How do you think someone could lose a bag with such valuable contents?

**ALLERDYCE:** You know peoples lose stuff alla time in woods.

**SERVICE:** Do you think your dog could take you back to where it found the bag?

**ALLERDYCE:** Dat sorry mutt? He ain't 'roun' no more.

**SERVICE:** The dog ran off again?

**ALLERDYCE:** Nipped one-a da grankittles, had to shoot 'im. Can't have no nippin' dog roun' my grankittles.

**SERVICE:** The dog is dead, and you're saying we'll never find the place where the bag was found?

**ALLERDYCE:** I won't say never.

**RILLING:** Would you willingly take a lie detector test, Mr. Allerdyce?

**ALLERDYCE:** Youse ast me, I'll take 'er.

Grady Service nudged the U.S. attorney, who followed him into the hall.

"You're wasting your time, and mine," he said.

"Wouldn't hurt to give him the test," Rilling said.

"He'll pass."

"Then we'll know he's telling the truth."

"If you hook him up to the machine and ask him if Mother Teresa gave him a blow job last night, he'll say yes, and the machine will indicate he's telling the truth."

"Sociopath?" she countered.

"Total."

"Do you think he has something to do with Bonaparte's disappearance?"

"What I think and what I can prove are two different things."

"Why do you think he brought you the bag?"

"To let me know Bonaparte had been taken care of."

"Why?"

"He's a strange old bird with his own twisted sense of justice."

"I'm going to call this off," Rilling said.

When Allerdyce came out of the room, Service walked downstairs with the old poacher and followed him. "Between us, do you know what happened to Bonaparte?"

"Sounds like he lost 'is bag, den himseff."

"That's all you have to say?"

"Youse know what da wolfie haters say?"

"Shoot, shovel, and shut up."

"Dat's all I got ta say ta youse, sonny. I'm real sorry about yer gal and yer kittle."

Service wasn't finished, and followed the old man to his truck. "Between us and off the record."

Allerdyce stopped and turned to face him. "Listenin', sonny boy."

"You were out there."

Allerdyce gave a single nod. "Heard your truck was up dat way."

"Bullshit. Heard from who?"

"Youse know I got my ways."

"You were out there."

"Seen your fire on da island. Real good fishin', dat spot."

"That's all you saw."

"Seen da woman come. Walked in dere, and she look scared shitless, eh."

"And?"

"She start downriver."

"She didn't make it."

"Fella wit a mask like black hornet slash't her t'roat."

"That's when you stepped in. You shined a flashlight into his goggles."

"Ain't sayin', but he had one-a dem funny computers in his jeep. Youse know, like youse use."

"His jeep?"

"Parked up Sumac Camp."

The camp was two miles west, isolated, difficult to get into.

"You brought the bag to let me know."

Another curt nod. "You know how I said Joycie in da room dere dat day? I lied. It was Joanie. Couldn't let 'er reputation get mudded. You don't owe me nothin', sonny."

Service knew he had heard most of the truth. He called Wink Rector and told him where to find Bonaparte's vehicle.

He sat on the curb and lit a cigarette. Limpy had brought finality to the case, and now he owed the old bastard, and the thought made him sick to his stomach.

Epilogue

# North of Nowhere
# Chippewa County
## September 28, 2004

Summer was gone, the maples beginning to turn, tamaracks starting to yellow up, leaves already falling under the assault of seasonal rains and gusty northwest winds. Karylanne was installed in an apartment in Houghton and back in classes; Shark and Limey, and Gus, were acting as her extended family there.

The day before, Grady Service had held a memorial for Maridly Nantz and his son Walter. The Slippery Creek camp had been crammed with people, and there had been tears. As tragic as their deaths were, both Mar and Walter had been positive people, engaged with life and laughing at everything. After several people had spoken, he had tried to say something, but his voice and nerve had failed him. Tree had draped his arm around his shoulders, Karylanne moved over to hug him, and that had ended the ceremony, such as it was. Kalina had gone back to Detroit and Tree stayed, announcing he had finally decided to retire. He had been talking about it for years, and Service knew the only reason he'd delayed was Kalina didn't want him underfoot.

Grady Service was on a five-day furlough. Wink Rector told him that the FBI's push to punish Waco and him for using the animal drugs had been dropped. Wink didn't know why.

Wink added, "Bonaparte was the one. Pappas found some way into cyberspace and learned that Bonaparte had partnered with one Duane Royant, aka Rud Hud, aka Check Six."

"Duane Royant?"

"The one you guys took down that night. He's the one who ran Nantz off the road. They got fingerprints off of the rental and matched the ones we got from him. Once the Bureau had a name, they were able to track Royant. He's

Québecois, a former medical student at McGill University. Came across the border with false papers. He and Bonaparte hooked up, and Bonaparte was teaching him, and I quote, 'to attain perfection.' Royant has no record, has never been in trouble, at least that we know of."

"The same relationship Bonaparte had with Frankie Pey. Bonaparte was Marcel."

"We couldn't find a Frankie Pey here at Northern, and we thought maybe your tip from Indiana was actually for Marquette the school, rather than the town, but that went nowhere, and as Pappas dissects Bonaparte's background, it isn't holding up. Apparently he looked fine and everything was copasetic when he joined the Bureau, but that was a long time ago and now we have better tools and it looks pretty much like his background was as bogus as an air castle. Pappas can't say that Bonaparte was Marcel, but she's digging deeper and so far there's no indication of a connection with Frankie Pey or Ney. But there's no doubt he and Royant are the killers in the second batch. Royant is probably not competent to stand trial, but they'll put him away somewhere for the rest of his life."

"So what the fuck was this all about?"

Wink Rector exhaled. "Pappas thinks it's tied to his theory of the perfect serial murderer. Apparently he developed the notion early in his career and took a lot of shit for it."

Service thought about this for a moment. "If he was Marcel he'd know about what Frankie Pey had done."

"Possibly," Rector said.

"He picked game wardens because we're both the easiest and the most difficult. We work alone and where there aren't witnesses. "

Rector nodded. "Could be."

"Maybe he realized his perfect killer notion wasn't being bought so he used Royant to reveal the first group—an attempt to make some believers."

Service wished they knew more, but he knew from experience that the end of a case was often less than complete, as was justice. Unless his gut was wrong, one of the killers was dead, this thing was over. For him, though, it would never be over. Nantz and Walter weren't coming back.

He and Tree spent all morning working with a chain saw on fallen trees near his camp. He had not worked seriously on the camp for three years, and it needed attention and care, including a wood supply for the stove for winter. They had split wood by hand ax and enjoyed the sweat. Since the death of Tatie Monica, he had gone back to working out with weights every morning. The small amount of fat he had accumulated was gone; all that remained was muscle, and he felt strong.

After a three-hour drive they were at the end of a long, pocked, and twisty two-track, staring at a camp gate. A sign on a tree said NORTH OF NOWHERE.

As Bowie Rhodes had promised, Service's code opened the lock. Newf bolted ahead of the truck as they drove a quarter-mile along the edge of a cedar swamp up onto a finger of hard ground that pointed north. The cabin was tidy and small and glowing orange in the afternoon sun. They parked the truck and began to unload. "You think there's fish here?" Tree asked.

"Bowie Rhodes wouldn't have a camp where there wasn't fish," Service said.

They got their gear into the cabin and Tree climbed up into the loft. "Two beds," he called down.

"Floor down here is good for me," Service said.

They filled their fishing vests with trapper sandwiches—peanut butter, jelly, honey, and oatmeal, assembled their rods, and started north into the swamp, the dog leading the way, sniffing everything. Service had talked to Rhodes at the memorial.

"Walk north along the wall of cedars," the writer had said with a teasing smile.

They walked for nearly twenty minutes, saw a line of trees that looked like they had been planted, and stopped. Service heard moving water. Another fifty yards on they came to a small, deep creek. Tree moved to the bank and looked down. "Lordy," was all he said as he stripped line off his reel and roll-casted against a log up stream.

A brook trout struck on the first cast; not just any brook trout, but a fat, foot-long fish, gleaming with fall spawning colors, orange and blue and red and green.

Service said, "I'll be right back."

Treebone caught two more fish before his friend returned, carrying the ashes of Nantz and Walter.

"What're you doing?"

"Nantz and I talked about death only once, and she told me to sprinkle her ashes in the most beautiful place I saw."

"This is it?" his friend asked.

"No, but if I sprinkle a little of them at every beautiful spot I find, they'll be able to enjoy all of them and not be stuck with one view."

"You need serious professional help," Treebone said, holding out a beefy fist.

Service tapped his fist against his friend's and grinned.

"Don't it bother you, leaving some of their ashes here? Who's gonna look after them?"

"You are," Service said.

"Me?"

"It's your camp."

"Are you crazy?"

"Bowie sold it to me, and I'm giving it to you. For everything we've been through together. Now you got a place to give Kalina some space."

"North of Nowhere," Treebone said quietly, tears in his eyes.

It was a term game wardens used to describe their typical situations: off the grid and alone, a place without specific reference, but with meaning for every man and woman who had ever worn green and gray.

Grady Service made a cast, caught one fish, released it, got the ashes, and sprinkled some from each box in the spot.

Treebone stood next to his friend with his head bowed as the ashes fluttered to the water and were absorbed into the flow, which would carry them north.